W9-BVE-916

BUSN¹¹

INTRODUCTION TO BUSINESS

MARCE KELLY

Santa Monica College

CHUCK WILLIAMS

Butler University

CENGAGE

Australia · Brazil · Canada · Mexico · Singapore · United Kingdom · United States

BUSN11

Marce Kelly and Chuck Williams

Senior Vice President, Higher Ed Product, Content, and Market Development: Erin Joyner

Product Manager: Heather Mooney

Content/Media Developer: Allie Janneck

Product Assistant: Tawny Schaad

Marketing Manager: Charisse Darin

Marketing Coordinator: Audrey Jacobs

Content Project Manager: Darrell E. Frye

Senior Art Director: Bethany Bourgeois

Internal Designer: Lou Ann Thesing/ Thesing Design

Cover Designer: Lisa Kuhn, Curio Press, LLC/Chris Miller, Cmiller design

Cover Image: Matelly/Getty Images

Intellectual Property Analyst: Diane Garrity

Intellectual Property Project Manager: Sarah Shainwald

Production Service: MPS Limited

© 2019, 2018 Cengage Learning, Inc.

Unless otherwise noted, all content is © Cengage

ALL RIGHTS RESERVED. No part of this work covered by the copyright herein may be reproduced or distributed in any form or by any means, except as permitted by U.S. copyright law, without the prior written permission of the copyright owner

For product information and technology assistance, contact us at **Cengage Customer & Sales Support, 1-800-354-9706** or **support.cengage.com.**

For permission to use material from this text or product, submit all requests online at **www.cengage.com/permissions.**

Library of Congress Control Number: 2017959000

Student Edition ISBN: 978-1-337-40713-7
Student Edition with MindTap ISBN: 978-1-337-40712-0

Cengage
200 Pier 4 Boulevard
Boston, MA 02210
USA

Cengage is a leading provider of customized learning solutions with employees residing in nearly 40 different countries and sales in more than 125 countries around the world. Find your local representative at **www.cengage.com.**

To learn more about Cengage platforms and services, register or access your online learning solution, or purchase materials for your course, visit **www.cengage.com.**

Printed in the United States of America
Print Number: 05   Print Year: 2021

KELLY/WILLIAMS
BUSN¹¹ BRIEF CONTENTS

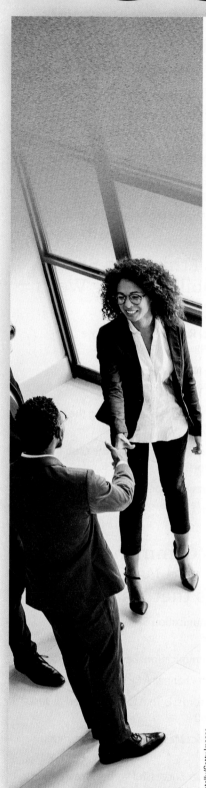

Matelly/Getty Images

CONTENTS

Part 1
THE BUSINESS ENVIRONMENT

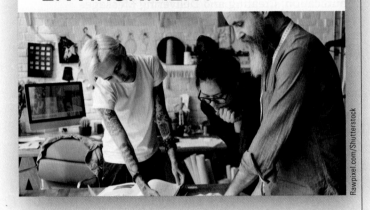

Rawpixel.com/Shutterstock

Part 2
CREATING A BUSINESS

Monkey Business Images/Shutterstock

Part 3
FINANCING A BUSINESS

Uber Images/Shutterstock

Part 4
MARKETING A BUSINESS

Ryan Pierse/Getty Images

Part 5
MANAGING A BUSINESS

Monkey Business Images/Shutterstock

With love and
appreciation
to Kathy,
the best friend imaginable!

—Marce Kelly

To Jenny,
the book is done, let's play!

—Chuck Williams

The idea for this book—a whole new way of learning—began with students like you across the country. We paid attention to students who wanted to learn about business without slogging through endless pages of dry text. We listened to students who wanted to sit through class without craving a triple espresso. We responded to students who wanted to use their favorite gadgets to prepare for tests.

So we are confident that BUSN will meet your needs. The short, lively text covers all the key concepts without the fluff. The examples are relevant and engaging, and the visual style makes the book fun to read. But the text is only part of the package. You can access a rich variety of study tools via computer or iPad—the choice is yours.

We did one other thing we hope you'll like. We paid a lot of attention to students' concerns about the high price of college textbooks. We made it our mission to ensure that our package not only meets your needs but does so without busting your budget!

This innovative, student-focused package was developed by the authors—Marce Kelly and Chuck Williams—and the experienced Cengage Learning publishers. The Cengage team contributed a deep understanding of students and professors across the nation, and the authors brought years of teaching and business experience.

Marce Kelly, who earned her MBA from UCLA's Anderson School of Management, spent the first 14 years of her career in marketing, building brands for Neutrogena and The Walt Disney Corporation. But her true love is teaching, so in 2000 she accepted a full-time teaching position at Santa Monica College. Professor Kelly has received seven Outstanding Instructor awards from the International Education Center and has been named four times to *Who's Who Among American Teachers*.

Chuck Williams' interests include employee recruitment and turnover, performance appraisal, and employee training and goal setting. Most recently, he was the Dean of Butler University's College of Business. He has taught in executive development programs at Oklahoma State University, the University of Oklahoma, Texas Christian University, and the University of the Pacific. Dr. Williams was honored by TCU's M.J. Neeley School of Business with the undergraduate Outstanding Faculty Teaching Award, was a recipient of TCU's Dean's Teaching Award, and was TCU's nominee for the U.S. Professor of the Year competition sponsored by the Carnegie Foundation for the Advancement of Teaching. He has written three other textbooks: *Management, Effective Management: A Multimedia Approach,* and *MGMT*.

We would appreciate any comments or suggestions you want to offer about this package. You can reach Chuck Williams at crwillia@butler.edu, and Marce Kelly at marcella.kelly@gmail.com. We wish you a fun, positive, productive term, and look forward to your feedback!

Marce Kelly

Chuck Williams

1 | Business Now:
Change Is the Only Constant

Rawpixel.com/Shutterstock.com

LEARNING OBJECTIVES

After studying this chapter, you will be able to:

1-1 Define business and discuss the role of business in the economy

1-2 Explain the evolution of modern business

1-3 Discuss the role of nonprofit organizations in the economy

1-4 Outline the core factors of production and how they affect the economy

1-5 Describe today's business environment and discuss each key dimension

1-6 Explain how current business trends might affect your career choices

Remember to visit
PAGE 17
for additional
STUDY TOOLS

1-1 BUSINESS NOW: MOVING AT BREAKNECK SPEED

Day by day, the business world simply spins faster. Industries rise—and sometimes fall—in the course of a few short months. Technologies forge instant connections across the globe. Powerful new trends surface and submerge, sometimes within less than a year. In this fast-paced, fluid environment, change is the only constant. According to Charles Darwin, it is not the strongest of the species that survive, nor the most intelligent, but the one most responsive to change. And so it is with business.

Successful firms lean forward and embrace the change. They seek the opportunities and avoid the pitfalls. They carefully evaluate risks. They completely understand their market, and they adhere to ethical practices. Their core goal: to generate long-term profits by delivering unsurpassed **value** to their customers.

Over the past decade, the explosive growth in social media has played a pivotal new role for businesses and consumers alike in today's dynamic business environment. Digging deeper into current culture, several leading-edge trendspotting experts have recently identified an array of key trends likely to shape the world's economies as we close out the turbulent teenage years of the twenty-first century. A few highlights:

■ **Sexual harassment:** 2017 was a year that shined bright light on sexual harassment and assault in the workplace. Hundreds of women in prominent positions came forward publicly with their stories

value The relationship between the price of a good or a service and the benefits that it offers its customers.

of harassment. Public opinion, the press, their employers, and in many cases, even the law, rallied behind them with strong support—punishing the perpetrators, and establishing new safeguards to prevent future abuse. Actress Alyssa Milano reactivated the #MeToo movement, in an effort to demonstrate the widespread prevalence of sexual assault and harassment—especially in the workplace—and to create empathy among victims. Facebook reported that less than 24 hours after Milano tweeted "Me Too," there were more than 12 million posts, comments, and reactions regarding #MeToo by 4.7 million users around the world. And Twitter confirmed that over 1.7 million tweets included the hashtag #MeToo, with 85 countries that had at least 1,000 #MeToo tweets. When Milano tweeted "Me Too," she apparently didn't realize that the movement had actually been launched more than a decade earlier by women's activist Tarana Burke to support survivors of sexual violence, mainly young women of color.[1]

- **Artificial intelligence (AI):** Visionary entrepreneur Elon Musk (founder of PayPal, Tesla, and SpaceX) issued ominous warnings in 2017 that artificial

> "You miss 100% of the shots you don't take."
>
> —WAYNE GRETZKY.
> HOCKEY STAR

intelligence may become dangerous to its creators. Meanwhile, business titans such as Google and Apple continued to pour millions of dollars into developing AI products and services. Apple CEO Tim Cook described the technology behind self-driving cars as "the mother of all AI product projects…a core technology that we view as very important." A slightly different twist on AI is augmented reality (AR). The hit AR game Pokémon Go was downloaded more than 750 million times in its first year and the company that created it plans to release a Harry Potter AR game in the near future—competitors are sure to jump into the lucrative AR field as its potential unfolds. Yet another twist on AI is the consumer push for virtual companionship. And no, this is not a dystopian movie come to life—72% of regular voice technology users say "I think brands should have unique voices and personalities for their apps and skills."[2]

- **Welcome Generation Z:** Over the last few years the millennial generation has received enormous attention and it's certainly been well deserved! Millennials—born between 1980 and 1995—shaped the Internet and changed popular culture. But Generation Z—also known as digital natives—outnumbers millennials by about a million people, and comprises about a quarter of America's population. Generation Z (born between 1996 and 2011) doesn't remember a world without the Internet and smart phones—the defining event in their lives was typically the Great Recession, which means that many of them simply don't trust business. They use their tactical technical prowess to actively seek the very best value and they tend to be great customers for no-frills, you-only-pay-for-what-you-get type services (Spirit Airlines, anyone?). Similar to millennials, Generation Z is open-minded but they have absolutely no tolerance for any sort of bigotry (actual or perceived). Their attention span is short (8 seconds on average), but their work ethic is strong.[3]

Kjpargeter/Shutterstock.com

- **Alibaba dominates retail:** Way back in 2009, China's goliath online retailer Alibaba created a tongue-in-cheek new "holiday," Singles' Day, designed for unmarried people to celebrate their single status by buying stuff for themselves. The date is November 11, 11/11, lots of ones—get it? Over the years the holiday has gained traction, spurred by special promotions such as a lifetime supply of baiju liquor for a one-time payment of 1,111 yuan, hammering in the joke about the nature of Singles' Day. In 2017 Singles' Day sales hit more than $25 billion—more than double the sales of Black Friday and Cyber Monday combined![8]

- **Federal tax reform:** In late 2017, the U.S. Congress passed the most sweeping rewrite of the tax code in more than 30 years. Although it is far too soon to determine the true impact of the changes, many analysts anticipate that the new tax code will dramatically alter the American economic landscape, which will

! OOPS! WHAT WERE THEY THINKING?

Not Every Dumb Move Is an Utter Disaster...

In the wake of disastrous mistakes and outrageous mismanagement across our economy, it might be tough to remember that some mistakes are actually pretty amusing. Several examples might help remind you.

- **Bad fabric, not fat thighs:** In early 2013, Lululemon Athletica was forced to recall its popular (and expensive) yoga pants, because many women found them utterly see-through. Later in the year, the founder of the firm was forced to resign after blaming the problem on women with fat thighs who rubbed the fabric too sheer with multiple uses.[4]

- **Apple angst:** In a rare display of new product development weakness, Apple released its Maps program before it was ready for the Big Time. Mostly harmless, the program baffled millions of trusting consumers. But in Fairbanks, Alaska, it directed hapless users onto active runways of the

international airport. Fortunately, there were no collisions— the worst harm done was to Siri's reputation as a navigator.[5]

- **Geography lessons needed:** In 2016, Coca-Cola sent a promotional tweet featuring an outdated map of Russia. Offended Russian patriots responded with pictures of themselves pouring the soft drink into toilets with the hashtag #BanCocaCola.[6]

- **Thank you, Captain Obvious!** A surprising number of firms just can't seem to credit their customers with even basic intelligence. Marks & Spencer's labeled one of their Bread Puddings, PRODUCT WILL BE HOT AFTER HEATING. On a Sears hairdryer, DO NOT USE WHILE SLEEPING. And on packaging for a Rowenta iron, DO NOT IRON CLOTHES ON BODY. While these warnings most likely have a legal backstory, it's hard for a reasonable consumer not to see them as silly goofs.[7]

be further discussed later in later in this text. Key changes:

- The corporate tax rate will drop permanently from 35% to 21%.
- Incentives will be available for corporations to bring money from foreign accounts back to the United States.
- Individual federal income taxes will drop at least through 2025.[9]

1-1a Business Basics: Some Key Definitions

While you can certainly recognize a business when you see one, more formal definitions may help as you read through this book. A **business** is any organization or activity that provides goods and services in an effort to earn a **Profit** is the financial reward that comes from starting and running a business. More specifically, profit is the money that a business earns in sales (or revenue), minus expenses such as the cost of goods and the cost of salaries. But clearly, not every business earns a profit all the time. When a business brings in less money than it needs to cover expenses, it incurs a **loss**. If you launch a music label, for instance, you'll need to pay your artists, lease a studio, and purchase equipment, among other expenses. If your label generates hits, you'll earn more than enough to cover all your expenses and make yourself rich. But a series of duds could leave you holding the bag. Just the possibility of earning a profit provides a powerful incentive for people of all backgrounds to launch their own enterprises. But unfortunately, the rate of new business start-ups has been decreasing over the past few years. As the economy has finally emerged from the Great Recession, and unemployment and financial ruin are less of a threat, fewer people have been motivated to risk starting new businesses.[10] People who do risk their time, money, and other resources to start and manage a business are called **entrepreneurs**.

Interestingly, as entrepreneurs create wealth for themselves, they produce a ripple effect that enriches everyone around them. For instance, if your new website becomes the next Facebook, who will benefit? Clearly, *you* will. And you'll probably spend at least some of that money enriching your local clubs, clothing stores, and car dealerships. But others will benefit, too, including your members, advertisers on your site and the staff who support them, contractors who build your facilities, and the government that collects your taxes. The impact of one successful entrepreneur can extend to the far reaches of the economy. In fact, fast-growing new firms generate about 10% of all new jobs in any given year.[11] Multiply the impact by thousands of entrepreneurs—each working in his or her own self-interest—and you can see how the profit motive benefits virtually everyone.

From a bigger-picture perspective, business drives up the **standard of living** for people worldwide, contributing to a higher **quality of life**. Businesses not only provide the products and services that people enjoy but also provide the jobs that people need. Beyond the obvious, business contributes to society through innovation—think cars, TVs, and tablet computers. Business also helps raise the standard of living through taxes, which the government spends on projects that range from streetlights to environmental cleanup. Socially responsible firms contribute even more by actively advocating for the well-being of the society that feeds their success.

1-2 THE HISTORY OF BUSINESS: PUTTING IT ALL IN CONTEXT

You may be surprised to learn that—unlike today—business hasn't always been focused on what the customer wants. In fact, business in the United States has changed rather dramatically over the past 200–300 years. Most business historians divide the history of American business into five distinct eras, which overlap during the periods of transition:

- **The Industrial Revolution:** Technological advances fueled a period of rapid industrialization in America from the mid-1700s to the mid-1800s. As mass production took hold, huge factories replaced skilled artisan workshops. The factories hired large numbers of semiskilled workers who specialized in a limited number of tasks. The result was unprecedented production

business Any organization or activity that provides goods and services in an effort to earn a profit.

profit The money that a business earns in sales (or revenue), minus expenses, such as the cost of goods and the cost of salaries. Revenue − Expenses = Profit (or Loss).

loss When a business incurs expenses that are greater than its revenue.

entrepreneurs People who risk their time, money, and other resources to start and manage a business.

standard of living The quality and quantity of goods and services available to a population.

quality of life The overall sense of well-being experienced by either an individual or a group.

Henry Ford's assembly line began operation on December 1, 1913. Initially developed for the Model T, this new production system allowed manufacturers of all kinds to output products like never before.

efficiency but also a loss of individual ownership and personal pride in the production process.

- **The Entrepreneurship Era:** Building on the foundation of the Industrial Revolution, large-scale entrepreneurs emerged in the second half of the 1800s, building business empires. These industrial titans created enormous wealth, raising the overall standard of living across the country. But many also dominated their markets, forcing out competitors, manipulating prices, exploiting workers, and decimating the environment. Toward the end of the 1800s, the government stepped into the business realm, passing laws to regulate business and protect consumers and workers, creating more balance in the economy.

- **The Production Era:** In the early part of the 1900s, major businesses focused on further refining the production process and creating greater efficiencies. Jobs became even more specialized, increasing productivity and lowering costs and prices. In 1913, Henry Ford introduced the assembly line, which quickly became standard across major manufacturing industries. With managers focused on efficiency, the customer was an afterthought. But when customers tightened their belts during the Great Depression

nonprofits Business-like establishments that employ people and produce goods and services with the fundamental goal of contributing to the community rather than generating financial gain.

and World War II, businesses took notice. The "hard sell" emerged: aggressive persuasion designed to separate consumers from their cash.

- **The Marketing Era:** After World War II, the balance of power shifted away from producers and toward consumers, flooding the market with enticing choices. To differentiate themselves from their competitors, businesses began to develop brands, or distinctive identities, to help consumers understand the differences among various products. The *marketing concept* emerged: a consumer focus that permeates successful companies in every department, at every level. This approach continues to influence business decisions today as global competition heats up to unprecedented levels.

- **The Relationship Era:** Building on the marketing concept, today, leading-edge firms look beyond each immediate transaction with a customer and aim to build long-term relationships. Satisfied customers can become advocates for a business, spreading the word with more speed and credibility than even the best promotional campaign. And cultivating current customers is more profitable than constantly seeking new ones. One key tool is technology. Using the Web and other digital resources, businesses gather detailed information about their customers and use these data to serve them better, "bringing a level of customer centricity that we've never seen before," according to Graeme Noseworthy, marketing director for IBM.

1-3 NONPROFITS AND THE ECONOMY: THE BUSINESS OF DOING GOOD

Nonprofit organizations play a critical role in the economy, often working hand in hand with businesses to improve the quality of life in our society. Focusing on areas such as health, human services, education, art, religion, and culture, **nonprofits** are business-*like* establishments, but their primary goals do not include profits. Chuck Bean, executive director of the Nonprofit Roundtable, explains: "By definition, nonprofits are not in the business of financial gain. We're in the business of doing good. However, nonprofits are still businesses in every other sense—they employ people, they take in revenue, they produce goods and services and contribute in significant ways to our region's economic stability and growth." Nationwide, nonprofits employ about one in ten workers, accounting for more paid workers than the entire construction industry

The Connection Economy

Success today no longer requires building great things, although there will always be big rewards for building the *best* new things (see Apple, Tesla, and Virgin, among other success stories). According to industry leaders, the most successful firms of the present rely on connection—either connecting buyers and sellers or connecting consumers and information. Uber, the largest ride-sharing company, owns no vehicles but connects people to rides and drivers to customers. Airbnb, the largest provider of accommodations, owns no real estate but connects people to lodging. Kickstarter and Indiegogo, both giants of crowdfunding, have no money to invest but may soon surpass traditional venture capital firms by connecting investors to opportunities. According to entrepreneur and author Seth Godin, the connection economy works best when the following four conditions are met:

1. *Coordination*. Without coordination, connections can't happen. In fact, the most significant business opportunities may lie in areas that currently appear chaotic.

2. *Trust*. Finding ways to connect and create value only works when the players share basic trust.

3. *Permission*. When you offer ideas to people who give you permission to do so, it's a resource. Without that permission, it's an annoyance. What's new and significant is that the permission must be earned, and not requested.

4. *The exchange of ideas*. True value emerges when people exchange ideas deliberately and with established purpose (at a meet-up or conference, for instance).

Godin also emphases the importance of generosity and art. No one wants to connect with a person who always takes but never gives back. You must add value to all of your interactions to make the connection worthwhile. Art is important, according to Godin, because forward-thinking people are looking for the extraordinary. Traditional systems are inherently boring and unremarkable. In the connection economy, people are seeking the *remarkable*—the things that are truly worthy of remark.[12]

---

and more than the finance, insurance, and real-estate sectors combined. And nonprofit museums, schools, theaters, and orchestras have become economic magnets for many communities, drawing additional investment.[13]

1-4 FACTORS OF PRODUCTION: THE BASIC BUILDING BLOCKS

Both businesses and nonprofits rely on **factors of production**—four fundamental resources—to achieve their objectives. Some combination of these factors is crucial for an economic system to work and create wealth. As you read through the factors, keep in mind that they don't come free of charge. Human resources, for instance, require wages, while entrepreneurs need a profit incentive.

- **Natural Resources:** This factor includes all inputs that offer value in their natural state, such as land, fresh water, wind, and mineral deposits. Most natural resources must be extracted, purified, or harnessed; people cannot actually create them. (Note that agricultural products, which people do create through planting and tending, are not a natural resource.) The value of all natural resources tends to rise with high demand, low supply, or both.

- **Capital:** This factor includes machines, tools, buildings, information, and technology—the synthetic resources that a business needs to produce goods or services. Computers and telecommunications capability have

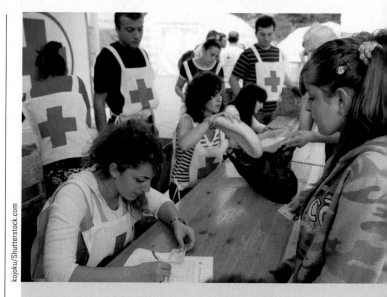

kojoku/Shutterstock.com

Many businesses work with nonprofits to boost their impact in the community.

become pivotal elements of capital across a surprising range of industries, from financial services to professional sports. You may be surprised to learn that in this context, capital does not include money, but, clearly, businesses use money to acquire, maintain, and upgrade their capital.

> **factors of production** Four fundamental elements—natural resources, capital, human resources, and entrepreneurship—that businesses need to achieve their objectives.

- **Human Resources:** This factor encompasses the physical, intellectual, and creative contributions of everyone who works within an economy. As technology replaces a growing number of manual labor jobs, education and motivation have become increasingly important to human resource development. Given the importance of knowledge to workforce effectiveness, some business experts, such as management guru Peter Drucker, break out knowledge as its own category, separate from human resources.

- **Entrepreneurship:** Entrepreneurs are people who take the risk of launching and operating their own businesses, largely in response to the profit incentive. They tend to see opportunities where others don't, and they use their own resources to capitalize on that potential. Entrepreneurial enterprises can kick-start an economy, creating a tidal wave of opportunity by harnessing the other factors of production. But entrepreneurs don't thrive in an environment that doesn't support them. The key ingredient is economic freedom: freedom of choice (whom to hire, for instance, or what to produce), freedom from excess regulation, and freedom from too much taxation. Protection from corruption and unfair competition is another entrepreneurial "must."

Clearly, all of these factors must be in place for an economy to thrive. But which factor is most important? One way to answer that question is to examine current economies around the world. Russia and China are both rich in natural resources and human resources, and both countries have a solid level of capital (growing in China, and deteriorating in Russia). Yet, neither country is wealthy; both rank relatively low in terms of gross national income per person. The missing ingredient seems to be entrepreneurship, limited in Russia largely through corruption and in China through government interference and taxes. Contrast those examples with, say, Hong Kong. The population is small, and the natural resources are severely limited, yet Hong Kong has consistently ranked among the richest regions in Asia. The reason: operating for many years under the British legal and economic system, the government actively encouraged entrepreneurship, which fueled the creation of wealth. Recognizing the potential of entrepreneurship, China has recently done more to relax regulations and support free enterprise. The result has been tremendous growth, which may yet bring China into the ranks of the wealthier nations.[14]

business environment The setting in which business operates. The five key components are economic environment, competitive environment, technological environment, social environment, and global environment.

1-5 THE BUSINESS ENVIRONMENT: THE CONTEXT FOR SUCCESS

No business operates in a vacuum. Outside factors play a vital role in determining whether each individual business succeeds or fails. Likewise, the broader **business environment** can make the critical difference in whether an overall economy thrives or disintegrates. The five key dimensions of the business environment are the economic environment, the competitive environment, the technological environment, the social environment, and the global environment, as shown in Exhibit 1.1.

1-5a The Economic Environment

In September 2008, the U.S. economy plunged into the worst fiscal crisis since the Great Depression. Huge, venerable financial institutions faced collapse, spurring unprecedented bailouts by the federal government and the Federal Reserve. By the end of the year, the stock

Exhibit 1.1
The Business Environment

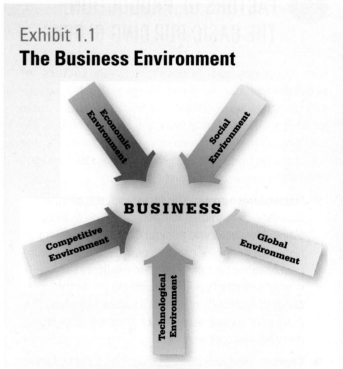

Each dimension of the business environment affects both individual businesses and the economy in general.

"A banker is a fellow who lends you his umbrella when the sun is shining, but wants it back the minute it begins to rain."

—MARK TWAIN, AMERICAN AUTHOR

market had lost more than a third of its value, and 11.1 million Americans were out of work. Housing prices fell precipitously, and foreclosure rates reached record levels. As fear swept through the banking industry, neither businesses nor individuals could borrow money to meet their needs. Economic turmoil in the United States spread quickly around the world, fueling a global economic crisis.

The U.S. economy continued to stagger through 2010 and 2011, with unemployment remaining stubbornly high, although signs of recovery began to emerge in late 2012, and certainly in 2013. The Federal Reserve—the U.S. central banking system—took unprecedented, proactive steps to encourage an economic turnaround. And President Barack Obama spearheaded passage of a massive economic stimulus package, designed not only to create jobs but also to build infrastructure—with a focus on renewable energy—to position the U.S. economy for stability and growth in the decades to come. (The price, of course, was more national debt, which will ultimately counterbalance some of the benefits.) Although the U.S. economic recovery continued through 2015, the entire world economy began to stagger in early 2016 as economic instability in China caused frightening ripples around the globe.

The government also takes active steps on an ongoing basis to reduce the risks of starting and running a business. The result: free enterprise and fair competition flourish. Despite the economic crisis, research suggests that most budding entrepreneurs still plan to launch their firms in the next three years. One government policy that supports business is the relatively low federal tax rate, both for individuals and businesses. A number of states—from Alabama to Nevada—make their local economies even more appealing by providing special tax deals to attract new firms. The federal government also runs entire agencies that support business, such as the Small Business Administration. Other branches of the government, such as the Federal Trade Commission, actively promote fair competitive practices, which help give every enterprise a chance to succeed.

Another key element of the U.S. economic environment is legislation that supports enforceable contracts. For instance, if you contract a baker to supply your health food company with 10,000 pounds of raw kale chips at $1.00 per pound, that firm must comply or face legal consequences. The firm can't wait until a day before delivery and jack up the price to $10.00 per pound because you would almost certainly respond with a successful lawsuit. Many U.S. businesspeople take enforceable contracts for granted, but in a number of developing countries—which offer some of today's largest business opportunities—contracts are often not enforceable (at least not in day-to-day practice).

Corruption also affects the economic environment. A low level of corruption and bribery dramatically reduces the risks of running a business by ensuring that everyone plays by the same set of rules—rules that are clearly visible to every player. Fortunately, U.S. laws keep domestic corruption mostly—but not completely—at bay. Other ethical lapses, such as shady accounting, can also increase the cost of doing business for everyone involved. But in the wake of corporate ethical meltdowns such as Enron, the federal government has passed tough-minded new regulations to increase corporate accountability. If the new legislation effectively curbs illegal and unethical practices, every business will have a fair chance at success.

Upcoming chapters on economics and ethics will address these economic challenges and their significance in more depth. But bottom line, we have reason for cautious (some would say very cautious) optimism. The American economy has a proven track record of flexibility and resilience, which will surely help us navigate this crisis and uncover new opportunities.

1-5b The Competitive Environment

As global competition intensifies yet further, leading-edge companies have focused on customer satisfaction like never before. The goal: to develop long-term, mutually beneficial relationships with customers. Getting current customers to buy more of your product is a lot less expensive than convincing potential customers to try your product for the first time. And if you transform your current customers into loyal advocates—vocal promoters of your product or service—they'll get those new customers for you more effectively than any advertising or discount program. Companies such as Amazon, Coca-Cola, and Northwestern Mutual life insurance lead their industries in customer satisfaction, which translates into higher profits even when the competition is tough.[15]

Most Valuable	Biggest Gainer	Percentage Growth
Apple	Facebook	+48%
Google	Amazon	+29%
Microsoft	Adobe	+19%
Coca Cola	Adidas	+17%
Amazon	Goldman Sachs	+16%
Samsung	Starbucks	+16%
Toyota	Huawei, Morgan Stanley	+14%
Facebook	Morgan Stanley	+14%
Mercedes Benz	FedEx	+12%
IBM	PayPal	+12%

Source: Best Global Brands 2017, Interbrand, http://interbrand.com/best-brands/best-global-brands/2017/ranking/, accessed April 13, 2018.

Customer satisfaction comes in large part from delivering unsurpassed value. The best measure of value is the size of the gap between product benefits and price. A product has value when its benefits to the customer are equal to or greater than the price that the customer pays. Keep in mind that the cheapest product doesn't necessarily represent the best value. If a 99-cent toy from Big Lots breaks in a day, customers may be willing to pay several dollars more for a similar toy from somewhere else. But if that 99-cent toy lasts all year, customers will be delighted by the value and will likely encourage their friends and family to shop at Big Lots. The key to value is quality, and virtually all successful firms offer top-quality products relative to their direct competitors.

A recent ranking study by consulting firm Interbrand highlights brands that use imagination and innovation to deliver value to their customers. Exhibit 1.2 shows the winners and the up-and-comers in the race to capture the hearts, minds, and dollars of consumers around the world.

Leading Edge versus Bleeding Edge Speed-to-market—the rate at which a firm transforms concepts into actual products—can be another key source of competitive advantage. And the pace of change just keeps getting faster. In this tumultuous setting, companies that stay ahead of the pack often enjoy a distinct advantage. But keep in mind that there's a difference between leading edge and bleeding edge. Bleeding-edge firms launch products that fail because they're too far ahead of the market. During the late 1990s, for example, in the heart of the dot.com boom, Webvan, a grocery delivery service, launched to huge fanfare. But the firm went bankrupt just a few years later in 2001, partly because customers weren't yet ready to dump traditional grocery stores in favor

Nadalina/Shutterstock.com

Workforce Magazine named American Express as its top company for HR management in 2016. Google, Accenture, USAA, and AT&T rounded out the rest of the top five.

speed-to-market The rate at which a new product moves from conception to commercialization.

of cyber-shopping. Leading-edge firms, on the other hand, offer products just as the market becomes ready to embrace them.[16]

Apple provides an excellent example of leading edge. You may be surprised to learn that Apple—which controls about 70%[17] of the digital music player market—did not offer the first MP3 player. Instead, it surveyed the existing market to help develop a new product, the iPod, which was far superior in terms of design and ease-of-use. But Apple didn't stop with one successful MP3 player. Racing to stay ahead, they soon introduced the colorful, more affordable iPod mini. And before sales reached their peak, they launched the iPod Nano, which essentially pulled the rug from under the blockbuster iPod mini just a few short months before the holiday selling season. Why? If they hadn't done it, someone else may well have done it instead. And Apple is almost maniacally focused on maintaining its competitive lead.[18]

1-5c The Workforce Advantage

Employees can contribute another key dimension to a firm's competitive edge. Recent research suggests that investing in worker satisfaction yields tangible, bottom-line results. The researchers evaluated the stock price of *Fortune* magazine's annual list of the "100 Best Companies to Work for in America" to the S&P 500, which reflects the overall market. From 2009 to 2014, cumulative stock market returns for the "100 Best" were up +205%, compared to +121% for the S&P 500. On an annualized basis, this translates to a return of about +20.4% per year for the "100 Best," and about +14.1% per year for the S&P 500 over the same time period. While the critical difference in performance most likely stemmed from employee satisfaction, other factors—such as excellent product and superb top management—likely *also* played a role in both employee satisfaction and strong stock performance.[19]

Finding and holding the best talent will likely become a crucial competitive issue in the next decade as the baby boom generation begins to retire. The 500 largest U.S. companies anticipate losing about half of their senior managers over the next five to six years. Since January 1, 2011, approximately 10,000 baby boomers began to turn 65 (the traditional retirement age) every day, and the Pew Research Center anticipates that this trend will continue for 19 years. Replacing the skills and experience these workers bring to their jobs may be tough: baby boomers include about 77 million people, while the generation that follows includes only 46 million. Firms that cultivate human resources now will find themselves better able to compete as the market for top talent tightens.[18] However, job market contraction may not be an issue, because a growing number of baby boomers opt to either postpone retirement or continue working part-time during retirement, in the face of inadequate financial resources.

The Uber Syndrome

No doubt about it—senior executives make the most money in business. They also have the most to worry about, however. In a 2015 study of senior executives, one participant described her firm's biggest worry as "the 'Uber Syndrome'—where a competitor with a completely different business model enters your industry and flattens you." In today's tumultuous business world, this concern is completely understandable. Analyzing the research, *Fortune* magazine editor Geoff Colvin noticed that this year, for the first time, most business leaders expected new competitors to be outsiders. Business leaders know they must disrupt—or be disrupted. The solution to this impending threat, according to the small cohort of highly successful firms that the research dubs "torchbearers," seems to be to focus more on customers and less on competitors. When a disruptive player makes its move, loyal customers are less likely to defect and destroy your business.

According to a separate survey of CEOs released in 2016, the two largest concerns among chief executives around the world are the global economic environment and geopolitical tensions. The global economy is more integrated today than ever before, and a crisis within any major country can quickly spread around the world. We've seen this time and time again in recent years, from the Grecian debt crisis of 2009 to the Chinese stock market plunge of early 2016. Dennis Nally, global chairman of PwC Consultancy, explains why geopolitical tension is a threat to the global economy: "[If] you've got hot spots anywhere in the world, it creates instability . . . business leaders hate instability." The latest PwC survey of CEOs shows that among American CEOs in particular, there is widespread recognition that a strong corporate purpose is vital in the digital world. In addition, CEOs are focused on building stronger trust with employees and customers alike. So if your life goal is to reach the top rung at a major corporation, don't expect to leave your worries behind. It would seem that the higher you go, the more pressing the worries.[21]

1-5d The Technological Environment

The broad definition of **business technology** includes any tools that businesses can use to become more efficient and effective. But more specifically, in today's world, business technology usually refers to computers, telecommunications, and other digital tools. Over the past few decades, the impact of digital technology on business has been utterly transformative. New industries have emerged, while others have disappeared. And some fields—such as travel, banking, and music—have changed dramatically. Even in categories with relatively unchanged products, companies have leveraged technology to streamline production and create new efficiencies. Examples include new processes such as computerized billing, digital animation, and robotic manufacturing. For fast-moving firms, the technological environment represents a rich source of competitive advantage, but it clearly can be a major threat for companies that are slow to adopt or to integrate new approaches.

The creation of the **World Wide Web** has transformed not only business but also people's lives. Anyone, anywhere, anytime can use the Web to send and receive images and data (as long as access is available). One result is the rise of **e-commerce** or online sales, which allow businesses to tap into a worldwide community of potential customers. In the wake of the global economic crisis, e-commerce has slowed from the breakneck 20%+ growth rates of the past five years, but even so, analysts predict that solid growth will continue. Business-to-business selling comprises the vast majority of total e-commerce sales (and an even larger share of the profits). A growing number of businesses have also connected their digital networks with suppliers and distributors to create a more seamless flow of goods and services.[22]

Alternative selling strategies thrive on the Internet, giving rise to a more individualized buying experience. If you've browsed seller reviews on eBay or received shopping recommendations from Amazon, you'll have a sense of how personal web marketing can feel. Online technology also allows leading-edge firms to offer customized products at prices that are comparable to standardized products. On the Burton website, for instance, customers can "custom build" professional quality "Custom X" snowboards while sitting at home in their pajamas. Nike offers a similar service for NikeID shoes, clothing, and gear.

As technology continues to evolve at breakneck speed, the scope of change—both in everyday life and business operations—is almost unimaginable. In this environment, companies that welcome change and manage it well will clearly be the winners.

1-5e The Social Environment

The social environment embodies the values, attitudes, customs, and beliefs shared by groups of people. It also covers **demographics**, or the measurable characteristics of a population. Demographic factors include population size and density and specific traits such as age, gender, race, education, and income. Clearly, given all these influences, the social environment changes dramatically from country to country. And a nation as diverse as the United States features a number of different social environments. Rather than cover the full spectrum, this section focuses on the broad social trends that have the strongest impact on American business. Understanding the various dimensions of the social environment is crucial since successful businesses must offer goods and services that respond to it.

Diversity While the American population has always included an array of different cultures, the United States has become more ethnically diverse in recent years. Caucasians continue to represent the largest chunk of the population at 63%, but according to the director of the U.S. Census Bureau, "The next half century marks a turning point in continuing trends—the U.S. will become a plurality nation, where the non-Hispanic white population remains the largest single group, but no group is in the majority." This will probably happen in about 2043. The Hispanic and Asian populations will probably continue to grow faster than any other ethnic groups. By 2060, nearly one in three U.S. residents will be Hispanic, up from about one in six today. This will happen even though the overwhelming wave of immigration from Mexico to the United States has stalled and even begun to reverse in the past few years; nevertheless, among Mexican-born people worldwide, one in ten currently

business technology Any tools—especially computers, telecommunications, and other digital products—that businesses can use to become more efficient and effective.

World Wide Web The service that allows computer users to easily access and share information on the Internet in the form of text, graphics, video, apps, and animation.

e-commerce Business transactions conducted online, typically via the Internet.

demographics The measurable characteristics of a population. Demographic factors include population size and density, as well as specific traits such as age, gender, and race.

Do You Do It?

More than 1,000 times a minute, someone in America bites into a Jack in the Box taco—one of more than a million Jack in the Box tacos sold every day. With such numbers, you might think that Jack unearthed the secret to the perfect-tasting taco . . . but you'd be wrong. Jack's taco has been variously described by its fans as:

- "a wet envelope of cat food"
- "vile and amazing"
- "disgusting and delectable"
- "repulsive and yet irresistible"

So why does the Jack in the Box taco do so well? Food writer Sophie Egan offers three possible reasons. First, it's cheap. At two for $.99 it's a real deal. Second, it's fried. As much as we like the idea of fruits and vegetables—fried stuff tastes good! Finally, it's a metaphorical flip of the bird to the "food police," who many believe are attempting to exert too much control over our rights to eat whatever we please.[23]

Hurst Photo/Shutterstock.com

lives in the United States.[24] Exhibit 1.3 demonstrates the shifting population breakdown.

But the national statistics are somewhat misleading, since ethnic groups tend to cluster together. African Americans, for example, currently comprise about 37% of the Mississippi population, Asians comprise about 39% of the Hawaii population, and Hispanics comprise about 47% of the New Mexico population.[25]

Exhibit 1.3
U.S. Population Estimates

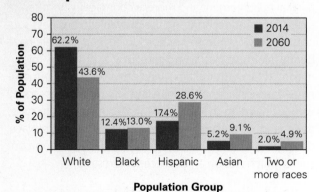

Source: Projections of the Size and Composition of the U.S. Population: 2014 to 2060, U.S. Census Bureau, March 2015, https://www.census.gov/content/dam/Census/library/publications/2015/demo /p25-1143 .pdf, accessed May 9, 2016.

So what does this mean for business? Growing ethnic populations offer robust profit potential for firms that pursue them. For instance, a number of major brands such as Coca-Cola, General Mills, Ford, Nestlé, Purina, and Walmart have invested heavily in the Hispanic market over the past five years. Recognizing the potential of the Hispanic market, Japanese automakers have begun actively targeting Latino customers. Because of these efforts, Hispanic customers are reportedly 15% more likely than any other group to buy a Japanese-made car. Toyota, in particular, has been the top-selling brand among Latinos for more than ten years thanks to its highly targeted marketing. Targeting an ethnic market can also yield remarkable results for products that cross over into mainstream culture. Music mogul and entrepreneur Russell Simmons, for example, initially targeted his music and clothing to the African American market, but his success quickly spilled over to mainstream culture, helping him build a hip-hop empire.[26]

Growing diversity also affects the workforce. A diverse staff—one that reflects an increasingly diverse marketplace—can yield a powerful competitive advantage in terms of both innovation and ability to reach a broad customer base. From global behemoths, such as Coca-Cola and Verizon, to local corner stores, companies have taken proactive steps to hire and nurture people from a broad range of backgrounds. And that doesn't just reflect racial or ethnic roots. True diversity also includes differences in gender, age, religion, and nationality, among other areas. Leading-edge firms have also taken proactive steps to train their entire workforce to manage diversity for top performance.[27]

Effectively managing diversity should only become easier as time goes by. Multiple studies demonstrate that young American adults are the most tolerant age group, and they are moving in a more tolerant direction than earlier generations regarding racial differences, immigrants, and homosexuality. As this generation gathers influence and experience in the workforce, they are likely to leverage diversity in their organizations to hone their edge in a fiercely competitive marketplace.[28]

Aging Population

As life spans increase and birthrates decrease, the American population is rapidly aging. The U.S. Census Bureau projects that the nation's population age 65 and older will more than double between 2005 and 2060. By 2060, older Americans will represent just over one in five residents, up from one in seven today. Also, the number of working-age Americans will shrink from 63% to 57% of the population, dramatically increasing the number of people who are depending on each working American. And the United States isn't alone in this trend. The population is aging across the developed world, from Western Europe to Japan. China faces the same issue, magnified by its huge population. Demographers estimate that in the next 20 years the number of people in China over the age of 60 will double, leading to a nation where the retired will outnumber the entire population of Western Europe. There are currently six workers to every retiree, but China's one-child policy suggests that the number of people providing for the old will rapidly collapse.[29]

The rapidly aging population brings opportunities and threats for business. Companies in fields that cater to the elderly—such as healthcare, pharmaceuticals, travel, recreation, and financial management—will clearly boom. But creative companies in other fields will capitalize on the trend as well by reimagining their current products to serve older clients. Possibilities include books and movies—maybe even video games—with mature characters; low-impact fitness programs such as water aerobics; and cell phones and PDAs with more readable screens. Again, the potential payoff of age diversity is clear: companies with older employees are more likely to find innovative ways to reach the aging consumer market.

But the larger numbers of retired people also pose significant threats to overall business success. With a smaller labor pool, companies will need to compete even harder for top talent, driving up recruitment and payroll costs. As state and federal governments stretch to serve the aging population, taxes may increase, putting an additional burden on business. And as mid-career workers spend more on elder care, they may find themselves with less to spend on other goods and services, shrinking the size of the consumer market.

> In Asia, the average person's living standards are currently set to rise by 10,000% in one lifetime!
>
> —NEWSWEEK

Rising Worker Expectations

Workers of all ages continue to seek flexibility from their employers. Moreover, following massive corporate layoffs in the early 2000s, employees are much less apt to be loyal to their firms. A study released in 2013 showed that on average, employees in Fortune 500 firms have a median tenure of only 3.68 years. As young people today enter the workforce, they bring higher expectations for their employers in terms of salary, job responsibility, and flexibility—and less willingness to pay dues by working extra-long hours or doing a high volume of "grunt work." Smart firms are responding to the change in worker expectations by forging a new partnership with their employees. The goal is a greater level of mutual respect through open communication, information sharing, and training. And the not-so-hidden agenda, of course, is stronger long-term performance.[30]

Ethics and Social Responsibility

With high-profile ethical meltdowns dominating the headlines in the past few years, workers, consumers, and government alike have begun to hold businesses—and the people who run them—to a higher standard. Federal legislation, passed in the wake of the Enron fiasco, demands transparent financial management and more accountability from senior executives. And recognizing their key role in business success, a growing number of consumers and workers have begun to insist that companies play a proactive role in making their communities—and often the world community—better places. Sustainability—doing business today without harming the ability of future generations to meet their needs—has become a core issue in the marketplace, driving business policies, investment decisions, and consumer purchases on an unprecedented scale.[31]

1-5f The Global Environment

The U.S. economy operates within the context of the global environment, interacting continually with other economies. In fact, over the past two decades, technology and free trade have blurred the lines between individual economies

Rawpixel.com/Shutterstock.com

around the world. Technology has forged unprecedented links among countries, making it cost effective—even efficient—to establish computer help centers in Mumbai to serve customers in Boston, or to hire programmers in Buenos Aires to make websites for companies in Stockholm. Not surprisingly, jobs have migrated to the lowest bidder with the highest quality—regardless of where that bidder is based.

Often, the lowest bidder is based in China or India. Both economies are growing at breakneck speed, largely because they attract enormous foreign investment. Over the past couple of decades, China has been a magnet for manufacturing jobs because of the high population and low wages—about $3.50 per hour (including government-mandated benefits) versus about $19.50 in the United States—although the gap is rapidly closing due to double-digit annual wage inflation in China. And India has been especially adept at attracting high-tech jobs, in part because of their world-class, English-speaking university graduates who are willing to work for less than their counterparts around the globe.[32]

The migration of jobs relates closely to the global movement toward **free trade**. In 1995, a renegotiation of the **General Agreement on Tariffs and Trade (GATT)**—signed by 125 countries—took bold steps to lower tariffs (taxes on imports) and to reduce trade restrictions worldwide. The result: goods move more freely than ever across international boundaries. Individual groups of countries have gone even further, creating blocs of nations with virtually unrestricted trade. Mexico, Canada, and the United States have laid the groundwork for a free-trade mega-market through the North American Free Trade Agreement (NAFTA), and 25 European countries have created a powerful free-trading bloc through the European Union, which has been weakened by a severe, ongoing financial crisis. The free-trade movement has lowered prices and increased quality across virtually every product category as competition becomes

truly global. We'll discuss these issues and their implications in more depth in Chapter 3.

A Multi-Pronged Threat In the past decade alone, war, terrorism, disease, and natural disasters have taken a horrific toll in human lives across the globe. The economic toll has been devastating as well, affecting businesses around the world. The 9/11 terrorist attacks in New York and Washington, D.C., decimated the travel industry and led to multibillion-dollar government outlays for Homeland Security. In 2002, a terrorist bombing at an Indonesian nightclub killed nearly 200 people, destroying tourism on the holiday island of Bali. Similarly, the 2015 terror attacks in Paris dealt a devastating blow to tourism throughout Europe, which was already struggling to handle an overwhelming refugee crisis. The 2003 deadly epidemic of the SARS flu dealt a powerful blow to the economies of Hong Kong, Beijing, and Toronto. And the Ebola outbreak of 2014 had a catastrophic impact on several impoverished African economies that could least afford the hit. Less than two years later, the Indian Ocean tsunami wiped out the fishing industry on long swaths of the Indian and Sri Lankan coastlines and crippled the booming Thai tourism industry. That same year, in 2005, Hurricane Katrina destroyed homes and businesses alike and brought the Gulf Coast oil industry to a virtual standstill. In 2012, Hurricane Sandy wreaked $50 billion of economic damage on the eastern seaboard states. And in 2013, Typhoon Haiyan decimated the Philippines. The wars in Afghanistan and Iraq—while a boon

> **free trade** An international economic and political movement designed to help goods and services flow more freely across international boundaries.
>
> **General Agreement on Tariffs and Trade (GATT)** An international trade agreement that has taken bold steps to lower tariffs and promote free trade worldwide.

to the defense industry—have dampened the economic potential of both areas. With nationalism on the rise, and growing religious and ethnic tensions around the world, the global economy may continue to suffer collateral damage.[33]

1-6 BUSINESS AND YOU: MAKING IT PERSONAL

Whatever your career choice—from video game developer to real-estate agent, to web designer—business will affect your life. Both the broader economy and your own business skills will influence the level of your personal financial success. In light of these factors, making the right career choice can be a bit scary. But the good news is that experts advise graduating students to "Do what you love." This is a hardheaded strategy, not softhearted puffery. Following your passion makes dollars and sense in today's environment, which values less-routine abilities such as creativity, communication, and caring. These abilities tend to be more rewarding for most people than routine, programmable skills that computers can easily emulate. Following your passion doesn't guarantee a fat paycheck, but it does boost your chances of both financial and personal success.[34]

THE BIG PICTURE

Business today is complex, global, and faster moving than ever before. Looking forward, the rate of change seems likely to accelerate yet further. Although the full impact of the global economic crisis is still unclear, China and India seem poised to gain economic clout, raising worldwide competition to a whole new level. Technology will continue to change the business landscape. And a new focus on ethics and social responsibility will likely transform the role of business in society. This book will focus on the impact of change in every facet of business, from management to marketing, to money, with an emphasis on how the elements of business relate to each other and how business as a whole relates to you.

CAREERS IN BUSINESS

Manager of New Media

Work with marketing team to determine what motivates and inspires consumers. Lead development and execution of digital marketing campaigns across a variety of platforms to build a deep, meaningful, and genuine relationship with consumers. Develop and manage interactive viral campaigns, integrate interactive media into the overall business strategy. According to Salary.com, the median base salary for social media marketing managers in 2016 was $93,659, although there was significant variation based on company, location, industry, experience, and benefits. Most new media positions require experience in the field and a four-year degree in either business or communication. Many also prefer a master's degree in business (an MBA).

STUDY TOOLS 1

LOCATED AT BACK OF THE TEXTBOOK

☐ Rip-Out Chapter Review Card

☐ Gain unique perspectives on key concepts with new concept videos in the e-book

☐ Increase your comprehension with online homework and quizzes

☐ Study with existing flashcards and make your own

2 | Economics:
The Framework for Business

Rawpixel.com/Shutterstock.com

LEARNING OBJECTIVES

After studying this chapter, you will be able to:

2-1 Define economics and discuss the evolving global economic crisis

2-2 Analyze the impact of fiscal and monetary policy on the economy

2-3 Explain and evaluate the free market system and supply and demand

2-4 Explain and evaluate planned market systems

2-5 Describe the trend toward mixed market systems

2-6 Discuss key terms and tools to evaluate economic performance

Remember to visit **PAGE 37** for additional **STUDY TOOLS**

2-1 ECONOMICS: NAVIGATING A CRISIS

In September 2008, the United States plunged into a deep economic crisis. The banking system hovered on the edge of collapse. Property values plummeted, and home foreclosure rates soared. Massive layoffs put more than a million Americans out of work. By the end of the year, the stock market had lost more than a third of its value, and financial turmoil in the United States had sparked sequential economic shocks from Europe to South America, to Asia and beyond. The outlook was grim.

economy A financial and social system of how resources flow through society, from production to distribution, to consumption.

economics The study of the choices that people, companies, and governments make in allocating society's resources.

macroeconomics The study of a country's overall economic dynamics, such as the employment rate, the gross domestic product, and taxation policies.

How did this happen? Why? How could the economy get back on track?

Understanding these issues—and how the government, businesses, and individuals responded to them—requires understanding some basic definitions: The **economy** is essentially a financial and social system. It represents the flow of resources through society, from production to distribution, to consumption. **Economics** is the study of the choices that people, companies, and governments make in allocating those resources. The field of economics falls into two core categories: macroeconomics and microeconomics. **Macroeconomics** is the study of a country's overall economic dynamics, such as the employment rate, the gross domestic product, and taxation policies. While macroeconomic issues may seem abstract, they directly affect your day-to-day life, influencing key variables such as what jobs will be available for you, how much cash you'll actually take home after taxes, or how much you can buy with that cash in any given month. **Microeconomics** focuses on smaller economic units such as individual consumers, families, and individual businesses. Both macroeconomics and microeconomics have played an integral role in the global economic crisis.

2-1a Global Economic Crisis: How Did This Happen?

The seeds of the crisis were planted more than a decade ago, during a time of prosperity. Through the last half of the 1990s, America enjoyed unprecedented growth. Unemployment was low, productivity was high, inflation was low, and the real standard of living for the average American rose significantly. The American economy grew by more than $2.4 trillion, a jump of nearly 33% in just five years. But the scene changed for the worse when the dot-com bubble burst in 2000, followed by the 9/11 terrorist attacks in 2001. As the stock market dropped and unemployment rose, economic experts

> "Economics is very useful as a form of employment for economists."
>
> —JOHN KENNETH GALBRAITH, ECONOMIST

feared that the country was hovering on the brink of a full-blown recession.[1]

In an effort to avert recession by increasing the money supply and encouraging investment, the Federal Reserve—the nation's central bank—decreased interest rates from 6.5% in mid-2000 to 1.25% by the end of 2002. As a result, the economy was awash with money, but opportunities to invest yielded paltry returns. This is when *subprime mortgage loans* came into play. Most experts define subprime mortgages as loans to borrowers with low credit scores, high debt-to-income ratios, or other signs of a reduced ability to repay the money they borrow.

These subprime mortgage loans were attractive to borrowers and lenders alike. For the borrowers, getting a loan suddenly became a cinch, and for the

microeconomics The study of smaller economic units such as individual consumers, families, and individual businesses.

A Trillion Dollars? Say What?

Between stimulating the economy and managing the federal debt, "a trillion dollars" is a figure you may have heard a lot lately. But getting your mind around what that actually means may be a little tricky, since it's just so much money. To understand the true magnitude of a trillion dollars, consider this:

- If you had started spending a million dollars a day—every day, without fail—at the start of the Roman Empire, you still wouldn't have spent a trillion dollars by 2016; in fact, you'd have more than $250 billion left over.

- One trillion dollars, laid end-to-end, would stretch farther than the distance from the earth to the sun. You could also wrap your chain of bills more than 12,000 times around the earth's equator.

- If you were to fly a jet at the speed of sound, spooling out a roll of dollar bills behind you, it would take you more than 14 years to release a trillion dollars. But your plane probably couldn't carry the roll, since it would weigh more than one million tons.

Turning the economy around may take even more than a trillion dollars, but make no mistake when you hear those numbers thrown around on the news—a trillion dollars is an awful lot of money![2]

iStock.com/Selensergen

first time ever, hundreds of thousands of people could afford homes. The lenders were all too willing to give them mortgage loans, sometimes with little or no documentation (such as proof of income), and sometimes with little or no money down. As demand for homes skyrocketed, prices continued to rise year after year. Borrowers took on adjustable-rate loans assuming that when their loans adjusted up—usually sharply up—they could simply refinance their now-more-valuable homes for a new low starter rate and maybe even pull out some cash.

Subprime loans were attractive to lenders because they provided a higher return than many other investments, and—given the growth in housing prices—they seemed relatively low risk. Banks and investment houses invented a range of stunningly complex financial instruments to slice up and resell the mortgages as specialized securities. Hedge funds swapped the new securities, convinced that they were virtually risk-free. With a lack of regulation—or any other government oversight—financial institutions did *not* maintain sufficient reserves in case those mortgage-backed funds lost value.

And they did indeed lose value. In 2006, housing prices peaked, and in the months that followed, prices began falling precipitously (see Exhibit 2.1), dropping nearly 35% from the market peak in 2006 through the market trough in 2009. Increasing numbers of subprime borrowers found

themselves "upside down"—they owed their lenders more than the value of their homes. Once this happened, they couldn't refinance to lower their payments. Foreclosure rates climbed at an increasing pace. RealtyTrac, a leading online marketplace for foreclosure properties, reported that foreclosure rates were 33% higher in 2010 than they were in all of 2009. In 2011, the foreclosure rate dropped to the lowest level since 2007, when the recession began. And by January 2014, the inventory of foreclosed homes had experienced 16 consecutive months of year-to-year double-digit declines, signaling that the fragile economic recovery had finally taken hold.[3]

As mortgage values dropped, financial institutions began to feel the pressure—especially firms such as Bear Stearns that specialized in trading mortgage-backed securities, and firms such as Washington Mutual that focused on selling subprime mortgages. When financial institutions actually began to face collapse, a wave of fear washed over the entire banking industry. Banks became unwilling to lend money to each other or to clients, which meant that funds were not available for businesses to finance either day-to-day operations or longer-term growth. Company after company—from General Motors to Yahoo!, to American Express, to countless small employers—began to announce layoffs. The December 2008 unemployment rate hit 7.2%. About 2.6 million Americans lost their jobs in 2008,

> "The financial crisis is a stark reminder that transparency and disclosure are essential in today's marketplace."
>
> —U.S. SENATOR JACK REED

Exhibit 2.1
House Price Index

Source: Housing's Rise and Fall in 20 Cities, December 27, 2011, *The New York Times* website, http://www
.nytimes.com/interactive/2011/05/31/business/economy/case-shiller-index.html#city/IND20, accessed
January 25, 2012.

making 2008 the worst year for jobs since 1945. And the unemployment rate continued to rise, hitting 9.3% in 2009 and 9.6% in 2010, leading to total Great Recession job losses of nearly 8 million, many of which will never come back as the economy continues to change and old skills become obsolete.[4] The national average unemployment rate began to drop in late 2011 and continued to trend down throughout 2014, 2015, and 2016, another sign that the economic recovery has taken hold.

2-1b Moving in a Better Direction

Although the benefits were not immediately obvious in the face of a downward trend, the federal government and the Federal Reserve—known as "the Fed"—intervened in the economy at an unprecedented level to prevent total financial disaster. In March 2008, the Fed staved off bankruptcy at Bear Stearns. In early September 2008, the U.S. Department of the Treasury seized Fannie Mae and Freddie Mac, which owned about half of the U.S. mortgage market. A week later, the Fed bailed out tottering global insurance giant AIG with an $85 billion loan. But the bleeding continued.

The negative spiral spurred Congress to pass a controversial $700 billion economic bailout plan in early October 2008, called TARP (the Troubled Assets Relief Program). By the end of the year, the Treasury had spent the first half of that money investing in banks, although early results were imperceptible for the economy. Just as the Treasury began to release funds to the banks, GM and Chrysler, two of the Big Three U.S. automakers, announced they also desperately needed a bailout. Both firms suggested that

bankruptcy was imminent without government assistance. (Ford, the other member of the Big Three, also admitted to financial problems but claimed that it was not in the dire straits faced by its domestic competitors.) Facing the loss of more than 2.5 million jobs related to the auto industry, the Treasury agreed to spend a portion of what remained of the $700 billion in a partial auto industry bailout.[5] Although much of the public railed against the expensive government bailout program, by 2010 it appeared likely that TARP could end up costing taxpayers far less than anticipated, or even nothing, as insurance companies and banks began to break even, or in many cases earn profits, and pay back their government loans.[6]

As the new administration began, President Obama proposed, and Congress passed, an $825 billion economic stimulus package called the American Recovery and Reinvestment Act, designed to turn the economy around over the next two years. The plan included cutting taxes, building infrastructure, and investing $150 billion in green energy. In late 2011, the economy began to turn around at a very slow pace. Employment grew slowly for 49 months in a row—the best run since at least World War II. Although employment numbers improved, many people traded good-paying jobs for part-time work and/or lower-paying positions. This has constrained incomes and restrained consumer spending in the years since.[7]

All of these moves by the federal government and the Federal Reserve are part of fiscal and monetary policy.

2-2 MANAGING THE ECONOMY THROUGH FISCAL AND MONETARY POLICY

While the free market drives performance in the American economy, the federal government and the Federal Reserve can help *shape* performance. During the recent crisis, both the government and the Fed have taken proactive—some say heavy-handed—roles to mitigate this economic

> "Government does not solve problems; it subsidizes them."
>
> —U.S. PRESIDENT RONALD REAGAN

contraction. The overarching goal is controlled, sustained growth, and both fiscal and monetary policy can help achieve this objective.

2-2a Fiscal Policy

Fiscal policy refers to government efforts to influence the economy through taxation and spending decisions that are designed to encourage growth, boost employment, and curb inflation. Clearly, fiscal strategies are closely tied to political philosophy. But regardless of politics, most economists agree that lower taxes can boost the economy by leaving more money in people's pockets for them to spend or invest. Most also agree that government spending can boost the economy in the short term by providing jobs, such as mail carrier, bridge repairer, or park ranger; and in the long term by investing in critical public assets, such as a national renewable energy grid. Done well, both taxation and spending can offer economic benefits. The tricky part is finding the right balance between the two approaches. As American economist Henry Hazlitt pointed out, it's important to keep in mind that "[e]ither immediately or ultimately, every dollar of government spending must be raised through a dollar of taxation; once we look at the matter in this way, the supposed miracles of government spending will appear in another light."

2-2b Debt Ceiling/Fiscal Cliff

In mid-2011, the U.S. economy shuddered again as the news headlines screamed with dire warnings about a national or even international economic meltdown when we hit the federal *debt ceiling*. What did this mean? The debt ceiling is the maximum amount Congress lets the government borrow. In theory, this is meant to limit the amount that the government can borrow, but in practice, voting on the debt ceiling happens separately from voting on taxes and spending, so the debt ceiling ends up being mostly about whether the federal government can pay for debts that it has already incurred. Typically, debt ceiling hikes are fairly routine; in fact, Congress has raised the debt ceiling 74 times since 1962, and ten times since 2001, all with little or no notice. But as federal debt began to nudge the ceiling in 2011, it garnered unprecedented political and journalistic attention because various political groups saw the issue as an opportunity to further their political agenda. Those who wanted to raise the debt ceiling portrayed others as irresponsible buffoons who were willing to shut down the government simply to make a point without any real long-term change in spending. Those who did not want to raise the debt ceiling argued that the others are spendthrift bureaucrats who must learn to live within their means like the Americans who elected them.

After weeks of high-profile wrangling, Congress finally agreed to raise the debt ceiling, which temporarily averted a shutdown crisis, but the deal they reached to do so created the fiscal cliff. The *fiscal cliff* was a package of draconian across-the-board spending cuts and sharp tax hikes scheduled to hit at the same time that could dramatically decrease the U.S. budget deficit. Going over the *fiscal cliff* could potentially cripple the U.S. economy, and possibly even cause the United States to default on some of its debt, which could send world markets into a tailspin. But once again, Congress could not reach a reasonable long-term agreement, so they simply passed last-minute legislation that pushed the really tough tax and spending decisions farther down the road. The federal government actually did shut down for 16 days in October 2013 after much congressional squabbling failed to produce a budget agreement. The government reopened with passage of another temporary agreement that again delayed the tough fiscal choices. If the country continues to fracture along political lines, it may become increasingly difficult to reach a federal budget agreement, leading to more regular government shutdowns, such as the two very brief shutdowns at the start of 2018.[8]

Every year, the government must create a budget, or a financial plan, that outlines expected revenue from taxes and fees, and expected spending. If revenue is higher than spending, the government incurs a **budget surplus** (rare in recent years, but usually quite welcome!). If spending is higher than revenue, the government incurs a **budget deficit** and must borrow money to cover the shortfall. The sum of all the money borrowed over the years and not yet repaid is the total **federal debt**. Exhibit 2.2 shows

fiscal policy Government efforts to influence the economy through taxation and spending.

budget surplus Overage that occurs when revenue is higher than expenses over a given period of time.

budget deficit Shortfall that occurs when expenses are higher than revenue over a given period of time.

federal debt The sum of all the money that the federal government has borrowed over the years and not yet repaid.

iStock.com/Talaj

Exhibit 2.2
Federal Government Revenue and Expenses

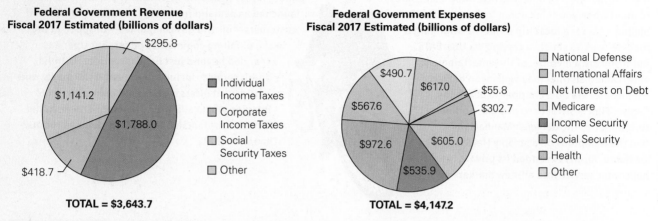

Federal Government Revenue
Fiscal 2017 Estimated (billions of dollars)

$295.8

$1,141.2

$1,788.0

$418.7

- ■ Individual Income Taxes
- □ Corporate Income Taxes
- □ Social Security Taxes
- □ Other

TOTAL = $3,643.7

Federal Government Expenses
Fiscal 2017 Estimated (billions of dollars)

$490.7

$617.0

$55.8

$567.6

$302.7

$972.6

$605.0

$535.9

- ■ National Defense
- □ International Affairs
- ■ Net Interest on Debt
- □ Medicare
- ■ Income Security
- □ Social Security
- □ Health
- □ Other

TOTAL = $4,147.2

Source: Economic Report of the president, 2017, Table B–19. Federal receipts and outlays, by major category, and surplus or deficit, fiscal years 1950–2017, https://www.whitehouse.gov/sites/default/files/docs /ERP_2016_Book_Complete%20JA.pdf, accessed April 19, 2018.

an estimate of key sources of revenue and key expenses for the federal government in 2017. Note that spending significantly outstrips receipts, creating a one-year budget deficit of more than a trillion dollars. Clearly, any additional spending without corresponding tax increases could dramatically increase the shortfall.

As of mid-2018, the total U.S. federal debt stood at more than $21 trillion and growing, a staggering $64,000+ for every U.S. citizen.[9]

The debt has only grown bigger every year since 1957, and the pace of growth will likely increase further in the wake of the economic crisis. This matters to each taxpayer because as the government repays the debt—not to mention paying the skyrocketing interest to finance this debt—less and less money will be available for other uses; services may be eliminated (e.g., student loans, veterans' benefits, housing subsidies), or taxes will soar, or perhaps even both.

Analysts agree that the federal tax reform that Congress passed in late 2017 will add an estimated $1.5 trillion to the deficit over ten years due to a decrease in corporate taxes from 35% to 21% and a decrease in individual income taxes.[10]

2-2c Monetary Policy

Monetary policy refers to actions that shape the economy by influencing interest rates and the supply of money. The Federal Reserve—essentially the central bank of the United States—manages U.S. monetary policy. For the first time in its history, the Fed has also taken an activist role in

bailing out and propping up shaky financial firms during the economic crisis. Other Fed functions include banking services for member banks and the federal government.

The Fed is headed by a seven-member Board of Governors. The president appoints each member of the Board to serve a single 14-year term—though a member can also complete a former member's unexpired term and still be appointed to a full term of his or her own. These terms are staggered, with one expiring every two years, so that no single president can appoint all of the members. This structure helps ensure that the Fed can act independently of political pressure.

In addition to setting monetary policy, the Board of Governors oversees the operation of the 12 Federal Reserve Banks that carry out Fed policies and perform banking services for **commercial banks** in their districts. Interestingly, the federal government does not own these Federal Reserve Banks. Instead, they're owned by the member commercial banks in their individual districts.

The president appoints one of the seven members of the Board of Governors to serve as its chair—a position so powerful that many consider him or her the second most powerful person on earth. For nearly 19 years, the chair was Alan Greenspan. When Greenspan retired in early 2006,

monetary policy Federal Reserve decisions that shape the economy by influencing interest rates and the supply of money.

commercial banks Privately owned financial institutions that accept demand deposits and make loans and provide other services for the public.

What Does It Really Mean to Call an Uber?

If you're like most people, the first thing that comes to mind when you think about "calling an Uber" is hailing a car for a local trip or maybe arranging a food delivery to satisfy a craving via UberEATS. But if you are a member of the entertainment elite, calling an Uber may well mean hailing a helicopter via UberChopper to get to the Cannes Film Festival or to avoid the bumper-to-bumper traffic between Manhattan and the Hamptons on a steamy New York weekend. Airbus expanded its private helicopter service into all-new markets by joining forces with Uber in 2016. The partnership was launched as demand from some of Airbus's traditional customers—oil and gas companies—dropped in the wake of falling commodity prices. But Uber has expanded beyond just helicopter rides. In India, Uber's services include on-demand rickshaws, and in Turkey, it offers on-demand boats. It's fun to imagine what calling an Uber might mean in the future—on-demand drones? On-demand robots? Time will tell.[11]

www.hollandfoto.net/Shutterstock.com

President Bush appointed economist Ben Bernanke to the chair role. Bernanke led the Fed's proactive efforts to turn the ailing economy around. In early 2014, the Senate confirmed economist Janet Yellen as new chair of the Fed. Yellen is the first female chair, and she has focused primarily on fighting unemployment by encouraging economic expansion. In late 2017, President Trump appointed Jerome Powell to succeed Janet Yellen as new chair of the Fed. Although analysts anticipate that Powell will continue Yellen's policies, he is quite different from recent Fed Chairs because he has a business background, rather than an academic background.

The core purpose of the Fed is to influence the size of the **money supply**—or the total amount of money within the overall economy. Clearly, you know what money is. But the formal definition of **money** is anything generally accepted as a medium of exchange, a measure of value, or a means of payment. The two most commonly used definitions of the money supply are M1 and M2:

- **M1:** All currency—paper bills and metal coins—plus checking accounts and traveler's checks.

- **M2:** All of M1 plus most savings accounts, money market accounts, and certificates of deposit (low-risk savings vehicles with a fixed term, typically less than one year).

By mid-2016, the M1 money supply totaled about $3.18 trillion, and the M2 version of the money supply totaled about $12.7 trillion. In practice, the term "money supply" most often refers to M2. (Note that credit cards are not part of the money supply, although they do have an unmistakable impact on the flow of money through the economy.)[12]

When the economy contracts, the Fed typically increases the money supply. If more money is available, interest rates usually drop, encouraging businesses to expand and consumers to spend. But when prices begin to rise, the Fed attempts to reduce the money supply. Ideally, if less money is available, interest rates will rise. This will reduce spending, which should bring inflation under control. Specifically, the Fed uses three key tools to expand and contract the money supply: open market operations, discount rate changes, and reserve requirement changes.

Open Market Operations This is the Fed's most frequently used tool. **Open market operations** involve buying and selling government securities, which include treasury bonds, notes, and bills. These securities are the IOUs the government issues to finance its deficit spending.

How do open market operations work? When the economy is weak, the Fed *buys* government securities on the open market. When the Fed pays the sellers of these securities, money previously held by the Fed is put into circulation. This directly stimulates spending. In addition, any of the additional funds supplied by the Fed that are deposited in banks will allow banks to make more loans, making

money supply The total amount of money within the overall economy.

money Anything generally accepted as a medium of exchange, a measure of value, or a means of payment.

M1 money supply Includes all currency plus checking accounts and traveler's checks.

M2 money supply Includes all of M1 money supply plus most savings accounts, money market accounts, and certificates of deposit.

open market operations The Federal Reserve function of buying and selling government securities, which include treasury bonds, notes, and bills.

Looking to Multiply Your Money? Look No Further Than Your Local Bank!

Everyone knows that banks help people save money, but most people don't realize that banks actually create money. While the process is complex, a simplified example illustrates the point. Say you deposit $5,000 in the bank. How much money do you have? Obviously, $5,000. Now imagine that your neighbor Anne goes to the bank for a loan. In line with Federal Reserve requirements, the bank must hold onto about 10% of its funds, so it loans Anne $4,500. She uses the money to buy a used car from your neighbor Jake, who deposits the $4,500 in the bank. How much money does Jake have? Clearly, $4,500. How much money do you have? Still, $5,000. Thanks to the banking system, our "money supply" has increased from $5,000 to $9,500. Multiply this phenomenon times millions of banking transactions, and you can see why cold, hard cash accounts for only about 10% of the total U.S. M2 money supply. But what happens if everyone goes to the bank at once to withdraw their money? The banking system would clearly collapse. And in fact, in 1930 and 1931, a run on the banks caused wave after wave of devastating bank failures. Panicked customers lost all their savings, ushering in the worst years of the Great Depression. To restore public confidence in the banking system, in

1933 Congress established the **Federal Deposit Insurance Corporation (FDIC)**. The FDIC insures deposits in banks and thrift institutions for up to $100,000 per customer, per bank. In the wake of the banking crisis, the FDIC temporarily increased its coverage to $250,000 per depositor at the end of 2008. Since the FDIC began operations on January 1, 1934, no depositor has lost a single cent of insured funds as a result of a bank failure.

Syda Productions/Shutterstock.com

credit more readily available. This encourages even more spending and further stimulates the economy.

When inflation is a concern, the Fed *sells* securities. Buyers of the securities write checks to the Fed to pay for securities they bought, and the Fed withdraws these funds from banks. With fewer funds, banks must cut back on the loans they make, credit becomes tighter, and the money supply shrinks. This reduces spending and cools off the inflationary pressures in the economy.

Open market operations are set by the aptly named Federal Open Market Committee, which consists of the seven members of the Board of Governors and 5 of the 12 presidents of the Federal Reserve district banks. Each year, the Federal Open Market Committee holds eight regularly scheduled meetings to make decisions about open market operations, although they do hold additional meetings when the need arises. Both businesses and markets closely watch Open Market Committee rate setting and outlook statements in order to guide decision making.

Discount Rate Changes Just as you can borrow money from your bank, your bank can borrow funds from the Fed. And just as you must pay interest on your loan, your bank must pay interest on loans from the Fed. The **discount rate** is the interest rate the Fed charges on

its loans to commercial banks. When the Fed reduces the discount rate, banks can obtain funds at a lower cost and use these funds to make more loans to their own customers. With the cost of acquiring funds from the Fed lower, interest rates on bank loans also tend to fall. The result: businesses and individuals are more likely to borrow money and spend it, which stimulates the economy. Clearly, the Fed is most likely to reduce the discount rate during recessions. In fact, during the early months of the financial crisis, the Fed cut the rate to less than 1%. The Fed kept the rate well below 1% throughout the recovery, eventually nudging it up at the end of 2015 and again at the end of 2016. If the recovery continues, The Fed is expected to continue raising rates slowly—*very* slowly. But in response to inflation— usually a sign of a rapidly expanding economy—the Fed usually increases the discount rate. In response, banks raise the interest rates they charge their customers. Fewer businesses and individuals are willing to take loans, which ultimately slows down the economy and reduces inflation.[13]

Federal Deposit Insurance Corporation (FDIC) A federal agency that insures deposits in banks and thrift institutions for up to $250,000 per customer, per bank.

discount rate The rate of interest that the Federal Reserve charges when it loans funds to banks.

Reserve Requirement Changes The Fed requires that all of its member banks hold funds, called "reserves," equal to a stated percentage of the deposits held by their customers. This percentage is called the **reserve requirement** (or required reserve ratio). The reserve requirement helps protect depositors who may want to withdraw their money without notice. Currently, the reserve requirement stands at about 10%, depending on the size and type of a bank's deposits. If the Fed increases the reserve requirement, banks must hold more funds, meaning they will have fewer funds available to make loans. This makes credit tighter and causes interest rates to rise. If the Fed decreases the reserve requirement, some of the funds that banks were required to hold become available for loans. This increases the availability of credit and causes interest rates to drop. Since changes in the reserve requirement can have a dramatic impact on both the economy and the financial health of individual banks, the Fed uses this tool quite infrequently.

Other Fed Functions In addition to monetary policy, the Fed has several other core functions, including regulating financial institutions and providing banking services both for the government and for banks. In its role as a regulator, the Fed sets and enforces rules of conduct for banks and oversees mergers and acquisitions to ensure fairness and compliance with government policy. The Fed will likely become even more proactive regarding regulation in the wake of the financial crisis. In its role as a banker for banks, the Fed coordinates the check-clearing process for checks on behalf of any banks that

"The U.S. economy is 70% based on consumer spending."

—*TIME* MAGAZ

are willing to pay its fees. And as the government's bank, the Fed maintains the federal government's checking account and keeps the U.S. currency supply in good condition.

2-3 CAPITALISM: THE FREE MARKET SYSTEM

It's a simple fact—more clear now than ever before—no one can get everything they want all of the time. We live in a world of finite resources, which means that societies must determine how to distribute resources among their members. An **economic system** is a structure for allocating limited resources. Over time and around the globe, nations have instituted different economic systems. But a careful analysis suggests that no system is perfect, which may explain why there isn't one standard approach. The next sections of this chapter examine each basic type of economic system and explore the trend toward mixed economies.

The economic system of the United States is called **capitalism**, also known as a "private enterprise system" or a "free market system." Brought to prominence by Adam Smith in the 1700s, capitalism is based on private ownership, economic freedom, and fair competition. One core capitalist principle is the paramount importance of individuals, innovation, and hard work. In a capitalist economy, individuals, businesses, or nonprofit organizations privately own the vast majority of enterprises (with only a small fraction owned by the government). These private-sector businesses are free to make their own choices regarding everything from what they will produce to how much they will charge, to whom they will hire and fire. Correspondingly, individuals are free to choose what they will buy, how much they are willing to pay, and where they will work.

To thrive in a free enterprise system, companies must offer value to

reserve requirement A rule set by the Fed, which specifies the minimum amount of reserves (or funds) a bank must hold, expressed as a percentage of the bank's deposits.

economic system A structure for allocating limited resources.

capitalism An economic system—also known as the private enterprise or free market system—based on private ownership, economic freedom, and fair competition.

Heartland Arts/Shutterstock.com

ADAM SMITH

Adam Smith (1723–1790) has often been called the "father of modern economics."

their customers—otherwise, their customers will choose to go elsewhere. Businesses must also offer value to their employees and suppliers in order to attract top-quality talent and supplies. As companies compete to attract the best resources and offer the best values, quality goes up, prices remain reasonable, and choices proliferate, raising the standard of living in the economy as a whole.

2-3a The Fundamental Rights of Capitalism

For capitalism to succeed, the system must ensure some fundamental rights—or freedoms—to all of the people who live within the economy.

- *The right to own a business and keep after-tax profits:* Remember that capitalism doesn't guarantee that anyone will actually *earn* profits. Nor does it promise that there won't be taxes. But if you do earn profits, you get to keep your after-tax income and spend it however you see fit (within the limits of the law, of course). This right acts as a powerful motivator for business owners in a capitalist economy; the lower the tax rate, the higher the motivation. The U.S. government strives to maintain low tax rates to preserve the after-tax profit incentive that plays such a pivotal role in the free enterprise system.

- *The right to private property:* This means that individuals and private businesses can buy, sell, and use property—which includes land, machines, and buildings—in any way that makes sense to them. This right also includes the right to will property to family members. The only exceptions to private property rights are minimal government restrictions designed to protect the greater good. You can't, for instance, use your home or business to produce cocaine, abuse children, or spew toxic smoke into the air.

- *The right to free choice:* Capitalism relies on economic freedom. People and businesses must be free to buy (or not buy) according to their wishes. They must be free to choose where to work (or not work) and where to live (or not live). Freedom of choice directly feeds competition, creating a compelling incentive for business owners to offer the best goods and services at the lowest prices. U.S. government trade policies boost freedom of choice by encouraging a wide array of both domestic and foreign producers to compete freely for our dollars.

- *The right to fair competition:* A capitalist system depends on fair competition among businesses to drive higher quality, lower prices, and more choices. Capitalism can't achieve its potential if unfair practices—such

ValeStock/Shutterstock.com

Which of the four degrees of competition does the soft drink market represent?

as deceptive advertising, predatory pricing, and broken contracts—mar the free competitive environment. The government's role is to create a level playing field by establishing regulations and monitoring the competition to ensure compliance.

2-3b Four Degrees of Competition

Although competition is essential for the free market system to function, not all competition works the same. Different industries experience different degrees of competition, ranging from pure competition to monopolies.

- **Pure competition** is a market structure with many competitors selling virtually identical products. Since customers can't (or won't) distinguish one product from another, no single producer has any control over the price. And new producers can easily enter and leave purely competitive markets. In today's U.S. economy, examples of pure competition have virtually disappeared. Agriculture probably comes closest—corn is basically corn, for example—but with the dramatic growth of huge corporate farms and the success of major agricultural cooperatives such as Sunkist and Sun-Maid, the number of competitors in agriculture has dwindled, and new farmers have trouble

> **pure competition** A market structure with many competitors selling virtually identical products. Barriers to entry are quite low.

entering the market. Not only that, segments of the agriculture market—such as organic farms and hormone-free dairies—have emerged with hit products that command much higher prices than the competition.

- **Monopolistic competition** is a market structure with many competitors selling differentiated products. (Caution! Monopolistic competition is quite different from a *monopoly*, which we will cover shortly.) Producers have some control over the price of their wares, depending on the value that they offer their customers. And new producers can fairly easily enter categories marked by monopolistic competition. In fact, in monopolistic competition, a successful product usually attracts new suppliers quite quickly. Examples of monopolistic competition include the clothing industry and the restaurant business.

Think about the clothing business, for a moment, in local terms. How many firms do you know that sell T-shirts? You could probably think of at least 50 without too much trouble. And the quality and price are all over the board: designer T-shirts can sell for well over $100, but plenty of options go for less than $10. How hard would it be to start your own T-shirt business? Probably not hard at all. In fact, chances are strong that you know at least one person who sells T-shirts on the side. In terms of product and price variation, number of firms, and ease of entry, the T-shirt business clearly demonstrates the characteristics of monopolistic competition.

- **Oligopoly** is a market structure with only a handful of competitors selling products that can be similar or different. The retail gasoline business and the car manufacturing industry, for instance, are both oligopolies, even though gas stations offer very similar products, and car companies offer quite different models and features. Other examples of oligopoly include the soft drink industry, the computer

GongTo/Shutterstock.com

In April 2016, the European Union filed antitrust charges against Google for forcing manufacturers to load 11 undeletable apps onto their Android-based smartphones. If Google is found guilty, it faces up to $7.5 billion in fines.

business, and network television. Breaking into a market characterized by oligopoly can be tough because it typically requires a huge upfront investment.

You could start making T-shirts in your kitchen, for instance, but you'd need a pretty expensive facility to start manufacturing cars. Oligopolies typically avoid intense price competition, since they have nothing to gain—every competitor simply makes less money. When price wars do flare up, the results can be devastating for entire industries.

- **Monopoly** is a market structure with just a single producer completely dominating the industry, leaving no room for any significant competitors. Monopolies usually aren't good for anyone but the company that has control, since without competition there isn't any incentive to hold down prices or increase quality and choices. Because monopolies can harm the economy, most are illegal according to federal legislation such as the Sherman Antitrust Act of 1890 and the Clayton Antitrust Act of 1914. Microsoft is the latest example of an industry giant that ran afoul of antimonopoly laws due to its position and policies in the software business. Even though Microsoft is not an actual monopoly, it was convicted of "monopolistic practices" that undermined fair competition.

However, in a few instances, the government not only allows monopolies but actually encourages them. This usually occurs when it would be too inefficient for each competitor to build its own infrastructure to serve the public. A **natural monopoly** arises. Public utilities

monopolistic competition
A market structure with many competitors selling differentiated products. Barriers to entry are low.

oligopoly A market structure with only a handful of competitors selling products that can be similar or different. Barriers to entry are typically high.

monopoly A market structure with one producer completely dominating the industry, leaving no room for any significant competitors. Barriers to entry tend to be virtually insurmountable.

natural monopoly A market structure with one company as the supplier of a product because the nature of that product makes a single supplier more efficient than multiple, competing ones. Most natural monopolies are government sanctioned and regulated.

Exhibit 2.3
The Supply Curve and Demand Curve

Quantity of Pizza Supplied per Day (in Thousands)

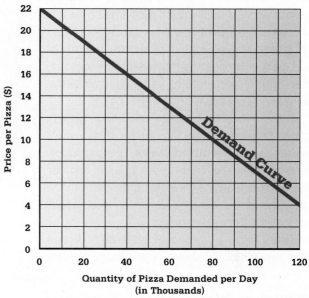

Quantity of Pizza Demanded per Day (in Thousands)

offer a clear example. Would it really make sense for even a handful of competitors to pipe neighborhoods separately for water? Clearly, that's not practical. Just imagine the chaos! Instead, the government has granted exclusive rights—or monopolies—to individual companies for limited geographic areas and then regulated them (with mixed results) to ensure that they don't abuse the privilege. In addition to natural monopolies, the government grants patents and copyrights, which create artificial monopoly situations (at least temporarily) to encourage innovation.

2-3c Supply and Demand: Fundamental Principles of a Free Market System

In a free market system, the continual interplay between buyers and sellers determines the selection of products and prices available in the economy. If a business makes something that few people actually want, sales will be low, and the firm will typically yank the product from the market. Similarly, if the price of a product is too high, low sales will dictate a price cut. But if a new good or service becomes a hit, you can bet that similar offerings from other firms will pop up almost immediately (unless barriers—such as government-granted patents—prevent new entrants). The concepts of supply and demand explain how the dynamic interaction between buyers and sellers directly affects the range of products and prices in the free market.

Supply **Supply** refers to the quantity of products that producers are willing to offer for sale at different market prices. Since businesses seek to make as much profit as possible, they are likely to produce more of a product that commands a higher market price and less of a product that commands a lower price. Think about it in terms of pizza. Assume it costs a local restaurant about $5 to make a pizza. If the market price for pizza hits, say, $20, you can bet that restaurant will start cranking out pizza. But if the price drops to $6, the restaurant has much less incentive to focus on pizza and will probably invest its limited resources in cooking other more pricey dishes.

The relationship between price and quantity from a supplier standpoint can be shown on a graph called the **supply curve**. The supply curve maps quantity on the *x*-axis (or horizontal axis) and price on the *y*-axis (or vertical axis). In most categories, as the price rises, the quantity produced rises correspondingly, yielding a graph that curves up as it moves to the right. Exhibit 2.3 shows a possible supply curve for pizza.

Demand **Demand** refers to the quantity of products that consumers are willing to buy at

supply The quantity of products that producers are willing to offer for sale at different market prices.

supply curve The graphed relationship between price and quantity from a supplier standpoint.

demand The quantity of products that consumers are willing to buy at different market prices.

different market prices. Since consumers generally seek to get the products they need (or want) at the lowest possible prices, they tend to buy more products with lower prices and fewer products with higher prices. Pizza and tacos, for instance, are both popular meals. But if pizza costs a lot less than tacos, most people will get pizza more often than tacos. Likewise, if the price of pizza were out of hand, people would probably order tacos (or some other option) more often, reserving their pizza-eating for special occasions.

The relationship between price and quantity from a demand standpoint can be shown on a graph called the **demand curve**. Like the supply curve, the demand curve maps quantity on the *x*-axis and price on the *y*-axis. But different from the supply curve, the demand curve for most goods and services slopes downward as it moves to the right, since the quantity demanded tends to drop as prices rise. Exhibit 2.3 shows how a demand curve for pizza could look.

Equilibrium Price It's important to remember that supply and demand don't operate in a vacuum. The constant interaction between the two forces helps determine the market price in any given category. In theory, market prices adjust toward the point where the supply curve and the demand curve intersect (see Exhibit 2.4). The price associated with this point of intersection—the point where the quantity demanded equals the quantity supplied—is called the **equilibrium price**, and the quantity associated with this point is called the "equilibrium quantity."

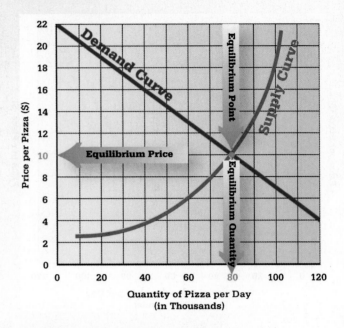

Exhibit 2.4
Equilibrium

Quantity of Pizza per Day
(in Thousands)

Price per Pizza ($)

Demand Curve

Supply Curve

Equilibrium Point

Equilibrium Price

Equilibrium Quantity

2-4 PLANNED ECONOMIES: SOCIALISM AND COMMUNISM

demand curve The graphed relationship between price and quantity from a customer demand standpoint.

equilibrium price The price associated with the point at which the quantity demanded of a product equals the quantity supplied.

socialism An economic system based on the principle that the government should own and operate key enterprises that directly affect public welfare.

In capitalist economies, private ownership is paramount. Individuals own businesses, and their personal fortunes depend on their success in the free market. But in planned economies, the government plays a more heavy-handed role in controlling the economy. The two key categories of planned economies are socialism and communism.

2-4a Socialism

Socialism is an economic system based on the principle that the government should own and operate key enterprises that directly affect public welfare, such as utilities, telecommunications, and healthcare. Although the official government goal is to run these enterprises in the best interest of the overall public, inefficiencies and corruption often interfere with effectiveness. Socialist economies also tend to have higher taxes, which are designed to distribute wealth more evenly through society. Tax revenues typically fund services that citizens in free enterprise systems would have to pay for themselves in countries with lower tax rates. Examples range from free childcare to free university education, to free public healthcare systems. Critics of the recent government intervention in the U.S. economy believe that the new moves have pushed us too far in a socialist direction.

Most Western European countries—from Sweden to Germany, to the United Kingdom—developed powerful socialist economies in the decades after World War II. But more recently, growth in these countries has languished. Although many factors have contributed to the slow-down, the impact of high taxes on the profit incentive and lavish social programs on the work incentive has

Waste Not, Want Not

For years upon years, parents and grandparents have counseled their children with this sage advice: "Waste not, want not." Yet somewhat ironically, this age-old wisdom applies just as much to the on-demand economy, which puts idle resources to work for the benefit of society. This growing trend has radically changed consumer expectations in regards to sustainability. According to trendspotting experts, younger consumers increasingly expect the companies they buy from to create new sources of value and to eliminate wasted resources in creative ways. The reason: "When you can pay to use cars by the minute, access office space by the hour, eat your food cooked by your neighbors and more, then 'traditional' business processes suddenly start to look even more wasteful." Trendwatching. com calls the upending of existing processes to reduce waste

capacity capture. As this trend grows, smart and dynamic businesses will need to use extraordinary creativity to reengineer their approach to sustainability— all while delivering ongoing profitability.[14]

---

clearly played a role. Potential entrepreneurs may migrate to countries that let them keep more of their profits, and workers with abundant benefits may find themselves losing motivation. In late 2010, many of these economies imposed stiff austerity measures to control government spending, eliminating some public benefits many took for granted.

2-4b Communism

Communism is an economic and political system that calls for public ownership of virtually all enterprises, under the direction of a strong central government. The communist concept was the brainchild of political philosopher Karl Marx, who outlined its core principles in his 1848 *Communist Manifesto*. The communism that Marx envisioned was supposed to dramatically improve the lot of the worker at the expense of the super-rich.

But countries that adopted communism in the 1900s—most notably the former Soviet Union, China, Cuba, North Korea, and Vietnam—did not thrive. Most imposed authoritarian governments that suspended individual rights and choices. People were unable to make even basic choices such as where to work or what to buy. Without the free market to establish what to produce, crippling shortages and surpluses developed. Corruption infected every level of government. Under enormous pressure from their own people and the rest of the world, communism began to collapse across the Soviet Union and its satellite nations. At the

end of the 1980s, it was replaced with democracy and the free market. Over the past two decades, China has also introduced significant free market reforms across much of the country, fueling a torrid growth rate that has only recently begun to slow. And in the 1990s, Vietnam launched free market reforms, stimulating rapid, sustained growth. The remaining communist economic systems—North Korea and Cuba—continue to falter, their people facing drastic shortages and even starvation.

2-5 MIXED ECONOMIES: THE STORY OF THE FUTURE

In today's world, pure economies—market or planned— are practically nonexistent, since each would fall far short of meeting the needs of its citizens. A pure market economy would make insufficient provision for the old, the young, the sick, and the environment. A pure planned economy would not create enough value to support its people over the long term. Instead, most of today's nations have **mixed economies**, falling somewhere along

communism An economic and political system that calls for public ownership of virtually all enterprises, under the direction of a strong central government.

mixed economies Economies that embody elements of both planned and market-based economic systems.

photocritical/Shutterstock.com

Big Brother Is Watching . . . or Is He?

One of the underlying principles of communism and socialism is that most people are willing to sacrifice self-interest for the good of the overall society. That may be true, but a new study suggests that may *only* be true if other people are watching. Researchers at the psychology department of a major university recently ran an experiment whereby they changed the price list at an honor system–based coffee bar in the faculty and staff break room. The prices themselves remained unchanged, but each week the photocopied picture above the prices varied between flowers and the eyes of real faces. The faces changed, but the eyes on the faces always looked directly at the observer. During the weeks with faces on the list, staff members paid nearly three times as much for their drinks as during the weeks with flowers. These results suggest that self-interest may be more natural and comfortable than fairness for most people. We're happy to be generous, but only when we think someone is watching—even if that someone is just a cutout picture of a face with observant eyes. Our deep-seated interest in our own well-being over everyone else's may be one reason why socialism and communism haven't created as much wealth over the long term as free enterprise has.[15]

rangizzz//Shutterstock.com

a spectrum that ranges from pure planned at one extreme to pure market at the other.

Even the United States—one of the most market-oriented economies in the world—does not have a *pure* market economy. The various departments of the government own a number of major enterprises, including the postal service, schools, parks, libraries, entire systems of universities, and the military. In fact, the federal government is the nation's largest employer, providing jobs for more than 4 million Americans. And—although the government does not directly *operate* firms in the financial sector—the federal government has become part owner in a number of financial institutions as part of the recent bailouts. The government also intervenes extensively in the free market by creating regulations that stimulate competition and protect both consumers and workers. Regulations are likely to become stronger in the wake of the economic crisis.[16]

Over the past 30 years, most economies of the world have begun moving toward the market end of the spectrum. Government-owned businesses have converted to private ownership via a process called **privatization**. Socialist governments have reduced red tape, cracked down on corruption, and created new laws to protect economic rights. Extravagant human services—from free healthcare to education subsidies—have shrunk. And far-reaching tax reform has created new incentives for both domestic and foreign investment in once-stagnant planned economies.[17]

Unfortunately, the price of economic restructuring has been a fair amount of social turmoil in many nations undergoing market reforms. Countries from France to China have experienced sometimes violent demonstrations in response to social and employment program cutbacks. Change is challenging, especially when it redefines economic winners and losers. But countries that have taken strides toward the market end of the spectrum—from small players such as the Czech Republic, to large players such as China—have seen the payoff in rejuvenated growth rates that have raised the standard of living for millions of people.

Ekaterina Bykova/Shutterstock.com

Karl Marx (1818–1883) was a Prussian-born theorist who helped develop the political ideology of communism.

privatization The process of converting government-owned businesses to private ownership.

What in the World Happened to Capitalism?

Recent research from Harvard University suggests that young people today no longer believe that the capitalist "American Dream" of prior decades will deliver for them. In fact, the research showed that only 42% of younger Americans said they support capitalism, and just 19% identified themselves as capitalists. One young student explained, "We don't trust capitalism because we don't see ourselves getting ahead." As capitalism has lost young people, socialism has gained an **increasing number of young followers. Perhaps this should not be surprising, given the passionate millennial support for the Bernie Sanders 2016 presidential campaign. But as the text highlights, every economic system has advantages and disadvantages. Perhaps Winston Churchill had it right when he said, "Capitalism is the worst economic system, except for all the others."[18]**

2-6 EVALUATING ECONOMIC PERFORMANCE: WHAT'S WORKING?

Clearly, economic systems are complex—very complex. So you probably won't be surprised to learn that no single measure captures all the dimensions of economic performance. To get the full picture, you need to understand a range of terms and measures, including gross domestic product, employment level, the business cycle, inflation rate, and productivity.

2-6a Gross Domestic Product

Real **gross domestic product**, or GDP, measures the total value of all final goods and services produced within a nation's physical boundaries over a given period of time, adjusted for inflation. (Nominal GDP does not include an inflation adjustment.) All domestic production is included in the GDP, even when the producer is foreign-owned. The U.S. GDP, for instance, includes the value of Hyundai Sonatas built in Alabama, even though Hyundai is a Korean firm. Likewise, the Indonesian GDP includes the value of Gap clothing manufactured in Indonesian factories, even though Gap is an American firm.

GDP is a vital measure of economic health. Businesspeople, economists, and political leaders use GDP to measure the economic performance of individual nations and to compare the growth among nations. Interestingly, GDP levels tend to be somewhat understated since they don't include any illegal activities—such as paying undocumented nannies and gardeners, or selling illegal drugs—which can represent a significant portion of some countries' production. The GDP also ignores legal goods that are not reported to avoid taxation, plus output produced within households.[19] Check out Chapter 3 for a survey of the world's key economies according to total GDP and GDP growth rate.

2-6b Employment Level

The overall level of employment is another key element of economic health. When people have jobs, they have money, which allows them to spend and invest, fueling economic growth. Most nations track employment levels largely through the **unemployment rate**, which includes everyone age 16 and older who doesn't have a job and is actively seeking one. The U.S. unemployment rate climbed precipitously through the Great Recession, rising from 5.8% in 2008 to 9.3% in 2009, then dropping to 8.1% in 2012 as the economy began its glacially slow turnaround. Unemployment didn't move below 8% until September of 2012, and then it dropped slowly throughout 2013 to end the year at an annual average of 7.4% as the recovery began to take hold. Unemployment continued dropping, hitting 4.7% in December 2016. The unemployment rate dropped throughout 2017, ending the year at 4.1%, and remaining at 4.1% through mid-2018.[20] But unfortunately, about half of the 8 million jobs

gross domestic product (GDP) The total value of all final goods and services produced within a nation's physical boundaries over a given period of time.

unemployment rate The percentage of people in the labor force over age 16 who do not have jobs and are actively seeking employment.

lost during the recession were middle-income jobs, and about half of the new jobs created since have been in low-wage sectors of the economy, leading to stagnant household incomes.[21]

Interestingly, some unemployment is actually good—it reflects your freedom to change jobs. If you have an awful boss, for instance, you may just quit. If you quit, are you unemployed? Of course you are. Are you glad? You probably are, and in normal times, the chances are good that you'll find another position that's a better fit for you. This type of job loss is called *frictional unemployment,* and it tends to be ultimately positive. *Structural unemployment*, on the other hand, is usually longer term. This category encompasses people who don't have jobs because the economy no longer needs their skills. In the United States, growing numbers of workers in the past decade have found themselves victims of structural unemployment as manufacturing jobs have moved overseas. Often their only option is expensive retraining. Two other categories of unemployment are *cyclical*, which involves layoffs during recessions, and *seasonal*, which involves job loss related to the time of year. In some areas of the country, construction and agricultural workers are seasonally unemployed, but the best example may be the department-store Santa who has a job only during the holiday season!

2-6c The Business Cycle

The **business cycle** is the periodic contraction and expansion that occur over time in virtually every economy. But the word "cycle" may be a little misleading, since it implies that the economy contracts and expands in a predictable pattern. In reality, the phases of the cycle are different each time they happen, and—despite the efforts of countless experts—no one can accurately predict when changes will occur or how long they will last. Those who make the best guesses stand to

business cycle The periodic contraction and expansion that occur over time in virtually every economy.

contraction A period of economic downturn, marked by rising unemployment and falling business production.

recession An economic downturn marked by a decrease in the GDP for two consecutive quarters.

depression An especially deep and long-lasting recession.

recovery A period of rising economic growth and employment.

expansion A period of robust economic growth and high employment.

Raising a child born in 2015 from birth to age 17 costs about $233,610 (not including college!)—almost $14,000 every year.

—U.S. DEPARTMENT OF AGRICULTURE

make fortunes, but bad bets can be financially devastating. The two key phases of the business cycle are contraction and expansion, shown in Exhibit 2.5.

■ **Contraction** is a period of economic downturn, marked by rising unemployment. Businesses cut back on production, and consumers shift their buying patterns to more basic products and fewer luxuries. The economic "feel-good factor" simply disappears. Economists declare an official **recession** when GDP decreases for two consecutive quarters. A **depression** is an especially deep and long-lasting recession. Fortunately, economies seldom spiral into severe depressions, thanks in large part to proactive intervention from the government.

The last depression in the United States was the Great Depression of the 1930s. Whether a downturn is mild or severe, the very bottom of the contraction is called the "trough," as shown in Exhibit 2.5.

■ **Recovery** is a period of rising economic growth and increasing employment following a contraction. Businesses begin to expand. Consumers start to regain confidence, and spending begins to rise. The recovery is essentially the transition period between contraction and expansion.

■ **Expansion** is a period of robust economic growth and high employment. Businesses expand to capitalize on emerging opportunities. Consumers are optimistic and confident, which fuels purchasing, which fuels production, which fuels further hiring. As Exhibit 2.5 demonstrates, the height of economic growth is called the peak of the expansion. The U.S. economy had the longest growth spurt on record during the ten-year period from 1991 to 2001. After a relatively mild slowdown in 2001–2002, the U.S. economy again expanded for several years before it plunged into a full-blown recession in 2008.[22]

Exhibit 2.5
The Business Cycle

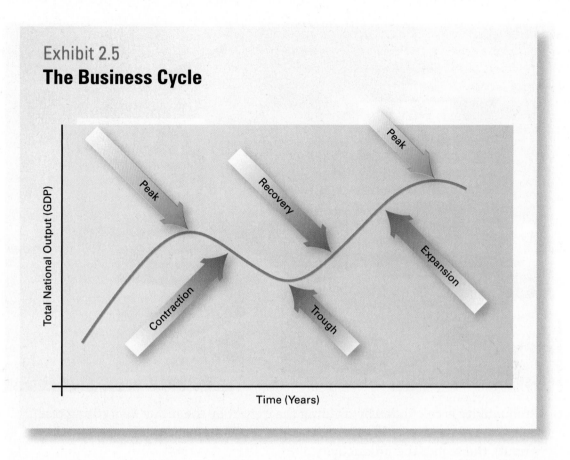

2-6d **Price Levels**

The rate of price changes across the economy is another basic measure of economic well-being. **Inflation** means that prices, on average, are rising. Similar to unemployment, a low level of inflation is not so bad. It reflects a healthy economy—people have money, and they are willing to spend it. But when the Federal Reserve—the nation's central bank—manages the economy poorly, inflation can spiral out of control, which can lead to **hyperinflation**, when average prices increase more than 50% per month. In Hungary, for example, inflation in its unstable, post–World War II economy climbed so quickly that prices doubled every 15 hours in 1946. More recently, prices in the war-torn former Yugoslavia doubled every 16 hours between October 1993 and January 1994.

When the rate of price increases slows down, the economy is experiencing **disinflation**, which was the situation in the United States in the mid-1990s and more recently in the second half of 2008. But when prices actually decrease, the economy is experiencing **deflation**, typically a sign of economic trouble that goes hand-in-hand with very high unemployment. People don't have money and simply won't spend unless prices drop. During the Great Depression in the 1930s, the U.S. economy experienced deflation, with prices dropping 9% in 1931 and nearly 10% in 1932. Despite some economic turmoil, inflation in the United States was relatively low from 2000 to 2007, hovering at around 3%. But inflation picked up in the first half of 2008, only to fall during the first months of the economic crisis, remaining low throughout 2009 and 2010. Inflation jumped to an annual average of 3.2% in 2011 but dropped to an annual average of 1.5% in 2013. The rate dropped further to 0.8% in 2014 and 0.7% in 2015, but rose to 2.1% in 2016.[23]

The government uses two major price indexes to evaluate inflation: the **consumer price index (CPI)** and the **producer price index (PPI)**. The

inflation A period of rising average prices across the economy.

hyperinflation An average monthly inflation rate of more than 50%.

disinflation A period of slowing average price increases across the economy.

deflation A period of falling average prices across the economy.

consumer price index (CPI) A measure of inflation that evaluates the change in the weighted-average price of goods and services that the average consumer buys each month.

producer price index (PPI) A measure of inflation that evaluates the change over time in the weighted-average wholesale prices.

Productivity is calculated by dividing the output by the input. Everything else being equal, the more chocolate pieces (output) produced per hour of work (input), the higher the productivity.

CPI measures the change in weighted-average price over time in a consumer "market basket" of goods and services that the average person buys each month. The U.S. Bureau of Labor Statistics creates the basket—which includes hundreds of items such as housing, transportation, haircuts, wine, and pet care—using data from more than 30,000 consumers. Although the market basket is meant to represent the average consumer, keep in mind that the "average" includes a lot of variation, so the CPI may not reflect your personal experience. For example, as a college student, you may be painfully sensitive to increases in tuition and the price of textbooks—a fact the authors of this particular textbook fully realize! But tuition and textbook prices aren't a big part of the "average" consumer's budget, so increases in these prices have a relatively small impact on the CPI.

The PPI measures the change over time in weighted-average wholesale prices, or the prices that businesses pay each other for goods and services. Changes in the PPI can sometimes predict changes in the CPI because producers tend to pass on price increases (and sometimes also price decreases) to consumers within a month or two of the changes.

2-6e Productivity

Productivity refers to the relationship between the goods and services that an economy produces and the resources needed to produce them. The amount of output—goods and services—divided by the amount of input (e.g., hours worked) equals productivity. The goal, of course, is to produce more goods and services, using fewer hours and other inputs. A high level of productivity typically correlates with healthy GDP growth, while low productivity tends to correlate with a more stagnant economy.

Over the past couple of decades, the United States has experienced strong productivity growth, due largely to infusions of technology that help workers produce more output, more quickly. But keep in mind that productivity doesn't measure quality. That's why it's so important to examine multiple measures of economic health rather than relying on simply one or two dimensions.

productivity The basic relationship between the production of goods and services (output) and the resources needed to produce them (input) calculated via the following equation: output/input = productivity.

THE BIG PICTURE

From a business standpoint, one key goal of economics is to guide your decision making by offering a deeper understanding of the broad forces that affect both your business and your personal life. Knowing even basic economic principles can help you make better business decisions in virtually every area—from production, to marketing, to accounting, to name just a few—regardless of your specific function or level within an organization.

But you won't find an economics department within many (if any) businesses—rather, you'll find people across the organization applying economic theories and trends to their work, even in the face of continual economic flux. As you read through the other chapters in this book, take a moment to consider both the macroeconomic and microeconomic forces that affect each area you study. You're likely to find a surprising number of examples.

CAREERS IN BUSINESS

Business Economist

Collect, analyze, and distribute data to explain economic phenomena and forecast economic trends, particularly with regard to supply and demand. Create and present clear, concise reports on economic trends to senior management on a monthly basis. Manage and motivate a small team of financial analysts and statisticians.

STUDY TOOLS 2

LOCATED AT BACK OF THE TEXTBOOK

☐ Rip-Out Chapter Review Card

☐ Gain unique perspectives on key concepts with new concept videos in the e-book

☐ Increase your comprehension with online homework and quizzes

☐ Study with existing flashcards and make your own

3 | The World Marketplace:
Business without Borders

LEARNING OBJECTIVES

After studying this chapter, you will be able to:

3-1 Discuss business opportunities in the world economy

3-2 Explain the key reasons for international trade

3-3 Describe the tools for measuring international trade

3-4 Analyze strategies for reaching global markets

3-5 Discuss barriers to international trade and strategies to surmount them

3-6 Describe the free-trade movement, and discuss key benefits and criticisms

Remember to visit
PAGE 56
for additional
STUDY TOOLS

3-1 AN UNPRECEDENTED OPPORTUNITY

As access to technology skyrockets and barriers to trade continue to fall, individual economies around the world have become more interdependent than ever before. The result is a tightly woven global economy marked by intense competition and huge, shifting opportunities. The long-term potential for U.S. business is enormous. Although the global economic crisis caused the world GDP to contract in 2009 for the first time since World War II, compared with average increases of about 3.5% per year since 1946, world GDP growth turned positive again in 2010 and 2011, continuing a slow, steady pace through 2016. The global upswing in the economic activity continued through 2017 with more growth forecast through 2018.[1] See Exhibit 3.1 for a sampling of some specific higher- and lower-growth countries.

A quick look at population trends validates the global business opportunity, especially in developing nations. In mid-2018, the world's population stands at about 7.6 billion people. With more than 326 million people, the United States accounts for less than 4.5% of the world's total population. More than 7.3 billion people live beyond our borders, representing more than 95% of potential customers for U.S. firms. But most of these nations remain behind the United States in terms of development and prosperity, posing considerable challenges for foreign firms. (In other words, most of their populations may not have the resources to buy even basic goods and services and their infrastructure and technology may not be developed

> "The world is more malleable than you think and it's waiting for you to hammer it into shape."
>
> —BONO, MUSICIAN AND HUMANITARIAN

EXHIBIT 3.1 SELECTED POPULATION AND GDP FIGURES

Nation	Population*	Per Capita GDP (U.S. Dollars)**	GDP Growth Rate***
China	1,413,990,958	$16,600	+6.8%
India	1,351,209,574	$7,200	+6.7%
European Union	516,195,432	$39,200	+1.9%
United States	326,325,888	$59,500	+2.2%
Indonesia	266,255,980	$12,400	+5.2%
Brazil	210,565,134	$15,500	+.7%

* China Population. (2018-01-23). Retrieved 2018-04-21, from http://worldpopulationreview.com/countries/china-population/, accessed April 21, 2018; India Population. (2018-01-23). Retrieved 2018-04-21, from http://worldpopulationreview.com/countries/india-population/, accessed April 21, 2018; United States Population. (2018-02-09). Retrieved 2018-04-21, from http://worldpopulationreview.com/countries/united states-population/ accessed April 21, 2018; Indonesia Population. (2018-01-23). Retrieved 2018-04-21, from http://worldpopulationreview.com/countries/indonesia-population/accessed April 21, 2018; Brazil Population. (2018-01-23). Retrieved 2018-04-21, from http://worldpopulationreview.com/countries/brazil-population/accessed April 21, 2018; CIA world factbook population 2017 estimate.

** *CIA World Factbook* GDP 2017 per capita estimates.

*** *CIA World Factbook* GDP 2017 growth estimates.[2]

The Next Big Thing

In early 2016, financial experts noticed that American-based global corporations, such as Alphabet (the parent corporation of Google), General Motors, and Apple, were hoarding enormous—even unprecedented—amounts of cash. To put it into context, with its $80 billion in cash reserves, Google could have bought Goldman Sachs, American Express, most of MasterCard, Costco, eBay, or a quarter of Amazon. So why was this happening? There are several possible reasons:

- **Tax avoidance:** Holding onto cashing and shifting it among subsidiaries can lower a firm's overall tax bill.

- **Acquisitions:** Buying the best firms and the best talent has become increasingly competitive. Rivals can be scared off if your firm seems to have limitless resources to spend.

- **Emergencies:** In a highly risky economic environment, extra cash is always helpful.

Even taken together, these three reasons don't come close to explaining the sheer size of the cash overload. So what gives? Some financial experts speculate that senior executives at these industries believe that the next big thing may be around the corner, and they are hoarding cash to invest in it. All of the transformative innovations of the past century—cars, for instance, or the emergence of the Internet—have required enormous investments in infrastructure, machinery, and technology. in many cases, the most successful companies were the ones that could make these investments early on. It's impossible to know if the corporate cash hoards are foreshadowing transformative innovation, but if they are, it bodes well for all of us. Jet packs, anyone? Flying cars? Or maybe something else yet to be imagined?[3]

ra2studio/Shutterstock.com

enough to support contemporary business.) Exhibit 3.1, a comparison of population, GDP growth rate, and per capita GDP for the world's six largest nations, highlights some of the discrepancies. Note that even though U.S. consumers clearly have money, China and India represent a much bigger opportunity in terms of both sheer size and economic growth.

3-1a Global Business's Momentum

Multinational businesses boomed throughout the 1990s and early 2000s. Powerful globe-spanning companies created economies of scale, dictated consumer trends in everything from movies to lingerie design, and crossed borders at will to create record-breaking profits. Many multinational corporations are still thriving—especially technology and consumer product superstars. In the past five years, however, the overall profits of multinationals have dropped by 25%. In 2017, however, solid global growth ignited across the global economy, and analysts expect momentum to continue through 2018 across both mature markets and emerging economies. Looking farther forward, an improvement in labor force skills, digitization, and especially stronger productivity growth may help sustain growth and provide better conditions for international businesses to thrive over the next decade.[4]

3-1b Emerging Economies

Analysts anticipate that emerging markets, which include most of South America, Africa, and Asia (with the exception of Japan) will experience even stronger growth in 2018 than they did in 2017. Emerging markets represent about 40% of the global economy, which is about twice as much as 25 years ago. And emerging market economies should grow faster than developed markets every year through 2021.

Several key factors will contribute to the economic growth. First, the population is rapidly growing in most emerging economies, with the dramatic exception of China. Second, many emerging economies are ripe for productivity growth (more output per worker) which in some cases may be as simple as installing lights so that workers can keep working after dark. Second, the middle class is growing explosively in key emerging markets—specifically, China and India. China may overtake the United States as having the largest middle class by 2020, and India just a year later. The middle class is economically important from a consumption standpoint because the middle class has more discretionary income and tends to spend it, which translates into significant business opportunities.[5]

Most experts seem to see a pattern of emergence in Southeast Asia and Africa. Vietnam, the Philippines, and Bangladesh are all benefitting from the migration of labor-intensive, low-wage manufacturing jobs away from China. As more jobs are created, these locations will likely begin to develop sturdy middle classes and stabilized economies. A number of sub-Saharan African nations, such as Nigeria, Kenya, and Angola, also represent an enormous opportunity for economic growth. According to a Standard Bank of Africa report, in the 11 countries that represent 50% of Africa's GDP, there are 15 million households in the middle class. The Standard Bank of Africa predicts that this number will grow to 42 million by 2030. This kind of prediction has spurred gigantic firms such as Kellogg's, Procter & Gamble, and Walmart to capitalize on the opportunity and make multimillion-dollar investments in Africa. Unfortunately, as is often the case, the opportunity comes hand in hand with massive challenges. Many African countries are rife with security risks, political instability, and flat-out civil war. Africa also faces seemingly intractable infrastructure problems, including insufficient access to fresh water and electricity. A silver lining, however, is that solving these infrastructure issues could itself be a new opportunity for investors and entrepreneurs.

3-1c Cell Phones and Economic Growth

The growing number of people with cell phones offers an interesting indicator of economic growth. Several recent studies have found that if a country increases cell phone penetration by 10 percentage points, GDP will likely increase by anywhere from +0.5% to +1.2%. That may seem small, but it equates to somewhere between $49 and $118 billion for an economy the size of China. In other words, when the percentage of the population with cell phones goes up, the entire economy benefits.

Not surprisingly, cell phone penetration in India and China is skyrocketing. China currently boasts the world's largest base of cell phone users—more than one billion—and the growth will likely continue. India's subscriber base just crossed the 1 billion mark; it has grown explosively over the past five years and seems likely to follow suit in the next decade. The growth may well continue until China and India hit the 100%+ cell phone penetration rates that characterize a number of developed nations, such as Taiwan, Hong Kong, Germany, and Argentina, which have more than one phone per person. In the United States, Europe, and Japan, cell phones followed landlines,

A teenage boy uses a cell phone in Salunkwadi, a rural village in central India.

Karves/Shutterstock.com

but large swaths of developing nations aren't bothering to build conventional phone service. Rather, they're moving directly to cell phone networks. This trend is particularly marked across Africa, where cell phone penetration rates continue to grow explosively. Most of the penetration growth involves basic-function phones, but smartphone penetration is growing as well, providing access to the Internet for the first time ever to huge swaths of the population. David Knapp, general director of Motorola Vietnam, points out that many developing nations "can leapfrog technology." And Vietnamese microentrepreneur Nguyen Huu Truc says, "It's no longer something that only the rich can afford. Now, it's a basic means of communication." As more people get the chance to get connected, better communication will likely feed economic growth. According to Muhammad Yunis, founder of Grameen Bank in Bangladesh, "A mobile phone is almost like having a

> 49.9% of households in India have a toilet, while more than 53% own a mobile phone.
>
> —CNN

card to get you out of poverty in a couple of years." The upshot is that millions of people worldwide will have a higher standard of living.[6]

3-2 KEY REASONS FOR INTERNATIONAL TRADE

Companies engage in global trade for a range of reasons beyond the obvious opportunity to tap into huge and growing new markets. The benefits include better access to factors of production, reduced risk, and an inflow of new ideas.

- *Access to factors of production:* International trade offers a valuable opportunity for individual firms to capitalize on factors of production that simply aren't present in the right amount for the right price in each individual country. India, China, and the Philippines, for example, attract multibillion-dollar investments because of their large cohort of technically skilled university graduates who work for about one-fifth the pay of comparable American workers. Russia and the OPEC nations offer a rich supply of oil, and Canada, like other forested nations, boasts an abundant supply of timber. The United States offers plentiful capital, which is less available in other parts of the world. International trade helps even out some of the resource imbalances among nations.

- *Reduced risk:* Global trade reduces dependence on one economy, lowering the economic risk for multinational firms. When the Japanese economy entered a deep, sustained slump in the 1990s, for instance, Sony and Toyota thrived through their focus on other, healthier markets around the world. But a word of caution is key: as national economies continue to integrate, an economic meltdown in one part of the world can have far-reaching impact. Major foreign banks, for example, were badly burned by the U.S. subprime market mess, due to heavy investments in U.S. mortgage markets.

- *Inflow of innovation:* International trade can also offer companies an invaluable source of new ideas. Japan, for instance, is far ahead of the curve regarding cell phone service. Japanese cell phone "extras," including games, ringtones, videos, and stylish new accessories, set the standard for cell service around the world. In Europe, meanwhile, consumers are showing a growing interest in traditional and regional foods, which allow them to picture where their ingredients come from. Companies with a presence in foreign markets experience budding trends like these firsthand, giving them a jump in other markets around the world.[7]

> Africa holds 40% of the world's strategic raw materials, including gold, iron ore, and oil.
>
> —*TIME* MAGAZINE

3-2a Competitive Advantage

Beyond individual companies, industries tend to succeed on a worldwide basis in countries that enjoy a competitive advantage. But to understand competitive advantage, you need to first understand how **opportunity cost** relates to international trade. When a country produces more of one good, it must produce less of another good (assuming that resources are finite). The value of the second-best choice—the value of the production that a country gives up in order to produce the first product—represents the opportunity cost of producing the first product.

A country has an **absolute advantage** when it can produce more of a good than other nations, using the same amount of resources. China, for example, has an absolute advantage in terms of clothing production, relative to the United States. But having an absolute advantage isn't always enough. Unless they face major trade barriers, the industries in any country tend to produce products for which they have a **comparative advantage**—meaning that they tend to turn out those goods that have the lowest opportunity cost compared to other countries. The United States, for instance, boasts a comparative advantage versus most countries in movie and television program production; Germany has a comparative advantage in the production of high-performance cars; and South Korea enjoys a comparative advantage in electronics.

But keep in mind that comparative advantage seldom remains static. As technology changes and the workforce evolves (through factors such as education and experience), nations may gain or lose comparative

opportunity cost The opportunity of giving up the second-best choice when making a decision.

absolute advantage The benefit a country has in a given industry when it can produce more of a product than other nations using the same amount of resources.

comparative advantage The benefit a country has in a given industry if it can make products at a lower opportunity cost than other countries.

advantage in various industries. China and India, for example, are both seeking to build a comparative advantage versus other nations in technology production by investing in their infrastructure and their institutions of higher education.

3-3 GLOBAL TRADE: TAKING MEASURE

After a decade of robust growth, global trade began slowing in 2007, due largely to turbulence in the worldwide financial markets. In 2008, the rate of growth in world trade slid below 5% as the global recession tightened its grip. In 2009, global trade plummeted nearly 25% in U.S. dollar terms, and 12% in terms of overall volume from the 2008 level, the largest single-year drop since World War II. In 2010, global trade volume surged 13.8% but expanded a more modest +5.0% in 2011. In 2012, the growth rate dropped to +2.3% but increased a modest +2.1% in 2013. Economists saw an increase of +4.7% in 2014, rather sluggish growth of +2.8% in 2015, and a further slowdown in 2016. All told, the past few years' numbers lag behind the turbo-charged growth rates of much of the past two decades. Measuring the impact of international trade on individual nations requires a clear understanding of balance of trade, balance of payments, and exchange rates.[8]

3-3a Balance of Trade

The **balance of trade** is a basic measure of the difference between a nation's exports and imports. If the total value of exports is higher than the total value of imports, the country has a **trade surplus**. If the total value of imports is higher than the total value of exports, the

Most apparel today is produced outside of the United States.

country has a **trade deficit**. Balance of trade includes the value of both goods and services, and it incorporates trade with all foreign nations. Although a trade deficit signals the wealth of an economy that can afford to buy huge amounts of foreign products, a large deficit can be destabilizing. It indicates, after all, that as goods and services flow into a nation, money flows out—a challenge with regard to long-term economic health. The United States has had an overall trade deficit since 1976, and as the American appetite for foreign goods has grown, the trade deficit has ballooned. But that growth may slow over the next few years if demand remains sluggish in response to the global economic crisis.

3-3b Balance of Payments

Balance of payments is a measure of the total flow of money into or out of a country. Clearly, the balance of trade plays a central role in determining the balance of payments. But the balance of payments also includes other financial flows such as foreign borrowing and lending, foreign aid payments and receipts, and foreign investments. A **balance of payments surplus** means that more money flows in than out, while a **balance of payments deficit** means that more money flows out than in. Keep in mind that the balance of payments typically corresponds to the balance of trade because trade is, in general, the largest component.

3-3c Exchange Rates

Exchange rates measure the value of one nation's currency relative to the currency of other nations. While the exchange rate does not directly measure global commerce, it certainly has a powerful influence on how global trade affects individual nations and their trading partners. The exchange rate of a given currency must be expressed in terms of another currency. The table below shows some

balance of trade A basic measure of the difference in value between a nation's exports and imports, including both goods and services.

trade surplus Overage that occurs when the total value of a nation's exports is higher than the total value of its imports.

trade deficit Shortfall that occurs when the total value of a nation's imports is higher than the total value of its exports.

balance of payments A measure of the total flow of money into or out of a country.

balance of payments surplus Overage that occurs when more money flows into a nation than out of that nation.

balance of payments deficit Shortfall that occurs when more money flows out of a nation than into that nation.

exchange rate A measurement of the value of one nation's currency relative to the currency of other nations.

examples of how the exchange rate can influence the economy, using the dollar and the euro. In 2012, for example, a number of currencies underwent value swings versus the U.S. dollar (e.g., the E.U. euro, the Japanese yen, the Brazilian real, the Indian rupee, the Australian dollar, and the Venezuelan bolivar). One result was multibillion-dollar earnings hits against U.S. corporations with a strong international presence, including automotive giants Ford and General Motors. Many firms opt to present their earnings reports stripped of the effects of currency translations, but in today's global economy, that clearly offers a misleading picture of performance.[9]

Strong Dollar versus Euro: Who Benefits? (Example: $1.00 = 1.20 euros)	Weak Dollar versus Euro: Who Benefits? (Example: $1.00 = 0.60 euros)
U.S. travelers to Europe: Their dollars can buy more European goods and services.	*European travelers to the United States:* Their dollars buy more American goods and services.
American firms with European operations: Operating costs—from buying products to paying workers—are lower.	*European firms with American operations:* Operating costs—from buying products to paying workers—are lower.
European exporters: Their products are less expensive in the United States, so Europe exports more, and we import more.	*American exporters:* Their products are less expensive in Europe, so we export more, and Europe imports more.

3-3d Countertrade

A complete evaluation of global trade must also consider exchanges that don't actually involve money. A surprisingly large chunk of international commerce—possibly as much as 25%—involves the barter of products for products rather than for currency. Companies typically engage in **countertrade** to meet the needs of customers who don't have access to hard currency or credit, usually in developing countries. Individual countertrade agreements range from simple barter to a complex web of exchanges that end up meeting the needs of multiple parties. Done poorly, countertrading can be a confusing nightmare for everyone involved. But done well, countertrading is a powerful tool for gaining customers and products that would not otherwise be available.[10] Not surprisingly, barter opportunities tend to increase during economic downturns. In 2009, for example, ads began to appear both in Russian newspapers and online, such as one that offered "2,500,000 rubles'

countertrade International trade that involves the barter of products for products rather than for currency.

worth of premium underwear for any automobile," and another that offered "lumber in Krasnoyarsk for food or medicine."[11]

3-4 SEIZING THE OPPORTUNITY: STRATEGIES FOR REACHING GLOBAL MARKETS

There is no one "right way" to seize the opportunity in global markets. In fact, the opportunity may not even make sense for every firm. While international trade can offer new profit streams and lower costs, it also introduces a higher level of risk and complexity to running a business. Being ready to take on the challenge can mean the difference between success and failure.

Firms ready to tap the opportunity have a number of options for how to move forward. One way is to seek foreign suppliers through outsourcing and importing. Another possibility is to seek foreign customers through exporting, licensing, franchising, and direct investment. These market development options fall in a spectrum from low cost–low control to high cost–high control, as shown in Exhibit 3.2. In other words, companies that choose to export products to a foreign country spend less to enter that market than companies that choose to build their own factories. But companies that build their own factories have a lot more control than exporters over how their business unfolds. Keep in mind that profit opportunity and risk—which vary along with cost and control—also play a critical role in how firms approach international markets.

Smaller firms tend to begin with exporting and move along the spectrum as the business develops. But larger firms may jump straight to the strategies that give them more control over their operations. Large firms are also likely to use a number of different approaches in different countries, depending on the goals of the firm and the

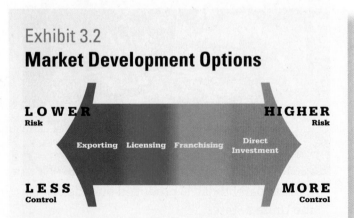

Exhibit 3.2
Market Development Options

LOWER Risk | HIGHER Risk

Exporting   Licensing   Franchising   Direct Investment

LESS Control | MORE Control

structure of the foreign market. Regardless of the specific strategy, most large companies—such as General Electric, Nike, and Disney—both outsource with foreign suppliers and sell their products to foreign markets.

3-4a Foreign Outsourcing and Importing

Foreign outsourcing means contracting with foreign suppliers to produce products, usually at a fraction of the cost of domestic production. H&M, for instance, relies on a network for manufacturers around the globe, mostly in less developed parts of the world, including Kenya, Cambodia, Indonesia, Myanmar, Sri Lanka, and Bangladesh. Apple depends on firms in China and Taiwan to produce the iPhone. And countless small companies contract with foreign manufacturers as well. The key benefit, of course, is dramatically lower wages, which drive down the cost of production.

But while foreign outsourcing lowers costs, it also involves significant risk. Quality control typically requires very detailed specifications to ensure that a company gets what it actually needs. Another key risk of foreign outsourcing involves social responsibility. A firm that contracts with foreign producers has an obligation to ensure that those factories adhere to ethical standards. Deciding what those standards should be is often quite tricky, given different cultures, expectations, and laws in different countries. And policing the factories on an ongoing basis can be even harder than determining the standards. But companies that don't get it right face the threat of significant consumer backlash in the United States and Europe. This has been a particular issue with products produced in China. In the recent past, for instance, product defects forced U.S. firms to recall a host of Chinese-produced toys, including Thomas the Tank Engine trains that were coated with toxic lead paint, ghoulish fake eyeballs that were filled with kerosene, and Polly Pocket dolls that posed a swallowing hazard. And in 2013, Greenpeace released a study that showed that the bulk of children's clothing produced in China—the world's largest exporter of textiles—contains hazardous levels of toxic chemicals.[12]

Many Americans have become personally familiar with the quality/cost tradeoff as a growing number of companies have outsourced customer service to foreign call centers. Research suggests that the approximate cost of offering a live, American-based, customer service agent averages about $7.50 per call, while outsourcing those calls to live agents in another country drops the average cost down to about $3.25 per call. But customers end up paying the difference in terms of satisfaction, reporting high levels of misunderstanding, frustration, and inefficiency. A number of firms—such as jetBlue and Amazon.com—have enjoyed the best of both worlds by outsourcing customer service calls to U.S. agents who work from their own homes.[13]

Importing means buying products from overseas that have already been produced, rather than contracting with overseas manufacturers to produce special orders. Imported products, of course, don't carry the brand name of the importer, but they also don't carry as much risk. Pier 1 Imports, a large retail chain, has built a powerful brand around the importing concept, creating stores that give the customer the sense of a global shopping trip without the cost or hassle of actually leaving the country.

3-4b Exporting

Exporting is the most basic level of international market development. It simply means producing products domestically and selling them abroad. Exporting represents an especially strong opportunity for small and mid-sized companies. In Tennessee, for instance, Heritage Glass, a small firm that has manufactured glass since the Civil War, plans to reopen a factory that was shuttered for two years, to capitalize on strong demand for patterned glass from the Philippines, Europe, and South America.[14]

3-4c Foreign Licensing and Foreign Franchising

Foreign licensing and foreign franchising, the next level of commitment to international markets, are quite similar. **Foreign licensing** involves a domestic firm granting a foreign firm the rights to produce and market its product or to use its trademark/patent rights in a defined geographical area. The company that offers the rights, or the *licensor*, receives

Dmitry Melnikov/Shutterstock.com

foreign outsourcing (also contract manufacturing) Contracting with foreign suppliers to produce products, usually at a fraction of the cost of domestic production.

importing Buying products domestically that have been produced or grown in foreign nations.

exporting Selling products in foreign nations that have been produced or grown domestically.

foreign licensing Authority granted by a domestic firm to a foreign firm for the rights to produce and market its product or to use its trademark/patent rights in a defined geographical area.

As the World Turns . . .

Around the world, people between the ages of 15 and 30 make up about a quarter of the population. Beyond their age, these individuals have a number of other factors in common. They grew up during the dawn of social media and the smartphone, and they witnessed the global financial meltdown of the late 2000s. As a group, they are wealthier and likely to live longer than any previous generation. They also tend to be brainier thanks to more advanced education and better nutrition practices. The elite among them, such as 29-year-old Dropbox co-founder Arash Ferdowsi, have changed the world. But many others face challenging hurdles. Globally, average youth unemployment sat at 13% in 2016, compared to an overall rate of 5.9%. And young people in some countries are facing even tougher numbers. A sampling:

Country	Youth Unemployment
Brazil	16%
France	25%
Italy	40%
Greece	48%
Spain	48%
South Africa	63%

Research shows that the effects of youth unemployment last well into adulthood in terms of both work habits and earning potential. Even more importantly, the talents and skills of this generation will be wasted if such high unemployment levels persist on a global level.[15]

Bogdan Khmelnytskyi/Shutterstock.com

a fee from the company that buys the rights, or the *licensee*. This approach allows firms to expand into foreign markets with little or no investment, and it also helps circumvent government restrictions on importing in closed markets. But maintaining control of licensees can be a significant challenge. Licensors also run the risk that unethical licensees may become their competitors, using information that they gained from the licensing agreement. Foreign licensing is especially common in the food and beverage industry. The most high-profile examples include Coke and Pepsi, which grant licenses to foreign bottlers all over the world.

Foreign franchising is a specialized type of licensing. A firm that expands through foreign franchising, called a *franchisor*, offers other businesses, or *franchisees*, the right to produce and market its products if the franchisee agrees to specific operating requirements—a complete package of how to do business. Franchisors also often offer their franchisees management guidance, marketing support, and even financing. In return, franchisees pay both a start-up fee and an ongoing percentage of sales

> **foreign franchising** A specialized type of foreign licensing in which a firm expands by offering businesses in other countries the right to produce and market its products according to specific operating requirements.

4kclips/Shutterstock.com

Foreign franchisers offer franchisees the rights to produce and market their products. According to Franchise Direct, hoteliers Marriott International, Wyndham Hotels & Resorts, and Hilton Hotels & Resorts were among the top global franchises for 2017.

to the franchisor. One key difference between franchising and licensing is that franchisees assume the identity of the franchisor. A McDonald's franchise in Paris, for instance, is clearly a McDonald's, not, say, a Pierre's Baguette outlet that also carries McDonald's products.

3-4d Foreign Direct Investment

Direct investment in foreign production and marketing facilities represents the deepest level of global involvement. The cost is high, but companies with direct investments have more control over how their business operates in a given country. The high-dollar commitment also represents significant risk if the business doesn't go well. Most direct investment takes the form of either acquiring foreign firms or developing new facilities from the ground up. Another increasingly popular approach is strategic alliances or partnerships that allow multiple firms to share risks and resources for mutual benefit.

Foreign acquisitions enable companies to gain a foothold quickly in new markets. In 2009, for example, Italian carmaker Fiat took over struggling U.S. auto giant Chrysler, with plans to more fully exploit the American market in the wake of the Great Recession. A number of other global giants, such as Microsoft, General Electric, and Nestlé, tend to follow a foreign acquisition strategy.[16]

Developing new facilities from scratch—or "offshoring"—is the most costly form of direct investment. It also involves significant risk. But the benefits include complete control over how the facility develops and the potential for high profits, which makes the approach attractive for corporations that can afford it. Intel, for instance, built a $2.5 billion specialized computer chip manufacturing plant in northeastern China. And foreign car companies, from German Daimler-Benz to Korean Hyundai, to Japanese Toyota, have built factories in the southern United States.[17]

Joint ventures involve two or more companies joining forces—sharing resources, risks, and profits, but not merging companies—to pursue specific opportunities. A formal, long-term agreement is usually called a **partnership**, while a less formal, less encompassing agreement is usually called a **strategic alliance**. Joint ventures are a popular, though controversial, means of entering foreign markets. Often a foreign company connects with a local firm to ease its way into the market. In fact, some countries, such as India and Malaysia, require that foreign investors have local partners. But research from Harvard finance professor Mihir Desai finds that joint ventures between multinational firms and domestic partners can be more costly and less rewarding than they initially appear. He and his team suggest that they make sense only in countries that require local political and cultural knowledge as a core element of doing business.[18]

> "Obstacles are those frightful things you see when you take your eyes off your goal."
>
> —HENRY FORD, FOUNDER OF FORD MOTOR COMPANY

3-5 BARRIERS TO INTERNATIONAL TRADE

Every business faces challenges, but international firms face more hurdles than domestic firms. Understanding and surmounting those hurdles is the key to success in global markets. Most barriers to trade fall into the following categories: sociocultural differences, economic differences, and legal/political differences. As you think about these barriers, keep in mind that each country has a different mix of barriers. Often countries with the highest barriers have the least competition, which can be a real opportunity for the first international firms to break through.

3-5a Sociocultural Differences

Sociocultural differences include differences among countries in language, attitudes, and values. Some specific, and perhaps surprising, elements that affect business include nonverbal communication, forms of address, attitudes toward punctuality, religious celebrations and customs, business practices, and expectations regarding meals and gifts. Understanding and responding to sociocultural factors are vital for firms that operate in multiple countries. But since the differences often operate at a subtle level, they can undermine relationships before anyone is aware that it's happening. The best way to jump over sociocultural barriers is to conduct thorough consumer research, cultivate firsthand knowledge, and practice extreme sensitivity. The payoff can be a sharp competitive edge. Hyundai, for instance, enjoys a whopping 18% share of the

direct investment (or foreign direct investment) When firms either acquire foreign firms or develop new facilities from the ground up in foreign countries.

joint ventures When two or more companies join forces—sharing resources, risks, and profits, but not actually merging companies—to pursue specific opportunities.

partnership A voluntary agreement under which two or more people act as co-owners of a business for profit.

strategic alliance An agreement between two or more firms to jointly pursue a specific opportunity without actually merging their businesses. Strategic alliances typically involve less formal, less encompassing agreements than partnerships.

sociocultural differences Differences among cultures in language, attitudes, and values.

passenger car market in India. It beats the competition with custom features that reflect Indian culture, such as elevated rooflines to provide more headroom for turban-wearing motorists.[19]

3-5b Economic Differences

Before entering a foreign market, it's critical to understand and evaluate the local economic conditions. Key factors to consider include population, per capita income, economic growth rate, currency exchange rate, and stage of economic development. But keep in mind that low scores for any of these measures don't necessarily equal a lack of opportunity. In fact, some of today's biggest opportunities are in countries with low per capita income. For example, the Indian division of global giant Unilever gets 50% of its sales from rural India by selling products to individual consumers in tiny quantities, such as two-cent sachets of shampoo. The rural Indian market has been growing so dramatically that in 2010, the chair of Hindustan Unilever declared, "What we have done in the last 25 years we want to do it in the next two years," scaling up the reach of its consumer products from about 250,000 rural retail outlets to about 750,000. In a recent TED Talk, the chair of Hindustan Unilever passionately argued that including value, purpose, and sustainability in top-level decision-making is not just savvy—it's the only way to run a twenty-first-century business responsibly. And Hewlett-Packard has recently joined forces with Unilever to give microdistributors in rural India the ability to check prices and place orders online from "what are now distinctively offline villages and regions." Also capitalizing on the rapid growth and increased demand, Samsung has introduced Guru, a mobile phone that can be charged with solar power, to rural India. Other mobile companies are scrambling to keep up.[20]

Effectively serving less developed markets requires innovation and efficiency. Emerging consumers often need different product features, and they almost always need lower costs. C. K. Prahalad, an influential business scholar, believed that forward-thinking companies can make a profit in developing countries if they make advanced technology affordable. Many markets are simply so large that high-volume sales can make up for low profit margins.

Overall, the profit potential is clear and growing. And as consumers in developing countries continue to gain income—although at a much slower pace in the wake of the economic crisis—companies that established their brands early will have a critical edge over firms that enter the market after them.

Infrastructure should be another key economic consideration when entering a foreign market. Infrastructure refers to a country's physical facilities that support economic activity. It includes basic systems in each of the following areas:

- Transportation (e.g., roads, airports, railroads, and ports)
- Communication (e.g., TV, radio, Internet, and cell phone coverage)
- Energy (e.g., utilities and power plants)
- Finance (e.g., banking, checking, and credit)

The level of infrastructure can vary dramatically among countries. In Africa, for instance, only 28.7% of the population has Internet access, compared to 88% in North America. In Vietnam and Thailand, many consumers buy products directly from vendors in small boats, compared to firmly grounded stores in Europe. Although credit card purchases are still relatively low in much of the world, particularly in Asia, recent growth has been explosive and will probably continue for the next few years.[21]

3-5c Political and Legal Differences

Political regimes obviously differ around the world, and their policies have a dramatic impact on business. The specific laws and regulations that governments create around business are often less obvious, yet they can still represent a significant barrier to international trade. To compete effectively—and to reduce risk—managers must carefully evaluate these factors and make plans to respond to them both now and as they change.

Laws and Regulations International businesses must comply with international legal standards, the laws of their own countries, and the laws of their host countries. This can be a real challenge since many developing countries change business regulations with little notice and less publicity. The justice system can pose another key challenge, particularly with regard to legal enforcement of ownership and contract rights. Since 2003, the World Bank has published a "Doing Business" report that ranks the ease of doing business for small and medium-sized companies in 190 different countries. The 2016 "Doing Business" report showed that New Zealand leads in the ease of doing business, followed by Singapore, Denmark, Hong Kong SAR, Korea, Norway, the United Kingdom, the United States, and Sweden. Brunei Darussalam was the individual economy that improved the most in terms of the ease of doing business. Overall, the Eastern Europe and Central Asia regions continued to show a faster rate of improvement than any other regions according to "Doing Business"

infrastructure A country's physical facilities that support economic activity.

Familiar Favorites with a Brand New Twist

Travel around the world, and you're likely to see American fast-food franchisees in virtually every city. Although you'll surely recognize the names of these fast-food behemoths, you may not be as familiar with the food that they serve, since many of the dishes have been completely changed in response to local culture.

Burger King:

- **Japan:** A limited-time offer of a Whopper with 15 strips of bacon added. Soon after, pigs were listed in the Endangered Species Registry in Japan (just kidding).

- **Austria:** X-tra Long Burger (sub sandwich–length burger with three beef patties topped with either chilli cheese or BBQ sauce AND onion rings).

- **Egypt:** Cheesy Whopper (a Whopper with a patty of deep-fried, breaded cheese on the beef).

- **United Kingdom:** Sprout Surprise Whopper. In case your Whopper tastes *too* good, this version adds a disk made of breaded Brussels sprouts and swiss cheese (surprise!).

Pizza Hut:

- **Japan:** Crust stuffed with shrimp nuggets and injected with mayonnaise.

- **South Korea:** Crust filled with sweet potato mousse.

- **China:** Lemon-flavored salmon pastry roll and scallop croquettes with crushed seaweed.

- **Middle East:** Crown Crust (a pizza/cheeseburger hybrid studded with "cheeseburger gems," which are cheeseburger sliders attached to the outside of a meaty pizza that's topped with lettuce and tomato and drizzled with "special sauce," served with a side of Pepto Bismol).

- **Singapore:** Double Decker Pizza: The second layer is comprised of turkey and ham rolls topped with mango mayonnaise (for the truly calorie deprived).

KFC:

- **China:** Spicy tofu chicken rice, rice porridge breakfast (congee).

- **India:** Chana Snacker (a chickpea burger topped with Thousand Island sauce).

- **Philippines:** Double Down Dog (a hot dog wrapped in a fried chicken bun).

McDonald's:

- **India:** Paneer Salsa Wrap (cottage cheese with Mexican-Cajun coating).

- **Australia:** Bacon and Egg Roll ("rashers of quality bacon and fried egg").

- **Brazil:** Cheese Quiche.

- **Kuwait:** Veggie Surprise Burger (no detailed description ... yikes!).[22]

- **Austria:** McItaly Adagio burger topped with "eggplant mousse" and chopped almonds.

- **Italy:** Nutella Burger (a sweet bun filled with a chocolate and hazelnut spread). This one sounds yummy!

Joe Raedle/Getty Images News/Getty Images

indicators. The "Doing Business" project examines the ease of doing business from ten different angles, including the ease of dealing with construction permits, paying taxes, and enforcing contracts.[23] The key benefit of an effective legal system is that it reduces risk for both domestic and foreign businesses.

Bribery, the payment of money for favorable treatment, and corruption, the solicitation of money for favorable treatment, are also major issues throughout the world. While bribery and corruption are technically illegal in virtually every major country, they are often accepted as a standard way of doing business. Regardless, U.S. corporations and American citizens are subject to prosecution by U.S. authorities for offering bribes in any nation. See Chapter 4 for more details.

Political Climate The political climate of any country deeply influences whether that nation is attractive to foreign business. Stability is crucial. A country subject to strife from civil war, riots, or other violence creates huge additional risk for foreign business. Yet, figuring out how to operate in an unstable environment, such as Russia, Bolivia, or the Middle East, can give early movers a real advantage. Grant Winterton, Coca-Cola's regional manager for Russia, commented to *Time* magazine that "the politics do concern us." But having snagged 50% of the $1.9 billion carbonated-soft-drink market, he concludes that "the opportunity far outweighs the risk." Poor enforcement of intellectual property rights across international borders is another tough issue for business. The Business Software Alliance's piracy-tracking study found that worldwide

Troubled Waters

Planet Earth does not produce more fresh water—it simply recycles what it has—which isn't nearly enough in light of the planet's exploding human population; in fact, according to the World Health Organization, more than 2.4 million people die every year from lack of access to clean water, which is not surprising, given that 1 in 10 people lack access to clean water. Amazingly, the problem only stands to worsen. By 2050, one in five developing countries will face water shortages, many of them severe. By 2030, China, the world's most populous country, may no longer be self-sufficient in terms of wheat and corn production. Clearly, the growing water shortage is a human crisis, but it also will be a business crisis. Obviously, food and beverage companies depend on water. But when it comes right down to it, every industry from pharmaceuticals to semiconductors, to mining, to clothing manufacturing depends on water at some point in its supply or usage chain. Investment in clean water can pay off—big time. According to Water .org, every $1 invested in water and sanitation provides a $4 economic return. *Fortune* magazine suggests that agricultural firms can begin preparing now by investing in the development of GMO crops, precision agriculture, and high-tech irrigation. According to brand consultancy *Interbrand*, other businesses would also be wise to prepare by designing and executing an enterprise-wide strategy for water stewardship—not just for their own operations but for their entire value chains.[24]

Fabien Monteil/Shutterstock.com

piracy rates hover at about 42%, with piracy rates in emerging markets towering over those in mature markets—68% versus 24%. The total value of software theft hit a record $63.4 billion. The highest-piracy countries are Georgia, Zimbabwe, Moldova, and Libya, all 90% or higher. Somewhat ironically, business decision makers admit to pirating software more frequently than other computer users do.[25]

International Trade Restrictions National governments also have the power to erect barriers to international business through a variety of international trade restrictions. The arguments for and against trade restrictions—also called **protectionism**—are summarized below. As you read, note that most economists find the reasons to eliminate trade restrictions much more compelling than the reasons to create them.

Just as trade restrictions have a range of motivations, they can take a number of different forms.

The most common trade restrictions are tariffs, quotas, voluntary export restraints, and embargoes.

- **Tariffs** are taxes levied against imports. Governments tend to use protective tariffs either to shelter fledgling industries that couldn't compete without help, or to shelter industries that are crucial to the domestic economy. In 2009, Egypt imposed tariffs on sugar, and the United States levied new tariffs on Chinese goods—including mattress springs and electrodes—that it contended were being dumped on the market at below-cost prices. In late 2014, the United States took steps toward imposing steep tariffs on Chinese-made tires, which it claimed were unfairly subsidized by the government.[26]

- **Quotas** are limitations on the amount of specific products that may be imported from certain countries during a given time period. Russia, for instance, has specific quotas for U.S. meat imports.

- **Voluntary export restraints (VERs)** are limitations on the amount of specific products that one nation will export to another nation. Although the government of the exporting country typically imposes VERs, they usually do so out of fear that the importing country would impose even more onerous restrictions. As a result, VERs often aren't as "voluntary" as the name suggests. The United States, for instance,

protectionism National policies designed to restrict international trade, usually with the goal of protecting domestic businesses.

tariffs Taxes levied against imports.

quotas Limitations on the amount of specific products that may be imported from certain countries during a given time period.

voluntary export restraints (VERs) Limitations on the amount of specific products that one nation will export to another nation.

insisted on VERs with Japanese auto exports in the early 1980s (which many economists believe ultimately precipitated the decline of the U.S. auto industry).

- An **embargo** is a total ban on the international trade of a certain item, or a total halt in trade with a particular nation. The intention of most embargoes is to pressure the targeted country to change political policies or to protect national security. The U.S. embargo against trade with Cuba offers a high-profile example.

Quotas, VERs, and embargoes are relatively rare compared to tariffs, and tariffs are falling to new lows. But as tariffs decrease, some nations are seeking to control imports through nontariff barriers such as:

- Requiring red-tape-intensive import licenses for certain categories

- Establishing nonstandard packaging requirements for certain products

- Offering less-favorable exchange rates to certain importers

- Establishing standards on how certain products are produced or grown

- Promoting a "buy national" consumer attitude among local people

Nontariff barriers tend to be fairly effective because complaints about them can be hard to prove and easy to counter.[27]

In October 2016, President Barack Obama lifted limits on cigars and rum imported from Cuba, easing the embargo imposed on the small Caribbean nation in 1962. Here, a woman prepares cigars for shipment at La Bodeguita del Medio in Havana, Cuba.

T photography/Shutterstock.com

Almost half the world—over three billion people—live on less than $2.50 a day.
—GLOBALISSUES.ORG

FREE TRADE: THE MOVEMENT GAINS MOMENTUM

Perhaps the most dramatic change in the world economy has been the global move toward **free trade**— the unrestricted movement of goods and services across international borders. Even though *complete* free trade is not a reality, the emergence of regional trading blocs, common markets, and international trade agreements has moved the world economy much closer to that goal.

3-6a GATT and the World Trade Organization

The **General Agreement on Tariffs and Trade (GATT)** is an international trade accord designed to encourage worldwide trade among its members. Established in 1948 by 23 nations, GATT has undergone a number of revisions. The most significant changes stemmed from the 1986–1994 Uruguay Round of negotiations, which took bold steps to slash average tariffs by about 30% and to reduce other trade barriers among the 125 nations that signed.

The Uruguay Round also created the **World Trade Organization (WTO)**, a permanent global institution to promote international trade and to settle international trade disputes. The WTO monitors provisions of the GATT agreements, promotes further reduction of trade barriers, and mediates disputes among members. The decisions of the WTO are binding, which means that all parties involved in disputes must comply to maintain good standing in the organization.

Ministers of the WTO meet every two years to address current world trade issues. As the world economy has shifted toward services rather than goods, the emphasis of WTO meetings has followed suit. Controlling rampant piracy of intellectual property is a key

embargo A complete ban on international trade of a certain item, or a total halt in trade with a particular nation.

free trade The unrestricted movement of goods and services across international borders.

General Agreement on Tariffs and Trade (GATT) An international trade treaty designed to encourage worldwide trade among its members.

World Trade Organization (WTO) A permanent global institution to promote international trade and to settle international trade disputes.

concern for developed countries. For less-developed countries, one central issue is U.S. and European agricultural subsidies, which may unfairly distort agricultural prices worldwide.

In fact, both the broader agenda and the individual decisions of the WTO have become increasingly controversial over the past ten years. Advocates for less-developed nations are deeply concerned that free trade clears the path for major multinational corporations to push local businesses into economic failure. A local food stand, for instance, probably won't have the resources to compete with a global giant such as McDonald's. If the food stand closes, the community has gained inexpensive hamburgers, but the entrepreneur has lost his livelihood, and the community has lost the local flavor that contributes to its unique culture. Other opponents of the WTO worry that the acceleration of global trade encourages developing countries to fight laws that protect the environment and workers' rights, for fear of losing their low-cost advantage on the world market. The concerns have sparked significant protests during the past few meetings of the WTO ministers, and the outcry may well grow louder as developing nations gain economic clout.

3-6b The World Bank

Established in the aftermath of World War II, the **World Bank** is an international cooperative of 188 member countries, working together to reduce poverty in the developing world. The World Bank influences the global economy by providing financial and technical advice to the governments of developing countries for projects in a range of areas, including infrastructure, communications, health, and education. The financial assistance usually comes in the form of low-interest loans. But to secure a loan, the borrowing nation must often agree to conditions that can involve rather arduous economic reform.

World Bank An international cooperative of 188 member countries, working together to reduce poverty in the developing world.

International Monetary Fund (IMF) An international organization of 188 member nations that promotes international economic cooperation and stable growth.

3-6c The International Monetary Fund

Like the World Bank, the **International Monetary Fund (IMF)** is an international organization accountable to the governments of its 188 member nations. The basic mission of the IMF is to promote international economic cooperation and stable growth. Funding comes from the member nations, with the United States contributing more than twice as much as any other country. To achieve these goals, the IMF:

- Supports stable exchange rates
- Facilitates a smooth system of international payments
- Encourages member nations to adopt sound economic policies
- Promotes international trade
- Lends money to member nations to address economic problems

Although all of its functions are important, the IMF is best known as a lender of last resort to nations in financial trouble. This policy has come under fire in the past few years. Critics accuse the IMF of encouraging poor countries to borrow more money than they can ever hope to repay, which actually cripples their economies over the long term, creating even deeper poverty.

At the end of 2005, the IMF responded to its critics by implementing a historic debt relief program for poor countries. Under this program, which has since been expanded to include other agencies, the IMF and its partners have extended 100% debt forgiveness to 35 poor countries, erasing about $76 billion in debt. The managing director of the IMF pointed out that the canceled

Hector Vivas/STR/Getty Images

Donald Trump's America-first stances on trade and immigration have tested the United States' relations with Mexico. Here, Donald Trump is greeted by Mexican President Mexico Enrique Pena Nieto during an August 31, 2016 meeting in Mexico City, Mexico.

debt will allow these countries to increase spending in priority areas to reduce poverty and promote growth (although some experts worry that debt cancellation sets a troubling precedent for future lending). The result should be a higher standard of living for some of the poorest people in the world.[28]

3-6d Trading Blocs and Common Markets

Another major development in the past decade is the emergence of regional **trading blocs**, or groups of countries that have reduced or even eliminated all tariffs, allowing the free flow of goods among the member nations. A **common market** goes even further than a trading bloc by attempting to harmonize all trading rules. The United States, Mexico, and Canada have formed the largest trading bloc in the world, and the 28 countries of the European Union have formed the largest common market.

NAFTA The **North American Free Trade Agreement (NAFTA)** is the treaty that created the free-trading zone among the United States, Mexico, and Canada. The agreement took effect in 1994, gradually eliminating trade barriers and investment restrictions over a 15-year period. Despite dire predictions of American jobs flowing to Mexico, the U.S. economy has grown significantly since the implementation of NAFTA. The Canadian and Mexican economies have thrived as well (although all three economies have slowed significantly during the global economic crisis).

But NAFTA critics point out that the U.S. trade deficit with both Mexico and Canada has skyrocketed. While exports to both nations have increased, imports have grown far faster; both countries are among the top ten contributors to the total U.S. trade deficit, threatening the long-term health of the American economy. Other criticisms of NAFTA include increased pollution and worker abuse. Companies that move their factories to Mexico to capitalize on lower costs also take advantage of looser environmental and worker-protection laws, creating major ethical concerns. But the full impact of NAFTA—for better or for worse—is tough to evaluate because so many other variables affect all three economies.[29]

A key message of President Trump's 2016 presidential campaign was that NAFTA was a "total disaster" for the

> "We must create a kind of globalization that works for everyone... and not just for a few."
>
> —NESTOR KIRCHNER, ARGENTINE POLITICIAN

U.S. economy (to Mexico's advantage). Trump vowed to renegotiate the treaty with more favorable terms for the United States. During his first ten days in office, he also floated the idea of a steep import tax on Mexican goods. While this tax has not yet been imposed as of publication, it could potentially trigger a trade war with Mexico if it comes to pass. This would have a disproportionately high impact on California's economy (the sixth largest economy in the world), driving up prices on Mexican goods across the country. Margaritas, anyone? Not if they cost twice as much as any other drink![30]

European Union Composed of 28 nations and more than half a billion people, and boasting a combined GDP of nearly $17 trillion, the **European Union (EU)** is the world's largest common market. Exhibit 3.3 shows a map of the 2016 EU countries plus six countries that have applied to join.[31]

The overarching goal of the EU is to bolster Europe's trade position and to increase its international political and economic power. To help make this happen, the EU has removed all trade restrictions among member nations and unified internal trade rules, allowing goods and people to move freely among EU countries. The EU has also created standardized policies for import and export between EU countries and the rest of the world, giving the member nations more clout as a bloc than each would have had on its own. Perhaps the EU's most economically significant move was the introduction of a single currency, the euro, in 2002. Of the 15 EU members at the time, 12 adopted the euro (exceptions were the United Kingdom, Sweden, and Denmark). The EU also affects the global economy with its leading-edge approach to environmental protection, quality production, and human rights.

trading bloc A group of countries that have reduced or even eliminated tariffs, allowing for the free flow of goods among the member nations.

common market A group of countries that have eliminated tariffs and harmonized trading rules to facilitate the free flow of goods among the member nations.

North American Free Trade Agreement (NAFTA) The treaty among the United States, Mexico, and Canada that eliminated trade barriers and investment restrictions over a 15-year period starting in 1994.

European Union (EU) The world's largest common market, composed of 28 European nations.

Exhibit 3.3
European Union 2018

*Note: The United Kingdom is scheduled to depart the European Union on March 29, 2019.

Reasons to Create Trade Restrictions	Reasons to Eliminate Trade Restrictions
Protect domestic industry (e.g., the U.S. steel industry)	Reduce prices and increase choices for consumers by encouraging competition from around the world
Protect domestic jobs in key industries (but perhaps at the cost of domestic jobs in other industries)	Increase domestic jobs in industries with a comparative advantage versus other countries
Protect national security interests	Increase jobs—both at home and abroad—from foreign companies
Retaliate against countries who have engaged in unfair trade practices	Build exporting opportunities through better relationships with other countries
Pressure other countries to change their policies and practices	Use resources more efficiently on a worldwide basis

In 2010 and 2011, hobbled by overwhelming debt and slow growth, several of the weaker EU countries—most notably Greece—spiraled into economic crisis. Fearing a financial domino effect, due to the close ties among the nations, the economically stronger EU countries cobbled together several bailout packages. But many economists still fear that its weaker members could drag the EU overall into a deep, damaging recession and that one or more countries could default on its debt, withdraw from using the euro as currency, or

A Problem? An Opportunity? Or Both?

Between 2014 and 2016, approximately 3 million refugees poured into the European Union (EU) from Syria and other war-torn conflict zones in the Middle East. The overwhelming majority of those refugees sought a safe haven for themselves and their families—an opportunity to work hard and build a better future. They also sought to capitalize on the generous European social system, which provides education, healthcare, and ideally a chance at a fresh start. But not every country offered these newcomers a warm welcome. With economic growth rates slowing across Europe, many expressed concern about the high cost of integrating refugees. Others predicted a cultural clash between the refugees and current residents. Still others worried that the refugees would take their jobs. Despite these concerns, chances are good that the refugee influx will prove to be less of a crisis and more of an opportunity for the European Union. According to International Monetary Fund (IMF) research, host countries will experience a long-term increase in their GDPs as the refugees integrate into the workforce.

This workforce boost may be especially meaningful given that the populations of many EU countries are aging rapidly. The refugee population is relatively young, so they stand to replace workers who may soon be retiring in record numbers. Still, the IMF study emphasizes that *rapid* labor market integration is critical. EU governments may need to spend large sums of money to deal with the influx of refugees, but the impact of those expenses will be "short-lived and temporary." People who respond fearfully to the refugee crisis might do well to remember that co-founder of Apple Steve Jobs was the son of a Syrian immigrant to the United States.[32]

both, with devastating financial consequences for both the EU and the world economy.

In mid-2016, the United Kingdom, which includes England, Scotland, Wales, and Northern Ireland, held a referendum on whether to exit the European Union. After an intense and divisive campaign, the UK public voted to leave the EU in a very close vote. Dubbed *Brexit* (a combination of the words "British" and "exit"), the decision to leave was quite unexpected.[33] Many political and economic analysts have voiced deep concerns about the impact that Brexit will have on the United Kingdom as well as the rest of the world—especially in light of London's position as an international banking center. The initial vote is likely to be final, but the implementation of Brexit will not be immediate. There will be an initial two-year negotiation with the EU about the terms of withdrawal. This negotiation is unlikely to be favorable toward Britain, in part so that

the EU can discourage other countries from withdrawing. The EU has leverage with regard to items such as terms of trade.

So why did Britain want out? The two major issues at play were immigration and self-determination. Many British citizens, especially older and more rural populations in England, were concerned that the country's unemployment and social services would be swamped under the weight of new immigrant arrivals as mandated by the EU. Many Brits were also concerned that that the country's identity and direction would increasingly be determined by the EU and become fused into a continental identity. The ultimate impact of the British exit will be unclear for months, and likely years, to come. The next several years in particular will be critical to the shape, size, and structure of the European economy. The UK voted to leave the European Union and is scheduled to depart on March 29, 2019.[34]

The past decade has been marked by extraordinary changes in the world economy. The boundaries between individual countries have fallen lower than ever before, creating a new level of economic connectedness. The growing integration has created huge opportunities for visionary companies of every size. But integration also means risk. The dangers became clear in 2008, when the economic crisis in the United States rapidly reverberated around the globe, fueling a deep, worldwide recession.

To succeed abroad—especially in tough economic times—individual firms must make the right choices about how to structure their operations, surmount barriers to trade, meet diverse customer needs, manage a global workforce, and handle complex logistics. Human rights and environmental protection continue to be especially critical for international businesses. Both are vital components of social responsibility and will only gain importance as advocates raise awareness around the world. In the face of economic, political, and social flux, effective global business leaders must master both strategy and implementation at a deeper level than ever before.

CAREERS IN INTERNATIONAL BUSINESS

International Sports Marketing Manager

Implement marketing plans outside the United States with a focus on Europe, Australia, and New Zealand. Work with global brand marketing team to develop and execute events that incorporate athletes. Participate in the scouting process to identify and pursue up-and-coming athletes in relevant sports. Provide support for the endorsement contract negotiation process.

STUDY TOOLS 3

LOCATED AT BACK OF THE TEXTBOOK

☐ Rip-Out Chapter Review Card

☐ Gain unique perspectives on key concepts with new concept videos in the e-book

☐ Increase your comprehension with online homework and quizzes

☐ Study with existing flashcards and make your own

4 | Business Ethics and Social Responsibility:
Doing Well by Doing Good

Remember to visit
PAGE 74
for additional
STUDY TOOLS

LEARNING OBJECTIVES

After studying this chapter, you will be able to:

4-1 Define ethics and explain the concept of universal ethical standards

4-2 Describe business ethics and ethical dilemmas

4-3 Discuss how ethics relates to both the individual and the organization

4-4 Define social responsibility and examine the impact on stakeholder groups

4-5 Explain the role of social responsibility in the global arena

4-6 Describe how companies evaluate their efforts to be socially responsible

4-1 ETHICS AND SOCIAL RESPONSIBILITY: A CLOSE RELATIONSHIP

Ethics and social responsibility—often discussed in the same breath—are closely related, but they are definitely not the same. Ethics refers to sets of beliefs about right and wrong, good and bad; business ethics involve the application of these issues in the workplace. Clearly, ethics relate to individuals and their day-to-day decision making. Just as clearly, the decisions of each individual can affect the entire organization.

Social responsibility is the obligation of a business to contribute to society. The most socially responsible firms feature proactive policies that focus on meeting the needs of all their stakeholders—not just investors but also employees, customers, the broader community, and the environment. The stance of a company regarding social responsibility sets the tone for the organization and clearly influences the decisions of individual employees.

Although this chapter discusses ethics and social

responsibility separately, keep in mind that the two areas have a dynamic, interactive relationship that plays a vital role in building both profitable businesses and a vibrant community.

4-1a Defining Ethics: Murkier than You'd Think

In the most general sense, **ethics** refer to sets of beliefs about right and wrong, good and bad. While your individual ethics stem from who you are as a human being, your family, your social group, and your culture also play a

ethics A set of beliefs about right and wrong, good and bad.

significant role in shaping your ethics. And therein lies the challenge: in the United States, people come from such diverse backgrounds that establishing broad agreement on specific ethical standards can be daunting. The global arena only amplifies the challenge.

A given country's legal system provides a solid starting point for examining ethical standards. The function of laws in the United States (and elsewhere) is to establish and enforce ethical norms that apply to everyone within our society. Laws provide basic standards of behavior. But truly ethical behavior goes beyond the basics. In other words, your actions can be completely legal, yet still unethical. But since the legal system is far from perfect, in rare instances your actions can be illegal, yet still ethical. Exhibit 4.1 shows some examples of how business conduct can fall within legal and ethical dimensions. Clearly, legal and ethical actions should be your goal. Legality should be the floor—not the ceiling—for how to behave in business and elsewhere.

Do all actions have ethical implications? Clearly not. Some decisions fall within the realm of free choice with no direct link to right and wrong, good and bad. Examples might include what color T-shirt you choose to wear, what levels your game development company includes in its new video game, or what sunglasses you decide to purchase.

> "Corporate responsibility is the best strategic as well as financial path that most businesses can follow."
>
> —JEFFREY HOLLENDER, ENTREPRENEUR AND BUSINESS CONSULTANT

4-1b Universal Ethical Standards: A Reasonable Goal or Wishful Thinking?

Too many people view ethics as relative. In other words, their ethical standards shift depending on the situation and how it relates to them. Here are a few examples:

- "It's not okay to steal paper from the office supply store…*but* it's perfectly fine to 'borrow' supplies from the storage closet at work to use at home. Why? The company owes me a bigger salary."

- "It's wrong to lie…*but* it's okay to call in sick when I have personal business to take care of. Why? I don't want to burn through my limited vacation days."

EXHIBIT 4.1 | LEGAL-ETHICAL MATRIX

Legal and Unethical	Legal and Ethical
Promoting high-calorie/low-nutrient foods with inadequate information about the risks	Producing high-quality products
Producing products that you know will break before their time	Rewarding integrity Leading by example
Paying nonliving wages to workers in developing countries	Treating employees fairly Contributing to the community Respecting the environment
Illegal and Unethical	**Illegal and Ethical**
Embezzling money	Providing rock-bottom prices *only* to distributors in underserved areas
Engaging in sexual harassment	Collaborating with other medical clinics to guarantee low prices in low-income counties (collusion)
Practicing collusion with competitors	
Encouraging fraudulent accounting	

■ "Everyone should have a level playing field...*but* it's fine to give my brother the first shot at my company's contract. Why? I know he really needs the work."

This kind of two-faced thinking is dangerous because it can help people rationalize bigger and bigger ethical deviations. But the problem can be fixed by identifying **universal ethical standards** that apply to everyone across a broad spectrum of situations. Some people argue that we could never find universal standards for a country as diverse as the United States. But the nonprofit, nonpartisan Character Counts organization has worked with a diverse group of educators, community leaders, and ethicists to identify six core values, listed in Exhibit 4.2, that transcend political, religious, class, and ethnic divisions.

universal ethical standards
Ethical norms that apply to all people across a broad spectrum of situations.

business ethics The application of right and wrong, good and bad, in a business setting.

ethical dilemma A decision that involves a conflict of values; every potential course of action has some significant negative consequences.

 4-2

BUSINESS ETHICS: NOT AN OXYMORON

Quite simply, **business ethics** is the application of right and wrong, good and bad in a business setting. But this isn't as straightforward as it may initially seem. The most challenging business

decisions seem to arise when values are in conflict...when whatever you do will have negative consequences, forcing you to choose among bad options. These are true **ethical dilemmas**. (Keep in mind that ethical *dilemmas* differ from ethical *lapses*, which involve clear misconduct.) Here are three examples of ethical dilemmas:

■ Imagine that you did a great job on a recent project at your company. Your boss has been very vocal about acknowledging your work and the increased revenue that resulted from it. Privately, she said that you clearly earned a bonus of at least 10%, but due to company politics, she was unable to secure the bonus for you. She also implied that if you were to submit inflated expense reports for the next few months, she would look the other way, and you could pocket the extra cash as well-deserved compensation for your contributions.

■ Uber: Are Uber drivers employees of the Uber Corporation, or are they their own bosses (independent contractors)? It depends on who you ask. According to the Uber Corporation, its drivers are definitely independent contractors. In fact, the company requires all new drivers to sign a form acknowledging as much. This means that drivers do not get access to benefits or other protections such as workers' compensation and unemployment insurance, which leaves them financially vulnerable as they continue to contribute to the enormous value of the world's largest private venture-backed

Who Should Die? And Who Should Decide?

Imagine that your driverless robotic car blows a tire while careening down a lovely mountain road. Your car still has some degree of control, but it is quickly becoming clear that this is not going to end well. On one side of you is oncoming traffic (several cars and a family of bicyclists), and on the other is a very, very steep cliff. Should the car slam into the oncoming traffic to save your life, or send you careening over the cliff to save others? This is not just an abstract question—it's an authentic ethical dilemma that businesses will increasingly need to face as more and more consumer machinery takes on a superhuman ability to react to danger.

A major hurdle in programming a robot to make ethical decisions is anticipating the virtually endless number of scenarios that the robot might face. One possible solution is to randomize the robot's response, but that approach complete evades human responsibility and negates the potential positive power of human judgment. Courts, insurance companies, and governments around the world will certainly weigh in on how robots are and should be programmed. Clearly, contemporary "moral math" is nothing if not complex.

Martial Red/Shutterstock.com

start-up. Is this fair? Not so much. In 2015, driver groups in Massachusetts and California sued Uber to be reclassified as employees. The two parties eventually reached a settlement that gave drivers some concessions but left them as independent contractors. In 2016, however, a federal judge rejected the settlement, declaring that it was "not fair, adequate, and reasonable." The two parties are currently preparing to go to a jury trial. The outcome of this trial will affect not only the Uber Corporation and its drivers but also the overall structure of the gig economy that so many of us have come to rely on in one way or another.[1]

- Facebook: For one week in 2012, Facebook changed the content mix in the News Feeds of more than half a million users—without asking their permission—in an effort to gauge their emotional response. Although the manipulation was covered under Facebook's terms of service, many users were outraged at what they considered an unethical psychological experiment without their permission. Facebook COO Sheryl Sandberg issued a classic nonapology: "It was poorly communicated. And for that communication we apologize." In actuality, the experiment was not communicated at all.

Juli Hansen/Shutterstock.com

4-3 ETHICS: MULTIPLE TOUCHPOINTS

Although each person must make his or her own ethical choices, the organization can have a significant influence on the quality of those decisions.

4-3a Ethics and the Individual: The Power of One

Ethical choices begin with ethical individuals. Your personal needs, your family, your culture, and your religion all influence your value system. Your personality traits—self-esteem, self-confidence, independence, and sense of humor—play a significant role as well. A recent study suggested that personal empathy— "identification with and understanding of another's situation, feelings, and motives"—is another strong predictor of ethical leadership. In fact, business leaders who scored highest on empathy also exhibited the highest levels of ethical leadership. These factors all come into play as you face ethical dilemmas. The challenge can be overwhelming, which has led a range of experts to develop frameworks for reaching ethical decisions. While the specifics vary, the key principles of most decision guides are very similar:

- Do you fully understand each dimension of the problem?

- Who would benefit? Who would suffer?

- Are the alternative solutions legal? Are they fair?

- Does your decision make you comfortable at a "gut feel" level?

- Could you defend your decision on the nightly TV news?

- Have you considered and reconsidered your responses to each question?[2]

The approach seems simple, but in practice it really isn't. Workers—and managers, too—often face enormous pressure to do what's right for the company or right for their career, rather than simply what's right. And keep in mind that it's completely possible for two people to follow the framework and arrive at completely different decisions, each feeling confident that he or she has made the right choice.

4-3b Ethics and the Organization: It Takes a Village

Although each person is clearly responsible for his or her own actions, the organization can influence those actions to a startling degree. Not surprisingly, that influence starts at the top, and actions matter far more than words. The president of the Ethics Resource Center states, "CEOs in particular must communicate their personal commitment to high ethical standards and consistently drive the message down to employees through their actions." Any other approach—even just the *appearance* of shaky ethics—can be deeply damaging to a company's ethical climate. Here are a couple of examples from the wake of the Great Recession:

- High Flyers: When the CEOs of the Big Three automakers—two of them hovering on the edge of bankruptcy—went to Washington to request a $25 billion bailout package, they flew in three separate corporate jets at an estimated cost of $20,000 per round-trip flight. All three were operating in line with official corporate travel policies, but it just didn't look right. One lawmaker pointedly asked, "Couldn't you all have downgraded to first

EXHIBIT 4.2	UNIVERSAL ETHICAL STANDARDS
Trustworthiness	Be honest. Don't deceive, cheat, or steal. Do what you say you'll do.
Respect	Treat others how you'd like to be treated. Be considerate. Be tolerant of differences.
Responsibility	Persevere. Be self-controlled and self-disciplined. Be accountable for your choices.
Fairness	Provide equal opportunity. Be open-minded. Don't take advantage of others.
Caring	Be kind. Be compassionate. Express gratitude.
Citizenship	Contribute to the community. Protect the environment. Cooperate whenever feasible.

Source: © 2009 Josephson Institute. Reprinted from the Josephson Institute's Report Card on the Ethics of American Youth Summary with permission.

class or jet-pooled or something to get here? It would have at least sent a message that you do get it." Not surprisingly, the execs left empty-handed.[3]

- Beach Junket: A few days after the Fed committed $85 billion to keep AIG out of bankruptcy, the insurer spent more than $440,000 on a sales "retreat" at a luxury resort in California. Expenditures included $150,000 for food, $23,000 in spa charges, and $7,000 for golf. Rather than apologizing, CEO Edward Liddy only commented that the company would examine its expenses.[4]

- Gross Excess: In 2009, ousted Merrill Lynch CEO John Thain agreed—under pressure from President Obama—to reimburse federal bailout recipient Bank of America for an expensive, and fully approved, renovation of his office that had been done before the crisis hit. The somewhat outrageous expenses included an $87,000 area rug, a $5,000 mirror, and a $35,000 commode.

Are these decisions wrong? Unethical?[5] How do you feel about the business decisions described in Exhibit 4.3?

> "Our philosophy is that we care about people first."
>
> —MARK ZUCKERBERG, FACEBOOK FOUNDER

Pierre Omidyar eBay creator Omidyar has contributed $100 million to the Tufts University Micro Finance Fund. His goal is to give economic power to poor people around the world through small business loans. Ultimately, he hopes to create entrepreneurial self-sufficiency as eBay has done for so many avid users.

Sherron Watkins Despite intense pressure and high personal stakes, Watkins, a former vice president of Enron, reported the accounting irregularities that led to the discovery of staggering corporate fraud.

Stanley O'Neal As investment house Merrill Lynch began racking up losses that led to its collapse, CEO O'Neal announced his "retirement" and walked away with a compensation package worth more than $160 million.

Scott Thompson After less than six months as CEO of Yahoo!, Thompson left under a murky cloud when activist shareholders pointed out that an entry on his résumé was inaccurate, claiming a degree in computer science that he does not have.

Bill Gates As Microsoft CEO, Bill Gates made some ethically shaky moves, but he and his wife also established the Bill and Melinda Gates Foundation, by far the largest U.S. charity. Working for the foundation, Gates applies his famous problem-solving skills to global health, global development, and American education.

Jessica Alba: As a follow-up to her successful acting career, Alba launched The Honest Company to promote health products that were "honestly free" of dangerous chemicals. However, Alba faced a number of lawsuits from disgruntled consumers who claimed that her products contained unnatural ingredients and that her firm engages in deceptive marketing.

4-3c Creating and Maintaining an Ethical Organization

Research from the Ethics Resource Center (ERC) suggests that organizational culture has more influence than any other variable on the ethical conduct of individual employees. According to the ERC, key elements of a strong culture include displays of ethics-related actions at all levels of an organization and accountability for actions. The impact of these elements can be dramatic. Consider, for example, the following research results:

- A 61-percentage-point favorable difference in the level of observed misconduct when employees say they work in a strong ethical culture.

- When employees felt that the Great Recession negatively impacted the ethical culture of their company, misconduct rose by 16 percentage points.

- ERC research showed that companies behave differently during economic difficulties. The decisions and behaviors of their leaders are perceived by employees as a heightened commitment to ethics. As a result, employees adopt a higher standard of conduct for themselves.[7]

Robert Lane, former CEO of Deere, a highly performing, highly ethical corporation, believes in the importance of senior management commitment to ethics, but he points out that the "tone at the top" must be reinforced by the actual behavior observed by suppliers, dealers, customers, and employees. At Deere, this is summed up in highly visible, frequently referenced shorthand known as "the how." Lane

declares that to establish an ethical culture, ethical words must be "backed up with documented practices, processes, and procedures, all understood around the globe."[8]

ERC research further supports the need for senior manager commitment by showing that when employees perceive more management commitment, they tend to be more fully engaged. More-engaged employees are much less likely to behave badly, and much more likely to

Every year, the Ethisphere Institute publishes a list of the world's most ethical companies. Ethisphere's 2017 list featured 124 honorees from 19 countries and across 52 industry sectors, including 3M, Ford, Microsoft, Starbucks, T-Mobile, Target, and UPS. For the complete list, visit worldsmostethicalcompanies.ethisphere.com.

report others who do, which dramatically lowers the risk for the company.[9]

A strong organizational culture works in tandem with formal ethics programs to create and maintain ethical work environments. A written **code of ethics** is the cornerstone of any formal ethics program. The purpose of a written code is to give employees the information they need to make ethical decisions across a range of situations. Clearly, an ethics code becomes even more important for multinational companies, since it lays out unifying values and priorities for divisions that are rooted in different cultures. But a written code is worthless if it doesn't reflect living principles. An effective code of ethics flows directly from ethical corporate values and leads directly to ongoing communication, training, and action.

Specific codes of ethics vary greatly among organizations. Perhaps the best-known code is the Johnson & Johnson Credo, which has guided the company profitably—with a soaring reputation—through a number of crises that would have sunk lesser organizations. One of the striking elements of the credo is the firm focus on fairness. It carefully refrains from overpromising financial rewards, committing instead to a "fair return" for stockholders.

To bring a code of ethics to life, experts advocate a forceful, integrated approach to ethics that virtually always includes the following steps:

1. Get executive buy-in and commitment to follow through. Top managers need to communicate—even overcommunicate—about the importance of ethics. But talking works only when it's backed up by action: senior management must give priority to keeping promises and leading by example.

2. Establish expectations for ethical behavior at all levels of the organization, from the CEO to the nighttime cleaning crew. Be sure that outside parties such as suppliers, distributors, and customers understand the standards.

3. Integrate ethics into mandatory staff training. From new-employee orientation

BortN66/Shutterstock.com

to ongoing training, ethics must play a role. Additional, more specialized training helps employees who face more temptation (e.g., purchasing agents, overseas sales reps).

4. Ensure that your ethics code is both global and local in scope. Employees in every country should understand both the general principles and the specific applications. Be sure to translate it into as many languages as necessary.

5. Build and maintain a clear, trusted reporting structure for ethical concerns and violations. The structure should allow employees to seek anonymous guidance for ethical concerns and to report ethics violations anonymously.

6. Establish protection for **whistle-blowers**, people who report illegal or unethical behavior. Be sure that no retaliation occurs, in compliance with both ethics and the Sarbanes-Oxley Act (see discussion later in the chapter). Some have even suggested that whistle-blowers should receive a portion of the penalties levied against firms that violate the law.

7. Enforce the code of ethics. When people violate ethical norms, companies must respond immediately and—whenever appropriate—publicly to retain employee trust. Without enforcement, the code of ethics becomes meaningless.

4-4 DEFINING SOCIAL RESPONSIBILITY: MAKING THE WORLD A BETTER PLACE

Social responsibility is the obligation of a business to contribute to society. Similar to ethics, the broad definition is clear, but specific implementation can be complex. Obviously, the number-one goal of any business is long-term profits; without profits, other contributions are impossible. But once a firm achieves a reasonable return, the balancing act begins: How can a company balance the need to contribute against the need to boost profits, especially when the two conflict? The answer depends on the business's values, mission, resources, and management philosophy, which lead in turn to its position on social responsibility. Business approaches fall across the spectrum, from no contribution to proactive contribution, as shown in Exhibit 4.4.

code of ethics A formal, written document that defines the ethical standards of an organization and gives employees the information they need to make ethical decisions across a range of situations.

whistle-blowers Employees who report their employer's illegal or unethical behavior to either the authorities or the media.

social responsibility The obligation of a business to contribute to society.

Exhibit 4.4
The Spectrum of Social Responsibility

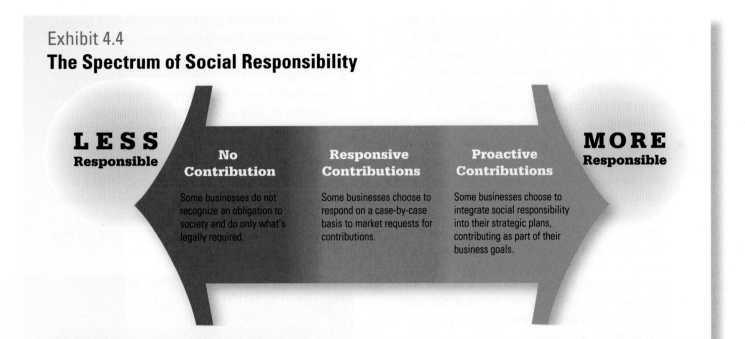

LESS Responsible	No Contribution	Responsive Contributions	Proactive Contributions	MORE Responsible
	Some businesses do not recognize an obligation to society and do only what's legally required.	Some businesses choose to respond on a case-by-case basis to market requests for contributions.	Some businesses choose to integrate social responsibility into their strategic plans, contributing as part of their business goals.	

4-4a The Stakeholder Approach: Responsibility to Whom?

Stakeholders are any groups that have a stake—or a personal interest—in the performance and actions of an organization. Different stakeholders have different needs, expectations, and levels of interest. The federal government, for instance, is a key stakeholder in pharmaceutical companies but a very minor stakeholder in local art studios. The community at large is a key stakeholder for a coffee shop chain but a minor stakeholder for a web design firm. Enlightened organizations identify key stakeholders for their business and consider stakeholder priorities in their decision making. The goal is to balance their needs and priorities as effectively as possible, with an eye toward building their business over the long term. Core stakeholder groups for most businesses are employees, customers, investors, and the broader community.

Responsibility to Employees: Creating Jobs that Work Jobs alone aren't enough. The starting point for socially responsible employers is to meet legal standards, and the requirements are significant. How would you judge the social responsibility of the firms listed in Exhibit 4.5? Employers must comply with laws that include equal opportunity, workplace safety, minimum-wage and overtime requirements, protection from sexual harassment, and family and medical unpaid leaves. We will discuss these legal requirements (and others) in Chapter 15 on Human Resource Management.

But socially responsible employers go far beyond the law. They create a workplace environment that respects the dignity and value of each employee. They ensure that hard work, commitment, and talent pay off. They move beyond minimal safety requirements to establish proactive protections, such as ergonomically correct chairs and computer screens that reduce eyestrain. And the best employers respond to the ongoing employee search for a balance between work and personal life. With an increasing number of workers facing challenges such as raising kids and caring for elderly parents, responsible companies are stepping in with programs such as on-site day care, company-sponsored day camp, and referral services for elder care.

Responsibility to Customers: Value, Honesty, and Communication One core responsibility of business is to deliver consumer value by providing quality products at fair prices. Honesty and communication are critical components of this equation. **Consumerism**—a widely accepted social movement—suggests that consumer rights should be the starting point. In the early 1960s, President Kennedy defined these rights, which most businesses respect in response to both consumer expectations and legal requirements:

■ The Right to Be Safe: Businesses are legally

stakeholders Any groups that have a stake—or a personal interest—in the performance and actions of an organization.

consumerism A social movement that focuses on four key consumer rights: (1) the right to be safe, (2) the right to be informed, (3) the right to choose, and (4) the right to be heard.

responsible for injuries and damages caused by their products—even if they have no reason to suspect that their products might cause harm. This makes it easy for consumers to file suits. In some cases, the drive to avert lawsuits has led to absurdities such as the warning on some coffee cups: "Caution! Hot coffee is hot!" (No kidding...)

■ The Right to Be Informed: The law requires firms in a range of industries—from mutual funds, to groceries, to pharmaceuticals—to provide the public with extensive information. The Food and Drug Administration, for instance, mandates that most grocery foods feature a very specific "Nutrition Facts" label. Beyond legal requirements, many firms use the Web to provide a wealth of extra information about their products. KFC, for example, offers an interactive Nutrition Calculator that works with all of its menu items (and it's fun to use, too).

■ The Right to Choose: Freedom of choice is a fundamental element of the capitalist U.S. economy. Our economic system works largely because consumers freely choose to purchase the products that best meet their needs. As businesses compete, consumer value increases. Socially responsible firms support consumer choice by

following the laws that prevent anticompetitive behavior such as predatory pricing, collusion, and monopolies.

■ The Right to Be Heard: Socially responsible companies make it easy for consumers to express legitimate complaints. They also develop highly trained customer service people to respond to complaints. In fact, smart businesses view customer complaints as an opportunity to create better products and stronger relationships. Statistics suggest that 1 in 50 dissatisfied customers takes the time to complain. The other 49 quietly switch brands. By soliciting feedback, you're not only being responsible but also building your business.[10]

> "In this era of corporate scandals, we must refocus our energies on corporate ethics and encourage individuals to report wrongdoing."
>
> —JORDAN THOMAS, CHAIR, WHISTLEBLOWER REPRESENTATION PRACTICE, LABATON SUCHAROW

EXHIBIT 4.5   SOCIAL RESPONSIBILITY AT WORK

How Would You Judge the Actions of These Firms?[11]

The Clorox Company In early 2008, Clorox introduced a line of "99% natural" cleaning products called Green Works. This was the first such effort from a major consumer products company, and also the first time that the Sierra Club endorsed a product line by allowing the use of its logo on the labels. In return, Clorox makes an annual contribution to the Sierra Club, the amount based on total Green Works sales.

Facebook For one week in 2012, Facebook changed the content mix in the News Feeds of more than half a million users—without asking their permission—in an effort to gauge their emotional response. Although the manipulation was covered under Facebook's terms of service, many users were outraged at what they considered an unethical psychological experiment without their permission. Facebook COO Sheryl Sandberg issued a classic nonapology: "It was poorly communicated. And for that communication we apologize." In actuality, the experiment was not communicated at all.

Kraft As obesity among kids spirals out of control, Kraft has taken a brave stand: a pledge to stop advertising unhealthy—yet highly profitable—foods to young children. Kraft also plans to eliminate in-school marketing and drop some unhealthy snacks from school vending machines. As the king of the food business, Kraft has chosen what's right for kids over what's right for its own short-term profits.

Enron/Arthur Andersen (now defunct) Enron, once hailed as a shining example of corporate excellence, collapsed in late 2001 due to massive accounting fraud, which bilked employees and other small investors out of millions of dollars. Arthur Andersen, hired to audit Enron's accountings, participated in the scandal by masking the issues and shredding documents containing potential evidence.

Subway Eating "fresh" may not sound so appetizing once you learn that Subway's chicken products could be made from less than 50% actual chicken. According to tests performed at Trent University in Canada, the remainder of a Subway chicken breast patty consists of soy and other filler ingredients. Subway denies the allegations. In 2014, however, Subway customers learned that a food-grade material also found in yoga mats was used to make the company's bread. Subway removed the ingredient and pledged to remove all artificial ingredients from its food in North America by 2017.[12]

AIG After the U.S. government pulled AIG from the brink of bankruptcy in 2008 with a bailout that topped $182 billion, the AIG board of directors voted in early 2013 about whether to join a lawsuit against the government, which claimed that the interest rate on the initial loan was excessive and the rescue was unfair to shareholders. Faced with public wrath and ridicule, they ultimately opted out of the lawsuit, but not before they further damaged their reputation among the general public.

Delivering quality products is another key component of social responsibility to consumers. **Planned obsolescence**—deliberately designing products to fail in order to shorten the time between consumer repurchases—represents a clear violation of social responsibility. In the long term, the market itself weeds out offenders. After all, who would repurchase a product that meets a premature end? But in the short term, planned obsolescence thins consumer wallets and abuses consumer trust.

When businesses do make mistakes, apologizing to consumers won't guarantee renewed sales. But a sincere apology can definitely restore a company's reputation, which can ultimately lead to greater profits. Here are some examples:

■ *Going with the Flow*: In late 2010, Johnson & Johnson discontinued the popular o.b. Ultra tampons. Loyal users stripped the shelves of remaining stock (bidding the price of a box of Ultras up to more than $100 on eBay) and bombarded the manufacturer with complaints. In late 2011, Johnson & Johnson announced that Ultras would be back on shelf by late 2012, and offered an apology video rife with every cliché imaginable, including a handsome, male singer. The music video was customizable; viewer names appeared throughout the video, and the video closed with a

Taylor Swift boycotted Apple's music streaming service after the company announced it wouldn't pay artists during a free three-month trial period. Apple made a quick fix by reversing the policy and announcing the change on Twitter.

Source: Lululemon

coupon offer. The video represented a masterful attempt to regain loyalty for a product that had yet to reappear on the shelf.[13]

Investors count on companies to spend money wisely and fully disclose all key facts.

■ *Apple Angst*: Apple introduced the iPhone on June 29, 2007, to rave reviews and stellar sales, despite the $599 price tag. But two months later, Apple dropped the price of the phone by $200 to expand the user base further. Not surprisingly, early adopters were livid—why, they demanded, did Apple repay their trust and support by ripping them off? CEO Steve Jobs quickly apologized and offered every $599 iPhone customer a $100 Apple store credit. The response seemed to work. In 2008, Apple's ranking in the American Customer Satisfaction Index climbed 8%, a full 10 percentage points ahead of its nearest competitor, maintaining a dramatic lead through 2011.[14]

■ *More Apple Angst:* In September 2012, Apple released an updated version of its mobile Maps program, which iPhone users quickly realized was a hot mess that featured too many wrong directions, misplaced locations, and bizarre satellite images. CEO Tim Cook sent a contrite apology to customers, but basically referred them to archrival Google Maps, after acknowledging that Apple's Maps was not up to par. He ended the apology with some puffery about how Apple aims to make all their products "the best in the world." The following Christmas, iPhone sales underperformed analyst expectations, and the stock price plummeted, which may have been completely unrelated to the Maps debacle.[15]

■ Even More Apple Angst: In 2015, Apple demonstrated that actions speak louder than words—and actions taken quickly enough can mitigate the need for an apology altogether. When Taylor Swift boycotted the company's new music streaming service after the company announced it wouldn't pay artists during a free three-month trial period, Apple made a quick fix by reversing the policy and announcing the change on Twitter: "#AppleMusic will pay artist for streaming, even during customer's free trial period," and a minute later, "We hear you @taylorswift13 and indie artists. Love, Apple."

Responsibility to Investors: Fair Stewardship and Full Disclosure

The primary responsibility of business to investors is clearly to make money—to create an ongoing stream of profits. But companies achieve and maintain

planned obsolescence
The strategy of deliberately designing products to fail in order to shorten the time between purchases.

Profits and So Much More

If the corporation you're dealing with does not have profits as a first priority, it may well be a B-Corp, or benefit corporation. B-Corps are a new corporate structure that value profits, but not more than other priorities such as employees, suppliers, the community, and the environment. Benefit corporations do not receive special tax treatment, but B-Corp status, like the food producer's organic certification, can offer a real advantage, especially for firms competing in crowded markets. Tim Frick, a B-Corp executive at MightyBytes, says that being a benefit corporation is "being part of a larger global movement of making sure that business is being used as a force for good and not for evil." It can also keep companies focused on what makes them different, especially since firms must undergo comprehensive annual audits to keep their status. Current B-Corps fall across a range of industries and include businesses of all different sizes. One example is Little Pickle Press, which publishes children's books, apps, and media. The firm is dedicated to fostering kindness in young people through both the messages of its books and the environmentally friendly way it produces and distributes its books. Little Pickle forges

partnerships with—and makes significant donations to—organizations that help children and teens in meaningful ways. For instance, when Little Pickle Press was launching a new book about ending hunger, the company teamed up with a nonprofit that feeds the hungry. Little Pickle then donated 15% of its net sales to that group over a ten-month period.[16]

Lotus Images/Shutterstock.com

long-term earnings in the context of responsibility to *all* stakeholders, which may mean trading short-term profits for long-term success. Responsibility to investors starts by meeting legal requirements, and in the wake of recent corporate scandals, the bar is higher than ever. The 2002 **Sarbanes-Oxley Act** limits conflict-of-interest issues by restricting the consulting services that accounting firms can provide for the companies they audit. Sarbanes-Oxley also requires that financial officers and CEOs personally certify the validity of their financial statements. (See Chapter 8 for more detail on the Sarbanes-Oxley Act.)

But beyond legal requirements, companies have a number of additional responsibilities to investors. Spending money wisely would be near the top of the list. For instance, are executive retreats to the South Pacific on the company tab legal? They probably are. Do they represent a responsible use of corporate dollars? Now that seems unlikely. Honesty is another key responsibility that relates directly to financial predictions. No one can anticipate exactly how a company will perform, and an overly optimistic or pessimistic assessment is perfectly legal. But is it socially responsible? It probably isn't, especially if it departs too far from the objective facts—which is, of course, a subjective call.

Responsibility to the Community: Business and the Greater Good

Beyond increasing everyone's standard of living, businesses can contribute to society in two main ways: philanthropy and responsibility. **Corporate philanthropy** includes all business donations to nonprofit groups, including both money and products. The Giving USA Foundation reported that total corporate donations increased 3.9% in 2015, another banner year for giving across all sources (perhaps due to the robust economy).[17] Corporate philanthropy also includes donations of employee time; in other words, some companies pay their employees to spend time volunteering at nonprofits. Patagonia, for example, allows workers after one year of service to apply for two-month internships with environmental not-for-profits, during which time they're still paid by Patagonia.[18]

Some companies contribute to nonprofits through **cause-related marketing**. This involves a partnership

Sarbanes-Oxley Act
Federal legislation passed in 2002 that sets higher ethical standards for public corporations and accounting firms. Key provisions limit conflict-of-interest issues and require financial officers and CEOs to certify the validity of their financial statements.

corporate philanthropy
All business donations to nonprofit groups, including money, products, and employee time.

cause-related marketing
Marketing partnerships between businesses and nonprofit organizations, designed to spike sales for the company and raise money for the nonprofit.

between a business and a nonprofit, designed to spike sales for the company and raise money for the nonprofit. Unlike outright gifts, these dollars are not tax deductible for the company, but they can certainly build the company's brands.

Corporate responsibility relates closely to philanthropy but focuses on the actions of the business itself rather than donations of money and time. Starbucks has joined nearly 50 leading U.S. companies in a campaign to hire 1 million "Opportunity Youth" (16-to 24-year-olds who are neither employed nor in school—an estimated 5.4 million young Americans) by 2021.[19] Taking a different approach to corporate responsibility, A to Z Wineworks in Oregon pays its workers 43% over the local living wage and guarantees its growers fair prices in both good and bad years. Chocolatier Madécasse noticed that Africa grows 70% of the world's cocoa, yet produces less than 1% of the world's chocolate. The company decided to change this statistic by making its chocolate entirely in Africa. Madécasse now empowers Madagascar's cocoa farmers with skills training and higher wages to make its chocolate right on the island. So far, the company has created meaningful income for more than 200 people in Madagascar across a wide variety of specialties, including chocolate making, packaging, shipping, and of course the

> "Consumers, investors, entrepreneurs, and policymakers have recognized that business is the most powerful man-made force on the planet and it can be used as a powerful force for good."
>
> —JAY COEN, FOUNDER OF B-LAB

Minerva Studio/Shutterstock.com

Protecting the environment has become the most crucial element of responsibility to businesses across the globe.

farming of the cocoa, spices, and fruits. And Madécasse's chocolate tastes delicious, too![20]

Responsibility to the Environment Protecting the environment is perhaps the most crucial element of responsibility to the community. Business is a huge consumer of the world's limited resources, from oil to timber, to fresh water, to minerals. In some cases, the production process decimates the environment and spews pollution into the air, land, and water, sometimes causing irreversible damage. And the products created by business can cause pollution as well, such as the smog generated by cars and the sometimes-toxic waste caused by junked electronic parts.

The government sets minimum standards for environmental protection at the federal, state, and local levels. But a growing number of companies are going further, developing innovative strategies to build their businesses while protecting the environment. Many have embraced the idea of **sustainable development**: doing business to meet the needs of this generation without harming the ability of future generations to meet their needs. This means weaving environmentalism throughout the business decision-making process. Since sustainable development can mean significant long-term cost savings, the economic crisis may even push forward environmentally friendly programs.

The results of sustainability programs have been impressive across a range of industries. McDonald's, for instance, produces mountains of garbage each year, as do virtually all major fast-food chains. But the Golden Arches stands above the others in its attempts to reduce the problem. Following are some encouraging statistics:

- By the end of 2008, McDonald's UK was recycling 100% of its used cooking oil for biodiesel to fuel delivery trucks. This equates to 1,500 family cars being removed from the road each year.

- On average, U.S. company–owned McDonald's restaurant recycles more than 17 tons of corrugated cardboard per year and approximately

corporate responsibility
Business contributions to the community through the actions of the business itself rather than donations of money and time.

sustainable development
Doing business to meet the needs of the current generation, without harming the ability of future generations to meet their needs.

13,000 pounds of used cooking oil per year.[21]

Reducing the *amount* of trash is better than recycling, but recycling trash clearly beats dumping it in a landfill. McDonald's participates in this arena as well, through their extensive recycling programs, but more importantly as a big buyer of recycled products.

Taking an even broader perspective, some firms have started to measure their carbon footprint, with an eye toward reducing it. **Carbon footprint** refers to the amount of harmful greenhouse gases that a firm emits throughout its operations, both directly and indirectly. The ultimate goal is to become carbon neutral—either to emit zero harmful gases or to counteract the impact of emissions by removing a comparable amount from the atmosphere through projects such as planting trees. Dell Inc. became fully carbon neutral in mid-2008, fulfilling its quest to become "the greenest technology on the planet." More recently, PepsiCo calculated the carbon footprint for its Tropicana orange juice brand and was surprised to learn that about a third of its emissions came from applying fertilizer to the orange groves. According to the Conference Board, business leaders have begun to see their carbon footprint— both measurement and reduction—as a burgeoning opportunity.[22] Many large corporations track three different types of emissions. The first, called Scope 1, refers to direct emissions produced by corporate operations. The second, called Scope 2, refers to emissions that result from purchased electricity, heat, and steam. Scope 3 emissions, which are more complex to track, are emissions that occur outside a company's boundary, but over which it has some control. This category includes areas such as employee commutes, supplier emissions, and product-use emissions. When Stonyfield Farms, maker of organic yogurt and other dairy products, examined their Scope 3 emissions, they came to the rather startling (and somewhat gross!) conclusion that most of their emissions did not come from manufacturing or transporting their products, but from the methane gas produced by the cows back at their suppliers' farms! Interest in Scope 3 emissions is still somewhat new but seems sure to grow as environmental accounting methods become more sophisticated.[24]

A growing number of companies use **green marketing** to promote their businesses. This means marketing environmental products and practices to gain a competitive edge. Patagonia, for example, markets outdoor clothing using 100% organic cotton and natural fibers such as hemp. But green marketing represents a tough challenge: while most people support the idea of green products, the vast majority won't sacrifice price, performance, or

Sorry! So, So Sorry!

Why is it so compelling to watch the rich and powerful squirm? It's hard to explain, but when CEOs of big companies apologize for their mistakes, people love to watch, and their apologies often go viral. Sometimes the apologies are sincere and heartfelt, and everyone moves on; and sometimes they become targets of ridicule. Here are a few noteworthy examples. You be the judge.

- In 2013, Chip Wilson, former CEO and co-founder of Lululemon, stated to the press that "some women's bodies just don't actually work" for Lululemon's yoga pants. He apologized via a YouTube video in which he declared, "I'm really sad. I'm sad for the repercussions of my actions." He didn't even bother to address his offended customers.

- In mid-2014, Snapchat founder and CEO Evan Spiegel was dismayed to learn that graphic emails from his party days as a Stanford undergrad were published online. In them, Spiegel wrote about getting sorority girls drunk and peeing on his date, among other offensive stories. In response, he issued a statement saying, "I'm obviously mortified and embarrassed that my idiotic emails during my fraternity days were made public. I have no excuse. I'm sorry I wrote them at the time and I was jerk to have written them. They in no way reflect who I am today or my views towards women."

- Two days after Volkswagen was faulted for using software to cheat an industry-standard emissions test, CEO Martin Winterkorn declared that he was deeply sorry and that the company would "do everything necessary to reverse the damage this has caused. This matter has first priority for me, personally." First priority apparently wasn't enough to save Winterkorn's job, since the maligned CEO resigned soon after. Winterkorn announced that he would accept responsibility to clear the way for a fresh start for the company and win back the public's trust. Only time will tell if Winterkorn's resignation wins back sales for Volkswagen, which saw its stock tank after the emissions scandal broke.[23]

carbon footprint Refers to the amount of harmful greenhouse gases that a firm emits throughout its operations, both directly and indirectly.

green marketing Developing and promoting environmentally sound products and practices to gain a competitive edge.

Does the Gender of Your Business Leaders Matter?

Many people would say absolutely not. But a recent study published in *Harvard Business Review* suggests that gender

michaeljung/Shutterstock.com

could make a real difference to profitability. A new global study of nearly 22,000 firms found that in 2014, almost 60% of these firms had no female board members. Just over half had no female C-suite executives, and fewer than 5% had a female CEO—although there was considerable variation among countries and industries. The study also showed that *these numbers matter to the bottom line*. Going from having no women in corporate leadership to a 30% share of women is associated with a 1% increase in net margin, which translates to a 15% increase in profitability for a typical firm—wow! This performance improvement seems to come from two key factors: (1) increased skill diversity within top management and (2) less gender discrimination throughout the management ranks, which helps the company recruit, promote, and retain talent. The key question is *how* to best achieve the goal of more talented women in executive leadership.[25]

convenience to actually buy those products. Sometimes, however, green marketing can be quite consistent with profitability. The Toyota Prius hybrid car offers an interesting example. The Prius costs several thousand dollars more than a standard car, but as gas prices skyrocketed through the summer of 2008, consumers flooded the dealerships, snapping up Prius hybrids faster than Toyota could ship them. Yet, when the economy dropped in late 2008, Toyota sales plummeted along with the rest of the industry, suggesting that the environment may be a fair-weather priority for consumers. But by 2012, Prius sales again were soaring, especially with the introduction of the plug-in hybrid version.[26]

4-5 ETHICS AND SOCIAL RESPONSIBILITY IN THE GLOBAL ARENA: A HOUSE OF MIRRORS?

Globalization has made ethics and social responsibility even more complicated for workers at every level. Bribery and corruption are among the most challenging issues faced by companies and individuals that are involved in international business. Transparency International, a leading anticorruption organization, published its yearly index of "perceived corruption" across 168 countries in 2015. No country scored a completely clean 100 out of 100, and the United States scored a troubling 76, which was quite a bit higher than India at 38 and China at 37, but lower than most of the European countries that dominated the top of the list. Not surprisingly, the world's poorest countries fall largely in the bottom half of the index, with African and Central Asian countries clustered at the very bottom, suggesting that rampant corruption is part of their business culture.[27]

Corruption wouldn't be possible if companies didn't offer bribes, so Transparency International also researched the likelihood of firms from industrialized countries to pay bribes abroad. The 2011 results indicated that firms from export powers Russia, China, and Mexico rank among the worst, with India following close behind. U.S. corporations, forbidden to offer bribes since 1977 under the Foreign Corrupt Practices Act, showed a disturbing inclination to flout the law. In fact, in 2012, Avon Corporation was accused of bribing Chinese officials to gain a permit to engage in direct sales; Walmart was accused of bribing Mexican officials to speed development of their stores in Mexico; and Ralph Lauren Corporation was accused of bribing Argentine customs officials to allow merchandise into that country. Other U.S. corporations that have recently found themselves in the crosshairs of government bribery investigations include Johnson & Johnson, Hewlett-Packard, and Disney. Overall, the United States scored 8.1 out of a possible 10, falling well below many Western European countries.[28]

These statistics raise some thought-provoking questions:

- When does a gift become a bribe? The law is unclear, and perceptions differ from country to country.

Choosing between a Loaf of Bread and a Packet of Shampoo

Three-quarters of the world's population—nearly 4 billion people—earn less than $2 per day. But C. K. Prahalad, a well-respected consultant and economist, claims that if the "aspirational poor" had a chance to consume, they could add about $13 trillion in annual sales to the global economy. Unilever, a global marketing company headquartered in Europe, has aggressively pursued this market with consumer products. Their customers might not have electricity, running water, or even enough for dinner, but many of them do have packets of Sunsilk shampoo and Omo detergent. Unilever's success stems from local knowledge gained over decades of operating in developing markets—Unilever has been in Indonesia since 1933 and India since 1888. Electronics companies

iStock.com/Sheriar Irani

have experienced marketing success as well. In Dharavi, for instance—one of the largest urban slums in India—more than 85% of households own a television.

Critics suggest that the corporate push to reach impoverished consumers will enrich multinationals at the expense of their customers, representing exploitation of the world's poorest people. Ashvin Dayal, East Asia director for the antipoverty group Oxfam UK, expressed concern to *Time* magazine that corporate marketing might unseat locally produced products or encourage overspending by those who truly can't afford it. Citing heavily marketed candy and soda, he points out that "companies have the power to create needs rather than respond to needs."

But Prahalad counters that many people at the bottom of the economic pyramid accept that some of the basics—running water, for instance—are not likely to ever come their way. Instead, they opt to improve their quality of life through affordable "luxuries," such as single-use sachets of fragrant shampoo. He argues, "It's absolutely possible to do very well while doing good." Furthermore, he suggests that corporate marketing may kick-start the poorest economies, triggering entrepreneurial activity and economic growth. Since globalization shows no signs of slowing, let's hope that he's right.[29]

What do you think? Is targeting the poor with consumer goods exploitation or simply smart marketing?

■ How can corporations monitor corruption and enforce corporate policies in their foreign branches?

■ What are other ways to gain a competitive edge in countries where bribes are both accepted and expected?

Other challenging issues revolve around business responsibility to workers abroad. At minimum, businesses should pay a living wage for reasonable hours in a safe working environment. But exactly what this means is less clear-cut. Does a living wage mean enough to support an individual

> In 2014, the Chinese government declared a "war on pollution" in response to devastating levels of air pollution, water pollution, and rapid water depletion.
>
> —CHINA OUTLOOK

or a family? Does "support" mean enough to subsist day to day or enough to live in modest comfort? Should American businesses ban child labor in countries where families depend on their children's wages to survive? Companies must address these questions individually, bringing together their own values with the laws of both the United States and their host countries.

The most socially responsible companies establish codes of conduct for their vendors, setting clear policies for human rights, wages, safety, and environmental impact. In 1991, Levi Strauss became the first global company to establish a comprehensive code of conduct for its contractors. Over the years, creative thinking has helped it maintain its high standards, even in the face of cultural clashes. An example from Bangladesh, outlined in the *Harvard Business Review*, illustrates its preference for win–win solutions. In the early 1990s, Levi Strauss "discovered that two of its suppliers in Bangladesh were employing children under the age of 14—a practice that violated the company's principles but was tolerated in Bangladesh. Forcing the suppliers to fire the children would not have ensured that the children received an education, and it would have caused serious hardship for the families depending on the children's wages. In a creative arrangement, the suppliers agreed to pay the children's regular wages while they attended school and to offer each child a job at age 14. Levi Strauss, in turn, agreed to pay the children's tuition and provide books and uniforms." This creative solution allowed the suppliers to maintain their valuable contracts from Levi Strauss, while Levi Strauss upheld its values and improved the quality of life for its most vulnerable workers.[30]

Clearly, codes of conduct work best with monitoring, enforcement, and a commitment to finding solutions that work for all parties involved. Gap Inc. offers an encouraging example. In 1996, Gap published a rigorous Code of Vendor Conduct and required compliance from all of its vendors. Its vendor-compliance officers strive to visit each of its 3,000 factories at least once a year.

Investors count on companies to spend money wisely and fully disclose all key facts.

The company has uncovered a troubling number of violations, proactively pulling contracts from serious violators and rejecting bids from suppliers who don't meet its standards.

Gap and Levi Strauss seem to be doing their part, but the world clearly needs universal standards and universal enforcement to ensure that the benefits of globalization don't come at the expense of the world's most vulnerable people.[31]

4-6 MONITORING ETHICS AND SOCIAL RESPONSIBILITY: WHO IS MINDING THE STORE?

Actually, many firms are monitoring themselves. The process is called a **social audit**, which is a systematic evaluation of how well a firm is meeting its ethics and social responsibility objectives. Establishing goals is the starting point for a social audit, but the next step is to determine how to measure the achievement of those goals, and measurement can be a bit tricky. As You Sow, an organization dedicated to promoting corporate social responsibility, recommends that companies measure their success by evaluating a "double bottom line," one that accounts for traditional financial indicators, such as earnings, and one that accounts for social-responsibility indicators, such as community involvement.

Other groups are watching as well, which helps keep businesses on a positive track. Activist customers, investors, unions, environmentalists, and community groups all play a role. In addition, the threat of government legislation keeps some industries motivated to self-regulate. One example is the entertainment industry, which uses a self-imposed rating system for both movies and TV, largely to fend off regulation. Many people argue that the emergence of salads at fast-food restaurants represents an effort to avoid regulation as well.

social audit A systematic evaluation of how well a firm is meeting its ethics and social responsibility goals.

Clearly, the primary goal of any business is to earn long-term profits for its investors. But profits alone are not enough. As active participants in society, firms must also promote ethical actions and social responsibility throughout their organizations and their corresponding customer and supplier networks. Although every area matters, a few warrant special mention:

- In tough economic times, effective business leaders focus more than ever on integrity, transparency, and a humane approach to managing the workforce—especially during cutbacks.

- Building or maintaining a presence in foreign markets requires particularly careful attention to human rights and local issues.

- Sustainable development and other environmentally sound practices are not only fiscally prudent and customer-friendly but also crucial for the health of our planet.

CAREERS IN BUSINESS ETHICS AND SOCIAL RESPONSIBILITY

Ethics Officer

Work with senior management to provide leadership, advice, and guidance in all matters pertaining to ethics, including training, enforcement, financial disclosure, and gift rules. Ensure that the company's code of ethics remains in strict compliance with all relevant laws. Model the highest standards of honesty and personal ethics at all times to foster an ethical climate in the organization. Arrange and facilitate employee ethics training. Work with HR to examine ethics complaints and to ensure that all investigations of employee misconduct are handled fairly and promptly. Assist in the resolution of ethical dilemmas wherever needed throughout the organization.

STUDY TOOLS 4

LOCATED AT BACK OF THE TEXTBOOK

☐ Rip-Out Chapter Review Card

☐ Gain unique perspectives on key concepts with new concept videos in the e-book

☐ Increase your comprehension with online homework and quizzes

☐ Study with existing flashcards and make your own

5 | Business Communication: Creating and Delivering Messages That Matter

Remember to visit
PAGE 91
for additional
STUDY TOOLS

LEARNING OBJECTIVES

After studying this chapter, you will be able to:

5-1 Explain the importance of excellent business communication

5-2 Describe the key elements of nonverbal communication

5-3 Compare, contrast, and choose effective communication channels

5-4 Choose the right words for effective communication

5-5 Write more effective business memos, letters, and emails

5-6 Create and deliver successful verbal presentations

5-1 EXCELLENT COMMUNICATION SKILLS: YOUR INVISIBLE ADVANTAGE

Much of your success in business will depend on your ability to influence the people around you. Can you land the right job? Close the deal that makes the difference? Convince the boss to adopt your idea? Motivate people to buy your products? Excellent communicators are not only influential but also well liked, efficient, and effective. Great communication skills can dramatically boost your chance for success, while poor communication skills can bury even the most talented people.

So what exactly are "excellent communication skills"? Many students believe that great business communication equates to a knack for speaking or a flair for writing. But if that's where you stop, you're likely to hit a brick wall again and again as you attempt to achieve your goals. Effective **communication** happens only when you transmit meaning—*relevant* meaning—to your audience.

communication The transmission of information between a sender and a recipient.

Communication must be dynamic, fluid, and two-way, which includes listening. Seeking and understanding feedback from your audience—and responding appropriately—form the core of successful business communication. And it isn't as easy as you may think. American novelist Russell Hoban neatly summarized the issue: "When you come right down to it, how many people speak the same language even when they speak the same language?"

5-1a Communication Barriers: "That's Not What I Meant!"

Why is effective communication so challenging? The key issue is **noise**, which is any interference that causes the message you send to be different from the message your audience understands. Some experts define noise in terms of **communication barriers**, which arise in a number of different forms. As you read the definitions, keep in mind that with a bit of extra effort, most are surmountable, and we'll discuss strategies and tips as we move through the chapter.

- **Physical Barriers:** These can range from a document that looks like a wall of type to a room that's freezing cold, to chairs in your office that force your visitors to sit at a lower level than you.

- **Language Barriers:** Clearly, if you don't speak the language, you'll have trouble communicating. But even among people who do share the same language, slang, jargon, and regional accents can interfere with meaning.

- **Body Language Barriers:** Even if your words are inviting, the wrong body language can alienate and distract your audience so completely that they simply won't absorb the content of your message.

> "If a leader can't get a message across clearly, and motivate others to act on it, then having a message doesn't even matter."
>
> —GILBERT AMELIO, CEO, JAZZ SEMICONDUCTOR CORP.

- **Perceptual Barriers:** How your audience perceives you and your agenda can create a significant obstacle to effective communication. If possible, explore their perceptions—both positive and negative—in advance!

- **Organizational Barriers:** Some companies have built-in barriers to effective communication, such as an unspoken rule that the people at the top of the organization don't talk to the people at the bottom. These barriers are important to understand but hard to change.

noise Any interference that causes the message you send to be different from the message your audience understands.

communication barriers Obstacles to effective communication, typically defined in terms of physical, language, body language, cultural, perceptual, and organizational barriers.

Where In the World?

According to former Secretary General of the United Nations Dag Hammarskjold, the *unspoken* dialogue between two people can never be put right by anything they say. To avoid making devastating gaffes when engaging in international business, consider researching other cultures where you hope to do business. And don't just read books and articles—seek out and interact with people who are part of the target culture. Some examples of intercultural communication differences that you may encounter:

- Time: Arriving late is shockingly rude from a Swedish perspective, while tardiness is almost expected in many Central American countries. Don't be caught by surprise!

- Greetings: In Saudi Arabia, male acquaintances kiss on the cheek, and some even walk through the streets holding hands. In Germany and China, on the other hand, most businesspeople actively avoid unnecessary touching.

- Gestures: When Japanese colleagues nod their heads and say, "hai," it doesn't necessarily mean that they agree with you, but rather that they hear you—big difference! When people in some parts of the Middle East give you the thumbs-up, it doesn't mean "good job." Quite the opposite—it's equivalent to flipping the bird in the United States.

- Directness: U.S. culture deeply values directness, which can lead people from other countries to view Americans as abrupt and crass. When doing business in countries such as Lebanon and India, an indirect approach can be much more effective.

- Business practices: From giving gifts to exchanging business cards, business practices vary widely from culture to culture. As in each of the other cultural arenas, advanced preparation definitely pays off!

graphbottles/Shutterstock.com

- **Cultural Barriers:** These can include everything from how you greet colleagues and establish eye contact to how you handle disagreement, eat business meals, and make small talk at meetings. As globalization gains speed, **intercultural communication** will become increasingly pivotal to long-term business success. Identifying and understanding communication barriers is a vital first step toward dismantling them in order to communicate more effectively with any audience.

5-2 NONVERBAL COMMUNICATION: BEYOND THE WORDS

intercultural communication
Communication among people with differing cultural backgrounds.

nonverbal communication
Communication that does not use words. Common forms of nonverbal communication include gestures, posture, facial expressions, tone of voice, and eye contact.

Most of us focus on what we want to say, but *how* we say it matters even more. In fact, studies cited in *The Wall Street Journal's Career Journal* suggest that during face-to-face communication, only 7% of meaning comes from the verbal content of the message—38% comes from tone of voice, and 55% comes from body language such as facial expressions, gestures, and posture.[1]

The goal of **nonverbal communication** should be to reinforce the meaning of your message. Random facial expressions and disconnected body language—arbitrary arm thrusts, for example—are at best distracting, and at worst clownish. But strong, deliberate nonverbal communication can dramatically magnify the impact of your messages. Here are a few examples of how this can work (but keep in mind that these examples do not necessarily translate from culture to culture):

- **Eye Contact:** Within American culture, sustained eye contact (different from a constant cold stare) indicates integrity, trust, and respectful attention, whether you're communicating with a subordinate, a superior, or a peer.

- **Tone of Voice:** Variation is the key to effectiveness, since paying attention to a monotone takes more concentration than most people are willing to muster. Also, even when you're angry or frustrated, try to keep your voice in a lower pitch to encourage listeners to stay with your message.

- **Facial Expressions:** People vary widely in terms of how much emotion they show on their faces, but virtually everyone communicates, whether or not they

If You See It in the News, It's Got to Be True . . . Psych!!!

Satirical news shows have long had a prominent seat in the spectrum of American entertainment. However, *fake news* rose to new prominence toward the end of the 2016 election cycle as each side accused the other of planting fake news stories to sway the election. Fake news catapulted to a whole new level of prominence when President Trump began labeling legitimate news organizations—such as The New York Times and CNN—as "fake news."

Outside of politics, more and more businesses depend on world events, filtered through the news, to guide their decision making. Millions of dollars hang in the balance, so the credibility of the news is crucial. But since mock news programs and websites enjoy more popularity than ever, business decision makers must make sure that they are in on the joke instead of the butt of the joke, which can't be as easy as it sounds, given the number of times legitimate news outlets and high-profile individuals have mistaken stories on *The Onion* website, a blatantly farcical mock news site, as real news. Some examples:

- China's *People's Daily Online* exuberantly reported that North Korea's short, pudgy leader, Kim Jong-un, was the "Sexiest Man Alive" based on a fake story in *The Onion*.

- During the government shutdown of 2013, a Fox News co-host falsely stated that President Obama offered to pay out of his own pocket for the museum of Muslim culture, a claim that originated from another satire website called the *National Report*.

- On April Fool's Day 2016, Yahoo's news service published an article reporting that Trader Joe's would close its more than 450 grocery stores in 2017. Furious Trader Joe's fans took to Twitter in a firestorm of fury and outrage—even though the end of the article clarified that it was just a joke.

The lesson here is NOT that you shouldn't believe everything you read, but rather that if something seems too silly to be true, it may not be, and it certainly merits further investigation. Otherwise, it may be the jokers who get the last laugh![2]

Skylines/Shutterstock.com

---

know it, through a wide range of expressions that include shy smiles, focused frowns, clenched jaws, squinted eyes, and furrowed brows.

- **Gestures and Posture:** How you handle your body speaks for you. For example, leaning forward can indicate interest, shrugging can suggest a lack of authority, and fidgeting can imply either impatience or nervousness. To increase the power of your message, both your gestures and your posture should be confident, open, and coherent.

When disgraced cyclist Lance Armstrong confessed to doping in a 2013 interview with Oprah Winfrey, body language expert Tonya Reiman noticed that despite the confidence of his words, he betrayed anxiety nonverbally by not meeting Ms. Winfrey's eyes, biting his lip, and repeatedly touching his face. She also pointed out that he "'fig-leafed,' or nervously covered his groin with his hands, several different times…That's a sign of somebody who's under pressure."[3] Reiman has also pointed out that when people swallow hard after making strong assertions, they are clearly lying. As silly as it sounds, one of the easiest, most effective ways to improve your body language is to practice nonverbal communication in front of the mirror. Check out your gestures, notice your facial expressions, and focus on eye contact. If you have the

time and ability, it's also helpful (though humbling!) to videotape yourself delivering both a formal and informal message, and ask a trusted friend to dissect the results with you.

Accurately discerning the body language of others is another powerful business communication tool. But keep in mind that you must evaluate others in the context of common sense. When your boss keeps yawning, she may be bored, *or* she may just be tired. When your colleague crosses his arms, he may be indicating defensiveness, *or* he might just normally stand that way.

5-2a Active Listening: The Great Divider

How we listen (or don't listen) also sends a high-impact, nonverbal message. In fact, an old Chinese proverb asserts that to listen well is as powerful a means of influence as to talk well. Those who do both are unstoppable.

Strong listening skills—**active listening**—play an obvious role in business success. The higher you go in an organization, the more you find that people are listening. Hourly employees may spend 30% of their time listening, while managers often spend 60%, and executives might spend

> **active listening** Attentive listening that occurs when the listener focuses his or her complete attention on the speaker.

EXHIBIT 5.1 TIPS FOR BETTER LISTENING

Listening Dos	Listening Don'ts
Use your extra mental capacity to summarize (to yourself!) what the speaker is saying. Ask yourself: Why does this matter? What's the key point?	Don't even glance at your emails or text messages. You won't fool anyone with those surreptitious peeks.
Take a few notes. It will not only help you concentrate but will also communicate to the speaker that his or her thoughts really matter.	Don't begin speaking the moment the person stops talking. Take a brief pause to indicate that you're absorbing the message.
Listen with both your ears and your eyes. Notice any inconsistency between the speaker's words and body language.	Don't get overly comfortable. If your body is too relaxed, your mind may wander more easily.
Use nonverbal communication—nods, smiles, leaning forward—to indicate interest in the speaker.	Don't pick up your phone—or even look at your phone—when you're listening. And whenever it's practical, set your cell phone to vibrate when others are speaking.
Use verbal feedback and questions to indicate understanding and empathy: "So you're saying that…," or "Why do you think that?"	Don't interrupt or finish other people's sentences. There are few better ways to cut off future communication.

75% or more. Interestingly, top salespeople also tend to spend about 75% of their communication time listening.[4]

According to the International Listening Association website, 85% of our learning is derived from listening, yet listeners are distracted, forgetful, and preoccupied 75% of the time. If listening is so crucial, why do most of us have such a hard time engaging completely? One reason may be that people *listen* at about 125 to 250 words per minute, but *think* at about 1,000 to 3,000 words per minute—that's a significant gap. Common ways to fill the void include daydreaming, thinking about the past (e.g., last night), and planning for the future (e.g., later in the day).[5]

When you listen, try to use the extra thinking time to make yourself pay closer attention to the speaker. You'll find that people tend to tell more to those who listen better, so if you polish your listening skills, you're also likely to buff up the quality of what you know and when you know it. Exhibit 5.1 highlights some listening dos and don'ts (specific to American culture).[6]

 5-3 CHOOSE THE RIGHT CHANNEL: A RICH ARRAY OF OPTIONS

Figuring out the right way to send a message can be a daunting challenge, especially in light of the growing number of choices. The various options are called **communication channels**. Understanding the impact of each channel will help you make the best decision regarding which to use.

Communication channels differ from one another in terms of how much information—or richness—they

communication channels
The various ways in which a message can be sent, ranging from one-on-one in-person meetings to Internet message boards.

communicate to the recipient. Exhibit 5.2 provides a brief overview of key channels. Other channels might include intranet postings, WebEx, Facebook, and instant messaging. Where would these additional channels fall on the spectrum? Why?

5-3a Consider the Audience: It's Not about You!

Clearly, the needs and expectations of your audience play a crucial role in your choice of communication channel. Even if the recipient's preferences seem absurd—for example, we probably all know someone who refuses to check email or voice mail—remember that your first priority is to communicate your message. If you send it through a channel that the audience doesn't expect, understand, or like, you've crippled your chance for successful communication.

Analysis and consideration of your audience should also be a top priority after you choose your communication channel. Meeting the needs of your audience will give you a crucial edge in developing a message that works.

 5-4 PICK THE RIGHT WORDS: IS THAT CAR PRE-LOVED OR JUST PLAIN USED?!

Mark Twain once said, "The difference between the right word and almost the right word is the difference between lightning and the lightning bug." Perhaps that's a little extreme, but it may not be too far from the truth. In the business world, where your messages are competing with so many others for the all-too-limited attention

EXHIBIT 5.2   COMMUNICATION CHANNELS

Communication Channel	Channel Richness	When Should You Use This Channel?
Texting	Very low: Because so many of us text with as few words as possible, your audience will pick up only the basics.	When your content is uncontroversial When you want a quick response regarding relatively simple issues When you know that your audience won't be annoyed by it
Memos/Reports	Very low: Your audience won't gain any information from your tone or your body language.	When your content is uncontroversial When you must reach a number of people with the same message When you must communicate lengthy or detailed information
Email	Very low: Here, too, your audience learns nothing beyond your words themselves.	When your content is uncontroversial When you must reach a number of people with the same message
Voice Mail	Low: Your audience has the benefit of hearing your tone but not seeing your body language.	When your content is uncontroversial When you don't need a record of your message (but don't forget that the recipient can easily save or forward your voice mail)
Telephone Conversation	Moderate: Your audience benefits from hearing your tone and how it changes through the call.	When you need to either deliver your message or get a response quickly When your content is more personal or controversial When you need or want a spontaneous, dynamic dialogue with the recipient
Videoconferencing	High: Especially with state-of-the-art equipment, the channel conveys much of the richness of actually being there.	When you need to reach multiple people with complex or high-priority content When you need or want a spontaneous, dynamic dialogue with an audience that you cannot reach in person
In-Person Presentation	High: Your audience directly experiences every element of your communication, from verbal content to tone, to body language.	When you need to reach a large audience with an important message When you need or want to experience the immediate response of your audience
Face-to-Face Meeting	Very high: Your audience experiences your full message even more directly.	When your message is personal, emotional, complex, or high priority (but if the recipient might be volatile, consider using a less immediate channel) When you need or want instant feedback from your audience

of the recipient, the right words can encourage your audience to stay with you long enough to absorb your message.

5-4a Analyze Your Audience

To find the right words, begin with the needs of your audience. Consider:

■ **Expectations:** What kind of language do most people use in the organization? Is it formal or informal? Is it direct or roundabout? Should you differ from the norm? Why or why not?

■ **Education:** The education level of the audience should drive the level of vocabulary and the complexity of the message.

■ **Profession:** Some professions (e.g., website development) are rife with jargon and acronyms. How should this influence your message?

5-4b Be Concise

Comedian Jerry Seinfeld once said, "I will spend an hour editing an eight-word sentence into five." While Jerry might be going a bit too far, it pays to be clear and concise in business communication. But don't be concise at the expense of completeness; include all information that your audience may need. (It'll save you time down the road.)

5-4c Avoid Slang

Unless you're absolutely certain that your audience will understand and appreciate it, do not use slang in either written or verbal communication. The risk of unintentionally alienating yourself from your audience is simply too high.

5-4d Avoid Bias

Intentionally or unintentionally, words can communicate biases that can interfere with your message, alienate your

OOPS! WHAT WERE THEY THINKING?

Ooops! Flushthatjobdownthetoilet

Common sense dictates that your work friends should not be your Facebook friends, especially if your private life is not suitable for your work realm (and in most cases—even if it isn't as racy as you might prefer—it simply isn't appropriate), but you might be surprised to learn that Twitter grew more than 60% between 2012 and 2014. And unlike Facebook posts, tweets are in the public arena, which means that workers must know, understand, and carefully follow their companies' social media policies or risk fairly certain consequences. Job seekers should be particularly careful about what they post on social media.

Forty-three percent of employers use social networking sites to research job candidates, according to a recent Career-Builders.com national survey, and 51% of them said they've found content that caused them to not hire the candidate. Here are some of the key reasons:

- Job candidate posted provocative or inappropriate photographs or information (46%).
- Job candidate posted information about him- or herself drinking or using drugs (41%).
- Job candidates bad-mouthed their previous company or fellow employee (36%).
- Job candidate had poor communication skills (32%).
- Job candidate had discriminatory comments related to race, gender, religion, and so on. (28%).

Potential employers also found some items that were just plain strange:

- Candidate's profile included links to an escort service.

- Candidate posted a photo of a warrant for his arrest.
- Candidate posted an exercise video for grandmothers.
- Candidate had sued his wife for shooting him in the head.
- Candidate featured a pig as his closest friend.
- Candidate posted his dental exam results.
- Candidate bragged about driving drunk and not getting caught on several occasions.
- Candidate was actively involved in a demonic cult.
- Candidate posted Sasquatch pictures he had taken.[7]

What do you think? Is it reasonable for employers to use social media to screen applicants? Why or why not? Does it represent a violation of privacy?

Denys Prykhodov/Shutterstock.com

---

audience, and call your own character into question. As a result, you will be less effective in achieving the immediate goals of your communication (and possibly any future communication as well). Three kinds of **bias** are common.

Gender Bias Gender bias consists of words that suggest stereotypical attitudes toward a specific gender. Avoiding bias becomes tricky when you simply don't know the gender of your audience, which often happens when you apply for a job in writing. The best solution, of course, is to find out the recipient's name, but if you can't do that, do not address your

> **bias** A preconception about members of a particular group. Common forms of bias include gender bias; age bias; and race, ethnicity, or nationality bias.

> **"Improvement in a firm's communication effectiveness is associated with a nearly 16% increase in its market value."**
>
> —WATSON WYATT, CONSULTING FIRM

message to "Dear Sir" or "Dear Madam"; rather, use the title of the position (e.g., "Dear Hiring Manager").

Another common challenge is to establish agreement in your sentences without creating gender bias. Consider the following example:

The manager who loses his temper must apologize.

Technically, this sentence is correct, but it implies that all managers are men. A simple solution would be to convert to plural:

Managers who lose their temper must apologize.

This approach almost always works to help you sidestep the gender bias issue. In the rare case that it doesn't, you can simply use the "his or her" option:

The manager who loses his or her temper must apologize.

Age Bias Age bias refers to words that suggest stereotypical attitudes toward people of specific ages. In American culture, older people tend to experience negative age bias much more often than younger people. This happens despite specific federal legislation outlawing employment discrimination against people over 40 years old. The reason may be that American culture associates youth with highly valued qualities such as creativity, speed, independence, and individualism. This bias will become increasingly detrimental as the workforce ages. Here is an example of age bias:

We need someone young and dynamic in this position!

You could easily eliminate the negative bias by simply deleting the word "young" or by replacing it with the word "energetic." One clear benefit of eliminating bias in this case would be a broader applicant pool that might include an older person who is more dynamic than any of the younger applicants.

Race, Ethnicity, and Nationality Bias Words can also suggest stereotypical attitudes toward specific races, ethnicities, and nationalities. Leaving aside prejudice—which is clearly wrong—the problems in this area are usually unintentional and stem from un-articulated assumptions about a person's attitudes, opinions, and experiences. Your best plan for avoiding bias is to forgo any references to race, ethnicity, or nationality unless they are directly relevant and clearly necessary. And, of course, never simply assume that one person embodies the attitudes, opinions, and experiences of a larger group. If you communicate with each person as an individual, you will not only avoid bias but also develop deeper, more effective channels of communication.

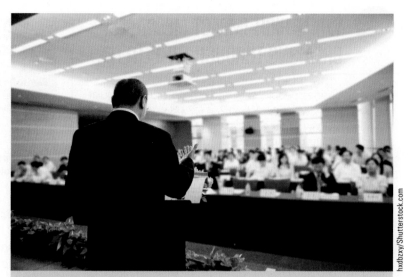

Effective business communication requires an analysis of the audience.

hxdbzxy/Shutterstock.com

5-4e Use the Active Voice Whenever Possible

Active voice facilitates direct, powerful, concise communication. You have used the **active voice** when the subject of your sentence *is* doing the action described by the verb. You have used the **passive voice** when the subject of your sentence *is not* doing the action described by the verb.

Here's an example of a sentence that uses the active voice:

Our team did not hit our sales goal.

Our team, the subject of the sentence, did the action described by the verb (missing the sales goal). The same sentence in the passive voice would read as follows:

The sales goal was not reached.

In this version, the subject of the sentence is the sales goal, which clearly did not do the action. As you can see from these examples, another benefit of active voice is accountability, which can create deeper trust between you and your audience.

active voice Sentence construction in which the subject performs the action expressed by the verb (e.g., The accountant did the taxes.). The active voice works better for the vast majority of business communication.

passive voice Sentence construction in which the subject does not do the action expressed by the verb; rather, the subject is acted upon (e.g., The taxes were done by our accountant.). The passive voice tends to be less effective for business communication.

> "What you do speaks so loud that I cannot hear what you say."
> —RALPH WALDO EMERSON

5-5 WRITE HIGH-IMPACT MESSAGES: BREAKING THROUGH THE CLUTTER

For many businesspeople, checking email—or even regular mail—is like approaching a fire hose for a sip of water. Goal number one is to crank down the pressure to get what you need without being knocked over by all the rest. To attain this goal, many people simply press the delete button.

Your challenge as a writer is to make your message a must-read, and the starting point should be the needs of your audience. Consider how the audience will respond to your message—think about how they will feel, not what they will do—and use that information to guide your writing. But keep in mind that it's hard to know for sure how the recipient will respond. For instance, each of the responses in Exhibit 5.3 could be reasonable for different people.

How do you know how your audience will respond? In most cases, you must simply guess based on as much evidence as you can find. The value of making a thoughtful guess is that the chances of achieving your goal will soar if you happen to be correct.

The anticipated audience response should directly affect how you structure your writing.

- If the recipient will feel positive or neutral about your message, the memo or email should begin with your bottom line. What is your request or

recommendation or conclusion? Why should the audience care? After you've clarified those points, follow up with your rationale and explanations (keeping in mind that less is usually more for time-starved businesspeople).

- If the recipient will feel negative about your message, start the memo or email with a couple of lines that present the rationale before you give the bottom line. Follow up with alternatives if there are any, and be sure to end on a positive note (rather than an apology). This structure is less straightforward, but it's a more effective way to communicate your message.

See Exhibit 5.4 for sample emails based on different anticipated responses to messages in an Internet game development firm.

EXHIBIT 5.3 MESSAGES AND RESPONSES

Message	Channel Richness
Please note the new computer password procedures.	**Positive:** *Great! We've really needed this.* **Neutral:** *Okay, no big deal.* **Negative:** *Not another change....*
The company plans to re-assign your project team at the end of the year.	**Positive:** *I can hardly wait to work with new people!* **Neutral:** *It's all part of the job ...* **Negative:** *Not another change!*

What's the Trick to Getting More People to Respond to Your Emails?

Do you often find yourself left hanging after sending an email? One helpful trick may be changing your sign-off. According to a recent study on email written to request help or advice, fewer than half received a response (47.5%). However, the response rate increased a whopping 36% on average when email had a "thankful closing" such as "thanks in advance," "thanks," or "thank you." Overall, email with a thankful closing garnered a 62% response rate. Other popular sign-offs were total duds in comparison:

- **Cheers: 54% response rate**
- **Regards: 54% response rate**
- **Best: 51% response rate**

So always keep in mind: if you want your email to result in action, a little thanks goes a long way.[8]

AFANASEV IVAN/Shutterstock.com

Mind Your Digital Manners! Not as Easy as You Might Think...

Technology today makes almost everything easier. We can use navigation programs to find even the most obscure address and never struggle with an uncooperative paper map. We can use cheap or free video chat programs to see the faces of friends and family around the world. We can use health apps to monitor our own heart rate and sleeping patterns.

But technology doesn't make it easier to mind our manners as we communicate with each other—or with our devices—in the rapidly changing digital world. In fact, Kevin Sintumuang, columnist for *The Wall Street Journal*, noted, "More devices will have us talking (or yelling) into the air—crying out, as if to the Almighty, 'Please play the workout mix!'" Sintumuang points out that it's rude to text at a nice restaurant and to take selfies at disaster sites. He also comments that while some people are absolutely fluent in emojis, others swear that the cute cartoon symbols are destroying "real" human language. British researchers and other digital etiquette experts tried to help by developing a list of golden etiquette rules for the digital age. A sampling:

■ Don't overshare on Facebook.

■ Don't look for hook-ups on LinkedIn or any other professional platform.

■ Don't even *glance* at your phone or smartwatch when you're having a face-to-face conversation—it's rude, and you're not fooling anyone.

■ Use your email client's vacation responder so people won't be left hanging when you're out of town.

■ Never text, email, or use social media while drunk, angry, or emotional.

■ Never end a relationship by text or social media.

■ Don't look through your partner's phone.

So what are the right answers? Well, until technology stops—which we hope won't be anytime soon—and the proper etiquette sorts itself out, all of us should probably let common sense and old-fashioned consideration be our guides.[9]

Rommel Canlas/Shutterstock.com

5-5a Strike the Right Tone

Good business writing sounds natural—it flows like spoken language and reads like a conversation on paper. To strike the right tone for any given message, remember that you can choose from a wide variety of conversational styles, from formal to chatty. Imagine yourself speaking to the recipient of your message, and you'll find that the right tone emerges naturally. A few guidelines will also help:

■ Use common words in most situations (e.g., *use* versus *utilize*).

■ Use the active voice (e.g., *We made a mistake* versus *A mistake was made*).

■ Use personal pronouns (*I*, *you*) whenever appropriate.

■ Use contractions (*I'll, don't, here's*) as often as you would when speaking.

5-5b Don't Make Grammar Goofs

Grammatical errors distract your reader from your writing and undermine your credibility. Most businesspeople are aware of the more common grammatical errors, so they tend to jump off the page before the content of the message. But if you're uncertain about a particular point, look at how professionally edited publications handle similar issues. Finally, don't be afraid to do a commonsense check on any grammatical question.

Edward P. Bailey, noted professor and business communication author, points out that many writers make grammar mistakes based on phantom knowledge—"mythical" grammar rules that aren't even in grammar handbooks. His research firmly reassures us that:

■ It is okay to end a sentence with a preposition when doing so sounds natural and does not involve excess words (e.g., *Where is this book from?* is much better than *From where is this book?*).

■ It is okay to begin sentences with "And" or "But" (e.g., *Most teens enjoy video games with a moderate level of violence. But a small, vocal minority strongly advocates a more clean-cut approach.*).

■ It is okay to split infinitives (e.g., *Try to effectively film the next scene* is a perfectly acceptable sentence, even though "effectively" is inserted between "to" and "film.").

Exhibit 5.4
Sample Emails: Same Message, Different Approach

If the recipient will feel neutral ...

Subject line specifies the key issue

Main point in the first sentence

Inbox

TO: Online Poker Team
FROM: Yumi Tanaka, VP Product Development
RE: Game Development Team Restructuring

To help meet our goal of developing three more innovative games this year, I plan to reassign each member of the online poker team to a new team that needs to brainstorm more effectively. Please let me know sometime in the next two days if you have a preference regarding your new assignment.

Thank you for arranging to present the new version of your online poker game to the sales force last week. I am confident that this game your team developed will be a huge hit with our key customers.

Positive close reinforces goodwill

If the recipient will feel negative ...

Neutral subject line–informative but not alarming

Opening establishes goodwill

The reasons for the restructuring precede the announcement

Inbox

TO: Online Poker Team
FROM: Yumi Tanaka, VP Product Development
RE: Game Development Teams

Thank you for arranging to present the new version of online poker to the sales force next week. I am confident that this game your team developed will be a huge hit with our key customers.

Looking forward, we hope to develop at least three more innovative games this year. To best use the expertise that your team has developed in this area, I plan to reassign each member to a new team that needs to brainstorm more effectively. Please let me know sometime in the next two days if you have a preference regarding your new assignment. I'd be glad to answer any questions.

Positive close reinforces goodwill

If you follow these principles, your writing not only will sound more natural but also will flow more easily. Winston Churchill, a renowned writer and speaker, was on-board with this commonsense approach decades ago, as we can see from his joking comment that poked fun at tortured writing: "From now on, ending a sentence with a preposition is something up with which I will not put."[10]

5-5c Use Block Paragraphs

There are three elements to block paragraphs: (1) use single spacing, (2) double space between paragraphs, and (3) do not indent the first sentence of your paragraphs. This approach has become standard for business writing over the past decade, as writers have begun to include an increasing number of additional elements such as headings and illustrations. The block paragraphs create a more organized look for your page, guiding the reader's eye through the key elements of your structure.

5-5d Use Headings and Bulleted Lists Wherever Appropriate

Both headings and bulleted lists guide your reader more easily through your writing. And the easier it is for your

> "Technology of late has been so fun, so easily engrossing, that it's amplified the jerkitude of the average American."
>
> —KEVIN SINTUMUANG, THE WALL STREET JOURNAL

reader, the more likely that he or she will absorb your message, which is, of course, your ultimate goal.

- **Headings:** A heading is not a title; rather, it is a label for one of several parts. If you have only one part, skip the heading, and use a title or a subject line. Consider using informative headings (e.g., "Recruitment has stalled," rather than simply "Recruitment") or question headings (e.g., "Have we met our recruitment goals for this campaign?"). And remember, headings are just as effective for letters and emails as they are for memos, and they are perfectly okay in one-page documents.

- **Bulleted Lists:** A bulleted list is an invaluable tool that you can use to engage your reader's attention whenever you have more than one of

> "The single biggest problem in communication is the illusion that it has taken place."
>
> —GEORGE BERNARD SHAW

anything in your writing (e.g., next steps, similar sections, questions). By formatting your lists with bullets, you are directing your reader's eye through your writing.

5-6 CREATE AND DELIVER SUCCESSFUL VERBAL PRESENTATIONS: HOOK 'EM AND REEL 'EM IN!

What do people fear most? The *Book of Lists* asserts that public speaking ranks number one for the majority of people, high above the fear of death at number four. So, when people say they would rather die than give a speech, they may really mean it! This section is designed to mitigate any fear you might have about public speaking by giving you guidance on how to create and deliver a high-impact verbal presentation.

As with most communication, the needs of the audience are the best place to begin. How does your audience feel about you and your topic? Are they interested? Hostile? Positive? What were they doing before your presentation? Dragging themselves out of bed after a late night at a sales meeting? Eating lunch? Use this information to guide how you develop your presentation. For instance, an eager, educated audience might not need as much background as a more lethargic, less-interested audience.

5-6a Opening

The opening of your presentation gives you a chance to grab the attention of the audience. If your opening hooks them, you've boosted the likelihood that you will hold their attention throughout the presentation. But developing that hook can be a challenge. The following are some suggestions for effective hooks:

- **An Interesting or Startling Statistic:** In a presentation from a nonprofit foodbank seeking to partner with a grocery chain, you could open by sharing that "the U.S. has the largest number of homeless women and children of any industrialized nation, and 57% of homeless kids spend at least one day a month completely without food. How could we improve these devastating numbers?"

- **Audience Involvement:** Pulling the audience into your opening can be very effective. For instance, in a presentation for a clothing company: "Imagine yourself with me at 11 P.M. on a Friday night, standing in line for admission to the hottest club in New York. As we inch forward, we suddenly realize that three other women in line are wearing the exact same dress as you…."

- **A Compelling Story or Anecdote:** This approach works best when it's completely genuine, using specific details that are directly relevant to the audience. For

---

EXHIBIT 5.5 | TEN TIPS FOR EXCELLENT EMAIL

1. Consider both your primary and secondary readers. In other words, never forget that your reader may forward your email without considering the potential impact on you.

2. Keep it short! Many readers won't scroll down past whatever shows on their screen, so be sure to get your bottom line close to the top of your message.

3. Don't forget to proofread. This is especially important if you're asking someone to do something for you. And remember that your spell-checker won't catch every mistake.

4. Use standard writing. Smiley faces, abbreviations, and five exclamation points are all fine if you're emailing your buddies, but in more formal messages they can make you look silly (or like you just don't care).

5. Avoid attachments if possible. They take time and space to open, and they don't always translate well to cell phones and PDAs. Instead, cut and paste relevant sections of the attachment into your email.

6. Don't assume privacy. Think of your emails as postcards that anyone (especially computer system administrators and managers) can read along the way. In that light, try not to use email to communicate negative or critical messages.

7. Respond promptly to emails. If you don't have time to respond to the email itself, consider sending a message such as "Sorry, but I'm swamped right now—will get back to you early next week."

8. Assume the best. Because emails are often brief, they can cause unintentional offense. If you receive an off-key message, don't be afraid to inquire: "I'm not sure what you mean . . . could you please explain?"

9. Create a compelling subject line. Make your reader want to open your message. Briefly communicate the topic of your message and why your reader should care.

10. Think before you write, and think again before you send! Too many people send messages in an emotional moment that they later regret. Take time to think and think again.

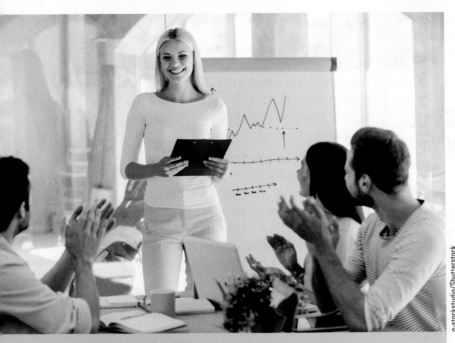

Giving great presentations may be easier than you think.

with visual reinforcement. Then as you move to each new point, you can refer to the blueprint that you established upfront. A clear, explicit structure will help the audience track with you as you move through your material.

5-6c Close

Ideally, the close of your presentation will summarize your key points. Then circle back to your introduction, so that the beginning and the end serve as "bookends" for the body of your presentation. For instance, if you began by asking questions, end by answering them. If you began with an anecdote, end by referring to the same story. As an alternative (or maybe an addition), consider sharing a quotation or a bit of humor relevant to your content.

Also, keep in mind that you should verbally signal to your audience that you are about to conclude. After you do so—by saying, "In summary," for instance—be sure that you actually do conclude. Nothing alienates an audience more quickly than launching into another point after you've told them you're finished! Your body language will support your conclusion if you turn off your projector and move toward the audience to answer questions. And even if you aren't so eager to field questions, try to paste a receptive look on your face—it'll increase your credibility and set a positive tone for the Q&A session.

5-6d Questions

At the start of your presentation, decide whether you want to handle questions throughout your talk or save them for the end. Tell your audience your preference upfront; most of the time they will respect it. But if you do receive unwanted questions in the middle of your presentation, don't ignore them. Simply remind the questioner that you'll leave plenty of time for questions at the end.

Not surprisingly, the best tip for handling questions is to be prepared. Since it's tough to anticipate questions for your own presentation, you may want to enlist the help of a trusted colleague to brainstorm the possibilities. And don't just come up with the questions—prepare the answers, too!

5-6e Visual Aids

Studies suggest that three days after a presentation, people retain 10% of what they heard from an oral

instance, in a presentation about employee benefits, you might want to share the story of a colleague who beat cancer using the company's innovative healthcare program.

- **A Relevant Simile or Metaphor:** Patricia Fripp, an award-winning keynote speaker, shares a simile that worked well to open a presentation for a colleague: "Being a scientist is like doing a jigsaw puzzle in a snowstorm at night …you don't have all the pieces …and you don't have the picture to work from."
- **Engaging Questions:** In a presentation about customer service, you could open by asking: "How many of you have spent far too long waiting on hold for customer service that was finally delivered by a surly agent who clearly knew nothing about your question?"

5-6b Body

The most common presentation mistake is to include too many key ideas in the body of your presentation. Audiences simply cannot absorb more than two to four main points, and three are ideal. Specific examples and vivid comparisons will illustrate your points and bring them to life, while trusted sources, specific data, and expert quotations will increase your credibility and persuasiveness. Regardless of the length of your presentation, be sure to use clear transitions as you move from point to point.

Just before launching into the body of your presentation, you should tell the audience your key points, ideally presentation, 35% from a visual presentation, and 65% from a combined visual and oral presentation. The numbers are compelling: visual aids matter. Depending on your audience, effective, high-impact visual aids could range from props to charts to mounted boards. But in business communication, PowerPoint slides are the most common option. If you use PowerPoint, consider these suggestions:

- **Showing Works Better Than Simply Telling:** Use pictures and other graphics whenever possible.

- **Less Is More:** Keep this helpful guideline in mind: no more than seven words per line, no more than seven lines per slide.

- **Don't Just Read Your Slides Aloud:** Instead, paraphrase, add examples, and offer analysis and interpretation.

- **Go Easy on the Special Effects:** Too many sounds and too much animation can be painfully distracting.

- **Don't Let Your Slides Upstage You:** Look at your audience, not at the slides. And dim the screen when you're not specifically using it.[11]

5-6f Google Presentations

Although Microsoft PowerPoint remains the software option of choice for business presentations, Google Presentations software is swiftly gaining ground. Google Presentations is one of a growing number of applications based in "the cloud." Another popular option is Prezi, which includes pan and zoom features that give presentations an engaging cinematic feel. Cloud-based presentation software means that when you buy a new computer, you don't need to spend hundreds of dollars buying PowerPoint. You simply log into your Google account, for instance; use the Google Presentations software; and save your finished product on Google's servers. Since your work is stored on the Internet, you can access it from any device with a web connection—you don't need to email it to yourself, or store it on a temperamental local drive, or worry about saving your changes as you move from work to home, to school.

But cloud-based software is far from perfect. If you temporarily lose your Internet connection—while on a plane or a bus, for instance—you cannot access your work. Security might be a worry, since web-based data may be vulnerable to hackers. If Google disables your account for any reason, your work is lost. And Google Presentations does not yet include all the features available in PowerPoint, such as chart-making tools and advanced slide animations. The price, though, for both Google Presentations and Prezi is pretty attractive: free! And that includes new versions and updates.

From a long-term perspective, another key benefit of Google Presentations—and all other cloud computing applications—is environmental. *Newsweek* writer Brian Braiker points out that "conducting affairs in the cloud is not only convenient, it's also greener: less capital and fewer printouts means less waste." All of which suggests that the forecast for Google Presentations is far from cloudy.[12]

5-6g Handling Nerves

Believe it or not, most experts agree that nervousness can be useful before a presentation. A little adrenalin can help you perform better, think faster, and focus more completely. But we all know that out-of-control nerves can interfere with effectiveness. Here are some ideas to mitigate speech anxiety:

- Send yourself positive messages; visualize success. Examples: "I will be dynamic and engaging." "They will completely support my new product idea."

- Take ten slow, deep breaths—use the yoga approach of breathing in through your nose and out through your mouth.

  - Take a sip of water to loosen your throat muscles and mitigate a shaking voice. (Water also gives you a way to fill pauses.)

    - Pick a friendly face or two in the audience, and imagine yourself speaking only to those people (but don't fix them down with a cold stare!).

    - Remind yourself that the audience wants you to succeed. Focus on their needs rather than your own nerves.

      If possible, have a handful of one-on-one conversations with audience members before your presentation. This will almost certainly reinforce that they want you to succeed, which will likely take the edge off your nerves.

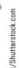

PathDoc/Shutterstock.com

5-6h Handling Hostility

We've all seen hostile questioners who seem determined to undermine presenters. It can be awful to watch, but it's surprisingly easy to handle. Here are a few tips:

- Stay calm and professional. Rightly or wrongly, the hostile questioner has won the day if you get defensive or nervous.

- Don't be afraid to pause before you answer to gather your thoughts and allow the hostility to diffuse. (A sip of water can provide good cover for a thought-gathering moment.)

- Once you've answered the question, don't reestablish eye contact with the questioner. Doing so would suggest that you are seeking approval for your response, which only invites further hostile follow-up.

- If the questioner insists on follow-up, you may need to agree to disagree. If so, be decisive: "Sounds like we have two different points of view on this complex issue."

- Use body language to reinforce that you are done interacting with the questioner. Take a couple of steps away, and ask another part of the group whether they have any questions.

5-6i Incorporating Humor

Everyone likes to be funny, but incorporating humor in a business presentation can be risky. Only do it if you're very, very sure that it's funny. Even so, double-check that your jokes are appropriate and relevant. You should never, ever laugh at the expense of any member of your audience. Even laughing at yourself is chancy, since you risk diminishing your credibility. (But a joke at your own expense is always effective if you make a mistake; there's no better way to recover the goodwill of your audience.)

dynamic delivery Vibrant, compelling presentation delivery style that grabs and holds the attention of the audience.

5-6j A Spot on the Back Wall?

Many people have heard the old myth that no one will know the difference if you calm your nerves by looking at a spot on the back wall rather than at the audience. Don't do it! While *you* may be more comfortable, your audience will be mystified . . . more often than not, they'll keep turning around to find out what's so interesting back there!

5-6k Delivery

Some people are naturals, but for the rest of us, **dynamic delivery** is a learned skill. It begins and ends with preparation, but keep in mind that practice doesn't always make perfect—in fact, practice more often just makes permanent. So be sure that you practice with an eye toward improvement. If possible, you should set up a practice situation that's close to the real thing. If you'll be standing to present, stand while you practice, since standing makes many people feel more vulnerable. Consider practicing in front of a mirror to work on eye contact and gestures. Also, try recording your voice to work on a lively tone.

Finally, practice in front of a trusted friend or two who can give you valuable feedback. See Exhibit 5.6 for Ten Tips for Dynamic Delivery.

EXHIBIT 5.6 **TEN TIPS FOR DYNAMIC DELIVERY**

1. PRACTICE!

2. Know your material, but never memorize it word for word.

3. Look directly at members of your audience at least 50% of the time.

4. Vary your voice, your facial expressions, and your body language.

5. Use selective notes (but keep them inconspicuous).

6. Stick to your allotted time.

7. Slow down and listen to yourself.

8. Don't apologize (unless you really did something wrong!).

9. Remember to use natural gestures.

10. PRACTICE!

THE BIG PICTURE

Effective communication saves time and money—boosting performance and morale—across every area of business. But one vital principle holds true regardless of the more specific nature of your communication: the best way to achieve your goals is to focus on your audience, not on yourself. If you understand the goals, expectations, and needs of your audience, you can tailor your communication to boost your chances (sometimes dramatically) of accomplishing your objectives.

As globalization and technological change continue to accelerate, new communication challenges will likely develop across the spectrum of business. To ensure that your communication continues to be effective, keep an open mind. Pay attention to differences among cultures, to language usage in professional publications, and to new communication technology. And don't be afraid to consult an up-to-date communication website or handbook every so often. When other resources aren't available, rely on courtesy, consideration, and common sense—valuable tools to guide your communication in any situation.

CAREERS IN BUSINESS COMMUNICATION

Public Relations Manager

Plan and implement strategies to build and maintain a positive image for the organization. Build strong relationships and open channels of communication with relevant members of the press. Write and distribute compelling press releases about the organization via both traditional and digital media. Respond to requests for information from the media. Work with senior management to develop crisis management plans when necessary. Work with marketing to create events and stunts that build the company's public image. Perform an effective liaison role with an outside public relations agency when there is one.

STUDY TOOLS 5

LOCATED AT BACK OF THE TEXTBOOK

☐ Rip-Out Chapter Review Card

☐ Gain unique perspectives on key concepts with new concept videos in the e-book

☐ Increase your comprehension with online homework and quizzes

☐ Study with existing flashcards and make your own

6 | Business Formation:
Choosing the Form That Fits

LEARNING OBJECTIVES

After studying this chapter, you will be able to:

6-1 Describe the characteristics of the four basic forms of business ownership

6-2 Discuss the advantages and disadvantages of a sole proprietorship

6-3 Evaluate the pros and cons of the partnership as a form of business ownership

6-4 Explain why corporations have become the dominant form of business ownership

6-5 Explain why limited liability companies are becoming an increasingly popular form of business ownership

6-6 Evaluate the advantages and disadvantages of franchising

Remember to visit

PAGE 111

for additional

STUDY TOOLS

6-1 BUSINESS OWNERSHIP OPTIONS: THE BIG FOUR

One of the most important decisions entrepreneurs make when starting a new business is the form of ownership they'll use. The form they choose affects virtually every aspect of establishing and operating their firm, including the initial cost of setting up the business, the way the profits are distributed, the types of taxes (if any) the business must pay, and the types of regulations it must follow. Choice of ownership also determines the degree to which each owner is personally liable for the firm's debts and the sources of funds available to the firm to finance future expansion. Finally, choosing the right business form helps entrepreneurs battle the steep odds against survival. Eighty percent of new businesses close within five years, and even 37% of large, established, and highly successful Fortune 500 and S&P 500 firms can be expected to fail every five years.[1]

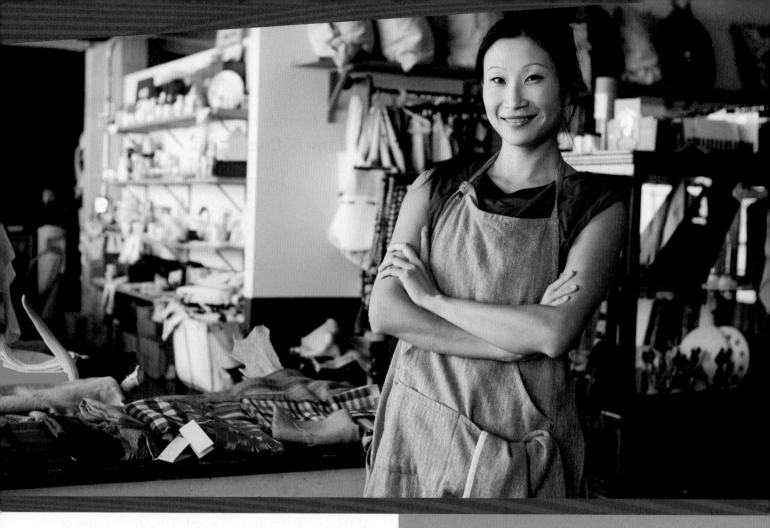

The vast majority of businesses in the United States are owned and organized under one of the four forms:

1. A **sole proprietorship** is a business that is owned, and usually managed, by a single individual. As far as the law is concerned, a sole proprietorship is simply an extension of the owner. Company earnings are treated just like the owner's income; likewise, any debts the company incurs are considered to be the owner's personal debts.

2. A **partnership** is a voluntary agreement under which two or more people act as co-owners of a business for profit. As we'll see later in the chapter, there are several types of partnerships. In its most basic form, known as a **general partnership**, each partner has the right to participate in the company's management and share in profits—but also has unlimited liability for any debts the company incurs.

3. A **corporation** is a business entity created by filing a form (known in most states as the **articles of incorporation**) with the appropriate state agency, paying the state's incorporation fees, and meeting other requirements. (The specifics vary among states.) Unlike a sole proprietorship or a partnership, a corporation is considered to be a legal entity that is separate and distinct from its owners. In many ways, a corporation is like an artificial person. It can legally engage in virtually any business activity a natural person can pursue. For example, a corporation can enter into binding contracts, borrow money, own property, pay taxes, and initiate legal actions (such as lawsuits) in its own name. It can even be a partner in

> "The limited liability corporation is the *GREATEST* single discovery of modern times."
>
> —NICHOLAS MURRAY BUTLER, PRESIDENT OF COLUMBIA UNIVERSITY, 1902–1945

sole proprietorship A form of business ownership with a single owner who usually actively manages the company.

partnership A voluntary agreement under which two or more people act as co-owners of a business for profit.

general partnership A partnership in which all partners can take an active role in managing the business and have unlimited liability for any claims against the firm.

corporation A form of business ownership in which the business is considered a legal entity that is separate and distinct from its owners.

a partnership or an owner of another corporation. Because of a corporation's status as a separate legal entity, the owners of a corporation have **limited liability**—meaning they aren't personally responsible for the debts and obligations of their company.

4. A **limited liability company (LLC)** is a hybrid form of business ownership that is similar in some respects to a corporation while having other characteristics that are similar to a partnership. Like a corporation, a LLC is considered a legal entity separate from its owners. Also like a corporation—and as its name implies—an LLC offers its owners limited liability for the debts of their business. But it offers more flexibility than a corporation in terms of tax treatment; in fact, one of the most interesting characteristics of an LLC is that its owners can elect to have their business taxed either as a corporation *or* a partnership. Many states even allow individuals to form single-person LLCs that are taxed as if they were sole proprietorships.

Sole proprietorships, partnerships, and corporations have been around in some form since the beginning of our nation's history, but limited liability companies are a relatively new form of ownership in the United States. In 1977, Wyoming passed the first state statute allowing LLCs, and Florida became the second state to do so in 1982. But it wasn't until a ruling by the IRS in 1988 clarifying the tax treatment of LLCs that most other states followed suit. Today every state has enacted LLC legislation, and the LLC has become a very popular ownership option. In many states, filings to form LLCs now outnumber filings to form corporations.[2]

Exhibits 6.1 and 6.2 provide some interesting insights about the relative importance of each form of ownership. As shown in Exhibit 6.1, the sole proprietorship is by far the most common type of business organization in the United States. In 2016, 24.07 million individuals reported operating nonfarm sole proprietorships. This represented nearly 72% of the total number of business enterprises. As a group, these sole proprietorships reported $1.3 trillion in revenue and $305 billion in net income (profit). But while these figures are impressive in the aggregate, most

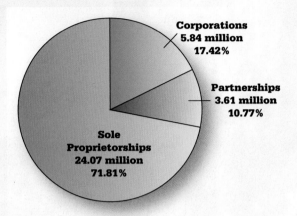

Exhibit 6.1
Total Number of Businesses by Form of Ownership

Corporations
5.84 million
17.42%

Partnerships
3.61 million
10.77%

Sole Proprietorships
24.07 million
71.81%

Source: "Table 12: Number of Business Tax Returns, by Size of Business for Income Years, 1990-2014 [1] Expanded," Internal Revenue Service, https://www.irs.gov/uac/soi-tax-stats-historical-table-12, accessed January 16, 2017.

individual sole proprietorships are quite small. According to data released by the IRS in 2016, about 70% of all sole proprietorships reported annual revenue of less than $25,000, while less than 1% reported receipts in excess of $1 million.[3] So while sole proprietorships make up nearly 72% of all businesses, they only account for 3.64% of total revenue and 10.32% of total profit. Still, 59% of sole proprietorships break even or are profitable.[4]

As Exhibit 6.2 shows, when it comes to economic impact, the corporate form of ownership rules. Though corporations comprised only 17.42% of all business entities, in 2016 they reported 82.17% of all business revenues and 63.35% of all business profits. Corporations such as Apple (technology), JP Morgan Chase (banking) Berkshire Hathaway (investing), Wells Fargo (banking), and Gilead (pharmaceuticals) have annual sales revenues measured in the billions (sometimes hundreds of billions) of dollars.[5] But not all corporations are multibillion-dollar enterprises. In fact, 24.1% of all corporations reported total revenues of less than $25,000.[6]

articles of incorporation The document filed with a state government to establish the existence of a new corporation.

limited liability When owners are not personally liable for claims against their firm. Owners with limited liability may lose their investment in the company, but their other personal assets are protected.

limited liability company (LLC) A form of business ownership that offers both limited liability to its owners and flexible tax treatment.

> "Corporation: an ingenious device for obtaining profit without individual responsibility."
>
> —AMBROSE BIERCE, 19TH-CENTURY COMPILER OF *THE DEVIL'S DICTIONARY*

Exhibit 6.2

Total Revenue and Net Income by Form of Ownership

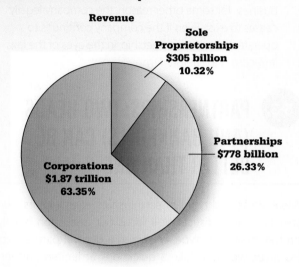

Revenue

Sole Proprietorships $305 billion 10.32%

Partnerships $778 billion 26.33%

Corporations $1.87 trillion 63.35%

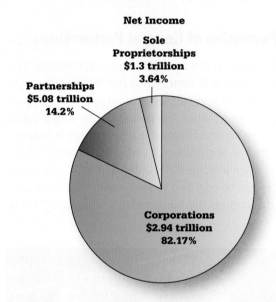

Net Income

Sole Proprietorships $1.3 trillion 3.64%

Partnerships $5.08 trillion 14.2%

Corporations $2.94 trillion 82.17%

Source: "Table 1. Number of Returns, Total Receipts, Business Receipts, Net Income (less deficit), Net Income, and Deficit by Form of Business, Tax Years 1980-2012," Internal Revenue Service, https://www.irs.gov/pub/irs-soi/12otidb1.xls, accessed January 16, 2017.

As you can see from Exhibit 6.1, partnerships are less common than sole proprietorships or corporations. Still, more than 3.61 million businesses were classified as partnerships in the United States. And partnerships tend to be both larger and more profitable than sole proprietorships. As Exhibit 6.2 shows, in the aggregate, partnerships earned 2.55 times more total net income than sole proprietorships, despite the fact that sole proprietorships outnumbered partnerships by a ratio of almost seven

to one![7] Altogether, partnerships earned 14.2% of business revenues and 26.33% of business profits.

You've probably noticed that Exhibits 6.1 and 6.2 don't include specific information about limited liability companies. That's because these exhibits are based on information taken from annual tax returns submitted to the IRS. The IRS doesn't track LLC information separately. Instead, it classifies each LLC based on the tax treatment the company selects. LLCs that choose to be taxed as partnerships are classified as partnerships, while those choosing to be taxed as corporations are classified as corporations. (The vast majority of LLCs elect to be taxed as partnerships, so most LLC earnings are reported in the partnership category.)

We'll see that each form of ownership has distinct advantages and disadvantages. As a company grows and matures, the form of ownership that's best suited to its needs may change. Fortunately, the form of ownership for a business isn't set in stone. For example, it is possible—and in fact quite common—for business owners to convert from a sole proprietorship to a corporation, or from a corporation to a LLC.

6-2 ADVANTAGES AND DISADVANTAGES OF SOLE PROPRIETORSHIPS

Our look at Exhibits 6.1 and 6.2 raises two questions about sole proprietorships. First, why is this form of ownership so popular? Second, why do sole proprietorships usually remain relatively small? A look at the advantages and disadvantages of sole proprietorships can help answer these questions.

6-2a Advantages

Sole proprietorships offer some very attractive advantages to people starting a business:

- **Ease of Formation:** Compared to the other forms of ownership we'll discuss, the paperwork and costs involved in forming a sole proprietorship are minimal. No special forms must be filed, and no special fees must be paid. Entrepreneurs who are eager to get a business up and running quickly can find this a compelling advantage.

- **Retention of Control:** As the only owner of a sole proprietorship, you're in control. You have the ability to manage your business the way you want. If you want to "be your own boss," a sole proprietorship might look very attractive. Nicholas Hollows, sole proprietor of Hollows Leather in Eugene, Oregon, says, "I definitely don't intend to switch my role from a person who makes things to a person who manages people. Being hands on is the whole reason I do this."[8]

- **Pride of Ownership:** One of the main reasons many people prefer a sole proprietorship is the feeling of pride and the personal satisfaction they gain from owning and running their own business.

- **Retention of Profits:** If your business is successful, all the profits go to you—minus your personal taxes, of course.

- **Possible Tax Advantage:** No taxes are levied directly on the earnings of sole proprietorships as a business. Instead, the earnings are taxed only as income of the proprietor. As we'll see when we discuss corporations, this avoids the undesirable possibility of double taxation of earnings.

6-2b Disadvantages

Entrepreneurs thinking about forming sole proprietorships should also be aware of some serious drawbacks:

- **Limited Financial Resources:** Raising money to finance growth can be tough for sole proprietors. With only one owner responsible for a sole proprietorship's debts, banks and other financial institutions are often reluctant to lend it money. Likewise, suppliers may be unwilling to provide supplies on credit. This leaves sole proprietors dependent on their own wealth plus the money that their firms generate.

- **Unlimited Liability:** Because the law views a sole proprietorship as an extension of its owner, the debts of the firm become the owner's personal debts. The owner of Erie County Farms, a grocery store in Erie, Pennsylvania, never incorporated his business, so the store operated as a sole proprietorship. Accordingly, when Erie County Farms went bankrupt, the bankruptcy court seized the owner's home and personal assets to pay $650,000 in unpaid bills.[9] Likewise, if someone sues your business and wins, the court can seize your personal possessions—even those that have nothing to do with your business—and sell them to pay the damages. This unlimited personal liability means that operating as a sole proprietorship is a risky endeavor.

- **Limited Ability to Attract and Maintain Talented Employees:** Most sole proprietors are unable to pay the high salaries and substantial perks that highly qualified, experienced employees get when they work for big, well-established companies.

- **Heavy Workload and Responsibilities:** Being your own boss can be very rewarding, but it can also mean very long hours and a lot of stress. Sole proprietors—as the ultimate authority in their business—often must

perform tasks or make decisions in areas where they lack expertise.

- **Lack of Permanence:** Because sole proprietorships are just extensions of their owners, they lack permanence. If the owner dies, retires, or withdraws from the business for some other reason, the company legally ceases to exist. Even if the company continues to operate under new ownership, in the eyes of the law, it becomes a different firm.

6-3 PARTNERSHIPS: TWO HEADS (AND BANKROLLS) CAN BE BETTER THAN ONE

There are several types of partnerships, each with its own specific characteristics. We'll focus our discussion mainly on the most basic type, known as a general partnership. However, we'll also take a quick look at limited partnerships and limited liability partnerships (LLPs).

6-3a Formation of General Partnerships

There is no limit on the number of partners who can participate in a general partnership, but most partnerships consist of only a few partners—often just two. The partnership is formed when the partners enter into a voluntary partnership agreement. It is legally possible to start a partnership on the basis of a verbal agreement, but doing so is often a recipe for disaster. It's much safer to get everything in writing and to seek expert legal assistance when drawing up the agreement. A typical partnership

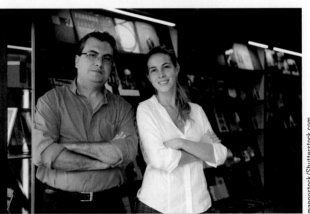

mangostock/Shutterstock.com

Sharing responsibilities and complementary skills are one of the advantages of general business partnerships.

"It is rare to find a business partner who is selfless. If you are lucky it happens once in a lifetime."

—MICHAEL EISNER, FORMER DISNEY CEO

agreement spells out details, such as the initial financial contributions each partner will make, the specific duties and responsibilities each will assume, how they will share profits (and losses), how they will settle disagreements, and how they will deal with the death or withdrawal of one of the partners. Well-written agreements can prevent common misunderstandings.

6-3b Advantages of General Partnerships

Partnerships offer some key advantages relative to both sole proprietorships and corporations:

- **Ability to Pool Financial Resources:** With more owners investing in the company, a partnership is likely to have a stronger financial base than a sole proprietorship.

- **Ability to Share Responsibilities and Capitalize on Complementary Skills:** Partners can share the burden of running the business, which can ease the workload. Tasks and jobs can also be divided based on complementary skills, using each partner's talents to best advantage.

- **Ease of Formation:** In theory, forming a partnership is easy. As we've already noted, it's possible (but not advisable) to establish a partnership based on a simple verbal agreement. But we shouldn't overemphasize this advantage. Working out all of the details of a partnership agreement can sometimes be a complex and time-consuming process.

- **Possible Tax Advantages:** Similar to a sole proprietorship, the earnings of a partnership "pass through" the business—untouched by the IRS—and are taxed only as the partners' personal income. Again, this avoids the potential for double taxation endemic to corporations.

6-3c Disadvantages of General Partnerships

General partnerships also have some serious disadvantages. Well-written partnership agreements, however, can mitigate some of these major drawbacks:

- **Unlimited Liability:** As a general partner, you're not only liable for your own mistakes but also for those of your partners. In fact, all general partners have unlimited liability for the debts and obligations of their business. So, if the assets they've invested in the business aren't sufficient to meet these claims, the personal assets of the partners are at risk. When someone sues a general partnership, the lawsuit can target *any* individual partner or group of partners. In fact, lawsuits often go after the partners with the deepest pockets, even if they did not personally participate in the act that caused the legal action. In other words, if you have more personal wealth than the other partners, you could lose more than they do even if they were the ones at fault!

- **Potential for Disagreements:** If general partners can't agree on how to run the business, the conflict can complicate and delay decision making. A well-drafted partnership agreement usually specifies how disputes will be resolved, but disagreements among partners can create friction and hard feelings that harm morale and undermine the cooperation needed to keep the business on track.

- **Lack of Continuity:** If a current partner withdraws from the partnership, the relationships among the participants will clearly change, potentially ending the partnership. This creates uncertainty about how long a partnership will remain in business.

- **Difficulty in Withdrawing from a Partnership:** A partner who withdraws from a partnership remains personally liable for any debts or obligations the firm had *at the time of withdrawal*—even if those obligations were incurred by the actions of other partners.

6-3d Limited Partnerships

The risks associated with unlimited liability make general partnerships unattractive to many individuals who would otherwise be interested in joining a business partnership. Fortunately, two other types of partnerships allow some partners to limit their personal liability to some extent, although each comes with particular requirements.

The first of these, known as a **limited partnership**, is a partnership arrangement that includes at least one general partner *and* at least one limited partner. Both types of partners contribute financially to the company and share in its profits. But in other respects they play different roles:

- General partners have the right to participate fully in managing their partnership, but they also assume unlimited personal liability for any of its debts—just like the partners in a general partnership.

- Limited partners *cannot* actively participate in its management, but they have the

> **limited partnership** A partnership that includes at least one general partner who actively manages the company and accepts unlimited liability and one limited partner who gives up the right to actively manage the company in exchange for limited liability.

Senior Home Care: Today's Biggest Franchise Opportunity

A key to franchise success is serving fast-growing markets. McDonald's and Dunkin' Donuts began franchising in the 1950s when gasoline and automobiles were inexpensive, thousands of miles of new interstate roads were being built, and it was too expensive for typical American families (with three or four children) to eat at restaurants. Thanks to low costs, fast service, standardized menus, and thousands of convenient locations, McDonald's and Dunkin' Donuts grew rapidly as consumers grabbed inexpensive coffee and donuts for breakfast, or burgers, fries, and shakes for lunch and dinner.

Today's baby boomers, the children born in the 1950s who grew up eating at McDonald's and Dunkin' Donuts, are retiring at a rate of 10,000 per day. The U.S. Census Bureau now predicts that there will be 38% more Americans age 65 and older (66 million

Rob Marmion/Shutterstock.com

in all, up from 47.8 million) by 2025, and 78% more (85 million in all) by 2050. As they age, boomers will increasingly need help with home care, such as meals, laundry, and cleaning; personal care, such as dressing and grooming; medical care, such as rehabilitation following surgery; and daily care among those suffering from chronic diseases, memory loss, and immobility.

Just as they did with fast food in the 1950s, baby boomers' health and retirement needs are driving today's franchise business opportunities. Claudine Halpern, COO of senior home care franchise My Elder Advocate LLC, says, "There is no way to lose with the demographics we see. All of us are planning on living to 100." Indeed, the senior home care industry is growing by 6.6% a year, compared to 2.6% average growth among all other kinds of franchises.

In addition to their steady growth, senior home care franchises have low initial costs and strong profitability margins. For example, the initial cost to establish a BrightStar home care franchise (315 locations in 38 states) is $92,371 to $174,032. The cost to establish a Home Instead Inc. home care franchise (1,110 locations in 12 countries) is $155,000 to $125,000. By contrast, the initial cost of launching a sit-down restaurant franchise is roughly $1 million.

Eric Stites, CEO of Franchise Business Review, a market research firm specializing in franchise business opportunities, says senior care franchises garner 44% higher annual profits than other franchises on average ($118,000 vs. $82,000). Stites says, "Of all the sectors we look at, it has one of the highest returns on investment."[10]

---

protection of limited liability. This means that, as long as they do not actively participate in managing the company, their personal wealth is not at risk.

6-3e Limited Liability Partnerships

The **limited liability partnership (LLP)** is another partnership arrangement that is attractive to partners who want to limit their personal risk. It is similar to a limited partnership in some ways, but it has the advantage of allowing *all* partners to take an active role in management while also offering *all* partners some form of limited liability. In other words, there's no need to distinguish between limited and general partners in an LLP.

The amount of liability protection offered by LLPs varies among states. In some states, LLPs offer "full-shield" protection, meaning

> **limited liability partnership (LLP)** A form of partnership in which all partners have the right to participate in management and have limited liability for company debts.

that partners have limited liability for all claims against their company, except those resulting from *their own* negligence or malpractice. In other states, partners in LLPs have a lesser "partial-shield" protection. In these states, each partner has limited liability for the negligence or malpractice of other partners but still has unlimited liability for any other debts. Another drawback is that some states only allow specific types of professional businesses to form LLPs. For example, California law allows only accountants, lawyers, and architects to form LLPs.

6-4 CORPORATIONS: THE ADVANTAGES AND DISADVANTAGES OF BEING AN ARTIFICIAL PERSON

There are several types of corporations. The most common is called a **C corporation**; when people use the term "corporation" without specifying which type, they

EXHIBIT 6.3 | STOCK OWNERSHIP IN SELECTED MAJOR U.S. CORPORATIONS

Corporation	Shares of Common Stock Outstanding (Billions)	Total Number of Stockholders	Percentage of Shares Owned by Institutional Investors
Apple	5.53	25,641	60.20
Coca-Cola	4.31	224,780	63.20
Ford	3.90	137,858	60,00
GE	8.85	458,000	56.60
IBM	0.951	444,582	59.90
McDonald's	0.830	1,579,000	69.30
Microsoft	7.78	106,534	72.60
Walmart	3.07	243,327	30.60

Sources: Shares outstanding and percentage of institutional ownership are from the Key Statistics for each corporation reported in Yahoo! Finance (http://finance.yahoo.com/); Information about the number of shareholders is found in Item 5 (Market for the Company's Common Equity) of each firm's 2015/2016 10-K annual report filed with the SEC accessed through the Edgar database (http://www.sec.gov/edgar.shtml) accessed January 18, 2017.

are generally referring to a C corporation. Because it's the most common, we'll devote most of our discussion to C corporations. However, we'll also describe three other types of corporations: S corporations, statutory close (or closed) corporations, and nonprofit corporations.

6-4a Forming a C Corporation

As mentioned earlier, the formation of a corporation requires filing articles of incorporation and paying filing fees. It also requires the adoption of **corporate bylaws**, which are detailed rules that govern the way the corporation is organized and managed. Because of these requirements, forming a corporation tends to be more expensive and complex than forming a sole proprietorship or partnership. The requirements, however, vary among the states. Some states are known for their simple forms, inexpensive fees, low corporate tax rates, and "corporation-friendly" laws and court systems. In those states, forming a corporation is not much harder or more expensive than setting up a sole proprietorship and sometimes can be simpler than forming a partnership. Not surprisingly, many large companies choose to incorporate in states with such favorable environments—even if they intend to do the majority of their business in other states. Delaware, in particular, has been very successful at attracting corporations. You may not think of Delaware as the home of corporate power, but more than half of all publicly traded corporations—and 64% of the firms listed in the *Fortune 500*—are incorporated in Delaware.[11]

6-4b Ownership of C Corporations

Ownership of C corporations is represented by shares of stock, so owners are called "**stockholders**" (or "shareholders"). Common stock represents the basic ownership interest

in a corporation, but some firms also issue preferred stock. One key difference between the two types of stock involves voting rights; common stockholders normally have the right to vote in stockholders' meetings, while preferred stockholders do not. As shown in Exhibit 6.3, many large corporations issue billions of shares of stock and have hundreds of thousands—or even millions—of stockholders.

Stock in large corporations is usually publicly traded, meaning that anyone with the money and inclination to do so can buy shares—and that anyone who owns shares is free to sell them. But many smaller corporations are owned by just a handful of stockholders who don't actively trade their stock. It's even possible for individuals to incorporate their business and be the sole shareholder in their corporation.[12]

Stockholders don't have to be individuals. **Institutional investors**, such as mutual funds, insurance companies, pension funds, and endowment funds, pool money from a large number of individuals and use these funds to buy stocks and other securities. As Exhibit 6.3 illustrates, such institutional investors own the majority of stock in many large corporations.

6-4c The Role of the Board of Directors

It's not practical for all of the stockholders of a large corporation to actively

C corporation The most common type of corporation, which is a legal business entity that offers limited liability to all of its owners, who are called stockholders.

corporate bylaws The basic rules governing how a corporation is organized and how it conducts its business.

stockholder An owner of a corporation.

institutional investor An organization that pools contributions from investors, clients, or depositors and uses these funds to buy stocks and other securities.

LLCs: Philanthropy without Foundation

Wealthy families often form charitable nonprofit foundations to direct how their tax deductible philanthropic gifts are used. A nonprofit foundation must pay out 5% of its endowment each year, establish a board of directors, annually report strategic and financial information to the government and the public, and only support activities related to its charitable mission. But when Facebook founder Mark Zuckerberg and wife

Adam Berry/Getty Images Entertainment/Getty Images

Dr. Priscilla Chan gave away their $45 billion fortune, they established a LLC instead of a nonprofit because it gave them more control and privacy.

According to Zuckerberg, "By using an LLC instead of a traditional foundation, we receive no tax benefit from transferring our shares to the Chan Zuckerberg Initiative (CZI), but we gain flexibility to execute our mission more effectively." Being an LLC means that the CZI can spend its funds as quickly (or slowly) as needed (no annual 5% payout), change how it spends funds over time, and not have to disclose who it works with or how it invests its endowment funds. The CZI can even make political contributions and invest in for-profit businesses, all in support of its mission of encouraging "personalized learning, curing disease, connecting people and building strong communities." In short, by deploying their wealth through an LLC and not a traditional foundation, Chan and Zuckerberg believe that they can "help hundreds of millions of children get an education and save millions of lives by helping people avoid disease."[13]

participate in the management of their company. Besides, most stockholders don't have the time, management skills, or desire to effectively manage such a complex business enterprise. Thus, in accordance with corporate bylaws, the stockholders elect a **board of directors** and rely on this board to oversee the operation of their company and protect their interests.

The board of directors establishes the corporation's mission and sets its broad objectives. But board members seldom take an active role in the day-to-day management of their company. Instead, again in accordance with corporate bylaws, the board appoints a chief executive officer (CEO) and other corporate officers to manage the company on a daily basis. The board also sets the level of compensation for these officers and monitors their performance to ensure that they act in a manner consistent with stockholder interests. When Apple's sales and profits came in at 3.7% and 0.5%, respectively, below target in 2016, Apple's Board of Directors cut CEO Tim Cook's pay by 15% and cut the pay of other top executives by 9.6%.[14] It also provides advice to these officers on broad policy issues, approves their major proposals, and ensures that the company adheres to major regulatory requirements.

6-4d Advantages of C Corporations

Corporations have become the dominant form of business ownership for several reasons:

- **Limited Liability:** As already explained, stockholders are not personally liable for the debts of their company. If a corporation goes bankrupt, the stockholders might find that their stock is worthless, but their other personal assets are protected.

- **Permanence:** Unless the articles of incorporation specify a limited duration, corporations can continue operating as long as they remain financially viable and the majority of stockholders want the business to continue. Unlike a sole proprietorship or partnership, a general corporation is unaffected by the death or withdrawal of an owner.

- **Ease of Transfer of Ownership:** It's easy for stockholders of publicly traded C corporations to withdraw from ownership—they simply sell their shares of stock.

- **Ability to Raise Large Amounts of Financial Capital:** Corporations can raise large amounts of financial capital by issuing shares of stock or by selling formal IOUs called corporate bonds. The ability to raise money by issuing these securities gives corporations a major financial advantage over most other forms of ownership.

- **Ability to Make Use of Specialized Management:** Large corporations often find it easier to hire highly qualified professional managers than proprietorships and partnerships. Major corporations can typically offer attractive salaries and benefits, and their permanence and potential for growth offer managers opportunities for career advancement.

6-4e Disadvantages of C Corporations

In addition to their significant benefits, C corporations have a number of drawbacks:

- **Expense and Complexity of Formation and Operation:** As we've already seen, establishing a

board of directors The individuals who are elected by stockholders of a corporation to represent their interests.

corporation can be more complex and expensive than forming a sole proprietorship or partnership. Corporations are also subject to more formal operating requirements. For example, they are required to hold regular board meetings and keep accurate minutes.

- **Complications When Operating in More Than One State:** When a business that's incorporated in one state does business in other states, it's called a "*domestic* corporation" in the state where it's incorporated, and a "*foreign* corporation" in the other states. A corporation must register (or "qualify") as a foreign corporation in order to do business in any state other than the one in which it incorporated. This typically requires additional paperwork, fees, and taxes. But registration as a foreign corporation is only necessary if the company is involved in substantial business activities within the state. Businesses that only engage in minor business activities typically are exempt from the registration requirement. For example, a firm operating a production facility or maintaining a district office in a state other than its corporate home would need to register as a foreign corporation, but a firm that simply held a bank account or solicited sales to customers in that state through the mail would not be required to do so.

- **Double Taxation of Earnings and Additional Taxes:** The IRS considers a C corporation to be a separate legal entity and taxes its earnings accordingly. Then, as shown in Exhibit 6.4, any dividends (earnings the corporation distributes to stockholders) are taxed *again* as the personal income of the stockholders. This double taxation can take a big bite out of earnings

that are distributed to shareholders. But note that corporations often reinvest some or all of their profits back into the business. Shareholders don't pay income taxes on these *retained earnings*. Many states also impose separate income taxes on corporations. Most states also impose an annual franchise tax on both domestic and foreign corporations that operate within their borders.

- **More Paperwork, More Regulation, and Less Secrecy:** Corporations are more closely regulated and are required to file more government paperwork than other forms of business. Large, publicly traded corporations are required to send annual statements to all shareholders and to file detailed quarterly and annual reports with the Securities and Exchange Commission (SEC). The annual report filed with the SEC (called a Form 10-K) is often hundreds of pages long and includes a wealth of information about the company's operations and financial condition. Anyone can look at these forms, making it difficult to keep key corporate information secret from competitors.

> "General Electric, one of the largest corporations in America, filed a whopping 57,000-page federal tax return ...[which] would have been 19 feet high if printed out and stacked."
>
> — *WEEKLY STANDARD*

Exhibit 6.4
How Double Taxation Reduces Earnings for Stockholders

| Pre-Tax Corporate Earnings | Corporate Taxes | After Tax Corporate Earnings | Stockholders | Personal Income Taxes | Stockholders' After-Tax Income |

EXHIBIT 6.5   CHARACTERISTICS OF S, STATUTORY CLOSE, AND NONPROFIT CORPORATIONS

Type	Key Advantages	Limitations
S Corporation	■ The IRS does not tax earnings of S corporations separately. Earnings pass through the company and are taxed only as income to stockholders, thus avoiding the problem of double taxation associated with C corporations. ■ Stockholders have limited liability.	■ It can have no more than 100 stockholders. ■ With only rare exceptions, each stockholder must be a U.S. citizen or permanent resident of the United States (no ownership by foreigners or other corporations).
Statutory Close (or Closed) Corporation	■ It can operate under simpler arrangements than conventional corporations. For example, it doesn't have to elect a board of directors or hold an annual stockholders' meeting. ■ All owners can actively participate in management while still having limited liability.	■ The number of stockholders is limited. (The number varies among states but is usually no more than 50.) ■ Stockholders normally can't sell their shares to the public without first offering the shares to existing owners. ■ Not all states allow formation of this type of corporation.
Nonprofit (or Not-for-Profit) Corporation	■ Earnings are exempt from federal and state income taxes. ■ Members and directors have limited liability. ■ Individuals who contribute money or property to the nonprofit can take a tax deduction, making it easier for these organizations to raise funds from donations.	■ It has members (who may pay dues) but cannot have stockholders. ■ It cannot distribute dividends to members. ■ It cannot contribute funds to a political campaign. ■ It must keep accurate records and file paperwork to document tax-exempt status.

■ **Possible Conflicts of Interest:** The corporate officers appointed by the board are supposed to further the interests of stockholders. But some top executives pursue policies that further their *own* interests (such as prestige, power, job security, high pay, and attractive perks) at the expense of the stockholders. The board of directors has an obligation to protect the interests of stockholders, but in recent years the boards of several major corporations have come under criticism for continuing to approve high compensation packages for top executives, even when their companies performed poorly.

6-4f Other Types of Corporations: Same but Different

Now that we've described C corporations, let's take a quick look at three other types of corporations: **S corporations, statutory close corporations**, and **nonprofit corporations**. Like C corporations, each is created by filing the appropriate paperwork with a government agency. Also like general corporations, these corporations are considered legal entities that stand apart from their owners and can enter into contracts, own property, and take legal action in their own names. But in other key respects they are quite different from C corporations—and from each other. Exhibit 6.5 summarizes the basic features of these corporations.

6-4g Corporate Restructuring

Large corporations constantly look for ways to grow and achieve competitive advantages. Some corporations work to achieve these goals, at least in part, through mergers, acquisitions, and divestitures. We'll close our discussion of corporations by taking a quick look at these forms of corporate restructuring.

Mergers and Acquisitions In the news and casual conversation, the terms "merger" and "acquisition" are often used interchangeably. However, there's a difference between the two. An **acquisition** occurs when one firm buys another firm. The firm making the purchase is called the "acquiring firm," and the firm being purchased is called the "target firm." After the acquisition, the target firm ceases to exist as an independent entity while the purchasing firm continues in operation, and its stock is still traded. But not all acquisitions are on friendly terms. When the acquiring firm buys the target firm despite the opposition of the target's board and top management, the result is called a "hostile takeover."

S corporation A form of corporation that avoids double taxation by having its income taxed as if it were a partnership.

statutory close (or closed) corporation A corporation with a limited number of owners that operates under simpler, less formal rules than a C corporation.

nonprofit corporation A corporation that does not seek to earn a profit and differs in several fundamental respects from C corporations.

acquisition A corporate restructuring in which one firm buys another.

EXHIBIT 6.6 | TYPES OF MERGERS AND ACQUISITIONS

Type of Merger	Definition	Common Objective	Example
Horizontal Merger	A combination of firms in the same industry.	Increase size and market power within the industry. Improve efficiency by eliminating duplication of facilities and personnel.	U.S.-based Sherwin-Williams, which makes paints and paint-related products, acquired U.S.-based Valspar, a paint, coating, and finishes company, for $11.3 billion.
Vertical Merger	A combination of firms that are at different stages in the production of a good or service, creating a "buyer-seller" relationship.	Provide tighter integration of production and increased control over the supply of crucial inputs.	China National Chemical Corporation, a Fortune 500 firm and the largest chemical firm in China, acquired Swiss-based Sygenta AG, which sells pesticides and soybean seeds, for $43 million.
Conglomerate Merger	A combination of firms in unrelated industries.	Reduce risk by making the firm less vulnerable to adverse conditions in any single market.	Chinese-based Midea, a maker of consumer appliances and heating, ventilation, and air-conditioning systems, acquired Kuka AG, a German-based robotics and automation systems company, for $5 billion.

In a **merger**, instead of one firm buying the other, the two companies agree to a combination of equals, joining together to form a new company out of the two previously independent firms. Exhibit 6.6 describes the three most common types of corporate combinations.

Divestitures: When Less Is More Sometimes corporations restructure by subtraction rather than by addition. A **divestiture** occurs when a firm transfers total or partial ownership of some of its operations to investors or to another company. Firms often use divestitures to rid themselves of a part of their company that no longer fits well with their strategic plans. This allows them to streamline their operations and focus on their core businesses. In many (but not all) cases, divestitures involve the sale of assets to outsiders, which raises financial capital for the firm.

One common type of divestiture, called a "spin-off," occurs when a company issues stock in one of its own divisions or operating units and sets it up as a separate company—complete with its own board of directors and corporate officers. It then distributes the stock in the new company to its existing stockholders. After the spin-off, the stockholders end up owning two separate companies rather than one. They can then buy, sell, or hold either (or both) stocks as they see fit. While a spin-off allows a corporation to eliminate a division that no longer fits in its plans, it doesn't actually generate any additional funds for the firm.

A "carve-out" is like a spin-off in that the firm converts a particular unit or division into a separate company and issues stock in the newly created corporation. However, instead of distributing the new stock to its current stockholders, it sells the stock to outside investors, thus raising additional financial capital. In many cases, the firm sells only a minority of the total shares, so that it maintains majority ownership.

In February 2017, Time Warner shareholders voted overwhelmingly in favor of an $85.4 billion merger with telecom giant AT&T. Shareholder approval was largely expected. Governmental approval, on the other hand, could prove more challenging.

Drop of Light/Shutterstock.com

horizontal merger A combination of two firms that are in the same industry.

vertical merger A combination of firms at different stages in the production of a good or service.

conglomerate merger A combination of two firms that are in unrelated industries.

merger A corporate restructuring that occurs when two formerly independent business entities combine to form a new organization.

divestiture The transfer of total or partial ownership of some of a firm's operations to investors or to another company.

Divestiture: HP Spins Off HP Enterprises

Companies use divestiture to transfer total or partial ownership of some of their operations to investors or to another company. When a part of a company no longer fits strategically, divesting allows the firm to streamline operations and refocus on its core business. A common divestiture, called a *spin-off*, occurs when a company sets up a division as a separate company—complete with its own board of directors, corporate officers, and stock. The parent company then distributes stock in the new company to its existing stockholders. After the spin-off, the stockholders own shares of two separate companies, which they can buy, sell, or hold like any other stock.

Silicon Valley was born in 1938, when David Packard and Bill Hewlett shared the rent of a home at 367 Addison Avenue in Palo Alto, California. Packard and his wife, Lucile, lived in

the first-floor apartment, while Bill Hewlett slept in a shed in the backyard. Their start-up company used the property's single-car garage as an office and workshop. The resulting business, Hewlett-Packard, became one of Silicon Valley's oldest and most successful companies.

But after eight decades in business, Hewlett-Packard announced in 2014 that it would spin off into two separate, publicly held companies. Today, HP Inc. makes and sells personal computers and printers. Hewlett Packard Enterprise (HPE) sells large computer servers, data storage and networking equipment, software, and consulting services. The primary reason for the divestiture was strategic. Hewlett-Packard CEO Meg Whitman (who became HPE CEO) explained, "We're leaving behind a company that was very large, running two businesses that were very different. We're creating two new big companies, not bite-sized morsels, with real capabilities to change things."

The spin-off took a year of planning, as a team of 500 created, cloned, and tested 2,800 computer applications and 75,000 computer interfaces to ensure that each company's operations would not be affected by the change.

In the wake of the spin-off, the two companies have independent boards of directors and issue different shares of stock. As of January 2017, HP Inc. (stock symbol HPQ) has 1.71 billion shares outstanding for a total market capitalization of $25.12 billion, while HPE (stock symbol HPE) has 1.66 billion shares outstanding and a total market capitalization of $38.09 billion.[15]

drserg/Shutterstock.com

6-5 THE LIMITED LIABILITY COMPANY: THE NEW KID ON THE BLOCK

As the newest form of business ownership, state laws concerning the legal status and formation of LLCs are still evolving. Several states have recently revised their statutes to make forming LLCs simpler and to make transfer of ownership easier. Other states have kept more restrictive requirements intact. This diversity of state requirements, and the continuing evolution of LLC statutes, makes it difficult to provide meaningful generalizations about this form of ownership.[16]

6-5a Forming and Managing an LLC

In many respects, forming an LLC is similar to forming a corporation. As with corporations, LLCs are created by filing a document (which goes by a variety of names, such as *certificate of organization* or *articles of organization*) and paying filing fees in the state where the business is organized. Organizers of most LLCs also draft an operating agreement, which is similar to the bylaws of a corporation. Some states also require LLCs to publish a notice of intent to operate as a LLC.

Because LLCs are neither corporations nor partnerships, their owners are called *members* rather than stockholders or partners. Members of LLCs often manage their own company under an arrangement similar to the relationship among general partners in a partnership. However, some LLCs hire professional managers who have responsibilities much like those of the CEO and other top officers of corporations.

6-5b Advantages of LLCs

Why are LLCs becoming so popular? This form of ownership offers significant advantages:

- **Limited Liability:** Similar to a corporation, all owners of an LLC have limited liability.

- **Tax Pass-Through:** As mentioned at the beginning of this chapter, for tax purposes the owners of LLCs may elect to have their companies treated as either a corporation or a partnership—or even as a sole proprietorship if owned by a single person. The default tax classification for LLCs with more than one owner—and the one most LLCs choose—is the partnership option. Under this arrangement, there is no separate tax on the earnings of the company. Instead, earnings "pass through" the company and are taxed only as income of the owners. This eliminates the double taxation of profits that is endemic to general corporations. However, there are some cases where it makes sense for LLCs to elect to be taxed as a corporation. For example, the owner of a single-person LLC can avoid paying self-employment taxes by electing to have the LLC treated as a corporation rather than as a sole proprietorship.

- **Simplicity and Flexibility in Management and Operation:** Unlike corporations, LLCs aren't required to hold regular board meetings. Also, LLCs are subject to less paperwork and fewer reporting requirements than corporations.

- **Flexible Ownership:** Unlike S corporations, LLCs can have any number of owners. Also unlike S corporations, the owners of LLCs can include foreign investors and other corporations. However, some states do make it difficult to transfer ownership to outsiders.

6-5c Limitations and Disadvantages of LLCs

Despite their increasing popularity, LLCs have some limitations and drawbacks:

- **Complexity of Formation:** Because of the need to file articles of organization and pay filing fees, LLCs can take more time and effort to form than sole proprietorships. In general, forming an LLC is also more difficult than creating a partnership. But as we mentioned earlier, the formation of a partnership requires a "meeting of the minds" of the partners, which isn't always easy to achieve. So in some cases, the formation of a partnership can prove to be every bit as challenging as the formation of an LLC.

- **Annual Franchise Tax:** Even though they may be exempt from corporate income taxes, many states require LLCs to pay an annual franchise tax.

dizain/Shutterstock.com

Running Your Own Business: Start Fresh or Franchise?

While millions dream of running their own businesses, cost and inexperience are two big reasons one-third to one-quarter of small businesses fail within two years. Inexperienced entrepreneurs often struggle to get customers to buy from them rather than from existing businesses, and small business owners typically need a great deal of start-up capital to pay for offices, facilities, transportation, insurance, and salaries (but probably not for themselves until the business establishes itself financially). It's not easy!

Aspiring entrepreneurs don't need to build new businesses from scratch, however. With franchising, a franchisor licenses the franchisee to use its name, trademark, products, and business methods. In short, franchising allows a businessperson to launch a new business with the support of a successful brand and backed by a proven business model. Moreover, starting a franchise often costs less than starting a fresh new business.

iStock.com/Skyhobo

Thanks to crowded franchise markets, many franchisors have begun discounting initial franchisee fees and royalties. For example, Cincinnati-based sports restaurant chain Buffalo Wings & Rings sold just three franchises in 2013. After cutting its franchisee fee from $35,000 to $5,000, however, the restaurant went on to sell 17 new franchises in 2014. Buffalo Wings & Rings' Director of Franchise Development Dan Doulen says, "In the grand scheme of things, $30,000 doesn't seem like a huge amount—but it is to those investors . . . [who] think about every penny they spend."

And once a franchise is successful, franchisors often offer even bigger discounts. Denny's restaurant chain, for instance, offers up to $1 million in discounts on fees for current franchisees who commit to opening six restaurants in untapped markets. Again, not an easy task by any means, but certainly easier than opening six new restaurants from scratch.[17]

- **Foreign Status in Other States:** Like corporations, LLCs must register or qualify to operate as "foreign" companies when they do business in states other than the state in which they were organized. This results in additional paperwork, fees, and taxes.

- **Limits on Types of Firms that Can Form LLCs:** Most states do not permit banks, insurance companies, and nonprofit organizations to operate as LLCs.

- **Differences in State Laws:** As we've already mentioned, LLC laws are still evolving—and their specific requirements vary considerably among the states. In 2006, the National Conference of Commissioners on Uniform State Laws created a Revised Uniform Limited Liability Company Act that could be used as a model by all states. To date, only a few states have adopted this law. Until there is more uniformity in state laws, operating LLCs in more than one state is likely to remain a complex endeavor.[18]

6-6 FRANCHISING: PROVEN METHODS FOR A PRICE

franchise A licensing arrangement under which a franchisor allows franchisees to use its name, trademark, products, business methods, and other property in exchange for monetary payments and other considerations.

franchisor The business entity in a franchise relationship that allows others to operate its business using resources it supplies in exchange for money and other considerations.

franchisee The party in a franchise relationship that pays for the right to use resources supplied by the franchisor.

distributorship A type of franchising arrangement in which the franchisor makes a product and licenses the franchisee to sell it.

business format franchise A broad franchise agreement in which the franchisee pays for the right to use the name, trademark, and business and production methods of the franchisor.

A **franchise** is a licensing arrangement under which one party (the **franchisor**) allows another party (the **franchisee**) to use its name, trademark, patents, copyrights, business methods, and other property in exchange for monetary payments and other considerations. Franchising has become a very popular way to operate a business and an important source of employment and income. A 2016 study conducted by Global Insight for the International Franchising Association's Education Foundation reported that 783,000 franchise establishments operated in the United States, employing more than 8.83 million workers. And according to another

While franchises are usually associated with restaurants, any kind of business can be operated as a franchise. Some non-restaurant franchises in the United States include convenience store 7 Eleven, hotel chain Marriott International, Chem-Dry Carpet Cleaning, and car rental service Hertz.

charnsitr/Shutterstock.com

franchising study published by the Bureau of the Census, franchise establishments dominate several major markets such as fast food, auto dealerships, convenience stores, and private mail distribution centers.[19]

The two most popular types of franchise arrangements are **distributorships** and **business format franchises**. In a distributorship, the franchisor makes a product and grants distributors a license to sell it. The most common example of this type of franchise is the arrangement between automakers and the dealerships that sell their cars. In a business format franchise, the franchisor grants the franchisee the right to both make *and* sell its good or service. Under this arrangement, the franchisor usually provides a wide range of services to the franchisee, such as help with site selection, training, and help in obtaining financing, but also requires the franchisee to follow very specific guidelines while operating the business. You're no doubt very familiar with business format franchises; examples include Wendy's, Supercuts, Jiffy Lube, and Massage Envy.

6-6a Franchising in Today's Economy

Franchising is now a well-established method of operating a business—but that doesn't mean it's static. Let's look at some ways the world of franchising is changing.

One of the biggest trends in franchising for the past several years has been an expansion into foreign markets. Franchisors in a variety of industries have found that opportunities for franchise growth are greater in foreign countries because competition is less intense, and markets are less saturated than in the United States. In 2016, McDonald's had 17,389 franchise outlets in foreign countries (4,411 more than it had in the United States), Subway had 17,950, and 7–11 had 50,712.[20] Of course, operating in foreign countries can pose special challenges. Differences in culture, language, laws, demographics, and economic development mean that franchisors, like other types of business owners, must adjust their business methods—and the specific products they offer—to meet the needs of foreign consumers.

Another notable trend has been the growth in the number of women franchisees. Reliable statistics on women in franchising are difficult to find, but the International Franchising Association (IFA) estimates that women now own about 45% of all franchises, and anecdotal evidence suggests that the trend toward more women-owned franchises is continuing. A number of women, such as Dzana Homan (founder of School of Rock music lesson franchises), and Eileen Huntington, co-founder of Huntington Learning Centers, also have become very successful franchisors.[21] But, despite these highly visible success stories, the number of women franchisors hasn't grown nearly as fast as the number of women franchisees.[22]

Minority participation in franchises, both as franchisees and franchisors, has been relatively low. African Americans, Hispanics, Asian Americans, and Native Americans make up about a third of the population, and that share is expected to steadily grow over the next several decades. Indeed, 20.5% of franchises are minority-owned, which is roughly 50% higher than 14.2% for nonfranchised businesses.[23] One of the main reasons for such low minority involvement in franchising is a lack of awareness of franchising opportunities within minority communities. But many franchisors are now making a strong effort to actively recruit minority franchisees.[24]

Two major initiatives have given the efforts to reach minority franchising a boost in recent years. The first, known as the National Minority Franchising Initiative (NMFI), was founded in 2000. The NMFI's website currently maintains a directory of more than 500 franchisors who actively promote minority franchise ownership. The second initiative, called DiversityFran, was established in early 2006 by the IFA. This initiative has the cooperation of a variety of organizations interested in promoting minority business ownership, including the National Urban League, the Association of Small Business Development Centers, the U.S. Pan Asian American Chamber of Commerce, and the Minority Business Development Agency. Franchisors participating in the program receive information and marketing materials designed to help them reach potential minority franchisees more effectively. As of April 2015, DiversityFran had 119 participating franchisors, including such major players as Chick-fil-A, Dunkin' Donuts, and KFC-YUM! Brands (which owns KFC, Taco Bell, and Pizza Hut), all pledging to actively recruit minority franchisees.[25]

6-6b Advantages of Franchising

Both the franchisee and the franchisor must believe they'll benefit from the franchise arrangement; otherwise, they wouldn't participate. The advantages of franchising for the franchisor are fairly obvious. It allows the franchisor to expand the business and bring in additional revenue (in the form of franchising fees and royalties) without investing its own capital. Also, franchisees—business owners who are motivated to earn a profit—may have a greater incentive than salaried managers to do whatever it takes to maximize the success of their outlets.

From the franchisee's perspective, franchising offers several advantages:

- **Less Risk:** Franchises offer access to a proven business system and product. The systems and methods offered by franchisors have an established track record. People who are interested in buying a franchise can do research to see how stores in the franchise have performed and can talk to existing franchisees before investing.

- **Training and Support:** The franchisor normally provides the franchisee with extensive training and support. For example, Subway offers two weeks of training at its headquarters and additional training at meetings.

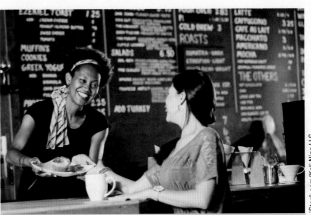

The National Minority Franchising Initiative (NMFI) and DiversityFran are two programs founded to promote minority business ownership.

EXHIBIT 6.7 | FRANCHISEE COSTS FOR SELECTED FRANCHISES

Franchise	Type of Business	Initial Franchisee Fee	Ongoing Royalty*	Estimated Minimum Initial Investment
Coffee News	Newspaper distributed at restaurants	$8,500	$25 to $80/wk.	$9,750 to $10,750
Anytime Fitness	24/7 Fitness club	$19,000 to $37,500	$549/mo.	$80,020 to $490,100
Subway	Fast food	$15,000	8%	$116,600 to $263,150
Papa John's	Pizza delivery	$25,000	5%	$129,910 to $844,210
Great Clips	Hair styling	$20,000	6%	$132,250 to $253,100
The UPS Store	Mailing and business	$29,950	5%	$159,224 to $434,521
The Joint	Chiropractic care	$39,900	7%	$216,200 to $331,700
Jiffy Lube	Automobile maintenance	$10,000	3%	$219,000 to $400,000

*Royalty is expressed as a percentage of gross revenues unless otherwise specified.
Source: Individual franchise opportunity pages for each listed franchise on the Entrepreneur.com website, http://www.entrepreneur.com/franchiseopportunities/index.html, accessed January 19, 2017.

The franchisor also sends out newsletters, provides Internet support, maintains a toll-free number for phone support, and provides on-site evaluations.[26]

■ **Brand Recognition:** Operating a franchise gives the franchisee instant brand-name recognition, which can be a big help in attracting customers.

■ **Easier Access to Funding:** Bankers and other lenders may be more willing to lend money if the business is part of an established franchise than if it is a new, unproven business.

6-6c Disadvantages of Franchising

Franchising also has some drawbacks. From the franchisor's perspective, operating a business with perhaps thousands of semi-independent owner–operators can be complex and challenging. With such a large number of owners, it can be difficult to keep all of the franchisees satisfied, and disappointed franchisees sometimes go public with their complaints, damaging the reputation of the franchisor. In fact, it isn't unusual for disgruntled franchisees to sue their franchisors.

Franchisees are also likely to find some disadvantages:

■ **Costs:** The typical franchise agreement requires franchisees to pay an initial franchise fee when they enter into the franchise agreement and an ongoing royalty (usually a percentage of monthly sales revenues) to the franchisor. In addition, the franchisor may assess other fees to support national advertising campaigns or for other purposes. These costs

> "In business for yourself, not by yourself."
>
> —RAY KROC, FOUNDER, MCDONALD'S RESTAURANTS

vary considerably, but for high-profile franchises, they can be substantial. Exhibit 6.7 compares the initial franchise fees, ongoing royalties, and minimum initial investment for several well-established franchises. (Initial investment reflects the fact that the cost of starting a franchise generally requires the franchisee to invest in property, equipment, and inventory in addition to paying the franchise fee. The actual total investment that franchisees make is often substantially higher than the estimated minimum investment cited in Exhibit 6.7.)

■ **Lack of Control:** The franchise agreement usually requires the franchisee to follow the franchisor's procedures to the letter. People who want the freedom and flexibility to be their own boss can find these restrictions frustrating.

■ **Negative Halo Effect:** The irresponsible or incompetent behavior of a few franchisees can create a negative perception that adversely affects not only the franchise as a whole but also the success of other franchisees.

■ **Growth Challenges:** While growth and expansion are definitely possible in franchising (many franchisees own multiple outlets), strings are attached. Franchise agreements usually limit the franchisee's territory and require franchisor approval before expanding into other areas.

■ **Restrictions on Sale:** Franchise agreements normally prevent franchisees from selling their franchises to other investors without prior approval from the franchisor.

Large Fries: McDonald's Moves Toward Multiple-Store Franchisees

If you're trying to decide whether franchising is a good opportunity, know that the millions of business people who bought and run franchises did so because franchising offers reduced risk, training and support from the franchisor, the advantage of instant brand recognition (as opposed to building a new brand from scratch), and easier access to funding as bankers and other lenders have greater confidence that a franchise business will succeed. Akram Khan, a KFC franchisee in the United Kingdom (UK) says, "When the opportunity to buy a franchise came up, I jumped at it. I like the structure of franchising—I haven't got the confidence to open my own restaurant. This way, you have the autonomy of your own restaurant but you have access to expertise."

While most franchisees start with one store and one location, many enter franchising with the aim of owning multiple franchises. Indeed, Akron Khan now owns 15 KFC franchises.

Sorbis/Shutterstock.com

Mike Guerin, who bought his first McDonald's franchise in the UK 23 years ago, now owns 12.

Today, however, it is increasingly difficult for a small franchisee to succeed. Ted Lezotte, who owned McDonald's franchises for more than three decades, sold his six stores because of large remodeling costs, which can run from $600,000 for an interior makeover of an existing store to as high as $1 million to $2 million for a complete tear down and rebuild of an old McDonald's. Common additional costs include $125,000 to install touchscreen ordering systems that let diners customize orders, $13,000 for McCafé espresso machines, $4,500 for the special equipment that bakes fresh muffins, and anywhere from $500 to $5000 for the additional equipment needed to serve all day breakfast (which McDonald's now offers). Lezotte says, "In today's financial world, it's becoming necessary to have more than a couple [of stores] to survive. Ten [stores] kind of gives you a good footing." Five of Lezotte's stores were sold to larger McDonald's franchisees, while the sixth was closed.

Rob Hunziker, who runs a restaurant brokerage called advanced restaurant sales, says that McDonald's is, "encouraging the smaller franchisees to sell out." When you have thousands of franchisees that you need to keep monitored or updated, it's just difficult and expensive for the parent company." The percentage of McDonald's franchisees who own five or fewer restaurants has dropped 4.6% since 2014, while the number running 10 or more stores has increased by 12%. CEO Steve Easterbrook says, "Does that give us fewer, [but] stronger operators and a stronger balance sheet and their ability to invest in scale? It could."[27]

■ **Poor Execution:** Not all franchisors live up to their promises. Sometimes the training and support are of poor quality, and sometimes the company does a poor job of screening franchisees, leading to the negative halo effect we mentioned previously.

These considerations suggest that before buying a franchise, potential owners should carefully research the franchise opportunity.

6-6d Entering into a Franchise Agreement

To obtain a franchise, the franchisee must sign a **franchise agreement**. This agreement is a legally binding contract that specifies the relationship between the franchisor and the franchisee in great detail. There's no standard form for the contract, but some of the key items normally covered include the following:

■ **Terms and Conditions:** The franchisee's rights to use the franchisor's trademarks, patents, and signage, and any restrictions on those rights. It also covers how long the agreement will last and under what terms (and at what cost) it can be renewed.

> **franchise agreement**
> The contractual arrangement between a franchisor and franchisee that spells out the duties and responsibilities of both parties.

- **Fees and Other Payments:** The fees the franchisee must pay for the right to use the franchisor's products and methods, and when these payments are due.

- **Training and Support:** The types of training and support the franchisor will provide to the franchisee.

- **Specific Operational Requirements:** The methods and standards established by the franchisor that the franchisee is required to follow.

- **Conflict Resolution:** How the franchisor and franchisee will handle disputes.

- **Assigned Territory:** The geographic area in which the franchisee will operate and whether the franchisee has exclusive rights in that area.

Franchise Disclosure Document (FDD) A detailed description of all aspects of a franchise that the franchisor must provide to the franchisee at least 14 calendar days before the franchise agreement is signed.

It's vital for anyone thinking about entering into a franchise agreement to know all the facts before signing on the dotted line. Fortunately, the Federal Trade Commission (FTC) requires franchisors to provide potential franchisees with a document known as a **Franchise Disclosure Document (FDD)**. This long, complex document (covering 23 separate major topics and sometimes running well over 100 pages) can be an invaluable source of information about virtually every aspect of the franchise arrangement. For example, the FDD must provide contact information for at least 100 current franchisees. (If the franchisor has fewer than 100 current franchisees, it must list all of them.) This gives a potential franchisee the ability to contact other franchisees and ask them about their experiences with the franchisor. As an added bonus, the FTC requires the FDD to be written in "plain English" rather than in the complex legal jargon that often characterizes such documents. This rule means you actually have a chance to understand what you're reading![28]

Under FTC rules, the franchisor must give the franchisee at least 14 calendar days to review the FDD before the franchise agreement can be signed. A careful study of the FDD can go a long way toward ensuring that the franchisee makes an informed decision. Even though the FDD is written in "plain English," it's a good idea to have a lawyer who is knowledgeable about franchise law review it. You'll have to pay for any legal advice, but entering into a bad franchise agreement can be a lot more expensive (and stressful) than a lawyer's fees.

THE BIG PICTURE

This chapter discusses the four major forms of business ownership. Each form of ownership has both advantages and limitations, so no single form of ownership is the best in all situations.

Sole proprietorships are appealing to entrepreneurs who want to start a business quickly, with few formalities or fees, and who want to be their own boss. But sole proprietorships aren't well suited for raising financing from external sources, so growth opportunities are limited. And sole proprietors have unlimited liability for their company's debts and obligations.

General partnerships allow two or more owners to pool financial resources and take advantage of complementary skills. But each owner must assume the risk of unlimited liability, and disagreements among partners can complicate and delay important decisions.

Corporations are more complex and expensive to create than other forms of business. Another potentially serious drawback is the double taxation of earnings. But corporations have the greatest potential for raising financial capital and provide owners with the protection of limited liability.

The limited liability company (LLC) is a relatively new form of business ownership that offers many of the advantages of corporations without as many regulations. One major advantage of LLCs compared to corporations is that its earnings can be taxed as if the company is a partnership, thus avoiding double taxation. But the laws governing limited liability companies vary considerably among states, making it a challenge to operate an LLC in multiple states.

CAREERS IN FRANCHISING

Franchise Store Manager

Responsible for running day-to-day retail store operations. Required to open and close the store; manage schedules and productivity; provide world-class customer service; monitor cost control, payroll, and expenses; provide weekly and monthly reports to the franchise owner; recruit, train, and coach employees; and develop and implement store marketing program. Ultimately accountable for profit/loss, continuous improvement, service delivery levels, personnel management, and business development. The ideal candidate has a college degree, a dynamic personality, two years of retail store operations experience, strong management skills, excellent computer knowledge, and is a good listener who can motivate a team and run good meetings.

STUDY TOOLS 6

LOCATED AT BACK OF THE TEXTBOOK

☐ Rip-Out Chapter Review Card

☐ Gain unique perspectives on key concepts with new concept videos in the e-book

☐ Increase your comprehension with online homework and quizzes

☐ Study with existing flashcards and make your own

7 | Small Business and Entrepreneurship:
Economic Rocket Fuel

Remember to visit
PAGE 126
for additional
STUDY TOOLS

LEARNING OBJECTIVES

After studying this chapter, you will be able to:

 7-1 Explain the key reasons to launch a small business

7-2 Describe the typical entrepreneurial mindset and characteristics

7-3 Discuss funding options for small business

7-4 Analyze the opportunities and threats that small businesses face

7-5 Discuss ways to become a new business owner and tools to facilitate success

7-6 Explain the size, scope, and economic contributions of small business

---

7-1 ## LAUNCHING A NEW VENTURE: WHAT'S IN IT FOR ME?

Over time, the entrepreneurship rate has played a powerful, positive role in the U.S. economy. The new business creation rate in 2014 showed the largest year-over-year increase of the last two decades, but start-up activity still remains below historic norms. As the economy continued to gain momentum, unemployed workers were able to find jobs rather than turn to entrepreneurship.[1] The drop in entrepreneurship has been especially sharp among Generation Y (born between early 1980s and early 2000s). Despite their strong entrepreneurial spirit—65% have a desire to start their own business—many are struggling with heavy student debt and a challenging job market. Since the prime age for entrepreneurship is late 30s to early 40s, a burst of entrepreneurial activity may lie ahead as the huge Generation Y reaches that age range. Entrepreneurial activity may pick up even sooner since Generation Z, or digital natives, are intensely entrepreneurial—particularly in the digital realm—with nearly three-quarters of them planning to start their own business and a critical mass beginning the process while they are still in high school.[2]

Starting a new business can be tough—very tough. Yet, for the right person, the advantages of business ownership far outweigh the risk and hard work. Although people start their own ventures for a variety of reasons, most are seeking some combination of greater financial success, independence, flexibility, and challenge. Others are simply seeking survival.

7-1a Greater Financial Success

Although you can make a pretty good living working for someone else, your chances of getting really rich may be higher if you start your own business. The *Forbes* magazine annual list of the 400 richest Americans is dominated by **entrepreneurs**, such as Bill Gates and Paul Allen (founders of Microsoft), Phil Knight (founder of Nike), Michael Dell (founder of Dell Inc.), and Sergey Brin and Larry Page (founders of Google). And many people feel that their

> "In the end, a vision without the ability to execute it is probably a hallucination."
>
> —STEVE CASE, CO-FOUNDER AMERICA ONLINE, CHAIRMAN, STARTUP AMERICA PARTNERSHIP

chances of even moderate financial success are higher if they're working for themselves rather than someone else. The opportunity to make more money is a primary motivator for many entrepreneurs, although other factors clearly play a role as well.[3]

7-1b Independence

Being your own boss is a huge benefit of starting your own business. You answer to no one other than yourself and any investors whom you invite to participate in your business. Bottom line: You are the only one who is ultimately responsible for your success or failure. This setup is especially compelling for people who have trouble

entrepreneurs People who risk their time, money, and other resources to start and manage a business.

> "Obviously everyone wants to be successful, but I want to be looked back on as being very innovative, very trusted and ethical and ultimately making a big difference in the world."
>
> —SERGEY BRIN, CO-FOUNDER, GOOGLE

being subordinates because of their personalities (and we probably all know someone who fits that description!). But while independence is nice, it's important to keep in mind that every business depends on meeting the needs of its customers, who can be even more demanding than the toughest boss.

7-1c Flexibility

The ability to set your own hours and control your own schedule is a hugely appealing benefit for many business owners, especially parents seeking more time with

> "Whatever you're thinking, think bigger."
>
> —TONY HSIEH, FOUNDER, ZAPPOS.COM

their kids or retirees looking for extra income. Given current technological tools—from email to eBay—it's easy for small business owners to manage their firms on the go or after hours. Of course, there's often a correlation between hours worked and dollars earned. (It's rare to work less and earn more.) But when more money isn't the primary goal, the need for flexibility can be enough to motivate many entrepreneurs to launch their own enterprise.

7-1d Challenge

Running your own business provides a level of challenge unmatched by many other endeavors. Most business owners—especially new business owners—never find themselves bored! Starting a business also offers endless opportunities for learning that can provide more profound satisfaction for many people than grinding out the hours as an employee.

7-1e Survival

Although most entrepreneurs launch their business in response to an opportunity with hopes of improving their lives, some entrepreneurs—called "necessity entrepreneurs"—launch their business because they believe it is their *only* economic option. Necessity

Eccentric Entrepreneurs

Do quirky people become entrepreneurs, or does successful entrepreneurship breed quirkiness? Hard to know which comes first, but it's not hard to find quirky entrepreneurs. Some highlights:

- Mark Zuckerberg, founder of Facebook, personally butchered all the animals he ate in 2011.

- Automobile tycoon Henry Ford ate weeds from his garden, and even ate sandwiches filled with weeds.

- Dustin Moscovitz, Zuckerberg's college roommate at Harvard and Facebook's third employee, still rides his bicycle to work despite being the world's youngest billionaire at age 29.

- Marc Andreessen, founder of Netscape, blogs in his underwear.

- David Karp, CEO of Tumblr, prides himself on ignoring email.

- Paul Graham, founder of Y Combinator, wrote an essay titled "Why Nerds Are Unpopular."

- Co-founder of Apple Steve Jobs would eat only one type of food, such as carrots or apples, for weeks at a time. He reportedly ate so many carrots at one time that his skin turned bright orange. Jobs also believed that his restrictive, vegan diet meant that his body was free from body odor and allowed him to bathe only once per week.

- John Harvey Kellogg (pictured), founder of the cereal empire, began his career as a medical doctor, and was once the chief physician at the Western Health Reform Institute of Battle Creek, where he argued that people should have yogurt enemas on a daily basis. Perhaps we should all be thankful that his corn flakes went mainstream, rather than his other ideas about health.

AP Images

So if you're a quirky individual, you may want to consider nurturing your quirks, not hiding them. Who knows? Even if you're not the world's next billionaire, your quirks may give you a common interest with him or her, which could ultimately land you a great job![4]

entrepreneurs range from middle-aged workers laid off from corporate jobs, to new immigrants with limited English and heavy accents, to those who experience discrimination in the standard workplace. For each of these types of people, small business ownership can be the right choice in the face of few other alternatives.

 ## 7-2 THE ENTREPRENEUR: A DISTINCTIVE PROFILE

Successful entrepreneurs tend to stand out from the crowd in terms of both their mindset and their personal characteristics. As you read this section, consider whether you fit the entrepreneurial profile.

7-2a The Entrepreneurial Mindset: A Matter of Attitude

Almost every entrepreneur starts as a small businessperson—either launching a firm or buying a firm—but not every small businessperson starts as an entrepreneur. The difference is a matter of attitude. From day one, a true entrepreneur—such as Sam Walton of Walmart, Steve Jobs of Apple, or Jeff Bezos of Amazon—aims to change the world through blockbuster goods or services.

That isn't the case for all small business owners. Most people who launch new firms expect to better themselves, but they don't expect huge, transformative growth. In fact, nearly 70% of small business owners say they don't want to grow any larger.[5]

However, classic entrepreneurs who deliver on the promise of their best ideas can dramatically change the economic and social landscape worldwide. Examples of business owners who thought and delivered big include Henry Ford, founder of the Ford Motor Company and originator of assembly line production; Walt Disney, founder of The Walt Disney Company and creator of Mickey Mouse; Mary Kay Ash, founder of a cosmetics powerhouse; Martha Stewart, lifestyle innovator for the masses; Stephenie Meyer, creator of the *Twilight* franchise; and Mark Zuckerberg, founder of Facebook.

7-2b Entrepreneurial Characteristics

While experts sometimes disagree about the specific characteristics of successful entrepreneurs, virtually all include vision, self-reliance, energy, confidence, tolerance of uncertainty, and tolerance of failure. (See Exhibit 7.1.) Most successful entrepreneurs have all of these qualities and more, but they come in a huge variety of combinations that highlight the complexity of personality: there is no one successful entrepreneurial profile.

Exhibit 7.1
Entrepreneurial Characteristics

Vision

Self-Reliance

Energy

Confidence

Tolerance of Uncertainty

Tolerance of Failure

Arek Malang/Shutterstock.com

Vision Most entrepreneurs are wildly excited about their own new ideas, which many seem to draw from a bottomless well. Entrepreneurs find new solutions to old problems, and they develop new products that we didn't even know we needed until we had them. And entrepreneurs stay excited about their ideas, even when friends and relatives threaten to call the loony bin. For instance, Fred Smith, founder of the FedEx empire, traces the concept for his business to a term paper he wrote at Yale, which supposedly received a C from a skeptical professor. But that didn't stop him from creating a business logistics system that transformed the industry, and along with UPS, enabled e-commerce to flourish.

Self-Reliance As an entrepreneur, the buck stops with you. New business owners typically need to do everything themselves, from getting permits to motivating employees, to keeping the books—all in addition to producing the product or service that made them start the business in the first place. Self-reliance seems to come with an **internal locus of control**, or a deep-seated sense that the individual is personally responsible for what happens in his or her life. When things go well, people with an internal locus of control feel that their efforts have been validated, and when things go poorly, those same people feel that they need to do better next time. This sense of responsibility encourages positive action. In contrast, people with an **external locus of control** rely less on their own efforts, feeling buffeted by forces such as random luck and the actions of others, which they believe will ultimately control their fate.

Energy Entrepreneurs simply can't succeed without an enormous amount of energy. Six or seven 12-hour workdays are not atypical in the start-up phase of running a business. In fact, 61% of small business owners report working six or more days per week, compared to only 22% of workers in the general population. And for small business owners, even a day off isn't *really* off. Only 27% of small business owners define a day off as not working at all, while 57% of small business owners say they always or most of the time work on holidays. But Discover Financial Services also learned that many small business owners seem to find the grind worthwhile: 47% of small

> ## "A lot of times, people don't know what they want until you show it to them."
> —STEVE JOBS, CO-FOUNDER, APPLE

business owners said that if they won $10 million in the lottery, they would still work in their current job. Only 9% would stop working, and 8% would combine work, volunteering, and other areas of interest.[6]

Confidence Successful entrepreneurs typically have confidence in their own ability to achieve, and their confidence encourages them to act boldly. But too much confidence has a downside. Entrepreneurs must take care not to confuse likelihood with reality. In fact, many could benefit from the old adage "Hope for the best and plan for the worst." A study for the Small Business Administration Office of Advocacy confirmed that entrepreneurs are typically overconfident regarding their own abilities. As a result they're sometimes willing to plunge into a new business, but they don't always have the skills to succeed.[7]

Tolerance of Uncertainty More often than others, entrepreneurs see the world in shades of gray rather than simply black and white. They tend to embrace uncertainty in the business environment, turning it to their advantage rather than shying away. Uncertainty also relates to risk, and successful entrepreneurs tend to more willingly accept risk—financial risk, for instance, such as mortgaging their home for the business, and professional risk, such as staking their reputation on the success of an unproven product.

Tolerance of Failure Even when they fail, entrepreneurs seldom label themselves losers. They tend to view failure as a chance to learn rather than as a sign that they just can't do it (whatever "it" may be for them at any given moment). Interestingly, Isaac Fleischmann, director of the U.S. Patent Office for 36 years, pointed out: "During times of economic decline when unemployment increases, so does the number of patents. Dark days often force us to become more ingenious, to monitor and modify the ways we reached failure and reshape them into a new pattern of success." Failure can actually be an effective springboard for achievement.[8]

A surprising number of twentieth-century entrepreneurial stars experienced significant failure in their careers yet bounced back to create wildly successful ventures. Early in his career, for instance, Walt Disney was fired from an ad agency (in hindsight, a rather foolish ad agency) for a "singular lack of drawing ability." Ray Kroc, the man who made McDonald's into a fast-food empire, couldn't make a go of real estate, so he sold milkshake machines for much of his life. He was 52 years old, and in failing health, when he discovered the McDonald brothers' hamburger stand and transformed it into a fast-food empire. Steve Jobs, founder of

internal locus of control A deep-seated sense that the individual is personally responsible for what happens in his or her life.

external locus of control A deep-seated sense that forces other than the individual are responsible for what happens in his or her life.

Apple computer, found himself unceremoniously dumped by his board of directors less than ten years after introducing the world's first personal computer. After another decade, he returned in triumph, restoring Apple's polish with blockbuster new products such as the iPod and the iPhone. And JK Rowling, creator of the $15 billion Harry Potter empire, had her initial book rejected by 12 shortsighted publishers. So next time you fail, keep your eyes open for opportunity—your failure may be the first step of the next big thing.[9]

7-3 FINDING THE MONEY: FUNDING OPTIONS FOR SMALL BUSINESSES

For many entrepreneurs, finding the money to fund their business is the top challenge of their start-up year. The vast majority of new firms are funded with the personal resources of their founder. In fact, about 95% of entrepreneurs raise start-up funds from personal accounts, family, and friends. Other key funding sources include bank loans, angel investors, and venture capital firms.[11]

7-3a Personal Resources

While the idea of using just your own money to open a business sounds great, and more than three-quarters of small business owners spend their own savings as a source of start-up funding,[12] the financial requirements of most new firms typically force entrepreneurs to also tap personal resources such as family, friends, and credit cards. According to *Consumer Reports*, 68% of total start-up financing comes from personal resources.[13] If you do borrow from family or friends, virtually every small business expert recommends that you keep the relationship as professional as possible. If the business fails, a professional agreement can preserve personal ties. And if the business succeeds, you'll need top-quality documentation of financing from family and friends to get larger-scale backing from outside sources.

Personal credit cards can be an especially handy—though highly risky—financing resource. In fact, a recent survey found that nearly half of all start-ups are funded with plastic. (It's no

Big Lies about Entrepreneurship

There's no shortage of advice about entrepreneurship in the business world. However, that doesn't mean that it's all *good* advice. Inc. magazine asked a handful of entrepreneurs and experts to share the biggest whoppers they ever heard about entrepreneurship. Here are some highlights:

- **All you need is a good idea.** "An excellent idea is an important first step, but your business will not take off as a success unless you have a smart strategy and put passionate effort behind it."—*Sherry Harnett, a marketing and leadership consultant, professor, and a judge for Get Started Pensacola 2016*

- **Being an entrepreneur is glamorous.** "Being an entrepreneur is harder than a 9–5 job. You must eat, sleep,

Ditty_about_summer/Shutterstock.com

and dream it. This ain't for the weary or weak."—*Duncan Kabinu, co-founder of Gainesville Dev Academy, a software training center; and a judge for Get Started Gainesville 2016*

- **Do what you love and the money will follow.** "No words have ever created more failed entrepreneurs than the notion that just because you love doing something, it will be a successful business and you will make tons of money. In fact, often times, a person's love for doing something becomes a problem because instead of running their business, they just focus on delivering the service they enjoy so much, as the business around them crumbles."—*Topher Morrison, executive director of Key Person of Influence, a growth accelerator that has worked with more than 2,000 entrepreneurs*

- **Entrepreneurship is a young person's game.** Not always. "Success is much more likely to find a mid-career professional who has identified a market opportunity through their own professional and life experience and has the financial capital and network required to take the risk, assemble the team, and network to advance a new venture."—*Garret Westlake, executive director of the da Vinci Center, a unique collegiate model that advances innovation and entrepreneurship through cross-disciplinary collaboration at Virginia Commonwealth University*

So, as always, don't believe everything you hear. A little extra research may serve you well before you turn your dream into reality.[10]

If You Don't Know Jack . . .

. . . chances are that you will soon. Jack Ma, founder and chairman of Alibaba group and one of China's richest men, is quickly rising to the forefront of the business world. Alibaba is a multifaceted e-commerce behemoth that is somewhat similar to Amazon, yet significantly more profitable. Although Alibaba carries enormous heft within China, it remains mysterious to most non-Chinese, because relatively few people outside China actually do business with Alibaba. But Jack Ma aims to change that.

In early 2017, Jack Ma met with President Trump and promised that Alibaba would help create 1 million jobs in the United States over five years. According to Ma, Alibaba will empower 1 million small US businesses to sell their goods in China using Alibaba's various e-commerce platforms. Each business that sells on Alibaba will hire one employee, resulting in the 1 million new jobs.

Ma is a powerful advocate—not just for Alibaba, but for globalism and business in general. He refers to globalism as a baby and says, "the baby is having growing pains. We should not kill the baby because he cries a lot." As to business in general, Ma

believes that businesspeople can accomplish what politicians cannot. "When you put 200 companies in the same room trying to realize something, it's impossible but when you put 200 business people in one room, we might work something out."[14]

Drew Angerer/Getty Images

wonder, given that those solicitations just keep on coming.) Credit cards do provide fast, flexible money, but watch out—if you don't pay back your card company fast, you'll find yourself socked with financing fees that can take years to pay off.[15]

7-3b Loans

Getting commercial loans for a new venture can be tough. Banks and other lenders are understandably hesitant to fund a business that doesn't have a track record. And when they do, they require a lot of paperwork and often a fairly long waiting period. Given these hurdles, only 20% of new business owners launch with commercial loans. Unfortunately, small business lending fell 78% in the five years following the Great Recession.[16] And virtually no conventional lending source—private or government—will lend 100% of the start-up dollars for a new business. Most require that the entrepreneur provide a minimum of 25% to 30% of total start-up costs from personal resources.[17]

Another source for loans may be the U.S. Small Business Administration (SBA). The SBA doesn't give free money to start-up businesses—neither grants nor interest-free loans—but it does partially guarantee loans from local commercial lenders. This reduces risk for the lenders, who are, in turn, more likely to lend money to a new business owner. The SBA also has a microloan program that lends small amounts of money—$13,000 on average—to start-up businesses through community nonprofit organizations.[18]

Peer-to-peer lending offers yet another potential funding source for new business start-ups. Websites such as Prosper.com and LendingClub.com bring together borrowers and investors so that both can benefit financially. Many entrepreneurs have found this is an easier way to get money, at more favorable terms, than through more-established sources.

7-3c Crowdfunding

Crowdfunding is the process of funding ventures by raising money from a large number of investors via the Internet. Crowdfunding began to appear in the mid-2000s, and quickly gained traction, becoming a nearly $35 billion funding source by 2016. Experts anticipate that global crowdfunding could grow to $96 billion by 2020.[19] Many crowdfunding sites are used to fund nonprofits. The largest crowdfunding sites in terms of traffic are gofundme.com, kickstarter.com, and indiegogo.com. Two examples of big crowdfunding successes are (1) the Pebble smart watch, which raised $1 million in just 28 hours and eventually went on to raise more than $10 million, and (2) the feature film *Veronica Mars*, which raised $4.7 million.

7-3d Angel Investors

Angel investors aren't as saintly—or as flighty—as they sound. They are wealthy individuals who invest in promising start-up companies for one basic reason: to make money

angel investors Individuals who invest in start-up companies with high growth potential in exchange for a share of ownership.

Should You Protect Your Startup from Hackers?

Not if the hackers are growth hackers! Growth hacking means using metrics, creative strategies, and state-of-the-art technology to accelerate the growth of your brand, service, or product far beyond the norm. Growth hackers know their customers inside and out, including their pain points. Perhaps more importantly, they also know which products and services will alleviate that pain. Often, growth hackers create blogs and other types of content that invite potential consumers to participate in conversations about the brand. And when people do participate, the growth hackers assiduously collect and massage the data, using it to generate leads, which they then transform into powerful growth. Growth hackers also test, test, test. Which works better—Strategy A or Strategy B? And after optimizing that choice, they move on to the next crossroads, and growth keeps booming. It's no surprise then that growth hacking has become a strategy of choice for new economic giants such as Facebook, Twitter, and scores of others. Perhaps as you enter the world of business, you should consider putting it work for you.[20]

alphaspirit/Shutterstock.com

---

for themselves. According to Jeffrey Sohl, director of the Center for Venture Research, angels look for companies that seem likely to grow at 30% to 40% per year and will then either be bought or go public. He estimates that 10% to 15% of private companies fit that description, but points out that finding those firms isn't easy. It doesn't help, he says, that "80% of entrepreneurs think they're in that 10% to 15%." In 2015, the angel investor market experienced a slight increase in investment dollars (+1.9%) and in deal size (+5.1%). Unfortunately, investment in new, first sequence investments was down 49% from 2014. "This decrease in new investments is a discouraging sign for our nation's start-ups," said Sohl.[21]

7-3e Venture Capital

Venture capital firms fund high-potential, new companies in exchange for a share of ownership, which can sometimes be as high as 60%. These deals tend to be quite visible, but keep in mind that only a tiny fraction of new businesses receive any venture capital money. The advice and guidance that come with the dollars can also be quite significant. David Barger, chief executive officer of jetBlue Airways, remembers that he and jetBlue's founder, David Neeleman, originally planned to call the airline Taxi and to fly bright yellow planes. But

> ## "Anything that's really awesome takes a lot of work."
>
> —MARK ZUCKERBERG, FOUNDER, FACEBOOK

an influential venture capitalist changed their minds. He called them into his office and said, "If you call this airline Taxi, we're not going to invest." The name changed, and the venture capitalist stayed.[22]

7-4 OPPORTUNITIES AND THREATS FOR SMALL BUSINESS: A TWO-SIDED COIN

Most small businesses enjoy a number of advantages as they compete for customers. But they also must defuse a range of daunting potential threats to succeed over the long term.

7-4a Small Business Opportunities

Small businesses enjoy a real competitive edge across a range of different areas. Because of their size, many small firms can exploit narrow but profitable **market niches**,

venture capital firms Companies that invest in start-up businesses with high growth potential in exchange for a share of ownership.

market niche A small segment of a market with fewer competitors than the market as a whole. Market niches tend to be quite attractive to small firms.

Founded in 2015 by entrepreneur Sky White, Wendigo Tea Co. offers imperial-grade loose-leaf teas named after mythic beasts like Bigfoot and Nessy (the Loch Ness Monster). Wendigo uses branding and marketing strategies modeled after the craft beer industry to reach the market niche of young, hip tea drinkers.

offer personal customer service, and maintain lower overhead costs. And due to advances in technology, small firms can compete more effectively than ever in both global and domestic markets.

Market Niches Many small firms are uniquely positioned to exploit market niches. These sparsely occupied spaces in the market tend to have fewer competitors because they simply aren't big enough—or high-profile enough—for large firms. They nonetheless offer more than enough potential for small, specialized companies. For example, Kazoo & Company, a relatively small toy store, competes effectively with Walmart, Target, and Kmart by stocking different—and complementary—products, deliberately zigging when the big players zag.[23]

Personal Customer Service With a smaller customer base, small firms can develop much more personal relationships with individual customers. Shel Weinstein, for instance, former owner of a Los Angeles corner pharmacy, knew his customers so well that they would call him at home in the middle of the night for help with medical emergencies. The personal touch can be especially beneficial in some foreign markets, where clients prize the chance to deal directly with top management.

Lower Overhead Costs With entrepreneurs wearing so many hats, from CEO to customer service rep, many small firms have lower overhead costs. They can hire fewer managers and fewer specialized employees. Perhaps more importantly, smaller firms—due to a lack of resources—tend to work around costs with tactics such as establishing headquarters in the owner's garage or offering employees flexible schedules instead of costly healthcare benefits.

Technology The Internet has played a powerful role in opening new opportunities for small businesses. Using a wealth of online tools, from eBay to eMachineshop, companies-of-one can create, sell, publish, and even manufacture goods and services more easily than ever before. The Internet has also created international opportunities, transforming small businesses into global marketers. The London-based Anything Left-Handed retail store, for instance, evolved into an award-winning global wholesaler of left-handed items within a year of launching its website. Founder Keith Milsom comments that "our website has allowed us to communicate with potential customers and market our business worldwide at very little cost, making international development possible."[24]

7-4b Small Business Threats

While small businesses do enjoy some advantages, they also face intimidating obstacles, from a high risk of failure to too much regulation.

High Risk of Failure Starting a new business involves risk—a lot of risk—but the odds improve significantly if you make it past the first five years. Check out the ten-year survival rate in Exhibit 7.2. Notice that it declines much more slowly in Years 7–10. Not surprisingly, new research also shows that the five-year survival rate depends fairly heavily on the industry, ranging from 51.3% at the high end for manufacturing to 36.4% at the low end for construction, as illustrated in Exhibit 7.3. So clearly, it pays to choose your industry carefully when you launch a new business.

Even though these numbers may look daunting, it's important to remember that owners shut down their businesses for many reasons other than the failure of the firm itself. The possibilities include poor health, divorce, better opportunities elsewhere, and interestingly, an unwillingness to make the enormous time commitment of running a business. Small business expert David Birch jokingly calls this last reason—which is remarkably common—the "I had no idea!" syndrome. It highlights the importance of anticipating what you're in for *before* you open your doors.[25]

Lack of Knowledge and Experience People typically launch businesses because they either have expertise in a particular area—such as designing websites or cooking Vietnamese food—or because they have a breakthrough idea—such as a new way to develop computer chips or run an airline. But in-depth knowledge in a specific area doesn't necessarily mean expertise in running a business. Successful business owners must know everything from finance to human resources, to marketing.

Too Little Money The media are filled with stories of business owners who made it on a shoestring, but lack of start-up money is a major issue for most new firms. Ongoing profits don't usually begin for a while, which means that entrepreneurs must plan on some lean months—or even years—as the business develops momentum. That means a real need to manage money wisely and to resist the temptation to invest in fixed assets, such as fancy offices and advanced electronics, before sufficient regular income warrants it. It also requires the nerve to stay the course despite initial losses.[26]

Bigger Regulatory Burden Complying with federal regulations can be challenging for any business, but it can be downright overwhelming for small firms. But relief may be on the way: Congress continues to examine ways to reduce the growing regulatory burden on small businesses—an urgent need in the face of the struggling economy.[27]

Higher Health Insurance Costs Administrative costs for small health plans are much higher than for large businesses, making it even tougher for small firms

EXHIBIT 7.3	NEW BUSINESS 4-YEAR SURVIVAL RATES BY INDUSTRY
Finance, Insurance, and Real Estate	58%
Education and Health	56%
Agriculture	56%
Services	55%
Wholesale	54%
Mining	51%
Manufacturing	49%
Construction	47%

Source: Here Are the Startup Failure Rates by Industry, by Kristin Pryor, January 12, 2016, Tech.co website, http://tech.co/startup-failure-rates-industry-2016-01, accessed May 18, 2016.

to offer coverage to their employees. Given skyrocketing healthcare costs in general, the best employees are likely to demand a great insurance plan, putting small business at a real disadvantage in terms of building a competitive workforce. But this may all change as Republicans and Democrats struggle to enact their own versions of healthcare reform. Currently, under the Affordable Care Act, all but the very smallest businesses are required to offer "affordable" health insurance to their full-time employees. Navigating the complexities of constantly changing legislation has been a significant challenge for many small business owners. However, they may find the whole ordeal worth it if they come out the other side being able to offer their workers top-quality health insurance at competitive rates.[28]

7-5 LAUNCH OPTIONS: REVIEWING THE PROS AND CONS

When you imagine starting a new business, the first thought that comes to mind would probably be the process of developing your own big idea from an abstract concept to a thriving enterprise. But that's not the only option. In fact, it may make more sense to purchase an established business, or even buy a franchise such as a Pizza Hut or Subway restaurant. Each choice, of course, involves pros and cons. The trick is finding the best fit for you: the combination that offers you the least harmful downsides and the most meaningful upsides. Broadly speaking, it's less risky to buy an established business or franchise, but it can be more satisfying to start from scratch. Exhibit 7.4 offers a more detailed overview of the pros and cons.

EXHIBIT 7.2	NEW BUSINESS SURVIVAL RATES	
Year in Business	**Survival Rate**	**Change vs. Prior Year (percentage points)**
Year 1	100.0%	—
Year 2	78%	−22
Year 3	66%	−12
Year 4	56%	−10
Year 5	50%	−6
Year 6	45%	−5
Year 7	42%	−3
Year 8	40%	−2
Year 9	37%	−3
Year 10	35%	−2

Source: Entrepreneurship and the U.S. Economy, Bureau of Labor Statistics website, http://www.bls.gov/bdm/entrepreneurship/bdm_chart3.htm, accessed May 18, 2016.

EXHIBIT 7.4 PROS AND CONS OF STARTING A BUSINESS FROM SCRATCH VERSUS BUYING AN ESTABLISHED BUSINESS

Starting Your Business from Scratch

Key Pros	Key Cons
It's all *you*: your concept, your decisions, your structure, and so on.	It's all *you*. That's a lot of pressure.
You don't have to deal with the prior owner's bad decisions.	It takes time, money, and sheer sweat equity to build a customer base.
	Without a track record, it's harder to get credit from both lenders and suppliers.
	From securing permits to hiring employees, the logistics of starting a business can be challenging.

Buying an Established Business

Key Pros	Key Cons
The concept, organizational structure, and operating practices are already in place.	Working with someone else's idea can be a lot less fun for some entrepreneurs.
Relationships with customers, suppliers, and other stakeholders are established.	You may inherit old mistakes that can range from poor employee relations to pending lawsuits.
Getting financing and credit is less challenging.	

Buying a Franchise

Key Pros	Key Cons
In most cases, you're buying your own piece of a well-known brand and proven way of doing business.	You have less opportunity for creativity since most agreements tie you to franchise requirements.
Typically, management expertise and consulting come with the franchise package.	If something goes wrong with the national brand (e.g., *E. coli* at a burger joint), your business will suffer, too.
Franchisers occasionally offer not just advice but also the financing that can make the purchase possible.	The initial purchase price can be steep, and that doesn't include the ongoing percent-of-sales royalty fee.
These advantages add up to a very low 5% first-year failure rate.	

Source: Five Reasons Why Franchises Flop, by Steve Strauss, February 28, 2005, USA Today Money website, http://www.usatoday.com/money/smallbusiness/columnist/strauss/2005-02-28-franchise_x.htm.

7-5a Making It Happen: Tools for Business Success

Whatever way you choose to become a small business owner, several strategies can help you succeed over the long term: gain experience in your field, learn from others, educate yourself, access **Small Business Administration (SBA)** resources, and develop a business plan.

Gain Experience Getting roughly three years of experience working for someone else in the field that interests you is a good rule of thumb. That way, you can learn what does and doesn't fly in your industry with relatively low personal risk (and you'd be making any mistakes on someone else's dime). You can also start developing a vibrant, relevant network before you need to ask for favors. But if you stay much longer than three years, you may get too comfortable to take the plunge and launch your own venture.

Learn from Others You should actively seek opportunities to learn from people who've succeeded in your field. If you don't know anyone personally, use your network to get introductions. And don't forget industry associations, local events, and other opportunities to build relationships. Also, remember that people who failed in your field may be able to give you valuable insights (why make the same mistakes they did?). As a bonus, they may be more willing to share their ideas and their gaffes if they're no longer struggling to develop a business of their own.

Educate Yourself The opportunities for entrepreneurial learning have exploded in the past decade. Many colleges and universities now offer full-blown entrepreneurship programs that help students both develop their plans and secure their initial funding. But education shouldn't stop there. Seek out relevant press articles, workshops, websites,

Small Business Administration (SBA) An agency of the federal government designed to maintain and strengthen the nation's economy by aiding, counseling, assisting, and protecting the interests of small businesses.

A business plan can help entrepreneurs stay focused.

Peshkova/Shutterstock.com

More than 30% of the richest people in the world do not have a college degree, but 57% of those who start a business in high-income countries do have a college degree.

—GLOBAL ENTREPRENEURSHIP MONITOR
AND *FORBES*

and blogs so that your ongoing education will continue to boost your career.

Access SBA Resources The SBA offers a number of resources beyond money (which we'll discuss in the next section). The SBA website, www.sba.gov, provides a wealth of information from industry-specific statistics, to general trends, to updates on small business regulations. The SBA also works hand in hand with individual states to fund local **Small Business Development Centers (SBDCs)**. SBDCs provide a range of free services for small businesses, from developing your concept to consulting on your business plan, to helping with your loan applications. And the SBA supports **SCORE**, the **Service Corps of Retired Executives**, at www.score.org. They provide free, comprehensive counseling for small businesses from qualified volunteers.

Develop a Business Plan Can a business succeed without a plan? Of course. Many do just fine by simply seizing opportunity as it arises, and changing direction as needed. Some achieve significant growth without a plan. But a **business plan** does provide an invaluable way to keep you and your team focused on success. And it's absolutely crucial for obtaining outside funding, which is why many entrepreneurs write a business plan after they've used personal funding sources (such as savings, credit cards, and money from family and friends) to get themselves up and running. Even then, the plan may be continually in flux if the industry is rapidly changing.

An effective business plan, which is usually 25 to 50 pages long, takes about six months to write. While the specifics may change by industry, the basic elements of any business plan answer these core questions:

- What service or product does your business provide, and what needs does it fill?
- Who are the potential customers for your product or service, and why will they purchase it from you?
- How will you reach your potential customers?
- Where will you get the financial resources to start your business?
- When can you expect to achieve profitability?

The final document should include all of the following information:

- Executive summary (two to three pages)
- Description of business (include both risks and opportunities)
- Marketing
- Competition (don't underestimate the challenge)
- Operating procedures
- Personnel
- Complete financial data and plan, including sources of start-up money (be realistic!)
- Appendix (be sure to include all your research on your industry)[29]

Check out the SBA business-planning site for more information on how to write your own

Small Business Development Centers (SBDCs) Local offices—affiliated with the Small Business Administration—that provide comprehensive management assistance to current and prospective small business owners.

SCORE (Service Corps of Retired Executives) An organization—affiliated with the Small Business Administration—that provides free, comprehensive business counseling for small business owners from qualified volunteers.

business plan A formal document that describes a business concept, outlines core business objectives, and details strategies and timelines for achieving those objectives.

Accidental Inventions

Every new business begins with a great idea, but not all great ideas begin with careful planning—a number of successful businesses have been built on inventions that happened by accident. But that doesn't mean that you shouldn't be prepared; first-century philosopher Seneca said, "Luck is what happens when preparation meets opportunity." A sampling of "accidental inventions":

- **Microwave Ovens:** When World War II scientist Percy Spencer was inspecting a magnetron tube at a Raytheon lab, he noticed that a candy bar in his pocket had melted, which sparked the idea of using microwaves for cooking. Today, more than 90% of households have microwave ovens.

- **Viagra:** The pills failed to achieve their original goal, but clinical trials did yield some startling secondary benefits, which gave rise to a brand new multibillion-dollar business for Pfizer.

- **Post-it Notes:** 3M scientist Spencer Silver developed the repositionable adhesive for Post-it Notes. But they didn't become a product until his co-worker, Art Fry, was looking for a sticky, reusable bookmark to replace the paper bookmarks that kept slipping out of his church hymnal. Fry proposed the product, which quickly became a worldwide hit for 3M.[30]

---

business plan and for samples of actual business plans (www.sba.gov/smallbusinessplanner/index.html). Other excellent resources (among many) on the Internet include the sample business plan resource center (www.bplans.com/) and the business plan pages of AllBusiness.com (www.allbusiness.com/).

 ## 7-6 SMALL BUSINESS AND THE ECONOMY: AN OUTSIZED IMPACT

The most successful entrepreneurs create goods and services that change the way people live. Many build blockbuster corporations that power the stock market and dominate pop culture through ubiquitous promotion. But small businesses—despite their lower profile—also play a vital role in the U.S. economy. Here are a few statistics from the U.S. Small Business Administration:

- Small businesses comprise 99.9% of all businesses in the United States

- Small businesses account for 48% of all private sector employees.

- Yet the opening of new businesses has accounted for over 40% of net new jobs in the U.S. economy over the past two decades.

The statistics, of course, depend on the definition of small business. For research purposes, the SBA defines small business as companies with up to 500 employees, including the self-employed. But the SBA also points out that the meaning of small business differs across industries. To officially count as "small," the number of employees can range from fewer than 100 to 1,500, and the average revenue can range from $0.75 million to $28.5 million, depending on the type of business. But regardless of the specific definition, the fact is clear: small business is a big player in the U.S. economy.

Beyond the sheer value of the goods and services they generate, small businesses make a powerful contribution to the U.S. economy in terms of creating new jobs, fueling innovation, and vitalizing inner cities.

- Creating New Jobs: Small businesses with employees start up at a rate of about 600,000 per year. Five years after they launch, about half of those businesses—and many of the jobs they create—remain viable. But while small businesses are quick to add new jobs, they're often the first to contract when times are tough; instability comes with the territory.[32]

- Fueling Innovation: Small businesses are much more likely to develop revolutionary new ideas. Small patenting firms produce about 16 times more patents per employee than their large-firm counterparts, and those patents are twice as likely to be found among the top 1% of highest-impact patents. Small firms tend to be effective innovators for a number of reasons. Perhaps most importantly, their very reason for being often ties to a brand-new idea. In the early years, they need innovation to simply survive. And they often display a refreshing lack of bureaucracy that allows new thinking to take hold.[33]

- Vitalizing Inner Cities: Research shows that small businesses are the backbone of urban economies, finding opportunity in niches that may not be worthwhile for larger firms. Small business comprises more than 99% of inner-city business establishments. In addition to creating new jobs, these small businesses generate 80% of total employment in American inner cities, providing a springboard for economic development.[34]

7-6a Entrepreneurship around the World

Research suggests that entrepreneurship has an economic impact in countries around the world. Societies need entrepreneurs to ensure that new ideas actualize and to ensure that people are able to self-employ when their economy does not provide for their basic needs. For the past 15 years, the Global Entrepreneurship Monitor (GEM) has measured the annual rate of new business start-ups across a range of countries across the globe. The 15th annual GEM study included 70 countries. According to GEM, the most effective way to evaluate entrepreneurship levels is by phase. A country's total early-phase entrepreneurship rate includes the percentage of adults who have been running their own business from three months to 3.5 years. The current entrepreneurship rate varies dramatically from country to country, ranging from a high of 39.9% in Nigeria and Zambia to a low of 3.4% in Italy, Russia, and Japan. (See Exhibit 7.5 for the ten nations with the highest and lowest entrepreneurship rates.) The differences among countries seem to depend largely on several key factors: What is the national per capita income? What will the entrepreneur need to give up (i.e., the opportunity costs)? How high is the risk of failure? How strongly do the national culture and political environment support business start-ups?

Per Capita Income In lower-income countries, such as China and Chile, a high percentage of entrepreneurs start their own businesses because they simply have no other options. This contributes heavily to the startlingly high overall level of entrepreneurship. The rate of such "necessity entrepreneurship" declines in higher-income countries, such as the United States and Japan, where entrepreneurs are more likely to strike out on their own in response to an opportunity that they spot in the marketplace.

Opportunity Costs Entrepreneurship rates are significantly lower in countries that provide a high level of employment protection (it's hard to get fired) and strong unemployment insurance (financial support if you do get fired). With these benefits in place, the sense of urgency regarding entrepreneurship tends to fall, in part because fear of failure is much lower. The European Union provides a number of clear examples.

EXHIBIT 7.5 EARLY PHASE ENTREPRENEURSHIP RATES 2016

Top Ten Entrepreneurship Rates		Bottom Ten Entrepreneurship Rates	
Country	Rate	Country	Rate
Burkina Faso	33.5%	Italy	4.4%
Ecuador	31.8%	Germany	4.6%
Belize	28.8%	Malaysia	4.7%
Cameroon	27.6%	Bulgaria	4.8%
Colombia	27.4%	France	5.3%
Peru	25.1%	Morocco	5.6%
Chile	24.2%	Greece	5.7%
Lebanon	21.2%	United Arab Emirates	5.7%
Guatemala	20.1%	Russian Federation	6.3%
Brazil	19.6%	Macedonia	6.5%

Source: Global Entrepreneurship Monitor 2016/2017 Global Report, http://www.gemconsortium.org/report/49812, accessed April 28, 2018.

Cultural/Political Environment Extensive, complex regulations can hinder entrepreneurship by raising daunting barriers. And a lack of cultural support only compounds the problem. These factors certainly contribute to the relatively low entrepreneurship rates in much of the European Union and Japan. Entrepreneurs in more supportive nations such as the United States and New Zealand get a boost from limited regulation and strong governmental support. A thriving "cowboy culture" helps, too—standout individuals who break free of old ways attract attention and admiration in many of the countries with higher entrepreneurship rates.[35]

violetkaipa/Shutterstock.com

THE BIG PICTURE

Successful entrepreneurs need more than simply a great idea. Bringing that idea to market—and earning a profit in the process—requires deep knowledge of every area of business. Finding money, attracting customers, and absorbing risk are only some of the challenges. But for the right person, the payoff can be huge in terms of everything from financial success to scheduling flexibility. The key is finding something you love to do that offers value to others. While that doesn't guarantee success, building on a passion suggests that you'll at least enjoy the journey. Looking forward from the global economic crisis, entrepreneurship seems likely to become a way of life, either part-time or full-time, for a growing swath of the population. The ideal result would be a higher standard of living—and a higher quality of life—for business owners and their customers worldwide.

CAREERS IN ENTREPRENEURSHIP

Clothing Company Founder

Design unique items that appeal to young people via innovative styles, attention-grabbing slogans, and distinctive fabrics. Build relationships with business funders. Oversee suppliers to ensure timely order delivery and ethical manufacturing practices. Build solid base of retail accounts. Develop a creative social media marketing campaign to boost sales. Meet profitability goals every quarter.

STUDY TOOLS 7

LOCATED AT BACK OF THE TEXTBOOK

- ☐ Rip-Out Chapter Review Card

- ☐ Gain unique perspectives on key concepts with new concept videos in the e-book
- ☐ Increase your comprehension with online homework and quizzes
- ☐ Study with existing flashcards and make your own

8 | Accounting:
Decision Making by the Numbers

LEARNING OBJECTIVES

After studying this chapter, you will be able to:

8-1 Define accounting and describe how accounting information is used by a variety of stakeholders

8-2 Identify the purposes and goals of generally accepted accounting principles

8-3 Describe the key elements of the major financial statements

8-4 Describe several methods stakeholders can use to obtain useful insights from a company's financial statements

8-5 Explain how the budget process can help managers plan, motivate, and evaluate their organization's performance

8-6 Explain the role of managerial accounting and describe the various cost concepts identified by managerial accountants

Remember to visit

PAGE 146

for additional

STUDY TOOLS

Uber Images/Shutterstock.com

8-1 ACCOUNTING: WHO NEEDS IT—AND WHO DOES IT?

Accounting is a system for recognizing, organizing, analyzing, and reporting information about the financial transactions that affect an organization. The goal of this system is to provide its users with relevant, timely information that helps them make better economic decisions.

Who uses the information that accounting provides? It's a long list; after all, everyone wants to make good decisions! In fact, a variety of business stakeholders rely so heavily on accounting information that it's sometimes called the "language of business."

8-1a Accounting: Who Uses It?

accounting A system for recognizing, organizing, analyzing, and reporting information about the financial transactions that affect an organization.

Key users of accounting information include:

- Managers: Marketing managers, for instance, need information

about sales in various regions and for various product lines. Financial managers need up-to-date facts about debt, cash, inventory, and capital.

- Stockholders: As owners of the company, most stockholders have a keen interest in its financial performance, especially as indicated by the firm's financial statements. Has management generated a strong-enough return on their investment? For instance, Ireland-based generic drug manufacturer Perrigo reported $1.09 billion in what it called "adjusted profit," while also reporting a net loss (using standard accounting procedures) of $33 million. Which number should stockholders believe?[1]

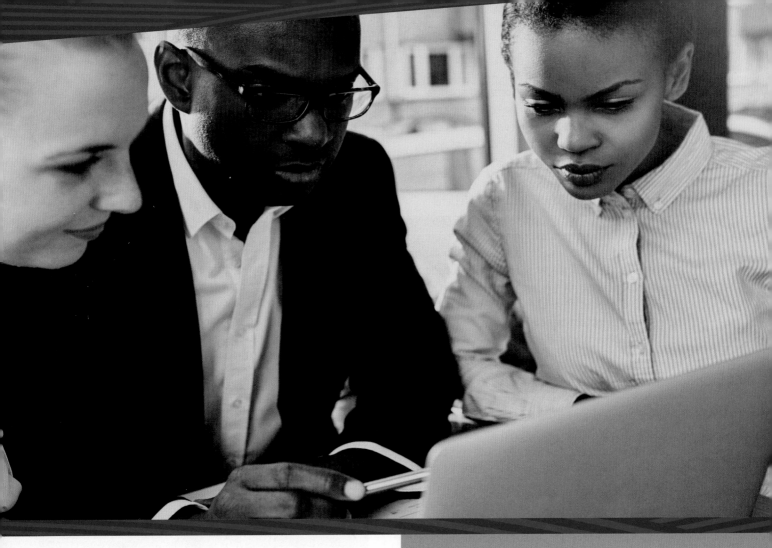

- Employees: Strong financial performance would help employees make their case for nice pay raises and hefty bonuses. But if earnings drop—especially multiple times—layoffs might be in the offing, so many employees might decide to polish their résumés!

- Creditors: The late, great comedian Bob Hope once defined a bank as a place that would only lend you money if you could prove you didn't really need it. That's a bit of an exaggeration, but it is true that before granting a loan, responsible bankers and other lenders want to assess a firm's creditworthiness by looking at its financial statements.

- Suppliers: Like bankers, companies that provide supplies want to know that the company can pay for the orders it places.

- Government agencies: Accurate accounting information is critical for meeting the reporting requirements of the Internal Revenue Service (IRS), the Securities and Exchange Commission (SEC), and other federal and state agencies.

> "The pen is mightier than the sword, but no match for the accountant."
>
> —JONATHAN GLANCEY,
> BRITISH JOURNALIST

A number of other groups—including the news media, competitors, and unions—might also have a real interest in a firm's accounting information—whether the firm wants them to have it or not! If you have any interest in managing, investing in, or working for a business, the ability to understand accounting information is extremely valuable.

8-1b Accounting: Who Does It?

Accountants work in a variety of positions to provide all of this information. Let's take a quick look at some of the roles accountants play:

- **Public accountants** provide services such as tax preparation, external auditing (a process we'll describe later in this chapter), and management consulting to clients on a fee basis.

- **Management accountants** work within a company and provide analysis, prepare reports and financial statements, and assist managers in their own organization. *Internal auditors* also work within their organizations to detect internal problems such as waste, mismanagement, embezzlement, and employee theft.

- **Government accountants** perform a variety of accounting functions for local, state, or federal government agencies. Some ensure that the government's own tax revenues and expenditures are recorded and reported in accordance with regulations and requirements. Others work for the IRS to audit tax returns or for other government agencies, such as the SEC or FDIC, to help ensure that our nation's banks and other financial institutions comply with the rules and regulations governing their behavior.

Many jobs performed by accountants require expertise in complex subject areas. For this reason, accountants who want to move up in their profession often seek certification in a particular field. But achieving such recognition isn't easy. For example, in order to be recognized as a *certified public accountant* in most states, a candidate must complete the equivalent of 150 semester hours (five years) of college education with a heavy emphasis in accounting and other business-related courses; must pass a rigorous two-day, four-part exam (very few candidates pass all four parts on their first try); and must complete at least one year of direct work experience in the field of accounting. Individuals seeking to become *certified management accountants* or *certified fraud examiners* must satisfy similarly challenging requirements.

8-2 FINANCIAL ACCOUNTING: INTENDED FOR THOSE ON THE OUTSIDE LOOKING IN

Financial accounting is the branch of accounting that addresses the needs of external stakeholders, including stockholders, creditors, and government regulators. These stakeholders are seldom interested in poring over detailed accounting information about the individual departments or divisions within a company. Instead, they're interested in the financial performance of the firm as a whole. They

financial accounting The branch of accounting that prepares financial statements for use by owners, creditors, suppliers, and other external stakeholders.

generally accepted accounting principles (GAAP) A set of accounting standards that is used in the preparation of financial statements.

often want to know how a firm's financial condition has changed over a period of several years, or to compare its results to those of other firms in the same industry. The major output of financial accounting is a set of financial statements designed to provide this broad type of information. We'll describe these statements in the next section.

8-2a Role of the Financial Standards Accounting Board

Imagine how confused and frustrated investors, creditors, and regulators would become if every firm could make its own financial accounting rules as it went along and change them whenever it wanted! To reduce confusion and provide external stakeholders with consistent and accurate financial statements, the accounting profession has adopted a set of **generally accepted accounting principles (GAAP)** that guide the practice of financial accounting. In the United States, the Securities and Exchange Commission (SEC) has the ultimate legal authority to set and enforce accounting standards. In practice, however, the SEC has delegated the responsibility for developing these rules to a private organization known as the

> "If my father had hugged me even once, I'd be an accountant right now."
>
> —*RAY ROMANO, COMEDIAN*

A variety of business stakeholders, managers, stockholders, employees, creditors, suppliers, and government agencies use accounting information.

Rawpixel/Shutterstock.com

Pfizer: Do Corporate Inversions Make Sense after Corporate Tax Changes?

In November 2015, Pfizer and Allergan announced a plan to merge so that Pfizer could move its registered domicile headquarters—the location that determines the corporation's primary laws and tax regulations—from New York to Allergan's home in Dublin, Ireland.

Why would Pfizer want to make such a move? All of Pfizer's global earnings—most other countries only tax domestic income—were subject to the United States' 35% corporate tax rate, then one of the highest in the world. Pfizer also paid a New York State corporate tax rate of 7.1%, bringing its total corporate tax rate to 42.1%—well above the 23.4% global tax rate it paid around the world and almost four times the Irish corporate tax rate of 12.5%. By reincorporating its headquarters to Ireland, it's estimated that Pfizer could reduce its overall global tax rate from 23.4% to 17% and save an estimated $2.1 billion a year.

After U.S. lawmakers strongly criticized Pfizer's attempt at a tax inversion (reincorporating to a country with a lower tax rate), Pfizer walked away from the deal.

But, with these major changes (shown below) to U.S. corporate tax laws effective January 1, 2018, does a tax inversion make sense for Pfizer anymore?

- Corporate tax rate drops from 35% to 21%.

- Only domestic income is taxed, not all foreign earnings, saving U.S.-based multinationals $22.5 billion a year.

- With all foreign earnings previously taxed at 35%, U.S. companies deferred repatriating nearly $2.5 trillion in profits. The new law gives firms a one-time opportunity to "bring home" foreign cash at a 15.5% tax rate and other assets at an 8% rate.

- Foreign income derived from goods and services based on U.S. patents, which certainly includes Pfizer's pharmaceutical business, will be taxed at 13.125%, down from 35%.

So, should Pfizer or other U.S.-based multinationals consider a tax inversion anymore? Probably not. Pfizer's repatriation of $86 billion of foreign earnings and assets, will only be taxed at 8.1%. Furthermore, Pfizer's U.S. tax rate, after deductions, is estimated at 17%, the same rate at which the company hoped to reduce its average global tax rate if it had merged with Allergan.

pio3/Shutterstock.com

Financial Accounting Standards Board (FASB). This board consists of seven members appointed by the Financial Accounting Foundation. Each member serves a five-year term and can be reappointed to serve one additional term. In order to preserve independence and impartiality, the members are required to sever all ties with any firms or institutions they served prior to joining the board.

Through GAAP, the FASB aims to ensure that financial statements are:

- Relevant: They must contain information that helps the user understand the firm's financial performance and condition.

- Reliable: They must provide information that is objective, accurate, and verifiable.

- Consistent: They must provide financial statements based on the same core assumptions and procedures over time; if a firm introduces any significant changes in how it prepares its financial statements, GAAP requires it to clearly identify and describe these changes.

- Comparable: They must present accounting statements in a reasonably standardized way, allowing users to track the firm's financial performance over a period of years and compare its results with those for other firms.

How well do companies adhere to GAAP practices? In 2015, only 5.7% of S&P 500 companies strictly reported GAAP-based results, down significantly from 25% in 2006. The remaining 94.3% of companies reported what's called "adjusted" or non-GAAP accounting in addition to their GAAP-based results. Fitbit's CFO Bill Zerella says, "I think non-GAAP [accounting results] can be valuable for investors, as long as it's not abused by management."[3] The problem with non-GAAP accounting is that the numbers may not be relevant, reliable, consistent, or comparable. Andrew Clarke, CFO of logistics company C.H. Robinson Worldwide, explains, "What one company says is adjusted might be different to what another

> **Financial Accounting Standards Board (FASB)**
> The private board that establishes the generally accepted accounting principles used in the practice of financial accounting.

company says is adjusted. . . . It lends itself to inconsistency. We believe in providing [stockholders] with a [GAAP-based] clean number as to how we perform so that they can make an informed decision."[4] For more on non-GAAP accounting, see "Profitable? Sure—As Long as You Don't Look at the GAAP!" later in this chapter.

8-2b Ethics in Accounting

Even clear and well-established accounting principles won't result in accurate and reliable information if managers and accountants don't use them. Caterpillar, $580 million; Waste Management, $1.5 billion; Olympus, $1.7 billion; HealthSouth, $2.7 billion; Autonomy, a software company purchased by Hewlett-Packard, $8.8 billion; and the biggest of them all, WorldCom, $11 billion, are all unfortunate examples of exorbitant accounting fraud where debts were hidden or earnings overstated by a half a billion to $11 billion or more. Once their accounting improprieties became known, most of these firms suffered severe financial difficulties.[5]

These scandals served as a wake-up call to the accounting profession that their ethical training and standards needed major improvement. In the wake of the scandals, many state accounting boards passed new ethics-related requirements.

 ## 8-3 FINANCIAL STATEMENTS: READ ALL ABOUT US

One of the major responsibilities of financial accounting is the preparation of three basic financial statements: the balance sheet, income statement, and statement of cash flows. Taken together, these financial statements provide external stakeholders with a broad picture of an organization's financial condition and its recent financial performance. Large corporations with publicly traded stock must provide an annual report containing all three statements to all stockholders. They also must file quarterly and annual reports, including financial statements, with the SEC. Let's take a look at the information each statement provides.

8-3a The Balance Sheet: What We Own and How We Got It

The **balance sheet** summarizes a firm's financial position at a specific point in time. Though the balance sheets of different firms vary in specifics, all of them are organized to reflect the most famous equation in all of accounting—so famous that it is usually referred to simply as the **accounting equation**:

Assets = Liabilities + Owners' Equity

Exhibit 8.1 shows a simplified balance sheet for McDonald's Corporation, which we'll use to illustrate the information provided by financial statements. Notice that the three major sectors of this statement reflect the key terms in the accounting equation. Once we've defined each of these terms, we'll explain the logic behind the accounting equation and how the balance sheet illustrates this logic.

- **Assets** are things of value that the firm owns. Balance sheets usually classify assets into at least two major categories. The first category, called *current assets,* consists of cash, $1.223 billion, and other assets that the firm expects to use up or convert into cash within a year. For example, in McDonald's balance sheet, the value for *accounts receivable,* $1.474 billion, refers to money owed to McDonald's by franchise restaurants who bought its goods on credit. (These receivables are converted into cash when the franchise restaurants pay their bills.) *Inventory,* also a current asset, represents the $58.9 million of burgers, fries, and other foods and ingredients used in McDonald's restaurants. If this strikes you as not very much, you're right. It isn't, because McDonald's never has more than three to four days of inventory on hand in its restaurants. McDonald's has $565.2 million of *prepaid expenses,* such as insurance, or prepaid advertising, that have been paid before they are due.

The other major category of assets on McDonald's balance sheets is *Property, plant, and equipment.* It lists the value, in this case $34.443 billion, of the company's land, buildings, machinery, equipment, and other long-term assets. With the exception of land, these assets have a limited useful life, so accountants subtract *accumulated depreciation,* $13.185 billion, from the original value of these assets, to reflect the fact that these assets are being used up over time.

Though not shown here, some companies list a third category of assets, called *intangible assets.* These are assets that have no physical existence—you can't see or touch them—but they still have value. Examples include patents, copyrights, trademarks, and even the goodwill a company develops with its stakeholders. McDonald's trademarks, such as Ronald McDonald and the golden arches, clearly have tremendous value to the company.

- **Liabilities** indicate what the firm owes to nonowners—in other words, the claims nonowners have against the firm's assets. Balance sheets usually

balance sheet A financial statement that reports the financial position of a firm by identifying and reporting the value of the firm's assets, liabilities, and owners' equity.

accounting equation
Assets = Liabilities + Owners' Equity

assets Resources owned by a firm.

liabilities Claims that outsiders have against a firm's assets.

Exhibit 8.1
The Balance Sheet for McDonald's Corporation

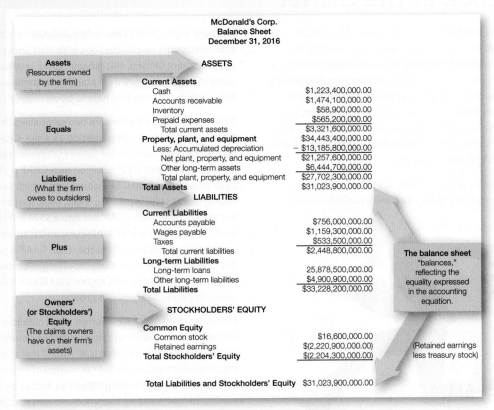

McDonald's Corp.
Balance Sheet
December 31, 2016

	Assets (Resources owned by the firm)			
	ASSETS			
	Current Assets			
	Cash		$1,223,400,000.00	
	Accounts receivable		$1,474,100,000.00	
	Inventory		$58,900,000.00	
Equals	Prepaid expenses		$565,200,000.00	
	Total current assets		$3,321,600,000.00	
	Property, plant, and equipment		$34,443,400,000.00	
	Less: Accumulated depreciation		− $13,185,800,000.00	
	Net plant, property, and equipment		$21,257,600,000.00	
	Other long-term assets		$6,444,700,000.00	
Liabilities (What the firm owes to outsiders)	Total plant, property, and equipment		$27,702,300,000.00	
	Total Assets		$31,023,900,000.00	
	LIABILITIES			
	Current Liabilities			
	Accounts payable		$756,000,000.00	
Plus	Wages payable		$1,159,300,000.00	
	Taxes		$533,500,000.00	
	Total current liabilities		$2,448,800,000.00	
	Long-term Liabilities			
	Long-term loans		25,878,500,000.00	
	Other long-term liabilities		$4,900,900,000.00	
	Total Liabilities		$33,228,200,000.00	
Owners' (or Stockholders') Equity (The claims owners have on their firm's assets)	**STOCKHOLDERS' EQUITY**			
	Common Equity			
	Common stock		$16,600,000.00	
	Retained earnings		$(2,220,900,000.00)	
	Total Stockholders' Equity		$(2,204,300,000.00)	
	Total Liabilities and Stockholders' Equity		$31,023,900,000.00	

The balance sheet "balances," reflecting the equality expressed in the accounting equation.

(Retained earnings less treasury stock)

Adapted from "McDonald's Corporation, Form 10-K," U.S. Securities and Exchange Commission, https://www.sec.gov/Archives/edgar/data/63908/000006390817000017 /mcd-12312016x10k.htm, accessed July 10, 2017. Because the accounting information found in the annual report is much more detailed than presented here, some of the accounting numbers in this balance sheet will differ from similar numbers shown in McDonald's balance sheets in the 10-K\ for the same time period.

organize liabilities into two broad categories: current liabilities and long-term liabilities. *Current liabilities*, totaling $2.448 billion for McDonald's, are debts that come due within a year of the date on the balance sheet. McDonald's has, for example, $756 million in accounts payable, that is, how much it owes suppliers on credit. Wages payable, $1.159 billion for McDonald's, what the firm owes to workers for work they have already performed, is another current liability, as are taxes, which amount to $533.5 million for McDonald's. *Long-term liabilities* are debts that don't come due until more than a year after the date on the balance sheet. McDonald's has $25.878 billion in long-term loans and $4.9 billion in other long-term liabilities.

- **Owners' (or Stockholders') equity** refers to the claims the owners have against their firm's assets. The specific accounts listed in the owners' equity section of a balance sheet depend on the form of business ownership. As Exhibit 8.1 shows, common stock is a key owners' equity account for corporations.

For corporations like McDonald's, the owners' equity section is usually titled *stockholders' equity*. Also notice that retained earnings, which are the accumulated earnings reinvested in the company (rather than paid to owners), are another major components of the owners' equity section. McDonald's has $16.6 million in common stock and negative $2.220 billion in retained earnings, which are typically put back into growing the company. In 2016, however, McDonald's incurred a $2.2 billion deficit in total stockholders' equity by virtue of a stock buy back of more than $11 billion (explained in the discussion of Exhibit 8.3 on McDonald's cash flows). Buying stock back from shareholders is another way, besides stock dividends (See Chapter 9), of returning earnings to shareholders. The large stock buy back, which was a strategic goal for the company, reduced

> **owners' equity** The claims a firm's owners have against their company's assets (often called "stockholders' equity" on balance sheets of corporations).

Profitable? Sure—As Long as You Don't Look at the GAAP!

While the Securities and Exchange Commission (SEC) is legally responsible for enforcing accounting standards, in practice, the SEC relies on the Financial Accounting Standards Board (FASB) to clarify and modify generally accepted accounting principles (GAAP) as new business practices and/or issues arise. GAAP exist so that financial statements are always relevant, reliable, consistent, and comparable, thus ensuring that managers and investors can track a firm's financial performance over time and accurately compare one firm's financial results to those of another.

Non-GAAP accounting is legal as long as both non-GAAP and GAAP results are reported. Many companies push things too far,

SFIO CRACHO/Shutterstock.com

however, highlighting favorable non-GAAP results in earnings announcements and discussions with Wall Street analysts while ignoring more modest, but reliable, GAAP results. Even worse, companies increasingly treat standard expenses as non-GAAP items, which they then exclude to boost non-GAAP profits.

Twitter and Salesforce.com are two companies that routinely treat executive stock compensation as a non-GAAP expense. For Twitter, not counting executive compensation was the difference between a $276 million non-GAAP profit and a $521 million GAAP loss. Salesforce.com, which sells customer management software and services, used the same approach to turn a $146 million GAAP loss into a $574 million non-GAAP profit. On average at profitable companies, adjusted, non-GAAP accounting profits are 44% higher than GAAP-based results. But at unprofitable companies reporting net losses, non-GAAP accounting results are 70% higher than GAAP-based results, often making losses look like profits!

Billionaire investor Warren Buffett often criticizes such tactics, saying, "The very name says it all: 'compensation.' If compensation isn't an expense, what is it? And, if real and recurring expenses don't belong in the calculation of earnings, where in the world do they belong?" Don't be fooled by non-GAAP results. Compare apples to apples, oranges to oranges, and GAAP financials to GAAP financials.[6]

---

retained earnings by $11 billion, and flipped retained earnings from positive to negative.

The logic behind the accounting equation is based on the fact that firms must finance the purchase of their assets, and owners and nonowners are the only two sources of funding. The accounting equation tells us that the value of a firm's assets must equal the amount of financing provided by owners (as measured by owners' equity) plus the amount provided by creditors (as indicated by the firm's liabilities) to purchase those assets. Because a balance sheet is based on this logic, it must *always* be in balance. In other words, the dollar value of the assets *must* equal the dollar value of the liabilities plus owners' equity. This is true for *all* firms, from the smallest sole proprietorship to the largest multinational

> **income statement** The financial statement that reports the revenues, expenses, and net income that resulted from a firm's operations over an accounting period.

> **revenue** Increases in a firm's assets that result from the sale of goods, provision of services, or other activities intended to earn income.

corporation. Notice in Exhibit 8.1 that the $31.023 billion in total assets listed on McDonald's balance sheet matches the $31.023 billion in liabilities plus owners' equity.

8-3b The Income Statement: So, How Did We Do?

The **income statement** summarizes the financial results of a firm's operations over a given period of time. The figure that attracts the most attention on the income statement is net income, which measures the company's profit or loss. In fact, another name for the income statement is the *profit and loss statement* (or, informally, the *P&L*). Just as with the balance sheet, we can use a simple equation to illustrate the logic behind the organization of the income statement:

$$\text{Revenue} - \text{Expenses} = \text{Net Income}$$

In this equation:

- **Revenue** represents the increase in the amount of cash and other assets (such as accounts receivable)

Does Apple Really Owe the European Union $14.5 Billion in Unpaid Taxes?

Does Apple, the world's most profitable company, owe Ireland $14.5 billion in unpaid taxes? The European Union (EU), of which Ireland is a member, says that it does. Apple and Ireland say it doesn't. Let's examine the issue.

Did Ireland give Apple special treatment? Apple established a factory in Cork, Ireland, in 1980. The EU said Ireland gave Apple special tax incentives then and several more times. Apple responded, "We never asked for, nor did we receive any special deals." But if Apple had asked for lower taxes, would that have been illegal or unethical? In most countries, no. But in the EU, tax incentives are forbidden if they help companies gain advantage over competitors.

Were Apple's taxes too low? At 12.5%, Ireland has one of the lowest corporate income tax rates in Europe. With standard tax deductions, the effective tax rate is 10.8%. But according to the EU, Apple's effective tax rate since 2003 was 0.005% to 1%. An Irish Department of Finance study, published two years before the EU ruling, showed that similar to Apple, other U.S.-owned, Irish-incorporated companies paid effective tax rates between 2.2% and 3.2%.

Did Apple or Ireland do anything illegal? Apple CEO Tim Cook said about the issue, "[W]e received guidance from Irish tax authorities on how to comply correctly with Irish tax law. . . . Apple follows the law and we pay all of the taxes we owe." A spokesperson for Ireland's Revenue Commission said, "It is emphatically the case that there was no departure from the applicable Irish tax law by Revenue. . . . and that full tax due was paid in accordance with the law."

Who determines the tax rate—Ireland or the EU? Irish Finance Minister Michael Noonan said Ireland would join Apple in appealing the ruling, "to defend the integrity of our tax system." Enda Kenny, Ireland's prime minister said, "I regard this matter as questioning Ireland's right as a sovereign nation to set out policies that are appropriate for Ireland." Apple argued that the EU is "effectively proposing to replace Irish tax laws with a view of what the [European] Commission thinks the law should have been."

What happened? In November 2017, Apple and Ireland agreed to pay the EU $14.5 billion in "allegedly unpaid taxes." Apple stated, "The debate over Apple's taxes is not about how much we owe but where we owe it. As the largest taxpayer in the world we've paid over $35 billion in corporate income taxes over the past three years plus billions of dollars more in property tax, payroll tax, sales tax and VAT. . . .At Apple, we follow the laws, and if the system changes we will comply. We strongly support efforts from the global community toward comprehensive international tax reform and a far simpler system, and we will continue to advocate for that."[7]

---

the firm earns in a given time period as the result of its business activities. For example, Exhibit 8.2 shows that McDonald's has $24.621 billion in revenues, with $15.295 billion coming from company-owned restaurants and $9.326 billion coming from franchised restaurants. With the goal of franchising 95% of it stores by 2019, revenues will shift significantly toward franchised restaurants in the near future. McDonald's has already sold 1,000 company-owned restaurants to franchises, and is now in the process of selling a significant part of its company-owned stores to franchises in Japan, China, and South Korea.[8] A firm normally earns revenue by selling goods or by charging fees for services (or both). Accountants use **accrual-basis accounting** when recognizing revenues. Under the accrual approach, revenues are recorded when they are earned, and payment is reasonably assured. It's important to realize that this is not always when the firm receives cash from its sales. For example, if a firm sells goods on credit, it reports revenue before it receives cash. (The revenue would show up initially as an increase in accounts receivable rather than as an increase in cash.)

■ **Expenses** indicate the cash a firm spends, or other assets it uses up, to carry out the business activities necessary to generate its revenue. Under accrual-basis accounting, expenses aren't necessarily recorded when cash is paid. Instead, expenses are matched to the revenue they help generate. The specific titles given to the costs and expenses listed on an income statement vary among firms—as do the details provided. But the general approach remains the same: costs are deducted from revenue in several stages to show how net income is determined. The first step in this process is to deduct *costs of goods sold*, $12.698 billion for McDonald's, which are costs directly related to buying, manufacturing, or providing the goods and services the company sells. (Manufacturing companies often use the term *cost of goods manufactured* for these costs.) The

> **accrual-basis accounting**
> The method of accounting that recognizes revenue when it is earned and matches expenses to the revenues they helped produce.
>
> **expenses** Resources that are used up as the result of business operations.

Exhibit 8.2
Income Statement for McDonald's

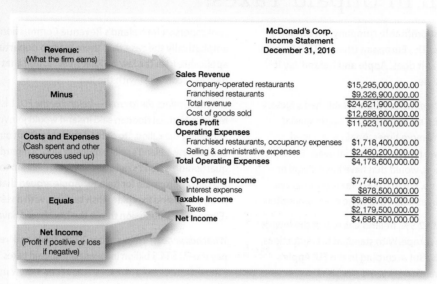

McDonald's Corp.
Income Statement
December 31, 2016

Sales Revenue	
Company-operated restaurants	$15,295,000,000.00
Franchised restaurants	$9,326,900,000.00
Total revenue	$24,621,900,000.00
Cost of goods sold	$12,698,800,000.00
Gross Profit	$11,923,100,000.00
Operating Expenses	
Franchised restaurants, occupancy expenses	$1,718,400,000.00
Selling & administrative expenses	$2,460,200,000.00
Total Operating Expenses	$4,178,600,000.00
Net Operating Income	$7,744,500,000.00
Interest expense	$878,500,000.00
Taxable Income	$6,866,000,000.00
Taxes	$2,179,500,000.00
Net Income	$4,686,500,000.00

Revenue: (What the firm earns)

Minus

Costs and Expenses (Cash spent and other resources used up)

Equals

Net Income (Profit if positive or loss if negative)

Adapted from "McDonald's Corporation, Form 10-K," U.S. Securities and Exchange Commission, https://www.sec.gov/Archives/edgar/data/63908/000006390817000017/mcd-12312016x10k.htm, accessed July 10, 2017.

difference between the firm's revenue and its cost of goods sold is its *gross profit*, which was $11.923 billion for McDonald's. The next step is to deduct *operating expenses*, totaling $4.178 billion for McDonald's, from gross profit. Operating expenses are costs the firm incurs in the regular operation of its business. Most income statements divide operating expenses into *selling expenses* (such as salaries and commissions to salespeople and advertising expenses) and *general* (or *administrative*) *expenses* (such as rent, insurance, utilities, and office supplies). McDonald's, however, typically owns the land and the building of franchised restaurants. So, it has another large, but specialized operating expense of $1.718 billion to pay for franchised restaurants' occupancy expenses. The difference between gross profit and operating expenses is *net operating income,* which is $7.744 billion for McDonald's. Finally, interest expenses and taxes are deducted from net operating income to determine the firm's net income. After paying $878.5 million in interest expenses and $2.179 billion in taxes, McDonald's net income is $4.686 billion.

net income The difference between the revenue a firm earns and the expenses it incurs in a given time period.

statement of cash flows The financial statement that identifies a firm's sources and uses of cash in a given accounting period.

> "It sounds extraordinary, but it's a fact that balance sheets can make fascinating reading."
>
> —BARONESS MARY ARCHER, CAMBRIDGE UNIVERSITY LECTURER AND CHAIRWOMAN OF THE NATIONAL ENERGY FOUNDATION

- **Net income** is the profit or loss the firm earns in the time period covered by the income statement. If net income is positive, the firm has earned a profit. If it's negative, the firm has suffered a loss. Net income is called the "bottom line" of the income statement because it is such an important measure of the firm's operating success.

8-3c The Statement of Cash Flows: Show Me the Money

The last major financial statement is the **statement of cash flows**. Cash is the lifeblood of any business organization. A firm must have enough cash to pay what it owes to workers, creditors, suppliers, and taxing authorities—hopefully, with enough left to pay a dividend to its owners!

Exhibit 8.3
McDonald's Statement of Cash Flows

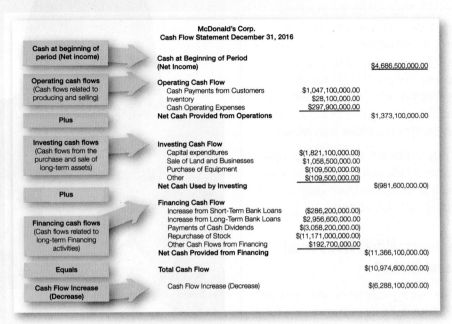

McDonald's Corp.
Cash Flow Statement December 31, 2016

Cash at Beginning of Period (Net Income)		$4,686,500,000.00
Operating Cash Flow		
Cash Payments from Customers	$1,047,100,000.00	
Inventory	$28,100,000.00	
Cash Operating Expenses	$297,900,000.00	
Net Cash Provided from Operations		$1,373,100,000.00
Investing Cash Flow		
Capital expenditures	$(1,821,100,000.00)	
Sale of Land and Businesses	$1,058,500,000.00	
Purchase of Equipment	$(109,500,000.00)	
Other	$(109,500,000.00)	
Net Cash Used by Investing		$(981,600,000.00)
Financing Cash Flow		
Increase from Short-Term Bank Loans	($286,200,000.00)	
Increase from Long-Term Bank Loans	$2,956,600,000.00	
Payments of Cash Dividends	$(3,058,200,000.00)	
Repurchase of Stock	$(11,171,000,000.00)	
Other Cash Flows from Financing	$192,700,000.00	
Net Cash Provided from Financing		$(11,366,100,000.00)
Total Cash Flow		$(10,974,600,000.00)
Cash Flow Increase (Decrease)		$(6,288,100,000.00)

Source: Adapted from "McDonald's Corporation," Form 10-K, U.S. Securities and Exchange Commission, https://www.sec.gov/Archives/edgar/data/63908/000006390817000017/mcd-12312016x10k.htm, accessed July 10, 2017. Because the accounting information found in the annual report is much more detailed than presented here, some of the accounting numbers shown here will differ from similar numbers shown in McDonald's cash flow statements in its 10-K.

So it's not surprising that a firm's stakeholders are very interested in how and why a company's cash balance changed over the past year. Cash flow statements commonly begin with net income. Why? Because it represents an increase (or decrease in the case of a loss) to the cash available to the company. Indeed, since McDonald's net income was $4.686 billion in 2016, we see that amount at the beginning of cash flow statement in Exhibit 8.3. The statement of cash flows identifies the amount of cash that flowed into and out of the firm from three types of activities:

1. Cash flows from *operating activities* show the amount of cash that flowed into the company from the sale of goods or services, as well as cash from dividends and interest received from ownership of the financial securities of other firms. It also shows the amount of cash used to cover expenses resulting from operations and any cash payments to purchase securities held for short-term trading purposes. Remember that under the accrual method, not all revenues and expenses on the income statement represent cash flows, so

> "Happiness is a positive cash flow."
> —*FRED ADLER*

operating cash flows may differ substantially from the revenues and expenses shown on the income statement. Exhibit 8.3 shows that McDonald's operating cash flow comes from three sources: $1.047 billion from cash payments from customers, $28.1 million for inventory sold to restaurants, and $297.9 million in cash received from its restaurants—all of which comes to $1.373 billion in net cash from operations.

2. Cash flows from *investing activities* show the amount of cash received from the sale of fixed assets (such as land and buildings) and financial assets bought as long-term investments. It also shows any cash used to buy fixed assets or make long-term financial investments. McDonald's had $1.058 billion from the sale of land and businesses, but spent $1.821 billion in cash on capital expenditures (primarily for building and opening new restaurants or remodeling existing restaurants) and an additional $109.5 million from cash on equipment for new restaurants or to upgrade existing restaurants, and an additional $109.5 million in cash on "other" investing activities.

3. Cash flows from *financing activities* show the cash the firm received from issuing additional shares of its own stock or from taking out short-term and long-term loans. McDonald's aggressively paid off short-term loans, thus reducing cash by $286.2 million. But thanks to long-term bank loans, cash flows increased by and $2.956 billion. Payments of dividends to shareholders reduced cash by $3.058 billion. McDonald's also decreased cash flow by spending $11.171 billion to repurchase shares of McDonald's stock. In all, cash flows from financing activities were negative for McDonald's at $11.366 billion more in cash outflows than inflows.

Exhibit 8.3 shows that McDonald's cash flows decreased in 2016 primarily because of cash dividends paid to shareholders and repurchasing of stock from shareholders, which together reduced cash flow by $14.229 billion.

8-3d Other Statements: What Happened to the Owners' Stake?

In addition to the three major statements we've just described, firms usually prepare either a statement of retained earnings or a stockholders' equity statement. Let's take a quick look at each.

The *statement of retained earnings* is a simple statement that shows how retained earnings have changed from one accounting period to the next. The change in retained earnings is found by subtracting dividends paid to shareholders from net income.

Firms that have more complex changes in the owners' equity section sometimes report these changes in notes to the financial statements in the annual report. But they often disclose these changes by providing a *stockholders' equity statement*. Like the statement of retained earnings, this statement shows how net income and dividends affect retained earnings. But it also shows other changes in stockholders' equity, such as those that arise from the issuance of additional shares of stock.

8-4 INTERPRETING FINANCIAL STATEMENTS: DIGGING BENEATH THE SURFACE

The financial statements we've just described contain a lot of important information. But they don't necessarily tell the whole story. In fact, the numbers they report can be misleading if they aren't put into proper context. Thus, in addition to looking at the statements, it's also important to check out the independent auditor's report and read the

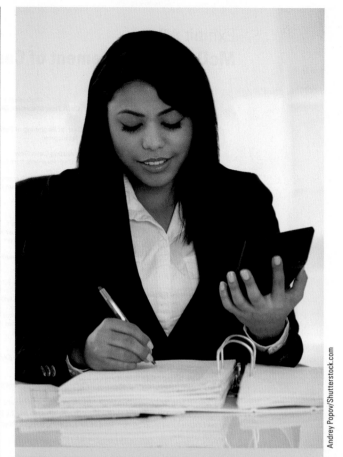

External auditors carefully examine a company's financial records before rendering their opinion.

Andrey Popov/Shutterstock.com

management discussion and footnotes that accompany these statements. It's also a good idea to compare the figures reported in current statements with those from earlier statements to see how key account values have changed.

8-4a The Independent Auditor's Report: Getting a Stamp of Approval

U.S. securities laws require publicly traded corporations in the United States to have an independent CPA firm (an accounting firm that specializes in providing public accounting services) perform an annual *external audit* of their financial statements. And many companies that aren't publicly traded also obtain external audits even though they aren't legally required to do so.

The purpose of an audit is to verify that a company's financial statements were properly prepared in accordance with generally accepted accounting principles and fairly present the financial condition of the firm. So external auditors don't just check the figures, they also examine the accounting *methods* the company used to *obtain* those figures. For

Should Your Business Quit Using Cash?

Tom O'Hara paid $13,000 in cash to buy a car at a used card dealership. O'Hara later said about the exchange, "You could do it by bank transfer. But most people just take out the cash and bring it over." While *you* probably wouldn't pay $13,000 in cash for a car, O'Hara is Swiss, and using cash for large purchases is common in Switzerland. Indeed, roughly 60% of all transactions are made with cash in the small Central European republic.

By contrast, only 22% of purchases are made with cash in the United States. Sweden leads the global trend toward cashless transactions, as only 20% of shop purchases and just 2% of all payments are made in cash. Louise Henriksson, a Swedish teaching assistant, says, "I don't use cash anymore, for anything.

You just don't need it. Shops don't want it; lots of banks don't even have it. Even for a candy bar or a paper, you use a card or phone." Indeed, 56% of Sweden's bank branches don't take cash deposits and don't even have cash on hand. Greg Birch, vice president of strategic initiatives for Ingenico Group, which makes secure e-payment systems for businesses, says, "What we've seen is a push toward electric payments because of convenience, especially for generations X and Y and onward. The phone has become more personal than the wallet has."

Given the trend toward cashless transactions, the question is: Should your business stop using cash?

After being robbed five times in three months, David Hart, the owner of Park Café and coffee bar in Baltimore, stopped accepting cash. Hart said, "I was very concerned, and I wanted to be thoughtful and explain to them [employees] what to say if the customers push back. But the customers didn't push back." Sales were unaffected.

With the exception of Massachusetts, there is no law that requires businesses to accept cash. As 7% to 8% of Americans don't have bank accounts, poorer customers may be affected. But in Sweden, even the poorest are cashless. Homeless people selling the Situation Stockholm magazine on the street to passersby have credit card swipe readers. Stefan Wikberg says, "Now people can't get away. When they say, 'I don't have change,' I tell them they can pay with card or even by SMS."[9]

example, auditors interview the company's accounting and bookkeeping staff to verify that they understand and properly implement procedures that are consistent with GAAP. They also examine a sample of specific source documents (such as sales receipts or invoices) and verify that the transactions they represent were properly posted to the correct accounts. Auditors also look for signs of fraud or falsified records. They often conduct an actual physical count of goods or supplies in inventory to determine the accuracy of the figures reported in the company's inventory records and contact the company's banker to verify its account balances. The audit process is rigorous, but it's important to realize that in large, public companies, it would be impossible for auditors to check the accuracy of every transaction.

The results of the audit are presented in an *independent auditor's report*, which is included in the annual report the firm sends to its stockholders. If the auditor doesn't find any problems with the way a firm's financial statements were prepared and presented, the report will offer an *unqualified* (or *"clean"*) *opinion*—which is by far the most common outcome. If the auditor identifies some minor concerns but

believes that on balance the firm's statements remain a fair and accurate representation of the company's financial position, the report will offer a *qualified opinion*. But when auditors discover more serious and widespread problems with a firm's statements, they offer an *adverse opinion*. An adverse opinion indicates that the auditor believes the financial statements are seriously flawed and that they may be misleading and unreliable. (An adverse opinion must include an explanation of the specific reasons for the opinion.) Adverse opinions are very rare, so when an auditor renders one, it should set off alarm bells, warning stakeholders to view the information in the firm's financial statements with real skepticism.

For CPA firms to perform audits with integrity, they must be independent of the firms they audit. During the 1990s, many of the major CPA firms entered into very lucrative consulting contracts with some of the businesses they were auditing. It became increasingly difficult for these CPA firms to risk losing these high-paying contracts by raising issues about accounting practices when they audited the books of their clients. In other words, the auditors ceased to be truly independent and objective. The lack of rigorous

Google = Alphabet + Budgets

Since its initial stock offering in 2004, Google has been so profitable that it has never had to worry about financial discipline or budgets. The funds from Google's search-based advertising businesses (Google search and ads, YouTube, Android, and Chrome), which accounted for 90% to 95% of company revenues, were so large that they covered up significant problems and losses across the rest of Google.

FABRICE COFFRINI/Getty Images

Indeed, non–search-related businesses, which Google calls "Other Bets," such as Google X (long-shot research and business ideas), Nest (networked thermostats), Google Fiber (broadband), Calico (longevity research), life sciences, and Google Ventures (start-up investments) lost $3.6 billion in 2015 on revenues of $0.4 billion, compared to Google's search-related profit of $15.8 billion on revenues of $74.5 billion. A formal Google executive explained, "No one wants to face the reality that this is an advertising company with a bunch of hobbies."

Likewise, in 2016, Google's organizational structure was so undisciplined that it had two music subscription businesses, two venture capital groups, two mobile operating systems, and two research labs. But who cares about budgets or whether you have two of everything when your core business is growing by 20% a year for 20 straight quarters?

That all changed, however, when Google reorganized into Alphabet, Inc. (a holding company for Google's businesses) and hired Ruth Porat (pictured) from Morgan Stanley to be Chief Financial Officer (CFO). As Alphabet's CFO, Borat quickly set to work establishing budgets, encouraging cost-cutting and revenue growth, and breaking out financial performance measures for each of Google's divisions.

Former Alphabet Chairman Eric Schmidt said of the new direction, "The cost-cutting is real, and it's the right thing to be done, and it's driven by [Porat]. Before she was there, we had lost discipline." Now, 18 months after Borat established budgets, search accounts for just 86% of Alphabet's revenues, while Other Bet losses have declined by 10% thanks to a 75% increase in revenues.[10]

---

oversight by external auditors contributed to the accounting scandals we mentioned earlier in this chapter.

In the aftermath of the scandals, Congress passed the Sarbanes-Oxley Act of 2002 (commonly referred to as "SOX" or "Sarbox"). This law banned business relationships that might create conflicts of interest between CPA firms and the companies they audit. It also established a private-sector nonprofit corporation known as the Public Company Accounting Oversight Board (PCAOB). The PCAOB defines its mission as follows: "To protect the interests of investors and further the public interest in the preparation of informative, fair, and independent audit reports."[11]

Despite Sarbanes-Oxley and the U.S. Securities and Exchange Commission's strict enforcement of GAAP accounting rules, 71 class-action lawsuits were filed against companies for improper accounting statements, which are alleged to have cost investors $35 billion in losses.[12]

To encourage accountants and auditors to report illegal or unethical accounting practices, the International Ethics Standards Boards for Accountants (IESBA) developed a new code of ethics for professional accountants that went into effect in July 2017. Stavros Thomadakis, chairman of the IESBA, says, "The

standards clarify that professional accountants must be active and not turn a blind eye to noncompliance. It's trying to bring about early, early detection, if you will, but also early action by management or authorities."[13]

8-4b Checking Out the Notes to Financial Statements: What's in the Fine Print?

Some types of information can't be adequately conveyed by numbers alone. Annual reports include notes (often *many* pages of notes) that disclose additional information about the firm's operations, accounting practices, and special circumstances that clarify and supplement the numbers reported on the financial statements. These notes can be *very* revealing. As mentioned earlier, GAAP often allows firms to choose among several options when it comes to certain accounting procedures—and the choices the firm makes can affect the value of assets, liabilities, and owners' equity on the balance sheet and the revenues, costs, and net income on the income statement. The notes to financial statements explain the specific accounting methods used to recognize revenue, value inventory, and

> In 2004 a horse named "Read The Footnotes" ran in the Kentucky Derby.
>
> — SECURITIES AND EXCHANGE COMMISSION

depreciate fixed assets. They might also provide details about the way the firm funds its pension plan or health insurance for its employees. They must also disclose *changes* in accounting methods that could affect the comparability of the current financial statements to those of previous years. Even more interesting, the notes might disclose important facts about the status of a lawsuit against the firm or other risks the firm faces. Stakeholders who ignore these notes are likely to miss out on important information.

Another important source of information is the section of the annual report usually titled "Management's Discussion and Analysis." As its name implies, this is where the top management team provides its take on the financial condition of the company. SEC guidelines require top management to disclose any trends, events, or risks likely to have a significant impact on the firm's financial condition in this section of the report. For 2016, the most significant item was achieving its three-year target of returning $30 billion in cash to shareholders (via dividends and stock buy backs).

8-4c Looking for Trends in Comparative Statements

The SEC requires publicly traded corporations to provide *comparative financial statements*. This simply means that the balance sheet, income statement, and statement of cash flows must list two or more years of figures side by side, making it possible to see how account values have changed over a period of time. Many firms that aren't publicly traded also present comparative statements, even though they are not required to do so by GAAP.

Comparative balance sheets allow users to trace what has happened to key assets and liabilities over the past two or three years, and whether its owners' equity had increased. Comparative income statements show whether the firm's net income increased or decreased and what has happened to revenues and expenses over recent years. Using comparative statements to identify changes in key account values over time is called **horizontal analysis**.

8-5 BUDGETING: PLANNING FOR ACCOUNTABILITY

Management accountants also play an important role in the development of budgets. **Budgeting** is a management tool that explicitly shows how a firm will acquire and allocate the resources it needs to achieve its goals over a specific time period. The budgetary process facilitates planning by requiring managers to translate goals into measurable quantities and identify the specific resources

iStock.com/Dean Mitchell

Budgeting encourages communication and coordination among managers and employees.

needed to achieve these goals. But budgeting offers other advantages as well. If done well, budgeting:

- Helps managers clearly specify how they intend to achieve the goals they set during the planning process. This should lead to a better understanding of how the organization's limited resources will be allocated.

- Encourages communication and coordination among managers and employees in various departments within the organization. For example, the budget process can give middle and first-line managers and employees an opportunity to provide top managers with important insights about the challenges facing their specialized areas—and the resources they need to meet those challenges. But, as we will explain in the next section, the extent to which this advantage is realized depends on the specific approach used in the budgeting process.

- Serves as a motivational tool. Good budgets clearly identify goals *and* demonstrate a plan of action for acquiring the resources needed to achieve them. Employees tend to be more

horizontal analysis Analysis of financial statements that compares account values reported on these statements over two or more years to identify changes and trends.

budgeting A management tool that explicitly shows how a firm will acquire and use the resources needed to achieve its goals over a specific time period.

highly motivated when they understand the goals their managers expect them to accomplish and when they view these goals as ambitious but achievable.

■ **Helps managers evaluate progress and performance.** Managers can compare actual performance to budgeted figures to determine whether various departments and functional areas are making adequate progress toward achieving their organization's goals. If actual performance falls short of budgetary goals, managers can look for reasons and, if necessary, take corrective action.

8-5a Preparing the Budget: Top-Down or Bottom-Up?

There are two broad approaches to budget preparation. In some organizations, top management prepares the budget with little or no input from middle and supervisory managers—a process known as *top-down budgeting*. Supporters of this approach point out that top management knows the long-term strategic needs of the company and is in a better position to see the big picture when making budget decisions.

The other approach to budgeting is called *bottom-up (or participatory) budgeting*. Organizations that use a participatory process allow middle and supervisory managers to participate actively in the creation of the budget. Proponents of this approach maintain that it has two major advantages. First, middle and supervisory managers are likely to know more about the issues and challenges facing their departments—and the resources it will take to address them—than top management. Second, middle and first-line managers are likely to be more highly motivated to achieve budgetary goals when they have a say in how those goals are developed. On the negative side, the bottom-up approach is more time consuming and resource intensive to carry out than the top-down approach. Also, some middle managers may be tempted to overstate their needs or set low budget goals in order to make their jobs easier—an outcome known as *budgetary slack*.[14] Despite these drawbacks, the participatory approach currently is more common than the top-down process.

operating budgets Budgets that communicate an organization's sales and production goals and the resources needed to achieve these goals.

financial budgets Budgets that focus on the firm's financial goals and identify the resources needed to achieve these goals.

master budget A presentation of an organization's operational and financial budgets that represents the firm's overall plan of action for a specified time period.

8-5b Developing the Key Budget Components: One Step at a Time

The budgeting process actually requires the preparation of several different types of budgets. But all of these individual budgets can be classified into two broad categories: operating budgets and financial budgets.

Operating budgets are budgets that identify projected sales and production goals and the various costs the firm will incur to meet these goals. These budgets are developed in a specific order, with the information from earlier budgets used in the preparation of later budgets.

The preparation of operating budgets begins with the development of a *sales budget* that provides quarterly estimates of the number of units of each product the firm expects to sell, the selling price, and the total dollar value of expected sales. The sales budget *must* be created first because many of the production and cost figures that go into other operating budgets depend on the level of sales. Once the sales budget is complete, the budgeted sales level can be used to develop the production budget, the administrative expenses, and the selling expenses budgets. And once the production budget is completed, the information it contains is used to prepare budgets for direct labor costs, direct materials costs, and manufacturing overhead. The final stage in the preparation of operating budgets is the creation of a *budgeted income statement*. This budget looks much like the income statement we described earlier, but instead of describing the actual results of the firm's past operations, it combines the revenue projections from the sales budget and the cost projections from the other operating budgets, to present a forecast of *expected* net income.

Financial budgets focus on the firm's financial goals and identify the resources needed to achieve these goals. The two main financial budget documents are the *cash budget* and the *capital expenditure budget*. The cash budget identifies short-term fluctuations in cash flows, helping managers identify times when the firm might face cash flow problems—or when it might have a temporary surplus of cash that it could invest. The capital expenditure budget identifies the firm's planned investments in major fixed assets and long-term projects. The information from these two financial budgets and the budgeted income statement are combined to construct the *budgeted balance sheet*. This is the last financial budget; it shows how the firm's operations, investing, and financing activities are expected to affect all of the asset, liability, and owners' equity accounts.

The firm's **master budget** organizes the operating and financial budgets into a unified whole, representing the firm's overall plan of action for a specified time period. In other words, the master budget shows how all of the pieces fit together to form a complete picture. Exhibit 8.4

Exhibit 8.4
Development of the Master Budget

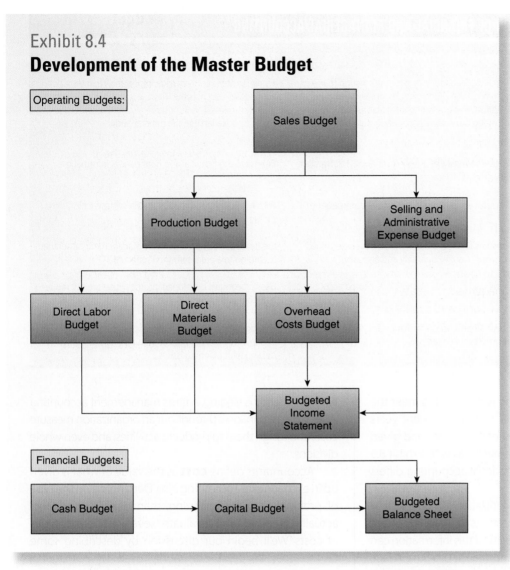

Operating Budgets:

Sales Budget

Production Budget

Selling and Administrative Expense Budget

Direct Labor Budget

Direct Materials Budget

Overhead Costs Budget

Budgeted Income Statement

Financial Budgets:

Cash Budget

Capital Budget

Budgeted Balance Sheet

shows all of the budget documents that are included in a typical master budget. The arrows indicate the order in which the budgets are developed, starting with the sales budget and ending with the budgeted balance sheet.

8-5c Being Flexible: Clearing Up Problems with Static

The budget process, as we've described it so far, results in a *static* budget, meaning that it is based on a single assumed level of sales. Static budgets are excellent tools for planning, but they have weaknesses when they are used to measure progress, evaluate performance, and identify problem areas that need correcting.

The problem with a static budget is that real-world sales can (and often do) vary considerably from their forecasted value—often for reasons that aren't under the control of the firm's management. For example, consumers are increasingly turning to online purchases—even for home

hardware purchases such as tools, parts, appliances, and cabinetry. As a result, big box hardware and home improvement chain Lowes announced in January 2017 that it was cutting 3,000 jobs and using information technology and in-store video cameras to properly match store staffing to store traffic trends. Lowes CEO Robert Niblock said, "We've got to make sure that as the consumer is changing the ways they engage with us, we continue to be nimble."[15]

As we mentioned earlier, many cost figures in budgets are based on the level of sales specified in the sales budget. When actual sales differ significantly from the sales volume assumed in a static budget, all of these related budget figures will be erroneous. Using these inaccurate figures to evaluate real-world performance is likely to result in very poor assessments!

One common way managerial accountants avoid this problem is to develop a *flexible budget* for control purposes. A flexible budget is one that isn't based on a single assumed level of sales. Instead, it is developed over a *range* of possible sales levels, and is designed to show the appropriate budgeted level of costs for each different level of sales. This flexibility enables managers to make more meaningful comparisons between actual costs and budgeted costs.

 8-6 ### INSIDE INTELLIGENCE: THE ROLE OF MANAGERIAL ACCOUNTING

Now that we've looked at financial accounting, let's turn our attention to the other major branch of accounting, **managerial (or management) accounting**. As its name

managerial (or management) accounting The branch of accounting that provides reports and analysis to managers to help them make informed business decisions.

EXHIBIT 8.5 | COMPARISON OF FINANCIAL AND MANAGERIAL ACCOUNTING

	Financial Accounting	Managerial Accounting
Purpose	Primarily intended to provide information to external stakeholders, such as stockholders, creditors, and government regulators. Information provided by financial accounting is available to the general public.	Primarily intended to provide information to internal stakeholders, such as the managers of specific divisions or departments. This information is proprietary—meaning that it isn't available to the general public.
Type of Information Presented	Focuses almost exclusively on financial information.	Provides both financial and nonfinancial information.
Nature of Reports	Prepares a standard set of financial statements.	Prepares customized reports to deal with specific problems or issues.
Timing of Reports	Presents financial statements on a predetermined schedule (usually quarterly and annually).	Creates reports upon request by management rather than according to a predetermined schedule.
Adherence to Accounting Standards?	Governed by a set of generally accepted accounting principles (GAAP).	Uses procedures developed internally that are not required to follow GAAP.
Time Period Focus	Summarizes past performance and its impact on the firm's present condition.	Provides reports dealing with past performance but also involves making projections about the future when dealing with planning issues.

implies, this branch of accounting is designed to meet the needs of a company's managers, though in recent years many firms have empowered other employees and given them access to some of this information as well. Exhibit 8.5 identifies several ways that managerial accounting differs from financial accounting.

Managers throughout an organization rely on information created by managerial accountants to make important decisions. The accuracy and reliability of this information can make a huge difference in the performance of a firm. In fact, many firms view their management accounting systems as a source of competitive advantage and regard the specifics of these systems as highly valuable company secrets.[16]

It's impossible to describe all the functions performed by managerial accountants in a single chapter. So we'll be selective and focus on only two of them—but the two we'll discuss often play a crucial role in managerial decision making: measuring and assigning costs, and developing budgets.

8-6a Cost Concepts: A Cost for All Reasons

Without good information on costs, managers would be operating in the dark as they try to set prices, determine the most desirable mix of products, and locate areas where efficiency is lagging. A firm's management accounting system helps managers throughout an organization measure costs and assign them to products, activities, and even whole divisions.

Accountants define **cost** as the value of what is given up in exchange for something else. Depending on the type of problem they are analyzing, managerial accountants actually measure and evaluate several different types of costs. We'll begin our discussion by describing some of the cost concepts commonly used by managerial accountants.

At the most basic level, accountants distinguish between out-of-pocket costs and opportunity costs. **Out-of-pocket costs** (also called *explicit costs*) are usually easy to measure because they involve actual expenditures of money or other resources. The wages a company pays to its workers, the payments it makes to suppliers for raw materials, and the rent it pays for office space are examples.

But accountants realize that not all costs involve a monetary payment; sometimes what is given up is the *opportunity* to use an asset in some alternative way. Such opportunity costs are often referred to as **implicit costs**. For example, suppose a couple of lawyers form a partnership and set up their office in a building one of the partners already owns. They feel good about their decision because they don't have to make any out-of-pocket payments for rent. But a good managerial accountant would point out to the partners that they still incur an implicit cost, because

cost The value of what is given up in exchange for something.

out-of-pocket cost A cost that involves the payment of money or other resources.

implicit cost The opportunity cost that arises when a firm uses owner-supplied resources.

The bricks, the mortar, the gloves, and the wages paid for the labor are all out-of-pocket costs.

by using the building themselves they forgo the opportunity to earn income by renting the office space to someone else.

Managerial accountants also distinguish between fixed costs and variable costs. As the name implies, **fixed costs** don't change when the firm changes its level of production. Examples of fixed costs include interest on a bank loan, property insurance premiums, rent on office space, and other payments that are set by a contract or by legal requirements. Many fixed costs are really only fixed for some "relevant range" of output. For example, if a company sees a dramatic rise in sales, it might have to move into bigger facilities, thus incurring a higher rent.

Variable costs are costs that rise (vary) when the firm produces more of its goods and services. As a company ramps up its production, it is likely to need more labor and materials and to use more electrical power. Thus payments for many types of labor, supplies, and utilities are variable costs.

8-6b Assigning Costs to Products: As (Not So) Simple as ABC?

Finally, accountants often want to assign costs to specific *cost objects*, such as one of the goods or services their firm produces. When they assign costs to specific cost objects, accountants distinguish between *direct costs* and *indirect costs*. **Direct costs** are those that can be directly traced to the production of the product. For example, the wage payments made to workers directly involved in producing a good or service would be a direct cost for that product. On the other hand, the costs

a firm incurs for plant maintenance, quality control, or depreciation on office equipment are usually classified as **indirect costs** since they tend to be the result of the firm's general operation rather than the production of any specific product.

Direct costs for labor and materials are usually easy to measure and assign, since they have an easily identifiable link to the object. Unfortunately, indirect costs aren't tied in such a simple and direct way to the production of a specific product. In the past, managerial accountants usually relied on simple rules to assign indirect costs to different products—and in some cases they still do. One such approach is to allocate indirect costs in proportion to the number of direct labor hours involved in the production of each product. Under this method, products that require the most labor to produce are assigned the most indirect costs. But while this approach is simple, it can provide very misleading information. There is simply no logical reason for many types of indirect costs to be related to the amount of direct labor used to produce a product.

In recent years, managerial accountants have developed more sophisticated ways to allocate costs. One relatively new method is called **activity-based costing (ABC)**.

This approach is more complex and difficult to implement than the direct labor method. Basically, it involves a two-stage process. The first stage is to identify specific activities that create indirect costs, and then determine the factors that "drive" the costs of these activities. The second stage is to tie these cost drivers to the production of specific goods (or other cost objects). Once the relationships between cost drivers and specific products are identified, they can be used to determine how much of each indirect cost is assigned to each product.

Clearly, ABC is much more complex to implement than a system that assigns costs based on a simple "one size fits all" rule, such as the direct labor method. However, it's likely to provide more meaningful results because it is based on a systematic examination of how indirect costs are related to individual goods.

fixed costs Costs that remain the same when the level of production changes within some relevant range.

variable costs Costs that vary directly with the level of production.

direct cost Costs that are incurred directly as the result of some specific cost object.

indirect costs Costs that are the result of a firm's general operations and are not directly tied to any specific cost object.

activity-based costing (ABC) A technique to assign product costs based on links between activities that drive costs and the production of specific products.

Accounting provides vital information to both the internal and external stakeholders of a firm. The balance sheet, income statement, and statement of cash flows that are the main output of financial accounting help external stakeholders, such as owners and creditors, evaluate the financial performance of a firm.

And managerial accounting helps managers throughout an organization make better decisions by providing them with relevant and timely information about the costs and benefits of the choices they have to make. Clearly, a basic knowledge of accounting concepts will help you succeed in just about any career path you choose.

Staff Accountant

Responsible for daily cash reconciliation, preparation of monthly financial reports, including balance sheets and profit and loss statements, preparing spreadsheets and financial forecasts and analyses for the accounting manager and/or controller, and ensuring compliance with GAAP

and Sarbanes-Oxley requirements. The ideal candidate has a bachelor's or master's degree in accounting, technical accounting knowledge, strong oral and written communication skills, a problem-solving attitude, the ability to prioritize tasks and work under deadlines, pays close attention to detail, and is eligible to sit for the CPA exam or is CPA certified.

STUDY TOOLS 8

LOCATED AT BACK OF THE TEXTBOOK

☐ Rip-Out Chapter Review Card

☐ Gain unique perspectives on key concepts with new concept videos in the e-book

☐ Increase your comprehension with online homework and quizzes

☐ Study with existing flashcards and make your own

9 | Finance:
Acquiring and Using Funds to Maximize Value

Remember to visit

PAGE 168

for additional

STUDY TOOLS

LEARNING OBJECTIVES

After studying this chapter, you will be able to:

9-1 Identify the goal of financial management, and explain the issues financial managers confront as they seek to achieve this goal

9-2 Describe the tools financial managers use to evaluate their company's current financial condition and develop financial plans

9-3 Evaluate the major sources of funds available to meet a firm's short-term and long-term financial needs

9-4 Identify the key issues involved in determining a firm's capital structure

9-5 Describe how financial managers acquire and manage current assets

9-6 Explain how financial managers evaluate capital budgeting proposals to identify the best long-term investment options for their company

---

9-1 WHAT MOTIVATES FINANCIAL DECISIONS?

Financial capital refers to the funds a firm uses to acquire its assets and finance its operations. Firms use some of their capital to meet short-term obligations, such as paying bills from suppliers, meeting payroll, repaying loans from banks, and paying taxes owed to the government. Other funds are used to finance major long-term investments, such as the purchase of a plant and equipment or the launch of a new product line. And firms need some funds to pay a return to the owners for their investment in the company.

Billionaire entrepreneur Elon Musk leads three companies—SolarCity, SpaceX, and Tesla Motors—worth more than $50 billion. It's estimated that in the last few years, Musk has invested $300 million of his personal funds to purchase additional shares in Tesla and SolarCity (figures are not available for SpaceX, which is privately funded). Musk said, "If I ask investors to put money in, then I feel morally I should put money in as well. I should not ask people to eat from the fruit bowl if I have not myself been willing to eat from the fruit bowl."[1] In addition to direct contributions from owners

financial capital The funds a firm uses to acquire its assets and finance its operations.

Diego Cervo/Shutterstock.com

like Elon Musk, companies can also acquire financial capital through reinvestment of earnings, loans from banks, credit provided by suppliers, and (for corporations) newly issued stocks or bonds. This isn't a complete list by any means—in fact, we'll discuss additional sources later in the chapter—but you get the idea: firms often have several ways to raise money.

In a nutshell, **finance** is the functional area of business that is responsible for finding, among all these alternatives, the best sources of funds and the best ways to use them. But which sources and uses are "best" depends on the goals of the financial managers. Historically, the most widely accepted goal of financial management has been to *maximize the value of the firm to its owners*. For corporations with publicly traded stock, this translates into finding the sources and uses of financial capital that will maximize the market price of the company's common stock. After all, the stockholders are the ones with their money at risk.

Financial managers emphasize the goal of maximizing the market price of stock because they have a legal and ethical obligation (called a *fiduciary duty*) to make decisions consistent with the financial interests of their firm's owners. The legal foundation of this fiduciary duty

> "Money is like a sixth sense— and you can't make use of the other five without it."
>
> —WILLIAM SOMERSET MAUGHAM, ENGLISH PLAYWRIGHT, NOVELIST, AND SHORT STORY WRITER

was established in a famous 1919 court case, *Dodge v. Ford Motor Co.*, in which the court ruled that "a business corporation is organized and carried on primarily for the profit of the stockholders."[2] Recent legal rulings and scholarship reaffirm this fiduciary duty.[3]

Another reason for emphasizing shareholder wealth is more pragmatic. Firms that fail to create shareholder wealth are unlikely to be viewed as attractive investments. So, to continue attracting the financial capital needed to achieve its other goals, a firm must provide value to its stockholders.

finance The functional area of business that is concerned with finding the best sources and uses of financial capital.

Exhibit 9.1

Risk-Return Trade-Off Average, High and Low Financial Returns, 1928–2016

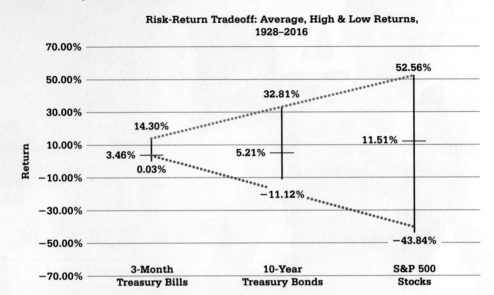

Risk-Return Tradeoff: Average, High & Low Returns, 1928–2016

Sources: A. Damodaran, "Annual Returns on Stock, T.Bonds and T.Bills: 1928– Current," Stern School of Business, New York University, January 5, 2017, http://pages.stern.nyu.edu/~adamodar/New_Home_Page/datafile/histretSP.html, accessed February 2, 2017; Risk and Return: An Introduction, Bogleheads, August 1, 2016, https://www.bogleheads.org/wiki/Risk_and_return:_an_introduction#cite_note-7, accessed February 2, 2017.

But finding the mix of sources and uses of funds that maximize shareholder value isn't a simple process. Let's look at two major issues that confront financial managers as they seek to achieve their primary goal.

9-1a Shareholder Value and Social Responsibility: Does Good Behavior Pay Off?

The emphasis that financial managers place on maximizing shareholder value may seem to conflict with the modern view that a socially responsible firm has an obligation to respect the needs of *all* stakeholders—not just its owners, but also its employees, customers, creditors, suppliers, and even society as a whole. The good news is that being socially responsible *can* be (and often is) a good strategy for also achieving the goal of shareholder wealth maximization—especially if managers take a *long-term* perspective.

When a company respects the needs of customers by providing high-quality goods and services at competitive prices, and when it listens and responds fairly to their concerns, those customers are more likely to keep coming back—and to recommend the company to friends and relatives.

Similarly, when a firm provides its employees with a good work environment, those employees are likely to have better morale and greater loyalty, resulting in higher productivity and lower employee turnover. And when a company supports its local community through corporate philanthropy or cause-related marketing, the resulting goodwill may boost sales and create a more favorable business climate. All of these outcomes suggest that a commitment to meeting social responsibilities can contribute to a more profitable company and an increase in shareholder value.[4]

But things aren't always that simple. Being socially responsible requires a long-term commitment to the needs of many different stakeholders. Incentives for top executives (in the form of raises, bonuses, and other perks), however, are often tied to their firm's *short-term* performance. In such cases, some managers focus on policies that make their firm's stock price rise in the short run, but which are unsustainable over the long haul. And when managers fix their attention on raising the market price of the company's stock in the next year (or next quarter), concerns about social responsibility sometimes get lost in the shuffle.

It is also worth noting that responding to the needs of all stakeholders isn't always a simple and straightforward task. Diverse stakeholder groups can have very different goals, and finding the right balance among the competing interests of these groups can be difficult. For example, a firm's managers might believe they can increase profits (and the value of its stock) by shutting down a plant in the United States and outsourcing the work to China. While this might benefit shareholders, it would clearly be detrimental to its U.S. workforce and the community in which that current plant is located. When conflicts arise between the long-term interests of owners and those of other stakeholders, the fiduciary duty required of financial managers generally leads them to make decisions that are most consistent with the interests of ownership.

9-1b Risk and Return: A Fundamental Trade-Off in Financial Management

One of the most important lessons in financial management is that there is a trade-off between risk and return. In financial management, **risk** refers to the degree of uncertainty about the actual outcome of a decision. The **risk-return trade-off** suggests that sources and uses of funds that offer the potential for high rates of return tend to be riskier than sources and uses of funds that offer lower returns.

Financial managers want to earn an attractive rate of return for shareholders. But they also must realize that the higher the expected return they seek, the more they expose their company to risk. Exhibit 9.1 illustrates the risk-return trade-offs of three kinds of investments from 1928 to 2016. As discussed in section 9-5a, treasury bills, or "T-bills," are backed by the U.S. government and are basically risk-free. They are often considered a "cash equivalent." Because of their short-term nature and nearly zero risk, the average return on T-bills is just 3.46%. Given their extremely low risk, T-bills have the smallest range of returns, from a low of 0.03% to a high of 14.30%. Ten-year treasury bonds generally produce higher returns because of the increased risk of holding the bond for such a long time. Therefore, not only is the average return from 10-year treasury bonds higher at 5.21%, the range of returns (the risk) is greater, with a low return of –11.12% and a high of 32.81%. (Section 10-3c explains why bond yields or returns vary from year to year.) Investing in stocks produces the highest average return at 11.51%. That higher return comes with much more risk. Indeed, annual stock returns ranged from a low of –43.84% to a high of 52.56%. The risk-return relationship is expressed in this exhibit via the green dotted line (representing highest returns) and red dotted line (representing lowest returns). The vertical distance between the green- and red-dotted lines represents the risk, or range of returns. This distance increases as the average return rises from left to right via T-bills, treasury bonds, and stocks.[5]

iStock.com/sshaw75

We can analyze McDonald's strengths and weaknesses by comparing the company's financial ratios to industry averages.

9-2 IDENTIFYING FINANCIAL NEEDS: EVALUATION AND PLANNING

Before financial managers can determine the best financial strategies for their firm, they must identify existing strengths and weaknesses. Then they must devise financial plans that provide a roadmap the firm can use to improve financial performance and acquire the resources needed to achieve its short-term and long-term objectives.

9-2a Using Ratio Analysis to Identify Current Strengths and Weaknesses

One way financial managers evaluate a firm's current strengths and weaknesses is by computing ratios that compare values of key accounts listed on their firm's financial statements—mainly its balance sheet and income statement. This technique is called **financial ratio analysis**. Over the years, financial managers have developed an impressive array of specific ratios. The most important fall into four basic categories: liquidity, asset management, leverage, and profitability. Because financial needs differ across industries,

> **risk** The degree of uncertainty regarding the outcome of a decision.
>
> **risk-return trade-off** The observation that financial opportunities that offer high rates of return are generally riskier than opportunities that offer lower rates of return.
>
> **financial ratio analysis** Computing ratios that compare values of key accounts listed on a firm's financial statements.

for example, the automobile industry is capital intensive (it takes billions of dollars to design new cars and build or refurbish factories), whereas the software industry is not (the marginal cost of producing another copy of a software program or app is close to zero); it's standard practice is to compare a firm's financial ratios to industry averages. We'll do just that as we work through the financial ratios below by continuing our financial analysis of McDonald's, which we began in Chapter 8 on accounting, where you learned the basics of income statements, balance sheets, and cash flows.[6]

1. **Liquidity ratios:** In finance, a **liquid asset** is one that can be quickly converted into cash with little risk of loss. **Liquidity ratios** measure the ability of an organization to convert assets into the cash it needs to pay off liabilities that come due in the next year.

   One of the simplest and most commonly used liquidity ratios is the *current ratio*, which is computed by dividing a firm's current assets by its current liabilities. Current assets include cash and other assets expected to be converted into cash in the next year, while current liabilities are the debts that must be repaid in the next year. The larger the current ratio, the easier it is for a firm to pay its short-term debts. A current ratio below 1.0 signifies that a company does not have enough current assets to pay short-term liabilities. In January 2017, McDonald's current ratio was 1.39 compared to the industry average of 1.54. So while McDonald's has 39% more current assets than liabilities the industry has a stronger financial liquidity ratio with 54% more current assets than liabilities. When we discuss how firms manage cash and other liquid assets, you'll learn that it is also possible to have too much liquidity.

iStock.com/Mgkaya

2. **Asset management ratios:** **Asset management ratios** (also sometimes called *activity ratios*) measure how effectively an organization uses its assets to generate net income. For example, the *inventory turnover ratio*—computed by dividing the firm's cost of goods sold by average inventory levels—measures how many times a firm's inventory is sold and replaced each year. For example, if a company keeps an average of 100 finished widgets in inventory each month, and it sold 1,000 widgets this year, then it turned its inventory ten times. A high turnover ratio is good because it indicates that a firm can continue its daily operations with a small amount of inventory on hand. It's expensive to have unsold inventory sitting on shelves, that is, low inventory turns. Companies with high inventory turns, which replenish inventory levels more frequently, have less cash tied up in inventory, which means those funds can be used elsewhere. However, inventory turnover ratios can be *too* high. When that happens, the company isn't keeping enough goods in stock, causing stockouts, which frustrates customers and results in lost sales if they take their business elsewhere.

   In January 2017, McDonald's inventory turnover ratio of 181 was much stronger than the industry average of 67. In other words, McDonald's carries 2.02 days' worth of inventory on average, compared to the average fast-food restaurant, which carries 5.45 days of inventory.

   For firms that sell a lot of goods on credit, the *average collection period* is another important asset management ratio. This ratio is computed by dividing accounts receivable by average daily credit sales. A value of 45 for this ratio means that customers take 45 days (on average) to pay for their credit purchases. In general, the smaller the ratio, the better, since a lower value indicates that the firm's customers are paying for their purchases more quickly. But we'll see in our discussion of working capital management that low collection periods can also have drawbacks. In January 2017, McDonald's average collection period was 20 days, compared to the fast-food industry average of 9 days. Typically, average collection periods under 30 days are considered to be very strong.

3. **Leverage ratios:** **Financial leverage** is the use of debt to meet a firm's financing needs; a *highly*

---

liquid asset An asset that can quickly be converted into cash with little risk of loss.

liquidity ratios Financial ratios that measure the ability of a firm to obtain the cash it needs to pay its short-term debt obligations as they come due.

asset management ratios Financial ratios that measure how effectively a firm is using its assets to generate revenues or cash.

financial leverage The use of debt in a firm's capital structure.

EXHIBIT 9.2 KEY FINANCIAL RATIOS

Ratio Name	Type	What It Measures	How It Is Computed
Current	Liquidity: measures ability to pay short-term liabilities as they come due.	Compares current assets (assets that will provide cash in the next year) to current liabilities (debts that will come due in the next year).	$\dfrac{Current\ Assets}{Current\ Liabilities}$
Inventory Turnover	Asset management: measures how effectively a firm is using its assets to generate revenue.	How quickly a firm sells its inventory to generate revenue.	$\dfrac{Cost\ of\ Goods\ Sold}{Average\ Inventory}$
Average Collection Period	Asset management: measures how effectively a firm is using its assets to generate revenue.	How long it takes for a firm to collect from customers who buy on credit.	$\dfrac{Accounts\ Receivable}{\left(\dfrac{Annual\ Credit\ Sales}{365}\right)}$
Debt to Asset	Leverage: measures the extent to which a firm relies on debt to meet its financing needs.	Similar to debt to equity, but compares debt to assets rather than equity. This is another way of measuring the degree of financial leverage, or debt, the firm is using.	$\dfrac{Total\ Debt}{Total\ Assets}$
Return on Equity	Profitability: compares the amount of profit to some measure of resources invested.	Indicates earnings per dollar invested by the owners of the company. Since common stockholders are the true owners, preferred stockholders' dividends are deducted from net income before computing this ratio.	$\dfrac{Net\ Income - Preferred\ Dividend}{Average\ Common\ Stockholders\ Equity}$
Earnings per Share	Profitability: compares the amount of profit to some measure of resources invested.	Measures the net income per share of common stock outstanding.	$\dfrac{Net\ Income - Preferred\ Dividend}{Average\ Number\ of\ Common\ Shares\ Outstanding}$

leveraged firm is one that relies heavily on debt. While the use of leverage can benefit a firm when times are good, a high degree of leverage is very risky. As we mentioned earlier, the extensive use of debt financing by big banks and major Wall Street firms played a major role in the financial meltdown that began during the latter part of the past decade.

Leverage ratios measure the extent to which a firm uses financial leverage. One common measure of leverage is the *debt-to-asset ratio* (sometimes just called the *debt ratio*), which is computed by dividing a firm's total liabilities by its total assets. If a firm financed half its assets with debt and half with owners' equity, its debt ratio would be 0.5 (or 50%). The higher the debt-to-asset ratio, the more heavily leveraged the firm is. In January 2017, McDonald's debt-to-asset ratio was 83.7%, compared to Starbucks' ratio of 25.1%. This indicates that McDonald's was leveraged with nearly 3.3 times the debt that Starbucks had.

4. **Profitability ratios:** Firms are in business to earn a profit, and **profitability ratios** provide measures of how successful they are at achieving this goal. There are many different profitability ratios, but we'll look at just a couple of examples. *Return on equity* (ROE), calculated by

dividing net income (profit) by owners' equity, measures the income earned per dollar invested by the stockholders. In January 2017, McDonald's ROE was a very strong 192%, compared to an industry average of 24.8%, so a dollar invested in McDonald's produces a larger return to shareholders than the fast-food industry on average.

Another profitability ratio, called *earnings per share* (EPS), indicates how much net income a firm earned per share of common stock outstanding. It is calculated by dividing net income minus preferred dividends by the average number of shares of common stock outstanding. In January 2017, McDonald's EPS was 5.44, compared to Starbucks' EPS of 1.90. So EPS shows that McDonald's earned greater net income per share of stock than Starbucks during this time.

Exhibit 9.2 defines each of the ratios we've just described and shows how it is computed. As you look at the exhibit, keep in mind that it represents only a sample of the financial ratios used by financial managers.

leverage ratios Ratios that measure the extent to which a firm relies on debt financing in its capital structure.

profitability ratios Ratios that measure the rate of return a firm is earning on various measures of investment.

9-2b Planning Tools: Creating a Road Map to the Future

Ratio analysis helps managers identify their firm's current financial strengths and weaknesses. The next step is to develop plans that build on the firm's strengths and correct its weaknesses. Financial planning is an important part of the firm's overall planning process. Assuming that the overall planning process has established appropriate goals and objectives for the firm, financial planning must answer the following questions:

- What specific assets must the firm obtain to achieve its goals?
- How much additional financing will the firm need to acquire these assets?
- How much financing will the firm be able to generate internally (through additional earnings), and how much must it obtain from external sources?
- When will the firm need to acquire external financing?
- What is the best way to raise these funds?

The planning process involves input from a variety of areas. In addition to seeking input from managers in various functional areas of their business, financial managers usually work closely with the firm's accountants during the planning process.

9-2c Basic Planning Tools: Budgeted Financial Statements and the Cash Budget

budgeted income statement A projection showing how a firm's budgeted sales and costs will affect expected net income. (Also called a pro forma income statement.)

budgeted balance sheet A projected financial statement that forecasts the types and amounts of assets a firm will need to implement its future plans and how the firm will finance those assets. (Also called a pro forma balance sheet.)

cash budget A detailed forecast of future cash flows that helps financial managers identify when their firm is likely to experience temporary shortages or surpluses of cash.

The budgeting process provides financial managers with much of the information they need for financial planning. The **budgeted income statement** and **budgeted balance sheet** are two key financial planning tools. Also called *pro forma financial statements*, they provide a framework for analyzing the impact of the firm's plans on the financing needs of the company.

- The budgeted income statement uses information from the sales budget and various cost budgets (as well as other assumptions) to develop a forecast of net income for the planning period. This can help the firm evaluate how much internal financing (funds generated by earnings) will be available.

- The budgeted balance sheet forecasts the types and amounts of assets a firm will need to implement its future plans. It also helps financial managers determine the amount of additional financing (liabilities and owners' equity) the firm must arrange to acquire those assets.

The **cash budget** is another important financial planning tool. Cash budgets normally cover a one-year period and show projected cash inflows and outflows for each month. Financial managers use cash budgets to get a better understanding of the *timing* of cash flows within the planning period. This is important because most firms experience uneven inflows and outflows of cash over the course of a year, which can lead to cash shortages and cash surpluses. For example, the video game industry experiences sizable increases in cash flows when Sony and Microsoft introduce new versions of their PlayStation and Xbox gaming platforms (typically every 3–4 years); when new blockbuster games (such as Madden NFL) are released; and in November and December, during which holiday sales often exceed sales from the rest of the year.[7] Projecting cash flows helps financial managers determine when the firm is likely to need additional funds to meet short-term cash shortages, and when surpluses of cash will be available to pay off loans or to invest in other assets.

Even firms with growing sales can experience cash flow problems, especially if many of their customers buy on credit. To meet increasing sales levels, a growing firm must hire more labor and buy more supplies. These workers and suppliers may expect to be paid long before the company's customers pay their bills, leading to a temporary cash crunch.

Exhibit 9.3 illustrates this type of situation by presenting a partial cash budget for a hypothetical firm called Oze-Moore. The cash budget shows that, despite its increasing sales, Oze-Moore will have cash shortages in March and April. Knowing this in advance gives financial managers time to find the best sources of short-term financing to cover these shortages. The cash budget also shows that Oze-Moore will experience a big cash surplus in May as the customers start paying for the purchases they made in March and April. Knowing this ahead of time helps managers forecast when they will be able to repay the loans they took out to cover their previous cash shortages. It also gives

Exhibit 9.3
Cash Budget for Oze-Moore

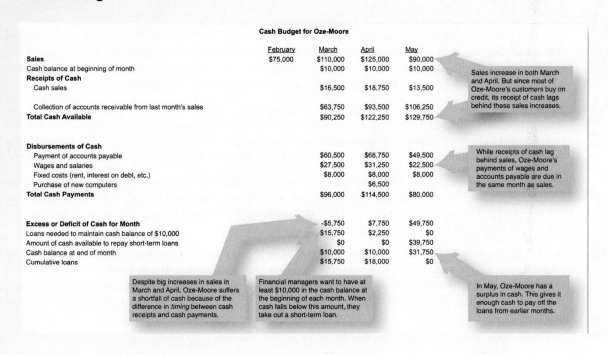

Cash Budget for Oze-Moore

	February	March	April	May
Sales	$75,000	$110,000	$125,000	$90,000
Cash balance at beginning of month		$10,000	$10,000	$10,000
Receipts of Cash				
Cash sales		$16,500	$18,750	$13,500
Collection of accounts receivable from last month's sales		$63,750	$93,500	$106,250
Total Cash Available		$90,250	$122,250	$129,750
Disbursements of Cash				
Payment of accounts payable		$60,500	$68,750	$49,500
Wages and salaries		$27,500	$31,250	$22,500
Fixed costs (rent, interest on debt, etc.)		$8,000	$8,000	$8,000
Purchase of new computers			$6,500	
Total Cash Payments		$96,000	$114,500	$80,000
Excess or Deficit of Cash for Month		-$5,750	$7,750	$49,750
Loans needed to maintain cash balance of $10,000		$15,750	$2,250	$0
Amount of cash available to repay short-term loans		$0	$0	$39,750
Cash balance at end of month		$10,000	$10,000	$31,750
Cumulative loans		$15,750	$18,000	$0

Sales increase in both March and April. But since most of Oze-Moore's customers buy on credit, its receipt of cash lags behind these sales increases.

While receipts of cash lag behind sales, Oze-Moore's payments of wages and accounts payable are due in the same month as sales.

Despite big increases in sales in March and April, Oze-Moore suffers a shortfall of cash because of the difference in *timing* between cash receipts and cash payments.

Financial managers want to have at least $10,000 in the cash balance at the beginning of each month. When cash falls below this amount, they take out a short-term loan.

In May, Oze-Moore has a surplus in cash. This gives it enough cash to pay off the loans from earlier months.

them time to evaluate short-term interest-earning investments they could make to temporarily "park" their surplus cash.

9-3 FINDING FUNDS: WHAT ARE THE OPTIONS?

Once financial managers have identified the amount of financial capital needed to carry out their firm's plans, the next step is to determine which sources of funds to tap. The most appropriate sources of funds for a business depend on several factors. One of the most important considerations is the firm's stage of development. Start-up firms face different challenges and have different needs than more established firms. Another factor is the reason the funds are needed. Funds used to meet short-term needs, such as meeting payroll, paying suppliers, or paying taxes, typically come from different sources than funds used to finance major investments in plants, property, and equipment.

The financing options available to new firms are generally much more limited than those available to more mature firms with an established track record. In fact, for start-up firms the main source of funds is likely to be the personal wealth of the owner (or owners), supplemented by loans from relatives and friends. Given how risky new business ventures are, banks and other established lenders often hesitate to make loans to new, unproven companies. (In some cases, the Small Business Administration overcomes this reluctance by guaranteeing loans for start-ups and other small businesses that satisfy its criteria.) As the firms grow and become more established, they typically are able to obtain financing from other sources.

Some start-ups with the potential for generating rapid growth may be able to attract funds from wealthy individuals, called *angel investors*, or from venture capital firms. Both angel investors and venture capitalists typically invest in risky opportunities that offer the possibility of high rates of return. Both also typically provide funds in exchange for a share of ownership.

9-3a Sources of Short-Term Financing: Meeting Needs for Cash

Firms that have survived the start-up phase of the business life cycle often have several sources of short-term financing. Let's take a look at some of the most common options.

Investing in a Better Future for Bigger Returns? Almost...

Of the $11 trillion in investment funds held today, $83 billion is held in socially responsible funds that invest in businesses with environmental, social, and corporate governance (ESG) missions and products. These funds not only invest in socially responsible companies; they actively avoid investing in firms that sell products that green investors see as detrimental to the environment or to society (such as guns, cigarettes, alcohol, and gambling).

The knock on ESG investing is that green products are more expensive and less profitable, so investors often reap lower returns. Critics argue that 65% of ESG funds have achieved below average returns over the last decade, but proponents counter that ESG companies have performed much better in recent years. Indeed, the MSCI KLD Social Index fund has averaged a 15.4% return the last three years, compared to 15.2% for the S&P 500, a standard investment benchmark.

So if you wanted to invest in ESG companies and investment funds, what should you expect? Morningstar analyst David Kathman says, "There isn't really strong evidence that it hurts or helps. It's basically neutral." Calvert Investments is one of the earliest ESG investment funds. It's CEO, John Steur, agrees with Kathman's analysis: "If you invest sustainably, you've got just as good a chance of beating the market or not."

In short, ESG companies are just as likely as other companies to make a profit, but they're also just as likely to produce losses. On top of that, sustainable companies are not always what they seem. British Petroleum, Volkswagen, and Chipotle were all known as socially responsible companies before BP caused a massive oil spill in the Gulf of Mexico; VW cheated on diesel engine pollution testing; and Chipotle spurred *Escherichia coli* (*E. coli*) outbreaks across the country.[8]

Trade Credit One of the most important sources of short-term financing for many firms is **trade credit**, which arises when suppliers ship materials, parts, or goods to a firm without requiring payment at the time of delivery. By allowing the firms to "buy now, pay later," they help the firm conserve its existing cash, thus avoiding the need to acquire funds from other sources.

In most cases, the terms of trade credit are presented on the invoice the supplier includes with the shipment. For example, the invoice might list the terms as 2/10 net 30. The "net 30" indicates that the supplier allows the buyer 30 days before payment is due. But the "2/10" tells the buyer that the supplier is offering a 2% discount off the invoice price if the buyer pays within 10 days.

At first glance, the 2% discount in our example may not seem like a big deal. But failing to take the discount can be very costly. Consider the terms we mentioned above: 2/10, net 30. If the firm fails to pay within 10 days, it loses the discount and must pay the full amount 20 days later. Paying 2% more for the use of funds for only 20 days is equivalent to an *annual* finance charge of over 37%![9]

Suppliers will grant trade credit only after they've evaluated the creditworthiness of the firm. But once they've granted this credit to a company, they generally continue offering it as long as the firm satisfies the terms of the credit arrangements. Trade credit is sometimes called **spontaneous financing** because it is granted when the company places its orders without requiring any additional paperwork or special arrangements. The level of trade credit automatically adjusts as business conditions change and the company places larger or smaller orders with its suppliers.

Although firms of all sizes use this type of financing, trade credit is a particularly important source of financing for small businesses. The Federal Reserve Board's *Survey of Small Business Finances* indicates that about 60% of small firms rely on trade credit as a major source of short-term financial capital.[10]

Factoring The money that customers owe a firm when they buy on credit shows up in accounts receivable on the company's balance sheet. A **factor** buys the accounts receivables of other firms. The factor makes a profit by purchasing the receivables at a discount and collecting the full amount from the firm's customers.

Although firms that use factors don't receive the full amount their customers owe, factoring offers some definite

trade credit Spontaneous financing granted by sellers when they deliver goods and services to customers without requiring immediate payment.

spontaneous financing Financing that arises during the natural course of business without the need for special arrangements.

factor A company that provides short-term financing to firms by purchasing their accounts receivables at a discount.

advantages. Instead of having to wait for customers to pay, the firm gets its money almost immediately. Also, since the factor is responsible for collection efforts, the firm using the factor may be able to save money by eliminating its own collection department. Finally, the factor typically assumes the risk for bad debts on any receivables it buys. However, factors typically perform a careful evaluation of the quality of accounts receivable before they buy them and may refuse to buy receivables that are high risk. Taiwan-based Foxconn Technology Group, which manufactures iPhones for Apple, has used factoring to provide $157 million in loans to its parts suppliers. Managing director Jack Lee explained why this is a good business risk for Foxconn, saying, "We know the suppliers' business status better than anyone because we are their customer."[11] According to the Commercial Finance Association, factoring has typically provided more than $216 billion in short-term funds on an annual basis to American businesses in recent years.[12]

Short-Term Bank Loans Banks are another common source of short-term business financing. Short-term bank loans are usually due in 30 to 90 days, though they can be up to a year in length. When a firm negotiates a loan with a bank, it signs a *promissory note*, which specifies the length of the loan, the rate of interest the firm must pay, and other terms and conditions of the loan. Banks sometimes require firms to pledge collateral, such as inventories or accounts receivable, to back the loan. That way, if the borrower fails to make the required payments, the bank has a claim on specific assets that can be used to pay off the amount due.

Rather than going through the hassle of negotiating a separate loan each time they need more funds, many firms work out arrangements with their bankers to obtain pre-approval so that they can draw on funds as needed. One way they do this is by establishing a **line of credit**. Under this arrangement, a bank agrees to provide the firm with funds up to some specified limit, as long as the borrower's credit situation doesn't deteriorate, and the bank has sufficient funds—conditions that aren't always met, as the recent financial meltdown clearly illustrated.

A **revolving credit agreement** is similar to a line of credit, except that the bank makes a formal, legally binding commitment to provide the agreed-upon funds. In essence, a revolving credit agreement is a *guaranteed* line of credit. In exchange for the binding commitment to provide the funds, the bank requires the borrowing firm to pay a commitment fee based on the *unused* amount of funds. Thus, under the terms of a revolving credit agreement, the firm will pay interest on any funds it borrows, and a commitment fee on any funds it does not borrow. The commitment fee is lower than the interest on the borrowed funds, but it can amount to a fairly hefty charge if the firm has a large unused balance. Because of the energy industry's well-known

goodluz/Shutterstock.com

Banks are a common source of short-term business financing. When a firm negotiates a loan with a bank, it signs a *promissory note*, which specifies the length of the loan, the rate of interest the firm must pay, and other terms and conditions of the loan.

boom and bust business cycles, oil and gas producers use funds from revolving credit agreements to pay expenses as they explore and develop energy reserves. They pay those funds down once production starts and revenues flow. In 2016, after oil prices dropped to $26 a barrel—one of the lowest prices in decades—many firms were unable to repay their revolving credit agreements. As a result, 51 US oil and gas producers filed for bankruptcy, while another 175 firms were at risk of not being able to repay their loans.[13]

Commercial Paper Well-established corporations have some additional sources of short-term financial capital. For instance, many large corporations with strong credit ratings issue **commercial paper**, which consists of short-term promissory notes (IOUs). Historically, commercial paper issued by corporations has been unsecured—meaning it isn't backed by a pledge of collateral. Because it is normally unsecured, commercial paper is only offered by firms with excellent credit ratings; firms with less than stellar financial reputations that try to issue unsecured commercial paper are

line of credit A financial arrangement between a firm and a bank in which the bank pre-approves credit up to a specified limit, provided that the firm maintains an acceptable credit rating.

revolving credit agreement A guaranteed line of credit in which a bank makes a binding commitment to provide a business with funds up to a specified credit limit at any time during the term of the agreement.

commercial paper Short-term (and usually unsecured) promissory notes issued by large corporations.

unlikely to find buyers. In recent years, a new class of commercial paper has emerged, called *asset-backed commercial paper*, which, as its name implies, is backed by some form of collateral.

Commercial paper can be issued for up to 270 days, but most firms typically issue it for much shorter periods—typically 30 days, but sometimes for as little as two days. One key reason commercial paper is popular with companies is that it typically carries a lower interest rate than commercial banks charge on short-term loans. By far the biggest issuers of commercial paper are financial institutions, but other large corporations also use this form of financing.

Why use commercial paper? According to the Consumerist, "The commercial paper market works like a credit card for big companies. Some days they have money, and some days they do not. So if they need money Tuesday, but will have money Friday, they'll go to the commercial paper market and borrow some money. Then on Friday they will pay back the money, plus interest."[14] According to the U.S. Federal Reserve, the average rate for 30-day commercial paper was 0.63% in February 2017.[15] That means a firm would pay $6,300 interest to use $1 million over 30 days. Commercial paper is sold at a discount, so the interest cost is deducted up front. In this instance, the firm would get $993,700 for 30 days, after which it would need to pay back $1,000,000 ($993,700 + $6,300 = $1,000,000). Commercial paper accounted for 6.4% of all short-term corporate cash assets in October 2016 down from 11% in 2013 and 8% in 2015.[16]

9-3b Sources of Long-Term Funds: Providing a Strong Financial Base

The sources of financial capital we've looked at so far have been appropriate for dealing with cash needs that arise from short-term fluctuations in cash flows. But financial managers typically seek more permanent funding to finance major investments and provide a secure financial base for their company. Let's take a look at some of the more common sources of long-term funds.

Direct Investments from Owners One key source of long-term funds for a firm is the money the owners themselves invest in their company. For corporations, this occurs when it sells *newly issued* stock—and it's important to realize that the *only* time the corporation receives financial capital from the sale of its stock is when it is initially issued. If Google issued new shares of stock, which you bought, the funds would go to Google. But once you own Google's stock, if you decide to sell your shares to another investor, Google gets nothing.

retained earnings The part of a firm's net income it reinvests.

Another way firms can meet long-term financial needs is by reinvesting their earnings. The profits that a firm reinvests are called **retained earnings**. This source isn't a pool of cash; it simply reflects the share of the firm's earnings used to finance the purchase of assets, pay off liabilities, and reinvest in the business. If you want to know how much cash a firm has, check the figure in the cash account at the top of its balance sheet. You'll typically find that the value in the firm's cash account is quite different from the amount listed as the retained earnings! For example, at the end of 2016, Google had 105.1 billion in retained earnings compared to $12.9 billion in cash and cash equivalents.[17]

Retained earnings are a major source of long-term capital for many corporations, but the extent to which they are used depends on the state of the economy. When the economy is booming and profits are high, retained earnings tend to soar. But when the economy slides into a recession, most corporations find they have few earnings to reinvest. For instance, in the recession year of 2008, corporate retained earnings fell to −$65.2 billion from $335.2 million in 2006 (negative retained earnings occur when the loss in any one year exceeds the accumulated retained earnings from previously profitable years). However, as the economic recovery ensued, retained earnings rebounded dramatically to a positive $879.3 billion in 2010. The most recent data showed that retained earnings were $706.9 billion in the third quarter of 2016.[18]

The decision to retain earnings involves a trade-off because firms have another way to use their earnings: they can pay out some or all of their profits to their owners by declaring a dividend. You might think that stockholders would be unhappy with a firm that retained most of its earnings, since that would mean they would receive a smaller dividend. But many stockholders actually prefer their companies to reinvest earnings—at least if management invests them wisely—because doing so can help finance their firm's growth. And a growing, more profitable firm usually translates into an increase in the market price of the firm's stock.

Billionaire Warren Buffett's company, Berkshire Hathaway, has never paid dividends, choosing to reinvest all of its substantial profits. This strategy paid off handsomely for stockholders. During the 12-year period between February 3, 2004, and February 2, 2017, Berkshire's stock soared from $90,800 to $244,330 per share.[19] Despite the fact that it paid them no dividend, you can bet that most of Berkshire's shareholders were pleased with the capital gains that resulted from this strategy!

Long-Term Debt In addition to contributions from owners, firms can also raise long-term funds by borrowing from banks and other lenders or by issuing bonds.

Term Loans There are many different types of long-term loans, but the most typical arrangement—sometimes simply called a *term loan*—calls for a regular schedule of fixed payments sufficient to ensure that the principal (the amount initially borrowed) and interest are repaid by the end of the loan's term.

Lenders often impose requirements on long-term loans to ensure repayment. Most lenders require that the loans be backed by a pledge of some type of collateral. Banks and other lenders also often include *covenants* in their loan agreements. A **covenant** is a requirement a lender imposes on the borrower as a condition of the loan. One common covenant requires the borrower to carry a specified amount of liability insurance. Another requires the borrower to agree not to borrow any *additional* funds until the current loan is paid off. Covenants sometimes even restrict the size of bonuses or pay raises the firm can grant to employees. The purpose of covenants is to protect creditors by preventing the borrower from pursuing policies that might undermine its ability to repay the loan. While covenants are great for lenders, borrowers often view them as highly restrictive.[20]

Corporate Bonds Rather than borrow from banks or other lenders, corporations sometimes issue their own formal IOUs, called *corporate bonds*, which they sell to investors. Bonds often have due dates (maturities) of ten or more years after issuance. Like corporate stock, bonds are marketable, meaning that bondholders can sell them to other investors before they mature. But it is important to realize that unlike shares of stock, which represent ownership in a corporation, bonds are certificates of debt.

9-4 LEVERAGE AND CAPITAL STRUCTURE: HOW MUCH DEBT IS TOO MUCH DEBT?

Most firms use a combination of **equity** and **debt financing** to acquire needed assets and to finance their operations. Owners provide equity financing, while creditors (lenders) provide debt financing. Thus, when a company issues and sells new stock or uses retained earnings to meet its financial needs, it is using equity financing. But when it takes out a bank loan, or issues and sells corporate bonds, it is relying on debt financing.

> " When you combine ignorance and leverage, you get some pretty interesting results."
> —WARREN BUFFETT

Both equity and debt financing have advantages and drawbacks. The extent to which a firm relies on various forms of debt and equity to satisfy its financing needs is called that firm's **capital structure**. To simplify our discussion, we'll focus mainly on the capital structure of corporations, but many of the basic principles apply to other forms of ownership.

9-4a Pros and Cons of Debt Financing

When a firm borrows funds, it enters into a contractual agreement with the lenders. This arrangement creates a *legally binding* requirement to repay the money borrowed (called the principal) *plus interest*. These payments take precedence over any payments to owners. Lenders often require the firm to pledge collateral, such as real estate, financial securities, or equipment, to back the loan. Should the firm be unable to make the required payments, the lenders can use this collateral to recover what they are owed. When Arch Coal, the second largest coal mining company in the United States, went bankrupt, shareholders were completely wiped out. According to the company, "Arch's existing stock will be canceled and the senior lenders will receive the substantial majority of the new stock in the reorganized Arch Coal." In other words, lenders' financial concerns took precedence over owners (that is, shareholders).[21]

Debt financing used to be less expensive because every dollar of interest payments made on debt was tax-deductible. Companies could raise needed funds and lower taxes. But because of U.S. corporate tax law changes in 2018, firms may now only deduct interest expenses up to 30% of earnings before interest, taxes, depreciation, and amortization (EBITDA). In addition, with the top corporate tax rate lowered to 21% from 39%, interest payment tax deductions are roughly half as valuable as before. Together, these changes make debt financing significantly more expensive.

Another advantage of debt was that firms acquired more funds without asking existing stockholders for more money or issuing new stock to new investors.

covenant A restriction lenders impose on borrowers as a condition of providing long-term debt financing.

equity financing Funds provided by the owners of a company.

debt financing Funds provided by lenders (creditors).

capital structure The mix of equity and debt financing a firm uses to meet its permanent financing needs.

In September 2016, Dell Inc., maker of computers, servers, and network technologies, completed a $60 billion acquisition of EMC Corporation, a manufacturer and provider of data storage technology and services. So how did Dell fund this enormous deal using cash, equity, and debt financing?

Dell Inc. didn't have $60 billion in cash. But together, Dell and EMC had somewhere between $12 billion and $21 billion in cash on their balance sheets. Dell Inc. and the resulting company, Dell Technologies, are private, so these are estimates. We do know, however, that founder and CEO Michael Dell and his personal investment partners contributed $4.25 billion in cash and that Dell Inc. and EMC began selling nonstrategic parts of their businesses hoping to raise $13 billion in cash.

What about equity financing? Because Dell was privately owned (with no stock), it couldn't swap Dell stock for EMC stock (EMC was publicly owned). Likewise, because Dell intended to remain private following the acquisition, it couldn't raise funds by selling new stock reflecting the value of the newly combined companies. With equity

financing not an option, Dell turned to debt financing (that is, bonds).

Bond investors were concerned about Dell's existing junk bonds. In 2013, Dell was publicly owned. To become privately owned, it sold $15 billion in junk bonds to help purchase the $24 billion in outstanding stock owned by all shareholders. Junk bonds, like credit cards, require a much higher interest payment because of a higher default risk. With $15 billion in existing junk bonds, investors wanted assurance that new Dell bonds would be a sound investment. Working with its bankers, Dell showed bond investors that the strong cash flows of the combined companies would easily pay the additional interest associated with new bonds. This permitted Dell to issue investment-grade bonds, which have significantly lower interest payments.

In summary, Dell's $60 billion acquisition of EMC was financed with roughly $20 billion in cash and $40 billion in debt financing. The new company, Dell Technologies, has 140,000 employees and estimated revenue of $74 billion a year.

Dell's interest payments on that $40 billion debt are approximately $2 billion a year, which, before 2018, were completely tax deductible. Under a 39% corporate tax, reducing taxable income by $2 billion was worth $780 million a year to Dell's bottom line.

But 2018 changes to U.S. corporate tax law limited interest payment deductions to 30% of earnings before interest, taxes, depreciation (EBITDA). This 30% limitation will cut Dell's interest deduction to an estimated $1.64 billion a year. With corporate tax rates reduced to 21% under the new law, the value of Dell's corporate interest deduction falls 56% to $344.4 million a year.

So, Dell is now exploring ways to go public via equity financing, which it would use to pay off a significant amount of its $40 billion in bonds.[22]

majestic b/Shutterstock.com

So, assuming proper investment of the borrowed funds, debt financing improved shareholders' return on equity by not diluting existing shares of stock. But, because of much higher costs stemming from changes in U.S. tax laws, debt financing is less likely to increase shareholders' return on equity. We'll further illustrate these issues in section 9-4c's discussion of using debt financing to leverage or magnify financial gains and losses.

One obvious disadvantage of debt is the requirement to make fixed payments. This can create real problems when the firm finds itself in an unexpectedly tight financial situation. In bad times, required interest payments can eat up

most (or all) of the earnings, leaving little or no return to the firm's owners. And if the firm is unable to meet these payments, its creditors can force it into bankruptcy.

As we mentioned earlier, another disadvantage of debt financing is that creditors often impose covenants on the borrower. These covenants can hamper the firm's flexibility and might result in unintended problems. For example, a covenant that restricts bonuses and pay raises to employees might undermine the morale of key workers and tempt them to seek employment elsewhere. Similarly, restrictions on dividends or on the ability of the firm to borrow additional funds may make it difficult for the firm to raise more money.

9-4b Pros and Cons of Equity Financing

For corporations, equity financing comes from two major sources: retained earnings and money directly invested by stockholders who purchase newly issued stock. Equity financing is more flexible and less risky than debt financing. Unlike debt, equity imposes no required payments. A firm can skip dividend payments to stockholders without having to worry that it will be pushed into bankruptcy. And a firm doesn't have to agree to burdensome covenants to acquire equity funds.

On the other hand, equity financing doesn't yield the same tax benefits as debt financing. In addition, existing owners might not want a firm to issue more stock, since doing so might dilute their share of ownership. Finally, a company that relies mainly on equity financing forgoes the opportunity to use financial leverage. But as we've already noted, leverage can be a two-edged sword. We'll illustrate the risks and rewards of leverage in our next section.

9-4c Financial Leverage: Using Debt to Magnify Gains (and Losses)

The discussion of financial ratios explained that firms using a lot of debt in their capital structure are highly leveraged. The main advantage of financial leverage is that it magnifies the return on the stockholders' investments. We'll illustrate how that works with two hypothetical companies, Eck-Witty and Oze-Moore, shown in Exhibit 9.4. The main disadvantage is that the cost of leverage or debt financing is now significantly higher because of changes to the 2018 U.S. corporate tax laws. We'll illustrate the real world consequences of those higher costs for First Data Corporation later in this section.

Exhibit 9.4 shows the revenues, expenses, and earnings that two firms—Eck-Witty Corporation and Oze-Moore International—would experience for two different levels of sales, one representing a strong year and the other a weak year. To make the impact of leverage easy to see, we'll assume that Eck-Witty and Oze-Moore are *identical* in all respects *except* their capital structure. In particular, our example assumes that the two companies have the same amount of assets and experienced exactly the same earnings before interest, taxes, depreciation and amortization (abbreviated as EBITDA). Thus, any differences in the net income of these firms results from differences in their use of debt and equity financing. We'll use return on equity (ROE) to measure the financial return each firm offers its stockholders. ROE is calculated by dividing after tax earnings by equity (funds supplied by owners).

Note that both firms have a total of $1 million in assets, but they've financed the purchase of their assets in very different ways. Eck-Witty used only common stock and retained earnings in its capital structure, so it has $1 million in equity financing and no debt. Oze-Moore's capital structure consists of $200,000 in owners' equity and $800,000 in debt, so it is highly leveraged. The interest rate on its debt is 10%, so Oze-Moore has to make required interest payments of $80,000 per year to its lenders. While the highest U.S. corporate tax rate is 21% as of 2018, we will use a 20% tax rate in Exhibit 9.4 to simplify the calculations.

As Exhibit 9.4 shows, debt financing significantly increases Oze-Moore's ROE compared to Eck-Witty's equity financing when sales are strong or weak. Why? Because Oze-Moore's interest payments are partially tax-deductible, its tax bill will be lower and its after tax income will be higher. Furthermore, those higher profits are based on a smaller amount of equity, $200,000 for Oze-Moore versus $1,000,000 for Eck-Witty, so Oze-Moore's ROE is naturally higher. Let's dig further into the specifics to see how this works.

When sales are strong, Oze-Moore's use of leverage results in a 68.8% ROE compared to Eck-Witty's 12.8%. Oze-Moore's interest payments are fixed. It pays its creditors $80,000 in interest—no more, no less—whether sales are strong or weak. With the interest deduction capped at 30% of EBITDA (earnings before interest, taxes, depreciation,

Exhibit 9.4
How Financial Leverage Affects the Return on Equity

Eck-Witty (Capital structure is all only equity)

Equity (Funds supplied by owners)		$1,000,000
Debt (Funds obtained by borrowing)		$0

	Strong Sales	Weak Sales
EBITDA	$160,000	$80,000
Deductible Debt Interest (Limited to 30% of EBITDA)	0.00	0.00
Taxable income	160,000	80,000
Taxes	32,000	16,000
After Tax Earnings	128,000	64,000
ROE	12.8%	6.8%

Oze-Moore (Capital structure is 20% equity and 80% debt)

Equity (Funds supplied by owners)		$200,000
Debt (Funds obtained by borrowing)		$800,000

	Strong Sales	Weak Sales
EBITDA	$160,000	$80,000
Deductible Debt Interest (Limited to 30% of EBITDA)	48,000	24,000
Taxable income	112,000	56,000
Taxes	22,400	11,200
After Tax Earnings	137,600	68,800
ROE	68.8%	34.4%

Saudi Arabia Invests $3.5 Billion toward Uber's Global Expansion

App-based ride sharing service Uber is in 460 cities in 69 countries. Every time it expands or enters a new market, Uber needs a considerable amount of cash to fund signing bonuses for new drivers (to give them time to build their businesses) and to woo first-time riders with sizable discounts.

ESB Professional/Shutterstock.com

Saudi Arabia's Public Investment Fund, a sovereign fund controlled by the Saudi government, invested $3.5 billion in Uber in 2016. Co-founder and former CEO Travis Kalanick said, "We appreciate the vote of confidence in our business as we continue to expand our global presence." Uber raises hundreds of millions of dollars several times a year to pay for its growing operations. Since its startup seven years ago, Uber has raised $11 billion from investors to fund its skyrocketing growth around the world.

As a result, Uber will invest $250 million to expand operations in Saudi Arabia to serve 15 cities in nine regions. By the end of 2016, Uber was already available in four more Saudi cities: Al-Qassim, Al-Kharj, Taif, and Al-Ahsa.[23]

---

and amortization), Oze-Moore can deduct $48,000 of its $80,000 of interest payments from earnings (30% of $160,000 in earnings is $48,000). This makes Oze-Moore's taxable income $112,000. By contrast, with no debt and no interest to deduct, Eck-Witty's taxable income is $160,000. In turn, Oze-Moore only pays $22,400 in taxes compared to $32,000 for Eck-Witty. That means that Oze-Moore's after-tax earnings are higher than Eck-Witty's, thanks to debt financing. Likewise, Oze-Moore's ROE of 68.8% ($137,600 in after tax earnings divided by $200,000 in equity) is much higher than Eck-Witty's ROE of 12.8% ($128,000 in after tax earnings divided by $1,000,000 in equity). So, compared to equity financing, debt financing leverages or magnifies financial gains.

This also happens when sales are weak. But, because of weaker sales, Oze-Moore can only deduct $24,000 of its $80,000 of interest payments from earnings (30% of $80,000 in earnings is $24,000). This makes Oze-Moore's taxable income $56,000. By contrast, with no debt and no interest to deduct, Eck-Witty's taxable income is $80,000. In turn, Oze-Moore only pays $11,200 in taxes compared to $16,000 for Eck-Witty. That again means that Oze-Moore's after-tax earnings are higher than Eck-Witty's, thanks to debt financing. Likewise, Oze-Moore's ROE of 34.4% ($68,800 in after tax earnings divided by $200,000 in equity) is much higher than Eck-Witty's ROE of 6.4% ($64,000 in after tax earnings divided by $1,000,000 in equity). So,

> ## "Debt is one person's liability, but another person's asset."
> — NOBEL PRIZE–WINNING ECONOMIST PAUL KRUGMAN

even when sales are weak, debt financing magnifies financial gains.

But what Exhibit 9.4's comparison of debt versus equity financing doesn't show is that debt financing has become significantly more expensive for highly leveraged firms under the 2018 tax laws. For example, First Data Corporation has $18.5 billion in debt, for which it pays $964 million in annual interest. Under prior tax law, it could deduct 100% of that interest, thus lowering its tax bill and increasing its after tax income. But with annual earnings of $2.7 billion, First Data can now only deduct $810 million of debt interest (30% of its $2.7 billion in annual earnings). As a result, First Data Corporation's taxes are now $154 million higher. Which is another way of saying that debt financing now costs First Data Corporation $154 million more a year under the new tax law. This shows how the cost of leveraging financial gains via debt financing is significantly more expensive than it used to be. For more on this issue, see Psst, Can you Lend Me $40 Billion—Cheap—for a Great Deal?

History offers another real world lesson about debt financing. Debt leverage not only magnifies financial gains, it magnifies financial losses! During the economic boom between 2003 and 2007, many companies used debt leverage to magnify their ROEs. When the economy slowed, the required interest and principal payments on their debt became a heavy burden. Many of those highly leveraged firms ended up in bankruptcy.

By late 2008, the highly leveraged firms that survived looked for ways to replace debt with equity—a strategy known as deleveraging. But most companies found deleveraging to be slow and painful. Poor financial performance during the financial meltdown meant earnings were low (or even negative), so they couldn't use retained earnings to build their equity capital. And the plummeting stock market and lack of investor confidence made it difficult to sell new stock. The moral of the story: if the financial returns of leverage seem too good to be true, over the long run they probably are. Sound financial management requires keeping a level head and balancing the risk and return of financial decisions.[24]

In the wake of the financial crisis, the federal government enacted the 2010 **Dodd-Frank Act**, which required large financial firms to hold more equity and less debt. The 2018 changes to U.S. corporate tax laws will also encourage less debt financing and more equity financing. Limiting deductions on debt-based interest payments to no more than 30% of EBITDA makes debt financing significantly more expensive than before and will likely reduce corporate profits. Likewise, reducing the corporate tax rate from 39% to 21% will significantly boost companies' retained earnings, leading to much greater use of this form of equity financing.[25]

9-5 ACQUIRING AND MANAGING CURRENT ASSETS

Let's turn our attention to how a firm determines the amount and type of current assets to hold. As we'll see, holding current assets involves trade-off; either too much or too little of these assets can spell trouble.

9-5a Managing Cash: Is It Possible to Have Too Much Money?

A company must have cash to pay its workers, suppliers, creditors, and taxes. Many firms also need cash to pay dividends. And most firms also want to hold enough cash

A U.S. Treasury bill's Treasury yield is its return on investment expressed as a percentage. In April 2017, the Treasury yield on a 10-year T-bill was 2.26%.

larry1235/Shutterstock.com

to meet unexpected contingencies. But cash has one serious shortcoming compared to other assets: it earns little or no return. If a firm holds much more cash than needed to meet its required payments, stockholders are likely to ask why the excess cash isn't being invested in more profitable assets. And if the firm can't find a profitable way to invest the money, the stockholders are likely to ask management why it doesn't use the excess cash to pay them a higher dividend—most shareholders can think of plenty of ways *they'd* like to use the cash!

In the narrowest sense, a firm's cash refers to its holdings of currency (paper money and coins issued by the government) plus demand deposits (the balance in its checking account). However, when most firms report their cash holdings on their balance sheet, they take a broader view, including **cash equivalents** along with their actual cash. Cash equivalents are very safe and highly liquid assets that can be converted into cash quickly and easily. Commercial paper, U.S. Treasury Bills (T-bills), and money market mutual funds are among the most popular cash equivalents. The advantage of these cash equivalents is that they offer a better financial return (in the form of interest) than currency or demand deposits.

As we explained in our discussion of short-term sources of funds, major

> "The Dodd-Frank Act was 2,319 pages in length. Apparently there was a lot about our financial system in 2010 that Congress wanted to change!"
>
> —DAVID SKEEL, IN *THE NEW FINANCIAL DEAL*

Dodd-Frank Act A law enacted in the aftermath of the financial crisis of 2008–2009 that strengthened government oversight of financial markets and placed limitations on risky financial strategies such as heavy reliance on leverage.

cash equivalents Safe and highly liquid assets that many firms list with their cash holdings on their balance sheet.

Stock Dividends: Don't Start—Because You Can't Stop

Financial managers have a fiduciary duty to act in the best interest of company ownership by increasing the value of the firm. In publicly-owned firms, financial managers accomplish that by increasing the firm's stock price in three ways.

First, earn higher profits. The stock of a company with consistently high profits is more valuable than the stock of a consistently less-profitable firm.

Second, buy back existing shares of publicly held (that is, outstanding) company stock. With fewer shares outstanding, earnings per share (EPS) will rise. Since EPS is a key metric in valuing stock performance, a rising EPS frequently leads to higher stock prices.

With corporate profits falling since 2014 and stock indices at all-time highs (making stock buybacks more expensive), companies are increasingly using a third method: paying cash dividends, that is, a portion of annual profits, directly to shareholders.

Young and struggling companies often don't pay dividends, choosing instead to invest profits (that is, retained earnings) back into the company to fund growth, develop new products, or increase quality. Once firms start paying dividends, there's a strong expectation that they won't stop. Simply put, investors see dividends as a long-term promise to share profits with shareholders. According to Howard Silverblatt at S&P Dow Jones Indices, "[Stock] buybacks can be turned on and off via the phone. [But once] you increase a dividend you have to keep paying the higher rate."

So, even though its EPS dropped 76% from 2015 to 2016, Caterpillar, which manufactures large earth-moving equipment, declared a $3.08 per share dividend in 2016, compared to $3.01 in 2015. A company spokesperson said, "Caterpillar has paid a cash dividend every year since the company was formed and has paid a quarterly dividend since 1933." Moreover, "Caterpillar has paid higher dividends to its shareholders for 23 consecutive years . . . ," including 2016.[26]

---

corporations with strong credit ratings often *sell* commercial paper to raise needed short-term funds. On the other side of such transactions are firms that *buy* commercial paper as part of their portfolio of cash equivalents because—at least under normal economic conditions—it is a safe and liquid way to earn some interest. But during economic downturns the appeal of commercial paper as a cash equivalent plummets due to increased risk.

U.S. Treasury Bills, or "T-bills," are short-term IOUs issued by the U.S. government. Most T-bills mature (come due) in 4, 13, or 26 weeks. There is a very active secondary market for T-bills, meaning that their owners can sell them to other investors before they mature. Thus, T-bills are highly liquid. And, unlike commercial paper, T-bills are backed by the U.S. government, so they are essentially risk-free. The safety and liquidity of T-bills make them very attractive cash equivalents even in times of economic distress.

Money market mutual funds raise money by selling shares to large numbers of investors. They then pool these funds to purchase a portfolio of short-term, liquid securities. (In fact, money market mutual funds often include

large holdings of commercial paper and T-bills.) Money market mutual funds are an affordable way for small investors to get into the market for securities, which would otherwise be beyond their means. This affordability also makes these funds a particularly attractive cash equivalent for smaller firms.

9-5b Managing Accounts Receivable: Pay Me Now or Pay Me Later

Accounts receivable represents what customers who buy on credit owe the firm. Allowing customers to buy on credit can significantly increase sales. However, as our discussion of the cash budget showed, credit sales can create cash flow problems because they delay the receipt of cash the firm needs to meet its financial obligations. Customers who pay late or don't pay at all only exacerbate the problem. So it's important for firms to have a well-thought-out policy that balances the advantages of offering credit with the costs. The key elements of this policy should include:

- Setting credit terms: For how long should the firm extend credit? What type of cash discount should the firm offer to encourage early payments?

- Establishing credit standards: How should the firm decide which customers qualify for credit? What type of credit information should it require? How strict should its standards be?

U.S. Treasury bills (T-bills) Short-term marketable IOUs issued by the U.S. federal government.

money market mutual funds A mutual fund that pools funds from many investors and uses these funds to purchase very safe, highly liquid securities.

- Deciding on an appropriate collection policy: How aggressive should the firm be at collecting past-due accounts? At what point does it make sense to take (or at least threaten to take) legal action against late-paying customers, or to turn over the accounts to collection agencies? When does it make sense to work out compromises?

In each area, financial managers face trade-offs. For example, a firm that extends credit for only 30 days will receive its payments sooner than a firm that allows customers 90 days. But setting short credit periods may also result in lost sales. Similarly, setting high credit standards reduces the likelihood a firm will have problems with customers who pay late (or not at all). However, strict standards may prevent many good customers from getting credit, resulting in lower sales. Finally, an aggressive collection policy may help the firm collect payments that it would otherwise lose. But an aggressive policy is costly, and it might alienate customers who make honest mistakes, causing them to take future business to competitors.

Some small businesses have found that being flexible and creative about the form of payment can help them get at least some of what they are owed. Barter arrangements sometimes work better than demanding cash—especially in troubled times such as the recent recession. At Molasses Books, a used book store in Brooklyn,

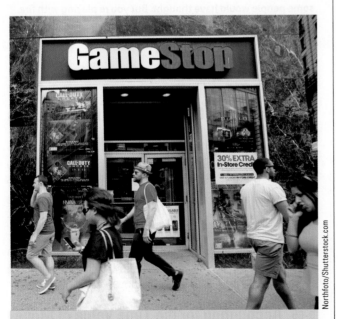

In 2016, GameStop invested $160 million in refurbishing and expanding 6,900 retail locations such as this New York City store.

New York, customers sometimes pay for books with coffee, wine, or beer. When asked how many books someone can buy with alcohol, employee Dave Morse said, "Depends how cheap the beer!"[27]

9-5c Managing Inventories: Taking Stock of the Situation

Inventories are stocks of finished goods, work-in-process, parts, and materials that firms hold as a part of doing business. Clearly, businesses must hold inventories to operate. For example, you'd probably be disappointed if you visited a Best Buy store and were confronted with empty shelves rather than with a wide array of electronic gadgets to compare and try out. Similarly, a manufacturing firm wouldn't be able to assemble its products without an inventory of parts and materials.

But for many firms, the costs of storing, handling, and insuring inventory items are significant expenses. In recent years, many manufacturing firms have become very aggressive about keeping inventories as low as possible in an attempt to reduce costs and improve efficiency. Such "lean" inventory policies can be very effective, but they leave the firm vulnerable to supply disruptions. Toyota had to shut down all of its Japanese auto assembly lines for six days in February 2016 after an explosion at Aichi Steel shut down production, depriving Toyota's factories of the steel needed to make key auto parts. If Toyota held larger inventories, it might have been able to continue operating its assembly lines until Aichi Steel resumed shipments.[28]

 9-6 ## CAPITAL BUDGETING: IN IT FOR THE LONG HAUL

We'll conclude the chapter with a look at how firms evaluate proposals to invest in long-term assets or undertake major new projects. **Capital budgeting** refers to the procedure a firm uses to plan for investments in assets or projects that it expects will yield benefits for more than a year. GameStop, an online and brick-and-mortar retailer of video games, pop culture collectibles, and consumer electronics, made $160 million in capital investments in 2016, to refurbish and expand its 6,900 stores across 14 countries.[29] The capital budgeting process evaluates proposals such as:

> **capital budgeting** The process a firm uses to evaluate long-term investment proposals.

- Replacing old machinery and equipment

The Alternative Universe of Negative Interest Rates

Banking is simple. Put money for living expenses in a checking account. Put the rest in a savings account so it can earn interest from the bank. Pay the bank interest when taking out loans.

But under negative interest rates, banking gets turned upside down. With negative rates, you pay the bank interest on your savings. Heike Hofmann, who runs a fruit and vegetable stand in Korschenbroich, Germany, considered it "madness" when negative rates *made her savings shrink* each month rather than grow. She said, "Every time I check my savings account, It makes me want to cry." Under negative interest rates, *the bank pays you interest when you borrow!* Hans Christensen of Aalborg, Denmark has a negative 0.0562% interest rate on his mortgage. So instead of paying interest each month, the bank pays him approximately 83 Kroner ($38).

To understand why negative interest rates exist, we have to distinguish between commercial banks (where consumers and businesses bank) and central banks run by governments. Commercial banks have accounts with central banks so they can borrow money or make deposits at rates determined by the central banks. When an economy is growing slowly, central banks lower the interest rates they charge commercial banks. Commercial banks then lower interest rates for consumer and business loans. At lower rates, more money is borrowed and then spent, hopefully growing the economy.

Central banks use negative interest rates when economies are not growing, or even worse, are shrinking. In these circumstances, think of negative interest rates as lower interest rates on steroids. Steroids, while bad for your health, amplify muscle growth and strength gains. Similarly, negative interest rates are supposed to amplify economic growth by shrinking savings and rewarding borrowing, both of which should encourage spending.

Do negative rates work? Or, like steroids, are there harmful side effects? US Federal Reserve Chair Janet Yellen says, "I would judge they seem to have mixed effects." But Lars Rhode, Governor of the Danish Central Bank (which has used negative rates since 2012), says, "There's no sharp, disruptive movement when you pass below zero. It's just working like very low interest rates." Still, in some countries, people are saving more even as their savings shrink. And mortgage loans, which pay borrowers, are fueling surges in house prices.

In the end, says Erik Nielsen, chief economist at Danish bank UniCredit, negative interest rates are "not the catastrophe that some people would have thought. But you're playing with fire."[30]

with new models to reduce cost and improve the efficiency of current operations

- Buying additional plant, machinery, and equipment to expand production capacity in *existing* markets

- Investing in plant, property, and equipment needed to expand into *new* markets

- Installing new, or modifying existing, plant and equipment to achieve goals not directly related to expanding production, such as reducing pollution or improving worker safety

The number of capital budgeting proposals a firm considers each year can be quite large. But it's unlikely that all proposals will be worth pursuing. How do financial managers decide whether or not to accept a proposal?

9-6a Evaluating Capital Budgeting Proposals

Financial managers measure the benefits and costs of long-term investment proposals in terms of the cash flows they generate. These cash flows are likely to be negative at the start of a project because money must be spent to get a long-term investment project up and running before it begins generating positive cash flows. But a project must eventually generate enough positive cash flows to more than offset these negative initial cash outflows if it is to benefit the company.

9-6b Accounting for the Time Value of Money

One of the most challenging aspects of the evaluation of a long-term project's cash flows is that they are spread out over a number of years. When financial

Exhibit 9.5

How a Present Value of $10,000 Grows to a Future Value of $11,255.09 in Four Years

Now
- Deposit $10,000.00 (present value)
- Earn 3% per year

After 1 year you have
- $10,000 + $300 interest earned over first year (3% of 10,000) =
- $10,300.00

After 2 years you have
- $10,300.00 + $309 interest earned over second year (3% of $10,300) =
- $10,609.00

After 3 years you have
- $10,609.00 + $318.27 interest earned over third year (3% of $10,609) =
- $10,927.27

After 4 years you have
- $10,927.27 + $327.82 interest earned over fourth year (3% of $10,927.27) =
- $11,255.09 (future value)

but also on *when* it is received. Financial managers compare cash flows occurring at different times by converting them to their present values. The **present value** of a cash flow received in a future time period is the amount of money that, if invested *today* at an assumed rate of interest (called the *discount rate*), would grow to become that future amount of money. Exhibit 9.5 shows that $10,000 invested today at 3% grows to a future value of $11,255.09 in four years. Thus, $10,000 is the present value of $11,255.09 received in four years.

managers compare cash flows that occur at different times, they must take the **time value of money** into account. The time value of money reflects the fact that, from a financial manager's perspective, a dollar received today is worth *more* than a dollar received in the future because the sooner you receive a sum of money, the sooner you can put that money to work to earn even *more* money.

Suppose, for example, that you were given the choice of receiving $1,000 either today or the same amount one year from today. If you think like a financial manager, this choice is a no-brainer! Let's be conservative and say that if you receive the money today you can deposit it in an insured one-year **certificate of deposit (CD)** at your local bank that pays 4% interest. (A CD is similar to a savings account, except that it requires the funds to remain on deposit for a fixed term; in our example, the term is one year. You would incur a penalty if you withdrew your funds early.) Investing in your 4% CD means that a year from today you would have $1,040 (the $1,000 you deposited plus $40 in interest). But if you wait until next year to receive the $1,000, you'll lose the opportunity to earn that $40 in interest. Clearly, receiving the cash today is the better option.

Because money has a time value, a cash flow's value depends not only on the *amount* of cash received

9-6c The Risk-Return Trade-Off Revisited

Unfortunately, financial managers don't have crystal balls, so they don't know the *actual* cash flows a proposed project will generate. Instead, they base their analysis on the cash flows the proposal is *expected* to generate. Once a company actually invests in a project, it may find that the *actual* cash flows are quite different from these estimated flows. This uncertainty means that capital budgeting decisions must consider risk.

In general, projects with the potential for high returns are also the projects with a high degree of uncertainty and risk. This is another example of the risk-return trade-off we introduced at the beginning of this chapter. Clearly, financial managers must take this trade-off into account when they compare different capital budgeting proposals; they must determine whether riskier

time value of money The principle that a dollar received today is worth more than a dollar received in the future.

certificate of deposit (CD) An interest-earning deposit that requires the funds to remain deposited for a fixed term. Withdrawal of the funds before the term expires results in a financial penalty.

present value The amount of money that, if invested today at a given rate of interest (called the discount rate), would grow to become some future amount in a specified number of time periods.

EXHIBIT 9.6 | DECISION RULE FOR CAPITAL BUDGETING

Result of NPV Calculation	Decision
NPV ≥ 0	Accept proposal ✔
NPV < 0	Reject proposal ✗

proposals generate a high enough expected return to justify their greater risk.

One common way financial managers try to do this is to use a higher discount rate when they compute the present values of cash flows for risky projects than when they compute present values for less risky projects. This reflects the idea that a higher return is required to compensate for the greater risk.

net present value (NPV) The sum of the present values of expected future cash flows from an investment, minus the cost of that investment.

9-6d Net Present Value: A Decision Rule for Capital Budgeting

The most common method financial managers use to evaluate capital budgeting proposals is to compute their **net present value (NPV)**. The NPV of an investment proposal is found by adding the present values of *all* of its estimated future cash flows and subtracting the initial cost of the investment from the sum. A positive NPV means that the present value of the expected cash flows from the project is greater than the cost of the project. In other words, the benefits from the project exceed its cost even after accounting for the time value of money. Financial managers approve projects with positive NPVs. A negative NPV means that the present value of the expected future cash flows from the project is less than the cost of the investment. This would indicate that the cost of the project outweighs its cash flow benefits. Financial managers would reject proposals with negative NPVs. (See Exhibit 9.6.)

THE BIG PICTURE

In this chapter, we described the tasks financial managers perform as they attempt to find the "best" sources and uses of financial resources—meaning those that will maximize the value of the firm to its owners. We saw that in their attempts to achieve this goal, financial managers face two challenges. The first is to balance the needs of owners against those of the other stakeholders; the second is to balance the potential rewards of their decisions against the risks.

Recent history illustrates how important sound financial management is to the success of a firm—and how devastating poor financial decisions can be. Indeed, the recent decline and fall of some of the biggest and best-known U.S. corporations can be traced in large measure to poor financial decisions—especially decisions that failed to adequately take risk into account, resulting in the use of too much leverage.

These lessons from the recent past will probably result in a different approach to financial management over the next several years. While memories of the Great Recession are still relatively fresh, firms may be more conservative in their view of what constitutes the best sources and uses of funds. In particular, they are likely to shy away from excessive debt and put more emphasis on equity financing. They also are less likely to use their funds to invest in highly risky or speculative assets. These more conservative tendencies are likely to be reinforced by the major regulatory reforms, designed to curb aggressive (and risky) behavior, introduced by the Dodd-Frank Act.

CAREERS IN FINANCE

Financial Analyst

Responsible for financial planning; preparing complex financial analyses and recommendations; establishing and maintaining internal financial controls; creating and analyzing monthly, quarterly, and annual reports; and ensuring financial information has been recorded accurately, working closely with business unit leaders to align company and financial goals, and performing Sarbanes-Oxley assessments and testing. The ideal candidate has a bachelor's or master's degree in finance, expert spreadsheet and analytical skills, strong oral and written communication skills, strong understanding of financial analysis and reporting, and effective time and project management skills including the ability to simultaneously manage multiple projects and priorities as well as to work under pressure to meet deadlines.

STUDY TOOLS 9

LOCATED AT BACK OF THE TEXTBOOK

☐ Rip-Out Chapter Review Card

☐ Gain unique perspectives on key concepts with new concept videos in the e-book

☐ Increase your comprehension with online homework and quizzes

☐ Study with existing flashcards and make your own

10 | Financial Markets:
Allocating Financial Resources

Remember to visit
PAGE 189
for additional
STUDY TOOLS

LEARNING OBJECTIVES

After studying this chapter, you will be able to:

10-1 Explain the role of financial markets in the U.S. economy, and identify the key players in these markets

10-2 Identify the key laws that govern the way financial markets operate, and explain the impact of each law

10-3 Describe and compare the major types of securities that are traded in securities markets

10-4 Explain how securities are issued in the primary market and traded on secondary markets

10-5 Compare several strategies that investors use to invest in securities

10-6 Interpret the information provided in the stock quotes available on financial websites

10-1 THE ROLE OF FINANCIAL MARKETS AND THEIR KEY PLAYERS

Financial markets perform a vital function: they transfer funds from savers (individuals and organizations willing to defer using some of their income to earn a financial return and build their wealth) to borrowers (individuals and organizations that need additional funds to achieve their financial goals). Without these markets, companies would find it difficult to obtain the financial resources needed to meet payrolls, invest in new facilities, develop new products, and compete effectively in global markets.

But it's not just businesses that benefit from these markets. You do, too, through your involvement in both sides of financial markets. You participate as a borrower when using your credit card to finance daily purchases or when taking out a loan for college tuition. You also participate as a saver. San Francisco–based marketing manager Jenn Chen uses Digit, a financial app that analyzes income and spending patterns, to automatically deduct savings from her checking account each month. When she has extra money or fewer expenses, Digit saves more. When her budget is tight, it saves less. Digit CEO Ethan Bloch says, "Digit tries to find the perfect amount you should save, money that you don't need to spend and that you won't feel you're missing."[1] Chen says, "Digit saves more at certain times and less at others. I kind of let it do its thing, knowing it's just running in the background."[2] Savers

> **financial markets** Markets that transfer funds from savers to borrowers.

like Jenn Chen participate in financial markets when using their savings to accumulate a down payment on a house or to invest in stocks and bonds to build a nest egg for retirement.

In the United States and other well-developed market economies, the vast majority of financing occurs indirectly, with *financial intermediaries* coming between the ultimate savers and borrowers. We'll see that they perform a variety of functions, but what they all have in common is that they help channel funds from savers to borrowers.

10-1a Depository Institutions

Depository institutions are financial intermediaries that obtain funds by accepting checking and savings deposits from individuals, businesses, and other institutions, and then lending those funds to borrowers.

■ Commercial banks are the most common depository institutions. When you make a deposit into a checking or savings account at your bank, you are providing funds that the bank can use for making loans to businesses, governments, or other individuals.

At the end of 2017, over half (57%) of total bank assets were in the form of loans, including over

"Sometimes your best investments are the ones you don't make."

—DONALD TRUMP

$5.1 trillion in real estate and mortgage loans, more than $1.8 trillion in consumer loans.[3]

■ **Credit unions** are cooperatives, meaning that they are not-for-profit organizations that are owned by their depositors. As not-for-profit organizations, they strive to pay higher interest rates on member deposits and charge lower interest rates on loans.

Credit unions are open to individuals who belong to a specific "field of membership." For example, membership in some credit unions is limited to the employees who work for a specific employer and their family members; other credit unions

> **depository institution** A financial intermediary that obtains funds by accepting checking and savings deposits and then lending those funds to borrowers.

> **credit union** A depository institution that is organized as a cooperative, meaning that it is owned by its depositors.

CHAPTER 10: Financial Markets: Allocating Financial Resources   171

Snap Up Snap's IPO Stock? Read the S-1 Registration First!

If you find social media app Snapchat confusing, you're not alone. The *Wall Street Journal's* Joanna Stern recently wrote, "Attention everyone born before 1986: It's not you, it's Snapchat." Snapchat has three components. Snaps are photos and 10-second videos that auto-delete after being viewed by the friends they're sent to. Stories are compiled photo sets or videos broadcast to everyone on Snapchat. Chats are one-to-one texts that auto-delete when you exit Snapchat or go elsewhere in the app. Snapchat is where all the cool kids are—cool as in the highly desired 18-to 34-year-old market segment whose work, play, and social activities revolve around their smartphones.

Snap Inc. which makes Snapchat, filed an S-1 Registration Statement with the U.S. Security and Exchange Commission in February 2017 for its initial public offering (IPO) of stock (see Exhibit 10.3). Snap hopes to raise $25 billion. Should investors snap up Snap's IPO stock as an investment? Fortunately, there's much to be learned about Snap's business by reading the S-1.

Christopher Penler/Shutterstock.com

Why Snap is a good investment . . .

- From 2015 to 2016, revenues grew by a factor of 6.9 (from $58.7 million to $404.5 million), while losses grew by a factor of 1.38 (from $372.9 million to $514.6 million).

- In the last two years, average daily revenue per user more than tripled, from $0.31 to $1.05, while the user base grew 48%, from 107 million to 158 million.

- Snap generates 90% of advertising sales from its sales force (a good thing), and it is transitioning to automated ad-buying systems (even better) similar to those used by Google and Facebook.

Why Snap is a risky investment . . .

- Users younger than age 25 use Snapchat 20 times a day for 30 minutes, while users older than age 25 use it 12 times a day for 20 minutes. So can Snapchat grow among older users, like Facebook? Being confusing and hard to learn won't help.

- Other potential threats include fickle user loyalty, the need to obtain U.S. Food and Drug Administration approval for its Spectacles (eyeglasses with video/audio recording capability), Facebook adding Snapchat-type features to its Instagram app, and not knowing whether the Chinese government would allow Snapchat to enter the Chinese market.

Snapchat users clearly value the privacy of having their videos, photographs, and chats auto-delete, never to be seen again. On the other hand, investors buying stock in Snap's IPO wouldn't be happy if the same thing happened to Snap's stock price.[4]

---

base membership on church or union affiliation or are open to people living in a certain geographic area.[5]

Credit unions are a much smaller player in financial markets than commercial banks, but in 2017 they held more than $428 billion in mortgage financing and $374 billion in consumer credit on their books.[6]

- **Savings and loan associations** (also called "S&Ls" or "thrifts") traditionally accepted only savings account deposits and used them to make mortgage loans. During the early 1980s, regulations on S&Ls were relaxed, allowing them to accept checking account deposits and make a broader range of loans. Still, the major focus of the savings and loan industry remains mortgage loans.

  - At the end of 2013 (the last year the Federal Reserve collected these data), S&Ls held $452 billion in mortgages—a big drop from 2006 when the figure peaked at $1.25 trillion.[7] In large part, this reflected the collapse of the housing market at the end of the past decade. But S&Ls began declining in importance well before the Great Recession.[8]

10-1b Nondepository Financial Institutions

In addition to banks and other depository institutions, a number of other financial intermediaries play important roles in financial markets.

savings and loan association A depository institution that has traditionally obtained most of its funds by accepting savings deposits, which have been used primarily to make mortgage loans.

- **Institutional investors** don't accept deposits but amass huge pools of financial capital from other sources and use these funds to acquire a portfolio of many different assets. Mutual funds obtain money by selling shares to investors; insurance companies obtain money by collecting premiums from policyholders; and pension funds obtain money by collecting funds employers and their employees contribute for the employees' retirement. These institutions invest heavily in corporate stock; institutional investors hold the majority of shares in most major U.S. corporations. They are also major holders of corporate bonds and government securities. Exhibit 10.1 lists the world's largest institutional investors, with New York-based BlackRock and Pennsylvania-based Vanguard Group topping the list with $2.98 and $1.97 trillion in holdings respectively.

- **Securities brokers** act as agents for investors who want to buy or sell financial securities, such as corporate stocks or bonds. In addition to handling the trades, many brokers provide their clients with additional services, such as financial planning and market research. Brokers are compensated by charging fees and commissions for the services they provide.

- **Securities dealers** participate directly in securities markets, buying and selling stocks and bonds for their own account. They earn a profit by selling securities for higher prices than they paid to purchase them. (The difference between the prices at which they buy and sell a security is called the *spread*.)

- **Investment banks** are financial intermediaries that help firms issue new securities to raise financial capital. Sometimes investment banks actually buy the newly issued securities themselves; in other cases, they simply help arrange for their sale. Today's investment banks aren't actually independent companies. Instead, they are typically divisions of huge bank holding companies that also own commercial banks.

10-2 REGULATING FINANCIAL MARKETS TO PROTECT INVESTORS AND IMPROVE STABILITY

Financial markets work well only when savers and borrowers have confidence in the soundness of key financial institutions and in the fairness of the market outcomes. When depositors lose confidence in their banks, or when

EXHIBIT 10.1 WORLD'S LARGEST INSTITUTIONAL INVESTORS

Institutional Investors	Headquarters Location	Financial Holdings (in U.S. millions)
BlackRock	New York, New York, USA	$2,984,720
Vanguard Group	Valley Forge, Pennsylvania, USA	$1,969,825
State Street Global Advisors	Boston, Massachusetts, USA	$1,812,627
BNY Mellon	New York, New York, USA	$1,404,170
Legal & General Investment	London, England, United Kingdom	$1,072,614
Fidelity Investments	Boston, Massachusetts, USA	$1,040,425
J.P. Morgan Asset Management	New York, New York, USA	$927,266
Wellington Management	Boston, Massachusetts, USA	$926,217
Prudential Financial	Newark, New Jersey, USA	$876,508
PIMCO	Newport Beach, California, USA	$760,245

Source: Y. Du, "Money managers by the Numbers," *Pensions & Investments*, May 30, 2016, http://www.pionline.com/article/20160530/INTERACTIVE/160529900/money-managers-by-the-numbers/F, accessed February 8, 2017.

investors discover that financial markets are rigged by practices such as insider trading or unethical and deceptive accounting, the financial system breaks down.

The financial crisis of 2008 is only the latest example of the disruptions that result when financial markets malfunction. From the early twentieth century to the present day, the U.S. economy has experienced several other major financial crises. The economy experienced massive bank failures in 1907 and in the early 1930s. It also weathered a savings and loan crisis in the late 1980s that brought the failure of over 1,000 S&Ls and required a federal bailout that cost over $120 billion.[9] And a variety of scandals involving ethical lapses (and in many cases outright fraud) roiled financial markets at the turn of the century.

securities broker A financial intermediary who acts as an agent for investors who want to buy and sell financial securities. Brokers earn commissions and fees for the services they provide.

securities dealer A financial intermediary who participates directly in securities markets, buying and selling stocks and other securities for its own account.

investment bank A financial intermediary that specializes in helping firms raise financial capital by issuing securities in primary markets.

10-2a Financial Regulation: Early Efforts

During most of the twentieth century, the federal government responded to financial upheavals by introducing new laws and regulations. This trend first emerged in the wake of the banking panic of 1907, which created pressure for Congress to find a way to stabilize the nation's banking system. The result was the **Federal Reserve Act of 1913**. As its name implies, this act created the Federal Reserve System (the Fed) to serve as the central bank in the United States. The law gave the Fed the primary responsibility for overseeing our nation's banking system.

Unfortunately, the creation of the Fed didn't solve all of the nation's banking problems. Another wave of bank failures occurred in the early 1930s as the economy sank into the Great Depression. Congress responded by passing the **Banking Act of 1933**, also known as the *Glass-Steagall Act*. This law established the Federal Deposit Insurance Corporation, which insured depositors against financial losses when a bank failed. The insurance initially covered only $2,500 of deposits—but $2,500 bought a lot more in the 1930s than it does today! Over the years, coverage has been increased several times. Today, the FDIC insures up to $250,000 in deposits.[10]

Another major provision of the Glass-Steagall Act banned commercial banks from dealing in securities markets, selling insurance, or otherwise competing with nondepository institutions such as insurance companies and investment banks. The rationale for these restrictions was

Federal Reserve Act of 1913 The law that established the Federal Reserve System as the central bank of the United States.

Banking Act of 1933 The law that established the Federal Deposit Insurance Corporation (FDIC) to insure bank deposits. It also prohibited commercial banks from selling insurance or acting as investment banks.

China's Skyscraper Curse

The basic function of financial markets is to transfer funds from savers, who invest to earn financial returns, to borrowers, who need funds to achieve financial goals. Toward the end of economic expansions (which typically last 6–7 years), however, savers and borrowers often become overly optimistic. When that happens, savers increasingly put funds into riskier investments, and borrowers, overconfident in themselves and their plans, borrow too much!

According to investment banker Andrew Lawrence, booms in skyscraper construction often occur at the ends of economic expansions or the starts of economic crashes. For example, planning for the Empire State Building coincided with the start of the Great Depression in 1929. In 1996, completion of the Petronas Towers in Malaysia preceded the 1997 Asian financial crisis. Dubai's Burj Khalifa, started in 2004 and completed in 2009, coincided with the end of an economic expansion and the start of the Great Recession in 2008. This *skyscraper curse* is ostensibly a sign of over-investing and over-borrowing.

Three of the six tallest buildings completed since 2014 are located in China, as are 12 of the 26 tallest buildings now under construction. With economic growth slowing (according to the Keqiang index, China's GDP grew 2.38% in 2015—not 6.9% as claimed by the Chinese government); an estimated 60% of Chinese bank loans used for buildings and real estate development; Chinese debt levels quadrupling to $28 trillion since 2007, far outpacing economic growth (Chinese debts are now 282% of GDP); a 20% decline in the yuan (China's currency) in two years; and a $5 trillion selloff of Chinese stocks in August 2015; the chances of a Chinese skyscraper curse don't seem so far-fetched.[11]

Sean Pavone/Shutterstock.com

that involvement in such activities exposed banks and their depositors to higher levels of risk.

Congress responded to the stock market crash that occurred in 1929 with two laws that are still the foundation of U.S. securities markets regulation. The first of these was the **Securities Act of 1933**, which dealt mainly with the process of issuing new securities. It prohibited misrepresentation or other forms of fraud in the sale of newly issued stocks and bonds. It also required firms issuing new stock in a public offering to file a registration statement with the SEC. The next year, Congress passed the **Securities Exchange Act of 1934**, which regulated the trading of previously issued securities. This law created the **Securities and Exchange Commission** (SEC) and gave it broad powers to oversee the securities industry. The law required that all publicly traded firms with at least 500 shareholders and $10 million in assets file quarterly and annual financial reports with the SEC, and that brokers and dealers register with the SEC.

The Securities Exchange Act also gave the SEC the power to prosecute individuals and companies that engaged in fraudulent securities market activities. For example, the SEC has the authority to go after individuals who engage in illegal *insider trading*, which is the practice of using inside information (important information about a company that isn't available to the general investing public) to profit unfairly from trading in a company's securities.

10-2b Deregulation During the 1980s and 1990s: Temporarily Reversing Course

The passage of these laws ushered in a period of more stable financial markets. But critics argued that the laws—especially the Glass-Steagall Act—represented an onerous government intrusion into the financial sector that stifled competition and impeded financial innovation. During the 1980s and 1990s Congress responded to these criticisms by easing restrictions on banks and other depository institutions. For instance, the **Financial Services Modernization Act of 1999**, also known as the *Gramm-Bliley-Leach Act*, reversed the Glass-Steagall Act's prohibition of banks selling insurance or acting as investment banks.

The financial sector initially seemed to prosper under its less regulated environment. It responded to its increased freedom with a variety of new services. Also, new technologies such as ATMs and online banking made financial transactions easier and more convenient.

10-2c Recent Developments: Reregulation in the Aftermath of Financial Turmoil

But the wave of deregulation didn't last. A series of accounting scandals at the beginning of the twenty-first century, followed by a near collapse of the financial system in 2008, created pressure for new laws.

Congress reacted to the accounting scandals in the first years of the new century by passing the Sarbanes-Oxley Act in 2002. This law included provisions to ensure that external auditors offered fair, unbiased opinions when they examined a company's financial statements. It also increased the SEC's authority to regulate financial markets and investigate charges of fraud and unethical behavior.[12]

Helga Esteb/Shutterstock.com

Elon Musk holds considerable sway at his companies, recently persuading 85% of shareholders to approve a merger between Tesla Motors and SolarCity. Here, Musk attends a Vanity Fair Oscar Party at the Wallis Annenberg Center for the Performing Arts in Beverly Hills, California.

Securities Act of 1933 The first major federal law regulating the securities industry. It requires firms issuing new stock in a public offering to file a registration statement with the SEC.

Securities and Exchange Act of 1934 A federal law dealing with securities regulation that established the Securities and Exchange Commission to regulate and oversee the securities industry.

Securities and Exchange Commission The federal agency with primary responsibility for regulating the securities industry.

Financial Services Modernization Act of 1999 An act that overturned the section of the Banking Act of 1933 that prohibited commercial banks from selling insurance or performing the functions of investment banks.

In the wake of the financial crisis of 2008–2009 Congress passed the Dodd-Frank Act of 2010. This far-reaching law expanded the Fed's regulatory authority over nondepository financial institutions, such as hedge funds and mortgage brokers that had previously operated with little regulatory oversight or accountability. It also created the Financial Stability Oversight Council to identify emerging risks in the financial sector so that action could be taken to rein in risky practices *before* they led to a crisis. The council was given the authority to recommend new rules to the Federal Reserve that would limit risky practices of the nation's largest, most complex financial institutions.[13]

 10-3 ## INVESTING IN FINANCIAL SECURITIES: WHAT ARE THE OPTIONS?

Financial securities markets are critical to corporations that rely on them to obtain much of their long-term financial capital. They also provide one of the most important venues that individuals can use to build their long-term wealth and earn significant financial returns.

10-3a Common Stock: Back to Basics

Common stock is the basic form of ownership in a corporation. Exhibit 10.2 shows a stock certificate for Berkshire Hathaway Inc. As owners of corporations, common stockholders have certain basic rights:

- **Voting Rights:** Owners of common stock have the right to vote on important issues at the annual stockholders' meeting. Under the most common arrangement, stockholders can cast one vote for each share of stock they own. One of the key issues that stockholders vote on is the selection of members to the corporation's board of directors, but they also may vote on other major issues, such as the approval of a merger with another firm or a change in the corporation's by-laws. Recall from Chapter 9 that billionaire entrepreneur Elon Musk is CEO of three companies. In 2016, Musk asked the shareholders of two of those companies, Tesla Motors, which makes luxury battery-powered cars, and SolarCity, which makes energy-generating solar panels, to approve a merger. Envisioning one brand selling to customers who valued clean energy

common stock The basic form of ownership in a corporation.

capital gain The return on an asset that results when its market price rises above the price the investor paid for it.

Robert Brown Stock/Shutterstock.com

Exhibit 10.2
Stock Certificates Represent Shares of Ownership in a Corporation

Common stock is the basic form of ownership in a corporation.

for their homes and vehicles, Musk said, "Would you go to an Apple store and expect to see six different [companies'] cellphones [for sale]?"[14] Eighty-five percent of shareholders across both companies subsequently approved the merger.[15]

- **Right to Dividends:** Dividends are a distribution of earnings to the corporation's stockholders. All common stockholders have the right to receive a dividend *if* their corporation's board of directors declares one. The "catch" is that the board has no legal obligation to declare a dividend. In fact, many rapidly growing companies routinely choose to skip dividends and reinvest most or all of their earnings to finance growth.

- **Capital Gains:** Stockholders receive another type of return on their investment, called a **capital gain**, *if* the price of the stock rises above the amount they paid for it. Capital gains can create very attractive financial returns for stockholders. Of course, there is no guarantee the stock's price will rise. If it falls, stockholders would experience a capital loss rather than a capital gain.

- **Preemptive Right:** If a corporation issues new stock, existing stockholders sometimes have a preemptive right to purchase new shares in proportion to their existing holdings before the stock is offered to the other investors. For example, if you own 5% of the existing shares of stock, then the preemptive right gives you the right to purchase 5% of the new shares. This could be important for large stockholders who want to maintain their share of ownership. However, the conditions under which existing stockholders have preemptive rights vary among the states. In several states, a preemptive right is only available if it is specifically identified in the corporation's charter.

- **Right to a Residual Claim on Assets:** The final stockholder right is a residual claim on assets. If the corporation goes out of business and liquidates its assets, stockholders have a right to share in the proceeds in proportion to their ownership. But note that this is a *residual* claim—it comes *after all other claims* have been satisfied. In other words, the firm must pay any back taxes, legal expenses, wages owed to workers, and debts owed to creditors before the owners get anything. By the time all of these other claims have been paid, nothing may be left for the owners.

10-3b Preferred Stock: Getting Preferential Treatment

Common stock is the basic form of corporate ownership, but some companies also issue **preferred stock**, so named because it offers its holders preferential treatment in two respects:

- **Claim on Assets:** Holders of preferred stock have a claim on assets that comes before common stockholders if the company goes out of business. This gives preferred stockholders a better chance than common stockholders of recovering their investment if the company goes bankrupt.

- **Payment of Dividends:** Unlike dividends on common stock, dividends on preferred stock are usually a stated amount. And a corporation can't pay *any* dividend to its common stockholders unless it pays the full stated dividend on its preferred stock. Still, it is important to note that a corporation has no *legal* obligation to pay a dividend to *any* stockholders, not even those who hold preferred stock.

Preferred stock sometimes includes a *cumulative feature*. This means that if the firm skips a preferred dividend in one

period, the amount it must pay the next period is equal to the dividend for that period *plus* the amount of the dividend it skipped in the previous period. Additional skipped dividends continue to accumulate, and the firm can't pay *any* dividends to common stockholders until *all* accumulated dividends are paid to preferred stockholders. In the midst of the lowest oil prices in two decades, Oklahoma-based Chesapeake Energy suspended its 2016 annual dividends to save $240 million. After significant restructuring and cost cutting, Chesapeake reinstated dividends in February 2017. But before resuming quarterly dividends, the company paid preferred stockholders the four quarterly dividends (that is, dividends in arrears) that it had missed in 2016.[16]

Preferred stock isn't necessarily "preferred" to common stock in all respects. For instance, preferred stockholders normally don't have voting rights, so they can't vote on issues that come up during stockholders' meetings. And even though preferred stockholders are more likely to receive a dividend, they aren't guaranteed a *better* dividend; the board can declare a dividend to common stockholders that offers a higher return.[17] Finally, when a company experiences strong earnings, the market price of its common stock can—and often does—appreciate more in value than the price of its preferred shares, thus offering common shareholders a greater capital gain.

10-3c Bonds: Earning Your Interest

A **bond** is a formal IOU issued by a corporation or government entity. Bonds come in many different varieties. Our discussion will focus on the basic characteristics of long-term bonds issued by corporations.

The date a bond comes due is called its **maturity date**, and the amount the issuer owes the bondholder at maturity is called the bond's **par value** (or face value). Long-term bonds issued by corporations usually mature ten to thirty years after issuance, but longer maturities are possible. In 2015, Brazilian oil company Petrobras sold $2.5 billion of century bonds that will mature in 2115—100 years later.[18]

Bondholders can sell their bonds to other investors before they mature, but the price they receive might not correspond to the bond's par value because bond prices fluctuate with conditions in the bond market. When a

> "One of the funny things about the stock market is that every time one person buys, another sells, and both think they are astute."
>
> —WILLIAM FEATHER

preferred stock A type of stock that gives its holder preference over common stockholders in terms of dividends and claims on assets.

bond A formal debt instrument issued by a corporation or government entity.

maturity date The date when a bond will come due.

par value (of a bond) The value of a bond at its maturity; what the issuer promises to pay the bondholder when the bond matures.

As of 2015, Berkshire Hathaway President and CEO Warren Buffett owned 37.99% of the company's Class A stock. At $244,560 a share, it's no wonder why Buffett is the second-wealthiest man in the United States.

bond's market price is above its par value, it is selling at a *premium*; when its price is below par value, it is selling at a *discount*.

Most bonds require their issuers to pay a stated amount of interest to bondholders each year until the bond matures. The **coupon rate** on the bond expresses the annual interest payment as a percentage of the bond's par value. For example, investors who own a bond with a par value of $1,000 and a coupon rate of 7.5% receive $75 in interest (7.5% of $1,000) each year until the bond reaches maturity—or until they sell their bonds to someone else. But since bonds can sell at a premium or a discount, the coupon rate doesn't necessarily represent the rate of return that investors earn on the amount they actually *paid* for the bond. The **current yield** expresses a bond's interest payment as a percentage of the bond's *current market price* rather than its par value. If the market price of the bond in our example was $833.33, then the current yield would be 9% (found by dividing the $75 interest payment by $833.33).

Unlike dividends on stock, a firm has a *legal obligation* to pay interest on

coupon rate The interest paid on a bond, expressed as a percentage of the bond's par value.

current yield The amount of interest earned on a bond, expressed as a percentage of the bond's current market price.

convertible security A bond or share of preferred stock that gives its holder the right to exchange it for a stated number of shares of common stock.

bonds—and to pay the bondholder the par value of the bond when it matures. Thus, bondholders are more likely to receive a financial return than stockholders. But that doesn't mean that bonds are without risk. Corporations that get into serious financial difficulties sometimes *default* on their bonds, meaning that they are unable to make required payments. When that happens, bankruptcy proceedings usually allow bondholders to recover some (but not all) of what they are owed; historically, the average amount recovered has been about 72 cents on the dollar.[19] While that is better than what stockholders can expect, it is far short of being risk free. In the 12 months ending in June 2016, 79 U.S. companies, mostly in the energy and mining industries, defaulted on their bonds.[20] Moody's, which provides credit ratings for companies, estimated that 2.1% of corporate debt would be defaulted in 2016, up from 1.7% in 2015 and 0.9% in 2014.[21]

10-3d Convertible Securities: The Big Switch

Corporations sometimes issue **convertible securities**, which are bonds or shares of preferred stock that investors can exchange for a given number of shares of the issuing corporation's common stock. A *conversion ratio* indicates the number of shares of common stock exchanged for each convertible security. Berkshire Hathaway's Class A stock was $244,560 per share when this was written. And yes, that's the most expensive share of stock in the world! Berkshire's Class B stock, however, traded for $163 on that same day. Each share of Berkshire's Class A stock can be converted into 1,500 Class B shares. At those prices, 1,500 shares of the Class B stock is worth $244,500, or $60 less than the class A stock. Because the conversion produces a $60 loss, Class A shareholders are not likely to convert their stock.[22] The ratio is set at the time the convertible securities are issued so that it is only financially desirable to convert the securities if the price of the common stock increases.

Owning a convertible security allows investors to gain from an increase in the price of common stock, while limiting their risk if the price of the stock falls. If the price of the common stock increases, the holders of convertible securities can convert them into the now more valuable stock. But if the price of the company's common stock falls, investors can continue to hold their convertible securities and collect their interest or preferred dividends.

The firm also can benefit from issuing convertible bonds, because the popularity of this feature with investors allows it to offer a lower coupon rate on convertible bonds (or a lower dividend on preferred stock), thus reducing its fixed payments. And if investors convert to common stock, the firm no longer has to make these fixed payments

My Bonds Got Called?

When buying a bond, you're lending an organization money for a specified period in exchange for interest payments (usually paid annually) until the bond maturity date, at which time you're paid the face (that is, par) value of the bond. For example, in February 2017, you could buy a 10-year bond from Microsoft with a coupon rate of 3.3%. If you bought $10,000 of Microsoft's bonds, the annual interest payments would be $330 per year (or $3,300 over 10 years). Then, after 10 years, Microsoft would pay you back the face value of your bonds, $10,000.

Unlike stock dividends, which are not guaranteed, firms are legally obligated to pay bond interest and the face value of the bond when it matures. But that doesn't mean that bonds are without risk. This is especially true when bonds are callable, which allows the firm to "call the bonds in" before the maturity date. For example, if Microsoft's 10-year bonds were callable after five years, then Microsoft could call the bonds in 2022, pay the face value for each bond, and then not have to pay the remaining five years of interest associated with the original maturity date in 2027.

Companies typically call bonds in early when interest rates drop. They pay off the more expensive, higher interest bonds and then issue new bonds with lower rates. Homeowners do the same thing when refinancing home mortgages from higher to lower rates.

While bond calls are a good deal for the corporation, investors are typically stuck with a smaller return than hoped for. So why buy callable bonds at all? Because they often come with a higher rate of return in exchange for their "call risk."[23]

---

at all. But there is one important group that may be unhappy with this arrangement; the corporation's existing stockholders may be displeased if the new stock issued to holders of convertible securities dilutes their share of ownership—and their share of profits!

Mutual Funds and ETFs: Diversification Made Easy

Financial diversification—the practice of holding many different securities in many different sectors—is generally considered a desirable strategy because it helps reduce (but not completely eliminate) risk. If you hold many different securities in different sectors of the economy, then losses on some securities may be offset by gains on others.

Many investors who want to hold diversified portfolios find that investing in large numbers of individual stocks and bonds is prohibitively expensive. And even if they could afford to do so, investors often lack the time and expertise to select a large number of individual securities. Faced with these limitations, many investors find that **mutual funds** and exchange-traded funds are attractive options.

Mutual Funds: Portfolios Made Easy

There are two ways mutual funds can be structured. A *closed-end fund* issues a fixed number of shares and invests the money received from selling these shares in a portfolio of assets. Shares of closed-end funds can be traded among investors much like stocks. An *open-end mutual fund* doesn't have a fixed number of shares, nor are its shares traded like stocks. Instead, the fund issues additional shares when demand increases and redeems (buys back) old shares when investors want to cash in.

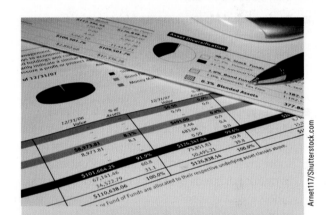

Arnet117/Shutterstock.com

Mutual funds are one of the best ways for individual investors to diversify investment portfolios across different sectors of the economy.

The price at which shares of an open-end mutual fund are issued and redeemed is based on the fund's **net asset value per share** (NAVPS), which is computed by dividing the total value of the fund's cash, securities, and other assets (less any liabilities) by the number of fund shares outstanding. Though the NAVPS is the basis for the price of a fund's shares, investors often also pay commissions and purchase fees.

financial diversification A strategy of investing in a wide variety of securities in order to reduce risk.

mutual fund An institutional investor that raises funds by selling shares to investors and uses the accumulated funds to buy a portfolio of many different securities.

net asset value per share The value of a mutual fund's securities and cash holdings minus any liabilities, divided by the number of shares of the fund outstanding.

> "All I ask is the chance to prove that money can't make me happy."
>
> —SPIKE MILLIGAN

Several features make mutual funds a popular choice for investors:

- **Diversification at Relatively Low Cost:** By pooling the funds of thousands of investors, mutual funds have the financial resources to invest in a broader portfolio of securities than individual investors could afford. This high level of diversification can help reduce risk. For instance Vanguard's Total Stock Market Index Fund allows investors to diversify because it holds more than 3,500 US stocks.[24]

- **Professional Management:** Most mutual funds are managed by a professional fund manager who selects the assets in the fund's portfolio. This can be appealing to investors who lack the time and expertise to make complex investment decisions.

- **Variety:** Whatever your investment goals and philosophy, you can probably find a fund that's a good match. There are many different types of funds; some invest only in certain types of securities (such as municipal bonds or stocks of large corporations), others invest in specific sectors of the economy (such as energy, technology, or healthcare), and yet others seek more balanced and broad-based portfolios. Some funds simply invest in a portfolio of stocks that matches those in a specific stock index, such as the Standard & Poor's 500 or the Wilshire 5000. These *index funds* have become very popular in recent years.

- **Liquidity:** It's easy to withdraw funds from a mutual fund. For a closed-end fund, you simply sell your shares. For an open-end fund, you redeem your shares from the fund itself. However, regardless of when you initiate your withdrawal, redemptions of an open-end fund are not carried out until its NAVPS is determined after the *next* trading session is completed.

Mutual funds do have some drawbacks. Perhaps the most serious is that the professional management touted by many funds doesn't come cheap. Investors in mutual funds pay a variety of fees that typically range from 1% to 3% of the amount invested. The fees charged by mutual funds can make a serious dent in the overall return received by the fund's investors. And funds assess these fees even when they perform poorly. One reason for the popularity of index funds is that they don't require professional management, so their fees are lower.

Another drawback of actively managed funds is that when their professional managers engage in a lot of trading, significant tax consequences are associated with those financial gains. It is also important to realize that some of the specialized mutual funds that invest in only one sector of the economy or only one type of security may not provide enough diversification to reduce risk significantly.

10-3e Exchange Traded Funds: Real Basket Cases (and We Mean That in a Good Way)

An **exchange-traded fund (ETF)** is similar to a mutual fund in some respects but differs in how it is created and how its shares are initially distributed. ETFs allow investors to buy ownership in what is called a *market basket* of many different securities. In fact, the market basket for most ETFs reflects the composition of a broad-based stock index, much like an index mutual fund. But in recent years more specialized ETFs that focus on narrower market baskets of assets have appeared on the market. Janus Capital Group, for example, sells an Obesity ETF to invest in companies that help 640 million obese people worldwide (up 600% in 40 years) control their weight by eating and exercising better, or otherwise treating health issues related to obesity.[25] Like closed-end mutual funds—but unlike the more common open-end funds—ETFs are traded just like stocks. Thus, you can buy and sell ETFs any time of the day.

Compared to most actively managed mutual funds, ETFs usually have lower costs and fees. However, since ETFs are bought and sold like stocks, you do have to pay brokerage commissions every time you buy or sell shares.

10-4 ISSUING AND TRADING SECURITIES: THE PRIMARY AND SECONDARY MARKETS

There are two distinct types of securities markets: the primary securities market and the secondary securities market. The **primary securities market** is where corporations raise additional financial capital by selling *newly*

exchange traded fund (ETF) Shares traded on securities markets that represent the legal right of ownership over part of a basket of individual stock certificates or other securities.

primary securities market The market where newly issued securities are traded. The primary market is where the firms that issue securities raise additional financial capital.

issued securities. The **secondary securities market** is where *previously issued* securities are traded.

10-4a The Primary Securities Market: Where Securities Are Issued

There are two methods of issuing securities in the primary market:

- In a **public offering**, securities are sold (in concept, at least) to anyone in the investing public who is willing and financially able to buy them.

- In a **private placement**, securities are sold to one or more private investors (who may be individuals or institutions) under terms negotiated between the issuing firm and the private investors.

Public Offerings Many corporations are initially owned by a small number of people who don't sell the stock to outsiders. But growing corporations often need to obtain more financial capital than such a small group can provide. Such firms may *go public* by issuing additional stock and offering it to investors outside their group. The first time a corporation sells its stock in a public offering, the sale is called an **initial public offering (IPO)**.

Going public is a complicated and high-stakes process; obtaining sufficient funds in an IPO is often critical to the firm's success. So, almost all firms that go public enlist the help and advice of an investment bank that specializes in helping firms issue new securities. The investment bank assists the firm at every step of the IPO, from the planning and market assessment phase until the actual securities are distributed to investors after the offering is conducted. Warrior Met Coal LLC, a coal mining company based in Brookwood, Alabama, hired investment bank Credit Suisse Group AG to lead an IPO from which it hopes to raise $3 billion.[26]

One of the key responsibilities of the investment bank is to arrange for the actual sale of the securities. The investment bank uses either a *best efforts* or a *firm commitment* approach. Under the best efforts approach, the bank provides advice about pricing and marketing the securities and assists in finding potential buyers. But it doesn't guarantee that the firm will sell all of its securities at a high enough price to meet its financial goals. The investment bank earns a commission on all of the shares sold under a best efforts approach.

Under a *firm commitment* arrangement, the investment bank **underwrites** the issue. This means that the investment bank itself purchases *all* of the shares at a specified price, thus guaranteeing that the firm issuing

"Investors must keep in mind that there's a difference between a good company and a good stock. After all, you can buy a good car but pay too much for it."

—RICHARD THALER, AMERICAN ECONOMIST

the stock will receive a known amount of new funds. The investment bank that underwrites the offer seeks to earn a profit by reselling the stock to investors at a higher price. For large public offerings, a group of investment banks, called an *underwriting syndicate*, may temporarily work together to underwrite the securities.

Before going public, a firm must file a **registration statement** with the Securities and Exchange Commission (SEC). Exhibit 10.3 shows the registration statement that Snap Inc., maker of the Snapchat social media app, filed regarding its IPO in 2017. This long, complex document must include the firm's key financial statements plus additional information about the company's management, its properties, its competition, and the intended uses for the funds it plans to obtain from the offering. The corporation cannot legally offer its new securities for sale until the SEC has examined this statement and declared it effective.

Private Placements In a private placement, the issuing firm negotiates the terms of the offer directly with a small number of **accredited investors**. These are individuals, businesses, or other organizations that meet specific financial requirements

secondary securities market The market where previously issued securities are traded.

public offering A primary market issue in which new securities are offered to any investors who are willing and able to purchase them.

private placement A primary market issue that is negotiated between the issuing corporation and a small group of accredited investors.

initial public offering (IPO) The first time a company issues stock that may be bought by the general public.

underwriting An arrangement under which an investment banker agrees to purchase all shares of a public offering at an agreed-upon price.

registration statement A long, complex document that firms must file with the SEC when they sell securities through a public offering.

accredited investor An organization or individual investor who meets certain criteria established by the SEC and so qualifies to invest in unregistered securities.

set by the SEC. Private placements are usually quicker, simpler, and less expensive than public offerings. The investment bank often helps the firm identify and contact accredited investors and assists the firm as it negotiates the terms of the private placement.

The main reason private placements are simpler and less expensive than public offerings is that privately placed securities are exempt from the requirement to register with the SEC. The ability to obtain financing without having to prepare complex registration documents can be a real attraction. But because the pool of potential investors is limited to accredited investors, private placements normally don't have the potential to raise as much money as public offerings. Another drawback is that securities that haven't been registered with the SEC can't be sold to anyone except other accredited investors.

10-4b Secondary Securities Markets: Let's Make a Deal

The firms that issue stocks and bonds don't receive any additional funds when their securities are traded in the secondary markets. But few investors would want to buy securities issued in the primary markets without the liquidity and possibility of earning capital gains provided by the opportunity to sell these securities in the secondary markets.

Stock (Securities) Exchanges The stocks of most large publicly traded corporations are listed and traded on a **stock (or securities) exchange**. A securities exchange provides an organized venue for stockbrokers and securities dealers to trade listed stocks and other securities. Each exchange establishes its own requirements for the securities it lists. The requirements vary among the exchanges, but they're typically based on the earnings of the company, the number of shares of stock outstanding, and the number of shareholders. In addition to meeting listing requirements, exchanges require firms to pay an initial fee at the time their securities are first listed, and an annual listing fee to remain listed on the exchange.

The New York Stock Exchange, owned by Intercontinental Exchange (which runs 12 exchanges across North America, Europe, and Asia), trades stock in 2,800 companies worth $26.5 trillion dollars, or three times larger than the next biggest exchange.[27] NASDAQ, the

stock (or securities) exchange An organized venue for trading stocks and other securities that meet its listing requirements.

Exhibit 10.3
Snap, Inc. Registration Statement for Initial Public Offering

UNITED STATES
SECURITIES AND EXCHANGE COMMISSION
WASHINGTON, D.C. 20549

FORM S-1
REGISTRATION STATEMENT
UNDER
THE SECURITIES ACT OF 1933

Snap Inc.
(Exact Name of Registrant as Specified in Its Charter)

7370
(Primary Standard Industrial Classification Code Number)

63 Market Street
Venice, California 90291
(310) 399-3359
(Address, Including Zip Code, and Telephone Number, Including Area Code, of Registrant's Principal Executive Offices)

Evan Spiegel
Chief Executive Officer
Snap Inc.
63 Market Street
Venice, California 90291
(310) 399-3359
(Name, address, including zip code, and telephone number, including area code, of agent for service)

Copies to:

Chris Handman
Atul Porwal
Snap Inc.
63 Market Street
Venice, California 90291
(310) 399-3359

Approximate date of commencement of proposed sale to the public:
As soon as practicable after this registration statement becomes effective.

Source: "Snap Inc. Form S-1 Registration Statement," US Securities and Exchange Commission, February 2, 2017, https://www.sec.gov/Archives/edgar/data/1564408/000119312517029199/d270216ds1.htm, accessed February 9, 2017.

second-largest stock exchange, is part of NASDAQ OMX, which runs exchanges in the United States and seven in Europe. NASDAQ began 45 years ago as the National Association of Securities Dealers, or NASD. Today, NASDAQ trades stock in 3,800 companies located in 35 countries, for a combined worth of $10.1 trillion.[28]

Trading on early stock exchanges occurred at physical locations where brokers met on trading floors to buy and sell securities for their clients. Some exchanges still maintain actual trading floors, but most trading on today's exchanges is done electronically. The participants in these markets carry out their trades mainly via computer networks.

The trend toward electronic trading began in 1971 with the establishment of NASDAQ, which initially was just a system used to report stock prices electronically. But over the years, it evolved into a complete market with formal listing requirements and fees. The stocks of many of today's high-profile technology companies, such as Apple, Google, and Microsoft, are traded on the NASDAQ market.

The key players in the NASDAQ market are known as **market makers**. These are securities dealers that make a commitment to continuously offer to buy and sell (make a market in) specific NASDAQ-listed stocks. Each NASDAQ stock has several market makers who compete against each other by posting two prices for each stock: the *bid price* indicates how much the market maker will pay per share to buy a stated quantity of the stock, while the *ask price* indicates the price per share at which it will sell the same stock. The ask price is higher than the bid price; the difference is called the *bid/ask spread* (or just the *spread*) and is the source of the market maker's profit.

The Over-the-Counter Market Many corporations with publicly traded stock don't meet the requirements to have their shares listed on an organized exchange; others choose not to list on exchanges because they don't want to pay the listing fees. The **over-the-counter market (OTC)** is where the stocks of such companies are traded. OTC stocks are traded through a system of market makers much like stocks are traded on the NASDAQ exchange. However, the market for most OTC stocks is much less active than for stocks listed on the major exchanges. Because of this, most stocks listed on the OTC have only a few market makers. The lack of competition often leads to much higher spreads between bid and ask prices for stocks traded in the OTC than normally exist for stocks traded on the NASDAQ exchange.

Electronic Communications Networks The newest development in stock market technology involves the rise of **electronic communications networks (ECNs)**. The SEC classifies ECNs as alternative trading systems because they represent an alternative to established stock exchanges as a venue for buying and selling securities. ECNs are entirely automated and computerized trading systems that allow traders to bypass the market makers used in the NASDAQ and OTC markets. However, individuals can only take advantage of this venue by opening an account with a broker-dealer that subscribes to an ECN.

If you place an order to buy a security on an ECN, the computer system checks to see if there is a matching order from another trader to sell the same security. If so, it immediately and automatically executes the transaction in a process that typically takes less than a second to complete. ECNs obviously speed up transactions. They also make it possible for investors to trade securities "after hours" when the U.S. exchanges are closed.

(10-5) **PERSONAL INVESTING**

Would investing in stocks, bonds, and other securities make sense for you? If so, how could you get started? What are the potential risks and rewards of various investment strategies?

Investing in securities requires you to think carefully about your specific situation, your personal goals, and your attitudes:

- What are your short-term and long-term goals?
- Given your budget, how much are you able to invest?
- How long can you leave your money invested?
- How concerned are you about the tax implications of your investments?
- How much tolerance do you have for risk?

Notice that the last question deals with your attitudes toward risk. Most people are not comfortable with high levels of risk. But no investment strategy completely avoids risk. And in general, the riskier the approach, the greater the *potential* rewards. To achieve your goals, you'll need to find the balance between risk and return that works for you.

10-5a Choosing a Broker: Gaining Access to the Markets

Members of the general public cannot directly trade stocks and other securities on the exchanges, the over-the-counter market, or the ECNs we described earlier in the chapter. Thus, most investors enlist the services of a brokerage firm to carry out their trades. Choosing the right broker is the first step in implementing your investment plans.

A *full-service broker* provides a wide range of services—such as market research, investment advice, and tax planning—in addition to carrying out your trades. *Discount brokers* provide the basic services needed to buy and sell securities but offer fewer additional services. They may also restrict your ability to trade certain types of securities. For example, some discount brokers don't offer the ability to buy and sell foreign securities. Discount brokers tend to charge significantly lower

market makers Securities dealers that make a commitment to continuously offer to buy and sell the stock of a specific corporation listed on the NASDAQ exchange or traded in the OTC market.

over-the-counter (OTC) market The market where securities that are not listed on exchanges are traded.

electronic communications network (ECN) An automated, computerized securities trading system that automatically matches buyers and sellers, executing trades quickly and allowing trading when securities exchanges are closed.

David Bowie: Rock 'n' Roll Icon and Businessman

Rock musician David Bowie's work spanned six decades—from his debut album *David Bowie* in 1967 to his 28th album, *Blackstar,* released days before his death on January 10, 2016. The musical highlights of Bowie's career include "Space Oddity" from the 1969 album of the same name, "Changes" from 1971's *Hunky Dory,* "Fame" from 1975's *Young Americans,* and "China Girl" and "Let's Dance" from the 1983 album *Let's Dance.* Bowie had less success as an actor but appeared in several films such as *The Man Who Fell to Earth* (1976), cult classic *Labyrinth* (1986), and comedy *Zoolander* (2001). He's also known for assuming various musical personalities while performing, such as the Thin White Duke, Ziggy Stardust, and Aladdin Sane (Google them!).

While you may be familiar with Bowie's artistic work, you may not know that he was also a financial innovator in the music industry. Reluctant to sell the rights to his music (a costly mistake the Beatles made), Bowie enlisted investment banker David Pullman to develop a better system. Pullman suggested that the future stream of earnings (that is, sales and royalties) from Bowie's first 25 albums be used to securitize (that is, pay the interest and principle of) 10-year *Bowie Bonds.* When issued in 1997, these bonds paid 7.9% interest. Bowie earned $55 million from the bond sale, and after 10 years, the full ownership rights to his music (as well as their subsequent earnings) reverted to him. While his music is timeless, the emergence of online music sharing services hurt music sales overall. Bowie Bonds were downgraded to junk status and then liquidated in 2007.[29]

JStone/Shutterstock.com

commissions than full-service brokers. In fact, many discount brokers charge flat fees of only a few dollars per trade for basic transactions. But brokerage firms also charge a variety of fees—sometimes including "inactivity fees" if you don't place enough orders! Once these fees are considered, brokerage firms that offer low commissions may not be as inexpensive as they first appear! To stop clients from defecting to discount brokers, many full-service firms have lowered commissions. At the same time, many discount brokers have begun offering a broader range of services. The result is that many brokerage firms offer investors the choice of either discount or full-service accounts.

With technology driving many of these changes, the financial planning industry now uses robo advisors to help people automatically set, track, stick to (that's the hard part), and eventually achieve their financial goals. Wealthfront and Betterment, two of the largest robo advisor services, use computer algorithms to automatically invest clients' wealth in a way that maximizes returns and minimizes taxes. Based on criteria set by the user, these services automatically deposit bank funds into retirement accounts each month; retrieve and then invest extra cash that would otherwise not earn a return; and rebalance stock portfolios by selling fast-moving stocks (capturing the gains) and investing in underweighted (and perhaps cheaper) stocks. Not only do robo advisors do all this automatically and based on individualized financial goals, they do so with lower annual fees than traditional advisors. Robo advisors typically charge 0.25% to 0.50% of assets, compared to 1% to 2% among human advisors.[30]

Once you've decided on a broker, you need to open an account. This is a fairly simple process; it requires filling out some forms (usually available online) and making an initial investment. The minimum initial investment varies, but $1,000 to $3,000 is fairly typical.

10-5b Buying Securities: Let's Make a Deal

Once you've set up your account, you can trade securities by contacting your broker and indicating the security you want to trade and the quantity you want to buy or sell. You can also specify the type of order you want to place. The most common types of orders are market orders and limit orders:

■ **Market orders** instruct the broker to buy or sell a security at the current market price. Placing a market order virtually guarantees that your order will be executed. The downside is that you may end up buying at a higher price than you expected to pay (or selling your stock for less than you expected to receive).

market order An order telling a broker to buy or sell a specific security at the best currently available price.

BREXIT AFFECTING EXCHANGE RATES, PRICING, AND PROFITS

If you've traveled abroad, you know that swings in currency exchange rates can make your trip significantly more or less expensive. In January 2012, a euro (€) was worth $1.27. But in January 2017, it was worth just $1.06. So if a Paris hotel charged €225 a night, the cost in U.S. dollars was $286 in 2012 and $239 (16% less) in 2017. Such significant currency changes affect product prices and firm profitability.

Since the citizens of the United Kingdom (U.K.) voted to leave the European Union (via Brexit, or British exit) on June 23, 2016, the British pound (£) has fallen 18.4% relative to the U.S. dollar, from $1.48 to $1.25. That's great if you're an American vacationing in London. But it's bad for American firms selling imported goods. These firms will see their U.K. revenue drop by 20% from the exchange rate alone.

In the short run, this leaves two bad options. First, raise prices aggressively to cover the entire currency fluctuation and watch sales drop as customers simply buy fewer of your products or buy cheaper products from a competitor instead. Second, raise prices modestly and take a direct hit to U.K. revenues. Either way, revenues and profits will likely drop—especially since the currency and prices changed so dramatically in so little time.

Because two-thirds of Apple's sales are outside the United States, its product pricing is strongly affected by exchange

rate swings. Due to strong product demand in the United Kingdom, Apple raised U.K. prices to cover the entire currency fluctuation. In most cases, that resulted in a 25% increase (18% to 20% higher because of currency fluctuations, followed by an additional 20% for the U.K.'s value added tax).

P&G, which imports household goods like Tide, Gillette shaving products, and Pampers diapers, competes in the United Kingdom against British and European firms. So, with less pricing power, it responded with a smaller 10% price increase.[31]

Koca Vehbi/Shutterstock.com

- **Limit orders** place limits on the prices at which orders are executed. A buy limit order tells a broker to buy a stock *only* if its price is at or below a specified value. You'd use this approach if you wanted to make sure you didn't pay more for the stock than you thought it was worth. A sell limit order tells your broker to sell the shares only if the price is at or above a specified value. This prevents your broker from selling your stock at a price you believe is too low.

10-5c Strategies for Investing in Securities

There are several strategies you can use to guide your investment decisions. We'll provide an overview of the more common approaches, but none of these

> "I will tell you how to become rich. Close the doors. Be fearful when others are greedy. Be greedy when others are fearful."
>
> —WARREN BUFFETT

approaches is foolproof—alas, there is no known strategy that is guaranteed to earn you millions.

Investing for Income Some investors focus on buying bonds and preferred stocks to generate a steady, predictable flow of income. This approach is popular with retirees who want to supplement their retirement income. But the return on such low-risk securities is relatively low, and their market value seldom increases much over time. Thus, it probably isn't the best strategy for younger investors who are trying to grow their wealth.

Market Timing Investors who rely on *market*

limit order An order to a broker to buy a specific stock only if its price is below a certain level, or to sell a specific stock only if its price is above a certain level.

CHAPTER 10: Financial Markets: Allocating Financial Resources   185

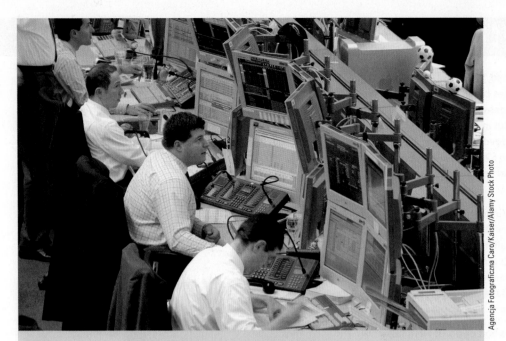

Stockbrokers place orders to buy and sell stocks and other securities for their clients.

Agencja Fotograficzna Caro/Kaiser/Alamy Stock Photo

Investing for Growth

Investors who focus on growth look for companies that have the potential to grow much faster than average for a sustained time, which they believe will lead to a steady (and sometimes spectacular) rise in the stock's price. Investors using this strategy often invest in stocks of relatively new companies with innovative products in a hot sector of the economy.

Investing for growth entails significant risk. Small new companies lack established track records. And rapidly expanding industries tend to attract many start-up companies, so competition can be intense. Finally, given the rapid pace of technological change, today's hot prospects may soon be dethroned by the next big thing. It's hard to predict which firms will be winners; even experts often make the wrong choice.

timing use a variety of analytical techniques to try to predict when prices of specific stocks are likely to rise and fall. Market timers try to make quick gains by buying low and selling high over a relatively short time horizon.

The problem with market timing is that so many factors can influence stock prices—some of them random in nature—that it's tough to consistently identify the timing and direction of changes in stock prices. Market timing also requires investors to make frequent trades. Given the commissions paid on trades and the taxes incurred on short-term capital gains, this approach may do a better job of enriching the broker than enriching the trader!

Value Investing Investors who favor *value investing* try to find stocks that are undervalued in the market. They believe that the market price will rise over time to reflect its true value, thus generating a capital gain. This approach requires intensive research to identify discrepancies between a company's true (or intrinsic) value and its current market price.

The drawback with value investing is that thousands of investors are all trying to do the same thing, so the competition to locate undervalued stocks is intense. Unless you're among the first to discover a good value, the investors who beat you to it will rush to buy up the stock, increasing demand and driving up the stock's price so that it is no longer undervalued.

Buying and Holding If you're a patient person with steady nerves, a buy-and-hold approach might appeal to you. This strategy involves purchasing a diversified set of securities and holding them for a long period of time. Buy-and-hold investors put their faith in the ability of the *overall market* to continue the long-run upward trend it has exhibited throughout its history. One way that many buy-and-hold investors do this is by investing in index mutual funds and ETFs. The buy-and-hold strategy seldom allows investors to "get rich quick," but it usually results in a solid financial return over the long haul.

Obviously, the buy-and-hold strategy will work only if you can afford to leave your money invested for a long time. When the stock market takes a dive, it can sometimes take years for stocks to recover and start to show solid returns. Some people who think they're comfortable with a buy-and-hold strategy end up getting "happy feet" after a few weeks of declining stock prices. They panic and sell off their stocks at exactly the wrong time, locking in big losses. For the buy-and-hold strategy to work, you've got to have the patience—and mental toughness—to ride out short-term downturns in the market. Michael Pagano, professor of finance at

Villanova University, explains why: "For a diversified equity portfolio of U.S. stocks, 10 to 15 years is long enough to overcome any bad timing in terms of entry points. Any shorter than that and you run the risk that you buy at a peak and then have to sell out at a trough."[32]

10-6 KEEPING TABS ON THE MARKET

Once you've begun to invest in securities, you'll want to keep track of how your investments are doing. Using the Internet, you can easily find information about both general market trends and the performance of specific securities.

10-6a Stock Indices: Tracking the Trends

One of the most common ways to track general market conditions and trends is to follow what's happening to various stock indices. A **stock index** tracks the prices of a large group of stocks that meet certain defined criteria. Many investors like to compare how the stocks in their own portfolio compare to the performance of these broad indices. Two of the best-known indices are the Dow Jones Industrial Average and the S&P 500.

- The **Dow Jones Industrial Average (DJIA)**: Often called just "the Dow," this is the most widely followed stock index. The Dow is based on the adjusted average price of 30 stocks picked by the editors of *The Wall Street Journal*. All of the Dow firms are large, well-established corporations, such as Apple, General Electric, Coca-Cola, McDonald's, Verizon, and Disney.

- The **Standard & Poor's 500**: With 500 stocks instead of just 30, the S&P 500 is a much broader index than the DJIA. Still, like the Dow, the companies Included in the S&P 500 are large, well-established American corporations such as 3M, Adobe Systems, Amazon, Google, Facebook, and Wells Fargo.

Exhibit 10.4 identifies several other well-known indices, including some that track prices of stocks in foreign securities markets.

10-6b Tracking the Performance of Specific Securities

Many financial websites offer detailed stock quotes that provide the current price of a company's stock and a wealth of related information. To check out a specific stock, you simply type its *stock symbol*—a short combination of letters that uniquely identifies a corporate security—into a "Get Quote" box. (Most sites have a lookup feature that finds the symbol if you type in the company's name.)

Exhibit 10.5 illustrates the information a popular financial website, Yahoo! Finance (http://finance.yahoo.com/), provides about McDonald's common stock. Some of the key figures reported for McDonald's include:

- *Last trade*: The price of McDonald's common stock for the most recent trade was $124.63.

- *Change*: The last trade of McDonald's stock was $0.04 lower than the closing price for the stock on the previous day.

- *Bid and Ask*: The highest price currently offered (bid) to buy McDonald's stock is $124.64 for 100 shares. The lowest price currently offered (asked) to sell the stock is $124.99 for 2,000 shares.

- *Day's range*: The highest price for the stock during the day was $124.98 and the lowest price was $124.36.

EXHIBIT 10.4	MAJOR STOCK PRICE INDICES
Index	**What It Tracks**
NASDAQ Composite	All of the domestic and foreign common stocks traded on the NASDAQ exchange.
Wilshire 5000	Stock prices of all U.S. corporations with actively traded stock. Despite the 5,000 in its name, this index actually includes well over 6,000 stocks. (The exact number changes frequently.)
Russell 2000	Stock prices of 2,000 relatively small but actively traded U.S. corporations.
FTSE 100	Stock prices of 100 of the largest and most actively traded companies listed on the London Stock Exchange.
Nikkei 225	Stock prices of 225 of the largest and most actively traded companies listed on the Tokyo Stock Exchange.
SSE Composite	Stock prices of all stocks listed on the Shanghai Stock Exchange.

stock index A statistic that tracks how the prices of a specific set of stocks have changed.

Dow Jones Industrial Average (DJIA) An index that tracks stock prices of 30 large, well-known U.S. corporations.

Standard & Poor's 500 A stock index based on prices of 500 major U.S. corporations in a variety of industries and market sectors.

EXHIBIT 10.5   YAHOO! FINANCE QUOTE FOR A STOCK

McDonald's Corp. Common St (NYSE: McD)
Real-time 124.63 ↓ 0.04 (0.03%) 2:30 PM EDT

Last Trade:	124.63	Day's Range:	124.36–124.98
Trade Time:	2:30 pm EDT	52wk Range:	110.33–131.96
Change:	↓ 0.04 (0.03%)	Volume:	1,420,703
Prev Close:	124.67	Avg Vol (3m):	3,882,779
Open:	124.47	Market Cap:	103.51B
Bid:	124.64 × 100	P/E (ttm):	23.42
Ask:	124.99 × 2,000	EPS (ttm):	5.32
1y Target Est:	125.32	Div & Yield:	3.76 (3.02%)

Source: Yahoo! Finance stock quote, accessed February 9, 2017.

- *52-Week range*: The highest price for McDonald's stock over the previous 52 weeks was $131.96 while its lowest price was $110.33.

- *Volume*: 1,420,703 shares of the stock have been traded up to this point in the current trading session—well below the average of 3,882,779 shares.

- *Market Cap*: The total market value of all shares of McDonald's common stock outstanding was 103.51 billion. This is found by multiplying the price per share times the number of shares of common stock outstanding.

- *P/E*: The price-to-earnings of 23.42 is found by dividing the stock's price per share by its earnings per share. In general, a higher P/E ratio means investors expect a greater growth in earnings over time.

- *EPS (earnings per share)*: McDonald's earned $5.32 per share of common stock outstanding. EPS is computed by dividing the net income available to common stockholders by the number of shares of common stock outstanding.

- *Div & Yield*: The sum of dividends paid by McDonald's over the past 12 months was $3.76 per share. Yield is found by dividing the dividend per share by the previous day's price per share. It tells us that at that price the dividend paid by McDonald's represented a 3.02% return to the investor. (But since the total return to stockholders may also include a capital gain or loss, this yield doesn't tell us the whole story.)

Financial websites also provide information about other types of securities such as mutual funds, ETFs, and bonds.

THE BIG PICTURE

Many different organizations participate in financial markets, including banks, finance companies, securities brokers and dealers, investment banks, and institutional investors such as mutual funds, insurance companies, and pension funds. Although they differ in their functions, each of these participants helps financial markets achieve their primary purpose of channeling funds from savers to borrowers.

In this chapter, we focused on one particular type of financial market, namely the market for financial securities. The financial capital that corporations raise when they issue stocks and bonds in these markets is critical to every functional area of their operations. Without these funds, the marketing department would lack the resources needed to develop new products; information technology professionals would be unable to update hardware and software; and operations managers would be unable to acquire the machinery and equipment needed to produce the goods and services the company sells to earn its profits.

On the other side of these markets, investors who buy corporate securities do so to acquire assets that they believe will help them achieve their own financial goals. But investing in securities involves risk. Over any short-run time period, there is simply no guarantee that stocks and bonds will provide investors with the returns they expect. The good news—at least if you plan to invest—is that history shows that, over the long run, the return on these securities is positive. Given enough time and patience, investing in stocks and other securities is likely to result in a substantial increase in wealth.

CAREERS IN BUSINESS

Stock Broker

Responsible for meeting and getting to know clients and their financial needs, offering financial advice on investment recommendations (for a diversified mix of stocks, fixed-income investments including bonds and certificates of deposit, mutual funds and annuities, as well as a wide range of insurance options, including life insurance, long-term disability, and long-term care), and placing trades. The ideal candidate has a bachelor's or master's degree, Series 7 license, a strong sales and/or management background, strong interpersonal skills that provide the ability to develop meaningful relationships, the drive to set and achieve goals in a performance-driven atmosphere, and the ability to work autonomously from your own neighborhood office.

STUDY TOOLS 10

LOCATED AT BACK OF THE TEXTBOOK

☐ Rip-Out Chapter Review Card

☐ Gain unique perspectives on key concepts with new concept videos in the e-book

☐ Increase your comprehension with online homework and quizzes

☐ Study with existing flashcards and make your own

CHAPTER 10: Financial Markets: Allocating Financial Resources   189

11 | Marketing: Building Profitable Customer Connections

LEARNING OBJECTIVES

After studying this chapter, you will be able to:

11-1 Discuss the objectives, the process, and the scope of marketing

11-2 Identify the role of the customer in marketing

11-3 Explain each element of marketing strategy

11-4 Describe the consumer and business decision-making process

11-5 Discuss the key elements of marketing research

11-6 Explain the roles of social responsibility and technology in marketing

Remember to visit
PAGE 207
for additional
STUDY TOOLS

11-1 MARKETING: GETTING VALUE BY GIVING VALUE

What comes to mind when you hear the term **marketing**? Most people think of the radio ad they heard this morning or the billboard they saw while driving to school. But advertising is only a small part of marketing; the whole story is much bigger. The American Marketing Association defines marketing as *the activity, set of institutions, and processes for creating, communicating, delivering, and exchanging offerings that have value for customers, clients, partners, and society at large.*

marketing An organizational function and a set of processes for creating, communicating, and delivering value to customers and for managing customer relationships in ways that benefit the organization and its stakeholders.

utility The ability of goods and services to satisfy consumer "wants."

The ultimate benefit that most businesses seek from marketing is long-term profitability. But attaining this benefit is impossible without first delivering value to customers and other stakeholders. A successful marketer delivers value by filling customer needs in ways that exceed their expectations. As a result, you get sales today and sales tomorrow and sales the next day, which—across the days and months and years—can translate into long-term profitability. Alice Foote MacDougall, a successful entrepreneur in the 1920s, understood this thinking early on: "In business you get what you want by giving other people what they want." **Utility** is the ability of goods and services to satisfy these wants. And since there is a wide range of wants, products can provide utility in a number of different ways:

- *Form utility* satisfies wants by converting inputs into a finished form. Clearly, the vast majority of products provide some kind of form utility. For example, Jamba Juice blends fresh fruits, juices, and vegetables into healthy and delicious smoothies, and UGG Australia stretches, treats, and sews sheepskins and wool into comfortable, stylish boots.

- *Time utility* satisfies wants by providing goods and services at a convenient time for customers. For example, Amazon Prime offers free same day delivery for qualifying orders in some areas, many dry cleaners offer one-hour service, 24 Hour Fitness is virtually always open, some fast-food restaurants offer 24-hour drive-through windows, and ATMs and online services have turned banking into an all-hours industry.

- *Place utility* satisfies wants by providing goods and services at a convenient place for customers. For example, Redbox makes DVDs and games available in front of a growing number of retailers, Denny's and Waffle House offer inexpensive food at the

> "A thrilled customer is the most potent marketing asset your organization can leverage."
>
> —JOHN JANTSCH, AUTHOR, *DUCT TAPE MARKETING*

bottom of many freeway off ramps, and vending machines refuel tired students on virtually every college campus.

- *Ownership utility* satisfies wants by smoothly transferring ownership of goods and services from seller to buyer. Virtually every product provides some degree of ownership utility, but some offer more than others. Consider that many car dealerships offer financing options. These dealerships and other lenders operate around the premise of ownership utility: if the borrower makes the specified number of payments, he or she will eventually own the product free and clear.

Satisfying customer wants—in a way that exceeds expectations—is a job that never ends. Jay Levinson, a recognized expert in breakthrough marketing, comments,

"Marketing is … a process. You improve it, perfect it, change it, even pause it. But you never stop it completely."

11-1a The Scope of Marketing: It's Everywhere!

For many years, businesspeople have actively applied the principles of marketing to goods and services that range from cars to fast food, to liquor, to computers, to movies. But within the past decade or two, other organizations have successfully adopted marketing strategies and tactics to further their goals.

Nonprofit organizations—in both the private and public sectors—play a significant role in our economy, employing more people than the federal government and all 50 state governments combined (not to mention an army of volunteers!). These organizations use marketing, sometimes quite assertively, to achieve their objectives. The U.S. Army's marketing communications budget, for example, sometimes approaches as much as $200 million per year. Your own college probably markets itself to both prospective students and potential alumni donors. Private-sector nonprofit organizations also use marketing strategies for everything from marshaling AYSO soccer coaches for kids to boosting attendance at the local zoo, to planning cultural events.[1]

Nonprofit organizations play a pivotal role in the expansion of marketing across our economy to include people, places, events, and ideas. But for-profit enterprises have also begun to apply marketing strategies and tactics beyond simply goods and services.

Graham R Prentice/Shutterstock.com

Athletic, cultural, and charitable events are all activities that rely on sponsorships as part of their event marketing approach.

- **People Marketing:** Sports, politics, and art dominate this category, but even some businesspeople merit mentioning. Top banking executives, for instance, took a beating from a marketing standpoint during the financial meltdown at the end of 2008. Also in 2008, President Barack Obama was named Ad Age Marketer of the Year, edging out powerhouse consumer brands that were also on the short list, such as Apple, Nike, and Coors. He became a living symbol of change in the minds of his supporters. President Trump took political people marketing to a whole new level during the 2016 presidential campaign when he marketed himself as the way to "Make America Great Again." Countless entertainers and athletes have used people marketing to their advantage as well. Consider, for example, Paris Hilton, who appeared to build her early career on promotion alone, eventually parlaying the media attention into a successful line of perfumes and fashion items. Hilton clearly has no doubt about her abilities, declaring, "I am a marketing genius." In fact, as you pursue your personal goals—whether you seek a new job, university admission, or a Friday night date—people marketing principles can help you achieve your objective. Start by figuring out what your "customer" needs, and then ensure that your "product" (you!) delivers above and beyond expectations.[2]

- **Place Marketing:** This category involves drawing people to a particular place. Cities and states use place marketing to attract businesses. Delaware, for instance, the second-smallest state in the Union, is home to more than half of the Fortune 500 firms because it deliberately developed a range of advantages for corporations. But more visibly, cities, states, and nations use place marketing to attract tourists. Thanks to powerful place marketing, most people have probably heard that "What happens in Vegas stays in Vegas." In late 2008, Las Vegas shelved the high-rolling campaign in favor of a more "recession-proof," but less successful strategy: the "Take a Break USA" campaign. By late 2009, Vegas had reverted to the "What Happens . . ." campaign that fueled visitors since its launch in 2003, leading to a record-breaking 42.9 million visitors in 2016.[3]

- **Event Marketing:** This category includes marketing—or sponsoring—athletic, cultural, or charitable events. Partnerships between the public and private sectors are increasingly common. Examples include the Olympics, the Super Bowl, and the FIFA World Cup.

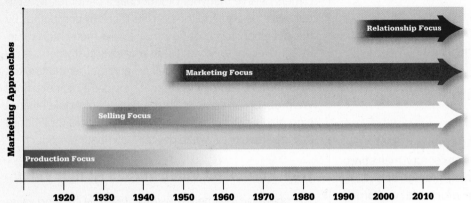

Exhibit 11.1
The Evolution of Marketing

The focus of marketing has evolved over time.

Marketing Approaches (vertical axis)

- Relationship Focus
- Marketing Focus
- Selling Focus
- Production Focus

1920 1930 1940 1950 1960 1970 1980 1990 2000 2010

While individual firms differ in their approach to marketing, the prevailing view at leading-edge firms has changed over time as shown here.

priority was to produce large quantities of goods as efficiently as possible.

Selling Era By the 1920s, production capacity had increased dramatically. For the first time, supply in many categories exceeded demand, which caused the emergence of the hard sell. The selling focus gained momentum in the 1930s and 1940s, when the Depression and World War II made consumers even more reluctant to part with their limited money.

Marketing Era The landscape changed dramatically in the 1950s. Many factories that had churned out military supplies converted to consumer production, flooding the market with choices in virtually every product category. An era of relative peace and prosperity emerged, and—as soldiers returned from World War II—marriage and birthrates soared. To compete for the consumer's dollar, marketers attempted to provide goods and services that met customer needs better than anything else on the market. As a result, the marketing concept materialized in the 1950s. The **marketing concept** is a philosophy that makes customer satisfaction—now and in the future—the central focus of the entire organization. Companies that embrace this philosophy strive to delight customers, integrating this goal into all business activities. The marketing concept holds that delivering unmatched value to customers is the only effective way to achieve long-term profitability.

Relationship Era The marketing concept has gathered momentum across the economy, leading to the current era, unfolding over the last decade, which zeros in on long-term customer relationships. Acquiring a new customer can cost five times more than keeping an existing customer. Retaining your current customers—and

- **Idea Marketing:** A whole range of public and private organizations market ideas that are meant to change how people think or act. Recycle, don't drink and drive, buckle your seatbelt, conserve water, support our political party, donate blood, and don't smoke are all examples of popular causes. Often, idea marketing and event marketing are combined, as we see in the annual Avon Walk for Breast Cancer. The planners actively market the idea of annual mammograms, as they solicit contributions for breast cancer research and participation in the event itself.

11-1b The Evolution of Marketing: From the Product to the Customer

The current approach to marketing evolved through a number of overlapping stages, as you'll see in Exhibit 11.1. But as you read about these eras, keep in mind that some businesses have remained lodged—with varying degrees of success—in the thinking of a past era.

Production Era Marketing didn't always begin with the customer. In fact, in the early 1900s, the customer was practically a joke. Henry Ford summed up the prevailing mindset when he reportedly said, "You can have your Model T in any color you want as long as it's black." This attitude made sense from a historical perspective, since consumers didn't have the overwhelming number of choices that are currently available; most products were purchased as soon as they were produced and distributed to consumers. In this context, the top business

> **marketing concept** A business philosophy that makes customer satisfaction—now and in the future—the central focus of the entire organization.

getting them to spend additional dollars—is clearly cost-effective. Moreover, satisfied customers can develop into advocates for your business, becoming powerful generators of positive "word of mouth."

11-2 THE CUSTOMER: FRONT AND CENTER

11-2a Customer Relationship Management (CRM)

Customer relationship management (CRM) is the centerpiece of successful, twenty-first-century marketing. Broadly defined, CRM is the ongoing process of acquiring, maintaining, and growing profitable customer relationships by delivering unmatched value. CRM works best when marketers combine marketing communication with one-on-one personalization. Amazon is a champion player at CRM, greeting customers by name, recommending specific products, and providing streamlined checkout. Clearly, information is an integral part of this process—you simply can't do CRM without collecting, managing, and applying the right data at the right time for the right person (and every repeat customer is the "right person"!).

Limited Relationships The scope of your relationships will depend not just on the data you gather but also on your industry. Colgate-Palmolive, for example, can't forge a close personal bond with every person who buys a bar of Irish Spring soap. However, the company does invite customers to call its toll-free line with questions or comments, and it maintains a vibrant website with music, an e-newsletter, special offers, and an invitation to contact the company. You can bet that the company actively gathers data and pursues a connection with customers who initiate contact.

Full Partnerships If you have a high-ticket product and a smaller customer base, you're much more likely to pursue a full partnership with each of your key clients. Colgate-Palmolive, for instance, has dedicated customer service teams working with key accounts such as Walmart and Costco. With a full partnership, the marketer gathers and leverages extensive information about each customer and often includes the customer in key aspects of the product development process.

Value You know you've delivered **value** when your customers believe that your product has a better relationship between the cost and the benefits than any competitor. By this definition, low cost does not always mean high value. In fact, a recent survey suggests that loyal customers are often willing to pay *more* for their products rather than switch to lower-cost competitors. Apple provides a clear example. We probably all know at least a handful of Apple fanatics who gladly pay far more for their PowerBooks (or iPhones or iPads) than they would pay for a competing product.

11-2b Perceived Value versus Actual Value

The operative idea here is *perceived*. Simply creating value isn't enough; you also must help customers believe that your product is uniquely qualified to meet their needs. This becomes a particular challenge when you're a new business competing against a market leader with disproportionately strong perceived value.

11-2c Customer Satisfaction

You know you've satisfied your customers when you deliver perceived value above and beyond their expectations. But achieving **customer satisfaction** can be tricky. Less savvy marketers frequently fall into one of two traps:

- The first trap is overpromising. Even if you deliver more value than anyone else, your customers will be disappointed if your product falls short of overly high expectations. The messages that you send regarding your product influence expectations—keep them real!

Perhaps in no other industry is there more customer loyalty than when purchasing a new vehicle.

Mangostock/Shutterstock.com

customer relationship management (CRM) The ongoing process of acquiring, maintaining, and growing profitable customer relationships by delivering unmatched value.

value A customer perception that a product has a better relationship than its competitors between the cost and the benefits.

customer satisfaction When customers perceive that a good or service delivers value above and beyond their expectations.

- The second trap is underpromising. If you don't set expectations high enough, too few customers will be willing to try your product. The result will be a tiny base of highly satisfied customers, which usually isn't enough to sustain a business.

Finding the right balance is tricky but clearly not impossible. According to their scores on the American Customer Satisfaction Index, Ford's Lincoln brand offered top customer satisfaction in 2016, edging out Honda to take the lead in the car category. Amazon's customer satisfaction continued to dominate among Internet retailers, while Walmart's score remains in the basement among all retailers. Wikipedia is the social media customer satisfaction winner. And among airlines, Jet Blue and Southwest tie for the top spot.[4]

11-2d Customer Loyalty

Customer loyalty is the payoff for delivering value and generating satisfaction. Loyal customers purchase from you again and again—and they sometimes even pay more for your product. They forgive your mistakes. They provide valuable feedback. They may require less service. They refer their friends (and sometimes even strangers). Moreover, studying your loyal customers can give you a competitive edge for acquiring new ones, since people with a similar profile would likely be a great fit for your products.[5]

 ## 11-3 MARKETING STRATEGY: WHERE ARE YOU GOING, AND HOW WILL YOU GET THERE?

In marketing terms, the questions become: Who is your target audience, and how will you reach them? Many successful firms answer this question by developing a formal **marketing plan**, updated on a yearly basis; other firms handle their planning on a more informal basis. But regardless of the specific approach, the first step in planning your marketing strategy should be to determine where to target your efforts. Who are those people who are most likely to buy your products? The first step is **market segmentation**—dividing your marketing into groups of people, or segments, that are similar to one another and different from everyone else. One or more of these segments will be your target market. Once you've identified your target market, your next step is to determine how you can best use marketing tools to reach them. And finally, you need to anticipate and respond to changes in the external environment. This section will define

Exhibit 11.2
Marketing Strategy

target market, explain market segmentation, introduce the marketing mix, and review the key factors in the marketing environment. Taken together, these elements will shape an effective marketing strategy, as shown in Exhibit 11.2.

The marketer creates the marketing mix but responds to the marketing environment with a single-minded focus on the target market.

11-3a Target Market

Your **target market** is the group of people who are most likely to buy your product. This is where you should concentrate your marketing efforts. But why not target your efforts toward everyone? After all, even if most middle-aged moms wouldn't buy purple polka-dotted miniskirts, an adventurous few just might do it. Well, you can always hope for the adventurous few, but virtually every business has limited resources, and marketing toward the

customer loyalty When customers buy a product from the same supplier again and again—sometimes paying even more for it than they would for a competitive product.

marketing plan A formal document that defines marketing objectives and the specific strategies for achieving those objectives.

market segmentation Dividing potential customers into groups of similar people, or segments.

target market The group of people who are most likely to buy a particular product.

people who are most likely to buy your flamboyant minis—say, teenage girls—will maximize the impact of each dollar you spend. A well-chosen target market embodies the following characteristics:

- Size: There must be enough people in your target group to support a business.

- Profitability: The people must be willing and able to spend more than the cost of producing and marketing your product.

- Accessibility: Your target must be reachable through channels that your business can afford.

- Limited competition: Look for markets with limited competition; a crowded market is much tougher to crack.

11-3b Consumer Markets versus Business Markets

Consumer marketers (B2C) direct their efforts to people who are buying products for personal consumption (e.g., granola bars, toothpaste, and clothing), whereas **business marketers (B2B)** direct their efforts to customers who are buying products to use either directly or indirectly to produce other products (e.g., lumber, insulation, and robots). But keep in mind that the distinction between the market categories is not in the products themselves; rather, it lies in how the buyer will use the product. For instance, shoes that you buy for yourself are clearly a consumer product, but shoes that a bowling alley buys for its customers are a business product. Similarly, a computer that you buy for yourself is a consumer product, but a computer that your school buys for the computer lab is a business product. Both B2C and B2B marketers need to choose the best target, but they tend to follow slightly different approaches.

consumer marketers (also known as business-to-consumer or B2C) Marketers who direct their efforts toward people who are buying products for personal consumption.

business marketers (also known as business-to-business or B2B) Marketers who direct their efforts toward people who are buying products to use either directly or indirectly to produce other products.

demographic segmentation Dividing the market into smaller groups based on measurable characteristics about people, such as age, income, ethnicity, and gender.

geographic segmentation Dividing the market into smaller groups based on where consumers live. This process can incorporate countries, cities, or population density as key factors.

psychographic segmentation Dividing the market into smaller groups based on consumer attitudes, interests, values, and lifestyles.

11-3c Consumer Market Segmentation

Choosing the best target market (or markets) for your product begins with dividing your market into segments, or groups of people who have similar characteristics. But people can be similar in a number of different ways, so, not surprisingly, marketers have several options for segmenting potential consumers.

Demographic B2C **demographic segmentation** refers to dividing the market based on measurable characteristics about people such as age, income, ethnicity, and gender. Demographics are a vital starting point for most marketers. Chapstick, for instance, targets young women with the Shimmer version of its lip balm, and Chevy Camaro targets young men with money. Sometimes the demographic makeup of a given market is tough to discern; African American artists, for instance, create the bulk of rap music, yet Caucasian suburban males form the bulk of the rap music market.

Geographic B2C **geographic segmentation** refers to dividing the market based on where consumers live. This process can incorporate countries, or cities, or population density as key factors. For instance, Ford Expedition does not concentrate on European markets, where tiny, winding streets and nonexistent parking are common in many cities. Cosmetic surgeons tend to market their services more heavily in urban rather than rural areas. And finding the perfect surfboard is easy in Hawaii but more challenging in South Dakota.

Psychographic B2C **psychographic segmentation** refers to dividing the market based on consumer attitudes, interests, values, and lifestyles. Toyota Prius, for instance, targets consumers who care about protecting the environment. A number of companies have found a highly profitable niche providing upscale wilderness experiences for people who seek all the pleasure with none of the pain

Who do you think is the target customer for the Chrysler Pacifica?

(you enjoy the great outdoors, while someone else lugs your gear, pours your wine, slices your goat cheese, and inflates your extra-comfy air mattress). Both magazine racks and the Internet are filled with products geared toward psychographic segments, including adventure travel sites, Adventure Center.com, shoe-selling mega site Zappos .com, and business and financial powerhouse WallStreet-Journal.com. *Note:* Marketers typically use psychographics to complement other segmentation approaches rather than to provide the core definition.

Behavioral B2C **behavioral segmentation** refers to dividing the market based on how people behave toward various products. This category includes both the benefits that consumers seek from products and how consumers use the product. The Neutrogena Corporation, for example, built a multimillion-dollar hair care business by targeting consumers who wanted an occasional break from their favorite shampoo. Countless products such as Miller Lite actively target the low-carbohydrate consumer. But perhaps the most common type of behavioral segmentation is based on usage patterns. Fast-food restaurants, for instance, actively target heavy users (who, ironically, tend to be slender): young men in their 20s and 30s. This group consumes about 17% of their total calories from fast food, compared to 12% for adults in general. Understanding the usage patterns of your customer base gives you the option of either focusing on your core users or trying to pull light users into your core market.

11-3d Business Market Segmentation

B2B marketers typically follow a similar process in segmenting their markets, but they use slightly different categories:

Geographic B2B geographic segmentation refers to dividing the market based on the concentration of customers. Many industries tend to be highly clustered in certain areas, such as technology in California and auto suppliers in the "auto corridor" that stretches south from Michigan to Tennessee. Geographic segmentation, of course, is especially common on an international basis, where variables such as language, culture, income, and regulatory differences can play crucial roles.

Customer-Based B2B customer-based segmentation refers to dividing the market based on the characteristics of customers. This approach includes a range of possibilities. Some B2B marketers segment based on customer size. Others segment based on customer type. Johnson & Johnson, for example, has a group of salespeople dedicated exclusively to retail accounts such as Target and Publix, while other salespeople focus solely on motivating doctors to recommend their products. Other potential B2B markets

Exhibit 11.3
Marketing Mix

include institutions—schools and hospitals, for instance, are key segments for Heinz Ketchup—and the government.

Product-Use–Based B2B product-use–based segmentation refers to dividing the market based on how customers will use the product. Small and midsized companies find this strategy especially helpful in narrowing their target markets. Possibilities include the ability to support certain software packages or production systems or the desire to serve certain customer groups, such as long-distance truckers or restaurants that deliver food.

11-3e The Marketing Mix

Once you've clearly defined your target market, your next challenge is to develop compelling strategies for product, price, distribution, and promotion. The blending of these elements becomes your **marketing mix**, as shown in Exhibit 11.3.

- ■ **Product Strategy:**
  Your product involves far more than simply a tangible good or

behavioral segmentation Dividing the market based on how people behave toward various products. This category includes both the benefits that consumers seek from products and how consumers use the products.

marketing mix The blend of marketing strategies for product, price, distribution, and promotion.

Color me ... hungry?!

Have you ever noticed that fast-food restaurants typically feature vivid shades of red, yellow, and orange in both their logos and their décor? Think McDonald's, KFC, Burger King, and Pizza Hut. The color choice is no coincidence.

Marketing researchers have learned that consumers in the United States associate red with energy, passion, and speed. Yellow suggests happiness and warmth, while orange suggests playfulness, affordability, and fun. A simulated cocktail party study found that partygoers in red rooms reported feeling hungrier and thirstier than others, and guests in yellow rooms ate twice as much as others. The implication? Surrounding customers with red, yellow, and orange encourages them to eat a lot quickly and leave, which aligns nicely with the goals of most fast-food chains.

Color psychology is a powerful—though often overlooked—marketing tool. Colors evoke emotions and trigger specific behaviors, which can dramatically influence how people buy your product. Here is a list of common colors and some of their associations in U.S. mainstream culture.

But there is more for marketers to consider than simply color associations. Research shows that the relationship between brands and color hinges on the perceived appropriateness of the color being used for the particular brand (in other words, the color must "fit" what is being sold). Purchasing intent is greatly affected by colors due to the impact that colors have on how a brand is perceived. This means that colors influence how consumers view the "personality" of the brand in question. For example, picture a stick of deodorant targeted at women, and then picture a stick of deodorant targeted at men. Research suggests that men prefer bold colors while women prefer softer ones. Interestingly, blue dominates as the favorite color for both men and women.

Keep in mind that while some color associations are universal, others can differ significantly among cultures. White, for instance, signifies death and mourning in Chinese culture, while purple represents death in Brazil.

RED – Love, passion, warmth, food, excitement, action, danger, need to stop

BLUE – Power, trustworthiness, calm, success, seriousness, boredom

GREEN – Money, nature, health, healing, decay, illness

ORANGE – Playfulness, affordability, youth, fun, low quality, cheap

PURPLE – Royalty, luxury, dignity, spirituality, nightmares, craziness

WHITE – Purity, innocence, simplicity, mildness

BLACK – Sophistication, elegance, seriousness, sexuality, mystery, evil

David P. Smith/Shutterstock.com

As a marketer, your goal should be to align your color choice with the perceptions of your target market and the features of your product. The result should be more green for your bottom line![6]

---

a specific service. Product strategy decisions range from brand name, to product image, to package design, to customer service, to guarantees, to new product development, and more. Designing the best product clearly begins with understanding the needs of your target market.

> "Don't find customers for your products, find products for your customers."
>
> —SETH GODIN, ENTREPRENEUR AND AUTHOR

■ **Pricing Strategy:** Pricing is a challenging area of the marketing mix. To deliver customer value, your prices must be fair, relative to the benefits of your product. Other factors include competition, regulation, and public opinion. Your product category plays a critical role as well. A low-cost desk, for instance, might be appealing, but who would want discount-priced knee surgery?

- **Distribution Strategy:** The goal is to deliver your product to the right people, in the right quantities, at the right time, in the right place. The key decisions include shipping, warehousing, and selling outlets (e.g., the Web versus network marketing versus brick-and-mortar stores). The implications of these decisions for product image and customer satisfaction can be significant.

- **Promotion Strategy:** Promotion includes all of the ways that marketers communicate about their products. The list of possibilities is long and growing, especially as the Internet continues to evolve at break-neck speed. Key elements today include advertising, personal selling, sales promotion, public relations, word of mouth, and product placement. Successful promotional strategies typically evolve in response to both customer needs and competition. A number of innovative companies are even inviting their customers to participate in creating their advertising through venues such as YouTube. Check out Exhibit 11.4 to see how easily you can analyze promotional strategies.

11-3f The Global Marketing Mix

As you decide to enter foreign markets, you'll need to reevaluate your marketing mix for each new country. Should it change? If so, how should it change? Many business goods simply don't require much change in the marketing mix, since their success isn't dependent on culture. Examples include heavy machinery, cement, and farming equipment. Consumer products, however, often require completely new marketing mixes to effectively reach their consumers.

Nike's approach to marketing in China offers an interesting example of how one firm managed the complex process of building a successful business in a foreign market. When Nike first entered China in the 1990s, the company seemed to face an insurmountable challenge: not only did a pair of Nike sneakers cost twice the Chinese average monthly salary, but most Chinese just didn't play sports, according to Terry Rhoads, then director of Nike sports marketing. So he boldly set out to change that. Rhoads created a Nike high-school basketball league, which has since spread to 17 cities. To loosen up fans, he blasted canned cheering during games and arranged for national TV coverage of the finals. He even leveraged connections with the NBA to bring Michael Jordan for visits.

The gamble quickly paid off, as the Chinese middle class emerged—along with more individualistic values, which are a strong fit with the Nike ethos. By 2001, Nike had dubbed its marketing approach "hip hoop," which they

Exhibit 11.4
Analyzing Promotional Strategies

Who is the target audience for each of these smartphone websites? How does each site position the product relative to the competition? Which strategy is most effective? Why?

Great features make all the difference

The most productive devices on the planet.

described as an effort to "connect Nike with a creative lifestyle." Sales in 2011 exceeded $2 billion, driven largely by basketball shoes, although sales began to soften in 2012 and 2013, due to fierce competition and deep discounting. In 2014, Nike continued to lose traction in China, due in part to fierce competition from Adidas. Analysts also pointed out that among other reasons, "Nike's branding is based on encouraging strong identification with iconic sports-stars it uses to endorse its products. In a culture where parents are excessively focused on academic achievement, such a strategy has limited appeal." Nike

Marketing to Millennials May Mean Melding with Pop Culture ...

... because millennials don't just shape pop culture—they actually create it through how they live their lives. A recent survey of millennials yielded the following interesting findings:

- 68% of millennials say: "Fans have at least some ownership of the things they're fans of."

- 70% say: "I choose activities that will give me things to post."

- 70% say: "We filter our social media feeds to only see what we want to see."

- 61% say: "I can influence popular culture."

- 51% say: "Messaging is just as personal as talking in person."

- 48% say: "I feel like I know my favorite celebrity."

- 29% say: "I post things that make my life look better than it really is."

In order for marketers to reach millennials, the United State's largest living generation, they should consider helping them in their quest to shape pop culture. One example of a brand that has done this successfully is Red Bull. The hugely popular energy drink periodically organizes "Flugtag" events in cities around the world. These events challenge participants to build and fly home-made, human-powered flying machines that are launched off a pier into the sea or another large body of water. Most competitors enter just for

DMITRY SEREBRYAKOV/Getty Images

fun, and the flying machines often don't fly at all. You can certainly see how this event would lead to a huge amount of posting, messaging, and other social media activity. Another high-impact option for marketers is to sponsor events that millennials care about. Bank of America, for example, is a top-level partner in Ocean Conservancy's International coastal cleanup, which sends hundreds of volunteers to remove debris from beaches—a hot-button issue for millennials. Partnering with celebrities or social media influencers can also yield strong results for marketers, assuming that there is a strong fit with their brands.[7]

---

emerged from its slump in 2015 with a powerful sales surge in China (despite the turbulence in the Chinese economy). Analysts anticipate that Nike's growth will continue because the NBA has begun investing in China—a move that will only help Nike.[8]

11-3g The Marketing Environment

While marketers actively influence the elements of the marketing mix, they must anticipate and respond to the elements of the external environment, which they typically cannot control. **Environmental scanning** is a key tool; the goal is simply to continually collect information from sources that range from informal networks to industry newsletters, to the general press, to customers, to suppliers, to the competition, among others. The key elements of the external environment include the following components:

environmental scanning The process of continually collecting information from the external marketing environment.

market share The percentage of a market controlled by a given marketer.

Competitive The dynamic competitive environment probably affects marketers on a day-to-day basis more than any other element. Understanding the competitive environment often begins with analysis of **market share**, or the percentage of the marketplace that each firm controls. To avoid ambushes—and to uncover new opportunities—you must continually monitor how both dominant and emerging competitors handle each element of their marketing mix. And don't forget indirect competitors, who meet the same consumer needs as you, but with a completely different product (e.g., Altoids vs. Scope).

Economic The only certainty in the economic environment is change, but the timing of expansions and contractions is virtually impossible to predict. Your goal as a marketer is to identify and respond to changes as soon as possible, keeping in mind that a sharp eye sees opportunity even in economic downturns. For instance, affordable luxuries and do-it-yourself enterprises can thrive during recessions.

Social/Cultural The social/cultural element covers a vast array of factors, including lifestyle, customs,

EXHIBIT 11.5 ELEMENTS THAT INFLUENCE THE CONSUMER DECISION-MAKING PROCESS

Influence	Description
Cultural	***Culture:*** The values, attitudes, and customs shared by members of a society
	Subculture: A smaller division of the broader culture
	Social Class: Societal position driven largely by income and occupation
Social	***Family:*** A powerful force in consumption choices
	Friends: Another powerful force, especially for high-profile purchases
	Reference Groups: Groups that give consumers a point of comparison
Personal	***Demographics:*** Measurable characteristics such as age, gender, or income
	Personality: The mix of traits that determines who you are
Psychological	***Motivation:*** Pressing needs that tend to generate action
	Attitudes: Lasting evaluations of (or feelings about) objects or ideas
	Perceptions: How people select, organize, and interpret information
	Learning: Changes in behavior based on experience

language, attitudes, interests, and population shifts. Trends can change rapidly, with a dramatic impact on marketing decisions. Anticipating and responding to trends can be especially important in industries such as entertainment, fashion, and technology. In late 2009, for instance, Facebook removed some key privacy controls from its News Feed. The social media giant did not anticipate the black eye it received from outraged consumers who believed that Facebook had violated their privacy. Facebook was also surprised that the privacy controls it implemented in May 2010, which required consumers to opt out of sharing, would not be enough to appease privacy advocates.[9]

Technological Changes in technology can be very visible to consumers (e.g., the introduction of the iPhone). However, technology often affects marketers in ways that are less directly visible. For example, technology allows mass customization of Levi's blue jeans at a reasonable price and facilitates just-in-time inventory management for countless companies that see the results in their bottom lines.

Political/Legal The political/legal area includes laws, regulations, and political climate. Most U.S. laws and regulations are clear (e.g., those declaring dry counties in certain states), but others are complex and evolving (e.g., qualifications for certain tax breaks). Political climate includes changing levels of governmental support for various business categories. Clearly, the political/legal issues affect heavily regulated sectors (e.g., telecommunications and pharmaceuticals) more than others.

11-3h The Global Marketing Environment

As the Internet has grown, the world market has become accessible to virtually every business. This boosts the importance of understanding each element of the marketing environment—competitive, economic, social/cultural, technological, and political/legal—in each of your key markets. Among the biggest global challenges are researching opportunities in other countries and delivering your product to customers in other countries.

11-4 CUSTOMER BEHAVIOR: DECISIONS, DECISIONS, DECISIONS!

If successful marketing begins with the customer, then understanding the customer is critical. Why do people buy one product, but not another? How do they use the products they buy? When do they get rid of them? Knowing the answers to these questions will clearly help you better meet customer needs.

11-4a Consumer Behavior

Consumer behavior refers specifically to how people act when they are buying products for their own personal consumption. The decisions they make often seem spontaneous (after all, how much thought do you give to buying a pack of gum?), but they often result from a complex set of influences, as shown in Exhibit 11.5.

> **consumer behavior**
> Description of how people act when they are buying, using, and discarding goods and services for their own personal consumption. Consumer behavior also explores the reasons behind people's actions.

Marketers, of course, add their own influence through the marketing mix. For instance, after smelling pretzels in the mall and tasting pretzel morsels from the sample tray, many of us would at least be tempted to cough up the cash for a hot, buttery pretzel of our own . . . regardless of any other factors! Similarly, changes in the external environment—for example, a series of hurricanes in Florida—dramatically affect consumer decisions about items such as flashlights, batteries, and plywood.

All these forces shape consumer behavior in each step of the process regarding purchase decisions. Exhibit 11.6 shows how the consumer decision process works.

Clearly, marketing can influence the purchase decision every step of the way, from helping consumers identify needs (or problems), to resolving that awful feeling of **cognitive dissonance** (or kicking oneself) after a major purchase. Some marketers attempt to avoid cognitive dissonance altogether by developing specific programs to help customers validate their purchase choices. One example might be post-purchase mailings that highlight the accolades received by an expensive product.

But does every consumer go through every step of the process all the time? That's clearly not the case! People make low-involvement decisions (such as buying that candy bar) according to habit . . . or even just on a whim. But when the stakes are high—either financially or socially—most people move through the five steps of the classic decision-making process. For example, most of us wouldn't think of buying a car, a computer, or the "right" pair of blue jeans without stepping through the decision-making process.

11-4b Business Buyer Behavior

Business buyer behavior refers to how people act when they're buying products to use either directly or indirectly to produce other products (e.g., chemicals, copy paper, computer servers). Business buyers typically have purchasing training and apply rational criteria to their decision-making process. They usually buy according to purchase specifications and objective standards, with a minimum of personal judgment or whim. Often, business buyers are integrating input from a number of internal sources, based on a relatively formal process. And finally, business buyers tend to seek (and often secure) highly customized goods, services, and prices.

Exhibit 11.6
Consumer Decision Process

Need Recognition
Your best friend suddenly notices that she is the only person she knows who still wears high-rise blue jeans to class ... problem alert!

Information Search
Horrified, your friend not only checks out your style but also notices what the cool girls on campus are wearing. AND she snitches your copy of *Cosmo* to leaf through the ads.

Evaluation of Alternatives
Your friend compares the prices and styles of the various brands of blue jeans that she identifies.

Purchase Decision
After a number of conversations, your friend finally decides to buy True Religion jeans for $215.

Post-Purchase Behavior
Three days later, she begins to kick herself for spending so much money on jeans because she can no longer afford her daily Starbucks habit.

11-5 MARKETING RESEARCH: SO WHAT DO THEY REALLY THINK?

If marketing begins with the customer, marketing research is the foundation of success. **Marketing research** involves gathering, interpreting, and applying information to uncover opportunities and challenges. The goal, of course, is better marketing decisions: more value for consumers and more profits for businesses that deliver. Companies use marketing research to:

- Identify external opportunities and threats (from social trends to competition).

- Monitor and predict customer behavior.

- Evaluate and improve each area of the marketing mix.

Most successful marketers rely on research to develop breakthrough products and effective marketing programs. But research will never replace the creative potential of the

---

cognitive dissonance Consumer discomfort with a purchase decision, typically for a higher-priced item.

business buyer behavior Describes how people act when they are buying products to use either directly or indirectly to produce other products.

marketing research The process of gathering, interpreting, and applying information to uncover marketing opportunities and challenges, and to make better marketing decisions.

OOPS! WHAT WERE THEY THINKING?

"If you can't be a good example, then you'll just have to serve as a horrible warning."

Even the heavy hitters make marketing gaffes. Their biggest mistakes are often entertaining, but they also serve as a powerful warning to consult with the customer *before* taking action. A few amusing examples:

- Polite men everywhere know it's never wise to talk to a woman about her weight. Too bad some big corporations don't seem to have gotten the message. In 2013, annoyed by the lack of larger clothing at retailer Abercrombie & Fitch, customers demanded an explanation. Apparently, the CEO "doesn't want his core customers to see people who aren't as hot as them wearing his clothing." Also in 2013, Target displayed a dress for sale, described as "Dark Heather Gray" for all but the plus size version, which was described as "manatee gray." Ouch!

- In late 2013, Burger King, in the wake of adding the French Fry Burger and reduced calorie Satisfries to their menu, pretended to change their name to Fries King, and uploaded a raft of photos to their Facebook page documenting the "new corporate I.D." The result was massive confusion, which mostly played out in a blizzard of baffled tweets.

- Another tough year for social media marketing was 2014. Union Street Guest House hotel in New York threatened to fine wedding parties $500 for every negative social media post and online review that their guests posted. And Minnesota retailer Global Village—showing a remarkable lack of sensitivity—commemorated Martin Luther King Day by offering "25% off everything black" via its Facebook page.

- In 2015, several large companies made news for being oddly oblivious to implications of date rape in their marketing. A Bloomingdale's Christmas catalog included an image of a man at a party leering at a woman who was laughing and looking the other direction. The image's caption read: "Spike your best friend's eggnog when they're not looking." Similarly, Anheuser-Busch used the tag line "The perfect beer for removing 'no' from your vocabulary for the night" on the labels of several Bud Light bottles. Both ads ignited a firestorm of criticism.

- In 2016, the U.S. State Department tweeted, "Not a '10' in the US? Then not a 10 overseas. Beware of being lured into buying expensive drinks or worse—being robbed. #springbreakingbadly," as part of its annual campaign to promote safe travel practices. The Tweet immediately offended followers, since it seemed to imply that if you're unattractive here, you're unattractive there—*and* you could be robbed. As if that weren't enough, it coldly punctured the time-honored vacation fantasy of overseas romance. Not surprisingly, the tweet sparked a number of parodies, including this tweet: "If you are a '3' in the United States you must carry a 'hand-written' letter of apology with you in order to travel"; and this Gawker headline: "The U.S. State Department Warns Americans That No One Could Possibly Find You Attractive."

These fiascos only highlight the importance of *marketing research* (combined with common sense). But sometimes, even research isn't enough to identify marketing issues before they hit. At that point, the priority should shift to dealing with the mistake openly, honestly, and quickly, which can help a company win the game, despite the gaffe.[10]

EXHIBIT 11.7 RESEARCH DATA COMPARISON

Secondary Data	Primary Data
Existing data that marketers gather or purchase	New data that marketers compile for the first time
Tends to be lower cost	Tends to be more expensive
May not meet your specific needs	Customized to meet your needs
Frequently outdated	Fresh, new data
Available to your competitors	Proprietary—no one else has it
Examples: U.S. Census, the *Wall Street Journal*, *Time* magazine, your product sales history	Examples: Your own surveys, focus groups, customer comments, mall interviews

gifted individual. Steve Jobs, founder of Apple, famously declared, "A lot of times, people don't know what they want until you show it to them."

11-5a Types of Data

There are two main categories of marketing research data—**secondary data** and **primary data**—each with its own set of benefits and drawbacks, as shown in Exhibit 11.7.

Clearly, it makes sense to gather secondary data before you invest in primary research. Look at your company's internal information. What does previous research say? What does the press say? What can you find on the Web? Once you've looked at the secondary research, you may find that primary research is unnecessary. But if not, your secondary research will guide your primary research and make it more focused and relevant, which ends up saving time and money.

secondary data Existing data that marketers gather or purchase for a research project.

primary data New data that marketers compile for a specific research project.

observation research Marketing research that does not require the researcher to interact with the research subject.

11-5b Primary Research Tools

There are two basic categories of primary research: observation and survey. **Observation research** happens when the researcher *does not* directly interact with the research subject. The key advantage of watching versus asking is that what people actually *do* often differs from what they *say*—sometimes quite innocently. For instance, if an amusement park employee stands

> "Marketing without data is like driving with your eyes closed."
>
> —DAN ZARRELLA, SOCIAL MEDIA SCIENTIST, HUB SPOT

There Is No "Me" in Sustainability—but Maybe There Should Be!

Recent research suggests that an overwhelming majority of people around the world care about sustainability. What's more, they are finally willing to put their money where their mouth is and actually buy eco-friendly products—even if they are a little pricier than conventional products or are not quite the same quality. Even so, a surprisingly small number of eco-friendly products have broken through into the mainstream in a significant way. One example of a big success is hybrid cars. The reason may be that hybrid cars answer the age-old question of "What's in it for me?" While most eco-friendly products offer broad planetary benefits such as cleaner oceans or more trees or cleaner air, they don't offer direct personal benefits. Hybrid cars offer planetary benefits, to be sure, but they *also* offer the direct personal benefits of better gas mileage and a highly visible symbol that tells the rest of the world that the driver has adopted an eco-friendly technology (and is paying a little extra to do so). There is much to be said for appealing to our better intentions and higher purpose, but perhaps there is more marketing success to be had in promising customers direct personal benefits. Unilever's *sustainable living* hub expands on this idea:

> Recycling is mainly a guilt-avoidance activity, but could it actually be a fun teachable moment with your kids? Eating sustainably can mean better tasting food and weight loss, with less pesticides or unhealthy food additives. Natural body care products may smell nicer and are gentle on sensitive skin. Washing your hair less or in a shorter shower maintains natural shine and prevents split ends. These are tiny benefits, but when was the last sustainability campaign that promised any direct personal benefits at all?[11]

Syda Productions/Shutterstock.com

outside an attraction and records which way people turn when they exit, he may be conducting observation research to determine where to place a new lemonade stand. Watching would be better than asking because many people could not honestly say which way they'd likely turn. Examples of observation research include:

- Scanner data from retail sales
- Traffic counters to determine where to place billboards
- Garbage analysis to measure recycling compliance

Observation research can be both cheap and amazingly effective. A car dealership, for instance, can survey the preset radio stations on every car that comes in for service. That information helps them choose which stations to use for advertising. But the biggest downside of observation research is that it doesn't yield any information on consumer motivation—the reasons behind consumer decisions. The preset radio stations wouldn't matter, for example, if the bulk of drivers listen only to their iPods in the car.

Survey research happens when the researcher *does* interact with research subjects. The key advantage is that you can secure information about what people are thinking and feeling, beyond what you can observe. For example, a carmaker might observe that the majority of its purchasers are men. They could use this information to tailor their advertising to men, or they could do survey research and possibly learn that even though men do the actual purchasing, women often make the purchase decision . . . a very different scenario! But the key downside of survey research is that many people aren't honest or accurate about their experiences, opinions, and motivations, which can make survey research quite misleading. Examples of survey research include:

- Telephone and online questionnaires
- Door-to-door interviews
- Mall-intercept interviews
- Focus groups
- Mail-in questionnaires

11-5c An International Perspective

Doing marketing research across multiple countries can be an overwhelming challenge. In parts of Latin America, for instance, many homes don't have telephone connections, so the results from telephone surveys could be very misleading. Door-to-door tends to

be a better approach. But in parts of the Middle East, researchers could be arrested for knocking on a stranger's door, especially if they aren't dressed according to local standards. Because of these kinds of issues, many companies hire research firms with a strong local presence (often based in-country) to handle their international marketing research projects.

11-6 SOCIAL RESPONSIBILITY AND TECHNOLOGY: A MAJOR MARKETING SHIFT

Two key factors have had a dramatic impact on marketing in the past couple of decades: a surge in the social responsibility movement, and the dramatic emergence of the Internet and digital technology. This section will cover how each factor has influenced marketing.

11-6a Marketing and Society: It's Not Just about You!

Over the past couple of decades, the social responsibility movement has accelerated in the United States, demanding that marketers actively contribute to the needs of the broader community. Leading-edge marketers have responded by setting a higher standard in key areas such as environmentalism, abolishment of sweatshops, and involvement in the local community. Starbucks, Target, and General Electric, for instance, all publish corporate responsibility reports that evaluate the social impact of how the companies run their businesses, and all highlight their programs on their corporate websites.

Green Marketing Companies employ **green marketing** when they actively promote the ecological benefits of their products. Toyota has been especially successful promoting the green benefits of its Prius (although, like all carmakers, Toyota has struggled during the global financial crisis and, more recently, during the Japanese earthquake and tsunami). Its strategy highlights fuel economy and performance, implying that

survey research Marketing research that requires the researcher to interact with the research subject.

green marketing Developing and promoting environmentally sound products and practices to gain a competitive edge.

Innovation: Unleashed!

In today's hyper-competitive marketplace, businesses must differentiate their products from an astonishing array of alternatives. While life-changing innovation is rare, many successful products simply provide a new twist on an existing product. Examples include Wish-Bone's salad dressing spritzers, Nike's neon-colored Flyknit athletic shoes, and Yoplait's squeezable, Go-gurt yogurt snack tubes.

To help you make those kinds of jumps, the game in this box uses rebus puzzles to stretch your creativity. Rebus puzzles present common words and phrases in novel orientation to each other. The goal is to determine the meaning. The puzzles are below, and the answers are at the bottom of the box.

| ARREST YOU'RE | HISTORY HISTORY HISTORY | SK8 iiiiiiiiiii iiiiiiiii | print | BAN ANA | Shut Sit |
| funny funny words words words words | ST4ANCE | herring | MEREPEAT | Jack | Symphon |

Answers: You're under arrest, too funny for words, history repeats itself, for instance, skate on thin ice, red herring, small print, repeat after me, banana split, Jack-in-the-box, sit down and shut up, unfinished symphony

Kues/Shutterstock.com

> ## 75% of the engagement on a Facebook post happens in the first five hours.
> —DIGITAL INSIGHTS

consumers can "go green" without making any real sacrifices. Environmentally friendly fashion offers another emerging example of green marketing. Over the past few years, a number of designers have rolled out their versions of upscale ecofashion. In addition to clothing made of organic cotton, recent entries include vegan stilettos with four-inch heels, bamboo dresses, biodegradable umbrellas, and solar-powered jackets. (These jackets feature solar cells, integrated into the collar, that collect solar energy and route it to charge devices.) Green marketing items are aimed at a growing number of consumers who make purchase decisions based (at least in part) on their convictions. But reaching these consumers may be an increasing challenge in tough economic times, when low prices trump all other considerations for a growing swath of the population.[12]

mass customization The creation of products tailored for individual consumers on a mass basis.

11-6b Technology and Marketing: Power to the People!

The emergence of the digital age has revolutionized every element of marketing. Perhaps the most dramatic change has been a shift in power from producers to customers. The Internet gives customers 24/7 access to information and product choices from all over the world. In response, competition has intensified as marketers strive to meet an increasingly high standard of value.

But technology has also created opportunities for marketers. The Internet has opened the door for **mass customization**: creating products tailored for individual consumers on a mass basis. Using sophisticated data collection and management systems, marketers can now collect detailed information about each customer, which allows them to develop one-on-one relationships and to identify high-potential new customers. Through the Web, marketers can tap into (or even create) communities of users that yield valuable information about their goods and services. Technology also helps marketers lower costs, so they can deliver greater value to their customers.

The digital boom has also created an abundance of promotional opportunities, as marketers reach out to consumers via new tools, such as interactive advertising, virtual reality displays, text messaging, and video kiosks. We'll discuss these tools in more detail in Chapter 12.

THE BIG PICTURE

Since the ultimate goal of most marketing is long-term profitability, a core marketing principle must infuse every facet of a successful organization: the need to deliver products that exceed customer expectations. The customer must come first for *every* department—including finance, accounting, engineering, manufacturing, and human resources—although the specifics of how that plays out will clearly differ for each organizational function. Competition in the future will only intensify. Customer choices will continue to multiply as globalization and technology march forward. While these forces will weed out the weaker players, firms with a deeply engrained marketing orientation and a strong customer focus will continue to flourish—delivering value to their stakeholders, and dollars to their bottom line.

CAREERS IN MARKETING

Brand Manager

Drive the overall performance and profitability of a brand or group of brands. Establish the brand image and position in relation to competitors. Formulate and implement creative and effective marketing strategies. Manage and motivate creative teams that support the brand's development. Understand and integrate overall corporate goals into brand strategies. Communicate brand performance to senior management. Communicate key brand information to both internal and external stakeholders.

STUDY TOOLS 11

LOCATED AT BACK OF THE TEXTBOOK

☐ Rip-Out Chapter Review Card

☐ Gain unique perspectives on key concepts with new concept videos in the e-book

☐ Increase your comprehension with online homework and quizzes

☐ Study with existing flashcards and make your own

12 Product and Promotion:
Creating and Communicating Value

Remember to visit

PAGE 234

for additional

STUDY TOOLS

Dean Drobot/Shutterstock.com

12-1 PRODUCT: IT'S PROBABLY MORE THAN YOU THOUGHT

When most people hear the term "product," they immediately think of the material things that we buy, use, and consume every day: for example, a can of Pepsi, or a pair of True Religion jeans. But from a marketing standpoint, product means much more. A **product** can be anything that a company offers to satisfy consumer needs and wants; the possibilities include not only physical goods but also services and ideas. A charity event, cosmetic surgery, and a cooking lesson all qualify as products.

When you buy a product, you also "buy" all of the attributes associated with the product. These encompass a broad range of qualities, such as the brand name, the image, the packaging, the reputation, and the guarantee. From a consumer standpoint, these attributes (or the lack of these attributes) are part of the product purchase, even if they don't add to its value. As a marketer, it's worth your while to carefully consider each element of your product to ensure that you're maximizing value without sacrificing profitability. With the introduction of the translucent, multicolored iMac computers in 1998, Apple established its reputation for creating value through product design—an attribute that other PC manufacturers completely overlooked as they churned out their inventories of boring, beige boxes. Over the years, Apple has continued to polish its reputation by introducing sleek, elegantly designed products such as its iPad tablet computers and its iPhones.

product Anything that an organization offers to satisfy consumer needs and wants, including both goods and services.

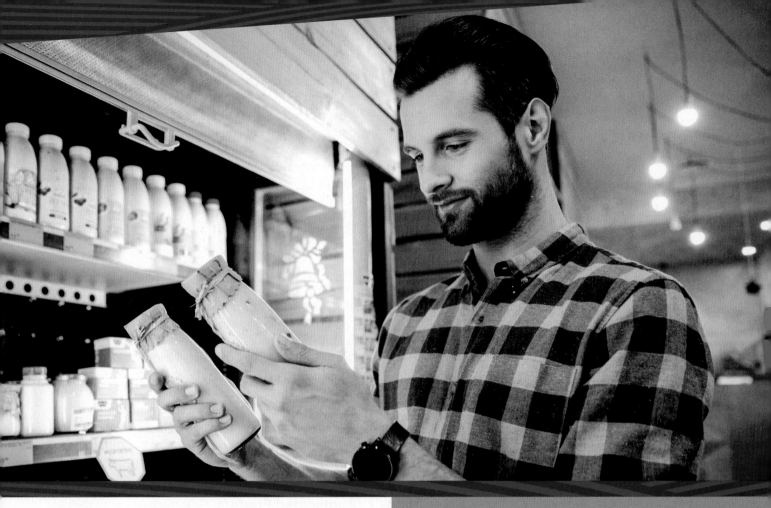

"Don't find customers for your products; find products for your customers."

—SETH GODIN, ENTREPRENEUR AND AUTHOR

12-1a Services: A Product by Any Other Name

If a "product" includes anything that satisfies consumer needs, services clearly fit the bill. But services have some obvious differences from tangible goods. You often cannot see, hear, smell, taste, or touch a service, and you can virtually never "own" it. After math tutoring, for example, you might possess sharper algebra skills, but you don't own the tutoring experience (at least not literally). Most services embody these qualities:

■ **Intangibility:** You typically cannot see, smell, taste, or touch a service before you buy it. Clearly, this creates a lot of uncertainty. Will the purchase really be worthwhile? Smart marketers mitigate the uncertainty by giving clues that suggest value. For example, the Culver hotel, a funky, old-time showbiz hotel and restaurant, plasters it's walls with pictures of movie stars, and fills its display space with moldering movie artifacts to provide "evidence" of its movie credentials.

■ **Inseparability:** Try as you might, you simply can't separate the buyer of a service from the person who renders it. Delivery requires interaction between the buyer and the provider, and the customer directly contributes to the quality of the service. Consider a trip to

the doctor. If you accurately describe your symptoms, you're likely to get a correct diagnosis. But if you simply say, "I just don't feel normal," the outcome will likely be different.

■ **Variability:** This one ties closely to inseparability. A talented massage therapist would probably help you relax, whereas a mediocre one might actually create tension. And even the talented massage therapist might give better service at the end of the day than at the beginning, or worse service on the day she breaks up with her boyfriend. Variability also applies to the difference among providers. A massage at a top-notch spa is likely to be better than a massage at your local gym.

■ **Perishability:** Marketers cannot store services for delivery at peak periods. A restaurant, for instance, only has so many seats; they can't (reasonably) tell their 8 P.M. dinner customers to come back the next day at 5 P.M. Similarly, major tourist destinations, such as Las Vegas, can't store an inventory of room service deliveries or performances of Cirque du Soleil. This creates obvious cost issues; is it worthwhile to prepare for a peak crowd but lose money when it's slow? The answer depends on the economics of your business.

12-1b Goods versus Services: A Mixed Bag

Identifying whether a product is a good or a service can pose a considerable challenge, since many products contain elements of both. A meal at your local Italian restaurant obviously includes tangible goods: you definitely own that calzone. But someone else took your order, brought it to the table, and (perhaps most importantly) did the dishes! Service was clearly a crucial part of the package.

A goods and services spectrum can provide a valuable tool for analyzing the relationship between the two. (See Exhibit 12.1.) At one extreme, **pure goods** don't include any services. Examples include a bottle of ketchup or a package of socks. At the other extreme, **pure services** don't include any goods. Examples include financial consulting or a piano lesson. Other products—such as a meal at Pizza Hut—fall somewhere between the poles.

12-1c Product Layers: Peeling the Onion

When customers buy products, they actually purchase more than just the good or service itself. They buy a complete product package that includes a core benefit, the actual product, and product augmentations. Understanding these layers is valuable, since the most successful products delight consumers at each one of them.

Core Benefit At the most fundamental level, consumers buy a core benefit that satisfies their needs. When you buy a smartphone, the core benefit is communication. When

you go to a movie, the core benefit is entertainment. And when you go to the doctor, the core benefit is better health. Most products also provide secondary benefits that help distinguish them from other goods and services that meet the same customer needs. A secondary benefit of a smartphone might include entertainment, since it probably plays your music, too.

12-1d Actual Product

The *actual product* layer, of course, is the product itself: the physical good or the delivered service that provides the core benefit. The Samsung Galaxy S8 is an actual good that provides the benefit of communication. A movie theater screening of *Wonder Woman* is an actual service that provides the benefit of entertainment. Identifying the actual product is sometimes tough when the product is a service. For example, the core benefit of visiting a doctor might be better health, but the actual product may be someone in a white coat pokingand prodding you. Keep in mind that the actual product includes all of the attributes that make it unique, such as the brand name, the features, and the packaging.

Augmented Product Most marketers wrap their actual products in additional goods and services, called the *augmented product*, that sharpen their competitive edge. Augmentations come in a range of different forms. Many upscale movie theaters in L.A. display props from movies that have played in that theater. Most smartphones come with warranties or insurance and offer at least some customer service. And some doctors might give you sample pills until you can get your prescription filled.

12-1e Product Classification: It's a Bird, It's a Plane...

Products fall into two broad categories—consumer products and business products—depending on the reason for the purchase. **Consumer products** are purchased for personal use or consumption, while **business products** are purchased to use either directly or indirectly in the production of another product. The shoes in your closet at home are a consumer product, while the shoes that you rent at the bowling alley are a business product.

pure goods Products that do not include any services.

pure services Products that do not include any goods.

consumer products Products purchased for personal use or consumption.

business products Products purchased to use either directly or indirectly in the production of other products.

Amero/Shutterstock.com

Exhibit 12.1
Goods and Services Spectrum

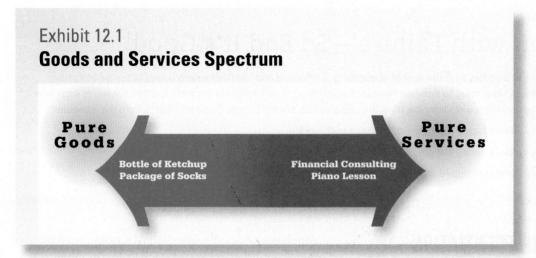

Pure Goods → **Pure Services**

Bottle of Ketchup
Package of Socks

Financial Consulting
Piano Lesson

Consumer Product Categories Marketers further divide consumer products into several different subcategories, as shown below. Understanding the characteristics of the subcategories can help marketers develop better strategies.

- *Convenience products* are the inexpensive goods and services that consumers buy frequently with limited consideration and analysis. Distribution tends to be widespread, with promotion by the producers. Examples include staples such as toothpaste and shampoo, impulse items such as magazines and candy bars, and emergency products such as headache tablets and plumbing services.

- *Shopping products* are the more expensive products that consumers buy less frequently. Typically, as consumers shop, they search for the best value and learn more about features and benefits through the shopping process. Distribution is widespread but more selective than for convenience products. Both producers and retailers tend to promote shopping products. Examples include cars, computers, and cell phone service.

- *Specialty products* are those much more expensive products that consumers seldom purchase. Most people perceive specialty products as being so important that they are unwilling to accept substitutes. Because of this, distribution tends to be highly selective. (Consumers are willing to go far out of their way for the "right" brand.) Both producers and retailers are apt to promote specialty products but to a highly targeted audience. Some specialty product examples are high-end sports cars, branded jewelry, and weight reduction surgery.

- *Unsought products* are the goods and services that hold little interest (or even negative interest) for consumers. Price and distribution vary wildly, but promotion tends to be aggressive to drum up consumer interest. Disability insurance and prepaid burial plots (especially for young people) and blood donations are some examples.

Business Product Categories Marketers also divide business products into subcategories. Here, too, understanding the subcategories can lead to better marketing strategies.

- *Installations* are large capital purchases designed for a long, productive life. The marketing of installations emphasizes personal selling and customization. Examples include industrial robots, new buildings, airplanes, and railroad cars.

- *Accessory equipment* includes smaller, movable capital purchases, designed for a shorter productive life than installations. Marketing focuses on personal selling but includes less customization than installations. Examples include personal computers, power tools, and furniture.

- The *maintenance, repair, and operating products* category consists of small-ticket items that businesses consume on an ongoing basis but don't become part of the final product. Marketing tactics emphasize efficiency. Examples include cleaning supplies, lightbulbs, and copy paper.

- *Raw materials* include the farm and natural products used in producing other products. Marketing emphasizes price and service rather than product differentiation. Examples include cotton, timber, and wheat.

- *Component parts and processed materials* include finished (or partially finished) products used in producing other products. Marketing emphasizes product quality as well as price and service. Examples include batteries and spark plugs for cars, aluminum ingots for soda cans, and Intel computer chips.

- *Business services* are those services that businesses purchase to facilitate operations. Marketing focuses on quality and relationships; the role of price can vary. Examples include payroll services, janitorial services, and legal services.

A Fascination with Failure—So Bad It's Good!

A brand-new museum is opening in Sweden, with the goal of celebrating "the absurd and hilarious wrong turns that companies have taken in their product development." According to museum founder Samuel West, "Every failure is uniquely spectacular, while success is nauseatingly repetitive. True innovation requires learning from the complexities of each failure."Some highlights from the museum:

- Toothpaste company Colgate offered frozen food like beef lasagna in the 1980s.
- Coca-Cola offered Coca-Cola BlaK—a coffee-flavored cola drink—from 2004 until 2006.
- Cult motorcycle brand Harley Davidson flopped delightfully with its "Hot Road" perfume.

 12-2

PRODUCT DIFFERENTIATION AND PLANNING: A MEANINGFUL DIFFERENCE

While some products have succeeded with little or no forethought, you'll dramatically boost your chance of a hit with careful planning. **Product differentiation** should be a key consideration. Winning products must embody a real or perceived difference versus the glut of goods and services that compete in virtually every corner of the market. But different alone isn't enough; different from, and better than, the competition are both critical in order to create the shortest path to success. A quick look at some high-profile product failures illustrates the point.

- **Vegetable Jello:** Few kids today would name Jello as their favorite dessert, and back in the 1960s, even fewer were fans of vegetable-flavored Jello (think celery, tomato, mixed vegetable, and Italian salad), which was soon yanked from the market.

- **Clear Beer:** In the 1990s, several companies introduced clear beers, reflecting an ill-fated obsession with clear products, including shampoo, soap, and the short-lived, clear Crystal Pepsi.

- **Lumia 900:** Nokia introduced the Lumia 900 phone in early 2012 for just $100 with a two-year contract. The price soon dropped to $50, but even that didn't spur sales, mostly due to a dearth of apps for its

Windows operating system. By 2013, Nokia, once the dominant player in cell phones, had sold its entire handset business to Microsoft.

- **Funky French Fries:** In 2002, Ore-Ida introduced Funky Fries. The flavors included cinnamon-sugar, chocolate, and "radical blue." Not surprisingly, they were off the market in less than a year.

- **Cocaine Energy Drink:** In 2006, Redux Beverages brought Cocaine Energy Drink to market, calling it a "legal alternative" to the illegal drug in form of an energy drink, and describing the beverage, which had no actual cocaine in it, as a "fruity, atomic fireball" drink. Redux was forced to pull Cocaine off the shelves in the United States in 2007 when the FDA declared that its producers were "illegally marketing their drink as an alternative to street drugs."[1]

12-2a Product Quality

Product quality relates directly to product value, which comes from understanding your customer. Peter Drucker, a noted business thinker, writer, and educator, declared:

Quality in a product or service is not what the supplier puts in. It's what the customer gets out and is willing to pay for. A product is not quality because it is hard to make and costs a lot of money . . . this is incompetence. Customers pay only for what is of use to them and gives them value. Nothing else constitutes quality.

In other words, a high-quality product does a great job meeting customer needs. Siemens, a huge electronics conglomerate, embodies this thinking in its approach to quality: "Quality is when our customers come back and our products don't."

> **product differentiation** The attributes that make a good or service different from other products that compete to meet the same or similar customer needs.

> "Give them quality. That's the best kind of advertising."
>
> —MILTON HERSHEY

EXHIBIT 12.2 — PRODUCT QUALITY INDICATORS

Product Category	Some Quality Indicators
Cell Phones	Design, brand, number of apps, graphics, memory, battery life, memory, and customer service
Kids' Toys	Safety, expert endorsements, and educational and entertainment value
Cars	Horsepower, design, fuel efficiency, brand, resale value, reliability, and awards
Water Parks	Thrill factor, design, cleanliness, variety, and setting
Coffee	Taste, brand, price, country of origin, and additives (or lack of)

But the specific definition of quality—and the attributes that indicate quality—changes across product categories. See Exhibit 12.2 for a few examples.

Regardless of product category, the two key aspects of quality are level and consistency. **Quality level** refers to how well a product performs its core functions. You might think that smart companies deliver the highest possible level of performance, but this is seldom profitable, or even desirable. For instance, only a tiny group of consumers would pay for a speedboat to go 200 mph, when 80 mph offers a sufficient thrill (at least for most of us!). The right level of product performance is the level that meets the needs of your consumers, and those needs include price. Decisions about quality level must also consider the competition. The goal is to outperform the other players in your category while maintaining profitability.

The second dimension of quality is **product consistency**. How consistently does your product actually deliver the promised level of quality? With a positive relationship between price and performance, consistent delivery can offer a competitive edge at almost any quality level.

Honda offers an excellent example. When most people consider the Accord, the Civic, and the CRV, all Honda-owned models, quality quickly comes to mind. And all three dominate their markets. But clearly, the quality *levels* (and price) are different for each. The Accord serves the upper, more conservative end of the market; the Civic tends to appeal to younger, hipper, more budget-minded consumers; the CRV tends to appeal to middle-of-the-road shoppers seeking a reliable, small SUV. In short, Honda succeeds at delivering product consistency at several markedly different quality levels.

12-2b Features and Benefits

Product features are the characteristics of the product you offer. If a product is well designed, each feature corresponds to a meaningful **customer benefit**. The marketer's challenge is to design a package of features that offers the highest level of value for an acceptable price. And the equation must also account for profitability goals.

One winning formula may be to offer at least some low-cost features that correspond to high-value benefits. Creating an "open kitchen" restaurant, for instance, has limited impact on costs but gives patrons an exciting, up-close view of the drama and hustle of professional food preparation. Exhibit 12.3 lists some other examples of product features and their corresponding customer benefits.

quality level How well a product performs its core functions.

product consistency How reliably a product delivers its promised level of quality.

product features The specific characteristics of a product.

customer benefit The advantage that a customer gains from specific product features.

EXHIBIT 12.3 — PRODUCT FEATURES AND CUSTOMER BENEFITS

Product	Product Feature	Customer Benefit
Subway Sandwiches	Lower fat	Looser pants
Costco	Rock-bottom prices on a huge range of higher end products and services	More cash for other needs
Whole Foods Market	Organic produce	A healthier planet
Stella McCartney Clutch	Highly fashionable	Feeling chic
Triple Latte	Caffeine, caffeine, caffeine	More time to, uh, study

12-2c Product Lines and the Product Mix

Some companies focus all of their efforts on one product, but most offer a number of different products to enhance their revenue and profits. A **product line** is a group of products that are closely related to each other in terms of either how they work or the customers they serve. Sony, for example, carries a wide range of digital cameras and accessories, to meet the needs of as many different customers as possible. A **product mix** is the total number of product lines and individual items sold by a single firm. Sony's product mix ranges from cameras to electronics, to phones, to music, to video game consoles, to entertainment (games, movies, music, etc.).

Decisions regarding how many items to include in each product line and in the overall product mix can have a huge impact on a firm's profits. With too few items in each line, the company may be leaving money on the table. With too many items, the company may be spending unnecessarily to support its weakest links.

One reason that firms add new product lines is to reach completely new customers. Gap, for instance, added Old Navy to reach younger, lower-income customers, and Banana Republic to reach older, higher-income customers. Each line includes a range of different products designed to meet the needs of their specific customers. But one risk of adding new lines—especially lower-priced lines—is **cannibalization**, which happens when a new entry "eats" the sales of an existing line. This is especially dangerous when the new products are lower-priced than the current ones. You could see the problem, for instance, if a $20 blue jean purchase from Old Navy replaces a $50 blue jean purchase from Gap; the company has lost more than half its revenue on the sale. Like other companies with multiple lines, Gap carefully monitors the cannibalization issue and works to differentiate its lines as fully as possible.

12-2d Branding

At the most basic level, a **brand** is a product's identity that sets it apart from other players in the same category. Typically, brands represent the combination of elements such as product name, symbol, design, reputation, and image. But today's most powerful emerging brands go far beyond the sum of their attributes. They project a compelling group identity that creates brand fanatics: loyal customers who advocate for the brand better than any advertising a marketer could buy. The overall value of a brand to an organization—the extra money that consumers will spend to buy that brand—is called **brand equity**.

Since 2001, *BusinessWeek* and Interbrand, a leading brand consultancy, have teamed up to publish a ranking of the 100 Best Global Brands by dollar value. The top ten brands are listed in Exhibit 12.4, but you can find the complete list at Interbrand's website.

Brand Name A catchy, memorable name is among the most powerful elements of your brand. While the right name will never save a bad business, it can launch a good business to new heights. But finding the right name can be tough. According to the respected Brighter Naming consulting group, the following characteristics can help:

1. Short, sweet, and easy to pronounce and spell: Examples include Sprite, H&M, GE, Nike, and Visa.

2. Unique within the industry: Think Caterpillar, Yahoo!, Starbucks, Zara, and Google.

3. Good alliteration, especially for long names: The words should roll off your tongue. Some examples are Coca-Cola, BlackBerry, Dunkin' Donuts, Weight Watchers, and Minute Maid.[2]

---

product line A group of products that are closely related to each other, either in terms of how they work or the customers they serve.

product mix The total number of product lines and individual items sold by a single firm.

cannibalization When a producer offers a new product that takes sales away from its existing products.

brand A product's identity—including product name, symbol, design, reputation, and image—that sets it apart from other players in the same category.

brand equity The overall value of a brand to an organization.

EXHIBIT 12.4	BUSINESSWEEK/INTERBRAND TOP TEN GLOBAL BRANDS 2017
Brand	**Country of Ownership**
Apple	United States
Google	United States
Microsoft	United States
Coca-Cola	United States
Amazon	United States
Samsung	South Korea
Toyota	Japan
Facebook	United States
Mercedes-Benz	Germany
IBM	United States

Source: Interbrand Website, http://interbrand.com/best-brands/best-global-brands/2016/ranking/, accessed May 4, 2018.

EXHIBIT 12.5 | BRAND NAME CATEGORIES

Category	Description	Examples
Location-Based	Refers to either the area served or the place of origin	Southwest Airlines, Bank of America, Best Western Hotels
Founder's Name	Can include first name, last name, or both	McDonald's, Dell Computer, Ford, Disney, Jenny Craig
Descriptive or Functional	Describes what the product is or how it works	eBay, U.S. News and World Report, Subway, Krispy Kreme
Evocative	Communicates an engaging image that resonates with consumers	Yahoo!, Craftsman, Virgin, Intel, Cosmopolitan, Starbucks, Apple, SpaceX, Oculus Rift

Brand names typically fall into four categories, as described in Exhibit 12.5.

Line Extensions versus Brand Extensions As companies grow, marketers look for opportunities to grow their businesses. **Line extensions** are similar products offered under the same brand name. Possibilities include new flavors, sizes, colors, ingredients, and forms. One example is Lays potato chips, which offers more than 45 versions, including BBQ, Baked, Flamin Hot, Chili Limon, Bacon Mac & Cheese, and Cheesy Garlic Bread. The marketing challenge is to ensure that line extensions steal market share from competitors rather than from the core brand.

Brand extensions, on the other hand, involve launching a product in a new category under an existing brand name. The Bic brand, for instance, is quite elastic, stretching nicely to include diverse products such as pens, glue, cigarette lighters, and disposable razors. The Virgin brand demonstrates similar elasticity, covering more than 350 companies that range from airlines to cell phones, to soft drinks, to cars. But the concept of brand extension becomes most clear (and most entertaining) through examining brand extension failures. Examples include Bic perfume, Budweiser Dry, Colgate (yes, the toothpaste brand!) frozen dinners, and Harley-Davidson Cologne. Apparently there is some mysterious link between lighter fluid and perfume. Zippo offers perfume, too.[3]

Licensing Some companies opt to license their brands from other businesses. **Licensing** means purchasing—often for a substantial fee—the right to use another company's brand name or symbol. The benefits are instant name recognition, an established reputation, and a proven track record. On a worldwide basis, the best-known licensing arrangements are probably character names, which range from Bart Simpson to SpongeBob and appear on everything from cereal to toys, to underwear. Many movie producers also do high-profile licensing, turning out truckloads of merchandise that features movie properties such as *Batman* and *Frozen*.

Another fast-growing area is the licensing of corporate or college names. Coca-Cola, for instance, claims to have more than 300 licensees who sell over a billion dollars of licensed merchandise each year. The potential benefits for Coca-Cola are clear: more promotion, increased exposure, and enhanced image. But the risk is significant. If licensed products are of poor quality or overpriced, the consumer backlash hits the core brand rather than the producer of the licensed product.

Cobranding Cobranding is when established brands from different companies join forces to market the same product. This cooperative approach has a long history but is currently enjoying a new popularity. Examples include:

- T.G.I. Friday's markets a broad (and very popular) range of Jack Daniel's-flavored foods.

- Dairy Queen worked with Girl Scouts to offer the hugely popular limited-edition Thin Mint Blizzard.

Cobranding can offer huge advantages to both partners, by leveraging their strengths to enter new markets and gain more exposure. But cobranding can be risky. If one partner makes a major goof, the fallout can damage the reputation of the other partner as well.

National Brands versus Store Brands National **brands**, also called *manufacturers' brands*, are brands that the producer owns and markets. Many are well known and widely available, such as Oreo cookies, Dial soaps, and Nutella. Although most retailers carry lots of national brands, an

line extensions Similar products offered under the same brand name.

brand extension A new product, in a new category, introduced under an existing brand name.

licensing Purchasing the right to use another company's brand name or symbol.

cobranding When established brands from different companies join forces to market the same product.

national brands Brands that the producer owns and markets.

Archer Farms, Target's high-quality food label, is one of the most popular and successful store brands.

increasing number have opted to also carry their own versions of the same products, called **store brands**, or *private label*. Deep discounters, such as Walmart and Costco, have had particular success with their private-label brands (e.g., Sam's Choice and Kirkland). *Private labels* play a growing role in grocery stores as well. In the United States, more than one out of four grocery purchases is private label, and the numbers are even higher in Europe, hitting half of all grocery sales in a number of markets. Since the global recession, private-label brand sales have grown more than twice as fast as national brand sales. The growing influence and increasing quality of low-end, private-label brands increase the pressure on national brands to continually innovate while holding down prices.[4]

At the upper end of the market—especially in the clothing business—key retailers specialize in private brands to create and protect a consistent, upscale image. Examples include Neiman Marcus, Coldwater Creek, and Saks Fifth Avenue.[5]

12-2e Packaging

Great packaging does more than just hold the product. It can protect the product, provide information, facilitate storage, suggest product uses, promote the product brand, and attract buyer attention. Great packaging is especially important in the crowded world of grocery stores and mass merchandisers. In the average supermarket, the typical shopper passes about 300 items per minute and makes anywhere from 20% to 70% of purchases on sheer impulse. In this environment, your package must call out to your target customers and

store brands Brands that the retailer both produces and distributes (also called private-label brands).

differentiate your product from all the others lined up beside it. Yet, in attracting consumer attention, a good package cannot sacrifice the basics such as protecting the product.[6]

Bottom line: great packaging stems from consumer needs, but it usually includes at least a smidge of creative brilliance. Examples include yogurt in a pouch that doesn't need a spoon, soup-to-go that can be microwaved in the can, "anti-theft" clear sandwich bags printed with mold-like green splotches (seriously!), and single-serving baby carrot packets that moms can toss into kids' lunches.

12-3 INNOVATION AND THE PRODUCT LIFE CYCLE: NUTS, BOLTS, AND A SPARK OF BRILLIANCE

For a business to thrive long term, effective new product development is vital. And the process works only if it happens quickly. As technological advances hit the market at breakneck speed, current products are becoming obsolete faster than ever before. The need for speed compounds as hungry competitors crowd every niche of the market. But the rush is risky, since new product development costs can be in the millions, and the success rate is less than a third. Marketers who succeed in this challenging arena devote painstaking effort to understanding their customers, but they also nurture the creativity they need to generate new ideas. An example of how this can work: the 3M Corporation—makers of Post-it Notes and Scotch Tape—introduces about 500 new products per year by pushing its employees to "relentlessly ask, 'What if?'" Some innovative firms, such as Google, Facebook, and LinkedIn, also encourage workers to spend 20% of their work time (paid work time!) on projects of personal interest.[7]

12-3a Types of Innovation

Clearly, the first personal computer represented a higher degree of newness than the first personal computer with a color screen. And the computer with a color screen represented a higher degree of newness than the first low-cost knockoff. Levels of innovation fall along a spectrum, as shown in Exhibit 12.6.

Discontinuous Innovation *Discontinuous innovations* are brand-new ideas that radically change how people live. Examples include the first car, the first television,

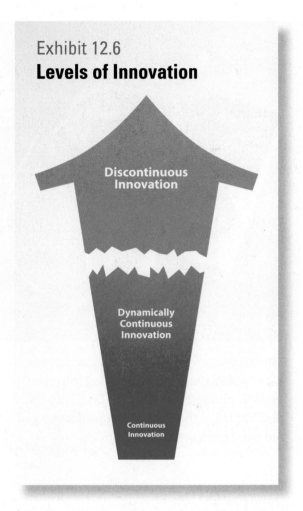

Exhibit 12.6
Levels of Innovation

Discontinuous Innovation

Dynamically Continuous Innovation

Continuous Innovation

new product success. The standard model includes six stages:

Each stage requires management to "green light" ideas before moving forward, to ensure that the company doesn't waste resources on marginal concepts.

- **Idea Generation:** Some experts estimate that it takes 50 ideas for each new product that makes it to market, so you should definitely cast a wide net. Ideas can come from almost anywhere, including customer research, customer complaints, salespeople, engineers, suppliers, and competitors.

- **Idea Screening:** The purpose of this stage is to weed out ideas that don't fit with the company's objectives and ideas that would clearly be too expensive to develop. The Walt Disney Company, for instance, would certainly eliminate the idea of an XXX cable channel because it just doesn't fit their mission.

- **Analysis:** The purpose of the analysis stage is to estimate costs and forecast sales for each idea to get a sense of the potential profit and of how the product might fit within the company's resources. Each idea must meet rigorous standards to remain a contender.

- **Development:** The development process leads to detailed descriptions of each concept with specific product features. New product teams sometimes also make prototypes, or samples, that consumers can actually test. The results help fully refine the concept.

- **Testing:** This stage involves the formal process of soliciting feedback from consumers by testing the product concept. Do they like the features? Are the benefits meaningful? What price makes sense? Some companies also test-market their products or sell them in a limited area to evaluate the consumer response.

and the first computer. These dramatic innovations require extensive customer learning, which should guide the marketing process.

Dynamically Continuous Innovation *Dynamically continuous innovations* are characterized by marked changes to existing products. Examples include cell phones, Blu-ray Discs, and digital cameras. These types of innovations require a moderate level of consumer learning in exchange for significant benefits.

Continuous Innovation A slight modification of an existing product is called a *continuous innovation*. Examples include new sizes, flavors, shapes, packaging, and design. The goal of continuous innovation is to distinguish a product from the competition. The goal of a knockoff is simply to copy a competitor and offer a lower price.

12-3b The New Product Development Process

An efficient, focused development process will boost your chances of

> "You can't wait for inspiration, you have to go after it with a club."
>
> —JACK LONDON, AUTHOR

- **Commercialization:** This stage entails introducing the product to the general market. Two key success factors are gaining distribution and launching promotions. But a product that tested well doesn't always mean instant success. The VW Beetle, for example, sold only 330 cars during its first year in the United States, but it later became a hit.

12-3c New Product Adoption and Diffusion

In order to become a commercial success, new products must spread throughout a market after they are introduced. That process is called *diffusion*. But diffusion clearly happens at different speeds, depending on the individual consumer and on the product itself.

Product Adoption Categories Some consumers like to try new things; others seem terrified of change. These attitudes clearly affect the rate at which individual people are willing to adopt (or begin buying and using) new products. The first adopters, about 2.5% of the total, are adventurous risk takers. The laggards, about 16% of the total, sometimes adopt products so late that earlier adopters have already moved to the next new thing. The rest of the population falls somewhere in between. Keep in mind that individuals tend to adopt new products at different rates. For instance, we probably all know someone who is an innovator in technology but a laggard in fashion, or vice versa.

Product Diffusion Rates Some new products diffuse into the population much more quickly than others. For example, Apple iPods and Segway Human Transporters appeared on the market around the same time; iPods became a pop culture icon, while Segways remained on the fringe. What accounts for the difference? Researchers have identified five product characteristics that affect the rate of adoption and diffusion. The more characteristics a product has, the faster it will diffuse into the population.

- **Observability:** How visible is the product to other potential consumers? Some product categories are easier to observe than others. If you adopt a new kind of car, the whole neighborhood will know, plus anyone else who sees you on the streets and highways.

- **Trialability:** How easily can potential consumers sample the new product? Trial can be a powerful way to create new consumers, which is why many markets fill their aisles with sample tables during popular shopping hours. Other examples of trial-boosting strategies include test-driving cars, sampling music, and testing new fragrances.

- **Complexity:** Can potential consumers easily understand what your product is and how it works? If

Ralph Gillen/Shutterstock.com

Fifteen years ago, portable media players like Apple's iPod were rocketing into the growth phase. Now, they are well into the decline stage thanks to the proliferation of always-connected smartphones.

your product confuses people—or if they find it hard to explain to others—adoption rates will slow. For example, many people who test-ride Segway Human Transporters love the experience, but they have trouble explaining to others how it works or why it beats other transportation options.

- **Compatibility:** How consistent is your product with the existing way of doing things? Cordless phones, for example, caught on almost instantly, since they were completely consistent with people's prior experiences—only better!

- **Relative Advantage:** How much better are the benefits of your new product compared to existing products? When gas prices climb, for example, the benefits of a hybrid car take on a much higher value relative to standard cars. As a result, demand skyrockets.

12-3d The Product Life Cycle: Maximizing Results over Time

When marketers introduce a new product, they hope it will last forever, generating sales and profits for years to come. But they also realize that all products go through

Exhibit 12.7
Product Life Cycle for a Typical Product Category

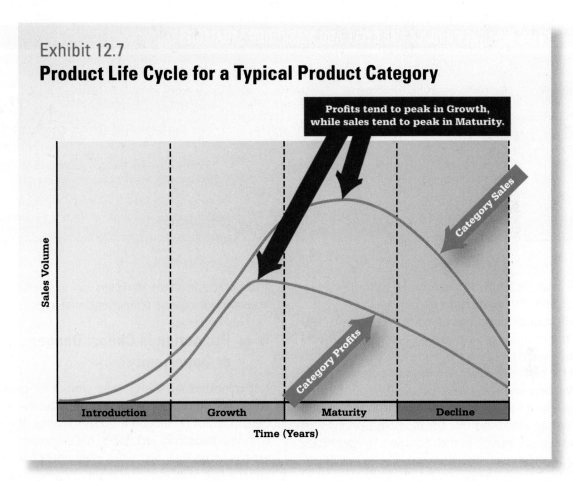

Profits tend to peak in Growth, while sales tend to peak in Maturity.

Category Sales

Category Profits

Sales Volume

Introduction | Growth | Maturity | Decline

Time (Years)

a **product life cycle**: a pattern of sales and profits that typically changes over time. The life cycle can be dramatically different across individual products and product categories, and predicting the exact shape and length of the life cycle is virtually impossible. But most product categories do move through the four distinct stages shown in Exhibit 12.7.

- **Introduction:** This is a time of low sales and nonexistent profits as companies invest in raising awareness about the product and the product category. Some categories, such as the microwave, languish in this phase for years, while other categories, such as computer memory sticks, zoom through this phase. And some categories never get beyond introduction. (Think clear beers.)

- **Growth:** During the growth period, sales continue to rise, although profits usually peak. Typically, competitors begin to notice emerging categories in the growth phase. They enter the market—often with new variations of existing products—which further fuels the growth. Electric cars, plug-in hybrids, personal drones, and driverless cars are currently in the

growth phase, and a number of competitors have recently entered the market.

- **Maturity:** During maturity, sales usually peak. Profits continue to decline as competition intensifies. Once a market is mature, the only way to gain more users is to steal them from competitors rather than to bring new users into the category. Weaker players begin to drop out of the category. Gasoline-powered cars, sugared soda, and network TV are in maturity in the United States.

- **Decline:** During this period, sales and profits begin to decline, sometimes quite rapidly. The reasons usually relate to either technological change or change in consumer needs. For instance, the introduction of word processing pushed typewriters into decline, and a change in consumer taste and habits pushed hot cereal into decline. Competitors continue to drop out of the category.

Familiarity with the product life cycle helps marketers plan effective strategies for existing products and identify profitable categories

product life cycle A pattern of sales and profits that typically changes over time.

EXHIBIT 12.8 | THE PRODUCT LIFE CYCLE AND MARKETING STRATEGIES

Phase	Examples	Sales/Profits	Key Marketing Strategies
Introduction	Virtual reality games, fuel cell technology, "smart" glasses	Low sales, low profits	Build awareness, trial, and distribution
Growth	Electric cars, eBook readers, mini tablets, fitness trackers	Rapidly increasing sales and profits	Reinforce brand positioning, often through heavy advertising
Maturity	Airlines, DVD players, personal computers, online stock trading, energy drinks	Flat sales and declining profits	Target competitors, while defending franchise with new product features, competitive advertising, promotion, and price cuts
Decline	Pagers, videocassettes	Declining sales and profits	Reduce spending and consider terminating the product

for new products. Exhibit 12.8 summarizes typical marketing strategies and offers examples for each phase.

Individual products also have life cycles that usually follow the category growth pattern but sometimes vary dramatically. Clearly, it's in the marketer's best interest to extend the profitable run of an individual brand as long as possible. There are several ways to make this happen: finding new uses for the product, changing the product, and changing the marketing mix. For example, *Dancing with the Stars* renews interest in their franchise by continually introducing new celebrity contestants.

12-4 PROMOTION: INFLUENCING CONSUMER DECISIONS

Promotion is the power to influence consumers—to remind them, to inform them, to persuade them. The best promotion goes one step further, building powerful consumer bonds that draw your customers back to your product again and again. But don't forget that great promotion only works with a great product. Bill Bernbach, an ad industry legend, captures this concept by noting, "A great ad campaign will make a bad product fail faster. It will get more people to know it's bad."

Marketers can directly control most promotional tools. From TV advertising to telephone sales, the marketer creates the message and communicates it directly to the target audience. But, ironically, marketers *cannot* directly control the most powerful promotional tools: publicity, such as a comment on *The View* or a review in *Consumer Reports*, and word-of-mouth, such as a recommendation from a close friend or even

promotion Marketing communication designed to influence consumer purchase decisions through information, persuasion, and reminders.

a casual acquaintance. Marketers can only influence these areas through creative promotional strategies.

12-4a Promotion in Chaos: Danger or Opportunity?

Not coincidentally, the Chinese symbol for crisis resembles the symbols for danger and opportunity—a perfect description of promotion in today's market. The pace of change is staggering. Technology has empowered consumers to choose how and when they interact with media, and they are grabbing control with dizzying speed. Digital TV and streaming movies continue to grow explosively. In 2015, people around the globe spent more than eight hours a day consuming media—much of it digital media—which continues to grow rapidly as a percentage of total media consumption. Meanwhile, more passive forms of entertainment, such as network television, are slowly losing their audience. And those people who do still watch TV are gleefully changing the schedules and zapping the ads with TiVo or similar devices. As media splinter across an array of entertainment options, usage patterns have changed as well: tech-savvy viewers are more prone to consume media in on-the-fly snacks rather than sit-down meals. Also, services such as Netflix streaming and Hulu Plus have led to an increase in binge viewing of entire seasons of TV shows. Rising consumer power and the breakneck pace of technology have created a growing need—and a stunning opportunity—for marketers to zero in on the right customers, at the right time, with the right message.[9]

12-4b Integrated Marketing Communication: Consistency and Focus

How many marketing messages have you gotten in the past 24 hours? Did you flip on the TV or radio? Surf the Web? Notice a billboard? Glance at the logo on a T-shirt or cap? Chat with a friend about some product he likes? Marketing exposure quickly snowballs: the typical consumer receives about 3,000 advertising messages each day. Some of those messages are hard to avoid as marketers find new, increasingly creative ways to promote their products to a captive audience. The venues include elevators, taxicabs, golf carts, and other surprising settings.[10]

Given the confounding level of clutter, smart companies use **integrated marketing communication** to coordinate their messages through every promotional vehicle—including their advertising, website, and salespeople—creating a coherent impression in the minds of their customers. Why bother coordinating all of these elements? The answer is clear. Consumers don't think about the specific source of the communication; instead, they combine—or integrate—the messages from *all* the sources to form a unified impression about your product. If the messages are out of sync or confusing, busy consumers won't bother to crack the code. They'll simply move on to the next best option.

Can you really control every message that every consumer sees or hears about your product? It's not likely. But if you accurately identify the key points of contact between your product and your target market, you can focus on those areas with remarkable effectiveness. For instance, the most common points of contact for McDonald's are probably advertising and the in-store experience. From upbeat commercials to smiling employees, to brightly striped uniforms, McDonald's spends millions of dollars to support its core message of fast, tasty food in a clean, friendly environment—heavily concentrated in the areas that are key to its brand.

Other companies are likely to encounter the bulk of their customers through different channels. You'd probably learn about Dell computers, for example, through either its website or word of mouth. Dell has invested heavily in both areas. The company maintains an innovative, user-friendly website that allows even novice users to create customized systems. And Dell delivers award-winning customer service and technical support, which gets its customers to recommend its products to family and friends.

12-4c Coordinating the Communication

Even after you've identified the key points of contact, coordinating the messages remains a challenge. In many companies, completely different teams develop the different promotional areas. Salespeople and brand managers often have separate agendas, even when the same executive manages both departments. Frequently, disconnected outside agencies handle advertising, web development, and sales promotion programs. Coordinating the messages will happen only with solid teamwork, which must begin at the top of the organization.

Information also plays a crucial role. To coordinate marketing messages, everyone who creates and manages them must have free access to knowledge about the customer, the product, the competition, the market, and the strategy of the organization. Some of this information, such as strategic goals, will come from the top down, but a fair amount, such as information about the customer, should come from the bottom up. Information must also flow laterally across departments and agencies. The marketing research department, for instance, might have critical information about product performance, which might help the web management agency create a feature page that might respond to competitive threats identified by the sales force. When all parties have access to the same data, they are much more likely to remain on the same page.

12-5 A MEANINGFUL MESSAGE: FINDING THE BIG IDEA

Your promotional message begins with understanding how your product is different from and better than the competition. But your **positioning statement**— a brief statement that articulates how you want your target market to envision your product relative to the competition—seldom translates directly into the

With so much clutter in the marketplace, coordinating messages can be a real challenge.

Joseph Sohm/Shutterstock.com

integrated marketing communication The coordination of marketing messages through every promotional vehicle to communicate a unified impression about a product.

positioning statement A brief statement that articulates how the marketer would like the target market to envision a product relative to the competition.

promotional message. Instead, it marks the beginning of the creative development process, often spearheaded by ad agency creative professionals. When it works, the creative development process yields a *big idea*—a meaningful, believable, and distinctive concept that cuts through the clutter. Big ideas are typically based on either a rational or an emotional premise. Here are a few examples from the last decade:

Rational:	Price:	Home Depot: "More saving. More doing."
	Engineering:	Bose: "Better sound through research"
	Ingredients:	Snapple: "Made from the best stuff on earth."
	Subway:	"Eat Fresh"
Emotional:	Imagination:	GE: "Imagination at work"
	Humor:	Virgin Atlantic: "More experience than our name suggests"
	Fear:	Cancer Patient's Aid Association: "Cancer Cures Smoking"
	Energy:	Nike: "Just do it"
	Self-Esteem:	L'Oréal "Because you're worth it."
	Patriotism:	Marines: "The few. The Proud. The Marines."

Not surprisingly, funny ads are a consumer favorite, although humor can be risky. For a record ten years in a row, from 1998 through 2008, Budweiser—known for using humor effectively—nabbed the top spot in *USA Today's* annual Ad Meter consumer ranking of Super Bowl ads. But in 2009, a very funny "Free Doritos" ad—created by talented amateurs in an online contest sponsored by Frito-Lay—knocked Budweiser off its pedestal. Budweiser regained the top spot in 2011, sharing the honor with Doritos, which, once again, took the top prize with a hilarious customer-created ad. Doritos used the same strategy to score a third win in 2012. In 2013, Budweiser held on to the top spot with a heart-warming spot about the bond between a trainer and his horse, while Doritos—again using the same strategy—fell to eighth place. In 2015, Budweiser again held the top spot with an ad about a puppy and a horse, while Doritos' customer-created ad took fifth place. In 2016, Doritos sported two ads in the top ten, while Budweiser dropped to ninth place. Hyundai snagged the top honors with a hilarious ad featuring an overprotective

In 2017, Kia Motors earned the top spot on *USA Today's* list of the best Super Bowl ads for "Hero's Journey." In this ad, Melissa McCarthy imagines herself taking on various eco-friendly causes—to disastrous results.

dad (played by comedian Kevin Hart) following his daughter on a first date. In 2017, Doritos opted out of advertising during the pricey Super Bowl. Budweiser's 2017 Super Bowl ad took fourth place. Kia Motors took the top spot with a hilarious ad featuring the ever-game comedian Melissa McCarthy. In 2018, Amazon celebrated its first ever Ad Meter victory with a hilarious thought about Alexa losing her voice. [11]

The best big ideas have entrenched themselves in popular culture. A small sampling:

- The Energizer Bunny
- "Got Milk?"
- Budweiser: "Whassssuuup?!?!"
- GE: "We bring good things to life."
- Motel 6: "We'll leave the light on for you."

12-5a An International Perspective

Some big ideas translate well across cultures. The Marlboro Man now promotes rugged individualism across the globe. But other big ideas don't travel as smoothly. DeBeers tried running ads in Japan using their proven strategy in the West: fabulously dressed women smiling and kissing their husbands who have just given them glittering diamonds. The ads failed in Japan because a Japanese woman would be more likely to shed a few tears and feign anger that her husband would spend so much money. The revised DeBeers campaign featured a hardworking husband and wife in their tiny apartment. Receiving a diamond, the wife chides her extravagant husband: "Oh, you stupid!" The campaign was a wild success. Taking a big idea to a foreign market can mean big money and a powerful brand, but careful research should still be your first step.[12]

12-6 THE PROMOTIONAL MIX: COMMUNICATING THE BIG IDEA

Once you've nailed your message, you need to communicate the big idea to your target market. The traditional communication tools—or **promotional channels**—include advertising, sales promotion, direct marketing, and personal selling. But more recently, a number of new tools have emerged, ranging from advergaming to Internet minimovies. The combination of communication tools that you choose to promote your product is called your "promotional mix."

12-6a Emerging Promotional Tools: The Leading Edge

In the past decade, the promotional landscape has changed dramatically. Consumer expectations and empowerment have skyrocketed. Consumer tolerance for impersonal corporate communication has fallen. And digital technology has surged forward at breakneck speed. As a result, new promotional tools have emerged, and previously minor tools have burst into the mainstream. This section covers several leading-edge promotional tactics, but keep in mind that other tools—such as mobile phone promotion, social media marketing, and widget-based marketing—are growing explosively, too.

Internet Advertising Internet advertising has been highly visible for more than a decade. But the industry has moved far beyond simple banner ads and annoying pop-up ads. The highest growth areas include paid search advertising, search engine optimization, and online video advertising.

Paid search advertising includes both sponsored links on Google that relate to the topic you've searched, and targeted Google text ads on a number of different websites—both of which are at the heart of Google's outsized financial success. Industry expert *eMarketer* estimates that paid search advertising, including both Google and other similar services, will top $40 billion by 2019, with much of that spending targeting mobile.[13] Paid search seems to be an especially attractive tactic during tough economic times, since it offers high accountability—marketers can tell exactly how well their limited advertising dollars are working.[14]

Search engine optimization (SEO) also demonstrated strong growth as the economy weakened. SEO involves taking specific steps to ensure that your website appears high on the list when customers look for your product or service via an Internet search engine such as Google or Yahoo!. Typically, the higher a firm appears, the more traffic that site will receive from potential customers. Analysis from *eMarketer* suggest that most marketers worldwide do desktop SEO as a matter of course, and will turn their efforts to mobile SEO over the next few years, since that is where consumers make most of their search queries.[15]

Online video advertising represents another high-growth area. This includes the increasingly popular "pre-roll" ads, the 15- to 30-second spots that viewers often sit through before watching an online video on YouTube, Hulu, or many other sites. According to *eMarketer* estimates, the growth will continue to increase at a spectacular rate, more than tripling from $4.14 billion in 2013 to nearly $15 billion in 2019.[16]

Social Media Clearly, social media—including Facebook, Twitter, Blogger, Tumblr, Foursquare, and many others—are not a fad, but rather a paradigm shift in how successful businesses market themselves. According to advertising heavyweight Alex Bogusky, "You can't buy attention anymore. Having a huge budget doesn't mean anything in social media. . . . The old media paradigm was PAY to play. Now you get back what you authentically put in." And the evidence is building that social media offer a truly impressive return on investment, especially compared to traditional media. A few examples compiled by social media expert Erik Qualman underscore the potential return on investment:

- Wetpaint/Altimeter study found companies that are both deeply and widely engaged in social media significantly surpass their peers in both revenues and profits. The study also found the company sales with the highest levels of social media activity grew on average by 18%, while those companies with the least amount of social activity saw their sales decline by 6%.

- BlendTec increased its sales five times by running the often humorous "Will It Blend" videos on YouTube, blending everything from an iPhone to a sneaker.

- Dell sold $3,000,000 worth of computers on Twitter.

- Ford Motor Company gave away 100 Fiestas to influential bloggers,

> **promotional channels**
> Specific marketing communication vehicles, including traditional tools, such as advertising, sales promotion, direct marketing, and personal selling, and newer tools such as product placement, advergaming, and Internet minimovies.

Social media offer marketers myriad opportunities to reach consumers.

resulting in 37% of Generation Y learning of the Ford Fiesta before it was launched in the United States.

■ Debt relief firm CareOne found that customers gained through social media completed their first payment through the company, at a higher rate of 732%.

■ Web host provider Moonfruit more than recouped its $15,000 social media investment as its website traffic soared 300% while sales increased 20%.

Looking ahead, smart marketers of both large and small businesses are investing their limited resources in social marketing and reaping an unprecedented return, forging the future of marketing promotion.[17]

Native Advertising Across all media, but especially Internet advertising and social media, native advertising is a burgeoning category of advertising specifically designed to mimic the user experience into which it is placed in terms of form and function (picture the "suggested posts" in your Facebook newsfeed that you as a user are much more likely to read and click on than a typical banner ad, or similarly, any of the first few options that come up on a typical Google search). Native ads are often fully integrated into a specific delivery platform, and are not always identified as advertising. They *do* look like the surrounding editorial content and they typically *are* relevant to it. Market research firm eMarketer projects that native advertising spending will increase nearly 75% between 2016 and 2018.

The company attributes this rapid growth to a demand for more engaging, less intrusive ads. Interestingly, nearly 90% of native advertising is purchased on

product placement The paid integration of branded products into movies, television, and other media.

mobile platforms. Overall, native advertising is still a relatively small part of marketers' spending plans due to concerns about ethics and budget.[18]

Product Placement Product placement—the paid integration of branded products into movies and TV—exploded into big-screen prominence in 1982, when Reese's Pieces played a highly visible role in Steven Spielberg's blockbuster film *E.T.* Reese's Pieces sales shot up 65% (a major embarrassment for the marketers of M&Ms, who had passed on the opportunity). Over the years, product placement in movies has moved rapidly into the limelight. A few notable examples are:

■ *Walking Dead*: Sponsor Hyundai played a starring role in this series about the zombie apocalypse, and the car somewhat oddly remains incongruously clean as the rest of the world decays.

■ *Modern Family* (2010): An entire episode of the hit TV show Modern Family revolved around the Apple iPad two days before the tablet hit the stores.

■ *James Bond*: This long-standing movie icon hawked so many products in recent movies (e.g., Omega watches, Heineken beer, British Airways, and most recently, in *Skyfall*, Macallan whiskey) that it triggered a backlash from annoyed moviegoers and critics.[19]

For many years, Apple took top honors in the movie product placement contest, with its products appearing in 34.3% of all number-one films at the U.S. box office. But in 2012, Mercedes-Benz became the most frequently placed brand in hit films, knocking Apple from the top spot. One reason may be that in 2012, many more number-one films were produced by Sony Studios than in the previous year, all of which featured Sony electronics—effectively shutting Apple out completely. But in 2014, Apple was back, showing up in 9 of the 35 number-one films. In 2015, Apple again lost the lead to Mercedes-Benz when the German auto maker appeared in 9 of the 31 top films. While Apple and Mercedes-Benz were battling it out, Lego may have won the greatest-ever product placement victory in 2014, when it generated an 11% increase in sales following the release of *The Lego Movie* (essentially a 2-hour ad for the product). Lego built on that success with the release of The Lego Batman Movie in March 2017.[20]

In an interesting combination of promotional tactics, product placement and online video have begun to merge. In 2010, Lady Gaga's YouTube smash hit video *Telephone* featured no fewer than ten product placements. Some of the placements, for instance, Miracle Whip, were paid, while others, such as Virgin Mobile and Polaroid, were extensions of existing partnerships with Gaga. In

International Intrigue—Not the 007 Kind!

For the past couple of decades, news headlines have been screaming about foreign countries as a seemingly endless source of cheap labor that sucks away American jobs. And millions of American jobs have indeed been exported overseas. But a closer look suggests that foreign markets may also be an intriguing source of new ideas—both new products and new customers. A couple of examples:

- **Crocs: Not the ultimate** *Fashion Don't*? While many customers love their unsurpassed comfort level, the brightly colored rubber clogs have been roundly ridiculed in the United States for their silly appearance, even spawning their own "I Hate Crocs" website and online store. But Crocs don't suffer the same reputation issues overseas. In China, consumers see Crocs more as "an American brand similar to Starbucks," and in Russia, consumers tend to gravitate more toward the brand's fur-lined boots. Who knew?

- **Pizza and a movie: Press play, call Dominos, and pull out your wallet, right?** Not so fast ... at least not in Brazil. You may be able to enjoy your pizza without spending an extra dollar. Ten video rental stores have partnered with Dominos to cover certain hit DVDs with thermal ink. As the disc spins, the ink melts to reveal the sight and smell of a Dominos pizza. Yum, yum!!

- **Shakey's: A new lease on life in Asia.** You may not remember it, but Shakey's Pizza was once a giant in the pizza parlor market, with locations dotting street corners across the United States. Although Shakey's is no longer the pizza mainstay it once was in America, the chain is a growth brand in Asia. Adapting to its new home, Shakey's now offers toppings like egg, fish flakes, and mackerel paste to suit local palates.[21]

2013, Avril Lavigne released her new single, "Rock N Roll," starting with a shot of her saying, "Oh, my new Sony phone is ringing." In 2014, 39 of the music videos on the Billboard top 100 included product placement, with Beats products appearing more than any other. Fans of the Netflix original series *House of Cards* have probably noticed placements for Samsung, Fiji water, and other products. Given its efficacy in reaching younger consumers, this approach seems sure to grow in the future.

Social media influencers are probably the biggest growth area for product placement today. These influencers, often YouTube or Instagram stars, promote products or services during their broadcasts in exchange for a fee. Since influencers tend to have an authentic relationship with their followers, they are more likely to disclose (and even joke about) the promotional relationship in order to maintain that authenticity. Product placement on TV has catapulted into the mainstream in response to the growing prominence of digital video recorders (DVRs) such as TiVo. Research suggests that 53% of U.S. households had at least one DVR in 2016, up from fewer than 10% in 2005. DVRs allow consumers not only to watch on their own schedule but also to zap ads. Worried marketers see product placement as a chance to "TiVo-proof" their messages by integrating them into the programming. Worldwide, the United States is the largest product placement market, but China is fastest growing. One notable example: Analysts estimate the media value of Macallan whiskey's appearance in the 2012 Bond film *Skyfall* at well over $9 million—plus a permanent place in Bond lore, which many brands would consider priceless . . .[22]

Product placement works best for marketers if the product seamlessly integrates into the show as a player rather than simply a prop. For instance, it was hard to miss Coke in *American Idol*. The judges were seldom without their Coca-Cola–emblazoned cups, and during the early years of the show a "Coke Couch" was used onstage. The price tag for this exposure—including commercial time and online content—was about $35 million. Media buyers often negotiate product placement deals as part of a package that includes regular ads, which reinforce the product that appeared in the program (unless, of course, the ads are zapped).[23]

Whether in TV or movies, product placement offers marketers huge sales potential in a credible environment, which may account for its huge growth rate. But product placement is risky—if your show is a dud, your placement is worthless. And the cost is high and growing, which only increases the financial risk. The benefits of product placement are tough to measure as well, especially for existing brands. But in the end, the only measure that really counts is consumer acceptance, which may disappear if product placement intrudes too much on the entertainment value of movies and TV.

Advergaming Interactive games have exploded into pop culture; about 67% of U.S. consumers play some kind of video game, and mobile gamers are the largest and most vibrant segment. Not surprisingly, marketers have followed closely behind, developing two promotional channels: **advergaming**, which involves video games created as a marketing tool, usually with brand

advergaming Video games created as a marketing tool, usually with brand awareness as the core goal.

Scandals Might Cut Hard, but They Don't Seem to Cut Deeply

You may remember a horrifying video from 2017 where a Vietnam-born doctor was roughly dragged off a United Airlines plane—blood running down his face—so that his seat could be used by a United employee. Given the consumer outrage directed at United, one would expect, and perhaps even hope, that the incident would have a financial impact on the company. But according to financial analysts, "Incidents like this rarely pose lasting or significant financial headwinds for major transportation companies." United stock fell a bit the day the video came out, but analysts attributed that to mixed operational data released that same morning.

You may also remember that Starbucks faced a call for a boycott in 2017 after CEO Howard Schultz announced that the coffee firm would hire 10,000 refugees globally. A few months later, Schultz addressed the issue directly at the company's annual stockholder meeting: "I can unequivocally tell you that there is zero, absolutely no evidence whatsoever that there is any dilution in integrity of the Starbucks brand, reputation, or our core business as a result of being compassionate."[24]

awareness as the core goal; plus advertising in the video games themselves.

According to Massive, an advertising network that specializes in video games, advergaming works for marketers. Gamers exposed to embedded ads show a 64% increase in brand familiarity, a 37% increase in brand rating, and a 41% increase in purchase consideration; furthermore, rather than despising the ads, 55% of gamers said they "look cool." But Massive isn't the only game in town. In early 2007, Google purchased AdScape, a nimble video game advertising company, and independent agency Double Fusion also provides fierce competition. Despite the strong research results, analysts anticipate that advergaming will move in a new direction over the next few years, with deals that link brands with tangible rewards for players. This approach still leaves room for purely promotional in-game ads to support the out-of-game campaigns. Given the explosive growth of mobile gaming, and the growing willingness of gamers to buy virtual goods (e.g., access to better game levels or to products for their online avatars), gamers may soon see a cyberworld filled with as much promotion as the real world.[25]

Buzz Marketing A recent study defined "buzz" as the transfer of information from someone who is in the know to someone who isn't. Buzz is essentially word of mouth, which now influences two-thirds of all consumer product purchases. And it makes sense. In a world that's increasingly complex, people turn to people they know and trust to help sort the garbage from the good stuff.

buzz marketing The active stimulation of word of mouth via unconventional, and often relatively low-cost, tactics. Other terms for buzz marketing are "guerrilla marketing" and "viral marketing."

Other popular terms for **buzz marketing** are "guerrilla marketing" and "viral marketing."

Not surprisingly, marketers have actively pursued buzz for their brands, especially with the rising cost and diminishing effectiveness of more traditional media channels. Innovative buzz campaigns are typically custom designed to meet their objectives, and they often cost significantly less than more traditional approaches. Here are some notable examples:

■ **Whopper Sacrifice:** Burger King has been among the most successful buzz marketers, using the Internet to develop quirky and creative campaigns that have quickly gone viral. In late 2009, Burger King invited customers to download their Whopper Sacrifice Facebook application and use it to drop ten Facebook friends in exchange for a free Angry Whopper coupon worth $3.69. The application then bluntly notified each friend that he or she had been dumped in exchange for about $0.37 worth of burger. Consumers responded in droves, apparently thankful for the excuse to purge their friend lists. Burger King terminated the campaign when Facebook requested that they terminate the "de-friending" notification. But Burger King could still loudly proclaim, "Your love for the Whopper sandwich proved to be stronger than 233,906 friendships."

90% of people trust online recommendations from people they know. Only 14% trust traditional TV advertisements.

—SOCIALNOMICS

Does Your Face Look Like a Taco?

Your face might have looked like a taco if you participated in Taco Bell's wildly successful 2016 Cinco de Mayo promotion with Snapchat. On May 5, 2016, Snapchat featured a special effects lens that allowed users across the country to change their faces into giant tacos. The result was 224 million views in one day, shattering Snapchat's previous record. Snapchat has been relatively slow to move into advertising. CEO Evan Spiegel has indicated some reluctance about sharing user information to better target ads, and parent company Snap insists on keeping some creative control of all advertising. The firm even retains the right to veto projects that it thinks look too much like basic advertising. This caveat has annoyed some brands in the past, but it helps to maintain the integrity of Snapchat itself. Meanwhile, Snapchat continues to innovate, quietly becoming the most-used augmented reality product in the world. If Snapchat remains open to creative advertising opportunities like the Taco Bell campaign, it may well scoop up a hefty portion of the billions of digital advertising dollars that marketers currently allocate to Facebook and Google.[26]

Source: Yum! Brands

■ **Fitness First:** This Dutch health club ambushed unsuspecting commuters by displaying their weight in neon lights when they took a seat at a bus bench in Rotterdam. Yikes. Chances are good that they both gained some new customers and scarred some other potential customers for life![27]

■ **ShareYourEars:** Unlike the previous two examples, some buzz campaigns are intended to spread *positive* energy. The Walt Disney Corporation, in partnership with the Make-A-Wish foundation, recently launched a campaign to raise awareness and funds for terminally-ill children. This campaign encouraged fans to share images and selfies featuring Disney's classic mouse ears on Twitter and Instagram using the #ShareYourEars hashtag. Disney pledged a $5 donation to the Make-A-Wish foundation for each participant, with a total cap of $1 million. The campaign was eventually so successful that Disney doubled its original pledge to $2 million.[28]

Sponsorships Sponsorships certainly aren't new, but they should experience healthy worldwide growth over the next few years, led by a vibrant emerging national sponsorship market, particularly in Central and South America, between the 2014 World Cup and the 2016 Olympic Games. Sponsorships provide a deep association between a marketer and a partner (usually a cultural or sporting event). Even though sponsors can't usually provide more than simply their logo or slogan, consumers tend to view them in a positive light, since they are clearly connected to events that matter to the target audience. The best sponsorship investments, of course, occur when the target audience for the marketer completely overlaps the target audience for

> "Doing business without advertising is like winking at a girl in the dark. You know what you are doing but nobody else does."
>
> —STEUART HENDERSON BRITT, MARKETING MANAGEMENT AND ADMINISTRATIVE ACTION

the event. The high level of integration between the sponsors and events can provide millions of dollars in valuable media coverage, justifying the hefty price.[29]

12-6b Traditional Promotional Tools: A Marketing Mainstay

Although new tools are gaining prominence, traditional promotional tools—advertising, sales promotion, public relations, and personal selling—remain powerful. In fact, many marketers use the new tools in conjunction with the traditional to create a balanced, far-reaching promotional mix.

Advertising The formal definition of **advertising** is paid, nonpersonal communication, designed to influence a target audience

sponsorship A deep association between a marketer and a partner (usually a cultural or sporting event), which involves promotion of the sponsor in exchange for either payment or the provision of goods.

advertising Paid, nonpersonal communication, designed to influence a target audience with regard to a product, service, organization, or idea.

EXHIBIT 12.9   2016 MEASURED MEDIA SPENDING BY MEDIUM (BILLIONS)

Measured Media	2016 Spending	Percentage of Total
TV	$78.9	35.7%
Internet	31.9	31.7
Newspapers	12.2	9.6
Radio	7.9	9.2
Magazines	18.8	8.7
Outdoors and Cinema	5.6	5.1
Total	$155.4	100%

Source: 2018 marketing Fact Pack, December 18, 2017. *Advertising Age.*

Note: TV includes broadcast, cable, spot, syndicated, and Spanish-language networks.

with regard to a product, service, organization, or idea. Most major brands use advertising not only to drive sales but also to build their reputation, especially with a broad target market. Television (network broadcasts and cable combined) remains the number-one advertising medium, with magazines and newspapers following. As mass media prices increase and audiences fragment, fringe media are roaring toward the mainstream. But measurement is tough, since alternative media tactics are buried in other categories, including magazines, outdoor, and Internet. The overall media spending patterns for 2016 are shown in Exhibit 12.9.

Each type of media offers advantages and drawbacks, as summarized in Exhibit 12.10. Your goal as a marketer should be to determine which media options reach your target market efficiently and effectively, within the limits of your budget.

Sales Promotion Sales promotion stimulates immediate sales activity through specific short-term programs aimed at either consumers or distributors. Traditionally, sales promotion has been subordinate to other promotional tools, but spending has accelerated in the past decade. Sales promotion falls into two categories: consumer and trade.

Consumer promotion is designed to generate immediate sales. Consumer promotion tools include premiums, promotional products, samples, coupons, rebates, and displays.

sales promotion Marketing activities designed to stimulate immediate sales activity through specific short-term programs aimed at either consumers or distributors.

consumer promotion Marketing activities designed to generate immediate consumer sales, using tools such as premiums, promotional products, samples, coupons, rebates, and displays.

- **Premiums** are items that consumers receive free of charge—or for a lower than normal cost—in return for making a purchase. Upscale cosmetics companies use the gift-with-purchase approach on a regular basis. Successful premiums create a sense of urgency—"Buy me now!"—while building the value of the brand.

- **Promotional** products are also essentially gifts to consumers of merchandise that advertises a brand name. Or pizza delivery places give away refrigerator magnets with their logo and phone number. Promotional products work best when the merchandise relates to the brand and it's so useful or fun that consumers will opt to keep it around.

- **Samples** reduce the risk of purchasing something new by allowing consumers to try a product before committing their cash. From 2009 to 2011, Muscle Milk hired hundreds of personal trainers to conduct promotions and distribute samples. Sampling also drives immediate purchases. At one time or another, most of us have probably bought food we didn't need after tasting a delicious morsel in the supermarket aisle. Costco and Trader Joe's do especially well with this angle on sampling.

- **Coupons** offer immediate price reductions to consumers. Instant coupons require even less effort, since they are attached to the package right there in the store. The goal is to entice consumers to try new products. But the downside is huge. Marketers who depend on coupons encourage consumers to focus on price rather than value,

EXHIBIT 12.10   **MAJOR MEDIA CATEGORIES**

Major Media	Advantages	Disadvantages
Broadcast TV	*Mass audience:* Top-rated shows garnered more than 15 million viewers in 2017. *High impact:* TV lends itself to vivid, complex messages that use sight, sound, and motion.	*Disappearing viewers:* The 100 million viewers for the top-rated show in 2012 was dwarfed by the 1983 record of 105 million viewers for the finale of M*A*S*H. *Jaded viewers:* Consumers who aren't zapping ads with their DVR are prone to simply tuning them out. *High cost:* A 30-second ad during Super Bowl 2013 cost a record $5.5 million, and a typical primetime ad cost $200,000 to $400,000, depending on the show.
Cable TV	*Targeted programming:* Cable helps advertisers target highly specialized markets (Zhong Tian Channel, anyone?). *Efficient:* The cost per contact is relatively low, especially for local buys. *High impact:* Cable offers the same sight, sound, and motion benefits as broadcast.	*DVRs:* As with broadcast TV, many viewers simply aren't watching ads. *Uneven quality:* Many cable ads are worse than mediocre, providing a seedy setting for quality products.
Newspapers	*Localized:* Advertisers can tailor their messages to meet local needs. *Flexible:* Turnaround time for placing and pulling ads is very short. *Consumer acceptance:* Readers expect, and even seek, newspaper ads.	*Short life span:* Readers quickly discard their papers. *Clutter:* It takes two or three hours to read the average metro paper from cover to cover. Almost no one does it. *Quality:* Even top-notch color newsprint leaves a lot to be desired.
Direct Mail	*Highly targeted:* Direct mail can reach very specific markets. *International opportunity:* Less jaded foreign customers respond well to direct mail. *Email option:* Opt-in email can lower direct mail costs.	*Wasted resources:* Direct mail uses a staggering amount of paper. And most recipients don't even read it before they toss it. *High cost:* Cost per contact can be high, although advertisers can limit the size of the campaign. *Spam:* Unsolicited email ads have undermined consumer tolerance for all email ads.
Radio	*Highly targeted:* In L.A., for example, the dial ranges from Vietnamese talk radio to urban dance music, each station with dramatically different listeners. *Low cost:* Advertisers can control the cost by limiting the size of the buy. *Very flexible:* Changing the message is quick and easy.	*Low impact:* Radio relies only on listening. *Jaded listeners:* Many of us flip stations when the ads begin.
Magazines	*Highly targeted:* From *Cosmopolitan* to *Computerworld*, magazines reach very specialized markets. *Quality:* Glossy print sends a high-quality message. *Long life:* Magazines tend to stick around homes and offices.	*High cost:* A full-page, four-color ad in *People* can cost nearly $400,000. *Inflexible:* Advertisers must submit artwork months before publication.
Outdoor	*High visibility:* Billboards and building sides are hard to miss. *Repeat exposure:* Popular locations garner daily viewers. *Breakthrough ideas:* Innovative approaches include cars and buses "wrapped" in ads, video billboards, and blimps.	*Simplistic messages:* Anything more than an image and a few words will get lost. *Visual pollution:* Many consumers object to outdoor ads. *Limited targeting:* It's hard to ensure that the right people see your ad.
Internet	*24/7 global coverage:* Offers a remarkable level of exposure. *Highly targeted:* Search engines are especially strong at delivering the right ad to the right person at the right time. *Interactive:* Internet ads can empower consumers.	*Intrusive:* The annoyance factor from tough-to-close pop-ups alienates consumers, infuriating many. *Limited readership:* Web surfers simply ignore the vast majority of ads.

Companies and stores work together to create a positive message through store displays.

Pio3/Shutterstock.com

which makes it harder to differentiate brands and build loyalty. In categories with frequent coupons (such as soap and cereal), too many consumers wait for the coupon in order to buy. They end up getting great deals, but marketers pay the price in reduced profits.

■ **Rebates**, common in the car industry and the electronics business, entice consumers with cash-back offers. This is a powerful tactic for higher-priced items, since rebates offer an appealing purchase motivator. And rebates provide an incentive for marketers as well: breakage. Most people who buy a product because of the rebate don't actually follow through and do the paperwork to get the money (some estimates suggest that breakage rates are as high as 90% to 95%). This means that marketers can offer hefty discounts without actually coughing up the cash, so it isn't surprising that rebates are a popular promotional tool!

■ **Displays** generate purchases in-store. Most experts agree that consumers make a hefty chunk of their purchase decisions as they shop, which means that displays can play a crucial role in sales success. Marketers of consumer products often give prefabricated display materials to grocery stores and mass merchandisers to encourage promotion.

Trade promotion is designed to stimulate wholesalers and retailers to push specific products more aggressively. Special deals and allowances are the most common form of trade promotion, especially for consumer products. The idea is that if you give your distributors a temporary price cut, they will pass the savings on to consumers via a short-term "special."

Trade shows are another popular form of trade promotion. Usually organized by industry trade associations, trade shows give exhibitors a chance to display and promote their products to their distributors. They typically attract hundreds of exhibitors and thousands of attendees. Trade shows are especially common in rapidly changing industries such as toys and consumer electronics. Every year the Consumer Electronics Association hosts "the world's largest annual trade show for consumer electronics!" in Las Vegas.

Other forms of trade promotion include contests, sweepstakes, and special events for distributors. A soda company might sponsor a contest to see which grocery store can build the most creative summer display for its soda brands. Or a cable TV programmer might take a group of system managers to Key West to "learn more about their programming" (really an excuse for a great party that makes the system managers more open to the programmer's pitch).

Public Relations In the broadest sense, **public relations (or PR)** involves the ongoing effort to create positive relationships with all of a firm's different "publics," including customers, employees, suppliers, the community, the general public, and the government. But in a more focused sense, PR aims to generate positive **publicity**, or unpaid stories in the media that create a favorable impression about a company or its products. The endgame, of course, is to boost demand.

For the most part, the media cover companies or products that they perceive as newsworthy. To get coverage, smart firms continually scan their own companies for potential news—a hot product or a major corporate achievement—and present that news to the media. But finding news on a regular basis can be tough. To fill the gaps, innovative PR people sometimes simply create "news." PR guru Bill Stoller offers some interesting ideas

trade promotion Marketing activities designed to stimulate wholesalers and retailers to push specific products more aggressively over the short term.

public relations (PR) The ongoing effort to create positive relationships with all of a firm's different "publics," including customers, employees, suppliers, the community, the general public, and the government.

publicity Unpaid stories in the media that influence perceptions about a company or its products.

Cheaters Never Prosper

In a massive, brand-breaking, environmentally damaging scandal, Volkswagen (VW) admitted in 2015 that it fit millions of cars with devices to mask the amount of pollutants that they spewed into the environment. In other words, VW knowingly cheated on standardized emissions tests so its cars would appear road-ready when they were anything but. Not surprisingly, this sizable scandal carried a sizable price for VW. Within a month of the cheating coming to light, Volkswagen sales plummeted −25%. What's more, the EPA levied fines against VW of up to $37,500 per car—more than the cost of each car affected—amounting to a total penalty of up to $18 billion. It's hard to imagine how the Volkswagen brand will recover, but it may take even longer for overall trust in automobile environmental claims to recover. [30]

Carsten Reisinger/Shutterstock.com

for how to invent stories that will grab media attention:

- **Launch a Hall of Fame:** Induct some luminaries from your industry, create a simple website, and send your press release to the media. Repeat each year, building your reputation along the way.

- **Make a List:** The best, the worst, the top ten, the bottom ten—the media loves lists, and the possible topics are endless! Just make sure that your list is relevant to your business.

- **Create a Petition:** The Web makes this tactic easy. Harness a growing trend or identify a need in your industry, and launch your petition. The more signatures you get, the better your chances for publicity.[31]

The biggest advantage of publicity is that it is usually credible. Think about it: Are you more likely to buy a product featured on the news or a product featured in a 30-second ad? Are you more likely to read a book reviewed by the *New York Times* or featured on a billboard? Publicity is credible because most people believe that information presented by the media is based on legitimate opinions and facts rather than on the drive to make money. And it also helps that publicity is close to free (excluding any fees for a PR firm).

But publicity has a major downside: the marketer has no control over how the media present the company or its products. For example, in an effort to protect

> "More than 85 percent of customers have a negative view of all salespeople."
>
> —BILL BROOKS, THE BROOKS GROUP

customers from a growing tide of solicitors in front of its stores, Target banned Salvation Army bell ringers in front of all its stores in 2004. The press cried foul, focusing not on the service to consumers, but rather on the disrespect to a venerable charity. Target's archrival Walmart, spotting an opportunity for itself at Target's expense, announced that it would match customer donations to the Salvation Army at all of its locations.

Personal Selling Personal selling—the world's oldest form of promotion—is person-to-person presentation of products to potential buyers. But successful selling typically begins long before the actual presentation and ends long afterward. In today's competitive environment, selling means building relationships on a long-term basis.

Creating and maintaining a quality sales force is expensive. Experts estimate that each business-to-business sales call costs nearly $400. So why are so many people employed in sales?[32] Because nothing works better than personal selling for high-ticket items, complex products, and high-volume customers. In some companies, the sales team works directly with customers; in other firms, the sales force works with distributors who buy large volumes of products for resale.

Salespeople fall along a spectrum that ranges from order takers who simply process sales to order

> **personal selling** The person-to-person presentation of products to potential buyers.

seekers who use creative selling to persuade customers. Most department stores hire order takers who stand behind the counter and ring up sales. But Nordstrom hires creative order seekers who actively garner sales by offering extra services such as tasteful accessory recommendations for a clothing shopper.

A separate category of salespeople focuses on *missionary selling*, which means promoting goodwill for a company by providing information and assistance to customers. The pharmaceutical industry hires a small army of missionary salespeople who call on doctors to explain and promote its products, even though the actual sales move through pharmacies.

The sales process typically follows six key stages. Keep in mind that well before the process begins, effective salespeople seek a complete understanding of their products, their industry, and their competition. A high level of knowledge permeates the entire selling process.

1. **Prospect and Qualify:** Prospecting means identifying potential customers. Qualifying means choosing those who are most likely to buy your product. Choosing the right prospects makes salespeople more efficient, since it helps them focus their limited time in areas that will yield results. Companies find prospects in a number of different ways, from trade shows to direct mail, to cold calling. In a retail environment, everyone who walks in the door is a prospect, so salespeople either ask questions or look for visual cues to qualify customers.

2. **Prepare:** Before making a sales call, research is critical, especially in a business-to-business environment. What are your prospect's wants and needs? What are his or her current product lines? Who are the key competitors? What are the biggest internal and external challenges? How much time is your prospect willing to give you? The answers to these questions will help you customize your presentation for maximum effectiveness.

3. **Present:** You've probably heard that you don't get a second chance to make a good first impression, and that's especially true in sales. With so many options and so little time, buyers often look for reasons to eliminate choices; a weak first impression provides an easy reason to eliminate you. Your presentation itself should match the features of your product to the benefits that your customer seeks (a chance to use all that preparation). Testimonials, letters of praise from satisfied current customers, can push forward the sale by reducing risk for your prospect. A demonstration can be the clincher. When test-driving cars,

a demonstration is a no-brainer. But in other categories, technology can help demonstrate products that are too big to move.

4. **Handle Objections:** The key to success here is to view objections as opportunities rather than criticism. Objections give you a chance to learn more about the needs of your prospects and to elaborate on the benefits of your product. You should definitely anticipate as many objections as possible and prepare responses. One response may be connecting prospects with others in your company who can better handle their concerns. This approach offers the additional benefit of deepening ties between your prospect and your company.

5. **Close Sale:** Closing the sale—or asking the prospect to buy—is at the heart of the selling process. The close should flow naturally from the prior steps, but often it doesn't—sealing the deal can be surprisingly tough. One approach may be a trial close: "Would you like the 15-inch screen or the 17-inch screen?" If your prospect is still reluctant to buy, you may want to offer another alternative or a special financial incentive. Even if the prospect doesn't actually make the purchase, remember that he or she may be willing in the future, so keep the door open.

6. **Follow-up:** The sales process doesn't end when the customer pays. The quality of service and support plays a crucial role in future sales from the same customer, and getting those sales is much easier than finding brand-new prospects. Great relationships with current customers also lead to testimonials and referrals that build momentum for long-term sales success.

Two personal selling trends are gathering momentum in a number of organizations: consultative selling and team selling. *Consultative selling* involves shifting the focus from the products to the customers. On a day-to-day basis, the practice involves a deep understanding of customer needs. Through lots and lots of active listening, consultative salespeople offer practical solutions to customer problems—solutions that use their products. While consultative selling generates powerful customer loyalty, it involves a significant—and expensive—time investment from the sales force.

Team selling tends to be especially effective for large, complex accounts. The approach includes a group of specialists from key functional areas of the company—not just sales but also engineering, finance, customer service, and others. The goal is to uncover opportunities and respond to needs that would be beyond the capacity of a single salesperson. In these situations, a key part of the salesperson's role is to connect and coordinate the right network of contacts.

12-6c Choosing the Right Promotional Mix: Not Just a Science

There are no fail-safe rules for choosing the right combination of promotional tools. The mix varies dramatically among various industries but also within specific industry segments. The best approach may simply be to consider the following questions in developing the mix that works best for your products.

- **Product Characteristics:** How can you best communicate the features of your product? Is it simple or complex? Is it high priced or inexpensive? A specialized, high-priced item, for example, might require an investment in personal selling, whereas a simple, low-cost product might lend itself to billboard advertising.

- **Product Life Cycle:** Where does your product stand in its life cycle? Are you developing awareness? Are you generating desire? What about driving purchases? And building loyalty? The answers will clearly affect your promotional focus. For instance, if you're developing awareness, you might focus more on advertising, but if you're aiming to drive immediate sales, you'll probably emphasize sales promotion.

- **Target Audience:** How big is your target audience? Where do they live and work? A small target audience—especially if it's geographically dispersed—would lend itself to personal selling or direct mail. A sizable target audience might suggest advertising as an effective way to reach large numbers. Audience expectations should also play a role in your promotional mix decisions.

- **Push versus Pull:** Does your industry emphasize push or pull strategies? A **push strategy** involves motivating distributors to "push" your product to the final consumers, usually through heavy trade promotion and personal selling. A **pull strategy** involves creating demand from your final consumers so that they "pull" your products through the distribution channels. Many successful brands use a combination of push and pull strategies to achieve their goals. P&G recently launched a consumer marketing campaign for Crest toothpaste featuring an "Irresistibility IQ" quiz for club-goers, but it also promotes heavily to dentists, hoping that those dentists will recommend Crest to their patients.

- **Competitive Environment:** How are your key competitors handling their promotional strategies? Would it make more sense for you to follow their lead or to forge your own promotional path? If all your competitors offer coupons, for instance, your customers may expect you to offer them as well. Or if the environment is cluttered, you might want to focus on emerging promotional approaches such as advergaming.

- **Budget:** What are your promotional goals? How much money will it take to achieve them? (Answering this question is tough, but it's clearly important.) How much are your competitors spending in each area of the mix? And how much money do you have for promotion? Even though available budget shouldn't drive the promotional mix, it plays a crucial role, especially for smaller businesses.

push strategy A marketing approach that involves motivating distributors to heavily promote—or "push"—a product to the final consumers, usually through heavy trade promotion and personal selling.

pull strategy A marketing approach that involves creating demand from the ultimate consumers so that they "pull" your products through the distribution channels by actively seeking them.

THE BIG PICTURE

The possibilities in both product development and promotional strategy have rapidly multiplied in the past few years alone. But companies can't deliver on the potential without well-oiled teamwork throughout the organization. For instance, the operations group must focus on quality, the accounting group must focus on cost, and the finance group must focus on funding—but from a big-picture standpoint, all groups must work toward the same overarching goal: maximizing customer value. Promotion also requires coordination within the organization and among the outside suppliers who provide promotional services. Finally, the best ideas for both product and promotion can come from any department. Marketers who stay ahead of the curve will only sharpen their competitive edge in the decade to come.

Pharmaceutical Sales Representative

Build effective long-term business relationships with healthcare providers. Develop and deliver sales presentations to healthcare professionals. Distribute product information and samples in order to encourage more prescriptions and recommendations. Answer questions from healthcare professionals in a timely manner. Keep current about clinical data, competitive offerings, and healthcare organizations, issues, and events, particularly in area of specialty. Organize group events for healthcare professionals. Create and maintain detailed records of all contacts and meetings.

STUDY TOOLS 12

LOCATED AT BACK OF THE TEXTBOOK

☐ Rip-Out Chapter Review Card

☐ Gain unique perspectives on key concepts with new concept videos in the e-book

☐ Increase your comprehension with online homework and quizzes

☐ Study with existing flashcards and make your own

13 | Distribution and Pricing:
Right Product, Right Person, Right Place, Right Price

Rawpixel.com/Shutterstock.com

LEARNING OBJECTIVES

After studying this chapter, you will be able to:

13-1 Define distribution and differentiate between channels of distribution and physical distribution

13-2 Describe the various types of wholesale distributors

13-3 Discuss strategies and trends in store and nonstore retailing

13-4 Explain the key factors in physical distribution

13-5 Outline core pricing objectives and strategies

13-6 Discuss pricing in practice, including the role of consumer perceptions

Remember to visit

PAGE 251

for additional

STUDY TOOLS

13-1 DISTRIBUTION: GETTING YOUR PRODUCT TO YOUR CUSTOMER

Next time you go to the grocery store, look around—the average U.S. supermarket carries about 50,000 different products.[1] Is your favorite brand of soda part of the mix? Why? How did it get from the factory to your neighborhood store? Where else could you find that soda? How far would you be willing to go to get it? These are marketing distribution questions that contribute directly to the **distribution strategy**: getting the right product to the right person at the right place at the right time.

distribution strategy A plan for delivering the right product to the right person at the right place at the right time.

channel of distribution The network of organizations and processes that links producers to consumers.

physical distribution The actual, physical movement of products along the distribution pathway.

direct channel A distribution process that links the producer and the customer with no intermediaries.

The distribution strategy has two elements: channels of distribution and physical distribution. A **channel of distribution** is the path that a product takes from the producer to the consumer, while **physical distribution** is the actual movement of products along that path. Some producers choose to sell their products directly to their customers through a **direct channel**. No one stands between the producer and the customer. Examples range from Dell computers to local farmers

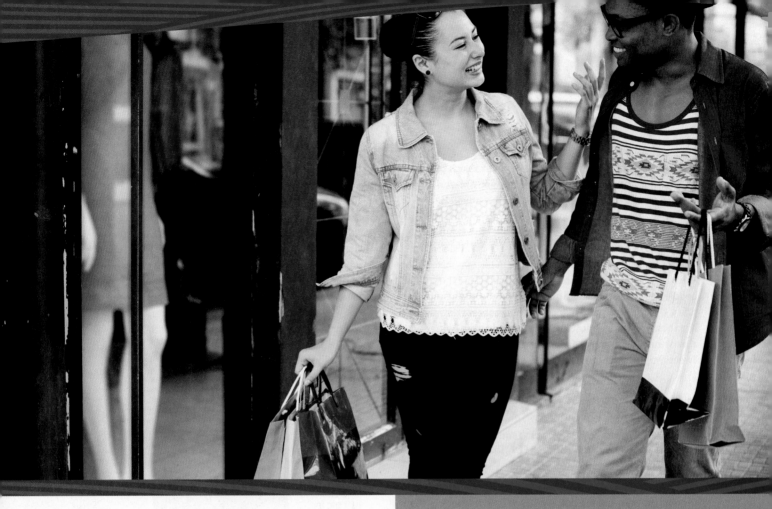

markets, to factory outlet stores. But most producers use **channel intermediaries** to help their products move more efficiently and effectively from their factories to their consumers. Hershey's, for example, sells chocolate bars to Sam's Club—a channel intermediary—which may, in turn, sell them to you.

13-1a The Role of Distributors: Adding Value

You might be asking yourself why we need distributors. Wouldn't it be a lot less expensive to buy directly from the producers? The answer, surprisingly, is no. Distributors add value—additional benefits—to products. They charge for adding that value, but typically they charge less than it would cost for consumers or producers to add that value on their own. When distributors add to the cost of a product without providing comparable benefits, the intermediaries don't stay in business. Fifteen years ago, for instance, most people bought plane tickets from travel agents. But when the Internet reduced the cost and inconvenience of buying tickets directly from airlines, thousands of travel agencies lost their customers.

One core role of distributors is to reduce the number of transactions—and the associated costs—for goods to flow

"We now live in an age of surreal abundance."

—JONAH LEHRER, AUTHOR

from producers to consumers. As you'll see in Exhibit 13.1, even one marketing intermediary in the distribution channel can funnel goods from producers to consumers, with far fewer costly transactions.

Distributors add value, or utility, in a number of different ways: form, time, place, ownership, information, and service. Sometimes the distributors deliver the value (rather than adding it themselves), but often they add new utility that wouldn't otherwise be present. As you read through the various types of utility, keep in mind that they are often interrelated, building on each other to maximize value.

Form utility provides customer satisfaction by converting inputs into finished products. Clearly, form utility is primarily a part of manufacturing. Pepsico, for instance,

channel intermediaries Distribution organizations that facilitate the movement of products from the producer to the consumer.

It's a Bird ... It's a Plane ... It's Superman ... Wait, No—It's a Drone!

In 2013, Amazon CEO Jeff Bezos made a media splash by announcing that the online giant is developing Amazon Prime Air, 30 minute deliveries via drone-like "octocopters." He cautioned that the service would not be in action until 2015 at the very earliest. The plan was for the drones to initially carry items up to five pounds, which is roughly 86% of all deliveries Amazon makes. Initial reaction from the public was mixed. Much of the public was concerned about safety and theft. Would people be shooting drones from the sky? And what about privacy? Others seemed to find the whole concept downright hilarious. The jokes almost instantly rippled across Twitter, which almost inevitably spawned parody accounts. A sampling of Tweets from the fictional Octobot to the Twitterverse:

- I see you have guests. You may also be interested in curtains.

- After your first drone arrives, five others will arrive bearing items we think you might also like.

- Want to show someone how much you hate them? Send me to their house with a Nickelback CD. #DroneRevenge

But not everyone was laughing—least of all the federal government. Although Amazon has tested its airborne delivery bots in Canada, the U.K., and the Netherlands, it cannot launch in the United States until the Federal Aviation Administration issues official commercial drone regulations. Until that happens, the FAA must approve each Amazon drone flight, and every drone must remain within its operator's line of site for the entire duration of the flight. With these restrictions in place, the Amazon Prime Air delivery project can't really get off the ground—so to speak. To increase the likelihood that the FAA's regulations will favor its operations, Amazon has begun dumping hundreds of thousands of dollars into political lobbying. Amazon is now Washington's fastest-growing tech lobby, pushing not only for delivery drone approval but also for larger trucks, more road improvements, and a closer partnership with the United States Postal Service. It may be quite some time before your next Amazon order floats down onto your porch from above, but if Amazon gets its way, drone delivery will one day be more than just pie in the sky.[2]

gualtiero boffi/Shutterstock.com

---

provides form utility by transforming water, chemicals, and aluminum into cans of soda. But retailers can add form utility as well. McDonald's, for instance, converts syrup, bubbly water, and paper into cups of soda.

Time utility adds value by making products available at a convenient time for consumers. In our 24/7 society, consumers feel entitled to instant gratification, a benefit that distributors can provide more easily than most producers. Consider one-hour dry cleaning, or vending machines at your school. These distributors provide options for filling your needs at a time that works for you.

Place utility satisfies customer needs by providing the right products in the right place. Gas stations and fast food, for instance, often cluster conveniently at the bottom of freeway ramps. ATMs—essentially electronic distributors— are readily available in locations that range from grocery stores to college cafeterias.

Ownership utility adds value by making it easier for customers to actually possess the goods and services that they purchase. Providing credit, cashing checks, delivering goods, and installing products are all examples of how distributors make it easier for customers to own their products.

chrisjohnsson/Shutterstock.com

Although Nintendo typically uses cargo ships to move products from Japan to the United States, the video game manufacturer changed its distribution method to airplane—to the tune of $45 per unit—to meet unexpectedly high demand for its new Switch console.

Exhibit 13.1
Reducing Transactions through Marketing Intermediaries

Information utility boosts customer satisfaction by providing helpful information. Zappos.com, for instance, hires customer service experts to guide its customers through its website to the perfect pair of shoes. Similarly, most skateboard stores hire skater salespeople who gladly help customers find the best board for them.

Service utility adds value by providing fast, friendly, personalized service. Examples include placing a special order for that part you need to customize your computer, or choosing just the right gift in your local clothing boutique. Distributors that provide service utility typically create a loyal base of customers.

The Members of the Channel: Retailers versus Wholesalers Many producers sell their goods through multiple channels of distribution. Some channels have many members, while others have only a few. The main distinction among channel members is whether they are retailers or wholesalers. **Retailers** are the distributors that most of us know and use on a daily basis. They sell products directly to final consumers. Examples include 7-Eleven markets, Starbucks, and Urban Outfitters. **Wholesalers**, on the other hand, buy products from the producer and sell them to businesses (or other nonfinal users, such as hospitals, nonprofits, and the government). The businesses that buy

from wholesalers can be retailers, other wholesalers, or business users. To complicate this fairly simple concept, some distributors act as both wholesalers and retailers. Costco, for example, sells directly to businesses *and* to consumers.

13-2 WHOLESALERS: SORTING OUT THE OPTIONS

Some wholesalers are owned by producers, while others are owned by retailers, but the vast majority—accounting for about two-thirds of all the wholesale trade—are **independent wholesaling businesses**. These companies represent a number of different producers, distributing their goods to a range of customers. Independent wholesalers fall into two categories: (1) **merchant wholesalers**, who take legal possession, or title, of the goods they distribute, and (2) **agents/brokers**, who don't take title of the goods.

13-2a Merchant Wholesalers

Merchant wholesalers comprise about 80% of all wholesalers. By taking legal title to the goods they distribute, merchant wholesalers reduce the risk of producers' products being damaged or stolen—or even that they just won't sell. Taking title also allows merchant wholesalers to develop their own marketing strategies, including pricing.

- Full-service merchant wholesalers provide a complete array of services to the retailers or business users who typically purchase their goods. This includes warehousing, shipping, promotional assistance, product repairs, and credit.

- Limited-service merchant wholesalers provide fewer services to their customers. For

retailers Distributors that sell products directly to the ultimate users, typically in small quantities, that are stored and merchandized on the premises.

wholesalers Distributors that buy products from producers and sell them to other businesses or nonfinal users such as hospitals, nonprofits, and the government.

independent wholesaling businesses Independent distributors that buy products from a range of different businesses and sell those products to a range of different customers.

merchant wholesalers Independent distributors who take legal possession, or title, of the goods they distribute.

agents/brokers Independent distributors who do not take title of the goods they distribute (even though they may take physical possession on a temporary basis before distribution).

example, some might warehouse products, but not deliver them. Others might warehouse and deliver, but not provide credit or marketing assistance. The specific categories of limited-service merchant wholesalers include the following:

- *Drop Shippers:* Drop shippers take legal title of the merchandise, but they never physically process it. They simply organize and facilitate product shipments directly from the producer to their customers. Drop shippers are common in industries with bulky products, such as coal or timber. Amazon, however, successfully pioneered the use of drop shipping in e-commerce, where it has become a standard shipping method for a number of major websites.

- *Cash and Carry Wholesalers:* These distributors service customers who are too small to merit in-person sales calls from wholesaler reps. Customers must make the trip to the wholesaler themselves and cart their own products back to their stores. Costco and Staples are both examples.

- *Truck Jobbers:* Typically working with perishable goods such as bread, truck jobbers drive their products to their customers, who are usually smaller grocery stores. Their responsibilities often include checking the stock, suggesting reorder quantities, and removing out-of-date goods.

13-2b Agents and Brokers

Agents and brokers connect buyers and sellers and facilitate transactions in exchange for commissions. But they do not take legal ownership of the goods they distribute. Many insurance companies, for instance, distribute via agents, while brokers often handle real estate and seasonal products such as fruits and vegetables.

13-3 RETAILERS: THE CONSUMER CONNECTION

Retailers represent the last stop on the distribution path, since they sell goods and services directly to final consumers. Given their tight consumer connection, retailers must keep in especially close touch with rapidly changing consumer needs and wants.

Smart retailers gain a competitive edge by providing more utility, or added

multichannel retailing
Providing multiple distribution channels for consumers to buy a product.

Shopping malls allow customers to visit several store retailers under one roof—but their days may be numbered in the wake of a dramatic retail restructuring.

value, than their counterparts. Low prices are only part of the equation. Other elements clearly include customer service, product selection, advertising, and location. The look and feel of the retailer—whether online or on-ground—is another critical element.

Retailing falls into two main categories: store and nonstore. But as we discuss each type, keep in mind that the lines between them are not always clear. In fact, **multichannel retailing**—or encouraging consumers to buy through different venues—is an emerging phenomenon. Some marketers have sold their products through multiple channels for many years. For example, on any given day, you could purchase a Coke from a grocery store, a restaurant, or a vending machine. But the emergence of the Internet has provided a host of new opportunities for firms that hadn't previously considered a multichannel approach. An active relationship between on-ground and online outlets has become pivotal for many retailers.

13-3a Store Retailers

While other retail channels are growing, traditional stores remain the 800-pound gorilla of the retail industry, accounting for well over 90% of total retail. Stores range in size from tiny mom-and-pop groceries to multi-acre superstores dwarfed only by their parking lots. Exhibit 13.2 highlights examples of different store types.

In early 2017, the retail industry began a period of dramatic restructuring. Brick-and-mortar stores began closing at a record pace while online shopping continued to grow explosively. But online shopping wasn't the only force at work. Some analysts also blamed the bursting of a retail bubble, similar to the housing bubble, for the sharp and sudden decline in retail. According to these analysts, the retail bubble

EXHIBIT 13.2   RETAIL STORE CATEGORIES

Store Type	Store Description	Examples
Category Killer	Dominates its category by offering a huge variety of one type of product.	OfficeMax, Best Buy, Staples, PetSmart, Toys R Us, Big 5 Sporting Goods
Convenience Store	Sells a small range of everyday and impulse products at easy-to-access locations with long hours and quick checkout.	7-Eleven, AM/PM markets, Circle K, and a wide range of local stores
Department Store	Offers a wide variety of merchandise (e.g., clothes, furniture, cosmetics), plus (usually) a high level of service.	Nordstrom, Macy's, Neiman Marcus
Discount Store	Offers a wide array of merchandise at significantly lower prices and with less service than most department stores.	Target, Walmart, Kmart
Outlet Store	Producer-owned store sells directly to the public at a huge discount. May include discontinued, flawed, or overrun items.	Nike, Versace, Quicksilver, Calvin Klein, Converse, GUESS
Specialty Store	Sells a wide selection of merchandise within a narrow category, such as auto parts.	Barnes & Noble, Victoria's Secret, Claire's, AutoZone, Lenscrafters, Bath & Body Works
Supermarket	Offers a wide range of food products, plus limited nonfood items (e.g., toilet paper).	Kroger, Safeway, Albertson's, Whole Foods, Trader Joe's
Supercenter	Sells a complete selection of food and general merchandise at a steep discount in a single enormous location.	Walmart Supercenters, Super Target
Warehouse Club	Sells discounted food and general merchandise to club members in a large warehouse format.	Costco, Sam's Club

began to inflate three decades ago, with thousands of new retail locations opening and rental prices soaring. As retailers overbuilt, an influx of fast fashion and low-priced chains arose, leading to a brutally competitive retail landscape. The confluence of all these forces led to the recent retail shakeout. According to financial services company Credit Suisse, the pace of retail closures in the first three months of 2017 suggested that more retailers would close in 2017 than during the Great Recession in 2008. It certainly doesn't help that mall traffic is down since consumers no longer view most malls as entertainment destinations.[3]

Both retailers and the producers who distribute through them must carefully consider their distribution strategy. The three key strategic options are intensive, selective, and exclusive.

Intensive Distribution Intensive distribution involves placing your products in as many stores as possible (or placing your stores themselves in as many locations as possible). This strategy makes the most sense for low-cost convenience goods that consumers won't travel too far to find. Marketers have chosen this strategy for Snickers candy bars, Dial soap, and *Sports Illustrated* magazine, among thousands of other items.

> In 2014, the average U.S. supermarket carried more than 42,000 different items.
> —FOOD MARKETING INSTITUTE

Selective Distribution Selective distribution means placing your products only with preferred retailers (or establishing your stores only in limited locations). This approach tends to work best for medium- and higher-priced products or stores that consumers don't expect to find on every street corner. Marketers have chosen this strategy for Neiman Marcus, Jones Soda, and most brands of paintball equipment, for instance.

Exclusive Distribution Exclusive distribution means establishing only one retail outlet in a given area. Typically, that one retailer has exclusive distribution rights and provides exceptional service and selection. This strategy tends to work for luxury-goods providers with a customer base that actively seeks their products. Examples include top-end cars such as Tesla and fashion trendsetters such as Raf Simons.

The **wheel of retailing** offers another key strategic consideration. The wheel is a classic theory that suggests retail firms—sometimes even entire retail categories—become more upscale as they go through their life cycles. For instance, it's easiest to enter a business on a shoestring, gaining customers by offering low prices. But eventually businesses trade up their selection, service, and facilities to maintain and build their customer base. Higher prices then follow, creating vulnerability to new, lower-priced competitors. And thus the wheel keeps rolling.

Although the wheel of retailing theory does describe many basic retail patterns, it doesn't account for stores that launch at the high end of the market (e.g., Whole Foods) and those that retain their niche as deep discounters (e.g., Dollar General or Taco Bell). But the wheel theory does underscore the core principle that retailers must meet changing consumer needs in a relentlessly competitive environment.

13-3b Nonstore Retailers

While most retail dollars flow through brick-and-mortar stores, a growing number of sales go through other channels, or nonstore retailers. The key players represent online retailing, direct-response retailing, direct selling, and vending.

Online Retailing Also known as "e-tailing," online retailing grew at the astonishing rate of nearly 25% per year for most of the early 2000s. But the torrid pace began to slow in 2008 with the onset of the recession. Online retailing grew only 1.6% in 2009, but growth bounced back to over 12% in 2011. Looking forward, experts at eMarketer predict that worldwide retail e-commerce sales will increase

> "Leaders win through logistics. Vision, sure. Strategy, yes. But when you go to war, you need to have both toilet paper and bullets at the right place at the right time. In other words, you must win through superior logistics."
>
> —TOM PETERS, BUSINESS WRITER

to $4.058 trillion by 2020, making up 14.6% of total retail spending that year. Analysts also predict that North American e-commerce sales will see consistent double-digit growth through 2020, fueled by increased spending from existing digital buyers, expansion into new categories such as grocery, and growing m-commerce (mobile commerce) sales.[4] Much of the growth will come at the expense of on-ground retail, as consumers shift more and more of their purchases to online channels. The bigger name brands—including online-only brands, such as Amazon, and on-ground brands with a strong web presence, such as Best Buy—seem poised to benefit most, since cautious consumers are most familiar with them.[5]

Online retailers, like their on-ground counterparts, have learned that great customer service can be a powerful differentiator. Simply "getting eyeballs" isn't enough, since—depending on the industry—fewer than 5% of the people visiting a typical website convert into paying customers. Optimizing one's conversion rate through excellent online customer service can dramatically increase both sales and profitability. One way of improving online service is by using a live chat greeting. You have likely encountered a box that pops up a few minutes after you've been browsing a retail website with a prompt asking if an agent can help you find what you need. Research suggests that visitors invited to chat are 6.3 times more likely to convert into customers than ones who aren't. What's more, 61% of those customers convert within the first chat! For higher-value products and services that entail greater levels of commitment, the conversation might start via chat and then move to a click-to-call channel when the visitor's interest in the product is confirmed. However, in the online environment—as in any business environment—a customer service agent's knowledge, training, and skills make all the difference between a satisfied customer and a dissatisfied one. Online retailers who invest in top-tier customer service in chat and beyond position themselves to achieve breakthrough success.[6]

wheel of retailing A classic distribution theory that suggests that retail firms and retail categories become more upscale as they go through their life cycles.

Kraska/Shutterstock.com

Despite the advantages, online retailers face two major hurdles. The first is that products must be delivered, and even the fastest delivery services typically take at least a couple of days. But the truly daunting hurdle is the lack of security on the Web. As online retailers and software developers create increasingly secure systems, hackers develop more sophisticated tools to crack their new codes.

Direct Response Retailing This category includes catalogs, telemarketing, and advertising (such as infomercials) meant to elicit direct consumer sales. Even though Victoria's Secret significantly cut back on its catalog circulation in 2016—including killing off the company's world-famous swimwear catalog—the catalog side of Victoria's Secret continues to thrive. According to Direct Marketing Association, 53% of consumers purchase from a catalog at least once a year, and 17% purchase monthly or more often.[7] Telemarketing, both inbound and outbound, also remains a potent distribution channel, despite the popular National Do Not Call list established in 2003.

Direct Selling This channel includes all methods of selling directly to customers in their homes or workplaces. Door-to-door sales has enjoyed a resurgence in the wake of the National Do Not Call list, but the real strength of direct selling lies in **multilevel marketing**, or **MLM**. Multilevel marketing involves hiring independent contractors to sell products to their personal network of friends and colleagues and to recruit new salespeople in return for a percentage of their commissions. Mary Kay Cosmetics and The Pampered Chef have both enjoyed enormous success in this arena, along with pioneering companies such as Tupperware.

Vending Until about a decade ago, vending machines in the United States sold mostly soft drinks and snacks. But more recently, the selection has expanded (and the machines have gone more upscale) as marketers recognize the value of providing their products as conveniently as possible to their target consumers. The Maine Lobster Game, for example, allows customers to catch their own fresh lobster dinner with a metal claw in restaurants and bars. But other countries are far ahead of the United States in the vending arena. In Japan, for instance, people buy everything from blue jeans to beef from vending machines. In China, a vending machine at a main subway station in Nanjing sells an average of 200 live hairy crabs every day. And vending machines in Puerto Rico dispense free tubes of Colgate along with candy bars, plus an LED message that says "Don't forget to brush."[8] As technology continues to roll forward, U.S. consumers are likely to see a growing number of vending machines for products as diverse as "fresh-baked" pizza, digital cameras, and specialty coffee drinks.

13-4 PHYSICAL DISTRIBUTION: PLANES, TRAINS, AND MUCH, MUCH MORE

Determining the best distribution channels for your product is only the first half of your distribution strategy. The second half is the physical distribution strategy: determining how your product will flow through the channel from the producer to the consumer.

The **supply chain** for a product includes not only its distribution channels but also the string of suppliers who deliver products to the producers. (See Exhibit 13.3.) Planning and coordinating the movement of products along the supply chain—from the raw materials to the final consumers—is called **supply chain management** or **SCM**. **Logistics** is a subset of SCM that focuses more on tactics (the actual movement of products) than on strategy.

At one time, relationships among the members of the supply chain were contentious. But these days, companies that foster collaboration, rather than competition, have typically experienced more success. Vendor-managed inventory is an emerging strategy—pioneered by Walmart—that allows suppliers to determine buyer needs and automatically ship product. This strategy saves time and money but also requires an extraordinary level of trust and information-sharing among members of the supply chain.

In our turbocharged 24/7 society, supply chain management has become increasingly complex. Gap, for instance, contracts with more than 3,000 factories in more than 50 different countries, and distributes its products to about 3,000 stores in eight different countries. The coordination requirements are mind-boggling. Key management decisions include the following considerations:

- **Warehousing:** How many warehouses do we need? Where should we locate our warehouses?

- **Materials Handling:** How should we move products within our

multilevel marketing (MLM) Involves hiring independent contractors to sell products to their personal network of friends and colleagues and to recruit new salespeople in return for a percentage of their commissions.

supply chain All organizations, processes, and activities involved in the flow of goods from the raw materials to the final consumer.

supply chain management (SCM) Planning and coordinating the movement of products along the supply chain, from the raw materials to the final consumers.

logistics A subset of supply chain management that focuses largely on the tactics involved in moving products along the supply chain.

Exhibit 13.3
Elements of the Supply Chain

The supply chain highlights the links among the various organizations in the production and distribution process.

Raw Materials

Logistics (transportation, coordination, etc.)

Warehouse/Storage

Production

Warehouse/Storage

Logistics (transportation, coordination, etc.)

Distributors—Marketing and Sales

facilities? How can we best balance efficiency with effectiveness?

- **Inventory Control:** How much inventory should we keep on hand? How should we store and distribute it? What about costs such as taxes and insurance?

- **Order Processing:** How should we manage incoming and outgoing orders? What would be most efficient for our customers and suppliers?

- **Customer Service:** How can we serve our customers most effectively? How can we reduce waiting times and facilitate interactions?

- **Transportation:** How can we move products most efficiently through the supply chain? What are the key tradeoffs?

- **Security:** How can we keep products safe from vandals, theft, and accidents every step of the way?

And fragile or perishable products require even more considerations.

13-4a Transportation Decisions

Moving products through the supply chain is so important that it deserves its own section. The various options—trains, planes, and railroads, for instance—are called **modes of transportation**. To make smart decisions, marketers must consider what each mode offers in terms of cost, speed, dependability, flexibility, availability, and frequency of shipments. The right choice depends on the needs of the business and on the product itself. See Exhibit 13.4 for a description of the transportation options.

Depending on factors such as warehousing, docking facilities, and accessibility, many distributors use several different modes of transportation. If you owned a clothing boutique in Las Vegas, for example, chances are that much of your merchandise would travel by boat from China to Long Beach, California, and then by truck from Long Beach to Las Vegas.

13-4b Proactive Supply Chain Management

A growing number of marketers have turned to supply chain management to build a competitive edge through greater efficiency. But given the complexity of the field, many firms choose to outsource this challenge to experts rather than handling it internally. Companies that

EXHIBIT 13.4 MODES OF TRANSPORTATION

Mode	Percentage of U.S. Volume Based on 2007 Ton-Miles	Cost	Speed	On-Time Dependability	Flexibility in Handling	Frequency of Shipments	Availability
Rail	39.5%	Medium	Slow	Medium	Medium	Low	Extensive
Truck	28.6%	High	Fast	High	Medium	High	Most extensive
Ship	12.0%	Lowest	Slowest	Lowest	Highest	Lowest	Limited
Plane	0.3%	Highest	Fastest	Medium	Low	Medium	Medium
Pipeline	19.6%	Low	Slow	Highest	Lowest	Highest	Most limited

Source: Table 1-46b: U.S. Ton-Miles of Freight (BTS Special Tabulation), 2007 data, Bureau of Transportation website, http://www.bts.gov/publications/national_transportation_statistics/html/table_01_46b.html, accessed September 5, 2017.

specialize in helping other companies manage the supply chain—such as UPS—have done particularly well in today's market.

13-5 PRICING OBJECTIVES AND STRATEGIES: A HIGH-STAKES GAME

Pricing strategy clearly has a significant impact on the success of any organization. Price plays a key role in determining demand for your products, which directly influences a company's profitability. Most people, after all, have a limited amount of money and a practically infinite number of ways they could spend it. Price affects their spending choices at a more fundamental level than most other variables.

But ironically, price is perhaps the toughest variable for marketers to control. Both legal constraints and marketing intermediaries (distributors) play roles in determining the final price of most products. Marketers must also consider costs, competitors, investors, taxes, and product strategies.

In today's frenetic environment, stable pricing is no longer the norm. Smart marketers continually evaluate and refine their pricing strategies to ensure that they meet their goals. Even the goals themselves may shift in response to the changing market. Common objectives and strategies include building profitability, boosting volume, matching the competition, and creating prestige.

Many firms express long-term profitability goals in terms of either return on investment or return on sales.

13-5a Building Profitability

Since long-term profitability is a fundamental goal of most businesses, profitability targets are often the starting point for pricing strategies. Many firms express these goals in terms of either return on investment (ROI) or return on sales (ROS). Keep in mind that profitability is the positive difference between revenue (or total sales) and costs. Firms can boost profits by increasing prices or decreasing costs, since either strategy will lead to a greater spread between the two. Doing both is tricky, but companies that succeed—such as Apple—typically dominate their markets.

13-5b Boosting Volume

Companies usually express volume goals in terms of market share—the percentage of a market controlled by a company or a product. Amazon.com, for example, launched with volume objectives. Its goal was to capture as many "eyeballs" as possible, in hopes of later achieving profitability through programs that depend on volume, such as advertising on its site. A volume objective usually leads to one of the following strategies.

Penetration Pricing Penetration pricing, a strategy for pricing new products, aims to capture as much of the market as possible through rock-bottom prices. Each individual sale typically yields a tiny profit; the real money comes from the sheer volume of sales. One key benefit of this strategy is that it tends to discourage competitors, who may be scared off by the slim margins. But penetration pricing makes sense only in categories that don't have a significant group of consumers who would be willing to pay a premium (otherwise, the marketer would be leaving money on the table). For obvious reasons, companies that use penetration pricing are usually focused on controlling costs. JetBlue is a key example. Its prices are often unbeatable, but it strictly controls costs by using a single kind of jet, optimizing turnaround times at the gate, and using many non-major airports.

Everyday-Low Pricing Also known as "sustained discount pricing," **everyday-low pricing (EDLP)** aims to achieve long-term profitability through volume.

modes of transportation The various transportation options—such as planes, trains, and railroads—for moving products through the supply chain.

penetration pricing A new product pricing strategy that aims to capture as much of the market as possible through rock-bottom prices.

everyday-low pricing (EDLP) Long-term discount pricing, designed to achieve profitability through high sales volume.

So What's the Trick to Getting College Students to Eat Healthier?

The answer may be in the pricing. A recent study at Belgium University found that increasing the price of meals sold with French fries significantly reduced the sale of fries, while offering discounts for choosing fruit for dessert increased fruit sales.

Before the experiment, more than half of students (53%) chose meals with French fries. During the experiment, the price of meals with French fries was raised 10% one week and 20% the next if students chose French fries instead of rice or mashed potatoes with lunch meals. About 42% of students chose French fries when the cost was 10% higher, and 31% chose them when the cost was 20% higher. A second experiment offered meals with fruit instead of pastries for dessert. Before the experiment, 37% of students chose meals with fruit. During the experiment, the price of meals with fruit was discounted 10% one week and 20% the next. About 62% of students chose fruit when it was discounted 10%, and about 79% chose fruit when the discount grew to 20%.

Interestingly, reducing the price of a healthy food had a greater impact on students' behavior than increasing the price of an unhealthy food. No gender differences were found. On campuses where students do more of their eating from vending machines, the lessons from this study could be applied quickly and effectively.[9]

pathdoc/Shutterstock.com

Walmart is clearly the king of EDLP with "Always low prices. *Always!*" But Costco uses the same strategy to attract a more-upscale audience. The difference between the two customer groups quickly becomes apparent by glancing at the cars, while strolling through the two parking lots. Costco customers are typically seeking everyday discounts because they want to, not because they need to. The product mix—eclectic and upscale—reflects the customer base. (Costco sells discounted fine wine, low-priced rotisserie chickens, fresh king crab legs, and high-end electronics.) While Costco posted years of healthy, sustained growth, the firm ran into trouble at the end of 2008. As the recession tightened its grip, sales began to soften, especially in non-food categories, suggesting that EDLP may be most effective for less-upscale products.[10] By 2010, Costco had recovered and returned to its historical growth trajectory.

High/Low Pricing The **high/low pricing** strategy tries to increase traffic in retail stores by special sales on a limited number of products, and higher everyday prices on others. Often used—and overused—in grocery stores, drug stores, and department stores, this strategy can alienate customers who feel cheated when a product they bought for full price goes on sale soon afterward. High/low pricing can also train consumers to buy only when products are on sale.

Loss-Leader Pricing Closely related to high/low pricing, **loss-leader pricing** means pricing a handful of items—or loss leaders—temporarily below cost to drive traffic. The retailer loses money on the loss leaders but aims to make up the difference (and then some) on other purchases. To encourage other purchases, retailers

---

high/low pricing A pricing strategy designed to drive traffic to retail stores by special sales on a limited number of products, and higher everyday prices on others.

loss-leader pricing Closely related to high/low pricing, loss-leader pricing means pricing a handful of items—or loss leaders—temporarily below cost to drive traffic.

> "If automobiles had followed the same development cycle as the computer, a Rolls-Royce would today cost $100, get a million miles per gallon, and explode once a year, killing everyone inside."
>
> —ROBERT CRINGELY, TECHNOLOGY JOURNALIST

Is Price Gouging Illegal? Is Price Gouging Immoral? Can Price Gouging Be a Good Thing?

Nobody loves the business that doubles the price of bottled water right after a hurricane or the individual who overcharges for generators in the wake of an earthquake. To discourage both businesses and individuals from raising prices after an emergency, many states have passed anti-price gouging laws. These laws are quite popular among consumers, but according to economists, they may exacerbate the supply problems that cause inconvenience—and even suffering—after natural disasters. For example, anti–price gouging laws tend to encourage hoarding. People at the front of the line may buy more cases of water than they actually need, leaving nothing for those at the back of the line. Anti–price gouging laws also remove the incentive for both businesses and individuals to replenish supply. Why go to the extra effort or incur the extra risks of bringing in extra inventory if you can't charge more to get extra profits? Nevertheless, most states *do* have anti–price gouging laws due to their overwhelming popularity with voters. If the price-gouging retailer finds himself at the wrong end of a natural disaster, he might end up being thankful for such laws as well.[11]

typically place loss leaders at the back of the store, forcing customers to navigate past a tempting array of more profitable items. The loss-leader strategy has been used effectively by producers, as well. Gillette, for instance, gives away some shavers practically for free but reaps handsome profits as consumers buy replacement blades. Similarly, Microsoft has sold its Xbox systems at a loss to increase potential profits from high-margin video games. But the loss-leader strategy can't be used everywhere, since a number of states have made loss leaders illegal for anti-competitive reasons.[12]

13-5c Matching the Competition

The key goal is to set prices based on what everyone else is doing. Usually, the idea is to wipe out price as a point of comparison, forcing customers to choose their product based on other factors. Examples include Coke and Pepsi, Honda and Toyota, Chevron and Mobil, and Delta and United. But sometimes one or two competitors emerge that drive pricing for entire industries. Marlboro, for instance, leads the pack in terms of cigarette pricing, with other brands falling into place behind.

13-5d Creating Prestige

The core goal is to use price to send consumers a message about the high quality and exclusivity of a product—the higher the price, the better the product. Of course, this strategy works only if the product actually delivers top quality; otherwise, nobody would buy more than once (and those who do so would clearly spread the word). Rolex watches, Mont Blanc pens, and Bentley cars all use prestige pricing to reinforce their image.

Skimming Pricing This new product pricing strategy is a subset of prestige pricing. **Skimming pricing** involves offering new products at a premium price. The idea is to entice price-insensitive consumers—music fanatics, for example—to buy high when a product first enters the market. Once these customers have made their purchases, marketers will often introduce lower-priced versions of the same product to capture the bottom of the market. Apple used this strategy with its iPod, introducing its premium version for a hefty price tag. Once it had secured the big spenders, Apple introduced the lower-priced iPod Nanos and Shuffles with a powerful market response. But keep in mind that skimming works only when a product is tough to copy in terms of design, brand image, technology, or some other attribute. Otherwise, the fat margins will attract a host of competitors.

13-6 PRICING IN PRACTICE: A REAL-WORLD APPROACH

At this point, you may be wondering about economic theory. How do concepts such as supply and demand and price elasticity affect pricing decisions?

Even though most marketers are familiar with economics, they often don't have the information they need to apply the theories to their specific pricing strategies. Collecting data for supply and demand curves is expensive and time consuming, which may be unrealistic for rapidly changing markets. From a real-world standpoint, most marketers consider market-based factors—especially customer expectations and competitive prices—but they rely

skimming pricing A new product pricing strategy that aims to maximize profitability by offering new products at a premium price.

Does Your Privacy Matter to You as Much as Cheap Prices?

Years ago, anyone willing to scour coupons, search for deals, and shop often could make use of the lowest prices at the grocery store. But those days are disappearing as quickly as your Internet privacy. A number of large grocers are now implementing personalized pricing programs that create unique offers and prices tailored to shoppers' individual behaviors and needs, ultimately bumping up the grocers' profit margins. Soon, such personalized pricing programs might well displace standardized price tags. For example, a shopper who has a history of purchasing alcohol and barbecue sauces may receive a coupon designed to encourage him or her to purchase a brand-new high margin Kentucky bourbon sauce. Some customized coupons are offered on-the-spot via mobile apps that are loaded with customer data, while others are sent in the mail. According to shopper Ainy Kazmi, "It's a little bit creepy, but I figure they're checking anything anyway—I might as well get a good deal out of it."[13]

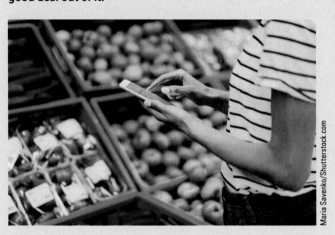

Maria Savenko/Shutterstock.com

on cost-based pricing. The key question is: What price levels will allow me to cover my costs and achieve my objectives?

13-6a Breakeven Analysis

Breakeven analysis is a relatively simple process that determines the number of units a firm must sell to cover all costs. Sales above the breakeven point will generate a profit; sales below the breakeven point will lead to a loss. The actual equation looks like this:

$$\text{Breakeven Point (BP)} = \frac{\text{Total fixed costs (FC)}}{\text{Price/unit (p)} - \text{Variable costs/unit (VC)}}$$

If you were selling customized nachos, for example, your fixed costs might be $400,000 per year. Fixed costs stay the same regardless of how many servings of nachos you sell. Specific fixed costs might include the mortgage, equipment payments, advertising, insurance, and taxes. Suppose your variable cost per serving—the cost of the ingredients and the cost of wages for the cook—were $5 per serving. If your customers would pay $12 per serving, you could use the breakeven equation to determine how many servings of nachos you'd need to sell in a year so that your total sales were equal to your total expenses. Remember: a company that is breaking even is not making a profit.

> **breakeven analysis**
> The process of determining the number of units a firm must sell to cover all costs.

Here's how the breakeven analysis would work for our nacho business:

$$\text{BP} = \frac{\text{FC}}{\text{P} - \text{VC}} = \frac{\$400,000}{\$12 - \$5} = \frac{\$400,000}{\$7} = 57,143 \text{ Servings Nachos}$$

Over a one-year horizon, 57,143 servings of customized nachos would translate to about 157 servings per day. Is that reasonable? Could you do better? If so, start thinking of some creative names! If not, you have several choices, each with its own set of considerations:

- **Raise Prices:** How much do other snack-like meals in your neighborhood cost? Are your nachos better in some way? Would potential customers be willing to pay more?

- **Decrease Variable Costs:** Could you use less expensive ingredients? Is it possible to hire less expensive help? How would these changes affect quality and sales?

- **Decrease Fixed Costs:** Should you choose a different location? Can you lease cheaper equipment? Would it make sense to advertise less often? How would these changes affect your business?

Clearly, there isn't one best strategy, but a breakeven analysis helps marketers get a sense of where they stand and the hurdles they need to clear before actually introducing a product.

Pricing Sleight of Hand

As a consumer, does it ever seem to you as though marketers use magic to separate you from your money? As a marketer, it may be helpful to know some pricing tricks that marketers use to maximize revenue. Here are some examples, used especially well by Apple:

- *Establish a high reference point:* Research suggests that most consumers need a reference point to determine whether a given price is reasonable. For instance, the iPhone cost $599 when it first launched, which helps make an iPhone today at $199 seem like a bargain.

- *Obscure the reference point:* Apple products look so unique that it's impossible to compare them accurately to anything else on the market. Similarly, candy and other treats in movie theaters are tough to accurately price-compare to goodies at other outlets, because they tend to come in unusual, large boxes that are shaped nothing like what you see at other stores.

- *Hide price components in bundles:* Not just Apple, but most electronic devices, count on downstream data fees over the course of a contract to supplement the cost of the device itself. For instance, computer printers are relatively cheap, but manufacturers rely on anticipated sales from proprietary ink cartridges. Ink revenue adds up quickly—especially over the full life of a printer.

Each of these strategies is legally sound, but they may be a bit ethically shaky. Being aware is a crucial part of being a smart consumer. And making pricing information transparent is part of being an ethical marketer.[14]

Ljupco Smokovski/Shutterstock.com

13-6b Fixed Margin Pricing

Many firms determine upfront how much money they need to make for each item they sell. The **profit margin**—which is the gap between the cost and the price on a per-product basis—can be expressed as a dollar amount but more often is expressed as a percent. There are two key ways to determine margins.

1. **Cost-Based Pricing:** The most popular method of establishing a fixed margin starts with determining the actual cost of each product. The process is more complex than it may initially seem, since fixed costs must be allocated on a per-product basis, and some variable costs fluctuate dramatically on a daily or weekly basis. But once the per-product cost is set, the next step is to layer the margin on the cost to determine the price. Costco, for instance, has a strict policy that no branded item can be marked up by more than 14%, and no private-label item by more than 15%. Supermarkets, on the other hand, often markup merchandise by 25%, and department stores by 50% or more. Margins in other industries can be much thinner.[15]

2. **Demand-Based Pricing:** This approach begins by determining what price consumers would be willing to pay. With that as a starting point, marketers subtract their desired margin, which yields their target costs. This

method is more market-focused than cost-based pricing, but it's also more risky, since profits depend on achieving those target costs. A number of Japanese companies, such as Sony, have been very successful with this approach, achieving extraordinarily efficient production.

13-6c Consumer Pricing Perceptions: The Strategic Wild Card

You just don't know if you've found the right price until you figure out how consumers perceive it. And those perceptions can sometimes defy the straightforward logic of dollars and cents. Two key considerations are price–quality relationships and odd pricing.

The link between price and perceived quality can be powerful. Picture yourself walking into a local sporting goods store, looking for a new snowboard. They have several models of your favorite brand, most priced at around $450. But then you notice another option— same brand, same style— marked down to $79. Would you buy it? If you

> There are two kinds of fools in any market. One doesn't charge enough. The other charges too much.
>
> —RUSSIAN PROVERB

profit margin The gap between the cost and the price of an item on a per-product basis.

were like most consumers, you'd probably assume that something was wrong with a board that cheap. Would you be right? It's hard to know. Sometimes the relationship between price and quality is clear and direct, but that is not always the case. Regardless, consumers will use price as an indicator of quality unless they have additional information to guide their decision. Savvy marketers factor this tendency into their pricing strategies.

Marketers also must weigh the pros and cons of **odd pricing**, or ending prices in numbers below even dollars and cents. A micro stereo system at Target, for instance, might cost $99.99 instead of an even $100. Gasoline uses odd pricing to 99/100ths of a cent. But wouldn't round numbers be easier? Does that extra penny really make a difference? While the research is inconclusive, many marketers believe that jumping up to the "next" round number sends a message that prices have hit a whole new level. In other words, they believe that the *perceived* gap between $99.99 and $100.00 is much greater than the *actual* gap of 0.0001%. And it certainly makes sense from an intuitive standpoint.

Odd prices have also come to signal a bargain, which is often—but not always—a benefit for the marketer. For instance, a big-screen TV for $999.99 might seem like a great deal, while knee surgery for $4,999.99 sounds kind of scary— you'd probably rather that

Olivier Le Moal/Shutterstock.com

Many marketers use odd pricing because the *perceived* gap between $1.00 and $0.99 is much greater than the *actual* gap between these two prices.

odd pricing The practice of ending prices in numbers below even dollars and cents in order to create a perception of greater value.

your doctor charge $5,000. Likewise, a fast-food joint might charge $3.99 for its value meal, while fine restaurants almost always end their prices in zeros. Marketers can determine whether odd pricing would work for them by evaluating the strategy in light of the messages it sends to the target market.

THE BIG PICTURE

Distribution and pricing are two fundamental elements of the marketing mix. In today's frenzied global economy, marketers are seeking a competitive edge through distribution management. Creating a profitable presence in multiple retail venues requires constant focus throughout the organization. And managing the supply chain—how products move along the path from raw materials to the final consumer—plays a crucial role in controlling costs and providing great customer service. Integrating effective technology during the entire process can separate the winners from the losers.

Pricing objectives and strategies are also pivotal since they directly impact both profitability and product image. As the market changes, successful companies continually reevaluate and modify their approach, working hand in hand with their accountants.

Looking ahead, a growing number of companies will probably move toward collaboration, rather than competition, as they manage their supply chains. And pricing will likely become even more dynamic in response to the changing market.

Warehouse Manager

Oversee the safe receipt, storage, retrieval, and timely transmission of goods. Oversee computerized inventory management system. Comply with federal, state, and local laws regarding warehousing, material handling, and shipping. Plan the arrangement of goods within the warehouse, and handle requirements for specialized stock (e.g., chilled goods or fragile products). Keep current with all relevant legislation and industry trends. Ensure security in all aspects of warehouse operation. Maintain physical condition of warehouse. Create and track warehousing budget to meet financial objectives. Hire, manage, and motivate warehouse staff.

STUDY TOOLS 13

LOCATED AT BACK OF THE TEXTBOOK

☐ Rip-Out Chapter Review Card

☐ Gain unique perspectives on key concepts with new concept videos in the e-book

☐ Increase your comprehension with online homework and quizzes

☐ Study with existing flashcards and make your own

Remember to visit
PAGE 269
for additional
STUDY TOOLS

LEARNING OBJECTIVES

After studying this chapter, you will be able to:

14-1 Discuss the role of management and its importance to organizational success

14-2 Explain key theories and current practices of motivation

14-3 Outline the categories of business planning and explain strategic planning

14-4 Discuss the organizing function of management

14-5 Explain the role of managerial leadership and the key leadership styles

14-6 Describe the management control process

14-1 BRINGING RESOURCES TO LIFE

To grow and thrive, every business needs resources—money, technology, materials—and an economic system that helps enterprise flourish. But those resources, or factors of production, are nothing without **management** to bring them to life. Managers provide vision and direction for their organizations, they decide how to use resources to achieve goals, and they inspire others—both inside and outside their companies—to follow their lead. By formal definition, managers achieve the goals of an organization through planning, organizing, leading, and controlling organizational resources, including people, money, and time.

> **management** Achieving the goals of an organization through planning, organizing, leading, and controlling organizational resources including people, money, and time.

> **planning** Determining organizational goals and action plans for how to achieve those goals.

> **organizing** Determining a structure for both individual jobs and the overall organization.

> **leading** Directing and motivating people to achieve organizational goals.

> **controlling** Monitoring performance and making adjustments as needed.

In simple terms, **planning** means figuring out where to go and how to get there. **Organizing** means determining a structure for both individual jobs and the overall organization. **Leading** means directing and motivating people to achieve organizational goals. And **controlling** means monitoring performance and making adjustments as needed. In today's chaotic, hyper-competitive business environment, managers face daunting challenges. But for the right people, management positions can provide an exhilarating—though sometimes exhausting—career.

As the business pace accelerates and the environment continues to morph—especially in the wake of economic turmoil—the role of management is also radically transforming. The successful manager has changed from boss to coach, from disciplinarian to motivator, from dictator to team builder. But the bottom-line goal remains the same: to create value for the organization.

In late 2017, management became more complex, with the reemergence of the #MeToo movement, which shined bright light on sexual harassment and assault in the workplace. Hundreds of women in prominent positions came forward publicly with their stories of harassment. Public opinion, the press, their employers, and in many cases, even the law, rallied behind them with strong support—punishing the perpetrators, and establishing new safeguards to prevent future abuse. Managers in today's workplace must be hyperaware of how they treat women and indeed, all employees—always keeping absolute fairness and transparency at the forefront of their actions and perspective. Please see Chapter 15 for more detail on this issue.

14-1a Management Hierarchy: Levels of Responsibility

Most medium-sized and large companies have three basic levels of management: **top management**, **middle management**, and **first-line (or supervisory) management**. The levels typically fall into a pyramid of sorts, with a small number of top managers and a larger number of supervisory managers. Responsibilities shift as managers move up the hierarchy, and the skills that they use must

> "If you can get those two things right—having a clear direction on what you are trying to do and bringing in great people who can execute on the stuff—then you can do pretty well."
>
> —MARK ZUCKERBERG, FOUNDER AND CEO, FACEBOOK

shift accordingly. Here are the differences between three key levels:

- **Top management** sets the overall direction of the firm. Top managers must articulate a vision, establish priorities, and allocate time, money, and other resources. Typical titles include chief executive officer (CEO), president, and vice president.

- **Middle management** manages the managers. (Say that three

top management Managers who set the overall direction of the firm, articulating a vision, establishing priorities, and allocating time, money, and other resources.

middle management Managers who supervise lower-level managers and report to a higher-level manager.

first-line (supervisory) management Managers who directly supervise nonmanagement employees.

Starting Early and Staying Strong

Some people seem compelled to succeed no matter what … and those are the folks who tend to drive the economy. A quick survey of some well-known super-achievers suggests that a high level of motivation was part of their personalities from the very beginning:

- *Mark Zuckerberg, Facebook founder*: Before he went to college, Mark was recruited to work for Microsoft and AOL. As a toddler, he found a screwdriver and dismantled his crib when he thought he was too old for a "baby bed."

- *Palmer Luckey, 23-year-old founder of Oculus Rift*: Luckey experimented with building coil guns in his parents' garage when he was a teenager. "Looking back," he says, "it's honestly a miracle I am not dead."

- *Oprah Winfrey, media mogul*: Winfrey (pictured) began working at the corner grocery store next to her father's barber shop, and she "hated every minute of it." Winfrey wasn't allowed to talk to the customers, which she understandably found "very, very, very hard."

- *Jeff Bezos, Amazon founder*: As a teenager, Jeff built amateur robots and an assortment of other electronic inventions.

- Warren Buffett, founder of Berkshire Hathaway and one of the richest people in the world, began delivering papers on his bicycle at the age of 13. By the time he finished high school in 1947, Buffett had earned $5,000, which is the equivalent of $54,000 today.

- *Richard Branson, Virgin Group CEO*: Branson attributes at least some of his motivation to his mom: When he was six, she would shove him out of the car and tell him to find his own way home.

- *Chris Rock, comedian*: Chris' first job was at Red Lobster. "The thing about Red Lobster is that if you work there, you can't afford to eat there," he once told Jay Leno. "You're making minimum wage. A shrimp costs minimum wage."

But keep in mind that some high achievers don't gear up until well after childhood. True motivation requires clear goals, which people can develop at any point in their lives. When meaningful goals merge with energy and determination, anything becomes possible.[1]

Krista Kennell//Shutterstock.com

---

times!) Middle managers must communicate up and down the pyramid, and their primary contribution often involves coordinating teams and special projects with their peers from other departments. Typical titles include director, division head, and branch manager.

- **First-line (supervisory) management** manages the people who do the work. First-line managers must train, motivate, and evaluate nonmanagement employees, so they are heavily involved in day-to-day production issues. Typical titles include supervisor, foreman, and section leader.

Smaller companies usually don't have a hierarchy of management. Often the owner must act as the top-, middle-, and first-line manager, all rolled into one. This clearly requires enormous flexibility and well-developed management skills.

technical skills Expertise in a specific functional area or department.

human skills The ability to work effectively with and through other people in a range of different relationships.

conceptual skills The ability to grasp a big-picture view of the overall organization, the relationships among its various parts, and its fit in the broader competitive environment.

14-1b Management Skills: Having What It Takes to Get the Job Done

Given the turbulence of today's business world, managers must draw on a staggering range of skills to do their jobs efficiently and effectively. Most of these abilities cluster into three broad categories: technical skills, human skills, and conceptual skills.

- **Technical Skills: Technical skills** refer to expertise in a specific functional area or department. Keep in mind that technical skills don't necessarily relate to technology. People can have technical skills—or specific expertise—in virtually any field, from sales, to copywriting, to accounting, to airplane repair, to computer programming.

- **Human Skills: Human skills** refer to the ability to work with and through other people in a range of different relationships. Human skills include communication, leadership, coaching, empathy, and team building. A manager with strong human skills can typically mobilize support for initiatives and find win–win solutions for conflicts.

- **Conceptual Skills: Conceptual skills** refer to the ability to grasp a big-picture view of the overall organization and the relationship between its various parts. Conceptual skills also help managers understand how their company fits into the broader competitive environment. Managers with strong conceptual skills typically excel at strategic planning.

All three categories of skill are essential for management success. But their importance varies according to the level of the manager. Front-line managers must have a high degree of technical skills, which help them hire, train, and evaluate employees; avoid mistakes; and ensure high-quality production. Middle-level managers need an especially high level of human skills. They typically act as the bridge between departments, coordinating people and projects that sometimes have mismatched priorities. Top-level managers must demonstrate excellent conceptual skills in order to formulate a vision, interpret marketplace trends, and plan for the future. To move up in an organization, managers must constantly learn and grow, nurturing skills that reflect their new tasks.

Across all three skill sets, critical thinking and decision-making abilities have become increasingly important. Critical thinking helps managers find value even in an overload of information. Part of how information overload plays out is in email management; according to *Fortune* magazine, the average knowledge worker now spends an astounding 28% of her work time managing email. Simply deleting unwanted emails could take more than 16 hours per year! Strong decision-making skills help managers respond wisely and rapidly to all this information, with an unwavering focus on customer satisfaction.

Managers who expect to grow in the company hierarchy must expect to foster new skills. Too often, workers get promotions because of great technical skills—for example, the top salesperson lands the sales manager slot—but they struggle to move further because they don't fully develop their human and conceptual skills.

 ## 14-2 MOTIVATION: LIGHTING THE FIRE

Standout managers motivate others to reach for their best selves—to accomplish more than they ever thought possible. Motivated workers tend to feel great about their jobs, and

---

OOPS! WHAT WERE THEY THINKING?

Bad Decisions, Big Impacts

Every day, managers around the globe make high-stakes decisions, from expanding overseas, to introducing new products, to closing factories. The great decisions have become the stuff of legends, shaping the business world as we know it today. Bad choices also abound. Consider these five business decisions that made history for their silliness:

- Faced with the opportunity to buy rights to the telephone in 1876, Western Union, the telegraph behemoth, rejected the newfangled device: "This 'telephone' has too many shortcomings to be seriously considered as a means of communication. The device is inherently of no value to us."

- In 1899, two young attorneys approached Asa Candler—owner of the briskly selling new fountain drink Coca-Cola—with an innovative proposal to bottle the beverage. Chandler sold them exclusive rights to bottle Coke across most of the United States for the grand sum of $1. Oops.

- In 1977, the executives at 20th Century Fox exhibited overconfidence in their deal-making abilities, and far too little confidence in director George Lucas's filmmaking and business savvy. In exchange for a paltry $20,000 pay cut, they signed over to Lucas all product merchandising rights for the current and all future *Star Wars* films. The combined revenue from merchandising is estimated to have exceeded $3 billion, and continues to grow annually, making it the most lucrative deal ever struck between an individual and a corporate studio in entertainment history. Seemed like a good idea at the time....

- In 1999, fledgling search engine Excite rejected an offer to buy Google because it considered the $1 million asking price to be too high. Google is now worth nearly $300 billion, and Excite is defunct.

- In 2016, Mylan pharmaceuticals raised the price of the EpiPen, a life-saving drug delivery system, from $57 to more than $500. After the news broke, Mylan's stock price dropped from almost $58 a share to around $38 per share—a loss of more than 34%—suggesting that sometimes increased profits just aren't worth as much as they may seem.

- Also in 2016, Samsung *twice* had to halt production and undergo a massive and expensive recall of its Galaxy Note 7 phone, which had the inconvenient and potentially deadly problem of heating up and catching fire. The cost of the recall may ultimately exceed $17 billion, which is potentially more than the phone would've attracted in the first place. Clearly, taking a product to market without thoroughly testing it first is not always worth the potential costs.

- Mike Smith, one of the executives in charge of evaluating new talent for the London office of Decca Records, rejected the Beatles in 1962 with the now infamous line: "Groups are out; four-piece groups with guitars particularly are finished." Not so much....

With the help of hindsight, momentous decisions may seem almost inevitable. But these bloopers clearly show that in the fog of the moment, the right choice can be anything but clear.[2]

EXHIBIT 14.1   MASLOW'S HIERARCHY OF NEEDS AND THE WORKPLACE

Maslow's Need	Description	Workplace Examples
Self-Actualization	Need for fulfillment—the need to realize one's fullest potential	Challenging, creative jobs; meaningful work that ties to a greater good; volunteer opportunities
Esteem	Need for self-respect and respect from others—recognition and status	Acknowledgment, feedback, promotions, perks, raises
Social (Belonging)	Need to feel connected to others—accepted by family and friends	Teamwork, positive corporate culture, company lunchroom, uniforms, department outings
Safety	Need to feel secure—free of harm and free of fear	Safety equipment, healthcare plans, life insurance, retirement plans, job security, gym membership
Physiological	Need for basic survival—food, water, clothing, and shelter	A job with enough pay to buy the basics

workers who feel great tend to produce more. But the thinking about *how* to motivate workers has changed dramatically over time. In the early 1900s, key management thinkers focused on efficiency and productivity, dictating precisely how workers should do each element of their jobs. But more recent research suggests that people's thoughts and feelings play a vital role in motivation, which leads to a range of new theories.

14-2a   Theories of Motivation

Maslow's Hierarchy of Needs Theory Noted psychologist Abraham Maslow theorized that people are motivated to satisfy only unmet needs. He proposed a hierarchy of human needs—from basic to abstract—suggesting that as each need is met, people become motivated to meet the next-highest need in the pyramid. Maslow's five specific needs are shown in Exhibit 14.1. While his theory was not based on the workplace, Maslow's ideas can illuminate the needs behind motivation at work.

From a workplace perspective, the idea that people are motivated only by unmet needs clearly holds true for the first two levels of the hierarchy. Finding a job that pays the bills, for instance, is the primary motivator for most people who don't have any job at all. People who have a job but no healthcare would find health insurance much more motivating than, say, a company picnic geared toward meeting social needs.

But after physiological and safety needs are met, the other needs are motivating to different degrees in different people. An employee with strong social connections outside work might be more motivated by a promotion that meets esteem needs than by a company outing that meets social needs. A number of firms actually use self-actualization needs as a starting point for motivating employees, by creating a mission statement that communicates the importance of the work. The House of Blues inspires employees through its lofty purpose: to promote racial and spiritual harmony through love, peace, truth, righteousness, and nonviolence.

14-2b   Theory X and Theory Y

Psychologist Douglas McGregor, one of Maslow's students, studied workplace motivation from a different angle. He proposed that management attitudes toward workers would directly affect worker motivation. His research suggested that management attitudes fall into two opposing categories, which he called **Theory X and Theory Y**, described in Exhibit 14.2.

McGregor proposed that managers should employ Theory Y assumptions to capitalize on the imagination and intelligence of every worker. In American business today, some organizations use a Theory X approach, but a growing number have begun to at least experiment with Theory Y, tapping into a rich pool of employee input.

Job Enrichment A number of researchers have focused on creating jobs with more meaningful content, under the assumption that challenging, creative work will motivate employees to give their best effort. **Job enrichment** typically includes the following factors:

1. **Skill Variety:** Workers can use a range of different skills.

2. **Task Identity:** Workers complete tasks with clear beginnings and endings.

Maslow's hierarchy of needs theory A motivation theory that suggests that human needs fall into a hierarchy and that as each need is met, people become motivated to meet the next-highest need in the pyramid.

Theory X and Theory Y A motivation theory that suggests that management attitudes toward workers fall into two opposing categories based on management assumptions about worker capabilities and values.

job enrichment The creation of jobs with more meaningful content, under the assumption that challenging, creative work will motivate employees.

EXHIBIT 14.2 THEORY X AND THEORY Y

Theory X Assumptions about Workers	Theory Y Assumptions about Workers
■ Workers dislike work and will do everything they can to avoid it.	■ Work is as natural as play or rest—workers do not inherently dislike it.
■ Fear is motivating—coercion and threats are vital to get people to work toward company goals.	■ Different rewards can be motivating—people can exercise self-direction and self-control to meet company goals.
■ People prefer to be directed, avoiding responsibility and seeking security.	■ People can accept and even seek responsibility.
	■ The capacity for imagination, creativity, and ingenuity is widely distributed in the population.
	■ The intellectual capacity of the average worker is underutilized in the workplace.

3. **Task Significance:** Workers understand the impact of the task on others.

4. **Autonomy:** Workers have freedom and authority regarding their jobs.

5. **Feedback:** Workers receive clear, frequent information about their performance.

Richard Branson, maverick founder of the Virgin Group, relies on job enrichment, especially autonomy and feedback, to keep people motivated at his 350-company empire (which includes a startling range of firms, such as Virgin Atlantic Airlines, Virgin Music, Virgin mobile phones, and Virgin Galactic space travel). Branson gives his managers a stake in their companies and then tells them "to run it as if it's their own." He says, "I have to be good at helping people run the individual businesses, and I have to be willing to step back. The company must be set up so it can continue without me." According to Virgin's website, "we pretty much practice a collaborative and supportive style of custodianship." Due in large part to Branson's motivational approach, the Virgin workforce is fully engaged with the company, contributing to its remarkable long-term success.[3]

Expectancy Theory Usually attributed to researcher Victor Vroom, **expectancy theory** deals with the relationship among individual effort, individual performance, and individual reward. The key concept is that a worker will be motivated if he or she believes that effort will lead to performance, and performance will lead to a meaningful reward.

$$\text{Effort} \rightarrow \text{Performance} \rightarrow \text{Reward}$$

The theory suggests that if any link in the chain is broken, the employee will not be motivated.

> "If we are not making mistakes, we're not trying hard enough."
>
> JAMES QUINCEY,
> CEO, COCA-COLA

Imagine if your professor announced on the first day of class that he or she had never given any student an A, as a matter of principle. Would you be motivated to perform in class? Not likely—the link between performance and reward would be broken. Retailer Hot Topic has done a particularly strong job implementing the link between effort and performance. A Hot Topic employee describes the connection, saying, "I've worked for HT for five years, and the best thing I've learned is that if you work hard enough and dedicate enough of yourself to something, you can achieve your goals!" Hot Topic has also established strong links between performance and rewards. Perhaps it's no coincidence that Hot Topic was one of the few retail chains that continued to perform well, even as the recession tightened its grip in late 2008 and early 2009.[4]

Equity Theory Pioneered by J. Stacy Adams, **equity theory** proposes that perceptions of fairness directly affect worker motivation. The key idea is that people won't be motivated if they believe that the relationship between what they contribute and what they earn is different from the relationship between what others contribute and what others earn. For example, if you worked ten-hour days, and earned less than the guy in the next cube who works seven-hour days, you'd probably think it was pretty unfair. To restore a sense of balance, you might:

■ Demand a raise

■ Start coming in late, leaving early, and taking extra-long lunch hours

expectancy theory A motivation theory that concerns the relationship among individual effort, individual performance, and individual reward.

equity theory A motivation theory that proposes that perceptions of fairness directly affect worker motivation.

Do You Have Hustle?

Today's business leaders didn't invent the concept of "hustle," but they are certainly putting a new spin on what hustle means. Jeff Sinelli, CEO of fast-growing restaurant chain Which Wich Superior Sandwiches, likes to joke that he emerged from the womb "naked and broke, sold his umbilical cord to the doctor, and hasn't stopped since." As CEO, Sinelli has kept Which Wich's focus on hustle, encouraging his team to maintain a "sense of urgency" in serving customers. Fortune describes the hustle culture as follows, especially in regard to tech driven start-ups: "Move first and move fast. Encourage

Mark Nazh/Shutterstock.com

internal competition. Test and learn. Always push relentlessly forward. Learn from your mistakes. Above all else, hustle." Under the direction of hard-driving CEO Travis Kalanick, ride share behemoth Uber took its hustle-oriented culture to an extreme, resulting in a toxic, macho environment that led to a raft of lawsuits, executive firings, disgruntled employees, and ultimately, a loss of revenue. According to some sources, hiring managers in the Bay Area have begun evaluating once highly sought-after applicants from Uber with a new degree of skepticism. More and more, a "hustle-oriented culture" has become something to be afraid of. Hustle clearly has value, but it also works best when it is balanced with empathy, respect, and sheer human decency.[5]

- Convince yourself that the other guy is about to be fired (or try to get him fired)
- Look for another job

The response to perceived inequity almost always involves trying to change the system, changing your own work habits, distorting your perceptions, or leaving the company.

But keep in mind that equity theory is based on perceptions, which are not always on the mark. People are all too prone to overestimate their own contributions, which throws perceived equity out of balance. The best way to combat equity issues is through clear, open communication from management.[6]

14-2c Motivation Today

Companies today use a range of approaches to motivation, although several key themes have emerged. Most firms no longer seek to make their employees happy; instead, they want their workers to be productive and engaged. Yet, for employees, work is about more than just productivity. University of Michigan business school professor David Ulrich points out that even in today's hyper-competitive environment, "people still want to find meaning in their work and in the institutions that employ them."[7]

A growing emphasis on corporate culture has captured the best of both worlds for companies that do it right. A look at *Fortune* magazine's 100 Best Companies to Work for in 2017 demonstrates that a distinctive, positive culture tends to create productive employees who are deeply attached to their work and their companies. The winners tend to emphasize the health and well-being of their employees and to offer strong commitments to make the world a better place. Google, which has been on the list for 11 years and in the number one slot for eight years, offers employees a famous set of perks at their Silicon Valley headquarters, including on-site haircutting, massage services, game facilities, and 25 cafés companywide, all free. As one happy Googler writes, "The company culture truly makes workers feel they're valued and respected as a human being, not as a cog in a machine." Despite—or perhaps in part *because of* the pricey perks—everything at Google is up: revenue, profits, share price, paid search clicks, and hiring. Googlers nearly uniformly praise the competence of their leadership, the support they receive as professionals, and the pride they take in the challenging work they accomplish together. "Simply by being here, I feel very naturally motivated to be (and also very proud to be) my best possible self," explains one employee. At a time when many Silicon Valley corporations are coming under fire for lack of diversity, Google has applied its rigorous analytical approach to creating a diverse, open work environment that employees describe as "safe and inclusive."

Many firms on the 2017 list seem to value teamwork deeply. Investment firm Baird, for example, maintains and enforces a rigorous "no a**holes" policy, calling for zero tolerance of those who don't play well with others at any level of the organization. Two-thirds of Baird's employees are also shareholders, which leads to a feeling among employees that "everyone is playing the same game and we are all equal contributors." Similarly, 100% employee-owned engineering, architecture, and construction firm Burns & McDonnell is frequently praised for its tightly knit,

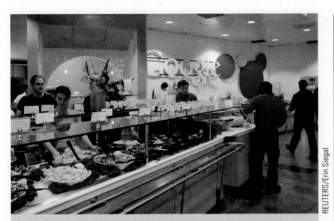

Many "Googlers" especially appreciate the top-quality free food that's always available for employees.

highly collaborative teams and its stance that "selfish behavior gets you nowhere."[8]

Many firms on the 2017 list also give their employees generous sabbaticals. Senior managers at Kimpton are eligible for month-long sabbaticals after seven years—but only if they promise to unplug from their work emails and phone calls. Adobe gives four weeks of paid time off after five years of service, five weeks after ten years, and six weeks after fifteen years. Genentech gives a six-week paid sabbatical after six years of service. Upscale home builder David Weekley Homes offers employees up to six weeks of paid sabbatical after ten years of service and even throws in a grant of $2,000 for travel and education expenses.[9]

A number of firms on the 2017 list have expanded their benefits programs to include a range of nontraditional services that employees love. At pet-friendly Kimpton Hotels & Restaurants, for example, employees are encouraged to bring their dogs to work. When a pet dies and employees need some time to grieve, "We make all the accommodations possible for that employee to show care for him/her during a difficult time." Professional services firm KPMG has an annual summer gift program, which it uses to celebrate success and thank employees for their contributions. In recent years, annual summer gifts have included barbecue and ice cream packages sent to all KPMGers' homes so they can share with their friends and family members. Technology company Workday offers its staffers a personal concierge service to help schedule appointments, run errands, go shopping, and more.[10]

Unique corporate cultures also contribute to employee motivation. Detroit-based Quicken Loans nurtures such an open culture that CEO Bill Emerson has given his personal cell phone number to each of the firm's 8,500 employees,

and has not received any prank calls, only a handful of "pocket calls." When Facebook went public, Mark Zuckerberg described the firm's "hack culture" as one of its assets, more specifically, an approach to building that involves continuous improvement and iteration. He added that "hackers believe that something can always be better, and that nothing is ever complete. They just have to go fix it—often in the face of people who say it's impossible or are content with the status quo." With the "Hacker Way," the best idea and implementation should always win—not the person who is best at lobbying for an idea or the person who manages the most people.[11]

Fortune also publishes a list of the hundred best companies for millennials to work for. Work-life balance, respecting employees, and time for fun are key themes among the companies that make this list. At digital marketing firm Elite SEM, the number-one company on the list, employees not only have unlimited paid vacation days, they are *required* to take a week of paid time off every year to ensure that they get a solid vacation. Listening to employees at every level is also important to millennials. At consulting firm Kimley-Horn, one employee remarks, "Although I have only been here a few years, my ideas, thoughts, issues, and solutions are always taken seriously." Kimley-Horn also sponsors monthly outings and events for employees, such as Metroplex kickball tournaments, ice cream socials, cooking contests, and pot luck dinners.

14-3 PLANNING: FIGURING OUT WHERE TO GO AND HOW TO GET THERE

The planning function—figuring out where to go and how to get there—is the core of effective management. A survey in the *Wall Street Journal* found that 80% of executives identify planning as their most valuable management tool. But even though planning is critical, it's also highly risky in light of cutthroat competition, rapid change, and economic uncertainty. The best plans keep the organization on track without sacrificing flexibility and responsiveness; they incorporate ways to respond to change both inside and outside the organization.[12]

Although all managers engage in planning, the scope of the process changes according to the manager's position, as shown in Exhibit 14.3. Top-level managers focus on **strategic planning**.

> **strategic planning**
> High-level, long-term planning that establishes a vision for the company, defines long-term objectives and priorities, determines broad action steps, and allocates resources.

EXHIBIT 14.3   MANAGERIAL PLANNING

Type of Planning	Management Level	Scope of Planning	Examples of Planning Questions and Concerns
Strategic Planning	Senior management	Typically five-year time frame	Should we acquire a new company? Should we begin manufacturing in China? Should we expand to overseas markets? Should we take our company public?
Tactical Planning	Middle management	Typically one-year time frame	Should we spend more time servicing each customer? Should we hire a public relations agency to handle PR? Should we spend fewer ad dollars on TV and more on the Web?
Operational Planning	First-line management	Daily, weekly, and monthly time frame	How should we schedule employees this week? When should we schedule delivery for each batch of product? How should customer service people answer the phones?

They establish a vision for the company, define long-term objectives and priorities, determine broad action steps, and allocate resources. Middle managers focus on **tactical planning**, or applying the strategic plan to their specific areas of responsibility. And first-line managers focus on **operational planning**, or applying the tactical plans to daily, weekly, and monthly operations. Successful firms often encourage a flow of feedback up and down the organization to ensure that all key plans are sound and that all key players "buy in." Some typical planning decisions and time frames are shown in Exhibit 14.3.

A fourth category of planning has gained new prominence in the past decade: **contingency planning**, or planning for unexpected events. Senior management usually spearheads contingency planning but with input from the other levels of management. Contingency plans consider what might go wrong—both inside the business and with the outside environment—and develop responses. Potential issues include:

- How should we respond if our competitors knock off our best-selling product?

- What should we do if the government regulates our industry?

- How should we respond if our data management/computer system fails?

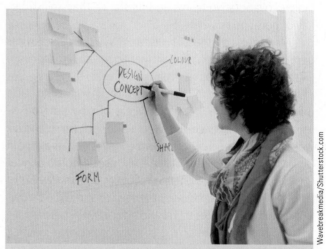

Effective planning can be complex and time-consuming.

- How can we restart our business if a natural disaster destroys our plant or supply channels?

- How will we evacuate employees if terrorists strike our headquarters?

Clearly, anticipating every potential problem is impossible (and impractical). Instead, effective contingency plans tend to focus only on the issues that are most probable, most potentially harmful, or both (see Exhibit 14.4). For example, a Southern California amusement park (e.g., Disneyland) might concentrate its contingency plans on earthquake response, while an online retailing firm might focus its plans on responding to a computer hacker attack.

tactical planning More specific, shorter-term planning that applies strategic plans to specific functional areas.

operational planning Very specific, short-term planning that applies tactical plans to daily, weekly, and monthly operations.

contingency planning Planning for unexpected events, usually involving a range of scenarios and assumptions that differ from the assumptions behind the core plans.

Exhibit 14.4
Contingency Planning Paradigm

Most Probable Issues

Most Harmful Issues

Focus Area for Contingency Plans

Businesses tend to focus their contingency plans on issues that are most probable *and* most potentially harmful.

EXHIBIT 14.5 | EXAMPLES OF MISSION STATEMENTS

Company	Mission Statement
Levi Strauss & Co.	We will market the most appealing and widely worn casual clothing in the world. We will clothe the world.
IKEA	To create a better everyday life for the many people. Our business idea supports this vision by offering a wide range of well-designed, functional home furnishing products at prices so low that as many people as possible will be able to afford them.
Google	To organize the world's information and make it universally accessible and useful.
Warby Parker	To offer designer eyewear at a revolutionary price, while leading the way for socially conscious businesses.

EXHIBIT 14.6 | SWOT ANALYSIS

Potential Internal Strengths	Potential External Opportunities
Premium brand name	Higher consumer demand
Proven management team	Complacent competitors
Lower costs/higher margins	Growth in foreign markets
Diverse workforce	New social trends

Potential Internal Weaknesses	Potential External Threats
Low employee satisfaction	A powerful new competitor
Inadequate financial resources	A deep recession
Poor location	New government regulations
Bad safety record	Significant new taxes

14-3a Strategic Planning: Setting the Agenda

Strategic planning is the most fundamental part of the planning process, since all other plans—and most major management decisions—stem from the strategic plan. The strategic planning process typically includes these steps:

1. Define the mission of the organization.
2. Evaluate the organization's competitive position.
3. Set goals for the organization.
4. Create strategies for competitive differentiation.
5. Implement strategies.
6. Evaluate results, and incorporate lessons learned.

Defining Your Mission The mission of an organization articulates its essential reason for being. The **mission** defines the organization's purpose, values, and core goals, providing the framework for all other plans (see Exhibit 14.5). Most large companies present their mission as a simple, vivid, compelling statement that everyone involved with the company—from the janitor to the CEO, from customers to investors—can easily understand. Mission statements tend to vary in their length, their language, and even their names, but they share a common goal: to provide a clear, long-term focus for the organization.

Evaluating Your Competitive Position Strategy means nothing in a vacuum—every firm must plan in the context of the marketplace. Many companies use a **SWOT analysis** (strengths, weaknesses, opportunities, and threats) to evaluate where they stand relative to the competition. Strengths and weaknesses are internal to the organization, and they include factors that would either build up or drag down the firm's performance. Opportunities and threats are external, and they include factors that would affect the company's performance but are typically out of the company's control. Exhibit 14.6 offers some examples.

mission The definition of an organization's purpose, values, and core goals, which provides the framework for all other plans.

SWOT analysis A strategic planning tool that helps management evaluate an organization in terms of internal strengths and weakness, and external opportunities and threats.

Managing Millennials

The millennial generation—roughly defined as people born in the 1980s and 1990s—is currently the largest generation in the workforce. Many businesses around the world are experiencing a great deal of stress over how to effectively manage millennials and keep them positive and productive. In fact, according to *The Wall Street Journal*, the concern has grown so intense that it has spawned a cottage industry of self-anointed experts who "decode" millennials for as much as $20,000 an hour. Yes, you read that right—$20,000 an HOUR!

But even with the help of pricey consultants, bosses continue to make mistakes as they manage millennials. Here are three common goofs:

- *Treating millennials like a different species.* Contrary to the stereotype, recent research shows that millennials seem to

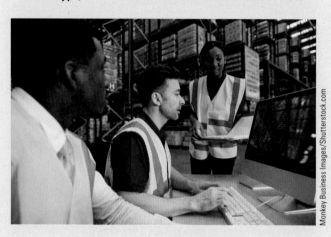

Monkey Business Images/Shutterstock.com

be more similar to than different from other generations. For example, millennial employees are less likely than Gen Xers to use personal social media accounts for work purposes. Perhaps even more surprising, millennials' preferred method of learning new work skills is face-to-face contact. So before you develop brand new tools and programs for millennial employees, consider rethinking and reintroducing the tools and programs that you already have.

- *Assuming that generational differences are more important than cultural differences.* American millennials have a reputation for always being on the lookout for the next best job. But this isn't the case everywhere—research shows that different cultures have different perspectives on company loyalty. In Peru, 82% of millennials expect to leave their employer in the next five years. In Belgium, only 51% do. Similarly, the share of millennials who have refused a work task because it conflicts with their values or ethics is generally high in Latin America—71% in Colombia—but only 20% in Japan.

- *Forgetting that millennials differ widely in terms of age and gender.* Born between 1982 and 2000, the millennial generation spans a wide range of ages and life cycle stages. A student in his late teens is just as much a millennial as a manager in her mid-thirties. Differences in experience, personal characteristics, and expectations are vast across the generation. Millennials also differ significantly by gender. For example, older and female millennials expect to stay in their current jobs longer than do younger and male millennials, say Bentley University researchers.

The most reasonable conclusion here is that millennials are a highly diverse group. Managing them effectively requires an openness to new perspectives and a wide range of thoughtful incentives.[13]

Initial information about internal strengths and weaknesses usually comes from careful analysis of internal reports on topics such as budget and profitability. But to better understand strengths and weaknesses, executives should actively seek firsthand information—on a personal basis—from key people throughout the company, from front-line workers to the board of directors.

Gathering information about external opportunities and threats can be more complex, since these areas include both current and potential issues (which can be tough to predict). Information about external factors can come from many different sources, including the news, government reports, customers, and competitors.

strategic goals Concrete benchmarks that managers can use to measure performance in each key area of the organization.

strategies Action plans that help the organization achieve its goals by forging the best fit between the firm and the environment.

Setting Your Goals **Strategic goals** represent concrete benchmarks that managers can use to measure performance in each key area of the organization. They must fit the firm's mission and tie directly to its competitive position. The three most effective goals are:

1. **Specific and Measurable:** Whenever possible, managers should define goals in clear numerical terms that everyone understands.

2. **Tied to a Time Frame:** To create meaning and urgency, goals should be linked to a specific deadline.

3. **Realistic but Challenging:** Goals that make people stretch can motivate exceptional performance.

Exhibit 14.7 offers examples of how weak goals can transform into powerful goals.

Creating Your Strategies **Strategies** are action plans that help the organization achieve its goals by

EXHIBIT 14.7	GOAL SETTING: GETTING IT RIGHT	
Weak Goal	**Powerful Goal**	
Become More innovative.	Introduce one new product each quarter for the next three years.	
Reduce Delinquent Accounts.	Reduce delinquent accounts to no more than 1% of the total by the next quarter.	
Increase Market Share.	Become the #1 or #2 brand in each market where we compete by the end of 2015.	

forging the best fit between the firm and the environment. The underlying aim, of course, is to create a significant advantage versus the competition. Sources of competitive advantage vary, ranging from better product quality to better technology, to more motivated employees. The most successful companies build their advantage across several fronts. Southwest Airlines, for example, has a more motivated workforce and a lower cost structure. H&M has lower prices and more fashionable clothing choices. And Procter & Gamble has more innovative new products and strong core brands.

The specifics of strategy differ by industry and by company, but all strategies represent a roadmap. The SWOT analysis determines the starting point, and the objectives signify the immediate destination. Since speed matters, you must begin mapping the next leg of the journey even before you arrive. For added complexity, you never know—given the turbulent environment—when you might hit roadblocks. This means that strategies must be dynamic and flexible. Top managers have responded to this challenge by encouraging front-line managers to participate in the process more than ever before.

Implementing Your Strategies Implementation should happen largely through tactical planning. Middle managers in each key area of the company must develop plans to carry out core strategies in their area. If the strategic plan, for example, calls for more new products, marketing would need to generate ideas, finance would need to find funding, and sales would need to prepare key accounts. And all of these steps would require tactical planning.

Evaluating Your Results and Incorporating Lessons Learned Evaluation of results should be a continual process, handled by managers at every level as part of their controlling function, covered further in this chapter. But for evaluation to be meaningful, the lessons learned must be analyzed objectively and factored back into the next planning cycle.

14-4 ORGANIZING: FITTING TOGETHER THE PUZZLE PIECES

The organizing function of management means creating a logical structure for people, their jobs, and their patterns of interaction. And clearly, the pieces can fit together in a number of different ways. In choosing the right structure for a specific company, management typically considers many factors, including the goals and strategies of the firm, its products, its use of technology, its size, and the structure of its competitors. Given the potential for rapid change in each of these factors, smart companies continually reexamine their structure and make changes whenever necessary. Microsoft, for instance, restructures its organization every couple of years as new challenges emerge.

But to be effective, reorganizations—and their purpose—must be clear to employees throughout the company. Xerox CEO Anne Mulcahy learned the hard way. Her comments: "During the 1990s, we had lots of consultants on organizational effectiveness. We sliced and diced the business into industries, product lines, and geographies . . . you name it. It looked good on paper, but fell apart in implementation. I found myself in a job where I couldn't look anybody in the eye and feel clear accountability for anything . . . I'll trade off organizational design for clarity and accountability any day of the week!"[14]

To help employees understand how they and their jobs fit within the broader organization, most firms issue an **organization chart**, or a visual representation of the company's formal structure, as shown in Exhibit 14.8.

Looking at the company represented by Exhibit 14.8, you would probably assume that the vice president of production has more power than a regular employee in the marketing department. And in terms of formal power, you'd be absolutely right. But if the marketing employee babysits on the weekend for the president's granddaughter, the balance of power may actually be a bit different than it seems. Make no mistake: The formal structure matters. But knowing how power flows on an informal basis could dramatically increase your effectiveness as well, by helping you target your ideas to the right managers and marshal the support of the most influential employees.

14-4a Key Organizing Considerations

In developing the organizational structure, management must make decisions

organization chart A visual representation of the company's formal structure.

Exhibit 14.8
Sample Organization Chart

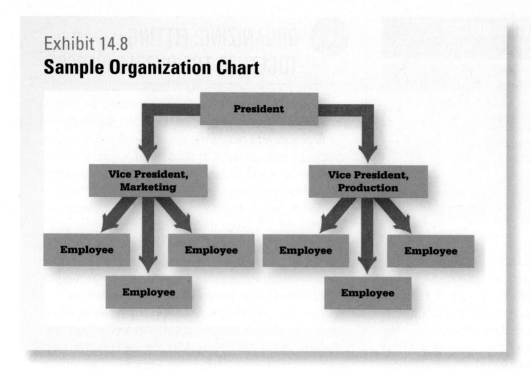

about the degree of centralization, the span of management control, and the type of departmentalization that makes the most sense at any given time.

Centralization The **degree of centralization** relates directly to the source of power and control. In centralized companies, a small number of people at the top of the organization have the power to make decisions. This approach is simple and efficient, and the result tends to be a strong corporate image and a uniform customer approach across the front lines. But the downside is that centralized companies typically respond more slowly to customer needs and have lower employee morale. The tradeoff may be worthwhile in steady, stable markets, but those are rare.

Faced with today's turbulent environment, most firms are moving toward greater decentralization, pushing power to the lower levels of the organization. Employees with the power to make decisions can respond to customer needs more quickly and effectively. They can also capitalize on opportunities that would likely vaporize in the time it would take to get permission to act. But for decentralization to work, every employee must fully

understand the firm's mission, goals, and strategy; otherwise, the company could develop a fragmented image, which would undermine its long-term strength. Also, active communication across departments is essential so that all employees can benefit from innovations in other parts of the organization.

Span of Control The **span of control**, or span of management, refers to the number of people a manager supervises. There is no ideal number for every manager. The "right" span of control varies, based on the abilities of both the manager and the subordinates, the nature of the work being done, and the location of the employees, and the need for planning and coordination. Across industries, the general trend has moved toward wider spans of control as a growing number of companies have pruned layers of middle management to the bare minimum.

Departmentalization Departmentalization means breaking workers into logical groups. A number of different options make sense, depending on the organization.

- **Functional:** Dividing employees into groups based on area of expertise, such as marketing, finance, and engineering, tends to be efficient and easy to coordinate. For those reasons, it works especially well for small- to medium-sized firms.

- **Product:** Dividing employees into groups based on the products that a company offers helps workers develop expertise about products that often results in especially strong customer relations.

- **Customer:** Dividing employees into groups based on the customers that a company serves helps companies focus on the needs of specific customer groups. Many companies have separate departments for meeting the needs of business and consumer users. This approach is related to product departmentalization.

- **Geographical:** Dividing employees into groups based on where customers are located can help different departments better serve specific regions

degree of centralization The extent to which decision-making power is held by a small number of people at the top of the organization.

span of control Span of management; refers to the number of people a manager supervises.

departmentalization The division of workers into logical groups.

Wanna Be More Productive? Relax!!

Ironically, a growing body of research suggests rather strongly that the best way to get more done may be to spend more time doing less, which may include daytime workouts, short afternoon naps, longer sleep hours at night, and longer, more frequent vacations. Despite misguided efforts to make it otherwise, time is definitely finite; energy, on the other hand, can be renewed. A recent study on the economic costs of insufficient sleep (less than six hours per night) found that a lack of sleep among the U.S. workforce is costing businesses about $411 billion in lost productivity each year. The study, which spanned the United States, the United Kingdom, Canada, Germany, and Japan, found that the United States sustained the highest economic losses due to sleep deprivation by far.

Studies of vacation show that taking more vacation days has a dramatic positive impact on worker performance. Unfortunately, whether it's obsession, dedication, or fear of unreasonable bosses, a recent study showed that the average American leaves four full days of paid vacation on the table each year. That's still better that South Korea, where workers throw an average 11 of their 15 available days of paid vacation away. Europeans, on the other hand, tend to use all of their 30 days of paid vacation—leading to a much healthier work-life balance.

Like sleep deprivation, not taking vacation days can be bad for the economy. Project: TimeOff estimates that servicing the needs of those unused American vacation days could have created 1.6 million jobs, resulting in $65 billion in additional income. If Americans used just one more day of vacation per year, the economy would see a $34 billion jump in total spending.

CEO Tony Schwartz attempts to run his business on the principle that the energy people bring to their jobs is more important than the number of hours they work. He and his management team have policies in place that reflect the idea that, "When we're renewing, we're truly renewing, so when we're working, we can really work." Partly because of this ethos, in the decade that his firm has been in business, no one has chosen to leave the company. If more CEOs communicated this message, chances are that more vacation time would actually be used. Eighty percent of employees surveyed by Project: TimeOff said that if they felt fully supported and encouraged by their boss, they would be more likely to take more time off. A growing number of high-profile companies, such as Virgin Group and Netflix, are offering employees unlimited or unmonitored vacation days to encourage time off and rejuvenation.[15]

Haveseen/Shutterstock.com

---

within one country. Similarly, many international firms create a separate department for each different country they serve.

- **Process:** Dividing into groups based on what type of work employees do is common in manufacturing, where management may divide departments by processes such as cutting, dyeing, and sewing.

As companies get larger, they usually adopt several different types of departmentalization at different levels of the organization. This approach, shown in Exhibit 14.9, is called "hybrid departmentalization."

14-4b Organization Models

Company structures tend to follow one of three different patterns: line organizations, line-and-staff organizations, and matrix organizations. But these organizational models are not mutually exclusive. In fact, many management teams build their structure using elements of each model at different levels of the organization.

Line Organizations A **line organization** typically has a clear, simple chain of command from top to bottom. Each person is directly accountable to the person immediately above, which means quick decision making and no fuzziness about who is responsible for what. The downside is a lack of specialists to provide advice or support for line managers. This approach tends to work well for small businesses, but for medium-sized and large companies, the result can be inflexibility, too much paperwork, and even incompetence, since experts aren't available to give their input on key decisions.

Line-and-Staff Organizations A **line-and-staff organization** incorporates the benefits of a line organization without all the drawbacks.

line organizations
Organizations with a clear, simple chain of command from top to bottom.

line-and-staff organizations
Organizations with line managers forming the primary chain of authority in the company, and staff departments working alongside line departments.

Exhibit 14.9

An Example of Hybrid Departmentalization

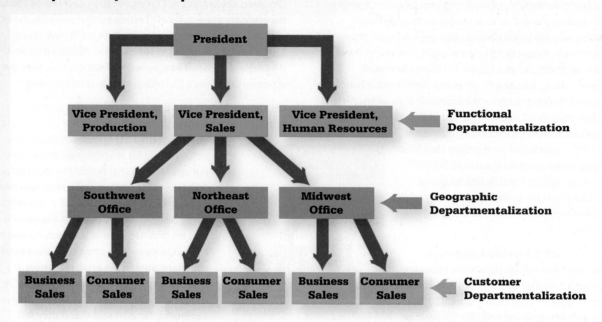

Line managers supervise the functions that contribute directly to profitability: production and marketing. **Staff managers**, on the other hand, supervise the functions that provide advice and assistance to the line departments. Examples include legal, accounting, and human resources. In a line-and-staff organization, the line managers form the primary chain of authority in the company. Staff departments work alongside line departments, but there is no direct reporting relationship (except at the top of the company). Since staff people don't report to line people, their authority comes from their know-how. This approach, which overlays fast decision making with additional expertise, tends to work well for medium-sized and large companies. But in some firms, the staff departments gain so much power that they become dictatorial, imposing unreasonable limitations on the rest of the company.

Matrix Organizations **Matrix organizations** build on the line-and-staff approach by adding a lot more flexibility. A matrix structure brings together specialists from different areas of the company to work on individual projects on a temporary basis. A new-product-development team, for instance, might include representatives from sales, engineering, finance, purchasing, and advertising. For the course of the project, each specialist reports to the project manager and to the head of his or her own department (e.g., the vice president of marketing). The matrix approach has been particularly popular in the high-tech and aerospace industries.

The matrix structure offers several key advantages. It encourages teamwork and communication across the organization. It offers flexibility in deploying key people. It lends itself to innovative solutions. And not surprisingly—when managed well—the matrix structure creates a higher level of motivation and satisfaction for employees. But these advantages have a clear flip side. The need for constant communication can bog down a company in too many meetings.

line managers Managers who supervise the functions that contribute directly to profitability: production and marketing.

staff managers Managers who supervise the functions that provide advice and assistance to the line departments.

matrix organizations Organizations with a flexible structure that brings together specialists from different areas of the company to work on individual projects on a temporary basis.

"Management is doing things right; leadership is doing the right things."

—PETER DRUCKER, MANAGEMENT RESEARCHER, WRITER, AND SPEAKER

The steady state of flux can be overwhelming for both managers and employees. And having two bosses can cause conflict and stress for everyone.

14-5 LEADERSHIP: DIRECTING AND INSPIRING

While most people easily recognize a great leader, defining the qualities of leaders can be more complex since successful leaders have a staggering range of personalities, characteristics, and backgrounds. Most researchers agree that true leaders are trustworthy, visionary, and inspiring. After all, we don't follow people who don't know where they're going, and we definitely don't follow people we don't trust. Other key leadership traits include empathy, courage, creativity, intelligence, and fairness.

14-5a Leadership Style

How a leader uses power defines his or her leadership style. While the range of specific styles is huge, most seem to cluster into three broad categories: autocratic, democratic, and free-rein. The categories fall along a continuum of power, with the manager at one end and the employees at the other, as shown in Exhibit 14.10.

Autocratic leaders hoard decision-making power for themselves, and they typically issue orders without consulting their followers. **Democratic leaders** share power with their followers. Even though they still make

The most effective leaders are typically comfortable using a range of different leadership styles.

Monkey Business/Fotolia LLC

final decisions, they typically solicit and incorporate input from their followers. **Free-rein leaders** set objectives for their followers but give them freedom to choose how they accomplish those goals.

Interestingly, the most effective leaders don't use just one approach. They tend to shift their leadership style, depending on the followers and the situation. When a quick decision is paramount, autocratic leadership may make the most sense. An army officer, for example, probably shouldn't take a vote on whether to storm a hill in the middle of a firefight. But when creativity is the top priority—during new-product brainstorming, for instance—free-rein management would probably work best. Likewise, a brand-new worker might benefit from autocratic (but friendly) management, while a talented, experienced employee would probably work best under free-rein leadership.

Another vital consideration is the customer. When the customer seeks consistency in the delivery of the product—in fast food, for instance—the autocratic leadership style may be appropriate. But when the customer needs flexibility and problem-solving assistance—a consulting client, for example—the free-rein leadership style may be most effective. The democratic leadership style typically provides customers with a balance of consistency and flexibility, which works across a wide range of industries.

autocratic leaders Leaders who hoard decision-making power for themselves and typically issue orders without consulting their followers.

democratic leaders Leaders who share power with their followers. While they still make final decisions, they typically solicit and incorporate input from their followers.

free-rein leaders Leaders who set objectives for their followers but give them freedom to choose how they will accomplish those goals.

Exhibit 14.10
The Continuum of Leadership and Power

Employee Power

Management Power

Free-Rein Leadership

Democratic Leadership

Autocratic Leadership

14-6 CONTROLLING: MAKING SURE IT ALL WORKS

Controlling may be the least glamorous of the management functions, but don't be fooled: It's critically important. Controlling means monitoring performance of the firm—or individuals within the firm—and making improvements when necessary. As the environment changes, plans change. And as plans change, the control process must change as well, to ensure that the company achieves its goals. The control process includes three key steps:

1. Establish clear performance standards.

2. Measure actual performance against standards.

3. Take corrective action if necessary.

Establishing clear standards—or performance goals—begins with planning. At every level of planning, objectives should emerge that are consistent with the company's mission and strategic plan. The objectives must be (1) specific and measurable, (2) realistic but challenging, and (3) tied to a time frame. Individual managers may need to break these goals into smaller parts for specific employees, but the subgoals should retain the same three qualities as the original objective.

Measuring performance against standards should happen well before the end of the time frame attached to the goal. A strong information-tracking system is probably management's best tool in this phase of the control process.

If the company or individual is not on track to meet the goals, management's first response should

> The control process includes three key steps:
>
> 1. **Establish clear performance standards**
>
> 2. **Measure actual performance against standards**
>
> 3. **Take corrective action if necessary**

Nerthuz/Shutterstock

> "Never accept or be too comfortable with the status quo, because the companies that get into trouble are historically the ones that aren't able to adapt to change and respond quickly enough."
>
> —TONY HSIEH, CEO, ZAPPOS.COM

be communication. Employees with full information are far more likely to improve their performance than employees who never learn that they're falling behind. But sometimes workers need more than information—they may need additional resources or coaching to meet their goals. Apple's Steve Jobs was often accused of being a tyrannical boss—especially in the employee-evaluation process—but he defended himself by saying, "My job is not to be easy on people. My job is to make them better." If they still don't succeed, perhaps the goals themselves need reexamination as part of a dynamic planning process. Given the expense in both human and financial terms, disciplining employees for poor performance should come only after exploring the reasons for not meeting goals and making changes if necessary.

THE BIG PICTURE

In the past decade, management has become more complex and demanding than ever before. Managers in every area of the business must carry out their roles—planning, organizing, leading, and controlling—in a relentlessly fast-paced world, seething with constant change. While management isn't for everyone, it's often a fit for people with vision, courage, integrity, energy, and a passionate commitment to their companies.

Looking forward, the role of management will continue to evolve in response to the environment. Regardless of how the changes unfold, several key factors will be absolutely vital for successful managers in the twenty-first century: a constant focus on the customer, a commitment to globalization, excellent judgment, and the right mix of talented, motivated employees.

Manager

Define strategic and tactical objectives for the organization or business unit. Develop plans to meet those objectives. Coach, counsel, motivate, and develop employees. Maintain and allocate resources as necessary to attain goals. Monitor achievement of objectives and make changes as necessary. Create and oversee a business unit budget. Ensure product and service quality by setting and enforcing standards. Foster a business culture that aligns with the broader organizational culture. Communicate and collaborate as appropriate throughout the organization. Maintain current professional and technical knowledge.

STUDY TOOLS 14

LOCATED AT BACK OF THE TEXTBOOK

☐ Rip-Out Chapter Review Card

☐ Gain unique perspectives on key concepts with new concept videos in the e-book

☐ Increase your comprehension with online homework and quizzes

☐ Study with existing flashcards and make your own

15 | Human Resource Management:
Building a Top-Quality Workforce

LEARNING OBJECTIVES

After studying this chapter, you will be able to:

 15-1 Explain the importance of human resources to business success

15-2 Discuss key human resource issues in today's economy

15-3 Outline challenges and opportunities that the human resources function faces

15-4 Discuss human resource planning and core human resources responsibilities

15-5 Explain the key federal legislation that affects human resources

Remember to visit

PAGE 285

for additional

STUDY TOOLS

Andrey_Popov/Shutterstock.com

15-1 HUMAN RESOURCE MANAGEMENT: BRINGING BUSINESS TO LIFE

As competition accelerates across the globe, leading firms in every business category have recognized that a quality workforce can vault them over the competition. Southwest Airlines was early to recognize the untapped potential of its people. Executive Chair Herb Kelleher declared, "We value our employees first. They're the most important, and if you treat them right, then they treat the customers right, and if you treat the customers right, then they keep coming back and shareholders are happy." His attitude has more than paid off. Southwest Airlines has posted profits for 44 consecutive years, even as other airlines have spiraled into decline.

As the Great Recession constricted the economy in 2009, managing human resources remained a top priority for Southwest CEO Gary Kelly. "We've never had a layoff. We've never had a pay cut. And we're going to strive mightily, especially this year, to avoid them once again." Instead, he says, "We're being more creative about encouraging employees to move about the company. We are not threatening people with their jobs." He points out, "We're known for being the greatest company to work for and at the top of the customer service rankings." He maintains, "There is a devotion to the people and a commitment to our people, once we hire them, that we have lived up to. We have proven many times that we're going to be there for our employees in the bad times." Even the union supports management, describing the naturally confrontational relationship as one of "the loyal opposition as opposed to death to the infidel. It's adversarial to get to a goal, not adversarial to hurt."[1]

Companies that get the most from their people often consider their human resources their biggest investment. They view the core goal of **human resource (HR) management** in a similar light: to nurture their human investment so that it yields the highest possible return. HR can achieve that goal by recruiting world-class talent, promoting career development, and boosting organizational effectiveness. But clearly, this can happen only in partnership with key managers throughout the company, especially senior executives. (In smaller companies, the owners usually handle HR management in addition to their other responsibilities.)

 15-2 **HUMAN RESOURCE MANAGEMENT CHALLENGES: MAJOR HURDLES**

Building a top-quality workforce can be tougher than it may initially seem. Human resource managers—and their counterparts throughout the company—face huge challenges. The best strategies still aren't clear,

> ## "If something goes wrong, it's my problem; if something goes *right*, it's their success."
>
> —PAMELA FIELDS, FORMER CEO, STETSON

but forward-thinking firms tend to experiment with new approaches.

15-2a Layoffs and Outsourcing

As high-tech, high-end jobs follow low-tech, low-end jobs out of the country—or even just to local contractors—human resources find themselves in turmoil. Many jobs have disappeared altogether as companies have contracted in response to the Great Recession. In 2011 and 2012, many economists were concerned about a "jobless recovery," as labor markets faltered, and unemployment rates began to rise again. How can businesses boost the morale and the motivation level

human resource (HR) management The management function focused on maximizing the effectiveness of the workforce by recruiting world-class talent, promoting career development, and determining workforce strategies to boost organizational effectiveness.

of the employees who are left behind? Does less job security translate to less worker loyalty? How can human resources continue to add value as the ground shifts beneath them—and as they wonder how long their own jobs will last?[2]

15-2b Wage Gap

Comparing CEO pay to worker pay demonstrates a startling wage gap, bigger in the United States than in any other developed country. In 2016, the average American CEO earned 271 times what the average employee earned. This This means that top CEOs make more in two days than an average employee does in one year.[3] Meanwhile, most other workers have faced stagnant wages.[4] As a point of comparison, 30 years ago, chief executives averaged only 30 to 40 times the average American worker's paycheck. In 2009, median CEO salaries at 200 large, publicly held U.S. firms fell by 0.9%, while net income decreased by 5%. Most observers don't object to the CEO-worker pay gap when top CEO pay is tied to top performance. But as the value of formerly high-flying corporations began to evaporate in 2008 and 2009, public rage over senior management salaries and bonuses hit new highs. But the tide turned in 2011, when data revealed CEO pay during 2011 was correlated to how well companies fared in the stock market, a change from 2010. The pay for performance trend continued through 2014, as investors gained more control over executive compensation. Although pay for performance appeals both to investors and to the general public, a recent article in the *Harvard Business Review* suggests that performance-based pay can actually have dangerous outcomes for the companies that implement it. In jobs that require learning and creativity—such as top management positions—tying pay to performance can actually harm the company. How so? Suppose a CEO's performance rating is tied to the company's stock price, so he cuts back on research and development spending in order to meet short-term stock price goals. This move is in the CEO's best interest personally, but it could devastate the company in the long run. Performance-based pay also increases the likelihood that a top-level manager is willing to cook the books to achieve his or her performance goals. Untangling these sorts of issues is a real strategic challenge for HR management.[5]

15-2c Older Workers

As the oversized baby boomer generation begins turning 60, their employers—which include virtually every major American company—face a potential crisis: the loss of key

> If forced to choose, 45% of millennial workers would choose workplace flexibility over increased pay.
>
> —MILLENNIAL BRANDING

talent and experience through massive retirements. Beginning January 1, 2011, every day more than 10,000 baby boomers reached the age of 65, and that will continue to happen every day until 2030.[6] Enlightened companies have responded with programs to retain their best employees through flexible schedules, training opportunities, and creative pay schedules. But as companies aggressively trimmed their payrolls in 2008 and 2009, the priority of these kinds of programs plummeted, which may leave some firms with a critical dearth of highly experienced workers when the economy revs back up. Pharmacy giant CVS Caremark views maintaining its older workers as a critical competitive advantage. The company offers a "snowbird" program whereby several hundred pharmacists and other employees from cold northern states are transferred to pharmacies in Florida and other warmer states each winter. According to one CVS executive, "A good number of our pharmacy customers are going to be mature customers, and as part of our focus on diversity, we want a workforce that reflects our customer base . . . so it was a no-brainer for us to have a lot of mature workers as part of our overall work force."[7]

15-2d Younger Workers

As twenty-somethings enter the workforce, they often bring optimism, open minds, technological know-how, a team orientation, a proven ability to multitask, and a multicultural perspective. But a number of them also bring an unprecedented sense of entitlement. This can translate into startlingly high expectations for their pay, their responsibilities, and their job flexibility, but little willingness to "pay dues." Many have no expectation that their employers will be loyal to them, and they don't feel that they owe their companies strong loyalty. Managing this group can sometimes be a challenge, but companies that do it well stand to deliver results for years to come.[8]

15-2e Women Workers

Over the past few decades, women have made enormous strides in terms of workplace equality. But several large-scale studies confirm that women continue to face daunting discrimination in terms of both pay and promotions. While unfair treatment has been an issue for many years, recent legal changes have made it easier for women to sue, costing companies millions of dollars in the past decade alone. And the flood of lawsuits shows no signs of slowing. Many women have responded to the unfriendly business environment by leaving the workforce; droves of highly

Women at Work and the Persistent Pay Gap

In 1980, women earned just $0.67 for every dollar that their male counterparts earned. Fortunately, the picture has improved quite a bit for women in the workforce. As of 2015 (the latest available data), women earned $0.83 for every dollar that men earned. Although the pay gap is better today than it was in 1980, it's still not ideal. At this rate, it would take a woman an extra 44 days of work to earn what a man does in one year. However, it's not all bad news. In 2015, *young* women saw a smaller pay gap than average, earning $0.90 for every dollar that their male counterparts earned. This still isn't perfect—but it's definitely better. So why, at this point in the twenty-first century, is there a pay gap at all between men and women? Experts identify several possible reasons:

- Women are more likely than men to either reduce hours or take time off to care for a child or another family member.
- Women are overrepresented in lower paying occupations and underrepresented in higher paying occupations.
- The #MeToo movement highlighted that sexual harassment and abuse continue to run rampant in the workplace, clearly hampering the pace of advancement for all too many women.

Looking forward, there is hope for even more improvement. According to a recent Pew Research Center study, 77% of women and 63% of men believe "this country needs to continue making changes to give men and women equality in the workplace."[9]

---

qualified, professional women step out of the workforce early—usually to raise children, start their own companies, or pursue other interests. As a result, we are experiencing a harmful, ongoing brain drain. Human resource managers can help mitigate this issue by implementing specific retention plans for valued women workers and by taking proactive steps to reintegrate returning women back into the workforce.[10]

In late 2017, the #MeToo movement made clear that women face issues of sexual harassment and assault in the workplace to a greater degree than most people realized. As awareness grew, human resources professionals took responsibility for training the workforce and establishing new safeguards to prevent future abuse. For the most part, absolute fairness and transparency have been at the forefront of their actions and perspective. Transparency can be a particularly tricky issue for human resources professionals with regard to sexual harassment. Employees who bring forward complaints would of course like to know what actions are being taken, but in fairness to the accused, HR must sometimes keep them in the dark, which can at times make HR appear insensitive.

15-2f Work–Life Balance

Over the past decade, workers across all ages and both genders have actively pursued more flexibility and work–life balance in their jobs. But as the recession deepened in 2009, companies began to cut back on these initiatives, describing them as "nice to have" programs in a time when "need to have" goals—such as meeting payroll each month—are tough to attain. Middle-level managers are also apt to demonstrate bias against worker flexibility, even when top management actively supports work–life balance

> ## Frivolous lawsuits cost American businesses over $865 billion per year.
> —PACIFIC RESEARCH INSTITUTE

programs. In spite of these issues, insightful HR managers try hard to offer enough flexibility to keep their best workers without jeopardizing their company's business goals.[11]

15-2g Lawsuits

The United States has become a wildly litigious society, with employees, customers, and shareholders levying lawsuit after lawsuit against firms of all sizes. Even though many of the lawsuits are legitimate—some profoundly important—a good number are just plain silly. But even if a lawsuit is frivolous, and even if it's thrown out of court, it can still cost a company millions of dollars. Even more importantly, a frivolous lawsuit can cost a business its reputation. Avoiding employee lawsuits by knowing the law and encouraging legal practices is a growing human resources challenge.

 15-3 ## HUMAN RESOURCES MANAGERS: CORPORATE BLACK SHEEP?

15-3a The Problem

The human resource management function is clearly critical, but human resources departments—and the people who work in them—face major challenges. Leading-edge

EXHIBIT 15.1 | JOB DESCRIPTION AND JOB SPECIFICATIONS: BAND MANAGER

Job Description	Job Specifications
Work with the music group to help make major decisions regarding the creative and business direction of the band	A bachelor's degree in music management
Negotiate recording contracts and engagement fees	A minimum of three years' experience managing a high-profile band
Help band members understand their rights and responsibilities	Excellent communication and networking skills

firms expect every department to offer "big picture," strategic contributions that boost company value. But a report in *Fast Company* suggests that most HR professionals lack sufficient strategic skills. Among other data, the report quotes a respected executive at a top U.S. company: "Business acumen is the single biggest factor that HR professionals in the U.S. lack today."[12]

But even highly qualified, strategically focused HR managers face daunting perception problems. A management professor at a leading school comments that "The best and the brightest just don't go into HR." Once in the workforce, many employees see the human resources department as irrelevant—or even worse, as the enemy. This perception clearly undermines their effectiveness.

15-3b The Solution

To gain respect from both senior management and their peers, human resources executives must earn a seat at the table. The first step is to know the company. What are the strategic goals? Who is the core customer? Who is the competition? Respected HR departments typically figure out ways to quantify their impact on the company in dollars and cents. They determine how to raise the value of the firm's human capital, which in turn increases the value of the firm itself. Effective HR people also remain open to exceptions even as they enforce broad company policies.

But clearly, these solutions will work only if senior management recognizes the potential value of effective human resource management. One simple test of senior management commitment is the reporting relationship. If the HR department reports to the CFO, it may be on the fast track to outsourcing. But if the HR department reports to the CEO, the strategic possibilities are unlimited.

job analysis The examination of specific tasks that are assigned to each position, independent of who might be holding the job at any specific time.

job description An explanation of the responsibilities for a specific position.

job specifications The specific qualifications necessary to hold a particular position.

 15-4 HUMAN RESOURCE PLANNING: DRAWING THE MAP

Great human resource management begins with great planning: Where should you go? And how should you get there? Your objectives should flow from the company's master plan, and your strategies must reflect company priorities.

One of the first steps in the HR planning process should be to figure out where the company stands in terms of human resources. What skills does the workforce already have? What skills does it need? A company-wide **job analysis** often goes hand in hand with evaluating the current workforce. Job analysis examines what exactly needs to be done in each position to maximize the effectiveness of the organization—independent of who might be holding each job at any specific time. Smaller companies often handle job analysis on an informal basis, but larger companies typically specify a formal **job description** and **job specifications** (or "specs").

A job description defines the jobholder's responsibilities, and job specs define the qualifications for doing the job. Consider the job of band manager. The job description might include finding engagements for the band and settling disputes among band members. The job specs might include the type of education and experience required. Taken together, the two might look something like Exhibit 15.1.

The next step is to forecast future human resource requirements. The forecasting function requires a deep understanding of the company's goals and strategies. HR managers must also assess the future supply of workers. Assessing supply can be a real challenge, since the size and quality of the workforce shift continually. But key considerations should include retirement rates, graduation rates in relevant fields, and the pros and cons of the international labor market.

A complete HR plan—which falls under the company's strategic planning umbrella—must cover each core area of human resource management (see Exhibit 15.2):

■ Recruitment

■ Selection

■ Training

- Evaluation
- Compensation
- Benefits
- Separation

15-4a Recruitment: Finding the Right People

Finding people to hire is easy—especially when the unemployment rate is high—but finding *qualified* employees is almost always a daunting challenge. The U.S. Census Bureau points out that a college degree typically doubles earning power, and the U.S. Bureau of Labor Statistics attests that most of the fastest-growing fields in the next five years will require college graduates. But only one-third of adults in America ages 25–29 have a college degree. And as highly trained, highly educated baby boomers hit retirement, HR recruiters may face a hiring crunch. In addition to finding qualified hires, recruiters also must find new employees who fit with the company culture in terms of both personality and style.[13]

New employees come from two basic sources: internal and external. **Internal recruitment** involves transferring or promoting employees from other positions within the company. This approach offers several advantages:

- Boosts employee morale by reinforcing the value of experience within the firm
- Reduces risk for the firm, since current employees have a proven track record
- Lowers costs of both recruitment and training

But companies often find that they don't have the right person within their organization. The firm may be too small, or perhaps no one has the right set of skills to fill the immediate needs. Or maybe the firm needs the fresh thinking and

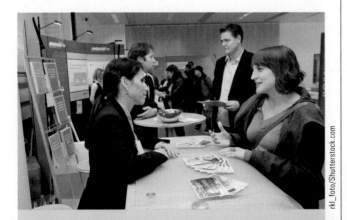

rkl_foto/Shutterstock.com

Job fairs are a popular external recruitment tool for companies looking to hire large numbers of entry-level employees.

Exhibit 15.2
Human Resource Management

STRATEGIC PLANNING

HUMAN RESOURCE MANAGEMENT

- Separation
- Recruitment
- Selection
- Training
- Evaluation
- Compensation/Benefits

energy that can come only from outside. When this is the case, companies turn to **external recruitment**.

External recruitment, or looking for employees outside the firm, usually means tapping into a range of different resources. The possibilities include employment websites, newspaper ads, job fairs, trade associations, college and university employment centers, and employment agencies. But the most promising source of new hires may be referrals from current employees. A growing number of organizations offer their current employees a cash bonus—typically $1,000 to $2,000—for each person they refer to the company who makes it past a probationary period. As an added benefit, employees who come through referrals have an excellent chance at success, since the person who recommended them has a stake in their progress. Employee-referral programs also represent a real bargain for employers, compared to the average cost per new hire of more than $4,000.

internal recruitment The process of seeking employees who are currently within the firm to fill open positions.

external recruitment The process of seeking new employees from outside the firm.

Not surprisingly, a higher level of employee referrals correlates to a higher level of shareholder returns, although lack of diversity may become a long-term problem with relying on employee referrals.[14]

15-4b Selection: Making the Right Choice

Once you have a pool of qualified candidates, your next step is to choose the best person for the job. This, too, is more easily said than done, yet making the right selection is crucial. The costs of a bad hire—both the direct costs such as placing ads, and the intangibles such as lost productivity and morale—can drain company resources. A typical selection process includes accepting applications, interviewing, testing, checking references and background, and making the job offer. Keep in mind that small businesses often follow a more streamlined process.

Applications Many companies use written applications simply as an initial screening mechanism. Questions about education and experience will determine whether a candidate gets any further consideration. In other words, the application is primarily a tool to reject unqualified candidates, rather than to actually choose qualified candidates.

Interviews Virtually every company uses interviews as a central part of the selection process. In larger companies, the HR department does initial interviews and then sends qualified candidates to the hiring manager for the actual selection. The hiring manager usually recruits coworkers to participate in the process.

Although employers frequently give interviews heavy weight in hiring decisions, interviews often say surprisingly little about whether a candidate will perform on the job. Too many managers use the interview as a get-to-know-you session rather than focusing on the needs of the position. To help ensure that interviews better predict performance, experts recommend a **structured interview** process: developing a list of questions beforehand and asking the same questions to each candidate. The most effective questions are typically behavioral: they ask the candidate to describe a situation that he or she faced at a previous job—or a hypothetical situation at the new job—and to explain the resolution. Interviewers should gear the specific questions toward

> "More than 70% of HR managers say that employee referral job candidates get high priority in job searches."
>
> —*LOS ANGELES TIMES*

behaviors and experiences that are key for the new position. Consider the following examples of how these questions could be worded:

- Describe a time when you had to think "outside the box" to find a solution to a pressing problem.
- Describe a situation that required you to do a number of things at the same time. How did you handle it? What was the outcome?
- If you realized that a coworker was cheating on his expense report, how would you handle the situation?
- What would you do if your boss asked you to complete a key project within an unreasonable time frame?

Cultural differences also affect interview performance. As the U.S. labor pool becomes more diverse, even domestic companies must be aware of cultural differences. And it isn't simply a matter of legality or ethics. Firms that hire the best people regardless of cultural background will gain a critical edge in our increasingly competitive world.

Most colleges and universities offer comprehensive career services. Especially in today's competitive labor market, you would be wise to visit your career center early in your college career and use those services to prepare yourself for a smooth transition into the workforce.

Testing Either before or after the interview process (and sometimes at both points), a growing number of companies have instituted employment testing of various sorts. The main categories include skills testing, personality testing, drug testing, and physical exams. Skills testing and personality testing carry a fair amount of legal risk, since these tests must measure skills and aptitudes that relate directly to the job itself. Virtually 100% of Fortune 500 companies conduct pre-employment drug testing, as do most other companies. Physical exams are also standard but are highly regulated by state and federal law to ensure that firms don't use them just to screen out certain individuals.

structured interviews
An interviewing approach that involves developing a list of questions beforehand and asking the same questions in the same order to each candidate.

> "External hires get paid 18–20% more than staff promoted from within."
>
> —MATTHEW BIDWELL, WHARTON BUSINESS SCHOOL

OOPS! WHAT WERE THEY THINKING?

Interview Gaffes: The Top Ten Things NOT to Do

As you get ready to interview for your dream job, you'll almost certainly find yourself awash in a torrent of advice from family and friends, and flooded with tips found on the Web and elsewhere. "Don't be late, don't be early ... Don't ask too many questions, don't ask too few ... Don't look too casual, don't look too stuffy .... And whatever you do, never let anyone see that you're nervous!" But however you actually feel—and whatever you actually say—take heart from knowing that you probably won't top these real-life interview blunders pulled from the annual CareerBuilder survey of employers and hiring managers:

1. Candidate said her hair was perfect when asked why she should become part of the team.

2. Candidate sang to a song on the radio playing overhead.

3. Candidate invited interviewer to dinner afterward.

4. Candidate stated that if the interviewer wanted to get to heaven, she would hire him.

5. Candidate ate crumbs off the table.

6. Candidate answered cell phone and asked the interviewer to leave her own office because it was a "private" conversation.

7. Candidate told the interviewer he wouldn't be able to stay with the job long because he thought he might get an inheritance if his uncle died—and his uncle "wasn't looking too good."

8. Candidate asked the interviewer for a ride home after the interview.

9. Candidate for an accounting position said she was a "people person," not a "numbers person."

10. Candidate flushed the toilet while talking to the interviewer during a phone interview.[15]

References and Background Checks Even if you feel absolutely certain that a candidate is right for the job, don't skip the reference check before you make an offer. Research from the Society for Human Resource Managers suggests that more than 50% of job candidates lie on their résumé in some way. Although it may be tough to verify contributions and accomplishments at former jobs, it's pretty easy to uncover lies about education, job titles, and compensation. And it's quite worthwhile, given that the costs of bringing an unethical employee on board can be staggering. Furthermore, if you happen to hire a truly dangerous employee, you can open the door to negligent-hiring lawsuits for not taking "reasonable care." But surprisingly—despite the high risk—employment expert James Challenger estimates that only about 25% of candidates are thoroughly vetted by the companies that consider them.[16]

Job Offers After you find the right person, the next hurdle is to design the right job offer and get your candidate to accept it. To hook an especially hot contender, you may need to get creative. A phone call from top management, the royal treatment, and special perks go a long way, but most superb candidates also want to know in very specific terms how their contributions would affect the business. And no matter how excited you are about your candidate, be certain to establish a **probationary period** up front. This means a specific time frame (typically three to six months) during which a new hire can prove his or her worth on the job. If everything works out, the employee will move from conditional to permanent status; if not, the company can fire the employee fairly easily.

Contingent Workers Companies that experience a fluctuating need for workers sometimes opt to hire **contingent workers**—or employees who don't expect regular, full-time jobs—rather than permanent, full-time workers. Specifically, contingent employees include temporary full-time workers, independent contractors, on-call workers, and temporary agency or contract agency workers. As a group, contingent workers accounted for just over 40% of U.S. employment in 2010—up from 30% in 2005.[17]

Employers appreciate contingent workers because they offer flexibility, which can lead to much lower costs. But the hidden downside can be workers who are less committed and less experienced. Too much reliance on contingent workers could unwittingly sabotage company productivity and the customer experience. Also, contingency workers tend to suffer from significantly higher poverty rates, meaning that they are more likely to face the damaging conditions that typically accompany poverty.[18]

probationary period A specific time frame (typically three to six months) during which a new hire can prove his or her worth on the job before he or she becomes permanent.

contingent workers Employees who do not expect regular, full-time jobs, including temporary full-time workers, independent contractors, and temporary agency or contract agency workers.

15-4c Training and Development: Honing the Competitive Edge

For successful companies in virtually every field, training and development have become an ongoing process rather than a one-time activity. Even in a recession, training and development must gather speed for companies and individuals to maintain their competitive edge. Experts offer five key reasons that relate directly to a healthy bottom line:

1. Increased innovation in strategies and products
2. Increased ability to adopt new technologies
3. Increased efficiency and productivity
4. Increased employee motivation and lower employee turnover
5. Decreased liability (e.g., sexual harassment lawsuits)

Training programs take a number of different forms, from orientation to skills training, to management development, depending on the specific employee and the needs of the organization.

Orientation Once you hire new employees, **orientation** should be the first step in the training and development process. Effective orientation programs typically focus on introducing employees to the company culture (but without sacrificing need-to-know administrative information). Research consistently shows that strong orientation programs significantly reduce employee turnover, which lowers costs.

The Boeing aerospace company has mastered the art of employee orientation. Boeing Military Aircraft and Missile Systems revamped its orientation process to include mentoring, meetings with senior executives, and an after-work social program. One highlight of the orientation—meant to crystallize the "wow" factor of working at Boeing—is the chance to take the controls of an F/A-18 fighter plane flight simulator. Management rightfully sees the program as a chance to develop "future leaders...the ones who will make sure that Boeing continues to be a great place to work."[19]

On-the-Job Training On-the-job training is popular because it's very low-cost. Employees simply begin their jobs—sometimes under the guidance of more experienced employees—and learn as they go. For simple jobs, this can make sense, but simple jobs are disappearing from the U.S. market due to the combined impact of offshoring and technology. On-the-job training can also compromise the customer experience. Have you ever waited much too long in a short line at the grocery store because the clerk couldn't figure out how to use the cash register? Multiplied across hundreds of customers, this kind of experience undermines the value of a company's brand.

Formal apprenticeship programs tend to be a more effective way of handling on-the-job training. **Apprenticeship** programs mandate that each beginner serve as an assistant to a fully trained worker for a specified period of time before gaining full credentials to work in the field. In the United States, apprenticeships are fairly common in trades such as plumbing and bricklaying. But in Europe, apprenticeships are much more common across a wide range of professionals, from bankers to opticians.

Off-the-Job Training Classroom training happens away from the job setting but typically during work hours. Employers use classroom training—either on-site or off-site—to teach a wide variety of topics from new computer programming languages, to negotiation skills, to stress management, and more. Going one step further than classroom training, some employers train workers off-site on "real" equipment (e.g., robots) similar to what they would actually use on the job. This approach is called "vestibule training." Police academies often use vestibule training for firearms. Job simulation goes even further than vestibule training, by attempting to duplicate the exact conditions that the trainee will face on the job. This approach makes sense for complex, high-risk positions such as astronaut or airline pilot.

On-the-job training often works best for relatively simple jobs.

orientation The first step in the training and development process, designed to introduce employees to the company culture and provide key administrative information.

on-the-job training A training approach that requires employees to simply begin their jobs—sometimes guided by more experienced employees—and to learn as they go.

apprenticeships Structured training programs that mandate that each beginner serve as an assistant to a fully trained worker before gaining full credentials to work in the field.

ESB Professional/Shutterstock.com

Computer-Based Training Computer-based training—mostly delivered via the Web—now plays a crucial role in off-the-job training. Broadband technology has turbocharged audio and visual capabilities, which support engaging and interactive online training programs. Online training also standardizes the presentation of the material, since it doesn't depend on the quality of the individual instructor. And the Web helps employers train employees wherever they may be in the world, at their own pace and convenience. But there is a key drawback: it takes a lot of discipline to complete an online program, and some people simply learn better through direct human interaction.

Evan Lorne/Shutterstock.com

Management Development As the bulk of top-level U.S. executives move toward retirement (or lose their jobs in the recession), developing new leaders has become a priority in many organizations. **Management development** programs help current and potential executives develop the skills they need to move into leadership positions. These programs typically cover specific issues that the business faces but also less-tangible—yet equally important—topics, such as communication, planning, business-analysis, change-management, coaching, and team-building skills.

15-4d Evaluation: Assessing Employee Performance

Straightforward, frequent feedback is a powerful tool to improve employee performance. The best managers provide informal feedback on a constant basis so that employees always know where they stand. But most companies also require that managers give formal feedback through periodic **performance appraisals**, usually every six months or once a year. Typically, managers conduct the appraisals by sitting down with each employee on a one-to-one basis and comparing actual results to expected results. The performance appraisal affects decisions regarding compensation, promotions, training, transfers, and terminations.

The HR role in performance appraisals begins with the strategic process of creating evaluation tools that tie directly into the company's big-picture objectives. Then, on a day-to-day basis, HR coordinates the actual appraisal process, which typically involves volumes of paperwork. HR must also ensure that managers are trained in providing relevant, honest, objective feedback, and that workers at every level know how to respond if they believe their appraisal is not fair.

Both giving and receiving evaluations tend to be awkward for everyone involved, and unfortunately, uncomfortable people tend to make mistakes. As you read the following list, you'll probably find that you've been on the receiving end of at least a couple of the most common appraisal goofs.

1. **Gotcha!** Too many managers use the performance appraisal as a chance to catch employees doing something wrong rather than doing something right.

2. **The Once-a-Year Wonder** Many companies mandate annual reviews, but some managers use that as an excuse to give feedback only once a year.

3. **Straight from the Gut** Although "gut feel" can have real value, it's no substitute for honest, relevant documentation of both expectations and accomplishments.

4. **What Have You Done for Me Lately?** Many managers give far too much weight to recent accomplishments, discounting the early part of the review period.

5. **The "Me Filter"** While appraisals are a bit subjective by their very nature, some managers filter every comment through their personal biases. Here are some examples:

   - **Positive Leniency:** "I'm a nice guy, so I give everyone great scores."

   - **Negative Leniency:** "I have high expectations, so I give everyone low scores."

   - **Halo Effect:** "I like this employee, so I'll give her top scores across the board."

For a performance appraisal to be effective, the manager must focus on fairness, relevance, objectivity, and balance. Equally important, the manager should give feedback on a continual basis to eliminate surprises and maximize performance.

management development Programs to help current and potential executives develop the skills they need to move into leadership positions.

performance appraisal A formal feedback process that requires managers to give their subordinates feedback on a one-to-one basis, typically by comparing actual results to expected results.

15-4e Compensation: Show Me the Money

The term **compensation** covers both pay and benefits, but when most people think about compensation, they think about cash. Yet your paycheck is only part of the picture. Many companies also offer noncash benefits such as healthcare, which can be worth up to 30% of each employee's pay. Researching, designing, and managing effective compensation systems are core HR functions.

From a company perspective, compensation—both cash and noncash—represents a big chunk of product costs, especially in labor-intensive businesses such as banks, restaurants, and airlines. Although many firms opt to cut labor costs as far as possible, others boost compensation above the norm to find and keep the best workers. In fact, research suggests that companies offering higher-than-average compensation generally outperform their competitors in terms of total return to shareholders—both stock price and dividend payouts.[20]

Regarding specific individuals and positions, companies typically base compensation on a balance of the following factors:

- **Competition:** How much do competing firms offer for similar positions?

- **Contribution:** How much does a specific person contribute to the bottom line?

- **Ability to Pay:** How much can the company afford?

- **Cost of Living:** What would be reasonable in light of the broader local economy?

- **Legislation:** What does the government mandate?

The most common compensation systems in the United States are wages and salaries. **Wages** refer to pay in exchange for the number of hours or days that an employee works. Variations can be huge, starting at the federal minimum wage of $7.25 per hour (as of May 2017) and ranging up to more than $50 per hour. Jobs that require less education—such as flipping burgers—typically pay hourly wages. Federal law requires companies to pay nonexempt wage earners overtime, 50% more than their standard wage, for every hour worked over 40 hours per week.

compensation The combination of pay and benefits that employees receive in exchange for their work.

wages The pay that employees receive in exchange for the number of hours or days that they work.

salaries The pay that employees receive over a fixed period, most often weekly or monthly.

benefits Noncash compensation, including programs such as health insurance, vacation, and childcare.

EXHIBIT 15.3 PERFORMANCE PAY OPTIONS

Variable Pay System	Description
Commission	Commission involves payment as a percentage of sales. Usually, larger commissions go with smaller base pay.
Bonuses	Bonuses are lump-sum payments, typically to reward strong performance from individual employees.
Profit Sharing	Profit-sharing plans reward employees with a share of company profits above and beyond predetermined goals.
Stock Options	Stock options are the right to buy shares of company stock at some future date for the price of the shares on the day that the company awarded the options.
Pay for Knowledge	This approach involves awarding bonuses and pay increases in exchange for increases in knowledge such as earning an MBA.

Salaries, on the other hand, cover a fixed period, most often weekly or monthly. Most professional, administrative, and managerial jobs pay salaries. While salaries are usually higher than wages, salaried workers do not qualify for overtime, which means that sometimes a low-level manager's overall pay may be less than the pay of wage-based employees who work for that manager.

Pay for Performance In addition to wages and salaries, many organizations link some amount of worker pay directly to performance. The idea is to motivate employees to excel. Exhibit 15.3 lists some common approaches.

As you look over the range of variable pay options, which would you find most motivating? Why? What type of business might use each form of variable pay? Why?

15-4f Benefits: From Birthday Cakes to Death Benefits

Benefits represent a significant chunk of money for employers, but for many years, workers took benefits for granted. No longer. As the unemployment rate skyrocketed in 2009, employees began to appreciate their benefits more than ever, recognizing that healthcare, dental care, paid sick days, retirement plans, and other perks add enormous value to their paychecks—and can be yanked at the discretion of their employer.[21]

In fact, a number of budget-minded employers already stick to the legally mandated basics: Social Security and Medicare contributions, payments to state unemployment and workers' compensation programs, and job

Come Back, Come Back, Wherever You Are!

In 2017, International Business Machines (IBM) dismantled its extensive employee telecommuting program. The company gave thousands of remote employees a choice: relocate to a regional office—sometimes hundreds of miles from their homes—or leave the company. The policy change was a rude shock to many employees because IBM was an early adopter of telecommuting and an outspoken advocate of its effectiveness—once boasting that more than 40% of its employees worked outside of traditional company offices. IBM defended the decision as a strategy to improve collaboration and accelerate the pace of work. Rebuilding the design and digital marketing teams in-house, it said, would allow the company to respond quickly to real-time data and customer feedback. However, because telecommuting employees report that they enjoy their jobs far more than on-site employees do, let's hope that IBM is not spurring a new trend with this move.[22]

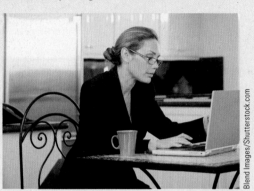

Blend Images/Shutterstock.com

protection per the Federal Family and Medical Leave Act. However, socially responsible employers—and companies that seek a competitive advantage through a top-notch workforce—tend to offer far more. Optional benefits usually include some or all of the following:

- Paid vacation days and holidays
- Paid sick days
- Health insurance
- Retirement programs
- Product discounts

A smaller number of companies also offer less traditional benefits such as backup childcare options, free massage, pet health insurance, tuition reimbursement, and paid time off for volunteering. Since the recession of 2009, companies that offered "extras" have focused extra attention on perks that would boost morale without an outrageous price tag.[23]

In the past decade, a growing number of companies have begun to offer **cafeteria-style benefits**. This approach involves giving their employees a set dollar amount per person that they must spend on company benefits. The key to these plans is choice, which allows employees to tailor their benefits to their individual needs.

Over the past couple of decades, employees across the U.S. economy have demanded more flexibility from their employers, and companies have responded. Flexible scheduling options include flextime, telecommuting, and job-sharing plans, discussed in detail below. But unfortunately, as massive, widespread layoffs swept across the economy in 2009, workers began to give up flexible schedules—or to stop even asking about them in the first place—out of fear that they would appear less committed to their jobs.[24]

Flextime A **flextime** plan gives workers some degree of freedom in terms of when they start and finish their workday, as long as they complete the required number of hours. Typically, companies with flextime scheduling oblige their employees to start work between mandated hours in the morning—say, anytime between 7 A.M. and 10 A.M.—to take lunch between certain hours in the middle of the day, and to complete work at the end of eight hours. This approach ensures that everyone is present during core hours for communication and coordination, but it provides choice outside those parameters. Flextime tends to increase employee morale and retention, but it makes less sense in jobs that entail extensive teamwork and customer interaction. It also requires careful management to avoid abuse.

The **compressed workweek**, another version of flextime scheduling, allows employees to work a full-time number of hours in less than the standard workweek. The most popular option is to work four ten-hour days rather than five eight-hour days. Major companies, such as Intel, have developed successful compressed workweek programs at a number of their facilities.

cafeteria-style benefits An approach to employee benefits that gives all employees a set dollar amount that they must spend on company benefits, allocated however they wish within broad limitations.

flextime A scheduling option that allows workers to choose when they start and finish their workdays, as long as they complete the required number of hours.

compressed workweek A version of flextime scheduling that allows employees to work a full-time number of hours in less than the standard workweek.

EXHIBIT 15.4   AN ANALYSIS OF TELECOMMUTING

	Benefits	Drawbacks
Organization	■ Lower costs for office space, equipment, and upkeep ■ Higher employee productivity due to better morale, fewer sick days, and more focused performance ■ Access to a broader talent pool (not everyone needs to be local)	■ Greater challenges maintaining a cohesive company culture ■ Greater challenges fostering teamwork ■ Greater challenges monitoring and managing far-flung employees
Employee	■ Much more flexibility ■ Zero commute time (less gas money) ■ Better work–family balance ■ Every day is casual Friday (or even pajama day!) ■ Fewer office politics and other distractions	■ Less fast-track career potential ■ Less influence within the organization ■ Weaker connection to the company culture ■ Isolation from the social structure at work

Source: Flexible Hours and Telecommuting—Not the Ticket to the Top of Corporate America, Five Questions for Susan DePhillips, Workforce Management, September 2005, http://www.workforce.com/section/02/article/24/14/66.html.

Telecommuting Despite clear benefits for employees, the environment, and many employers, telecommuting has not fully permeated the American workplace. Booming technological advances make it possible for many employees to "commute" to the office via phones, fax machines, and broadband networks. More than 60% of companies allow **telecommuting**, and 20–30% of Americans telecommute at least occasionally. The bottom-line benefits for companies that embrace the approach can be significant. Over two-thirds of employers report increased productivity among their telecommuters. Telecommuting employees are 35–40% more productive than their office-bound colleagues. And direct savings from decreased costs add up fast, as well. By establishing telecommuting programs, employers can realize annual cost savings of $20,000–$37,000 per employee, which adds up to hundreds of millions of dollars each year for big players. In fact, if every worker who *could* telecommute did so just half the time, the economic benefit would total more than $700 billion a year. Businesses would increase national productivity by 5 million human-years, or $270 billion worth of work. The nation would save almost 90,000 people from traffic-related injury or death. Accident-related costs would be reduced by more than $10 billion a year. And greenhouse gases would decrease by 54 million tons—the equivalent of taking almost 10 million cars (the entire New York State workforce) off the road for a year.[25]

While telecommuting sounds great at first glance, it offers benefits and drawbacks for organizations and employees alike, as you'll see in Exhibit 15.4.

telecommuting Working remotely—most often from home—and connecting to the office via phone lines and/or broadband networks.

Job Sharing Job sharing allows two or more employees to share a single full-time job. Typically, job-share participants split the salary equally, but they often need to allocate full benefits to just one of the partners. On a nationwide basis, fewer than 20% of employers (e.g., American Express, PricewaterhouseCoopers, and some departments of the U.S. federal government) offer job-sharing programs and reap the benefits such as higher morale and better retention.[26]

15-4g Separation: Breaking Up Is Hard to Do

Employees leave jobs for a number of different reasons. Experiencing success, they may be promoted or lured to another firm. Experiencing failure, they may be fired. Or in response to changing business needs, their employer might transfer them or lay them off. And employees also leave jobs for completely personal reasons such as family needs, retirement, or a change in career aspirations.

When companies terminate employees, they must proceed very carefully to avoid wrongful-termination lawsuits. The best protection is honesty and documentation. Employers should always document sound business reasons for termination and share those reasons with the employee.

But employees can still lose their jobs for reasons that have little or nothing to do with their individual performance. In response to the recession, employers eliminated 5.1 million jobs between December 2007 and March 2009. And while the economy regained its footing by 2015, many experts anticipate that it will not fully rebound for many years. As companies have become leaner, the remaining workers have experienced enormous stress. Managers can

What Your Boss REALLY Thinks of Your Tattoo

It doesn't really matter what your boss thinks of your tattoo—as long as your boss *can't see* your tattoo. But as climate change brings warmer temperatures, keeping your tattoo covered up may not always be an option, even if you are so inclined. Even in an age of relaxed attitudes about tattoos, this may pose a problem in the mainstream workplace. About 29% of the population (and 47% of millennials) sport at least one tattoo. However, 37% of HR managers cite tattoos as the third most likely physical attribute to limit career potential (behind bad breath and non-traditional piercings). There are currently no laws protecting people with tattoos from discrimination in the hiring process, but it's not all bad news if you're forced (or you choose) to show your ink. A number of top companies are known for being tattoo friendly, including Whole Foods, Google, Trader Joe's, Target, Home Depot, and Barnes &

Noble. Ninety-four percent of people with tattoos would hire someone with tattoos, so as ink becomes more common in the workplace, tattoo-based discrimination may soon be a thing of the past.[27]

FXQuadro/Shutterstock.com

---

mitigate the trauma most effectively by showing empathy and concern for their employees, and by treating any laid-off employees with visible compassion.[28]

15-5 LEGAL ISSUES: HR AND THE LONG ARM OF THE LAW

Even when the company is right—even when the company wins—employment lawsuits can cost millions of dollars and deeply damage the reputation of an organization, as we briefly discussed earlier in this chapter. To avoid employment lawsuits, most firms rely on HR to digest the complex, evolving web of employment legislation and court decisions, and to ensure that management understands the key issues.

The bottom-line goal of most employment legislation is to protect employees from unfair treatment by employers. Some would argue that the legislation goes so far that it hinders the ability of companies to grow. But regardless of your personal perspective, the obligation of an ethical employer is to understand and abide by the law as it stands—even if you're working within the system to change it.

The most influential piece of employment law may be the **Civil Rights Act of 1964. Title VII** of this act—which applies only to employers with 15 or more workers—outlaws discrimination in hiring, firing, compensation, apprenticeships, training, terms, conditions, or privileges of employment based on race, color, religion, sex, or

national origin. Over time, Congress has supplemented Title VII with legislation that prohibits discrimination based on pregnancy, age (40+), and disability.

Title VII also created the **Equal Employment Opportunity Commission (EEOC)** to enforce its provisions. And in 1972, Congress beefed up the EEOC with additional powers to regulate and to enforce its mandates, making the EEOC a powerful force in the human resources realm.

Here are some additional key pieces of employment legislation:

- **Fair Labor Standards Act of 1938:** Established a minimum wage and overtime pay for employees working more than 40 hours a week.

- **Equal Pay Act of 1963:** Mandated that men and women doing equal jobs receive equal pay.

- **Occupational Safety and Health Act of 1970:** Required safety equipment for employees and established maximum exposure limits for hazardous substances.

Civil Rights Act of 1964 Federal legislation that prohibits discrimination in hiring, firing, compensation, apprenticeships, training, terms, conditions, or privileges of employment based on race, color, religion, sex, or national origin.

Title VII A portion of the Civil Rights Act of 1964 that prohibits discrimination in hiring, firing, compensation, apprenticeships, training, terms, conditions, or privileges of employment based on race, color, religion, sex, or national origin for employers with 15 or more workers.

Equal Employment Opportunity Commission (EEOC) A federal agency designed to regulate and enforce the provisions of Title VII.

> ## About 12 workers are killed on the job in the United States every day.
>
> —OCCUPATIONAL SAFETY AND HEALTH ADMINISTRATION

- **Immigration Reform and Control Act of 1986:** Required employers to verify employment eligibility for all new hires.

- **Americans with Disabilities Act of 1990:** Prohibited discrimination in hiring, promotion, and compensation against people with disabilities and required employers to make "reasonable" accommodations for them.

- **Family and Medical Leave Act of 1993:** Required firms with 50 or more employees to provide up to 12 weeks of job-secure, unpaid leave on the birth or adoption of a child or the serious illness of a spouse, child, or parent.

15-5a Affirmative Action: The Active Pursuit of Equal Opportunity

The term **affirmative action** refers to policies meant to increase employment and educational opportunities for minority groups—especially groups defined by race, ethnicity, or gender. Emerging during the American civil rights movement in the 1960s, affirmative action seeks to make up for the systematic discrimination of the past by creating more opportunities in the present.

Over the past couple of decades, affirmative action has become increasingly controversial. Opponents have raised concerns that giving preferential treatment to some groups amounts to "reverse discrimination" against groups who do not get the same benefits. They claim that affirmative action violates the principle that all individuals are equal under the law. But supporters counter that everyone who benefits from affirmative action must—by law—have relevant and valid qualifications. They argue that proactive measures are the only workable way to right past wrongs and to ensure truly equal opportunity.

affirmative action Policies meant to increase employment and educational opportunities for minority groups—especially groups defined by race, ethnicity, or gender.

sexual harassment Workplace discrimination against a person based on his or her gender.

Recent U.S. Supreme Court decisions have supported affirmative action, pointing out that government has a "compelling interest" in ensuring racial diversity. But the Court has rejected "mechanistic" affirmative action programs that amount to quota systems based on race, ethnicity, or gender.

The long-term fate of affirmative action remains unclear, but achieving the underlying goal—a diverse workplace with equal opportunity for all—stands to benefit both business and society as a whole.

15-5b Sexual Harassment: Eliminating Hostility

Sexual harassment—which violates Title VII of the Civil Rights Act of 1964—involves discrimination against a person based on his or her gender. According to the EEOC, sexual harassment can range from requests for sexual favors to the presence of a hostile work environment. The EEOC also points out that a sexual harasser may be either a woman or a man, and the harasser doesn't need to be the victim's supervisor. The victim could be anyone affected—either directly or indirectly—by the offensive conduct. And clearly, to qualify as sexual harassment, the conduct must be unwelcome. The total number of sexual harassment charges filed with the EEOC in the past decade dropped 27% from 2001 to 2011. Interestingly, the number of charges filed by men rose from 13.7% to 17.1% in 2015, but dropped to 16.6% in 2016.[29]

Not just the perpetrator is liable for sexual harassment; employers may share accountability if they did not take "reasonable care" to prevent and correct sexually harassing behavior, or if they did not provide a workable system for employee complaints. Simply adopting a written policy against sexual harassment is not enough. Taking "reasonable care" also means taking proactive steps—such as comprehensive training—to ensure that everyone in the organization understands (1) that the firm does not tolerate sexual harassment and (2) that the firm has a system in place for complaints and will not tolerate retaliation against those who complain.[30]

The #MeToo movement in late 2017 highlighted the unfortunate prevalence of sexual harassment and assault in the workplace, and human resources is the first line of defense. Handling sexual harassment complaints can be especially thorny for human resources, particularly on behalf of younger workers—since the conventional understanding of sexual harassment does not typically match the legal definition of sexual harassment.

THE BIG PICTURE

Effective human resource management can create an unbeatable competitive edge—a fair, productive, empowering workplace pays off in bottom-line results. In good times, one core HRM goal is to find, hire, and develop the best talent. While that function remains crucial in tough economic times, the focus changes to managing HR costs while maintaining morale. Looking forward, a growing number of firms will most likely outsource traditional HR tasks such as payroll and benefits administration to companies that specialize in these areas. HR departments could then focus on their core mission: working with senior management to achieve business goals by cultivating the firm's investment in human resources.

CAREERS IN HUMAN RESOURCES

Human Resources Manager

Plan, organize, lead, and coordinate the personnel, or labor relations activities of an organization. Identify staff vacancies and recruit, interview, and select applicants, ensuring a strong match between personnel and positions. Establish, maintain, and implement a competitive pay and benefit structure, and insure that policies remain in compliance with federal, state, and local laws. Establish and conduct employee orientation and training programs. Provide current and prospective employees with information about company policies, pay, benefits, and promotional opportunities. Counsel and coach management as necessary on human resources issues. Maintain accurate human resources records. Keep current regarding professional and technical knowledge.

STUDY TOOLS 15

LOCATED AT BACK OF THE TEXTBOOK

☐ Rip-Out Chapter Review Card

☐ Gain unique perspectives on key concepts with new concept videos in the e-book

☐ Increase your comprehension with online homework and quizzes

☐ Study with existing flashcards and make your own

16 | Managing Information and Technology:
Finding New Ways to Learn and Link

LEARNING OBJECTIVES

After studying this chapter, you will be able to:

16-1 Explain the basic elements of computer technology—including hardware, software, and networks—and describe key trends in each area

16-2 Discuss the reasons for the increasing popularity of cloud computing

16-3 Describe how data become information and how decision support systems can provide high-quality information that helps managers make better decisions

16-4 Explain how Internet-based technologies have changed business-to-consumer and business-to-business commerce

16-5 Describe the problems posed by the rapid changes in Internet-based technologies, and explain ways to address these problems

Remember to visit

PAGE 305

for additional

STUDY TOOLS

Rus S/Shutterstock.com

16-1 INFORMATION TECHNOLOGY: EXPLOSIVE CHANGE

Over the past few decades, computer and communications hardware and software have changed dramatically. The capabilities of hardware have increased by orders of magnitude. In the late 1950s, for example, you would have needed fifty 24-inch disks—costing tens of thousands of dollars—to store 5 megabytes of data. Today you can buy a flash memory device, about the same size as a postage stamp, that stores 128 gigabytes of data—over 24,000 times more than that whole 1950s disk array—for under $30. And in terms of processing power and performance, Apple's iPad Pro, which performs nearly 5 billion mathematical operations per second, is not only faster than multimillion dollar super computers from the 1990s, it runs 10 hours on its battery and can be controlled via dictation, easy-to-learn touch screen commands, or the Apple Pencil, which can be used for handwritten notes and creating incredibly detailed drawings.[1] While more difficult to quantify with specific statistics, it's also clear that software has become more powerful, more flexible, and easier to use.

Perhaps an even more important development than the increased power of hardware and sophistication of software is the degree to which today's technology is linked by networks. These networks allow businesses to coordinate their internal functions, reach their customers, and collaborate with their suppliers and partners in ways that could not have been envisioned a quarter of a century ago. Networks have not only improved the efficiency and effectiveness of existing businesses, they've also opened up entirely new business opportunities. Pancreatic cancer often moves from stage I to stage IV in just a year. Because it grows so quickly and aggressively, it is often detected too late for surgical treatment. Just 25% of patients with untreatable pancreatic cancer survive after one year, and only 4% survive after five years.[2] However, by examining search logs mentioning pancreatic cancer ("I was just diagnosed with pancreatic cancer") on Microsoft's Bing.com search engine and then working backward to see if the same people had previously searched for information associated with symptoms of pancreatic cancer, researchers were able to identify 5% to 15% of people who later self-identified with the disease. Dr. Eric Horvitz, a study author, said, "We asked ourselves, 'If we heard the whispers of people online, would

"The Internet? Is that thing still around?"

—HOMER SIMPSON

it provide strong evidence or a clue that's something's going on?'"[3] The hope is that web search data might result in early detection, life-saving treatment, and higher survival rates.

Of course, these new linkages pose challenges and threats as well as benefits and opportunities. A quarter of a century ago, people hadn't heard of computer viruses, spyware, phishing, or spam (except for the Hormel meat product variety). Over the course of this chapter, we'll take a look at both sides of this rapidly changing story.

16-1a Hardware and Software

Hardware refers to the physical components used to collect, input, store, and process data, and to display and distribute information. This hardware includes

> **hardware** The physical tools and equipment used to collect, input, store, organize, and process data and to distribute information.

the various components of a computer system as well as communications and network equipment. Examples include barcode scanners, hard drives, printers, routers, and smartphones.

Software refers to the programs that provide instructions to a computer so that it can perform a desired task. There are two broad categories of software: system software and application software. Both types of software have used the tremendous increase in hardware capabilities to become more powerful and easier to use.

System software performs the critical functions necessary to operate a computer at the most basic level. The fundamental form of system software is the operating system, which controls the overall operation of the computer. It implements vital tasks, such as managing the file system, reading programs and data into main memory, and allocating system memory among various tasks to avoid conflicts.

Operating system software also provides the interface that enables users to interact with their computers. Early operating systems required users to type complex commands with very precise syntax to carry out tasks such as running programs or opening, saving, or deleting files. If you made an error while typing a command, your computer would just sit there until you typed the correct command. Today's operating systems are much simpler and more intuitive. The *graphical user interface* (or GUI— pronounced "gooey") allows users to enter commands by clicking on icons on the computer screen or by tapping or swiping them on devices with a touch screen.

Utility programs supplement operating system software in ways that increase the security or abilities of the computer system. Examples include firewalls, antivirus software, and antispyware programs. Over the years, operating systems have incorporated many features that were originally provided by such utility programs.

Applications software is software that helps users perform a desired task. Horizontal applications software, such as word processing, spreadsheet, and personal information management software, is used by many different businesses and occupations. Vertical applications software is designed for a specific industry or profession.

software Programs that provide instructions to a computer so that it can perform a desired task.

system software Software that performs the critical functions necessary to operate the computer at the most basic level.

applications software Software that helps a user perform a desired task.

Internet The world's largest computer network; essentially a network of computer networks all operating under a common set of rules that allow them to communicate with each other.

For many, the Internet is as much a social experience as it is an information-gathering one.

ProStockStudio/Shutterstock.com

For example, brokerage firms have special software that allows them to transact business on the stock exchanges, and product designers have computer-aided design (CAD) software that enables them to produce technical drawings in three dimensions.

16-1b Networks

Today, most firms (and households) use networks that allow users to communicate with each other and share both files and hardware resources. A network links computer resources, using either a wired or wireless connection. Firms usually want to prevent outsiders from obtaining access to their networks for privacy and security reasons, but they sometimes allow customers or suppliers partial access to their private networks to strengthen their relationships with these important stakeholders.

The Internet and the World Wide Web The development and growth of the **Internet** is one of the great networking stories of the past two decades. The Internet is often referred to as the world's largest computer network. It's actually a network of networks, consisting of hundreds of thousands of smaller networks operating under a common set of protocols (rules) so that they can communicate with each other.

One common way to experience the Internet is through the World Wide Web. But while the Internet supports the Web and provides access to it, only about 5% of the traffic on the Internet in North America involves the Web. Other traffic includes, but isn't limited to, real-time entertainment (70%) like Netflix, YouTube, and Amazon Prime streaming; marketplaces (7.2%) like eBay and iTunes; video and audio

Exhibit 16.1

Growth in Broadband and Smartphone Internet Access

Percentage of American Adults (Cell Phones & Smartphones) and Households (Broadband)

Cell phone: 62% ('02), 65% ('03), 67% ('04), 73% ('05), 75% ('07), 84% ('08), 83% ('09), 81% ('10), 87% ('11), 88% ('12), 92% ('13), 89% ('14), 91% ('15), 95% ('16)

Smartphone: 35% ('11), 45% ('12), 58% ('13), 59% ('14), 67% ('15), 77% ('16)

Broadband: 3% ('00), 6% ('01), 11% ('02), 16% ('03), 24% ('04), 33% ('05), 42% ('06), 47% ('07), 55% ('08), 63% ('09), 66% ('10), 62% ('11), 66% ('12), 66% ('13), 69% ('14), 70%, 73% ('16)

Legend: — Cell phone — Smartphone — Broadband

Year: '00 '01 '02 '03 '04 '05 '06 '07 '08 '09 '10 '11 '12 '13 '14 '15 '16

J. Horrigan and M. Duggan, "Home Broadband 2015," Pew Research Center, December 21, 2015, http://www.pewinternet.org/2015/12/21/home-broadband-2015/, accessed April 1, 2016; "Demographics of Internet and Home Broadband Usage in the United States," Pew Research Center, January 12, 2017, http://www.pewinternet.org/fact-sheet/internet-broadband/, accessed February 11, 2017.

communication (5%) like Skype; gaming services (4.3%) like Xbox Live and PlayStation Network; and social networking (3.9%) like Facebook.[4] Still, the Web is an incredibly rich environment; it consists of more than 46.7 billion pages of documents—the number grows every second—written and linked together using Hypertext Markup Language (HTML).[5]

The increased availability of broadband and wireless Internet connections have fueled the popularity of Internet applications. A **broadband Internet connection** has the capacity to transmit large amounts of data very quickly, allowing users to quickly download large files such as music, games, and movies. A survey by the Pew Internet and American Life Project, summarized in Exhibit 16.1, found that access to broadband Internet connections grew rapidly over the last two decades. As Exhibit 16.1 shows, only 1% of American adults had access to high-speed Internet at home in 2000, but by 2016 that figure had climbed to 73%.[6] Exhibit 16.1 also shows that while 95% of Americans have cell phones, 77% now have smartphones with fast cellular Internet service, up from 35% in 2011.[7] (It's worth noting that 10% of Americans who have smartphones do not have home broadband.)[8]

From a business perspective, the growth in high-speed Internet access via broadband and smartphones allows companies to offer richer, more interactive experiences to customers who visit their websites or use their apps, no matter where they're located.

But even today's broadband connections are too slow and inefficient for many business and scientific applications. Such projects often require high-definition video and audio files to be shared among multiple sites at the same time. Beginning in 1996, several leading research universities, corporations, and other organizations formed a coalition to create a new generation of Internet technology in the United States based on fiber-optic cable. The resulting network became known as **Internet2 (or "I2").**

broadband Internet connection An Internet connection that is capable of transmitting large amounts of information very quickly.

Internet2 (I2) A new high-tech Internet with access limited to a consortium of member organizations (and other organizations these members sponsor). I2 utilizes technologies that give it a speed and capacity far exceeding the current Internet.

Access to I2 was initially limited to dues-paying members of the Internet2 consortium, which today consists of over 317 major universities as well as 29 non-profit organizations, 83 leading high-tech corporations, 64 government agencies, 43 research and educational networks, and 65 international organizations.[9] But under an initiative begun in 2001, members of the I2 consortium can sponsor access to the network for other research and educational organizations that otherwise would be unable to qualify for membership. This initiative has given many elementary schools, high schools, community colleges, libraries, and museums access to I2 resources.[10]

Internet2 isn't simply a faster way to surf the Web or send email. In fact, such routine uses of the current Internet aren't even allowed. Instead, it is a noncommercial network that uses high-speed connectivity to improve education, research, and collaboration. Member organizations see Internet2 as a way to bring together their researchers, scientists, and engineers at various locations in a way that allows real-time collaboration on complex and important topics. It also allows corporations to collaborate with other companies, universities, and organizations located thousands of miles apart. One of the missions of the Internet2 consortium is to "facilitate the development, deployment and use of revolutionary Internet technologies."[11] So, the benefits of Internet2 will eventually become commonplace on the Internet that the rest of us use.

Exhibit 16.2
Igloo Software Intranet

Have You Been Pwned?

If founder and CEO of Facebook Mark Zuckerberg can be hacked, you can, too. Hackers breached Zuckerberg's LinkedIn, Twitter, and Pinterest accounts, across which he allegedly used the same password: "dadada." Online security consultant Graham Cluley said, "It shows it can happen to anyone—even geeks."

Zuckerberg found out about the infiltration when the hackers tweeted him saying, "We are just testing your security." Since hackers probably won't be contacting you, how can you find out when one of your accounts has been hacked?

One way is to use Have I Been Pwned? (HIBP, https://haveibeenpwned.com), a free website operated by Australian-born Microsoft security expert Troy Hunt. ("Pwned," an intentional misspelling of the word "owned," is slang for being defeated or embarrassed.) So far, HIBP has data from 191 pwned websites containing 2.1 billion user accounts. To check whether one or more of your accounts has been pwned, simply enter your email address or user name. HIBP shows whether your emails are associated with hacked accounts.

Hunt started HIBP after Adobe accounts were compromised and the hackers began selling email addresses and passwords. Says Hunt, "There is a massive trade in stolen data." The top five breaches thus far are MySpace (359 million), NetEase (235 million), LinkedIn (165 million), Adobe (152 million), and Badoo (112 million).

Have you been pwned? Probably. Check on HIBP. If so, use a password manager like LastPass (https://www.lastpass.com) to generate and store long, unique, randomly generated passwords for all of your accounts, and change key passwords every six months.

Be smart. Don't get pwned.[12]

F8 studio/Shutterstock.com

Intranets and Extranets An **intranet** is a private network that has the same look and feel as the Web and uses the same web browser software to display documents, but limits access to the employees of a single firm (or members of a single organization). When properly implemented, intranets enhance communication and collaboration among employees and provide an effective way to distribute information and applications throughout the organization. Employees can usually log onto their company's intranet from remote locations using password-protected Internet access, allowing them to use company resources when working on the road or from home from home. Exhibit 16.2 illustrates an example from Igloo Software, a leading provider of intranet software. On this screen, employees can find team members, communicate with them via social chat or Slack (a team communication tool), read and share news, see what activities are taking place, access and share files, and see what's coming up on the team calendar.

Firms sometimes also create **extranets** by giving key stakeholders, such as suppliers or customers, limited access to certain areas of their intranet. Extranets enable firms to provide additional services and information to their external stakeholders. For example, the firm might allow customers to check on the status of their order, or suppliers to check on the state of the firm's inventory to plan shipments of parts and materials.

16-1c The Role of the IT Department

Many business organizations have an information technology (IT) department to manage their information resources. But the role of this department varies significantly from one company to another. In some firms, the IT department plays a strategic role, making and implementing key decisions about the technologies the firm will use. In other organizations, the role of IT is largely operational; managers in functional departments make the key decisions about the computer and information resources their areas need, and the IT department simply maintains these resources and provides technical support to employees.

> **intranet** A private network that has the look and feel of the Internet and is navigated using a web browser, but which limits access to a single firm's employees (or a single organization's members).
>
> **extranet** An intranet that allows limited access to a selected group of stakeholders, such as suppliers or customers.

CLOUD COMPUTING: THE SKY'S THE LIMIT!

In most companies, employees use applications and access data stored on their own computers or their companies' servers. But "cloud computing" is challenging that approach. **Cloud computing** means using Internet-based storage capacity, applications, and processing power to supplement or replace internally owned computer resources.

You're already familiar with consumer-focused cloud computing services if you backup, organize, and share your photos on Google Photos; store your music on Apple's iCloud storage services; or use a service like Dropbox or Google Docs to access and share documents and files. These services clearly offer significant benefits, such as the ability to store large files without taking up valuable space on your computer's hard drive and the convenience of being able to access your documents, music, and photos from anywhere via any computer or mobile device with an Internet connection.

Until recently, most businesses were reluctant to embrace cloud computing, citing concerns about security and reliability. But that is changing. Two studies by global consulting company McKinsey & Co. indicate that while 77% of large companies now manage their own IT equipment and services in-house, this figure is expected to drop to 43% in 2018 as companies move to the cloud. McKinsey concludes, "More large enterprises are likely to move workloads away from traditional and virtualized environments toward the cloud—at a rate and pace that is expected to be far quicker than in the past."[13]

And for many organizations, moving to the cloud may actually increase data security. AWS (Amazon Web Services) is Amazon.com's quick, reliable IT backbone. But Amazon also sells the use of its AWS services to external companies. In fact, AWS has grown so quickly that it is now the world's largest provider of IT cloud services. AWS CEO Jason Anders says, "What's happened over the last three to four years is that most companies have figured out that they can have a much stronger security posture in AWS and the cloud than they can on-premises, because we're able to employ a lot more people to focus on security."[14] More specifically, the cloud offers to its users the ability to:

> **cloud computing** The use of Internet-based storage capacity, processing power, and computer applications to supplement or replace internally owned information technology resources.

- Access a vast array of computing resources without the need to invest heavily in expensive new hardware, software, and IT personnel. Thomas Publishing Co., which got its start more than

> "There are only two industries that refer to their customers as 'users.'"
>
> —EDWARD TUFTE, STATISTICIAN

Violetkaipa/Shutterstock.com

If you share photos on Facebook, store your music on Apple's iCloud storage services, or use Dropbox to access and share documents and files, you're already using cloud computing.

than a century ago publishing its "big green books," provides a comprehensive registry of U.S. manufacturers. Thomas moved its data online in 2006, running its own data centers and services. But now, Thomas is moving everything to AWS's cloud. Chief Technical Officer Hans Wald explains, "We want to be out of the business of running data centers."[15]

- Allow lower costs and excess capacity by only paying for the computer resources they need or use. When *Conde Nast*, the travel publisher, moved all of its data online, data costs dropped by 40%.[16]

- Encourage collaboration among employees and business partners. Cloud resources aren't confined to a specific platform or operating system, so it is easy for people using different computer systems to share files and programs. In addition, many cloud-based applications include tools specifically designed to facilitate collaboration.

- Take advantage of incredible gains in processing speed via *massively parallel computing* that simultaneously combines the processing power of hundreds (or even thousands) of computers. By combining computing power, data processing projects can be completed in 70–80% less time. For example, DNA2.0, using cloud computing and specialized software, can analyze and count the number of cells in 50,000 microscope images in just two years, a task that would have taken a team of scientists ten years to complete.[17]

16-3 INFORMATION TECHNOLOGY AND DECISION MAKING: A CRUCIAL AID

One of the vital functions of information technology—at least in relationship to business—is to transform data into useful information for decision makers. In order to make decisions, managers must have information about the current state of their business, their competitive environment, and the trends and market conditions that offer new opportunities. Where does this information come from? How can it be made more useful? How can managers process the information to make better decisions?

16-3a Data and Information

Let's start by distinguishing between data and information. **Data** are the facts and figures a firm collects. Data in their raw form have limited usefulness because they lack the context needed to give them meaning. Data become **information** when they are processed, organized, and presented in a way that makes them useful to a decision maker. Sometimes firms can obtain useful information from external sources, but sometimes they must create information by processing their own data. Given today's competitive environment, the speed with which managers obtain good-quality information can be a crucial competitive advantage.

Internally, every department of an organization generates facts and figures that the firm must store and track. Every time a financial transaction is completed, for example, the firm's accounting system must record the specific accounts affected. Similarly, a firm's human resources department must enter new data every time an employee is hired, fired, promoted, changes jobs, or retires. Firms must also keep track of the names, addresses, and credit information of each customer. This is hardly a complete list, but you get the picture; firms must store mountains of data and convert them into useful information.

"To err is human–and to blame it on a computer is even more so."
—ROBERT ORBEN, COMEDY WRITER AND SPEECHWRITER

Typically, today's businesses store their data in **databases**, which are files of related data organized according to a logical system and stored on hard drives or some other computer-accessible storage media. It isn't unusual for a company to have many different databases, each maintained by a different department or functional area to meet its specific needs. For example, the human resources department might have a database of employee pay rates, and the marketing department may have another database of customer history.

Once all these data are stored, the firm must convert them into information. One common method is to query a database. A query is a request for the database management software to search the database for data that match criteria specified by the user. Suppose, for instance, that a marketing manager plans to introduce a product upgrade. She can enter a query that asks for the email addresses of all customers who have purchased the product in the past year. She can use this information to send a targeted email message, promoting the upgrade to the customers who are most likely to buy it.

16-3b Characteristics of Good Information

We've seen that businesses have many sources of information. But not all information is of good quality. High-quality information is:

- Accurate: It should be free of errors and biases.
- Relevant: It should focus on issues that are important to decision makers.
- Timely: It should be available in time to make a difference.
- Understandable: It must help the user grasp its meaning.
- Secure: Confidential information must be secure from hackers and competitors.

data Raw, unprocessed facts and figures.

information Data that have been processed in a way that make them meaningful to their user.

database A file consisting of related data organized according to a logical system and stored on a hard drive or some other computer-accessible media.

16-3c Using Information Technology to Improve Decision Making

A company's information technology (IT) department frequently works closely with managers throughout the organization to support decision making. In fact, many companies develop **decision support systems (DSS)** that give managers access to large amounts of data and the processing power to convert the data into high-quality information quickly and efficiently. Over the past two decades, a new class of decision support system has evolved to take advantage of the dramatic increase in data storage and processing capabilities. Called **business intelligence systems**, these systems help businesses discover subtle and complex relationships hidden in their data. Such systems can be a source of competitive advantage for the businesses that develop them. Freight rail companies, which ship 40% of goods nationwide, use business intelligence systems to predict problems before they become safety issues. For example, a freight train can derail when one or more of the eight steel wheels on one of its freight cars breaks, possibly causing a massive loss of life and property. Every year, an average of 400 train wheels break, creating the possibility for 400 disasters. But with 12 million freight train wheels on 1.5 million freight rail cars in the United States, there is less than a 0.0033 percent chance of predicting when and where a wheel could break. Thanks to business intelligence systems, freight rail companies are frequently able to predict when a steel wheel needs fixing or replacing. As a result, the accident rate for freight trains has dropped 80% since 1980 and 45% since 2000.[18]

One of the most common approaches to implementing a business intelligence system is to create a data warehouse and use data mining to discover unknown relationships. A **data warehouse** is a very large, organization-wide database that provides a centralized location for storing data from both the organization's own databases and external sources. Why do companies need data warehouses? Because smart phones alone generate 18 exabytes of data each month. How big is that? An exabyte is 1,000 petabytes, which is 1,000 terabytes, which is 1,000 gigabytes. Most of us can conceptualize a gigabyte because of the gigabytes of storage on our smartphones, tablets, laptops, and gaming platforms.[19] Scott Dietzen is CEO of Pure, which makes data storage systems capable of holding five times more information than conventional technology. Dietzen says that the amount of data recorded today is so overwhelming that "[n]o one can look at all their data anymore; they need algorithm just to decide what to look at."[20]

Data mining uses powerful statistical and mathematical techniques to analyze vast amounts of data to identify useful information that had been hidden. In recent years, data mining has had considerable success in areas as diverse as fraud and crime detection and quality control and scientific research. New York City's Human Resources Administration used data mining to identify $46.5 million in fraudulent welfare claims, up 60% from before. Commissioner Steven Banks says data mining "allows us to zero in on likely fraud so we don't divert resources to finding what otherwise might be a needle in a haystack."[21]

16-3d Expert Systems

Managers who use decision support systems usually already know quite a bit about the problem and how they

An expert system helps managers make better decisions by asking a series of questions until enough information is gathered to reach a decision.

decision support system (DSS) A system that gives managers access to large amounts of data and the processing power to convert these data into high-quality information, thus improving the decision-making process.

business intelligence system A sophisticated form of decision support system that helps decision makers discover information that was previously hidden.

data warehouse A large, organization-wide database that stores data in a centralized location.

data mining The use of sophisticated statistical and mathematical techniques to analyze vast amounts of data to discover hidden patterns and relationships, thus creating valuable information.

Sergey Nivens/Shutterstock.com

want to solve it. They just need access to the right data and a system to "crunch the numbers" in a way that provides relevant, accurate, and timely information to help them make their decisions. But what happens when the problem is beyond the expertise of the manager? One way to deal with this problem is to set up an **expert system (ES)** to guide the manager through the decision-making process.

To develop expert systems, programmers ask experts in the relevant area to explain how they solve problems. They then devise a program to mimic the expert's approach, incorporating various rules or guidelines that the human expert uses. The finished program will ask a user a series of questions, basing each question on the response to the previous question. The program continues to ask questions until it has enough information to reach a decision and make a recommendation. Doctors at a large New York hospital system use an expert system to help determine if a coughing patient has pneumonia. The expert system asks the doctor whether the patient "has a fever and rapid heart rate," and if the doctor hears, "a 'crackle' in the lungs."[22] High scores indicate immediate treatment, while low scores suggest pneumonia isn't the issue.

Expert systems routinely solve problems in areas as diverse as medical diagnoses, fraud detection, and consumer credit evaluation. The troubleshooting systems that many companies have on the customer-support pages of their websites are another type of expert system. If your product doesn't work, the troubleshooter will ask a series of questions designed to diagnose the problem and suggest solutions. Based on your responses to each question, the system selects the next question as it starts narrowing down the possible reasons for the problem until it identifies the cause and offers a solution. Often you can solve your problem without waiting on hold to talk to a human expert over the phone.[23]

Despite impressive results in many fields, expert systems have their limitations. Programming thousands of decision rules into the system can be time-consuming, complicated, and expensive. In fact, it's sometimes impossible because the experts themselves can't clearly explain how they make their decisions—they just "know" the answer based on their years of experience. If the experts can't clearly explain how they reach their conclusions, then programmers can't include the appropriate decision rules in the system. Finally, an expert system has little flexibility and no common sense. It probably won't be able to find a solution to a problem that deviates in any significant way from the specific type of problem it was programmed to solve.[24]

 16-4 INFORMATION TECHNOLOGY AND THE WORLD OF E-COMMERCE

Over the past 20 years, advances in information technology have had a dramatic and widespread effect on how companies conduct their business. But in this chapter, we'll just concentrate on one key area: the growth and development of e-commerce.

E-commerce refers to marketing, buying, selling, and servicing of products over a network (usually the Internet). You're probably most familiar with **business-to-consumer (B2C) e-commerce**. You participate in this form of e-commerce when you purchase songs from iTunes, use Expedia to make travel arrangements, or buy stocks through an online broker such as Charles Schwab. However, **business-to-business (B2B) e-commerce**, which consists of markets where businesses sell supplies, components, machinery, equipment, or services to other businesses, actually accounts for a much larger volume of e-commerce.

While both B2C and B2B involve exchanging goods over the Internet, they differ in some important ways, as shown in Exhibit 16.3. Given these structural differences, it isn't surprising that the two markets operate so differently.

While B2B and B2C are the most obvious forms of e-commerce, they aren't the *only* forms. For example, inC2C (consumer-to-consumer) e-commerce, consumers buy from and sell to other consumers—think eBay and Craigslist. And in B2G (business-to-government), e-commerce businesses sell information, goods, and services to government agencies.

16-4a Using Information Technology in the B2C Market

Firms in the B2C market use information technology in a variety of ways. In this section, we'll describe how firms use technology in general (and the Internet in particular) to attract new customers and strengthen the loyalty of existing customers.

Web 2.0 One major goal for most firms today is to develop stronger relationships with their customers. The Internet has proven to be an excellent tool for

---

expert system (ES) A decision support system that helps managers make better decisions in an area where they lack expertise.

e-commerce The marketing, buying, selling, and servicing of products over a network (usually the Internet).

business-to-consumer (B2C) e-commerce E-commerce in which businesses and final consumers interact.

business-to-business (B2B) e-commerce E-commerce in markets where businesses buy from and sell to other businesses.

EXHIBIT 16.3 KEY DIFFERENCES BETWEEN B2C AND B2B E-COMMERCE

	B2C	B2B
Type of Customers	Individual final consumers	Other businesses
Number of Customers in Target Market	Very large	Often limited to a few major business customers
Size of Typical Individual Transaction	Relatively small (usually a few dollars to a few hundred dollars)	Potentially very large (often several thousand dollars, sometimes several million dollars)
Customer Behavior	May do some research, but many purchases may be based on impulse.	Usually does careful multiple research and compares vendors. May take bids.
Complexity of Negotiations	Purchase typically involves little or no negotiation. Customer usually buys a standard product and pays the listed price.	Often involves extensive negotiation over specifications, delivery, installation, support, and other issues.
Nature of Relationship with Customers	Firm wants to develop customer loyalty and repeat business but seldom develops a close working relationship with individual customers.	Buyers and sellers often eventually develop close and long-lasting relationships that allow them to coordinate their activities.

fostering such relationships—though it took a while for businesses to discover the best way to do so. In the early days of e-commerce, most companies tried to maintain tight control over the content presented on their websites. These websites presented information about products and allowed customers to place orders for goods and services, but offered little opportunity for user participation or involvement. However, by the early years of the twenty-first century, innovative businesses were developing ways to make e-commerce more interactive and collaborative. In doing so, they not only forged stronger relationships with the customers who posted this content, they also created a richer, more interesting, and more useful experience for *others* who visited the site. This new approach became known as **Web 2.0**.

Many Web 2.0 sites rely on users (or members) to provide most of their content. For instance, the online encyclopedia Wikipedia uses wiki software to allow users to comment on and contribute to its articles. And social networking sites such as Facebook and Twitter wouldn't exist without user-created material. The more users who participate on these sites, the more useful (and entertaining) they become—and the easier it is for them to attract even more visitors and contributors.

Interestingly, many companies have found that techniques used to encourage collaboration among their customers can be used to accomplish the same result with their employees. Major corporations such as HP, Wells Fargo, and Procter & Gamble now use Web 2.0 techniques to help their own employees work more effectively together. The use of Web 2.0 technologies within organizations is called Enterprise 2.0.[25]

Advertising on the Internet Many B2C companies have large target markets, so advertising is an important part of their marketing strategy. Internet advertising revenue grew rapidly in the early twenty-first century, increasing almost fourfold from 2002 to 2008. It dropped slightly in early 2009 (as did most types of advertising expenditures during the onset of the recession) but began rising again later that year.

By the end of 2009, it surpassed magazine advertising revenue for the first time, and in 2016 it increased to an estimated $70 billion. Annual Internet advertising revenues now exceed those from broadcast and cable TV, newspapers, radio, and magazines. Banner ads generated 10% of all Internet advertising revenues; ads placed on pages containing search results (such as those you see on Google or Bing) accounted for 27% of revenues; and for the second consecutive year, ads targeting mobile devices such as tablets and smartphones led the pack, generating 30% of Internet ad revenues.[26]

Firms in B2C markets also use opt-in email as an advertising medium. Opt-in emails are messages that the receiver has explicitly chosen to receive. Customers often opt in when they register their products online and click to indicate that they would like to receive product information from the company. Since the customer has agreed to receive the message, opt-in emails tend to reach interested consumers. And, because email requires no envelopes, paper, or postage, it's much less expensive than direct mail.

Web 2.0 Websites that incorporate interactive and collaborative features to create a richer, more interesting, and more useful experience for their users.

Hacking, Fraud, App Authing, and Tokenization: What You Need to Know

From malware to spyware, viruses, worms, spam, phishing, pharming, and SMiShing, Section 16-5 of this chapter explains how hackers can break into your email, online accounts, and other sources of data. Here are two more hacking methods, as well as ways to counter or prevent them.

App Authing: Letting Hackers in the Side Door

Ryan Holmes is CEO of Hootsuite, a firm that helps companies manage all of their social media marketing in one place. Holmes' Twitter account was hacked, but not by stealing his Twitter username and password. Holmes and his security team believe hackers got in via Foursquare, another social media app he had authorized to connect to his Twitter account (so that his Foursquare posts would automatically post to Twitter). App authorizations, which drive traffic and automatic cross-platform postings, are widely used. Holmes explains, "Most social platforms have multiple points of access through partner services—just think of how many apps, from Airbnb to WordPress, integrate into Facebook, for instance."

What's the solution? Go into your settings and revoke app authorizations for accounts you no longer use and for those with recent security issues. Don't let hackers in the "side door."

Chip and PIN Credit Cards Produce Surge in Online Credit Card Fraud

Thanks to chip and PIN credit cards (which require users to enter secret numbers into credit card scanners), credit card fraud in stores (known as "card present" transactions) is decreasing. On the other hand, online credit card fraud ("card-not-present" transactions) is up to 15%.

Tokenization, the use of one-time purchase codes, is an effective way to reduce online credit card fraud. Apple Pay, for example, uses secure fingerprint scanners on iPhones and iPads to authenticate your purchase approval. This is done on the device, not online, so it can't be hacked. Then, a one-time code or token is sent authorizing funds. Retailers—and hackers—never see your credit card, just the one-time token.

Tokenization has been possible in many brick-and-mortar and online stores for several years. But now, it also works on personal computers. Clicking the Apple Pay or Android Pay button in your computer's web browser securely prompts a fingerprint scan on your phone. When you scan your fingerprint, a secure token is sent to the retailer and the purchase on your computer's web browser is approved.

How long will revoking app authorizations and tokenization work? Stephen Coggeshall, chief analytics and science officer at identity-theft protection company Lifelock says, "Fraud is kind of like squeezing Jell-O. Stop it one place and it migrates to somewhere else."[27]

tuthelens/Shutterstock.com

Viral Marketing The Internet has also proven to be an effective medium for **viral marketing**, which attempts to get customers to communicate a firm's message to friends, family, and colleagues. Despite its name, legitimate viral marketing doesn't use computer viruses. Effective viral marketing campaigns can generate a substantial increase in consumer awareness of a product. As a strategy, viral marketing isn't unique to the Internet; even before the World Wide Web, marketers were adept at buzz marketing, the use of unconventional (and usually low-cost) tactics to stimulate word-of-mouth product promotion. But the Internet has made it possible

> **viral marketing** An Internet marketing strategy that tries to involve customers and others not employed by the seller in activities that help promote the product.

> The average American spends 50 minutes on Facebook every day.
>
> —FACEBOOK CEO, MARK ZUCKERBERG

(Whoa!)

A 2016 Smith & Forge ad featured an elite athlete who disguised himself as an old man, then showed up muscle-bound bodybuilders at Santa Monica's Muscle Beach. The ad quickly went viral, gaining more than 27 million views in 24 hours and 54 million views in less than a week.

to implement such strategies in clever ways and reach large numbers of people very quickly. Many viral marketing campaigns in recent years have used social media such as Facebook, Twitter, and YouTube.

Handling Payments Electronically B2C e-commerce normally requires customers to pay at the time the purchase is made. Clearly, the use of cash and paper checks isn't practical. In the United States, most payments in the B2C market are made by credit cards. To ensure that such transactions are secure, most sites transmit payment information using a secure socket layer (SSL) protocol. You can tell if a site on which you're doing business is using SSL in two fairly subtle ways. First, the URL will begin with https:// instead of simply http://. (Note the "s" after http in the address.) Also, a small closed lock icon will appear near the bottom of your web browser (the exact location depends on the specific browser you are using).

Another common method of payment is to use a **cybermediary**—an Internet-based company that specializes in the secure electronic transfer of funds. By far the best-known cybermediary is PayPal, which also operates Braintree (to handle companies' web and mobile payments), Venmo (to make payments to friends), and Xoom (to enable U.S. residents to send money, reload phones, and pay bills in 56 different countries). According to figures on its website, in 2016, PayPal had 197 million active accounts that handled $354 billion in annual payments in 203 countries and 100 currencies.[28]

There are two kinds of **electronic bill presentment and payment**, which is another form of electronic payments. With biller-direct, consumers receive email reminders and then pay their bills at the company website. But with bank-aggregator billing, you use the "bill-pay" service at your bank to automatically pay your monthly bills.

16-4b Using Information Technology in the B2B Market

B2B e-commerce generally requires a very different approach than B2C e-commerce. Not only do B2B transactions often involve much larger sums of money and require much more negotiation than B2C transactions, they also often result in long-term supply chain relationships that require close collaboration between buyer and seller. A *supply chain* is the network of organizations and activities needed to obtain materials and other resources, produce final products, and get those products to their final users. Forging tight and efficient supply chain relationships can be a key competitive advantage for firms.

An effective supply chain requires close coordination between a company and its suppliers. Information technology can provide the tools needed to foster this coordination. For example, the extranets we mentioned earlier can allow suppliers to keep tabs on their customers' inventories, thus anticipating when to make shipments of parts or materials.

Many firms involved in B2B business also make use of specialized Internet sites, called **e-marketplaces**, which provide a platform for businesses in specific B2B markets to interact. These platforms generally allow buyers in the market to solicit bids by posting requests for proposals (RFPs) on the site. Suppliers can then respond by bidding on RFPs that interest them.

E-marketplaces provide a number of advantages to their participants:

- Compared to older methods, they reduce the time, effort, and cost of doing business for both buyers and sellers.

- Because they are Internet-based, they don't require expensive dedicated connections between firms, so even smaller firms can afford to participate.

- They enable sellers and buyers to contact and negotiate with a large number of market participants on the other side of the market, thus maximizing the chances of finding good matches.

cybermediary An Internet-based firm that specializes in the secure electronic transfer of funds.

electronic bill presentment and payment A method of bill payment that makes it easy for the customer to make a payment, often by simply clicking on a payment option contained in an email.

e-marketplace A specialized Internet site where buyers and sellers engaged in business-to-business e-commerce can communicate and conduct business.

They often provide additional services—beyond simple trade—that allow firms to exchange information and collaborate, thus forging tighter supply chain relationships.

In recent years, many firms have begun using another information technology known as **radio frequency identification (RFID)** to improve the efficiency of their supply chains. This technology stores information on a microchip and transmits it to a reader when it's within range—up to several thousand feet. The chips can be extremely small—some are difficult to see with the naked eye—and can be embedded in most types of tangible products. The chips are usually powered by the energy in the radio signal sent by the reader, so they don't need batteries.

RFID chips can store and transmit all sorts of information, but most commonly they transmit a serial number that uniquely identifies a product, vehicle, or piece of equipment. This type of information can be used to help track goods and other resources as they move through a supply chain. Deliveries can be recorded automatically and electronically without the need to make manual records. The chips also can make taking inventory much quicker and simpler, since the items in stock identify themselves to readers. And the chips can be used to reduce the chances of theft. The results of these advantages are lower costs and a more efficient supply chain.

Disney World uses RFID chips in MagicBands, bracelets that serve as park visitors' admission tickets, hotel keys, and credit cards at shops and restaurants. Because they contain RFID chips, Disney can track where the park is busy and then add more staff at those rides and restaurants. And with the ability to shift staff precisely where they are most needed, Disney World can now easily admit 3,000 more people to the park each day. One example is faster food service. For instance, after park guests Jason and Melissa McInerney entered their lunch orders into a touch screen kiosk, the screen directed them to sit wherever they liked. Just after they sat down at

vetkit/Shutterstock.com

> "Getting information off the Internet is like taking a drink from a fire hydrant."
>
> —MITCHELL KAPOR, ENTREPRENEUR, FOUNDER OF LOTUS DEVELOPMENT CORPORATION

their table, their food server brought them their sandwiches and drinks. Thanks to the MagicBands, the kitchen and their server knew what they ordered and where they were sitting.[29]

16-5 CHALLENGES AND CONCERNS ARISING FROM NEW TECHNOLOGIES

So far, we've concentrated on the benefits of advances in information technology—and it's clear that these benefits are enormous. But rapid technological advances also pose challenges and create opportunities for abuse. These problems affect businesses, their customers, and their employees, as well as the general public. In this section, we'll look at annoyances, security concerns, and legal and ethical issues.

16-5a Malware

The Internet—for all its advantages—creates the possibility that unwanted files and programs may land on your computer. In many cases, this happens without your knowledge, much less your permission. Some of these files and programs are relatively benign (even useful), but others can create major problems. Software that is created and distributed with malicious intent is called **malware** (short for "malicious software"). Spyware, computer viruses, and worms are all examples of malware.

Spyware is software that installs itself on your computer without permission and then tracks your computer behavior in some way. It might track which Internet sites you visit to learn more about your interests and habits in order to send you targeted ads. Or, more alarmingly, it might log every keystroke (thus capturing

radio frequency identification (RFID) A technology that stores information on small microchips that can transmit the information when they are within range of a special reader.

malware A general term for malicious software, such as spyware, computer viruses, and worms.

spyware Software that is installed on a computer without the user's knowledge or permission to track the user's behavior.

Ransomware: Holding Your Data Hostage

Ransomware is a type of malware that works similarly to a traditional kidnapping—complete with a ransom demand. But instead of kidnapping a person, ransomware takes the data on your computer, your servers, and your systems hostage by encrypting it. Encrypted files look like scrambled code to the computer, so while the data are still there, they are virtually useless. Only after paying up do you receive a unique decryption key to unlock your files so that they're usable again.

Writing in the *New York Times*, Alina Simone described how CryptoWall ransomware locked down her mother's computer: "Your files are encrypted. To get the key to decrypt files you have to pay 500 USD." If she didn't pay within the week, the ransom would double to $1,000. The same thing happened at Houston-based Advantage Benefit Solutions, where ransomware spread from one computer to the company's file server and backup systems, encrypting the firm's financial and customer information. This time the ransom note said, "Pay $400 within 72 hours to unlock the data."

Much like other malware, ransomware can be activated by clicking on mail attachments from unknown senders. These attackers often try to make their emails look as normal as possible, even disguising their names and their attachments. California-based real estate agent Kevin Simpson was waiting for a client to email him some documents when he clicked on an email attachment that looked as if it had been sent by Federal Express (it had not). This activated ransomware that encrypted the data on his PC and his company's servers. On Apple computers, hackers embedded ransomware into the Transmission app, which ironically is used to encrypt sensitive files to protect them when sending them from one place to another. Anyone using the hacked Transmission app found their files encrypted and inaccessible, as well as a demand to pay $400 to regain access to the data.

Should you pay the ransom? If your backup data are current and easily retrieved, then probably not. But many people and firms are deciding it's just easier to pay. Advantage Benefits Solutions' Mark Stefanick says, "They set the ransom so low that, as violated as I felt and as much as I wanted to fight, at the end of the day I realized I can pay and get back to work."[30]

enterlinedesign/Shutterstock.com

---

passwords, account numbers, and user names to accounts as you enter them), allowing someone to steal your identity. Some spyware even goes beyond passive watching and takes control of your computer, perhaps sending you to websites you didn't want to visit.

Computer viruses are programs that install themselves on computers without the users' knowledge or permission and spread—sometimes very rapidly—by attaching themselves to other files that are transferred from computer to computer. Viruses are often attached to emails, instant messages, or files downloaded from the Internet. Some viruses are little more than pranks, but others can cause great harm. They can erase or modify data on your hard drive, prevent your computer from booting up, or find and send personal information you've stored on your computer to people who want to use it for identity theft. **Worms** are similar to viruses, except that they are independent programs that can spread across computer networks without being attached to other files.

computer virus Computer software that can be spread from one computer to another without the knowledge or permission of the computer users by attaching itself to emails or other files.

worm Malicious computer software that, unlike viruses, can spread on its own without being attached to other files.

How can you protect yourself from spyware, viruses, and worms? Take these commonsense steps:

- Perform regular backups. This can come in handy should a virus tamper with (or erase) the data on your hard drive. Store the backed-up data in a separate place.

- Install high-quality antivirus and antispyware software, and keep it updated. (Today's Internet security software usually has the ability to download and install updates automatically, but they may need to be configured to do so.)

- Update your operating system regularly so that any security holes it contains are patched as soon as possible.

- Don't open email messages or attachments if you don't know and trust the sender.

- Don't download files from websites unless you are sure they are legitimate. And be sure to read the licensing agreement of any programs you install—especially those of freeware you download from the Internet. The wording of these agreements will often indicate if other programs (such as spyware) will be installed along with your free program.

16-5b Spam, Phishing, and Pharming

Spam refers to unsolicited commercial emails, usually sent to huge numbers of people with little regard for whether they are interested in the product or not. It's estimated that 60% or more of all email traffic is spam. Some spam messages contain malicious email attachments that download ransomware to unknowing users' computers (see "Ransomware: Holding Your Data Hostage").[31] Spam filters are highly effective at screening the 205 billion emails sent every day. Google's Gmail, for instance, claims that that only 0.1% of spam gets past its spam filters to Gmail users. If all spam filters were that effective (they aren't), 205 million spam messages would still be delivered to email inboxes every day. And unfortunately, that would mean more false positives, whereby a spam filter wrongly screens out legitimate email messages (Gmail's false positive rate is 0.05%).[32]

The U.S. Congress enacted the Controlling the Assault of Non-Solicited Pornography and Marketing Act (usually called the CAN-SPAM Act) in 2003. This act requires senders of unsolicited commercial email to label their messages as ads and to tell the recipient how to decline further messages. It also prohibits the use of false or deceptive subject lines in email messages. But the rapid increase in the amount of spam in recent years suggests this law hasn't been an effective deterrent.

Phishing is another common use of spam. Phishers send email messages that appear to come from a legitimate business, such as a bank, credit card company, or retailer. The email attempts to get recipients to disclose personal information, such as their social security or credit card numbers, by claiming that there is a problem with their account—or sometimes simply that the account information needs to be verified or updated. The messages appear authentic; in addition to official-sounding language, they often include official-looking corporate logos. The email also usually provides a link to a website where the recipient is supposed to log in and enter the desired information. When the victims of the scam click on this link, they go to a website that can look amazingly like the site for the real company—but it's not. It's a clever spoof of the site where the phishers collect personal information and use it to steal identities. Exhibit 16.4 shows a highly sophisticated phishing attack using Google's Gmail service. A number of Gmail users received a convincing email that looked like it was sent from someone they knew. When the users clicked on an attachment included with the email (in the form of a Google-looking graphic), a new tab opened in their web browsers (Gmail is largely web-based). As Exhibit 16.4 shows, the Gmail users were then prompted to sign into their accounts again "to continue to Gmail." While careful email users would have noticed that the URL begins "data:text/html,https://accounts.google.com" instead of "https:accounts.google.

Exhibit 16.4
Gmail Phishing Example

Source: M. Maunder, "Wide Impact: Highly Effective Gmail Phishing Technique Being Exploited," Wordfence, January 12, 2017, https://www.wordfence.com/blog/2017/01/gmail-phishing-data-uri/#officialupdate, accessed February 13, 2017.

com," many Gmail users were fooled. When they mistakenly signed into their accounts again, what they were actually doing was giving hackers their Google account passwords. The result was that their Gmail and Google accounts were soon, if not immediately, compromised.[33]

One of the best ways to avoid such scams is to be skeptical of email requests for personal information; reputable businesses almost *never* ask you to divulge such information via email. Also, never click on a link in an email message to go to a website where you have financial accounts—if the message is from a phisher, that link is used to direct you to the fake site (as in the Gmail phishing attack shown in Exhibit 16.4) where the phishers hope that you'll mistakenly enter your username and password. Instead, use a link to the site that you've bookmarked, or type in the link to the real site yourself.

Not content with phishing expeditions, some scam artists have now taken to **pharming**. Like phishing, pharming uses fake websites

spam Unsolicited email advertisements usually sent to very large numbers of recipients, many of whom may have no interest in the message.

phishing A scam in which official-looking emails are sent to individuals in an attempt to get them to divulge private information such as passwords, usernames, and account numbers.

pharming A scam that seeks to steal identities by routing Internet traffic to fake websites.

Selfies and Face ID: The End of the Password?

The top five most popular passwords are: 123456, password, 12345678, qwerty, and 12345 (for those who found 12345678 too complex!). With easily guessed passwords like these, used across multiple accounts, no wonder companies are requiring new, longer passwords containing numbers, capital letters, and special characters every six months. Ironically, those security measures, which strengthen passwords and make them more difficult to hack, also make it more likely that users will forget their passwords (unless they use password management software).

Because weak passwords are the equivalent of leaving the keys in an unlocked car, some companies are doing away with passwords all together. For instance, Mastercard is replacing passwords (forgotten by more than half of its users each week) with selfie photos. When Mastercard's Identity Check system authenticates that the picture it just received from your phone

matches the digital photo it has of you in its system, it okays your Mastercard purchase.

Apple's iPhone X goes even further, using "Face ID" as the unique password for unlocking your phone and its secured banking and shopping apps. Look at the iPhone X screen and 30,000 invisible, infrared dots scan and compare a 3D face pattern to the infrared face scan created when the user set up Face ID. When they match, the iPhone and its apps unlock. With Face ID, only one face in a million is similar enough to unlock your phone, which is 20 times better than Touch ID based on fingerprints.[34]

Rus S/Shutterstock.com

---

to trick people into divulging personal information. But pharming is more sophisticated and difficult to detect than phishing because it doesn't require the intended victim to click on a bogus email link. Instead, it uses techniques to redirect Internet traffic to the fake sites. Thus, even if you type in the *correct* URL for a website you want to visit, you still might find yourself on a very realistic-looking pharming site. One way to check the validity of the site is to look for the indications that the site is secure, such as the https:// in the URL and the small closed lock icon mentioned earlier.[35]

Computers aren't the only devices plagued by these threats and annoyances. Cell phone users are facing increasing problems with spam delivered via text messaging. Even more alarming, some scammers have found ways to take their phishing expeditions to cell phones—a practice known as "SMiShing," or SMS phishing. One typical SMiShing ploy is to use text messaging to entice cell phone users to visit the scammer's fake website asking you to provide personal or financial information.[36]

16-5c Hackers: Break-Ins in Cyberspace

hacker A skilled computer user who uses his or her expertise to gain unauthorized access to the computer (or computer system) of others, sometimes with malicious intent.

firewall Software and/or hardware designed to prevent unwanted access to a computer or computer system.

Hackers are skilled computer users who have the expertise to gain unauthorized access to other people's computers. Not all hackers intend to do harm, but some—called "black hat hackers" (or "crackers")—definitely have malicious

intent. They may attempt to break into a computer system to steal identities or to disrupt a business.

Protecting against hackers requires individuals and businesses to be security conscious. Some of the precautions used against hackers, such as making frequent backups, are similar to those used to protect against viruses. Another key to protecting against hackers is to make sure that all data transmitted over a network are encrypted, or sent in encoded form that can only be read by those who have access to a key. Security experts also suggest that organizations restrict access to computer resources by requiring users to have strong passwords. According to Microsoft, strong passwords are at least 14 characters in length; include a mix of letters, numbers, and special characters; and don't contain any common words or personal information.[37] MIT researchers have found, however, that making passwords longer by "adding a word or two" is more effective than adding numbers or upper case letter. Their finding is that longer passwords are safer because they're much more difficult to crack.[38]

Unfortunately, users struggle to remember strong passwords, so they reuse one or two passwords. "Having the same password for everything is like having the same key for your house, your car, your gym locker, your office," says PayPal's Michael Barrett. With password management software, such as 1Password, users memorize just one master password. 1Password works with any browser on any computer, tablet, or smartphone. It generates unique, strong passwords, synchronizes encrypted data across devices, and autofills forms so you don't have to manually enter personal information or passwords.[39]

Firewalls are another important tool to guard against hackers and other security threats. A firewall uses

It's Thursday afternoon. You're off to the airport to join your spouse on a flight for a three-day weekend. As you come around a blind curve, you see four kids, none older than ten, walking on the shoulder of the road. Just as you drift toward the center line to avoid them, a semi-truck coming in the opposite direction suddenly swerves into your lane. What do you do? Swerve left into oncoming traffic? Stay in your lane, head on with the truck? Swerve right and hope you avoid the kids?

This classic scenario is based on the "Trolley Problem," in which the driver of a runaway trolley with no brakes has two choices: take the left track where only one person will be run over by the trolley, or take the right track where five people will be run over.

With self-driving cars in development, the Trolley Problem suddenly matters a great deal to car manufacturers who must program their cars to instantaneously make such decisions.

Mercedes-Benz's head of driver assistance and safety programs, Christoph von Hugo, says, "You could sacrifice the car, but then the people you've saved, you don't know what happens to them after that in situations that are often very complex, so you save the ones you know you can save. If you know you can save at least one person, at least save that one. Save the one in the car. If all you know for sure is that one death can be prevented, then that's your first priority."[40]

What Do YOU Think?

- If you were part of the programming team, do you program the self-driving car to save the children? Or the car passenger?

- What if there was only one child along the road, but five car passengers? What if the passengers were elderly?

- What do you think of Mercedes' subsequent clarification that "neither programmers nor automated systems are entitled to weight the value of human lives"?

---

hardware or software (or sometimes both) to create a barrier that prevents unwanted messages or instructions from entering a computer system. As threats from spyware, hackers, and other sources have developed, the use of firewalls has become commonplace.

16-5d Ethical and Legal Issues

Information technology raises a number of legal and ethical challenges, such as the need to deal with privacy issues and to protect intellectual property rights. These issues are controversial and don't have simple solutions.

Personal Privacy Firms now have the ability to track customer behavior in ways that were never before possible. This has advantages for you because it allows firms to offer better, more personalized service. But all this extra information comes at the expense of your privacy. Does the fact that firms know so much about your preferences and behavior make you a bit nervous?

Does it bother you that your email messages lack confidentiality? When you send an email, it could be stored on several computers: your personal computer, the server of your email provider, the server of your recipient's provider, and your recipient's own computer. If you send the email from your company's system, it's also likely to be stored when the company backs up its information. If you thought that deleting an email message from your

own computer erased it permanently and completely, you need to think again.

The list of other ways in which information technology can erode your personal privacy is long and getting longer. For example, RFID chips are now embedded in U.S. passports and in many states' driver's licenses. Some privacy experts are concerned that such chips will make it easy for government organizations to track individuals. One reason government officials gave for embedding RFID chips in passports and driver's licenses was to make it harder for criminals and terrorists to forge IDs. But in 2009, a hacker publicly demonstrated the ability to read the information in these chips from a distance of several yards, leading to fears that identity thieves could use similar techniques to obtain personal information and perhaps even create convincing copies of these important identification documents. Encryption and protective sleeves, however, can prevent unauthorized scanning. Furthermore, today's RFID chips use one-time transactions codes, which means that the number skimmed by a hacker is of limited value. And many card companies have replaced RFID chips with much more secure computer chip and PIN systems, making hacking that much more difficult.[41] The result is that thieves are more likely to successfully steal your actual ID or passport the old-fashioned way.[42]

The bottom line is that there's no simple way to solve privacy concerns. Privacy is an elusive concept, and there is no strong consensus about how much privacy is enough.

A growing trend in intellectual property crime is the illegal use of Internet protocol television (IPTV) to stream pay-per-view events, movies, and live television channels. Some black market retailers have even begun selling set-top boxes preconfigured to play illegal streams.

Kaspars Grinvalds/Shutterstock.com

Protecting Intellectual Property Rights

Intellectual property refers to products that result from creative and intellectual efforts. There are many types of intellectual property, but we'll focus on forms of intellectual property that are protected by copyright law, such as books, musical works, computer programs, video games, and movies. Copyright law gives the creators of this property the exclusive right to produce, record, perform, and sell their work for a specified time period.

intellectual property Property that is the result of creative or intellectual effort, such as books, musical works, inventions, and computer software.

Piracy of intellectual property occurs when someone reproduces and distributes copyrighted work without obtaining permission from—or providing compensation to—the owner of the copyrighted material. When piracy becomes widespread, creators of intellectual property receive much less income for their efforts. This can substantially reduce their incentive to continue developing creative material.

The Business Software Alliance estimates that, globally, 39% of all business software installed on personal computers in 2015 was pirated, resulting in the loss of over $52 billion in revenue to software companies. In several smaller countries, including Moldova, Armenia, and Zimbabwe, the rate of piracy was over 85%. Among larger nations, the piracy rate in China exceeded 70%, while in India it was 58%. The good news is that the piracy rate was much lower in the United States at 17%. But given the huge size of the U.S. software market, even this relatively low rate of piracy still resulted in losses of over $9.1 billion in revenue for software companies. Faced with such a widespread problem, many software publishers have become very aggressive at prosecuting firms and individuals engaged in software piracy.[43]

Music studios, video game developers, and motion picture producers also face significant problems with piracy.[44] Furthermore, software piracy costs companies 1.2 billion hours and $25 billion per year to identify, repair, and recover pirated software that is usually infected with malware designed to steal your personal and financial information.[45]

Given how lucrative piracy can be, it's unlikely that this problem will go away anytime soon. You can expect the companies hurt by these practices to continue aggressively prosecuting pirates and to work on new technologies that make pirating digital media more difficult.

THE BIG PICTURE

Information technology plays a vital role in virtually every aspect of business operations. For instance, marketing managers use information technology to learn more about customers, reach them in novel ways, and forge stronger relationships with them—as we showed in our discussion of Web 2.0. Operations managers use RFID technologies to coordinate the movement of goods within supply chains and to keep more accurate inventory records. And financial managers use IT to track financial conditions and identify investment opportunities. Managers in all areas of a business can use decision support systems to improve their decision making. They also can apply techniques such as data mining to obtain interesting new insights hidden in the vast streams of data that flow into their companies.

Cloud computing represents the newest and one of the most exciting new approaches to how companies acquire and utilize IT resources. The use of cloud-based resources has the potential to not only lower costs and increase flexibility but also significantly magnify computation power. If cloud computing can overcome concerns about security and stability, it is likely to continue growing in popularity, which could result in significant changes to the role IT departments play within their organizations.

The rapid changes in IT in recent years—especially those related to the rise of the Internet as a business venue—have opened up exciting new commercial opportunities. But these changes have also created a host of legal and ethical challenges and security questions. One thing is certain: business organizations that find ways to leverage the advantages of new IT developments while minimizing the accompanying risks are most likely to enjoy competitive success.

Information Technology Support Specialist

Responsible for installing and configuring software, responding to employee and customer issues within the ticket management system, interacting with sales, engineering, and product managers to address complex customer issues, escalating relevant problems to appropriate functional and management teams, contributing potential technical workarounds, and acting as a technical expert for IT solutions within a global IT team. The ideal candidate has a bachelor's degree in computer science or information technology, at least one year of experience with Windows and Unix/Linux administrative services, web services, configuration and release management, possesses strong analytical, problem solving, and customer communication skills, and is self-motivated and works effectively with little instruction.

STUDY TOOLS **16**

LOCATED AT BACK OF THE TEXTBOOK

☐ Rip-Out Chapter Review Card

☐ Gain unique perspectives on key concepts with new concept videos in the e-book

☐ Increase your comprehension with online homework and quizzes

☐ Study with existing flashcards and make your own

17 | Operations Management:
Putting It All Together

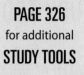

LEARNING OBJECTIVES
After studying this chapter, you will be able to:

17-1 Define operations management and describe how the role of operations management has changed over the last five decades

17-2 Discuss the key responsibilities of operations managers

17-3 Describe how operations managers face the special challenges posed by the provision of services

17-4 Explain how changes in technology have revolutionized operations management

17-5 Describe the strategies operations managers have used to improve the quality of goods and services

17-6 Explain how lean and green practices can help both the organization and the environment

Remember to visit
PAGE 326
for additional
STUDY TOOLS

17-1 OPERATIONS MANAGEMENT: PRODUCING VALUE IN A CHANGING ENVIRONMENT

Operations management is concerned with managing all of the activities involved in creating value by producing goods and services and distributing them to customers. When operations managers do their job well, their firms produce the *right* goods and services in the *right* quantities and distribute them to the *right* customers at the *right* time—all the while keeping quality high and costs low. Obviously, the decisions of operations managers can have a major impact on a firm's revenues and its costs, and thus on its overall profitability.

operations management
Managing all of the activities involved in creating value by producing goods and services and distributing them to customers.

efficiency Producing output or achieving a goal at the lowest cost.

17-1a Responding to a Changing Environment

The practice of operations management has changed dramatically over the past half century. New technologies, shifts in the structure of the economy, challenges posed by global competition, and concerns about the impact of production on the environment have fueled this revolution. Let's begin by identifying the key changes that have characterized the practice of operations management over the last five decades.

From a Focus on Efficiency to a Focus on Effectiveness To operations managers, **efficiency** means producing a product at the *lowest cost*. For example, passenger planes make money in the air, not sitting at the airport gate. So airlines strive to be as efficient as possible when "turning" planes. This means unloading the arriving passengers and luggage as quickly as possible, and then loading the departing passengers and luggage equally quickly. Ground crews must also hook the plane up to airport power and air conditioning, refuel the jet, and restock food and beverages before the plane can get back in the air. Turning planes efficiently is so critical to profitability that American Airlines awards each of its 113,000 employees a bonus of $150 if the company finishes among the top three airlines in key on-time rankings.[1]

Effectiveness means producing products that *create value* by providing customers with goods and services that offer a better relationship between price

> "Nothing is less productive than to make more efficient what should not be done at all."
>
> —PETER F. DRUCKER

> "Success is simple. Do what's *right*, the right way, at the right time."
>
> —ARNOLD H. GLASOW, AMERICAN PSYCHOLOGIST

and perceived benefits. In other words, effectiveness means finding ways to give customers more for their money—while still making a profit. Technological advances create value by allowing the development of faster, cheaper products with more features and functionality every year. For example, a 1998 desktop computer with 4MB (yes, megabytes, not gigabytes) of memory, a 720MB hard drive, a 14-inch VGA screen (640x480 resolution), and a bubble jet printer (4 pages per minute) would cost $3,225 in 2017 dollars. But today, a Dell desktop computer with 8GB of memory, a 1TB hard drive, a 23-inch HD monitor (1920x1080 resolution), and a wireless printer/scanner (20 pages per minute) costs just $600 at Best Buy. In

effectiveness Using resources to create value by providing customers with goods and services that offer a better relationship between price and perceived benefits.

other words, for just 18.6% of the cost of the 1998 computer package, today's consumer gets a 1,456 times larger hard drive, 256 times more memory, a 64% larger monitor that's much easier on the eyes, and a much cheaper, higher definition printer that is five times as fast. That's giving customers more for their money![2]

In the 1960s, the focus of operations management was mainly on efficiency. The goal was to keep costs low so the firm could make a profit while keeping prices competitive. In today's highly competitive global markets, efficiency remains important. But operations managers now realize that keeping costs (and prices) low are only part of the equation. Customers usually buy goods that offer the best value—and these aren't always the same as the goods that sell for the lowest price. A product that offers better features, more attractive styling, and higher quality may provide more value—and attract more customers—than a product with a lower price. Thus, today's operations managers have broadened their focus to look at benefits as well as costs.

From Goods to Services

Goods are tangible products that you can see and touch. *Durable goods* are expected to last three years or longer; examples include furniture, cars, and appliances. *Nondurable goods*, such as toothpaste, apples, and paper towels, are used up more quickly and are often perishable. **Services** are activities that yield benefits but don't directly result in a physical product. Examples include legal advice, entertainment, and medical care. Goods are consumed, while services are experienced.

In the 1960s, the U.S. economy was a manufacturing powerhouse, with more than a third of its labor force employed in the goods-producing sector. But over the last five decades, the American economy has experienced a fundamental shift away from the production of goods and toward the provision of services. By the beginning of 2017, less than 14% of the nonfarm labor force worked in the goods-producing sector. By contrast, employment in the service sector had risen to 86% of the labor force.[3]

From Mass Production to Mass Customization

Fifty years ago, one common production strategy was to keep costs low by producing large quantities of standardized products. The goal of this *mass production* strategy was to achieve reductions in average cost by taking

goods Tangible products.

services Intangible products.

advantage of specialization and the efficient use of capital. But today's technologies allow many firms to pursue *mass customization*—the production of small quantities of customized goods and services that more precisely meet the needs of specific customers—with very little increase in costs. Starbucks, for example, claims that there are 87,000 different drink combinations that a customer can order. Health reporter Julie Beck writes, "You've got your non-fat milk, full-fat milk, soy milk, and coconut milk; espresso shots; all the different flavored syrups, some of which are sugar-free; whipped cream; iced, hot, or "extra hot" if you've got a Kevlar tongue; different sizes; different roasts of coffee; and on and on and on."[4] Sophie Egan, program director at the Culinary Institute of America, says, "Mass customization [is] a desire within our hyper industrialized food system to have something that feels like it meets my personal taste profile. We have access to customized and personalized food experiences at the restaurant level, at the fast casual level, and at the packaged food level and it has only increased."[5]

From Local Competition to Global Competition

For the first 25 years after World War II, American firms dominated key markets. This strength was based partly on the fact that the United States possessed a rich base of natural resources, a growing and increasingly well-educated labor force, an excellent infrastructure, and the strong incentive system inherent in a market economy. But it also reflected the fact that the production facilities and infrastructure in many European and Asian nations had been severely damaged during the war.

By the early 1970s, the economies of Japan, Germany, and other war-ravaged nations had been rebuilt, with many of their major companies boasting efficient new production facilities with state-of-the-art technology. In addition, many Japanese firms had adopted new techniques that greatly improved the quality of their products. With lower labor costs, impressive technology, and world-class quality, these foreign producers quickly began to take market share from American firms. In more recent years, firms in Korea, India, and China have also become formidable competitors.

From Simple Supply Chains to Complex Value Chains

Over the last five decades, the increasingly competitive and global nature of markets has brought about major changes in how firms produce and distribute their goods and services. Many supply chains today span multiple organizations located in

Ikea: World Class Operations Management

When it comes to operations management, global home furnishings retailer Ikea is in a class by itself. Year after year, Ikea's products are better—and less expensive. Its Lack table, which cost $25 in 1985 ($56 adjusted for inflation), is only $10 today! Marty Marston, a public relations manager at Ikea, says, "On average, the prices would go down, from year to year, 1 percent overall." How does Ikea do it? Volume discounts, vertical integration, and products that meet customers' needs.

Being the world's largest wood furniture producer gives Ikea leverage. When Ikea guarantees its 978 suppliers (in 50 countries) huge production contracts, they in turn give Ikea huge volume discounts on pricing. How much does Ikea produce? To give you some idea, 7,689,600 units of the best selling Billy book cases are produced each year, or roughly 15 per minute. With its huge production volumes, Ikea's costs are significantly lower than those of its competitors'.

Vertical integration occurs when a firm develops the capability to carryout processes previously performed by its suppliers or distributors, or when it buys those external companies. Ikea uses 530 million cubic feet of wood each year—roughly 1% of the world's annual supply of lumber. To reduce costs and ensure access to sustainable wood, Ikea has begun vertically integrating its lumber supplies by buying forests in Romania, Bulgaria, Estonia, Lithuania, and Latvia.

A significant part of operations management is designing products that meet customers' needs. While Ikea has always designed products for tight living spaces (such as fold-up tables, sofas, and beds), it is now having to redesign many of

its products to accommodate modern apartment spaces, which have shrunk worldwide by 20% since 2001. Ikea tests new product ideas in a 600 square foot, 2-room apartment in Sweden. After living in the test apartment for 2 weeks with his three sons, Swede Robin Williams said, "The apartment felt much bigger than mine, which is actually 20 square meters bigger."

Ikea former-CEO Peter Agnefjäll says, "We're guided by a vision to create a better everyday life for the many people. That is what steers us, motivates us— that is our role. We feel almost obliged to grow."[6]

ValeStock/Shutterstock.com

many different countries. The shift from a cost perspective to a value perspective has led operations managers to extend their view beyond the traditional supply chain to encompass a broader range of processes and organizations known as a *value chain*.

From Exploiting the Environment to Protecting the Environment
In the 1960s, many operations managers viewed the natural environment as something to exploit. The emphasis on keeping costs low made it tempting to dispose of wastes as cheaply as possible—often by dumping them into rivers, lakes, or the atmosphere. But the serious consequences of environmental pollution became increasingly apparent. Operations managers at socially responsible companies responded by adopting a variety of green practices to produce goods and services in more environmentally responsible ways. Lisa Jackson, Apple's vice president of environment, policy, and social

initiatives, says, "If we had our preference, we'd just be able to say, 'We want 100 percent green power everywhere we use power.' The best would be if we could run every one of our stores, every one of our data centers, every office complex, every building we have, on 100 percent renewable—and if we didn't have to spend a whole bunch of our time and energy figuring out how to get that done." But since large sources of renewable energy are scarce, Apple made a long-term commitment to renewable energy by paying First Solar $848 million to buy half of the energy produced at its California Flats solar farm for 25 years.[7]

Exhibit 17.1 summarizes the discussion of the key ways in which operations management has changed over the last five decades. We'll look at these changes in greater detail as we move through this chapter. But first let's take a look at the some of the key tasks operations managers perform.

Exhibit 17.1
Operations Management: Five Decades of Change

Characteristics of Operations Management in 1962	Factors Promoting Change	Characteristics of Operations Management in 2016
• Focus on Minimizing Costs • Production of Goods • Mass Production • Simple Supply Chains • Exploit the Environment	• Improvements in Production and Information Technologies • Rise of Global Competition and Global Opportunities • Recognition of Quality as a Source of Competitive Advantage • Adoption of Marketing Perspective and Customer Focus • Recognition of Serious Environmental Problems	• Focus on Creating Value • Provision of Services • Mass Customization • Complex Value Chains • Sustain the Environment

17-2 WHAT DO OPERATIONS MANAGERS DO?

Understanding the marketing definition of *product* plays a pivotal role in understanding what operations managers do. A product consists of all of the tangible and intangible features (sometimes called the *customer benefit package*) that create value for consumers by satisfying their needs and wants. For example, when you purchase a car made by General Motors, you not only get the physical automobile, you also get (among other things) a warranty and (for many models) up to three years of OnStar services.[8] Likewise, when an airline purchases a Boeing passenger jet, it can include training in the purchase. Boeing trains pilots, mechanics, and flight crews on six continents with 80 full-flight simulators.[9]

Marketing research typically determines which features a product should include to appeal to its target customers. Although operations managers don't normally have the primary responsibility for designing these goods and services, they provide essential information and advice during the product-design process, especially regarding the challenges and constraints involved in creating actual products on time and within budget.

Once the actual goods and services are designed, operations managers must determine the processes needed to produce them and get them to the customer. A **process** is a set of related activities that transform inputs into outputs, thus adding value. Once these processes are designed, operations managers also play a key role in determining where they will be performed, what organizations will perform them, and how the processes will be organized and coordinated.

The most obvious processes are those directly involved in the production of goods and services. But there are many other processes that play necessary "supporting roles." For example, purchasing and inventory management processes ensure that the firm has an adequate supply of high-quality materials, parts, and components needed to produce the goods without delays or disruptions.

Let's take a closer look at some of the functions that operations managers perform to move goods and services from the drawing board to the final user.

17-2a Process Selection and Facility Layout

Once a product is designed, operations managers must determine the best way to produce it. This involves determining the most efficient processes, deciding the best sequence in which to arrange those processes, and designing the appropriate layout of production and distribution facilities. Well-designed processes and facility layouts enable a firm to

process A set of related activities that transform inputs into outputs, thus adding value.

Operations managers oversee the processes needed to produce products and get them to customers, including inventory control, project scheduling, and managing value chains.

produce high-quality products effectively and efficiently, giving it a competitive advantage. Poorly designed processes can result in production delays, quality problems, and high costs.

There are several ways to organize processes. The best approach depends on considerations such as the volume of production and the degree of standardization of the product.

- Firms often use a *product layout* when they produce goods that are relatively standardized and produced in large volumes. This type of layout organizes machinery, equipment, and other resources according to the specific sequence of operations that must be performed. The machinery used in this type of layout is often highly specialized, designed to perform one specific task *very* efficiently. One classic example of a product layout is an assembly line, where the product being produced moves from one station to another in a fixed sequence, with the machinery and workers at each station performing specialized tasks. Services that provide a high volume of relatively standardized products also use flow-shop processes. For example, fast-food restaurants often use a simple product layout to prepare sandwiches, pizzas, or tacos in a standard sequence of steps.

"The other part of outsourcing is this: It simply says where the work can be done outside better than it can be done inside, we should do it."
—ALPHONSO ROY JACKSON, FORMER U.S. SECRETARY OF HOUSING AND URBAN DEVELOPMENT

- A *process layout* is used by many firms that need to produce small batches of goods that require a degree of customization. This approach arranges equipment according to the type of task performed. For example, in a machine shop, all of the drills may be located in one area, all of the lathes in another area, and all of the grinders in yet another. Unlike assembly lines and other product layouts, a process layout doesn't require work to be performed in a specific sequence; instead, the product can be moved from one type of machinery to another in whatever sequence is necessary. Thus, process layouts can be used to produce a variety of products without the need for expensive retooling. But this flexibility sometimes comes at the cost of longer processing times and more complex planning and control systems. Also, because the machinery and equipment used in a process layout is usually more general-purpose in nature and may be used to produce a greater variety of goods, the process layout requires workers to be more versatile than those employed in a product layout.

- A *cellular layout* falls between the product layout and the process layout. It groups different types of machinery and equipment into self-contained cells. A production facility might have several cells, each designed to efficiently produce a family of parts (or entire products) that have similar processing requirements. Like an assembly line, the product moves from one station in the cell to the next in a specific sequence. However, unlike most assembly lines, cells are relatively small and are designed to be operated by a few workers who perform a wider array of tasks than assembly-line workers.

- A *fixed position layout* is used for goods that must be produced at a specific site (such as a building or a dam) or that are so large and bulky that it isn't feasible to move them from station to station (such as a ship or commercial airplane). Even some services, such as concerts or sporting events that are performed at a specific location, use this approach. In a fixed position layout, the good or service stays in one place, and the employees, machinery, and equipment are brought to the

EXHIBIT 17.2 FACTORS THAT AFFECT LOCATION DECISIONS

General Location Factors	Examples of Specific Considerations
Adequacy of Utilities	Is the supply of electricity reliable?
	Is clean water available?
Land	Is adequate land available for a facility?
	How much does the land cost?
Labor Market Conditions	Are workers with the right skills available?
	How expensive is labor?
Transportation Factors	Is the location near customers and suppliers?
	Is appropriate transportation nearby?
Quality-of-Life Factors	What is the climate like?
	Are adequate healthcare facilities available?
Legal and Political Environment	Does the local government support new businesses?
	What are the local taxes, fees, and regulations?

fixed site when needed during various stages of the production process.

17-2b Facility Location

There is an old saying in real estate that the three most important factors determining the value of a property are "location, location, and location." Location also matters to operations managers because the location of facilities strongly affects the efficiency and effectiveness of an organization's processes.

For some types of facilities, the location decision is dominated by one key consideration. A coal mine, for instance, must be located where there's coal. But for many other types of facilities, the decision is more complex. Exhibit 17.2 identifies some key factors that operations managers evaluate when they decide where to locate a facility, but the importance of each factor varies depending on the specific industry. For instance, many service firms place primary interest on locating close to their customers while manufacturing firms are often more concerned about the cost and availability of land and labor and access to highways, railways, and port facilities. For example, clothing designers like VF, Calvin Klein, and Tommy Hilfiger have begun locating new manufacturing facilities in Africa thanks to its growing infrastructure, lower wages, strong government support, and a free trade agreement with the US—not to mention rising wages and production costs in China and other parts of Asia. Fassill Tadesse, president of the Ethiopian Textile an Garment Manufacturers

inventory Stocks of goods or other items held by organizations.

Association, says of the shift, "Investors are coming here from Sri Lanka, Bangladesh, China, India and Turkey."[10]

17-2c Inventory Control: Knowing When to Hold 'Em

Inventories are stocks of goods or other items held by an organization. Manufacturing firms usually hold inventories of raw materials, components and parts, work in process, and finished goods. Retail firms don't normally hold work in process or raw materials, but they do hold inventories of the finished goods they sell as well as basic supplies that they need.

Deciding how much inventory to hold can be a real challenge for operations managers because increasing (or decreasing) the amount of inventory involves both benefits and costs. For example, the benefits of holding larger inventories include:

- **Smoother Production Schedules:** A candy maker might produce more candy than it needs in August and September and hold the excess in inventory so that it can meet the surge in demand for Halloween treats without investing in more production capacity.

- **Protection against Stock-Outs and Lost Sales:** Holding larger inventories reduces the chance of stock-outs and lost sales due to supply disruptions or unexpected surges in demand.

- **Reduced Ordering Costs:** Every time a company orders supplies, it incurs paperwork and handling costs. Holding a larger average inventory reduces

EXHIBIT 17.3 ACTIVITIES INVOLVED IN PRESENTING A PLAY

Activity	Description	Immediate Predecessor(s)	Estimated Completion Time (Weeks)
A	Select Play	None	2
B	Select Cast	A (must know play to know what roles are available)	4
C	Design Sets	A (must know play before sets can be designed)	4
D	Design Costumes	A (must know play to determine what costumes are needed)	5
E	Buy Materials for Sets	C (set must be designed to determine types and quantities of materials needed to build it)	2
F	Buy Materials for Costumes	D (costumes must be designed before materials for costumes are determined)	2
G	Build Sets	E (must have materials in order to build the sets)	4
H	Make Costumes	B, F (must have materials in order to make the costumes, and must know actors' sizes to ensure that costumes fit)	6
I	Initial Rehearsals	B (actors must be selected for each role before they can rehearse their parts)	2
J	Final (Dress) Rehearsal	G, H, I (costumes and sets must be completed, and initial rehearsals performed, before the final rehearsal can occur)	1
K	Perform Play (end of project)	J	N/A

the number of orders the firm must make and thus reduces ordering costs.

But holding larger inventories involves costs as well as benefits:

- **Tied-Up Funds:** Items in inventory don't generate revenue until they're sold, so holding large inventories can tie up funds that could be better used elsewhere within the organization.

- **Additional Holding Costs:** Bigger inventories require more storage space, which can mean extra costs for heating, cooling, taxes, insurance, and more.

- **Increased Risk:** Holding large inventories exposes the firm to the risk of losses due to spoilage, depreciation, and obsolescence.

Operations managers determine the optimal amount of inventory by comparing the costs and benefits associated with different levels of inventory. After several years of stocking additional inventory in their stores for online buyers to pick up, brick-and-mortar retailers like Home Depot, Target and Walmart are aggressively reducing in-store inventories. Home Depot's senior vice president of supply chain, Tom Shortt, says, "Get comfortable with days of inventory, not weeks." The risk, of course, is stock-outs—not having products that customers need.

To minimize stock-outs, Home Depot is changing supplier delivery schedules. For example, it might move from five truck deliveries two-days-a-week to two truck deliveries five-days-a-week. Finally, with less in-store inventory, store employees can quickly put new shipments directly onto lower store shelves instead of the slower, more expensive process of putting excess product inventory on top shelves via ladders and forklifts.[11]

17-2d Project Scheduling

Projects such as constructing a new production facility, developing a new commercial airliner, or filming a movie are complex and expensive endeavors. It's vital to monitor them carefully to avoid major delays or cost overruns. The **critical path method (CPM)** is one of the most important tools that operations managers use to manage such projects.

We can illustrate the basic idea behind this tool by looking at a simple example in which a theater company wants to stage a play. Exhibit 17.3 presents the steps involved in this project.

> **critical path method (CPM)** A project-management tool that illustrates the relationships among all the activities involved in completing a project and identifies the sequence of activities likely to take the longest to complete.

Exhibit 17.4
A CPM Network for Staging a Play

Notice that Exhibit 17.3 identifies **immediate predecessors** for all of the activities except activity A. *Immediate predecessors* are activities that must be completed before another activity can begin. For example, it is clear that the cast for the play cannot be determined until the play has been selected, so activity A (selecting the play) is an immediate predecessor to activity B (selecting the cast). Similarly, since sets can't be built without lumber, paint, and other materials, activity E (buying materials for the sets) is an immediate predecessor for activity G (building the sets).

Using the Critical Path Method to Focus Efforts Now look at Exhibit 17.4, which is a CPM network for the theater project. This network shows how all of the activities in the theater project are related to each other. The direction of the arrows shows the immediate predecessors for each activity. Notice that arrows go from activities B (selecting the cast) *and* F (purchasing material for the costumes) to activity H (making the costumes). This indicates that *both* of these activities are immediate predecessors for activity H—the costumes can't be made without material, and they must be made in the correct sizes to fit the actors. But also notice that no arrow

links activities B and C. This shows that these are independent activities; in other words, the theater company doesn't have to select the cast before it designs the sets (or vice versa).

We can use Exhibit 17.4 to illustrate some basic concepts used in CPM analysis. A *path* is a sequence of activities that *must be completed in the order specified by the arrows* for the overall project to be completed. You can trace several paths in our example by following a series of arrows from start to finish. For example, one path is A → B → I → J → K, and another path is A → C → E → G → J → K.

The **critical path** consists of the sequence of activities that takes the longest to complete. A *delay in any activity on a critical path is likely to delay the completion of the entire project.* Thus, operations managers watch activities on the critical path very carefully and take actions to help ensure that they remain on schedule. We've shown the critical path for the theater project (A → D → F → H → J → K) with red arrows on our diagram.

Distinguishing between the critical path and other paths can help operations managers allocate resources more efficiently. Activities that aren't on the critical path can be delayed without causing a delay in the overall completion of the project—as long as the delay isn't too great. In CPM terminology, these activities have *slack*. When operations managers see delays in critical path activities, they may be able to keep the project on track by diverting manpower and other resources from activities with slack to activities on the critical path.

immediate predecessors
Activities in a project that must be completed before some other specified activity can begin.

critical path The sequence of activities in a project that is expected to take the longest to complete.

17-2e Designing and Managing Value Chains

Perhaps the most important function of operations management is the design and management of value chains. A **value chain** is the network of relationships that channels the flow of inputs, information, and financial resources through all of the processes directly or indirectly involved in producing goods and services and distributing them to customers.

An organization's value chain clearly includes its supply chain, which consists of the organizations, activities, and processes involved in the physical flow of goods, from the raw materials stage to the final consumer. In fact, some organizations use the terms *value chain* and *supply chain* interchangeably. But a value chain is a broader concept; in addition to the supply chain, it includes activities and processes involved in *acquiring customers*—such as contract negotiations and customer financing—as well as activities and processes involved in *keeping customers* by providing services after the sale, such as performing warranty repairs, offering call center assistance, and helping customers recycle used goods. In a value chain, the main focus is on the customer; in contrast, the supply chain is more oriented toward traditional production relationships.[12]

One of the most important issues that operations managers examine when they design value chains is the trade-off between vertical integration and outsourcing. **Vertical integration** occurs when a firm attempts to gain more control over its value chain by either developing the ability to perform processes previously performed by other organizations in the chain or by acquiring those organizations. Netflix streams TV shows and movies to customers around the world, accounting for nearly a third of all downstream Internet traffic. To avoid bottlenecks, reduce how long it takes content to get to customers, and maximize the quality of its streamed data, Netflix installed hundreds of server boxes in the data warehouses of local Internet providers around the world. When asked whether Netflix should be more vertically integrated, Netflix CEO Reed Hastings answered, "no…[not with] the data transmission layer. We're a global company. We work with about 600 Internet service providers around the world. Netflix is an application on top of the Internet." On the other hand, Netflix began producing its own TV shows several years ago, such as *House of Cards*, *Orange is the New Black*, the *Unbreakable Kimmy Schmidt*, and nearly 50 others. According to Hastings, That is a form of vertical integration that's been very successful for us."[13]

Outsourcing is essentially the opposite of vertical integration; it involves arranging for other organizations to perform value chain functions that were previously performed internally. In recent years, the trend in value chain design has been to rely more on outsourcing and less on vertical integration. Outsourcing allows a firm to shed functions it doesn't perform well in order to focus on its areas of strength. It also frees people, money, and other resources that had been tied up in the outsourced activities, allowing these resources to be employed in more profitable ways. ways. Apple, based in Cupertino, California, designs but does not manufacture the iPads, iPhones, Mac computers, watches, and AirPods that it sells. Apple's products are manufactured in an outsourced global supply chain. The manufacture of the home button for the iPhone starts in Changsha, China where the top sapphire covers are made. Six hundred miles away in China's Jiangsu province, the sapphire covers are bonded to metal trim rings. Those combined parts are shipped to Taiwan, 1,000 miles away, to be attached to chips made in Shanghai, China and Touch ID sensors made in Europe. Final additions include button switches from Japan, flex circuits from Taiwan, and a 1,500 mile trip to Japan to be sealed and welded. Completed home buttons are finally installed in iPhones in Zhengzhou, China. Total travel distance for the parts involved—12,000 miles.[14]

Even when a firm decides to perform processes itself, it still faces a choice: Should it perform these functions domestically, or should it offshore these activities? **Offshoring** means moving processes previously performed domestically to a foreign location. It is important to realize that offshoring is *not* the same thing as outsourcing processes to other organizations. Offshoring doesn't require outsourcing; a firm often offshores processes by directly investing in its *own* foreign facilities. Similarly, outsourcing doesn't require a firm to go offshore; activities can be outsourced to other *domestic* firms. Despite this distinction, many firms have combined these approaches by hiring organizations in other countries to perform some of the processes that they previously performed at their own domestic facilities.

It is also worth noting that offshoring can go in both directions. Just as American firms offshore processes to other countries, some foreign companies offshore some of their processes to the United States. For example, several Japanese, European, and Korean automakers now have extensive design and production facilities in the United States.

One common reason for offshoring by U.S. firms

value chain The network of relationships that channels the flow of inputs, information, and financial resources through all of the processes directly or indirectly involved in producing goods and services and distributing them to customers.

vertical integration Performance of processes internally that were previously performed by other organizations in a supply chain.

outsourcing Arranging for other organizations to perform supply chain functions that were previously performed internally.

offshoring Moving production or support processes to foreign countries.

Offshoring involves moving activities previously performed domestically to a foreign location.

is to take advantage of less expensive labor. But other factors can also play a role. Land and other resources also may be less expensive in developing nations than in the United States. And some foreign governments, eager to attract American investments, may offer financial incentives or other inducements. In addition, many foreign markets are growing much more rapidly than the relatively mature U.S. market. Firms often find it advantageous to locate production facilities close to these rapidly growing markets.

While foreign outsourcing can often reduce costs, it also can complicate value chains and create coordination problems. And it can expose the firm to certain types of risks. When a firm outsources important functions, it may have to entrust others in its value chain with confidential information and intellectual property, such as copyrighted material or patented designs. These strategic assets have less legal protection in some countries than in the United States, so providing access to foreign firms may increase the risk that the firm's intellectual property will be pirated or counterfeited. This issue has been of greatest concern when firms have outsourced some of their supply chain functions to organizations in China.[15]

Given the trend toward offshoring and outsourcing, value chains (and the supply chains at their core) have become increasingly complex, often involving many different organizations and processes located in many different countries. Modern operations managers rely on sophisticated *supply*

chain management software* to streamline the communications among supply chain participants and to help them plan and coordinate their efforts.

The newest versions of **enterprise resource planning (ERP)** software take supply chain management to its highest level. ERP initially focused on integrating the flow of information among *all* aspects of a single organization's operations—accounting, finance, sales and marketing, production, and human resources. But the newest versions go beyond a single organization to help manage activities along an entire supply chain or value chain. The common information system makes it easier for organizations throughout the chain to communicate and coordinate their activities.

ERP systems do have some drawbacks. They are complex, expensive, and difficult to implement, and they require users to learn new ways to enter and access data. Productivity can actually fall until users become accustomed to these new methods. But despite these challenges, ERP systems have become very popular. And they continue to evolve and take advantage of new technologies. One of the newest developments is the arrival of Web-based ERP systems that can be "rented" from online providers—a strategy that reduces the need to invest in new hardware and software. The use of Web-based ERP services is an example of cloud computing discussed in Chapter 16.[16]

 17-3

IMPLICATIONS OF A SERVICE-BASED ECONOMY: RESPONDING TO DIFFERENT CHALLENGES

Exhibit 17.5 illustrates how services differ from tangible goods. These differences present a number of challenges to service providers. One key challenge arises because customers often participate in the provision of services, which means that service providers have less control over how the process is carried out, how long it takes to complete, and whether the result is satisfactory. For instance, the accuracy of a doctor's diagnosis depends on how honestly and completely the patient answers the doctor's questions. And the amount of time the doctor spends with each patient will depend on the seriousness of the problem and the complexity of the diagnosis and treatment.

17-3a Designing the Servicescape

Because of the interaction between customers and service providers, the design of service facilities often must take the experiences of the participants into account. A **servicescape** is the environment in which the customer and service provider interact. A well-designed servicescape

enterprise resource planning (ERP) Software-based approach to integrate an organization's (and in the sophisticated versions, a value chain's) information flows.

servicescape The environment in which a customer and service provider interact.

EXHIBIT 17.5 | DIFFERENCES BETWEEN GOODS AND SERVICES

Goods	Services
Are tangible: They have a physical form and can be seen, touched, handled, etc.	Are intangible: They can be "experienced," but they don't have a physical form.
Can be stored in an inventory.	Must be consumed *when* they are produced.
Can be shipped.	Must be consumed *where* they are provided.
Are produced independently of the consumer.	Often require the customer to be actively involved in their production.
Can have at least *some* aspects of their quality determined objectively by measuring defects or deviations from desired values.	Intangible nature means quality is based mainly on customer perceptions.

can have a positive influence on the attitudes and perceptions of both the customer and those who provide the service. A poor servicescape can have the opposite effect.[7]

The design of servicescapes centers on three types of factors: ambience; functionality; and signs, symbols, and artifacts.

- *Ambience* refers to factors such as decor, background music, lighting, noise levels, and even scents. For example, massage therapists often use low light, soothing background music, and pleasant scents to create a relaxing atmosphere for a massage.

- *Functionality* involves how easy it is for the customers to move through the facility and find what they are looking for.

- *Signs, symbols,* and *artifacts* convey information to customers and create impressions. Obviously, signs like "Place Your Order Here" and "Pick Up Your Order Here" provide useful information that helps consumers maneuver through the service encounter. But other signs and symbols can be used to create favorable impressions.

Taco Bell has significantly redesigned its servicescape to create new Taco Bell Cantina restaurants. These new locations are designed to compete with more upscale Chipotle Mexican restaurants. There are no drive-throughs at the Cantinas, which makes them easier to locate in city and urban locations. Menus, ordering, and payment are all digitized. Local architecture influences the interior and exterior design, thus differentiating each Cantina's look. Green design is emphasized with reclaimed materials and LED lighting. Open design

kitchens permit customers to see their food prepared as it is ordered. In addition to the standard Taco Bell menu, Cantinas will serve tapas-style shareable appetizers and alcohol (beer, wine, sangria, and frozen drinks).[17] R. J. Hottovy, a financial analyst at investment data and consultancy firm Morningstar, says, "Consumers have shown a willingness to pay up for fast-casual brands such as Chipotle, Five Guys, and Panera. I think this is Taco Bell attempting to play in that space."[18]

17-3b How Big Is Big Enough?

Because services are intangible and often must be experienced at the time they are created, service providers can't produce the service in advance and store it to meet temporary surges in demand. This can create challenges for operations managers because the demand for many types of services varies significantly, depending on the season, the day of the week, or the time of day. During peak lunch and dinner hours, popular restaurants tend to be very busy—often with crowds waiting to get a table. The same restaurants may be nearly empty during the mid-afternoon or late at night. Given such fluctuations in demand, the selection of *capacity*—the number of customers the service facility can accommodate per time period—becomes a crucial consideration.

If the capacity of a service facility is too small, customers facing long waits during periods of peak demand may well take their business elsewhere. But a facility large enough to handle peak capacity is more expensive to build; costs more to heat, cool, and insure; and may have substantial excess capacity during off-peak periods. Operations managers must weigh these drawbacks against the ability to handle a larger number of customers during peak hours.

Many service firms try to minimize this trade-off by finding ways to spread out demand so that big surges don't occur. One way to do this is to give customers an incentive to use the service at off-peak times. Many bars and restaurants have "happy hours" or "early-bird specials." Similarly, movie theaters have lower prices for matinée showings, and resort hotels offer reduced rates during their off seasons.

 17-4

THE TECHNOLOGY OF OPERATIONS

Now let's take a close look at how technology has revolutionized operations management. Some of the new technologies involve the increasing sophistication of machinery and equipment. Others involve advances in software and information technology. The impact of these technological advances is greatest when the automated machinery is directly linked to the new software running on powerful new computers.

17-4a Automation: The Rise of the Machine

For the past half century, one of the biggest trends in operations management has been increased **automation** of many processes. Automation means replacing human operation and control of machinery and equipment with some form of programmed control. The use of automated systems has become increasingly common—and increasingly sophisticated.

Automation began in the early 1950s with primitive programmed machines. But in recent decades, **robots** have taken automation to a whole new level. Robots are reprogrammable machines that can manipulate materials, tools, parts, and specialized devices in order to perform a variety of tasks. Some robots have special sensors that allow them to "see," "hear," or "feel" their environment. Many robots are mobile and can even be guided over rugged terrain.

Robots offer many advantages to firms:

- They often perform jobs that most human workers find tedious, dirty, dangerous, or physically demanding.

- They don't get tired, so they can work very long hours while maintaining a consistently high level of performance.

- They are flexible; unlike old dogs, robots *can* be taught new tricks because they are reprogrammable.

automation Replacing human operation and control of machinery and equipment with some form of programmed control.

robot A reprogrammable machine that is capable of manipulating materials, tools, parts, and specialized devices in order to perform a variety of tasks.

computer-aided design (CAD) Drawing and drafting software that enables users to create and edit blueprints and design drawings quickly and easily.

computer-aided engineering (CAE) Software that enables users to test, analyze, and optimize their designs.

Robots are most commonly used for tasks such as welding, spray painting, and assembling products, but they can do many other things ranging from packaging frozen pizza to disposing of hazardous waste. Robot use is expanding in manufacturing. Foxconn, which makes the iPhone for Apple, today uses robots to do the job of 60,000 factory workers. However, robots are also beginning to make a difference in restaurants and fast food chains as well.[19] In China, where restaurants are struggling with labor shortages and rising wages, robots are used for everything from slicing noodles to delivering food, to stopping at tables so that guests can clear their plates onto the robot's food and plate tray. Jiao Songhui, a manager at Beijing restaurant Fragrant Island Robot-Sliced Noodles, says, "Robot-sliced noodles are tastier . . . the texture is softer, more even."[20] Zume Pizza in Mountain View, California uses robots to spread sauce on pizza (employees add the other ingredients) and then put the pizzas into 850-degree ovens.[21] Cafe X in San Francisco combines digital ordering with robot baristas to create made-to-order lattes, cappuccinos, and other espresso-based coffee drinks.[22] Are we likely to see more robots and automation in restaurants? Yes. In China, labor savings allow restaurants to fully pay for the cost of a robot in 1.3 years.[23] McDonald's former CEO Ed Rensi said, "It's cheaper to buy a $35,000 robotic arm than it is to hire an employee who is inefficient, making $15 an hour bagging French fries."[24]

17-4b Software Technologies

Several types of software have become common in operations management, and as the processing power of computers has improved, the capabilities of these applications have become increasingly sophisticated. Some of the most common examples include:

- **Computer-aided design (CAD)** software provides powerful drawing and drafting tools that enable users to create and edit blueprints and design drawings quickly and easily. Current CAD programs allow users to create 3-D drawings.

- **Computer-aided engineering (CAE)** software enables users to test, analyze, and optimize their designs through

asharkyu/Shutterstock.com

"Customers don't expect you to be perfect. They do expect you to fix things when they go wrong."

—DONALD PORTER, VICE PRESIDENT, BRITISH AIRWAYS

computer simulations. CAE software can help engineers find and correct design flaws *before* production.

- **Computer-aided manufacturing (CAM)** software takes the electronic design for a product and creates the programmed instructions that robots and other automated equipment must follow to produce that product as efficiently as possible.

Today, **computer-aided design** and **computer-aided manufacturing** software are often combined into a single system, called **CAD/CAM**. This enables CAD designs to flow directly to CAM programs, which then send instructions directly to the automated equipment on the factory floor to guide the production process.

When a CAD/CAM software system is integrated with robots and other high-tech equipment, the result is **computer-integrated manufacturing (CIM)**, in which the whole design and production process is highly automated. The speed of computers, the ability to reprogram computers rapidly, and the integration of all these functions make it possible to switch from the design and production of one good to another quickly and efficiently. CIM allows firms to produce custom-designed products for individual customers quickly and at costs almost as low as those associated with mass-production techniques, thus allowing firms to pursue the strategy of mass customization mentioned at the beginning of this chapter.

17-5 FOCUS ON QUALITY

Almost everyone agrees that quality is important. But the concept of quality is tough to define—even expert opinions differ. For our purposes, we'll adopt the view that quality is defined in terms of how well a good or service satisfies customer preferences.

Why is quality so important? First, better quality clearly improves effectiveness (creates value) since consumers perceive high-quality goods as having greater value than low-quality goods. But finding ways to increase quality can also lead to greater efficiency because the cost

of poor quality can be very high. When a firm detects defective products, it must scrap, rework, or repair them. And the costs of poor quality can be even higher when a firm *doesn't* catch defects before shipping products to consumers. These costs include handling customer complaints, warranty repair work, loss of goodwill, and the possibility of bad publicity or lawsuits. In the long run, firms often find that improving quality reduces these costs by more than enough to make up for their investment.

These ideas aren't especially new. W. Edwards Deming, viewed by many as the father of the quality movement, first proposed the relationship between quality and business success in the early 1950s. His ideas, which came to be known as the *Deming Chain Reaction*, are summarized in Exhibit 17.6.

17-5a Waking Up to the Need for Quality

In the years immediately after World War II, most Japanese goods had a reputation for being cheap and shoddy. But during the 1950s, many Japanese firms sought advice from Deming and other U.S. quality gurus. They learned to view quality improvement as a *continuous* process that was the responsibility of all employees in the organization. During the 1950s and 1960s, the quality of Japanese goods slowly but steadily improved.

By the early 1970s, many Japanese firms had achieved a remarkable turnaround, with quality levels that exceeded those of companies in most other countries (including the United States) by a wide margin. This improved quality was a major reason why Japanese firms rapidly gained global market share, often at the expense of American firms that had faced little competition in years immediately following World War II.

17-5b How Global Firms Responded to the Quality Challenge

When operations managers realized how far they trailed the Japanese in quality, they made a real effort to

computer-aided manufacturing (CAM) Software that takes the electronic design for a product and creates the programmed instructions that robots must follow to produce that product as efficiently as possible.

computer-aided design/computer-aided manufacturing (CAD/CAM) A combination of software that can be used to design output and send instructions to automated equipment to perform the steps needed to produce this output.

computer-integrated manufacturing (CIM) A combination of CAD/CAM software with flexible manufacturing systems to automate almost all steps involved in designing, testing, and producing a product.

Mining 24 Hours a Day without People?

Using automation and robotics to replace human operation and control of equipment with some form of programmed control is one of the biggest trends in operations management today. Robots often perform jobs that people find tedious, dirty, dangerous, or physically demanding. And it's hard to think of a more dirty, dangerous, or physically demanding job than mining.

Australian mining company Rio Tinto uses self-driving trucks as big as two-story buildings to move iron ore. Not only are the driverless trucks 15% less expensive to run (drivers earn $250,000 per year), they're also more consistent in terms of operations, such as lining up for loading and unloading. Rio Tinto's Rob Atkinson says, "All those places where you could lose a few seconds or minutes by not being consistent add up." Thanks to these benefits and improved safety, Atkinson says, "We're going to continue as aggressively as possible down this [automation] path."

And with iron ore prices at $60 per ton (down from $136 in 2013 and $180 in 2011), Rio Tinto does need to cut costs. Which is why the company's *The Mine of the Future* program is driving automation into every corner of the business. The program's two main goals are "achieving massive productivity gains" and "extracting more ore from complex ore bodies."

Next steps include further development of an automated drilling system and AutoHaul, a fully automated long-distance rail system (1,056 miles) that will deliver iron ore to export terminals. By not having to change drivers, AutoHaul will add two hours of running time per day, yielding an immediate 8.3% increase in shipping volume.[25]

Plaksina/Shutterstock.com

---

change their ways. Like the Japanese a few decades earlier, business leaders began to view improving the quality of their goods and services as a key to regaining international competitiveness.

Total Quality Management The first result of this newfound emphasis on quality was the development of an approach called **total quality management (TQM)**, better known as TQM. There are several variations, but all versions of TQM share the following characteristics:

- **Customer Focus:** TQM recognizes that quality should be defined by the preferences and perceptions of customers. Since airlines started charging passengers to check luggage, travelers have brought more carry-on bags onto planes. Overhead bins don't have enough storage for every passenger, so frustrated late-boarding passengers often have to check their bags at the gate and pick them up at baggage claim. Customer and airline complaints prompted Boeing engineer Brent Walton to redesign overhead bins to make them tall enough to flip bags onto their narrower sides. With overhead bins now able to hold six bags rather than four, Boeing's bestselling 737-900 can now accomodate 174 roll-aboard bags—almost enough for the plane's 181 passengers.[26]

- **Emphasis on Building Quality throughout the Organization:** TQM views quality as the concern of every department and every employee.

- **Empowerment of Employees:** Most TQM programs give teams of workers the responsibility and authority to make and implement decisions to improve quality.

- **Focus on Prevention Rather than Correction:** The TQM philosophy agrees with the old adage that an "ounce of prevention is worth a pound of cure." Thus, TQM pursues a strategy of preventing mistakes that create defects. While Ikea is known for its low-cost self-assembly furniture, it is also strongly focused on quality. Karen Hopkinson Pflug, Ikea's global head of quality, says she was hired "to look at quality from the supply chain right through the customer satisfaction point of view. We're focusing on quality as an enabler of lower cost."[27] Under her leadership, Ikea runs two product testing labs, one in Sweden and the other in China. Together, these labs

total quality management (TQM) An approach to quality improvement that calls for everyone within an organization to take responsibility for improving quality and emphasizes the need for a long-term commitment to continuous improvement.

Exhibit 17.6

The Deming Chain Reaction: Improved Quality Helps the Business's Bottom Line

Improve quality

Costs decrease because of less rework, fewer mistakes, fewer delays and snags, and better use of time and materials

Productivity improves

Capture the market with better quality and lower price

Stay in business

Provide jobs and more jobs

conduct more than 100,000 quality tests each year. The focus of this product testing, Pflug says, is to "get things right at the very beginning."[28]

■ **Long-Run Commitment to Continuous Improvement:** TQM requires firms to adopt a focus on making improvements in quality a way of life.

In many cases, firms using TQM attempt to reduce defects by using **poka-yokes**—the Japanese term for "mistake proofing." Poka-yokes are simple procedures built into the production process that either prevent workers from making mistakes or help workers quickly catch and correct mistakes if they do occur. One simple example of a poka-yoke would be providing assembly workers with "kits" that contain exactly enough parts to complete one unit of work at a time. If the worker completes an assembly and sees a part left over, it's clear that a mistake has been made, and he or she can correct it on the spot.[29]

The Move to Six Sigma During the 1990s, another approach to quality improvement, known as **Six Sigma**, became increasingly popular. Six Sigma shares

some characteristics with TQM, such as an organization-wide focus on quality, emphasis on finding and eliminating causes of errors or defects (prevention rather than correction), and a long-term focus on continuous quality improvement. Also like TQM, it relies on teams of workers to carry out specific projects to improve quality. At any given time, a firm may have several Six Sigma projects under way, and the goal of each is to achieve the Six Sigma level of quality.

But Six Sigma differs from TQM in other respects. Unlike TQM, it has a single unifying measure: to reduce defects of any operation or process to a level of no more than 3.4 per million opportunities. Attaining this level of quality represents a rigorous and challenging goal. Six Sigma also differs from TQM in its reliance on extensive (and expensive) employee training and reliance on expert guidance. The techniques used in the Six Sigma approach are quite advanced, and their application requires a high level of expertise.

17-5c Quality Standards and Initiatives

Another way firms try to improve quality is to launch programs designed to achieve certification or recognition from outside authorities. Two common approaches are participation in the Baldrige National Quality Program and seeking certification under the International Organization for Standardization's ISO 9000 standards.

The Baldrige National Quality Program Congress passed the Malcolm Baldrige National Quality Improvement Act of 1987 in an effort to encourage American firms to become more competitive in the global economy by vigorously pursuing improvements in quality and productivity. Winners of the Baldrige Award must demonstrate excellence in seven areas: leadership; strategy; customers; measurement, analysis and knowledge management; workforce; operations; and results.

Firms that participate in the **Baldrige National Quality Program** receive benefits even if they don't win the award. Every participating firm receives a detailed report prepared by expert evaluators

poka-yokes Simple methods incorporated into a production process designed to eliminate or greatly reduce errors.

Six Sigma An approach to quality improvement characterized by very ambitious quality goals, extensive training of employees, and a long-term commitment to working on quality-related issues.

Baldrige National Quality Program A national program to encourage American firms to focus on quality improvement.

At UPS, Orion Refines the Delivery Process for Efficiency

Throughout its history, UPS has studied and dissected the process of package delivery down to the smallest detail. Drivers have long been trained to walk briskly (not run) and avoid left turns (they're less efficient than right turns).

From the receipt of a package to its delivery, having a refined process is critical for UPS. It is the world's largest package delivery company, operating in 200 countries and territories. Its drivers cover 55,000 routes per day in the United States alone.

As the number of routes is increasing, the type of delivery on each route is changing. Previously, UPS focused on commercial deliveries. Drivers would deliver and pick up multiple packages at a single business location. By 2018, however, UPS estimates that half of all deliveries will be residential (one package, one house) thanks to the explosion in e-commerce.

Gagliardilmages/Shutterstock.com

To add further complexity, UPS's "My Choice" service allows customers to choose the time and location of their deliveries. When any of the 12.9 million subscribers to My Choice makes a change in delivery preferences, it affects the route planned by the driver delivering the package. Each driver makes an average of 120 stops each day, so reshuffling deliveries throughout the day for each change wreaks havoc on the driver's schedule and efficiency.

At the same time, the company knows that it can save $50 million per year by reducing each of its routes by an average of just a single mile per day.

Enter ORION (On-Road Integrated Optimization and Navigation). A team of 50 UPS engineers wrote the 1,000-page algorithm that searches for the best possible way for drivers to organize their routes and calculates the most efficient path between a variety of points. Every time a change to a driver's route is needed, ORION considers up to 200,000 options before indicating the best scheduling alternative. ORION then reorganizes the entire route to accommodate the change and maintain efficiency and consistency.

Currently 40% of domestic UPS routes use ORION technology to schedule deliveries. By 2017, UPS expects all 55,000 routes to be using ORION, saving the company $300 million to $400 million annually—even with a few left turns.[30]

---

identifying areas of strength and areas where improvement is needed. Considering the normal fees that high-powered consulting firms charge for similar reports, the information and advice a firm gets for the fee charged to participate in the Baldrige program (which for manufacturing, service, and small businesses is $10,560 to $19,800 in 2017) are a tremendous bargain![31]

ISO 9000 Certification Founded in 1947, ISO is a network of national standards institutes from more than 161 nations that have worked together to develop over 21,000 international standards for a wide array of industries. ISO standards ensure that goods produced in one country will meet the requirements of buyers in another country. This benefits buyers by giving them the ability to purchase from foreign sellers with confidence, thus giving them

> **ISO 9000** A family of generic standards for quality management systems established by the International Organization for Standardization.

a wider array of choices. It also benefits sellers by allowing them to compete more successfully in global markets.[32]

Most of the standards established by the ISO are industry-specific. But in 1987, the ISO developed and published the **ISO 9000** family of standards. The goal of this effort was to articulate an international consensus on good quality-management practices that could be applied to virtually any company. Similar to the other quality initiatives we've discussed, ISO 9000 standards define quality in terms of the ability to satisfy customer preferences and require the firm to implement procedures for continuous quality improvement.

> "Quality is more important than quantity. One home run is much better than two doubles."
>
> —STEVE JOBS, CO-FOUNDER OF APPLE

Drones to the Rescue

Maintaining oil rigs is dangerous. Workers in harnesses attached to safety wires dangle from rigs as high as 40 stories tall as they look for cracks, rusting or broken parts, and nonfunctioning machinery that needs fixing or replacing. According to British Petroleum (BP) technology director Curt Smith, the old way to do maintenance inspections "was to shut everything down, put up scaffolding, have people climb around and see what is going on."

Now, however, the energy industry is saving time, money, and lives by replacing oil rig inspectors with flying drones equipped

think4hotop/Shutterstock.com

with high-definition thermal cameras. Industry analyst Michael Blades says, "Drones can do just about anything the energy companies don't want to send people to do."

During a standard drone inspection, an engineer and a drone operator fly a small drone around the oil rig, mapping the structure in 3D. Chris Blackford, COO of drone inspection company Sky Futures, says, "What we can capture in five days using a drone could take eight weeks with human inspectors." Moreover, inspections can occur without shutting down operation, saving as much as $4 million in otherwise lost production.

While drone operators are needed for more complex operations, automated drones can be used to continuously monitor sites and facilities. So-called boomerang self-piloted drones lift off, fly their routes, capture their data, and then return to their docking stations upload their information and automatically replace used batteries with charged batteries.[33]

There are several standards in the ISO 9000 family, but the most basic—and the only one for which organizations can be certified—is ISO 9001, which specifies the requirements for a quality-management system. (Other ISO 9000 standards are concerned with the documentation, training, and the economic and financial aspects of quality management.) As of 2016, over 1.03 million organizations worldwide had earned ISO 9001 certificates, but the number of U.S. firms with ISO 9001 certification lags that of several other nations. Only about 33,000 U.S. organizations had been certified in 2016, compared to over 292,000 in China and 132,000 in Italy.[34]

 ## 17-6 THE MOVE TO BE LEAN AND GREEN: CUTTING COST AND CUTTING WASTE

Lean production refers to a set of strategies and practices to eliminate waste, which is defined as any function or activity that uses resources but doesn't create value. Eliminating waste can lead to dramatic improvements in efficiency. For example, Louis Vuitton produces some of the most expensive handmade bags and purses in the world. To increase productivity, it switched to teams of 6 to 12 workers who learned to complete multiple production steps. So instead of having

three workers separately gluing, stitching, and finishing the edges of a flap over and over, one worker would do all three steps. Because of that, says CEO Ives Carcelle, "We were able to hire 300 new people without adding a factory."[35]

17-6a Reducing Investment in Inventory: Just-In-Time to the Rescue

One of the hallmarks of lean systems is a tight control on inventories. In part, this reflects recognition of the costs of holding large inventories that we discussed earlier. But the lean approach also offers another reason for minimizing inventories. Large inventories serve as a buffer that enables a firm to continue operations when problems arise due to poor quality, faulty equipment, or unreliable suppliers—making it easier for firms to live with these problems rather than correct them. Advocates of lean production argue that, in the long run, it is more efficient to improve quality, keep equipment in good working order, and develop reliable supply relationships than to continue compensating for these problems by holding large inventories.

Lean manufacturing avoids overproduction and holding large inventories of

lean production
An approach to production that emphasizes the elimination of waste in all aspects of production processes.

finished goods by using **just-in-time (JIT) production** methods. JIT produces only enough goods to satisfy current demand. This approach is called a *pull system* because actual orders "pull" the goods through the production process. The workers at the end of the production process produce just enough of the final product to satisfy actual orders and use just enough parts and materials from preceding stages of production to satisfy their needs. Workers at each earlier stage are expected to produce just enough output at their workstations to replace the amount used by the processes further along in the process—and in so doing they withdraw just the needed amount of parts and other supplies from even earlier processes.

JIT techniques obviously result in very small inventories of finished goods and work in process. But lean firms also hold only small inventories of materials and parts, counting on suppliers to provide them with these items as they need them to meet current demand. In a lean system, *all* organizations in the supply chain use the JIT approach, so that inventories are minimized at each stage. Clearly, this type of system requires incredible coordination among all parts of the supply chain; in fact, the movement toward JIT is a key reason why supply chain management has become so crucial. Spain-based Zara is a global clothing and accessories retailer. Zara's competitive advantage is fast fashion, meaning frequent introductions of new fashions that are made in small batches, delivered quickly to stores, and stocked as just-in-time inventory. It took just 25 days, for example, for a black, high collar women's wrap coat with a metal ring to end up in Zara's flagship store in New York City. The inspiration for the coat started with a Zara designer in Arteixo, Spain talking to store managers. The designer took five days to create a design prototype, which was handed over to a manufacturing pattern maker. Seamstresses at Zara's suppliers worked for 13 days to produce 8,000 coats. Six days were needed for ironing, labeling, quality checks, and transportation from Zara's distribution center in Zaragoza, Spain to the Barcelona airport to New York's JFK airport, and finally to the Zara's Fifth Avenue store. Industry analyst Anne Critchlow says, "Think of Zara not as a brand, but as speedy chameleon that adapts instantly to fashion trends."[36]

JIT does have some potential drawbacks. The most serious problem is that it can leave producers vulnerable to supply disruptions. If a key supplier is unable to make deliveries due to a natural disaster, labor strike, or other problem, the firms further along the supply chain may quickly run out of parts or materials and have to shut down production.

17-6b Lean Thinking in the Service Sector

Employing lean principles in the service sector can be quite a challenge because customers often participate in providing the service. This means a service firm usually has less control over how processes are conducted. But many service firms have benefited from creatively applying lean techniques. Kroger supermarkets used lean thinking to reduce checkout waiting times. Kroger uses Vision, a network of infrared sensors, to count the customers in a store and then determine how many checkout aisles should be opened now and in the next 30 minutes. The system dramatically slashed average checkout times from four minutes a few years ago to just 26 seconds today. As a result, customer satisfaction with checkout speed is up 42%, while sales are up nearly 10%. Kroger former Senior Vice President Marnette Perry said, "There are 7 million shoppers at Kroger stores today—we'll save them 25 million minutes today."[37]

17-6c Green Practices: Helping the Firm by Helping the Environment

Many of today's leading firms have also tried to become "greener" by finding environmentally friendly ways to carry out the processes needed to produce

Elxeneize/Shutterstock.com

Green practices aim to achieve sustainability by finding ways to meet the organization's current objectives while protecting and preserving the environment.

just-in-time (JIT) production
A production system that emphasizes the production of goods to meet actual current demand, thus minimizing the need to hold inventories of finished goods and work in process at each stage of the supply chain.

and distribute their goods and services. Green practices include designing facilities to be more energy efficient; using renewable energy sources such as wind, solar, or geothermal power when possible; making use of recyclable materials; switching to paints, lubricants, cleaning fluids, and solvents that are less harmful to the environment; and even providing labeling to help consumers find out which products are the most environmentally friendly. As part of a commitment to reduce carbon emissions by 50% by 2020, JPMorgan Chase & Co. is replacing 1.4 million lights with LEDs in its 5,300 bank branches. Chase will cut its lighting costs in half and use 184,000 fewer megawatts of electricity each year.[38]

The long-term goal of many green practices is to achieve *sustainability*, which means finding ways to meet the organization's current objectives while protecting and preserving the environment for future generations. One impediment to even greater acceptance of sustainability initiatives is that some sustainability efforts—such as switching to renewable sources of energy—add to costs. But many firms have found that other sustainability efforts can actually benefit the bottom line. A recent study by Aberdeen Group, a well-known technology research firm, found that firms employing best-in-class sustainability practices not only saw an 8% drop in sustainability-related costs but also experienced a 16% increase in customer retention. [39]

In the late 1990s, the International Organization for Standardization developed a set of standards called **ISO 14000**. This new set of standards focuses on environmental management. As with ISO 9000, the term "ISO 14000" actually refers to a family of standards. The broadest of these is ISO 14001. To receive ISO 14001 certification, a firm must:

- demonstrate the ability to identify and control the environmental impact of their activities;

- make a commitment to continually improve their environmental performance; and

- implement a systematic approach to setting environmental targets and to achieving those targets.

It is important to note that ISO 14000 standards do not establish specific goals for environmental performance; doing so would be very difficult, since ISO is intended to be a generic set of standards that apply to all industries, and each specific industry faces different environmental challenges.[40]

ISO 14000 A family of generic standards for environmental management established by the International Organization for Standardization.

THE BIG PICTURE

Operations managers are responsible for "putting it all together" by developing and implementing the processes needed to produce goods and services and distribute them to the target market. Their decisions affect both revenues and costs, going a long way toward determining whether a firm makes a profit or suffers a loss.

The responsibilities of operations managers require them to work closely with other managers throughout their organizations. For example, they must work with marketers and designers to ensure that the desired goods and services move from the drawing board to the final customer on time and within budget. They must work closely with financial managers to ensure that the company invests in the capital goods needed to produce goods and services in the most efficient manner. And they must work effectively with human resource managers to attract and develop workers who possess the knowledge and skills needed to become world-class competitors. Operations managers must even go beyond their own organization and work effectively with the suppliers and distributors who comprise the firm's value chain.

Operations managers must continuously adapt to changes in technology and in competitive conditions. Key challenges in recent years have centered on the need to continuously improve product quality while finding ways to reduce costs and protect the environment. You can expect the goals of becoming ever leaner—and ever greener—to remain a major focus of operations managers in years to come.

Plant Supervisor

Responsible for supervising production and warehouse crews, monitoring and maintaining a safe working environment, timely completion of paperwork and records, keeping lines of communication open between the plant, management, scheduling, and sales, coordinating overtime and reviewing production schedules to make sure each piece of equipment has the appropriate manpower, and cross-training employees for multiple tasks and jobs. The ideal candidate has a bachelor's degree, two to four years of manufacturing experience, strong interpersonal, communication, and team-building skills, good analytical and problem-solving skills, ability to analyze cost performance data to improve operations and reduce costs, and be willing to work evenings, night shifts, weekends, and holidays.

STUDY TOOLS 17

LOCATED AT BACK OF THE TEXTBOOK

☐ Rip-Out Chapter Review Card

☐ Gain unique perspectives on key concepts with new concept videos in the e-book

☐ Increase your comprehension with online homework and quizzes

☐ Study with existing flashcards and make your own

Personal Finance Appendix

Remember to visit

PAGE 340

for additional

STUDY TOOLS

LEARNING OBJECTIVES

After studying this appendix, you will be able to:

A-1 Apply the principles of budgeting to your personal finances

A-2 Identify strategies to help build a sufficient savings

A-3 Explain the importance of using credit wisely

A-4 Discuss key wealth-building principles and the financial instruments that may be part of a wealth-building strategy

Rawpixel.com/Shutterstock.com

Unfortunately, two-thirds of us can't pass a basic financial literacy test (see how well you do on the National Financial Capability Study at http://www.usfinancialcapability.org/quiz.php). Many struggle to calculate simple interest on loans. Only 45% of our parents or guardians taught us how to manage our finances. Only 31% of us have ever been offered the chance to take a class in personal finance. With financial illiteracy so widespread—and growing—it's not surprising that Americans report that money (61%), work (58%), and the economy (50%) are significant sources of stress.[1]

Personal financial management issues affect all of us, young and old alike. How successfully we manage our financial resources affects where we live, how well we can provide for our families, and when (or perhaps even if) we'll be able to retire comfortably. The financial decisions you make and the habits you develop now will affect your personal and financial future. Let's take a look at how budgeting, building your savings, managing your credit, and investing wisely can help you meet your financial goals, and hopefully reduce the money-related stress in your life.

> **budget (personal)** A detailed forecast of financial inflows (income) and outflows (expenses) to determine your net inflow or outflow for a given period of time.

A-1 YOUR BUDGET

One of the first steps in getting control over your financial situation is to develop a **budget**, which is a detailed forecast of your expected cash inflows (income) and cash outflows (expenditures). You can use your budget to develop your financial plan and to monitor your progress toward achieving your financial goals.

A-1a How Do I Get Started?

You can get a good handle on what should be included in your budget by carefully tracking and analyzing all of your financial transactions for several months. This takes discipline and careful record keeping, but once you know where your money comes from and where it goes, you'll have what you need to prepare your budget.

There are many approaches to setting up your budget. If you don't want to build your budget from scratch, you can check out several online personal finance sites that can help you get started.[2] For example, after you link your bank and financial accounts to Intuit's Mint.com, the online and app-based service will help you manage and pay bills, budget, and keep track of your credit score and investments. Northwestern Mutual's Mint Grad (http://

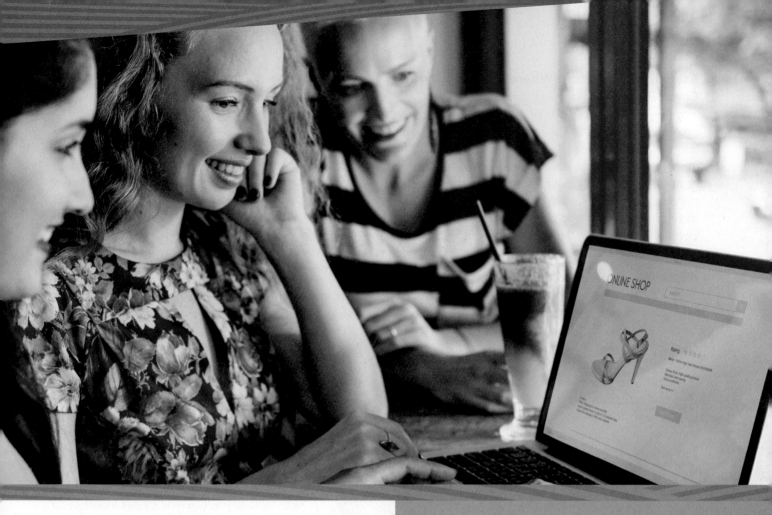

www.themintgrad.org/), developed specifically for college students and recent college grads, uses a four-step process to help young adults master personal finance:

- Learn (budgeting, spending, investing)
- Try it (quizzes, financial calculators, and budget worksheets)
- Plan (setting goals for saving, building positive credit, and paying down student debt)
- Online socializing (reading and discussing blog topics)

MassMutual Financial Group's Society of Grownups (https://www.societyofgrownups.com/) combines a range of online classes, labs (financial calculators), and blogs with face-to face classes and networking events. If you want more bells and whistles—and more support—you can purchase a commercial program such as Quicken, Moneydance, or AceMoney. Basic versions of these programs typically cost $40 to $75 and provide a wide range of features, such as online banking services, financial calculators, and stock quotes. Most also give you the ability to export data into tax preparation software, making tax filing much simpler. And if you prefer to work on the go, most also have corresponding apps for smartphones and tablets.

> "The safe way to double your money is to fold it once over and put it in your pocket."
>
> —FRANK "KIN" HUBBARD, CARTOONIST, HUMORIST, AND JOURNALIST

If you are comfortable with Excel (or other spreadsheet software), another option is to build your own budget. Microsoft's Templates and Themes for Office website (https://templates.office.com) has Excel budget templates for expenses, family budget planning, personal money tracking, college budgeting, and academic club budgeting to help you get started. These templates are generic, so you may want to tweak them to suit your own circumstances. You won't get all of the features provided by the commercial packages, but that isn't necessarily a bad thing. Some people actually find all of the bells and whistles in the commercial applications overwhelming and prefer the straightforward simplicity of a spreadsheet template. Also, the process of "building" the budget yourself may give you a sense of personal satisfaction and a greater appreciation for the budget relationships than you'd get using online sites or commercial software packages.

Assessing Revenues: Where Does My Money Come From? A budget starts with a forecast of your income—the money you bring in. This can come from many different sources. For many people, the paycheck from their job is their primary source of income. But the major source of income for entrepreneurs may be the profits they earn from their businesses. Some people also derive a substantial amount of income from financial investments, such as stocks and bonds, while others earn rental income. Retirees often depend on pensions, Social Security, and private investments for much of their income.

Assessing Expenses: Where Does It All Go?
Once you have identified the amount of income you expect to receive from various sources, you can turn your focus to the spending side of your budget. To set up your budget, you'll need to be very specific about where your money goes. As we've already mentioned, carefully tracking your expenditures over a period of several months can help you identify your spending patterns. Many people who do this are surprised by the habits they uncover. You may find that you're spending a lot more than you thought on video games, music downloads, or clothes. Once you discover your spending patterns, you'll be in a better position to determine the categories of spending to include in your budget and to estimate the amount you'll spend in each category. Mint.com, LearnVest, and YNAB (short for You Need a Budget) stand out as useful expense tracking tools.[3] They link to your financial accounts to track expenses and identify spending trends in various categories such as groceries, bills, clothes, and entertainment. Although Mint.com is free, Learn-Vest charges a $299 set up fee and $19 a month, while YNAB charges $6.99 a month (But anyone can try it free for a month. Students get an

additional 12 months free). Mint.com tracks your spending and suggests budget levels based on that spending (which might not work well if your spending is out of control), but LearnVest also provides a dedicated financial planner and a customized financial plan, while YNAB forces you to assign a spending or savings category for *every* dollar that goes in and out of your hands—and your various accounts. YNAB has you assign budget goals for each category, and then tracks your spending against each budget goal. Though more complicated, YNAB forces you to decide about your spending in order "to be intentional about what you want your money to do before you spend it."[4]

Understanding Your Spending Habits Your expenditures can be classified into discretionary and nondiscretionary categories. The payments you have the most control over are called your **discretionary payments**. Perhaps you like dining out, nightclubbing, or shopping. Perhaps you just have expensive taste in coffee. David Bach, author of *The Automatic Millionaire,* challenges us to look at our "latté factors," meaning the little vices we each find hard to resist. You'll find that something as seemingly minor as a $4 cup of coffee each workday costs you $1,040 each year ($4 × 5 days per week × 52 weeks). Once you realize the true cost of these "latté factors," you'll have a greater incentive to bring them under control.[5] Your budget can be helpful in imposing the discipline you need to accomplish this goal.

PathDoc/Shutterstock.com

Nondiscretionary payments are those you have little control over, such as your monthly rent or car payment, which are set by contract. Your lifestyle may also lock you into other costs that are at least partly nondiscretionary. Given your need to get to school and work, you may have to spend a significant amount of money on gas and car maintenance every month. But with a little flexibility and creativity, you may find that such costs aren't *completely* nondiscretionary. For instance, you might be able to significantly reduce your expenses for gas and car maintenance by carpooling or using public transportation.

discretionary payments
Expenditures for which the spender has significant control in terms of the amount and timing.

nondiscretionary payments Expenditures that the spender has little or no control over.

You may also want to consider your attitude toward spending. Are you most likely to spend too much money when you are depressed or stressed out? Look at this aspect carefully, and try to be as honest as possible with yourself. The final thing you should consider is who you are with when you spend money. You may find that you tend to spend much more money while hanging out with certain friends.

After you have prepared your budget, you'll need to keep track of your actual expenses and compare them to your budget. And you'll need to adjust your budget periodically to reflect significant changes in your lifestyle, employment status, and financial goals. It turns out that spending money the "right way" increases personal happiness. A study of 76,000 bank records matched to personality dimensions shows that people are happiest when spending their money on things that fit their personalities.[6] The study's lead author, Sandra Matz, explained, "Money enables us to lead a life we want."[7] But without keeping close track of how you spend your money, you may end up spending it in ways—and amounts—that don't fit who you are or your financial goals. Indeed, the study also found that spending money in ways contrary to personality resulted in less happiness.

> "Rather go to bed without dinner than to rise in debt."
>
> —BENJAMIN FRANKLIN

holiday gifts, or a large down payment on a car or home. However, it's even better to pay yourself first *twice* by automatically depositing money into savings *and* retirement accounts. Why twice? Retirement savings, discussed in section A-4e of this appendix, are often matched dollar for dollar by employers. If you put in $500 a month, your employer doubles it to $1,000—and that's before it grows through investing. The other advantage of retirement accounts is that the IRS usually adds a 10% penalty for early withdrawals, which is enough to discourage most people from trying to spend those funds.[9] By contrast, savings account are easily "raided" for impulsive, unplanned spending.

Interest rates on savings accounts vary from bank to bank, so you should shop around to find the best rate. In recent years, online savings banks have often provided higher interest rates than traditional banks. Just be sure to look for reputable banks that are insured by the **Federal Deposit Insurance Corporation (FDIC)**. The FDIC is an independent agency created by Congress to maintain stability and public confidence in the nation's financial system, primarily by insuring bank deposits. The FDIC insures individual deposits up to $250,000 per account in FDIC-insured banks.[10]

A-2 YOUR SAVINGS: BUILDING A SAFETY NET

A **savings account** is an interest-earning account that is intended to satisfy obligations that your checking account cannot handle. Think of your savings account as a "safety net" for unexpected financial challenges, such as a major plumbing repair, the need to replace your car's transmission, or even the loss of your job. Many financial experts suggest that you have enough money in your savings to cover six months of your expenses. The good news is that if you're lucky enough to avoid major problems, your savings account will earn you a bit of interest income.

One technique for establishing a sizable savings balance is to "pay yourself first." This concept, popularized by David Bach, suggests that you have a predetermined amount from each paycheck automatically deposited into your savings account. Once you've accumulated enough in your savings account to provide an adequate safety net, you can use the "pay yourself first" approach to achieve other financial goals.[8] For example, you can use your savings account to accumulate funds for vacations,

A-3 YOUR CREDIT: HANDLE WITH CARE!

Credit refers to your ability to obtain goods or resources without having to make immediate payment. One of the most important determinants of the amount of credit you can obtain is your **credit score**, which is a numerical indicator of your creditworthiness. Currently, the most commonly used credit scoring system is the Fair, Isaac and Company (FICO) scale. The FICO scale runs from 300 to 850.

Your individual FICO score is based on several factors, including your payment history, the amount

savings account An interest-bearing account holding funds not needed to meet regular expenditures.

Federal Deposit Insurance Corporation (FDIC) An independent agency created by Congress to maintain stability and public confidence in the nation's financial system, primarily by insuring bank deposits.

credit Allows a borrower to buy a good or acquire an asset without making immediate payment and to repay the balance at a later time.

credit score A numerical measure of a consumer's creditworthiness.

Score	Creditworthiness	Percentage of Consumers
Below 500	Very poor	5.7%
500–599	Poor to below average	18.5%
600–699	Below average to fair	22.3%
700–799	Fair to good	35%
800 or Better	Excellent	18.6%

you owe, the type of credit used, and the length of time you've held various credit accounts.[11] As Exhibit A.1 shows, about 57% of all Americans have scores between 600 and 800; only 5.7% have scores below 500, and 18.6% have scores above 800. A high score makes it easier to get credit on favorable terms.[12] On a $250,000, 30-year fixed mortgage, a borrower with a below-average credit score of 620 will pay $87,422 more interest because of higher interest rates than a borrower with a fair to good credit score of 780.[13]

A-3a Credit Cards: Boon or Bane?

Now let's look at a specific source of credit that is near and dear to many college students' hearts: the **credit card**. A credit card allows its holder to make a purchase now and pay the credit card issuer later.

There are several benefits to having and using credit cards. The most obvious is that credit cards are more convenient and safer than carrying a lot of cash. Credit cards also make it easy to track your expenditures, since you have access to a monthly summary of charges. And many cards offer perks, such as discounts on certain products, extended warranties on purchases, or frequent-flier miles.

Another benefit of the *responsible* use of credit cards is that it can improve your credit score by allowing you to establish a history of prompt payments. This can make it easier for you to borrow money when you really need it—such as when you want to buy a car or your first home.

One downside of having a credit card is that the "buy now, pay later" aspect of credit card use makes it hard for some people to maintain financial discipline. Another problem is that interest rates on unpaid card balances tend to be very high. Many card issuers also impose a variety of fees that can make a noticeable dent in your wallet. And making late payments or failing to pay what you owe can damage your credit history, hurting your chances of getting additional credit when you need it.

A-3b The Devil in the Details— Understanding Your Credit Card Agreement!

Before you accept a credit card, make sure you read the credit card agreement and understand the main conditions for using that card. Some things to look for include:

- **Grace period:** The period of time that you have to pay your balance before interest or fees are assessed. Some credit card companies expect to receive their payment within 21 days of the credit card statement date. So, it becomes very important to get these bills paid as soon as possible to avoid the interest and other fees.

- **APR (annual percentage rate):** The percentage financing cost charged on unpaid balances. The higher the APR, the greater your interest expense on unpaid balances. Your credit card company may charge different APRs for different types of transactions.

- **Late fees:** May also be assessed if a payment is not received within the grace period. Federal law now caps late fees at $27 for a first offense and $38 for additional late payments.[14]

- **Other fees:** Include *annual fees* (a charge just for the privilege of having a card, whether you use it or not), *over-the-credit-limit fees* if your charges exceed your credit limit, and *balance-transfer fees* if you transfer a balance from one card to another. This isn't a complete list, but it does reflect many of the most common types of fees you might incur. Not all cards

credit card A card issued by a bank or finance company that allows the cardholder to make a purchase now and pay the credit card issuer later.

grace period The period of time that the credit card holder has to pay outstanding balances before interest or fees are assessed.

annual percentage rate (APR) The interest expense charged on a credit card, expressed as an annual percentage.

are subject to all of these charges; the specific types and amounts of fees can vary considerably from one issuer to another—which is why reading the fine print is important!

A-3c Protection for Consumers: New Laws and Regulations

Two recent laws have had a significant impact on credit card practices. The Credit Card Accountability, Responsibility and Disclosure Act of 2009 (often called the CARD Act) requires issuers to give a 45-day notice before making significant changes to credit agreements and prohibits them from raising interest rates on existing balances unless the borrower is more than 60 days late in making required payments. It also requires anyone under the age of 21 who applies for a credit card to either verify proof of income or have an adult cosign the application. And it places caps on certain types of fees that credit card issuers can charge.[15]

New laws and regulations have changed the way many financial markets operate in recent years. The Dodd-Frank Wall Street Reform and Consumer Protection Act of 2010, passed in the wake of the financial crisis of 2008 and 2009, includes several provisions intended to protect the financial rights of consumers. One key provision of this Act is the establishment of the Consumer Financial Protection Bureau (CFPB) to eliminate confusing and potentially deceptive banking practices related to mortgages, credit cards, and other loan agreements.[16] The CFPB also makes it easier for consumers to compare the features and costs of various credit cards so that they can select the ones that best meet their needs. In addition to the creation of the CFPB, the Dodd-Frank Act also requires lenders, insurance companies, and others who reject your application to provide you with a free copy of your credit score.[17]

A-3d Using Credit Cards Wisely: The Need for Discipline

Although many young adults manage their credit cards without major problems, others are stunned when the credit card bill arrives. Many never read their credit card agreements, so they are taken by surprise by higher than expected interest charges and fees. Others simply lack discipline. They succumb to the temptations of a "buy now, pay later" mentality and run up big bills that they can't afford to pay.

> If you owe $5,000 on a credit card but only make minimum payments, you'll be repaying for 273 months, and pay $6,923 in interest!
>
> —BANKRATE.COM

The first rule when you have credit card difficulties is to "PUT THE CARD DOWN!" When you find yourself in trouble, stop using the card so you don't compound your difficulties. Make sure you don't use the card again until you've gotten your spending habits under control. If you're struggling to put the credit card down, use a task app or a reminder app to bolster your new spending habits. Researchers have found that when simple messages like "Don't swipe the small stuff. Use cash when it's under $20" are sent via email twice a month, displayed as a banner ad on one's banking Web site, and written on a refrigerator magnet, consumers spend 2% less over six months' time.[18] Activating alerts for daily spending summaries or purchases over a certain amount can also do wonders. The idea is to use reminders and alerts to strengthen your commitment to putting the card down.

Once you've eliminated the temptation to dig a deeper hole, the next step is to make sure you consistently pay a substantial amount each month toward retiring the debt on that card. Given how high APRs are on the unpaid balances for most credit cards, it is usually a good idea to place a *very* high priority on eliminating these balances as quickly as possible.

If you just can't seem to shake the habit of overspending, consider using cash or a **debit card** instead of a credit card. Although a debit card looks like a credit card, there is a big difference. When you use a debit card, money is immediately withdrawn from your bank account, so you "feel the pain" just as if you'd paid in cash. Many people spend less when they use cash or debit cards than when they use credit cards.

Andrey_Kuzmin/Shutterstock.com

debit card A card issued by the bank that allows the customer to make purchases as if the transaction involved cash. In a debit card purchase, the customer's bank account is immediately reduced when the purchase is made.

Monthly Savings	Starting Age			
	20	30	40	50
$30	$158,236	$68,816	$28,531	$10,381
$60	$316,472	$137,633	$57,062	$20,762
$90	$474,709	$206,449	$85,592	$31,143
$120	$632,945	$275,266	$114,123	$41,525
$150	$791,181	$344,082	$142,654	$51,906

Note: Figures in the table show the amount accumulated at age 65. Results are based on an assumed annual rate of return of 8% compounded monthly.

A-4 YOUR INVESTMENTS: BUILDING FOR THE FUTURE

Investing involves reducing consumption today in order to acquire assets that build future wealth. In a very real way, investing is like the concept of sowing and reaping. A farmer plants a seed (makes an investment) in anticipation of a harvest (return) that will be much larger than the seed that was planted. When it comes to investing, early is better than late—but late is better than never.

> "The best time to plant a tree was 20 years ago. The next best time is now."
> —CHINESE PROVERB

A-4a Building Wealth: The Key Is Consistency—And an Early Start!

Don't talk yourself out of investing just because you don't have much to invest. Even if you start with a small amount, your wealth will eventually grow to a significant amount as long as you stick with it. And the earlier you start, the better off you'll be. To see this, take a look at Exhibit A.2, which compares how big your retirement nest egg will be at age 65 for different monthly investment amounts beginning at different ages (and assuming you earn an annual return of 8%). A 30-year-old who invests $60 per month will end up with $137,633 at age 65. Compare this to someone who begins investing $60 per month at age 20, and the results are startling. The investor who starts at age 20 only directly invests $7,200 more ($60 per month for 120 more months) than the investor who starts at age 30. But the earlier investor ends up with a nest egg of $316,472—almost $179,000 more than that of the investor who started at age 30.

investing Reducing consumption in the current time period in order to build future wealth.

The reason for this result is that, over time, you earn interest not only on the money you directly invest but also on the *interest* you've earned in *previous* years—a process known as *compounding*. The earlier you begin investing, the more powerful the compounding effect becomes. By the time an investor reaches age 65, any dollars invested at age 20 have been compounded for a *very long* time, resulting in a big increase in the nest egg. The message of Exhibit A.2 is clear: an early start to investing can lead to dramatically more money when it comes time to retire.

Financial Securities: What Are My Investment Options? Now that we've demonstrated the importance of investing, let's look at some specific types of financial instruments you might want to include in your investment portfolio. Our brief discussion can't hope to cover all of the possibilities, so we'll focus only on some of the most common choices. Keep in mind that, in addition to the financial instruments we describe in this section, many people also hold much of their wealth in other assets. The largest single asset for many households is the equity they have in their home.

Let's begin by looking at *common stock*, which represents ownership in a corporation. Common stock offers the possibility of two types of financial returns. The first, called a *dividend*, is a distribution of profits paid out to the stockholders. Dividends are paid only if the corporation's board of directors declares them—and there is no legal requirement for them to do so. If a corporation is in poor financial shape, its board of directors may decide that it is unable to pay a dividend. But even if a company is highly profitable, its board may decide to reinvest (retain) its profits rather than pay dividends to stockholders.

Investors can earn a second type of return, called a capital gain, if the market price of their stock rises relative to the price they paid for it. But stock prices can go down as well as up—as many investors have painfully discovered in recent years! Thus, it is possible for investors to experience *capital losses* as well as capital gains. For example, while the average compound return from S&P 500 stocks was 9.83% a year from January 1988 to February 2017, the S&P 500 suffered a compound loss of –6.63% from March 2004 to March 2009.[19] Clearly, investing in common stock entails a significant degree of risk. But historically the average rate of return on stocks has been better than the return on many other types of investments.

In addition to common stock, some corporations also offer another type of stock, called *preferred stock*. The two types of stock have some important differences. From the perspective of many investors, the most important distinction is that owners of preferred stock are more likely to receive a dividend than owners of common stock. Preferred stock is normally issued with a stated dividend, and common stockholders can't be paid *any* dividend until the preferred dividend is paid in full. Still, even preferred stockholders have no guaranteed legal right to receive a dividend.

A *corporate bond* is another type of corporate security, but it is quite different from stock. A bond is a formal IOU issued by a corporation. While stockholders are the owners of a corporation, bondholders are its creditors. Most bonds are long-term debts that mature (come due) 10 to 30 years after they are issued, though bonds with shorter and longer maturities are sometimes issued.

As creditors, bondholders are legally entitled to receive interest payments from the issuing corporation every year until the bond matures, and to receive an amount known as the *principal* (or "face value") when the bond matures. But bondholders don't have to hold their bonds until they mature. Like stocks, bonds can be bought and sold on securities markets, and their price can rise and fall. So, like stockholders, bondholders can experience capital gains or losses.

Because the issuing corporation is legally required to pay interest and principal on a fixed schedule, the returns on bonds are more predictable than returns on stocks. However, even bonds pose some risk. During the recent economic downturn, many firms defaulted on (failed to make) their legally required bond payments.

Government securities are IOUs issued by government entities when they borrow money. As with corporate bonds, government securities normally pay their holders a stated rate of interest until they mature. State and local governments often issue bonds. In fact, many investors like to invest in municipal bonds because interest income earned on these bonds is usually exempt from federal income taxes. But the biggest single issuer of government securities is the federal government. The U.S. Treasury markets a variety of securities, from long-term bonds that mature in 30 years to short-term treasury bills (popularly called "T-bills") that can mature in as little as four weeks. Historically, securities issued by the federal government have been viewed as very safe investments. But in recent years, the rapid growth in federal debt has led some securities rating services to question this view.[20]

Certificates of deposit are offered by banks and other depository institutions like credit unions. They are similar to savings accounts but are issued for a fixed term—which could be as short as three months or as long as five years. The rate of interest paid on CDs is often higher than the rate on a regular savings account but usually lower than the interest rate on corporate bonds and most government securities. CDs with longer maturities typically earn a higher interest rate than CDs that have shorter terms. You can cash in a CD before it matures, but you'll incur a substantial penalty if you do.

One advantage of CDs is that they are insured by the FDIC. Because of this insurance and their predictable rate of return, CDs are considered to be among the safest investment options. The trade-off is that they offer lower returns than most other types of investments.

For many users today, a mobile app may be the most intuitive way to start investing. According to financial advice website NerdWallet, E-Trade and TD Ameritrade offer the best all-around mobile stock trading apps—for a price. Robinhood offers the best commission-free trading, while Acorns and Stash provide the best hands-off investing experience for new investors.

Mutual funds sell shares to investors and pool the resulting funds to invest in financial instruments such as corporate stocks, corporate bonds, government securities, or other assets. Some mutual funds invest mainly in bonds, others invest mainly in stocks, and others in government securities. Some invest in specific sectors of the economy, such as technology, energy, or healthcare, while others invest in broader portfolios.

Many mutual funds are professionally managed, with the fund's manager selecting the specific securities that the fund will hold. This professional management appeals to many investors who don't have the time or expertise to evaluate investment alternatives. But it is also expensive—mutual funds charge fees to cover the cost of managing the fund and to meet other expenses. Investors must pay these fees even if the funds perform poorly.

Exchange Traded Funds (ETFs) are similar to mutual funds in that they represent ownership in a broad portfolio of securities. However, unlike most mutual funds, they are bought and sold just like shares of corporate stock. ETFs are a relatively new investment vehicle (first marketed in 1993), but they have become quite popular in recent years.

A-4b Acquiring Financial Assets: The Role of a Broker

Investors normally acquire many of their financial assets, including shares of common and preferred stocks, corporate bonds, and certain other financial assets (such as ETFs), by purchasing them in securities markets. However, individual investors can't directly participate in these markets. Instead, they normally rely on the services of a brokerage firm to buy and sell securities.

When choosing a broker, it's important to consider both the costs and the level of service. In addition to carrying out your trades, a *full-service broker* provides a wide range of services—such as research to identify good investment opportunities, financial planning, and tax advice. Most full-service brokerage firms charge commissions based on the dollar value of the orders their clients place. They also charge fees for the services they provide. In contrast, *discount brokers* buy and sell securities for their clients but offer few additional services. The commissions and fees charged by discount brokers are usually significantly lower than those of full-service brokers. Many discount brokerage firms charge flat fees of a few dollars per trade for simple transactions.

Full-service brokers provide financial planning, tax advice, and research to identify good investment opportunities.

iStock.com/svetikd

In recent years, competition among brokerage firms has blurred the distinction between full-service and discount brokers. Many full-service firms have lowered their commissions, while many discount brokers have begun offering investment advice and other services. Most major brokerage firms now offer their clients both discount and full-service options.

Robo advisors are a third option for acquiring and managing financial assets. These automated advisors help people set, track, stick to (that's the hard part), and eventually achieve their financial goals. Wealthfront and Betterment, two of the largest robo advisor services, use computer algorithms to automatically invest clients' wealth in a way that maximizes returns and minimizes taxes. Based on criteria set by the user, these services automatically deposit bank funds into retirement accounts each month; retrieve and then invest extra cash that would otherwise not earn a return; and rebalance stock portfolios by selling fast-moving stocks (capturing the gains) and investing in underweighted (and perhaps cheaper) stocks. Not only do robo advisors do all this automatically and based on individualized financial goals, they do so with lower annual fees than traditional advisors. Robo advisors typically charge 0.25% to 0.50% of assets, compared to 1% to 2% among human advisors.[21]

Before entrusting a brokerage firm with your financial transactions, you should check out its background. The Financial Industry Regulatory Authority's (FINRA's) BrokerCheck website (http://www.finra.org/Investors/Tools Calculators/BrokerCheck/) is a good place to start. This site offers very detailed background information on more than

1.3 million current and former FINRA-registered brokers and more than 17,400 FINRA-registered brokerage firms.

A-4c Building a Portfolio: A Few Words about Diversification, Risk, and Return

The financial securities we've described are not mutually exclusive. It is possible—and usually desirable—to invest in a diversified financial portfolio consisting of a variety of stocks, bonds, CDs, government securities, and other assets.

The main advantage offered by diversification is that it reduces your risk. If you put a large part of your wealth into one specific investment, you could be wiped out if that investment goes sour. If you invest in several different assets, then losses in some are likely to be offset by gains in others. But diversification also has a downside—it not only reduces risk but also reduces the possibility of earning exceptionally high returns.

One widely accepted financial principle is that a trade-off exists between risk and return; in other words, investments with the potential for generating high returns tend to be riskier than investments that offer lower returns. For example, stock prices sometimes decline sharply, so investing in stocks is considered quite risky. But historically, the long-run average return on stocks has been significantly higher than the average return on bonds, which offer safer, more predictable returns.

In general, younger investors are less concerned about risk than older investors. When you are young, you have more time to recover from adverse results, so you may be willing to take more risks and be more aggressive in pursuit of higher returns. If you invest mostly in stocks when you are young, and the stock market crashes, you still have time to recoup your losses and take advantage of future increases in stock prices. But older investors who hold a lot of stock might find that the same crash wiped out much of the wealth just when they were counting on it to supplement their retirement income. Older investors often become more conservative, adjusting their portfolio to include a greater percentage of relatively safe assets such as government securities, bonds of corporations with strong credit ratings, and CDs.

A-4d But What Is My Best Investment? (Hint: Look in the Mirror!)

So far, we have focused on investing in financial assets. But in many ways, the most important investment you can make is in yourself, by devoting your time, effort, and money to your education, training, health, and fitness. The Bureau of Labor Statistics reports that the median weekly earnings of high-school graduates in the fourth quarter of 2016 was $698, while for workers with bachelor's degrees, the figure was $1,161—a difference of $463.[22] Over a typical worker's 40-year career, this amounts to a difference in earnings of over $963,000! And higher education not only increases your income, it also gives you more job security. In 2017, the unemployment rate for workers with a high-school education was 5.3% while the unemployment rate for workers with at least a bachelor's degree was 2.5%.[23]

Strategies to Become More Marketable One way to increase your marketability and your starting salary is to secure an internship during your college years. Such internships usually offer little or no monetary compensation, but they pay off in other ways. They give students a chance to gain firsthand experience that supplements what they learn in the classroom and helps them determine whether a specific career is right for them. And the internship experience looks great on a résumé. But in 2010, the U.S. Department of Labor issued a ruling that makes it more difficult for profit-seeking firms to offer unpaid or low-wage internships. Many educators, business leaders, and politicians have called on the Department of Labor to modify its stance to make internships easier to establish. But unless and until such modifications are adopted, internships may remain difficult to find.[24]

Other Work Opportunities Don't despair if you are unable to secure an internship. There are other ways to gain experience in your field of interest. Consider taking a (gulp) pay cut from your temporary *job* to get experience in your *career* field. Or perhaps consider doing volunteer work in that field—not only will you be doing a good deed, you'll also be learning the ropes in your chosen field. Taking a temporary pay cut to gain relevant work experience often pays for itself many times over when you leave college and pursue a full-time position.

kirill_makarov/Shutterstock.com

A-4e Investing for the Long Term: Planning for Your Retirement

One of the most important reasons people invest is to build up a nest egg for retirement. While your retirement might seem like it is a long way off, investing for your golden years now can really pay off, since it allows you to take advantage of the compounding effects we talked about earlier.

One of the most popular ways to build wealth for retirement is to set up an individual retirement account, or **IRA**. There are several types of IRAs; the two most popular are the *traditional IRA* and the *Roth IRA*. Both types of IRAs are individual investments—you make the decisions about how much to invest (subject to maximum allowable contributions) and what specific investments to make. You can put your IRA money into stocks, government securities, CDs, mutual funds, or other types of financial securities.

Both traditional and Roth IRAs offer tax advantages intended to provide an incentive for people to invest for their retirement. But the nature and timing of the tax advantages are different. With a traditional IRA, the contributions you make reduce your taxable income in the same tax year, and the earnings on your contributions are tax deferred, allowing them to grow more rapidly.[25] But you must pay taxes on the money received from a traditional IRA when you begin making withdrawals. On the other hand, the contributions you make to a Roth IRA are *not* tax deductible at the time you make them, but earnings on these contributions are tax-free, and you pay no taxes on the distributions you receive from a Roth IRA after you retire.

One drawback to both traditional and Roth IRAs is that the amount that individuals can contribute each year is relatively small. In 2016, the maximum contribution for both types of plans was $5,500. (Individuals over the age of 50 could contribute up to $6,500.)

The **401(k), 403(b), and 457 plans** are employee-contribution retirement plans that are named for the sections of the IRS tax code where they are described. These plans are similar in many respects; the main differences are in who qualifies for each type of plan. The 401(k) plans are offered to employees of private-sector businesses, while 403(b) plans are for employees of certain types of nonprofit organizations such as schools, religious organizations, and charities. The 457 plans are primarily for state and local government employees and nonprofit organizations. Some employees in the nonprofit sector qualify for both 403(b) and 457 plans.

Unlike IRAs, all of these plans are implemented through a payroll-deduction process. Also, these plans have much higher contribution limits than traditional and Roth IRAs. In 2017, for example, employees could contribute up to $18,000 in a 401(k) plan, with individuals over 50 allowed to contribute up to an additional $6,000 *if* their employer's plan contained a "catch-up" provision.[26] Other potential advantages of these plans include:

- **Tax advantages:** Any income employees invest in traditional 401(k), 403(b), and 457 plans is tax deductible, and the earnings on these investments are tax deferred. This reduces current taxes and allows the funds to grow more rapidly. However, retirees must pay taxes on funds distributed from their fund when they make withdrawals. As with IRAs, there are Roth versions of these plans. Employees who choose the Roth version pay taxes on the income they contribute, but earnings on these contributions and distributions after retirement are tax exempt.

- **Company matching:** Some employers match employee contribution either dollar for dollar or with a percentage of each dollar you contribute up to a limit. This can be a big advantage of these plans over IRAs. If your company matches your 401(k) or 403(b) or 457 contributions, you should consider contributing as much as you can up to the maximum your company will match—it's like getting free money for your retirement.

There are also some important restrictions on these plans. First, not all employers offer these plans. Second, if your employer does offer a plan that offers matching

Nattika/Shutterstock.com

IRA An individual retirement account that provides tax benefits to individuals who are investing for their retirement.

401(k), 403(b), and 457 plans Employee payroll-deduction retirement plans that offer tax benefits.

company matching An amount contributed by the employer to an employee's retirement account, matching the employee's retirement contributions either dollar-for-dollar or based on a percentage of each dollar contributed by the employee.

Venmo Me—But Don't Be a Jerk!

Venmo is a PayPal service that allows roommates, people sharing dinner, family members, and friends to share payments via an app—all without cash. Just link Venmo to your bank account or credit card, then "Venmo" money to a recipient using a phone numbers or email address—a Venmo account isn't needed to receive payments. If you'd like, you can post the payment to a social feed with commentary like "Here's my half of the rent, roomie!" or "This is the last time I bail you out of jail!" Venmo is free when using your bank account, debit card, a prepaid card, or your Venmo balance. Use your credit card with Venmo, however, and you'll be charged a standard 3% fee.

College Junior Caitlin McGorry explains why Venmo is so convenient: "When you're paying someone back with cash, it takes longer. You have to find time to go to the ATM, then find time to meet up, and then you start to feel bad it's taking so long to get your money back, so Venmo is easier and makes you feel better because you're paying someone back immediately."

But according to Quartz Media's Kari Paul, Venmo is "turning our friends into petty jerks." She cites the example of Friend A, who shared some wine at Friend B's house during an evening of Netflix binge-watching . . . only to be Venmoed a request from Friend B for $6, or half the cost of the wine. Friend A said, "I couldn't believe she was charging me for the glass of wine she poured me herself." Similarly, suppose Coworker C invites Coworker D for coffee, only to send a $3.79 Venmo request afterward (ignoring the office guideline that the person issuing the invitation pays)!

While Venmo makes it easy for everyone to pay their share, Paul warns not to put Venmo's convenience before friendship. "Buying a round of drinks, when you can afford it is a nice gesture and an increasingly lost art. And if you forgot your wallet on a trip to the coffee shop, I don't want you to send me $4.25. It's my treat—just get me back next time."[27]

Bloomberg/Getty Images

A key to a comfortable retirement is to start saving early.

EpicStockMedia/Shutterstock.com

vesting period A specified period of time for which an employee must work for an employer in order to receive the full advantage of certain retirement benefits.

contributions, you won't be entitled to all of the matching funds unless you've remained employed with the company for a stated period of time called the **vesting period**. The length of time for full vesting varies depending on the employer, but it is usually several years. Finally, keep in mind that these are *retirement* plans. There are restrictions on withdrawing the money in these plans prior to retirement, and you may pay significant penalties if you do.

THE BIG PICTURE

Making sound personal financial decisions requires careful thought and discipline. You should start by establishing a budget; doing so will help you understand your current financial situation, plan for the future, and monitor your progress toward achieving your goals. One of your first goals should be to set aside enough savings to provide adequate protection against unforeseen financial challenges. One good strategy to build your savings is to "pay yourself first." Another key to financial success is to make careful decisions with respect to your use of credit cards and other forms of credit. Next, you should turn your attention to investing to build your wealth over time. You'll discover many different investment opportunities, each with its own pros and cons. No single investment strategy is foolproof, but two principles that have stood the test of time are (1) start investing early to take full advantage of compounding, and (2) diversify your investments to protect against risk.

STUDY TOOLS APPENDIX

LOCATED AT BACK OF THE TEXTBOOK

☐ Rip-Out Chapter Review Card

☐ Gain unique perspectives on key concepts with new concept videos in the e-book

☐ Increase your comprehension with online homework and quizzes

☐ Study with existing flashcards and make your own

1

1. Me Too founder Tarana Burke: 'You have to use your privilege to serve other people' by Emma Brockes, January 15, 2018 the Guardian, https://www.theguardian.com/world/2018/jan/15/me-too-founder-tarana-burke-women-sexual-assault, accessed April 12, 2018; #MeToo reaches 85 countries with 1.7M tweets by Andrea Park, October 24, 2017, CBS News, https://www.cbsnews.com/news/metoo-reaches-85-countries-with-1-7-million-tweets/, accessed April 12, 2018.

2. Elon Musk says global race for A.I. will be the most likely cause of World War III by Ryan Browne, September 4, 2017, https://www.cnbc.com/2017/09/04/elon-musk-says-global-race-for-ai-will-be-most-likely-cause-of-ww3.html, accessed April 12, 2018; Tim Cook says Apple's car project is 'the mother of all AI projects' by Romain Dillet, June 13, 2017, https://techcrunch.com/2017/06/13/tim-cook-says-apples-car-project-is-the-mother-of-all-ai-projects/, accessed April's 12th 2018; Pokémon Go studio Niantic is making a Harry Potter AR game by Shannon Liao, November 8, 2017, https://www.theverge.com/2017/11/8/16623784/niantic-labs-pokemon-go-harry-potter-ar, accessed April 12, 2018; Pokemon GO clears 750 million downloads as Niantic prepares first anniversary celebrations by Ric Cowley, June 9, 2017, http://www.pocketgamer.biz/news/65944/pokemon-go-750-million-downloads/, accessed April 12, 2018.

3. Why Gen Z might signal the end of demographic targeting as we know it by Peter Adams, October 10, 2017, https://www.marketingdive.com/news/why-gen-z-might-signal-the-end-of-demographic-targeting-as-we-know-it/506796/, accessed April 12, 2018; 3 Things Generation Z Is Going to Do Better Than Millennials, Gen-Xers, and Baby Boomers Combined by Nicholas Cage, October 13, 2016, https://www.inc.com/nicolas-cole/3-things-generation-z-is-going-to-do-better-than-millennials-gen-xers-and-baby-b.html, accessed April 12, 2018; 8 Ways Generation Z Will Differ From Millennials In The Workplace by Deep Patel, September 21, 2017, https://www.forbes.com/sites/deeppatel/2017/09/21/8-ways-generation-z-will-differ-from-millennials-in-the-workplace/#4c575a5076e5, accessed April 12, 2018.

4. Leonid Bershidsky, "Here Comes Generation Z," *Bloomberg*, June 18, 2014, https://www.bloomberg.com/view/articles/2014-06-18/nailing-generation-z, accessed January 17, 2017; Elizabeth Segran, "Your Guide to Generation Z," Fast Company, September 8, 2016, https://www.fastcompany.com/3062475/most-creative-people/your-guide-to-generation-z-the-frugal-brand-wary-determined-anti-millen, accessed January 17, 2017.

5. "Improving Labor Market Could Be Cause of Drop in Total New Business Creation Rate in 2012," Kauffman Foundation, March 17, 2013, http://www.kauffman.org/newsroom/2013/04/entrepreneurial-activity-declines-as-jobs-rise-in-2012-according-to-kauffman-report, accessed February 2, 2015.

6. Cheryl Chumley, "Lululemon Athletica Chairman Quits After Firestorm Over His Fat-Thighs Comment," *Washington Times*, December 10, 2013, http://www.washingtontimes.com/news/2013/dec/10/lululemon-athletic-wear-chair-quits-over-firestorm/, accessed January 11, 2014.

7. "The Biggest Corporate Blunders of 2013," *CNBC*, http://www.cnbc.com/id/101283178/page/2, accessed February 2, 2015.

8. Sources: Alibaba smashes its Single's Day record once again as sales cross $25 billion by Jon Russell, November 11, 2017, https://techcrunch.com/2017/11/11/alibaba-smashes-its-singles-day-record/, accessed April 12, 2018; Alibaba's Singles' Day sale amassed $25.3 billion, doubling 2016 Black Friday and Cyber Monday sales combined by Natt Garun, November 11, 2017, https://www.theverge.com/2017/11/11/16637362/alibaba-singles-day-2017-sales-record-online-shopping-black-friday-cyber-monday, accessed April 12, 2018.

9. Tax Reform 2018 Explained, Brittney Laryea and Shen Lu, December 22, 2017, https://www.magnifymoney.com/blog/author/shen-lu/, accessed April 12, 2018.

10. "Mistakes in Advertising," *English Learning Network*, http://www.learnenglish.de/mistakes/HorrorMistakes.html, accessed February 2, 2015.

11. "State of Entrepreneurship Address," Kauffman Foundation, January 19, 2010, http://www.kauffman.org/newsroom/entrepreneurs-expect-to-limit-hiring-in-2010-according-to-new-kauffman-foundation-poll.aspx, accessed January 13, 2011.

12. Leonard Jacobs, "On the Nonprofit Sector and Community Solutions Act of 2010," The Clyde Fitch Report, June 18, 2010, http://www.clydefitchreport.com/2010/06/introducing-hr-5533-the-nonprofit-sector-and-community-solutions-act-of-2010/, accessed January 16, 2011; Suzanne Perry, "7.2% of Americans work for nonprofit groups, study finds," *The Chronicle of Philanthropy*, December 19, 2006, http://philanthropy.com/free/update/2006/12/2006121901.htm, accessed January 19, 2009; Amy Butler, "Wages in the Nonprofit Sector: Management, Professional, and Administrative Support Occupations," Bureau of Labor Statistics, October 28, 2008, http://www.bls.gov/opub/cwc/cm20081022ar01p1.htm, accessed January 19, 2008; "Occupational Employment and Wages, 2007," Bureau of Labor Statistics, May 9, 2008, http://www.bls.gov/news.release/pdf/ocwage.pdf, accessed January 19, 2009; Todd Cohen, "Nonprofit sector needs to be better understood," Inside Philanthropy Blog, *Philanthropy Journal*, February 22, 2010, http://philanthropyjournal.blogspot.com/2010/02/nonprofit-sector-needs-to-be-better.html, accessed March 23, 2010.

13. Ian Altman, "Top 10 Business Trends that Will Drive Success in 2016," *Forbes*, December 1, 2015, http://www.forbes.com/sites/ianaltman/2015/12/01/top-10-business-trends-that-will-drive-success-in-2016/#45212d2a5571, accessed January 25, 2016; "Seth Godin's Rules for Marketing in the New Economy," SAS, http://www.sas.com/en_us/insights/articles/marketing/seth-godins-rules-for-marketing-in-the-new-economy.html, accessed January 25, 2016.

14. "GNI Per Capita 2007," World Bank Data, October 17, 2008, http://siteresources.worldbank.org/DATASTATISTICS/Resources/GNIPC.pdf, accessed January 19, 2009; "East and Southeast Asia: China," The World Factbook, CIA," updated December 18, 2008, https://www.cia.gov/library/publications/the-world-factbook/geos/ch.html, accessed January 19, 2009; "Central Asia: Russia," The World Factbook, CIA, updated December 18, 2008, https://www.cia.gov/library/publications/the-world-factbook/geos/rs.html, accessed January 19, 2009; "East and Southeast Asia: Hong Kong," The World Factbook, CIA", updated December 18, 2008, https://www.cia.gov/library/publications/the-world-factbook/geos/hk.html, accessed January 19, 2009.

15. "American Customer Satisfaction Index, 2011 Results," *ACSI*, http://www.theacsi.org/index.php?option=com_content&view=article&id=12&Itemid=110, accessed January 14, 2012.

16. Joanna Glasner, "Why Webvan Drove Off a Cliff," *Wired News*, July 10, 2001, http://www.wired.com/techbiz/media/news/2001/07/45098.

17. Steven Levy, "Honey, I Shrunk the iPod. A lot.," *Newsweek* magazine, September 19, 2005; John Boddie, "Behind Apple's strategy: Be second to market," *Harvard Business School Working Knowledge*, August 29, 2005, http://hbswk.hbs.edu/item.jhtml?id=4970&t=technology; John Letzing, "What's to Become of Microsoft's Answer to the iPod?," Marketwatch, July 29, 2009, http://www.marketwatch.com/story/microsofts-zune-continues-to-struggle-2009-07-29, accessed April 1, 2010.

18. See note 17 above.

19. Andrew Chamberlain, "Does Company Culture Pay Off? Analyzing Stock Performance of 'Best Places to Work' Companies," GlassDoor, March 2015, https://glassdoor.app.box.com/s/49y1ulkftvbpsbqjgeo1zh3lvijbb9uo, accessed January 29, 2016.

20. "Baby Boomers Retire," Pew Research Center, January 17, 2011, http://pewresearch.org/databank/dailynumber/?NumberID=1150, accessed January 11, 2011.

21. Aza Wee Sile, "PwC's Dennis Nally Says Global Economy, Geopolitical Tensions Are CEOs' Top Worries," *CNBC*, January 20, 2016, http://www.cnbc.com/2016/01/20/pwcs-dennis-nally-says-global-economy-geopolitical-tensions-are-ceos-top-worries.html, accessed January 28, 2016; Geoff Colvin, "This Is What CEOs Are Worrying About the Most," *Fortune*, November 3, 2015, http://fortune.com/2015/11/03/ceos-worry-uber-syndrome/, accessed January 28, 2016.

22. Jeffrey Grau, "Retail E-Commerce Update," eMarketer, December 2008, http://www.emarketer.com/Reports/All/Emarketer_2000545.aspx, accessed January 19, 2009; David Kaplan, "eMarketer: E-Commerce Expected to Grow Double Digits through 2012," PaidContent, March 17, 2011, http://paidcontent.org/article/419-emarketer-e-commerce-expected-to-grow-double-digits-through-2012/, accessed January 15, 2012.

23. "In Trendy World of Fast Fashion, Styles Aren't Made to Last," *NPR*, March 11, 2013, http://www .npr.org/2013/03/11/174013774/in-trendy-world -of-fast-fashion-styles-arent-made-to-last, accessed February 3, 2015; Shannon Whitehead, "5 Truths the Fast Fashion Industry Doesn't Want You to Know," *The Huffington Post*, October 14, 2014, http://www.huffingtonpost.com/shannon-whitehead /5-truths-the-fast-fashion_b_5690575.html, accessed February 3, 2015.

24. "U.S. Census Bureau Projections Show a Slower Growing, Older, More Diverse Nation a Half Century from Now," *Census Bureau Press Release*, December 12, 2012. http://www.census .gov/newsroom/releases/archives/population/cb12 -243.html, accessed January 9, 2013; "Net Migration from Mexico Falls to Zero and Perhaps Less," Pew Hispanic Center Report, 2012, http://s3 .documentcloud.org/documents/346357/mexican -migration.pdf, accessed January 9, 2013; Jeffrey S. Passel and D'Vera Cohn, "U.S. Population Projections: 2005–2050," Pew Research Center, February 11, 2008, http://pewhispanic.org/files /reports/85.pdf, accessed January 17, 2011.

25. "New Mexico QuickFacts," U.S. Census, December 6, 2012, http://quickfacts.census.gov/qfd /states/35000.html; "Mississippi QuickFacts," U.S. Census, December 6, 2012, http://quickfacts.census. gov/qfd/states/28000.html; "Hawaii QuickFacts," U.S. Census, December 6, 2012, http://quickfacts.census. gov/qfd/states/15000.html, all accessed January 9, 2013; "State and County Quick Facts," Mississippi, U.S. Census Bureau, last revised February 23, 2010, http:// quickfacts.census.gov/qfd/states/28000.html, accessed March 30, 2010; "Hawaii's Asian Population at 55% is Highest Proportion in Nation," Hawaii 24/7, May 1, 2009, http://www.hawaii247.org/2009/05/01/hawaiis -asian-population-at-55-is-highest-proportion-in -nation/, accessed March 30, 2010; "State and County Quick Facts, New Mexico," U.S. Census Bureau, last revised February, 23, 2010, http://quickfacts.census. gov/qfd/states/35000.html, accessed March 30, 2010.

26. "Lynx Helped Panasonic Become a Major Player in the Hispanic Market," Lynx Hispanic Marketing Case Studies, 2013, http://www.lynxhispanicmarketing .com/case-studies/panasonic.php, accessed January 9, 2013; "Translating Hispanic Marketing Into Share-holder Value," Hispanic PR Wire/Business Wire, December 4, 2006, http://www.hispanicprwire.com /print.php?l =in&id=7660; Andrew Adam Newman, "Kraft Aims Kool-Aid Ads at a Growing Hispanic Market," *The New York Times*, May 26, 2011, http:// www.nytimes.com/2011/05/27/business /media/27adco .html, accessed January 16, 2012; Elli Bishop, "6 Brands That Succeed at Understanding Hispanic Marketing," *Business to Community*, October 7, 2014, http://www.business2community.com/marketing /6-brands-succeed-understanding-hispanic-marketing -01030311, accessed January 29, 2016.

27. "Diversity Awareness," Hershey Foods Corporation, https://www.hersheysjobs.com/Career /ControlPanel.aspx?ModuleCategoryID=1999999, accessed October 4, 2005.

28. "Attitudes of Young People Toward Diversity," CIRCLE fact sheet, February 2005, http://www .civicyouth.org/PopUps/FactSheets/Attitudes % 202.25.pdf.

29. "U.S. Census Bureau Projections Show a Slower Growing, Older, More Diverse Nation a Half Century from Now," *Census Bureau Press Release*, December 12, 2012, http://www.census.gov /newsroom/releases/archives/population/cb12-243

.html, accessed January 9, 2013; "China Seeks Ways to Manage Ageing Population Crisis," *BBC News*, September 21, 2012, http://www.bbc.co.uk/news /world-asia-china-19662365, accessed January 9, 2013; Jeffrey S. Passel and D'Vera Cohn, "U.S. Population Projections: 2005–2050," Pew Research Center, February 11, 2008, http://pewhispanic.org /files/reports/85.pdf, accessed January 17, 2011; Toshiko Kaneda, "China's Concern Over Population Aging and Health," Population Reference Bureau, http://www.prb.org/Articles/2006/ChinasConcern OverPopulation AgingandHealth.aspx, accessed January 17, 2011.

30. Taylor Soper, "Amazon, Google Employees Ranked as 'least loyal,'" *GeekWire*, July 24, 2013, http://www.geekwire.com/2013/amazon-google-employees-ranked-least-loyal/#disqus _thread, accessed January 9, 2014; Sue Shellenbarger, "Pending Job Flexibility Act Received Mixed Reviews," *WSJ Career Journal*, http://www.careerjournal.com /columnists/workfamily/20010426-workfamily.html, accessed October 4, 2005; Les Christie, "Bad Attitudes in the Workplace," *CNNMoney*, September 6, 2005, http://money.cnn.com/2005/08/24/pf/workplace _morale/?section=money_pf; John Ellis, "Inspiring Worker Loyalty One Tough Job," *East Bay Business Times*, July 1, 2005, http://www.bizjournals.com /eastbay/stories/2005/07/04/focus1.html; Laura Petrecca, "Employee Loyalty Is at a Three-Year Low," *USA Today*, March 28, 2011, http://www.usatoday .com/money/workplace/2011-03-26-employees-less -loyal.htm, accessed January 16, 2012.

31. "Sustainability: Balancing Opportunity and Risk in the Consumer Products Industry, 2007 Report," Deloitte, http://www.deloitte.com/dtt /cda/doc/ content/us_cb_sustainability-study_june2007opt. pdf, accessed January 20, 2009; Sarah Fister Gale, "While Everything Else Stops, Green Still Means Go," Green-Biz, January 19, 2009, http://www .planetthoughts.org/?pg=pt/Whole&qid=2675, accessed June 1, 2011.

32. Marc Weirsum, "China's Manufacturing Wages Rise to $7,000 Per Year: Baidu Benefits," Market Realist, April 22, 2014, http://marketrealist.com /2014/04/chinas-manufacturing-wages-rise-7000 -per-year-baidu-benefits/, accessed February 5, 2015; "Wages in China," China Labour Bulletin, June 10, 2013, http://www.clb.org.hk/en/content /wages-china, accessed January 10, 2014; Keith Bradsheir, "Even as Wages Rise, China Exports Grow," *The New York Times*, January 9, 2014, http:// www.nytimes.com/2014/01/10/business/international /chinese-exports-withstand-rising-labor-costs.html ?hpw&rref=business&_r=0, accessed January 10, 2014; "United States Average Hourly Wages in Manufacturing," *Trading Economics*, January 11, 2014, http://www .tradingeconomics.com/united -states/wages-in-manufacturing, accessed January 10, 2014; Louis Uchitelle, "Factory Jobs Gain But Wages Retreat," *The New York Times*, December 29, 2011, http://www.nytimes.com/2011/12/30/business/us -manufacturing-gains-jobs-as-wages-retreat.html ?pagewanted=all, accessed January 9, 2013; David Luhnow and Bob Davis, "For Mexico, an Edge on China," *The Wall Street Journal*, September 16, 2012, http://online.wsj.com/article/SB10000872396 390444318104577587191288101170.html, accessed January 9, 2013; Dexter Roberts, "How Rising Wages Are Changing the Game in China," *Business-Week*, March 27, 2006, http://www.businessweek .com/magazine/content/06_13/b3977049.htm, accessed January 20, 2009; Richard McCormack, "Good Luck Competing Against Chinese Labor

Costs, Mfg. Job Growth in China Is Headed Up, Not Down; 109 Million Mfg. Workers in China Dwarfs Number in U.S.," *Manufacturing and Technology News*, May 2, 2006, http://www .manufacturingnews.com/news/06/0502/art1.html, accessed January 20, 2009; Scott Tong, "Cost of Chinese Labor Is on the Rise," *Marketplace*, July 6, 2007, http://marketplace.publicradio.org/display /web/2007/07/06/cost_of_chinese_labor_is_on_the _rise/, accessed January 20, 2009; Judith Banister, "Manufacturing in China Today: Employment and Labor Compensation," The Conference Board, September 2007, http://www.conference-board.org /economics/workingpapers.cfm, accessed January 20, 2009; Bill Powell, "The End of Cheap Labor in China," *Time* magazine, June 26, 2011, http://www .time.com/time/magazine/article/0,9171,2078121,00 .html, accessed January 16, 2012.

33. Jason Beaubien, "Asian tsunami devastates Sri Lankan fishing industry," *NPR*, Morning Edition, January 10, 2005, http://www.npr.org/templates/story /story.php?storyId=4276161; Sally Pook, "Phuket tourism industry crippled by mass cancellations," Cyber Diver News Network, January 8, 2005, http://www.cdnn.info/news/travel/t050111.html; Veronique de Rugy, "Homeland security scuffle," *National Review*, October 15, 2004, http://www .nationalreview.com/comment/rugy 200410150840 .asp; "Bush brushes aside rebuilding cost concerns," Reuters News Service, *MSNBC*, September 19, 2005, http://www.msnbc.msn.com/id/9374106/.

34. Daniel Pink, "Pomp and Circumspect," *The New York Times*, June 4, 2005, http://select.nytimes. com/gst/abstract.html?res=F60C1FFD3F5C0C778 CDAF0894DD404482.

Pg. 14 Fact: http://www.thedailybeast.com/newweek /2007/12/22/the-rise-of-a-fierce-yet-fragile-superpower .html, accessed November 2012.

2

1. "B–1.—Gross Domestic Product, 1959–2008, Economic Report of the President: 2009 Spread-sheet Tables," Government Printing Office, updated January 14, 2009, http://www.gpoaccess.gov /eop/tables09.html, accessed January 20, 2009.

2. "How Much Is a Trillion Dollars?," *The Mansfield North Central Ohio Tea Party Association*, http:// americaneedsyounow.org/howmuch.htm, accessed July, 2013.

3. "U.S. Foreclosure Activity Decreases 14 Percent in June to Lowest Level Since December 2006 Despite 34 Percent Jump in Judicial Scheduled Fore-closure Auctions," *RealtyTrac*, July 11, 2013, http:// www.realtytrac.com/Content/foreclosure-market -report/midyear-2013-us-foreclosure-market-report -7794, accessed January 12, 2014; Amy Hoak, "More Foreclosures Expected in 2011," *The Wall Street Journal*, December 12, 2010, http://online .wsj.com/article/SB1000142405274870351860457 6014011451160994.html?mod=googlenews_wsj, accessed January 24, 2011; RealtyTrac Staff, "Re-altyTrac's James J. Saccacio to Discuss Foreclosure Crisis Fallout at AFSA State Government Affairs Forum," *RealtyTrac*, October 1, 2008, http://www .realtytrac.com/ContentManagement/pressrelease. aspx?ChannelID=9&ItemID=5284&a ccnt=64847, accessed January 22, 2009; RealtyTrac Staff, "REALTYTRAC® Year-end Report Shows Record 2.8 Million U.S. Properties With Foreclosure Filings in 2009," *RealtyTrac*, January 14, 2010,

http://www.realtytrac.com/contentmanagement /pressrelease.aspx?itemid=8333, accessed April 21, 2010; "RealtyTrac: 2011 National Foreclosure Rate Lowest Since 2007," *Commercial Record*, January 12, 2012, http://www.commercialrecord. com/news148166 .html, accessed January 18, 2012; *CoreLogic National Foreclosure Report*, CoreLogic, January 2014, http://www.corelogic.com/research /foreclosure-report/national-foreclosure-report -january-2014.pdf, accessed February 6, 2015.

4. Chris Isidore, "7.9 Million Jobs Lost—Many Forever," *CNNMoney*, July 2, 2010, http://money.cnn .com/2010/07/02/news/economy/jobs_gone_forever /index.htm, accessed January 24, 2011.

5. Credit Crisis—The Essentials, *The New York Times*, updated January 20, 2009, https://www .nytimes.com/topic/subject/economic-crisis-and -market-upheavals, accessed January 20, 2009; Sharon Silke Carty and Barbara Hagenbaugh, "Automakers Say If They Go, Millions of Jobs Will Vanish," *USA Today* website, http://www.usatoday. com/money/autos/2008-11-17-automakers-bailout -impact_N.htm, accessed January 21, 2009; "Auto Industry Bailout Overview," *The New York Times*, updated January 20, 2009, http://topics.nytimes .com/topics/reference/timestopics/subjects/c/credit _crisis/index.html, accessed January 21, 2009.

6. Jackie Calmes, "TARP Bailout to Cost Less Than Once Anticipated," *The New York Times*, October 1, 2010, http://dealbook.nytimes.com/2010/10/01 /tarp-bailout-to-cost-less-than-once-anticipated/.

7. Michael Grunwald, "One Trillion Dollars," January 26, 2009, *Time*, pp. 27–31, http://www.time .com/time/politics/article/0,8599,1871769,00.html, accessed February 5, 2011; Jeannine Aversa and Christopher S. Rugaber, "Economy Adds Jobs at Fastest Pace in Three Years," *Associated Press*, April 2, 2010, http://www.google.com/hostednews/ap/article /ALeqM5gNiyJ905Ho0Ur96V2TQhsBX19lGwD9 ER6P402, accessed April 20, 2010; Greg Robb, September "Bernanke Declares 'recession is very likely over,'" *MarketWatch*, September 15, 2009, http://www.marketwatch.com/story/bernanke -declares-the-recession-over-2009-09-15, accessed, April 20, 2010; Eric Morath, "Jobs Report: Solid Job Gains Belie Economic Unease," *The Wall Street Journal*, November 7, 2014, http://www.wsj.com /articles/jobs-report-economy-adds-214000-jobs -1415367269, accessed May 5, 2016.

8. Jeanne Sahadi, "Debt Ceiling FAQs: What You Need to Know," *CNN Money*, May 18, 2011, http://money.cnn.com/2011/01/03/news/economy /debt_ceiling_faqs/index.htm, accessed January 20, 2013; Michael Grunwald, "Cliff Dweller," *Time*, January 14, 2013, http://www.time.com/time /magazine/article/0,9171,2132749,00.html, accessed January 20, 2013.

9. US debt clock, US debt clock, http://www. usdebtclock.org/index.htmlhttp://www.usdebtclock. org/index.html, accessed April 19, 2018.

10. Will Tax Reform Add to US Debt Concerns? By VanEck, January 29, 2018, https://marketrealist. com/2018/01/will-tax-reform-add-u-s-debt-woes, accessed April 18, 2018.

11. Rebecca Blumenstein and Natalia Drozdiak, "Airbus to Join Forces with Uber for On-Demand Helicopter Service, CEO Says," *The Wall Street Journal*, January 18, 2016, http://www.wsj.com /articles/airbus-to-join-forces-with-uber-for-on -demand-helicopter-service-ceo-says-1453048668, accessed January 25, 2017.

12. Mike Juljenz, "A Message to Obama and Congress: Kill the Cent and Save a Pretty Penny," *Money News*, September 1, 2013, http://www.moneynews. com/MikeFuljenz/penny-cent-circulation-money /2013/09/01/id/523353, accessed January 15, 2014; Amy Bowen, "Is the Penny Going Away? Not Yet," *USA Today*, March 3, 2013, http://www.usatoday .com/story/news /nation/2013/03/02/penny-not -going-away-yet/1958995/, accessed January 15, 2014; "M1 Money Stock," Economic Research Federal Reserve Bank of St. Louis, https://research .stlouisfed.org/fred2/series/M1, accessed May 10, 2016.

13. "Historical Changes of the Target Federal Funds and Discount Rates," *Federal Reserve Bank of New York*, http://www.newyorkfed.org/markets /statistics/dlyrates/fedrate.html, accessed January 22, 2009.

14. "Workers on tap," *The Economist*, January 3, 2015, http://www.economist.com/news/leaders /21637393-rise-demand-economy-poses-difficult -question-workers-companies-and, accessed February 8, 2015.

15. Steven Levitt, "Scarecrows Work on People Too," *Freakonomics*, June 28, 2006, http:// freakonomics.com/2006/06/28/scarecrows-work-on -people-too/, accessed February 7, 2016.

16. "OK Federal Government, Excluding Postal Services," U.S. Department of Labor Bureau of Labor Statistics, March 12, 2008, http://stats.bls. gov/oco/cg/cgs041.htm, accessed August 16, 2008; "Postal Service Workers," U.S. Department of Labor Bureau of Labor Statistics, December 18, 2007, http://stats.bls.gov/oco/ocos141.htm, accessed August 16, 2008; "Job Opportunities in the Armed Forces," U.S. Department of Labor Bureau of Labor Statistics, December 18, 2007, http://stats.bls .gov/oco/ocos249.htm, accessed August 16, 2008.

17. Daniel J. Mitchell, "Russia's Flat Tax Miracle," The Heritage Foundation, March 24, 2003, http:// www.heritage.org/Press/Commentary/ed032403. cfm; Deroy Murdock, "Russians Do Taxes Right," *National Review Online*, March 1, 2002, http://www .nationalreview.com/murdock /murdock030102. shtml; "Russia: Income Taxes and Tax Laws," Worldwide-Tax, July 2005, http://www.worldwide -tax.com/russia/russia_tax .asp; "History of the U.S. Tax System," U.S. Department of the Treasury, https:// www.treasury.gov/resource-center/faqs/Taxes/Pages /historyroosevelt message.aspx, accessed May 21, 2017.

18. Socialism, Capitalism Seen in New Light by Younger Americans by By Eli Stokols, December 6, 2017, https://www.wsj.com/articles/socialism- capitalism-seen-in-new-light-by-younger-ameri- cans-1512561601, accessed April 19, 2018.

19. "Gross Domestic Product," Economic Research, Federal Reserve Bank of St. Louis, https:// research.stlouisfed.org/fred2/series/GDP, accessed May 10, 2016.

20. Bureau of Labor Statistics, https://data.bls.gov/ timeseries/LNS14000000, accessed April 19, 2018.

21. "Labor Force Statistics from the Current Population Survey," Bureau of Labor Statistics, http:// data.bls.gov/timeseries/LNU04000000?years _option=all_years&periods_option=specific _periods&periods=Annual+Data, accessed January 14, 2014; Rana Foroohar, "The Flat Paycheck Recovery," *Time* Magazine, January 13, 2014, http://content.time.com/time/magazine/article /0,9171,2161670,00.html, accessed January 14, 2014. Leslie Kwoh, "News and Trends in Manage-

ment," *The Wall Street Journal*, February 13, 2012, http://online.wsj.com/article/SB10001424052970 204642604577215372010543642.html, accessed January 21, 2013; Jeevan Vasagar, "Graduates Warned of Record 70 Applicants for Every Job," *The Guardian*, July 6, 2010, http://www.guardian.co.uk /education/2010/jul/06/graduates-face-tougher-jobs -fight, accessed January 26, 2011.

22. "Labor Force Statistics from the Current Population Survey: Unemployment Rate Table," U.S. Department of Labor, Bureau of Labor Statistics, http:// data.bls.gov/PDQ/servlet/SurveyOutputServlet?data _tool=latest_numbers&series_id=LNS14000000, accessed January 22, 2009.

23. "Table of Historical Inflation Rates by Month and Year (1914–2013)," U.S. Inflation Calculator, January 16, 2013, http://www.usinflationcalculator .com/inflation/historical-inflation-rates/, accessed January 21, 2013.

Pg. 26 Fact: Rana Foroohar, "Open the Door and Let 'Em In," *Time* Magazine, July 22, 2013, http:// content.time.com/time/magazine/article /0,9171,2147289,00.html, accessed September 2014.

Pg. 34 "Fact: Parents Projected to Spend $245,340 to Raise a Child Born in 2013, According to USDA Report," USDA News Report, August 18, 2014, http://www.usda.gov/wps/portal/usda/usdahome?c ontentidonly=true&contentid=2014/08/0179.xml, accessed September 2014.

3

1. "The World Economy Overview," The World Factbook, CIA, February 2011, https://www.cia .gov/library/publications/the-world-factbook /geos/xx.html, accessed February 5, 2011; "Global Economic Outlook 2012," The Conference Board, January 2012, http://www.conference-board.org /data/globaloutlook.cfm, accessed February 2, 2012; "World Economic Situation and Prospects 2014: Global Economic Outlook (Chapter 1)," United Nations, December 18, 2013, http://www.un.org/en /development/desa/publications/wesp2014-firstchapter .html, accessed February 22, 2015; World Economic Outlook, October 2017 Seeking Sustainable Growth https://www.imf.org/en/Publications/WEO/ Issues/2017/09/19/world-economic-outlook- october-2017, accessed April 21, 2018.

2. "Rank Order Estimates," The World Factbook, CIA, https://www.cia.gov/library/publications/the-world- factbook/rankorder/2003rank.html?countryName=In dia&countryCode=in&regionCode=sas&rank=35#in, https://www.cia.gov/library/publications/the-world -factbook/rankorder/2003rank.html?countryName =Algeria&countryCode=ag&regionCode=afr&rank =139#ag, https://www.cia.gov/library/publications /the-world-factbook/rankorder/2119rank.html?country Name=Angola&countryCode=ao&regionCode =afr&rank =59#ao, all accessed May 17, 2018.

3. Adam Davidson, "Why Are Corporations Hoarding Trillions?," *New York Times* Magazine, January 20, 2016, https://www.nytimes. com/2016/01/24/magazine/why-are-corporations -hoarding-trillions.html?_r=0, accessed January 27, 2017; Jeff Cox, "US Companies Are Hoarding $2.5 Trillion in Cash Overseas," *CNBC*, September 20, 2016, http://www.cnbc.com/2016/09/20/us -companies-are-hoarding-2-and-a-half-trillion -dollars-in-cash-overseas.html, accessed January 27, 2017.

4. Mature Economies are Solidifying Growth Path; Emerging Economies More Mixed November 13, 2017, https://www.conference-board.org/press/press-detail.cfm?pressid=7250, accessed April 21, 2018.

5. Emerging Markets: 3 Key Insights For 2018 By Edward Kerschner, Feb. 6, 2018, https://seekingalpha.com/article/4143365-emerging-markets-3-key-insights-2018, accessed April 26, 2018.

6. Natasha Lomas, "ABI: Africa's Mobile Market to Pass 80% Subscriber Penetration in Q1 Next Year; 13.9% of Global Cellular Market by 2017," TechCrunch, November 28, 2012, http://techcrunch.com/2012/11/28/abi-africas-mobile-market-to-pass-80-subscriber-penetration-in-q1-next-year-13-9-of-global-cellular-market-by-2017/, accessed January 24, 2013; Pia Heikkila, "1B Cell Phone Users and no Apple iPhone in India's Breakneck Mobile-Apps Market," International Business Times, September 15, 2012, http://www.ibtimes.com/1b-cellphone-users-and-no-apple-iphone-indias-breakneck-mobile-apps-market-789460, accessed January 24, 2013; Sumnina Udas, "Bringing Toilets and Dignity to India's Poor," CNN, September 17, 2012, http://www.cnn.com/2012/09/17/world/asia/india-open-toilets-udas/index.html, accessed January 24, 2013.

7. "Insperiences," Trendwatching, http://www.trendwatching.com/trends/insperience.htm, accessed January 12, 2006; "Ten Key Trends for Chocolate Products," Food and Drink Europe, January 23, 2012, http://www.foodanddrinkeurope.com/Consumer-Trends/10-key-trends-for-chocolateproducts?utm_source=copyright&utm_medium=OnSite&utm_campaign=copyright, accessed February 3, 2012.

8. "WTO Sees Gradual Recovery in Coming Months Despite Cut in Trade Forecasts," WTO press release, September 19, 2013, http://www.wto.org/english/news_e/pres13_e/pr694_e.htm, accessed January 16, 2014; "Trade to expand by 9.5% in 2010 after a dismal 2009," WTO press release, March 26, 2010, http://www.wto.org/english/news_e/pres10_e/pr598_e.htm, accessed February 9, 2010; "The World Economy: Overview," The World Factbook, CIA, updated February 2010, https://www.cia.gov/library/publications/the-world-factbook/geos/xx.html, accessed February 9, 2010; "Economy," The World Factbook, CIA, January 26, 2012, https://www.cia.gov/library/publications/the-world-factbook/geos/xx.html, accessed February 3, 2012; "Falling Import Demand, Lower Commodity Prices Push Down Trade Growth Prospects," WTO press release, September 30, 2015, https://www.wto.org/english/news_e/pres15_e/pr752_e.htm, accessed March 2, 2016.

9. Emily Chasan, "Currency Cost U.S. Companies at Least $4 Billion in Second Quarter," The Wall Street Journal, September 19, 2013, http://blogs.wsj.com/cfo/2013/09/19/currency-cost-u-s-companies-at-least-4-billion-in-second-quarter/, accessed January 16, 2014; Paul Ausick, "P&G Only One of Many Hit by Foreign Exchange Rates (PG, PEP, KMB, CL, KO, PM, MCD, F, CCL)," 24/7, The Wall Street Journal, June 20, 2012, http://247wallst.com/2012/06/20/pg-only-one-of-many-hit-by-foreign-exchange-rates-pg-pep-kmb-cl-ko-pm-mcd-f-ccl/, accessed January 25, 2013.

10. Neha Gupta, "What Is Countertrade?," Barter News Weekly, March 11, 2010, http://www.barternewsweekly.com/2010/03/11/what-is-counter-trade-1851/, accessed February 10, 2010; Dan West, "Countertrade—An Innovative Approach to Marketing," Chairman American Countertrade Association, BarterNews 36 (1996), http://barternews.com/approach_marketing.htm; Global Offset and Countertrade Association, http://www.globaloffset.org/index.htm, accessed January 27, 2006.

11. Ellen Barry, "Have Car, Need Briefs? In Russia, Barter Is Back," The New York Times, February 8, 2009, http://www.nytimes.com/2009/02/08/world/europe/08barter.html?pagewanted=all, accessed January 25, 2013.

12. Calum Macleod, "Greenpeace: China-made Kids' Clothes Carry Toxic Risk," USA Today, December 17, 2013, http://www.usatoday.com/story/news/world/2013/12/17/china-toxic-clothing-greenpeace/4049853/, accessed January 16, 2014; "Mattel Issues New Massive China Toy Recall," Associated Press, MSNBC, August 14, 2007, http://www.msnbc.msn.com/id/20254745/ns/business-consumer_news/, accessed February 10, 2010; Eric S. Lipton and David Barboza, "As More Toys Are Recalled, Trail Ends in China," The New York Times, June 19, 2007, http://www.nytimes.com/2007/06/19/business/worldbusiness/19toys.html, accessed January 29, 2009.

13. E. Yellin, Your Call Is (Not That) Important to Us (New York: Simon Schuster, 2009); Carolyn Beeler, "Outsourced Call Centers Return, to U.S. homes," NPR, August 25, 2010, http://www.npr.org/templates/story/story.php?storyId=129406588, accessed February 10, 2010.

14. Heesun Wee, "More Businesses Exporting 'Made in USA' Again," CNBC, May 12, 2014, http://www.cnbc.com/id/101646468, accessed March 2, 2015.

15. Robert Guest, "Generation Uphill," The Economist, January 23, 2016, http://www.economist.com/news/special-report/21688591-millennials-are-brainiest-best-educated-generation-ever-yet-their-elders-often, accessed January 27, 2017; "Global Unemployment Rate from 2007 to 2012 with a Forecast up to 2017," Statista, https://www.statista.com/statistics/279777/global-unemployment-rate/, accessed February 1, 2017.

16. Stacy Meichtry and John Stoll, "Fiat Nears Stake in Chrysler That Could Lead to Takeover," The Wall Street Journal, January 20, 2009, http://online.wsj.com/article/SB123238519459294991.html, accessed February 10, 2010; "eBay to acquire Skype," press release, Skype, September 12, 2005, http://www.skype.com/company/news/2005/skype_ebay.html, accessed February 10, 2010.

17. David Barboza, "Intel to Build Advanced Chip-Making Plant in China," The New York Times, March 27, 2007, http://www.nytimes.com/2007/03/27/technology/27chip.html, accessed January 30, 2009.

18. Cynthia Churchwell, "Rethink the value of joint ventures," Harvard Business School Working Knowledge, May 10, 2004, http://hbswk.hbs.edu/item.jhtml?id=4113&t=globalization.

19. Michael Schuman, "Hyundai Grows Up," Time Global Business, July 2005, http://www.time.com/time/globalbusiness/article/0,9171,1074141,00.html; Cathie Gandel, "At 5 Feet 10 Inches, I Was Too Tall for Tokyo," My Turn, Newsweek, December 12, 2005; Moon Ihlwan, "Hyundai Bets Big on India and China," BusinessWeek, January 30, 2008, http://www.businessweek.com/globalbiz/content/jan2008/gb20080130_061205.htm, accessed January 30, 2009; "Maruti, Hyundai, Tata Motors Lose Market Share to Smaller Firms in 2010," India Times, April 10, 2011, http://economictimes.indiatimes.com/automobiles/maruti-hyundai-tata-motors-lose-market-share-to-smaller-firms-in-2010-11/articleshow/7932281.cms, accessed February 6, 2012.

20. "Rural Market India Brand Equity Foundation," IBEF, December 10, 2010, http://www.ibef.org/artdispview.aspx?art_id=27581&cat_id=938&in=78, accessed February 10, 2010; "Selling to Rural India," Springwise Newsletter, June 2003, http://www.springwise.com/newbusinessideas/2003/06/shakti.html; "Red herring: selling to the poor," The Next Practice, April 11, 2004, http://www.thenextpractice.com/news/red_herring_selling_to_the_poor.php; Tim Weber, "Are you ready for globalization 2.0?," BBC News, January 28, 2005, http://news.bbc.co.uk/1/hi/business/4214687.stm.

21. Ted Burnham, "What Pizza Hut's Crown Crust Pizza Says about Global Fast Food Marketing," NPR, May 2, 2012, http://www.npr.org/sections/thesalt/2012/05/01/151781785/what-pizza-huts-crown-crust-pizza-says-about-global-fast-food-marketing, accessed January 25, 2013; Nina Africano, "McDonald's International: Top Ten Most Unusual Around the World," AOL Travel, September 3, 2010, http://news.travel.aol.com/2010/09/03/mcdonald-s-international-top-ten-most-unusual-around-the-world/, accessed January 25, 2013; "McDonald's country/market sites," http://www.mcdonalds.com/countries.html, accessed February 10, 2011; Domino's Pizza LLC [US], http://www.dominos.com/Public-EN/Site+Content/Secondary/Inside+Dominos/Pizza+Particulars/International+Speciality+Toppings/; Robyn Lee, "10 Crazy Asian Pizzas," http://slice.seriouseats.com/archives/2008/02/crazy-weird-asian-pizza-crusts-japanese-korean-hong-kong.html, accessed May 21, 2017; Editors of Publications International, "Favorite Pizza Toppings in 10 Countries," How Stuff Works Lifestyle, http://recipes.howstuffworks.com/fresh-ideas/dinner-food-facts/favorite-pizza-toppings-in-10-countries.htm, accessed May 21, 2017; William Mellor, "McDonald's No Match for KFC in China as Colonel Rules Fast Food," Bloomberg, January 26, 2011, http://www.bloomberg.com/news/2011-01-26/mcdonald-s-no-match-for-kfc-in-china-where-colonel-sanders-rules-fast-food.html, accessed February 6, 2012; Erik German, "Morocco Loving the McArabia," Global Post, May 30, 2010, http://www.globalpost.com/dispatch/morocco/090825/morocco-loving-the-mcarabia, accessed February 6, 2012.

22. "Internet World Stats," http://www.internetworldstats.com/stats.htm, accessed January 28, 2016.

23. World Bank, Doing Business 2017: Equal Opportunity for All (Washington, DC: World Bank). DOI: 10.1596/978-1-4648-0948-4. License: Creative Commons Attribution CC BY 3.0 IGO, accessed January 28, 2017.

24. Will Sarni, "Water Works," Interbrand, 2012, http://www.interbrand.com/en/best-global-brands/Best-Global-Green-Brands/2012-Report/water-works.aspx, accessed January 26, 2013; 2030: Brian Dumaine, "China's Coming Water Crisis," Fortune magazine, December 14, 2012, http://tech.fortune.cnn.com/2012/12/14/2030-chinas-coming-water-crisis/, accessed January 26, 2013; "WaterFacts," Water.Org, 2012, http://water.org/water-crisis/water-facts/water/, accessed January 26, 2013.

25. "Shadow Market: 2011 Global Software Piracy Study," Business Software Alliance, May 2012, http://portal.bsa.org/globalpiracy2011/downloads/study_pdf/2011_BSA_Piracy_Study-Standard.pdf, accessed January 26, 2013.

26. Wayne Ma, "China Levies 6.5% Tariff on U.S. Solar-Panel Materials," The Wall Street Journal,

September 18, 2013, http://online.wsj.com/news /articles/SB1000142412788732352700457907907057 2200630, accessed January 19, 2014; John W. Miller, "Nations rush to establish new barriers to trade," *The Wall Street Journal*, February 6, 2009, http:// online.wsj.com/article/SB123388103125654861.html, accessed January 26, 2013; William Mauldin, "U.S. Moves to Impose Tariffs on Chinese Tires," *The Wall Street Journal*, November 24, 2014, http://www.wsj .com/articles/u-s-moves-to-impose-tariffs-on -chinese-tires-1416866855, accessed March 2, 2015.

27. Richard Mills, "USTR Releases 2002 Inventory of Trade Barriers," press release, Office of the United States Trade Representative, April 2, 2002, https://ustr.gov/archive/Document_Library/Press _Releases/2002/April/USTR_Releases_2002 _Inventory_of_Trade_Barriers.html; "U.S. Targets Non-tariff Barriers to Global Trade," press release, Washington File, April 2, 2002, https://wfile.ait.org .tw/wf-archive/2002/020402/epf212.htm.

28. "Debt Relief Under the Heavily Indebted Poor Countries Initiative," Fact Sheet, International Monetary Fund, January 10, 2013, http://www.imf .org/external/np/exr/facts/hipc.htm, accessed January 26, 2013; "Debt Relief Under the Heavily Indebted Poor Countries (HIPC) Initiative," Fact-sheet, International Monetary Fund, December 16, 2010, http://www.imf.org/external /np/exr/facts/hipc .htm, accessed February 11, 2010.

29. Daniel Workman, "Top 10 Exporting Countries Causing the US Trade Deficit," Suite101, April 27, 2010, http://www.suite101.com/content/top-10 -exporting-countries-causing-the-us-trade-deficit -a226747, accessed February 11, 2011.

30. Eric Ting, "How a 20% Import Tax Could Affect California's Mexican Imports and Exports," San Francisco Gate, January 27, 2017, http://www .sfgate.com/politics/article/How-Trump-s-proposed -import-tax-will-impact-10887801.php, accessed January 31, 2017; "California Passes France As World's 6th-Largest Economy," June 18, 2016, http://fortune.com/2016/06/17/california-france -6th-largest-economy/, accessed January 31, 2017.

31. "European Union," The World Factbook, The Economy Overview: CIA, February 2011, https:// www.cia.gov/library/publications/the-world -factbook/geos/ee.html, accessed February 11, 2011.

32. Julie Kollewe, "IMF Says Refugee Influx Could Provide EU Economic Boost," *The Guardian*, January 20, 2016, http://www.theguardian.com /business/2016/jan/20/imf-refugee-influx-provide -eu-economic-boost, accessed March 10,2016; Jon Stone, "The Refugee Crisis Is Actually Having "Sizable" Economic Benefits in European Countries, EU Says," *The Independent*, November 5, 2015, http://www.independent.co.uk/news/world /europe/the-refugee-crisis-will-actually-have-a -sizable-positive-economic-impact-on-european -countries-eu-a6722396.html#gallery, accessed March 10, 2016.

33. Steven Erlanger, "'Brexit': Explaining Britain's Vote on European Union Membership," *The New York Times*, June 16, 2016, http://www .nytimes.com/interactive/2016/world/europe/britain -european-union-brexit.html?_r=1, accessed July 31, 2016; Everrett Rosenfeld, "Brexit 101: What Just Happened, and Why It's Important for Americans," June 24, 2016, http://www.cnbc.com /2016/06/24 /brexit-101-what-just-happened-and -why-its-important-for-americans.html, accessed July 31, 2016.

34. Rebecca Flood, "REVEALED: Which Countries Could Be Next to Leave the EU?," Express, October 2, 2016, http://www.express.co.uk/news /world/716421/EU-referendum-Brexit-leave-vote -country-Merkel-superstate-Italy, accessed January 31, 2017; Alex Hunt and Brian Wheeler, "Brexit: All you need to know about the UK leaving the EU," *BBC News*, June 21, 2018, https://www. bbc.com/news/uk-politics-32810887, accessed July 2, 2018.

Pg. 41 Fact: Sumnima Udas, "Bringing Toilets and Dignity to the Poor," *CNN*, September 17, 2012, http://www.cnn.com/2012/09/17/world/asia/india -open-toilets-udas/index.html, accessed November 2012.

Pg. 42 Fact: Stephen Gandel, "This Time for Africa?," *Time* magazine, November 1, 2010, http:// content.time.com/time/magazine/article/0,9171, 2026897,00.html, accessed October 19, 2016.

Pg. 51 Fact: Anup Shah, "Causes of Poverty," Global Issues, http://www.globalissues.org/issue/2 /causes-of-poverty, accessed November 2012.

4

1. Davey Alba, "Judge Rejects Uber's $100 Million Settlement with Drivers," Wired August 18, 2016,, https://www.wired.com/2016/08/uber-settlement -rejected/f, accessed March 25, 2017; Biz Carson, "Judge Grants Class-action Status to Uber Drivers Who Are Suing to Be Classified as Employees," BusinessInsider, September 1, 2015, http://www .businessinsider.com/judge-grants-class-action -status-to-uber-drivers-2015-9, accessed March 25, 2017; Rick McCormick, "Uber Settles Lawsuits to Keep Drivers as Independent Contractors in California and Massachusetts," The Verge Website, April 21, 2016, http://www.theverge.com/2016/4/21/11485424 /uber-suit-california-Massachusetts-drivers-employee -contractor, accessed March 25, 2017; David McCabe, "Uber Says More Drivers Holding Other Jobs," The Hill, December 7, 2015, http://thehill. com/policy/technology/262298-uber-says-more -working-for-company-on-the-side.

2. Craig Downden, "Forget Ethics Training: Focus on Empathy," *Financial Post*, June 21, 2013, http:// business.financialpost.com/2013/06/21/forget-ethics -training-focus-on-empathy/, accessed January 24, 2014.

3. Josh Levs, "Big Three Auto CEOs Flew Private Jets to Ask for Taxpayer Money," *CNN*, November 19, 2008, http://www.cnn.com/2008/US/11/19/autos .ceo.jets/, accessed February 2, 2009.

4. Ryan J. Donmoyer, "Lawmakers, Questioning Fed Bailout, Seek AIG 'Junket' Refund," *Bloomberg*, October 9, 2008, http://www.bloomberg.com /apps/news?pid=newsarchive&sid=aPlPYw6JXIBU &refer=us, accessed February 21, 2011.

5. Barney Gimbel, "Why We'll Miss the Disney Trial," *Fortune*, December 27, 2004, CNNMoney, http://money.cnn.com/magazines/fortune/fortune _archive/2004/12/27/8217949/index.htm; Peter Bart, "Disney's Basket Cases," *Variety*, March 7, 2004, http://www.variety.com/article/VR1117901299.html ?categoryid=1&cs=1.

6. "Pierre Omidyar: Tufts President Lawrence S. Bacow Awarded Pierre Omidyar an Honorary Degree During the University's 155th Commencement Ceremonies on Sunday, May 22, 2011, TuftsNow, February 24, 2013," http://now.tufts.edu/commencement-2011 /pierre-omidyar, accessed February 24, 2013; Walter

Hamilton and Kathy M. Kristof, "Merrill CEO departs with $160 million," *Los Angeles Times*, October 31, 2007, http://articles.latimes.com/2007 /oct/31/business/fi-merrill31, accessed February 24, 2013; Peter Edmonston, "Thain Says He'll Repay Remodeling Costs," *The New York Times*, January 26, 2009, http://www.nytimes.com/2009/01/27/business /27bank.html?_r=0, accessed February 24, 2013; David Kesmodel and John Wilke, "Whole Foods Is Hot, Wild Oats a Dud—So Said "Rahodeb", *The Wall Street Journal*, July 12, 2007, http://online.wsj .com/article/SB118418782959963745.html, accessed February 24, 2013.

7. "National Business Ethics Survey: How Employees View Ethics in Their Organizations, 1994–2005," Ethics Resource Center, October 12, 2005, http://www.ethics.org/research/2005-press -release.asp; "National Business Ethics Survey," Ethics Resource Center, 2009, http://www.ethics .org/nbes/files/nbes-final.pdf, accessed May 14, 2010; "2011 NBES Key Findings," Ethics, http:// www.ethics.org/nbes/findings.html, accessed February 26, 2012.

8. Bob Lane, "The Role of Tone from the Top," Ethisphere, December 28, 2009, http://ethisphere.com /the-role-of-tone-from-the-top/, accessed February 21, 2011.

9. "Supplemental Research Brief, Ethics and Employee Engagement, 2009 National Business Ethics Survey," Ethics Resource Center, http://www.ethics .org/files/u5/NBESResearchBrief2.pdf, accessed February 6, 2013.

10. Felicity Barringer, "Clorox Courts Sierra Club, and a Product Is Endorsed," *The New York Times*, March 26, 2008, http://www.nytimes.com/2008/03/26 /business/businessspecial2/26cleanser.html, accessed February 24, 2013; Tyson Foods home page, http://www.tyson.com/About-Tyson.aspx, accessed February 24, 2013; Andrea Tse, "Will Supreme Court Hear Farmer's Case Against Tyson Foods?," *The Street*, January 24, 2011, http://www.thestreet .com/story/10982877/1/will-supreme-court-hear-farmers -case-against-tyson-foods.html, accessed February 24, 2011; Sarah Ellison, "Kraft Limits on Kids' Ads May Cheese Off Rivals," *The Wall Street Journal*, January 13, 2005, http://www.aef.com/industry/news/data/2005 /3076, accessed February 24, 2013; Megan Chuchmach, "Bailed Out Bank of America Sponsors Super Bowl Fun Fest," *ABC News*, February 2, 2009, http:// abcnews.go.com/Blotter/story?id=6782719&page=1, accessed February 24, 2013; Jane Akre, "Crash That Led to Toyota Recall 'Inconclusive,'" Legal Examiner, December 8, 2009, http://news.legalexaminer.com /crash-that-led-to-toyota-recall-inconclusive.aspx ?googleid=275542, accessed February 24, 2013.

11. Bob Leduc, "Complaining Customers Are Good for Business," Virtual Marketing Newsletter, May 11, 2004, http://www.marketingsource.com /newsletter/05-11-2004.html.

12. Amanda MacMillan, "Is Subway Chicken Really 50% Filler?," *Time* Magazine, March 5, 2017, http://time.com/4686280/subway-chicken-fast-food -filler/, accessed March 25, 2017.

13. Jeannine Stein, "O.B. Ultra Tampons Are Coming Back, and the Company Apologizes with a Song," *Los Angeles Times*, December 8, 2011, http://articles.latimes.com/2011/dec/08/news /la-heb-ob-tampons-return-20111208, accessed February 29, 2012.

14. Open letter to iPhone customers, Apple, http:// www.apple.com/hotnews/openiphoneletter/, accessed February 3, 2009; Jeff Smykil, "Apple's customer satis-

faction up despite struggling industry," Ars Technica, August 19, 2008, http://arstechnica.com/apple/news /2008/08/apples-customer-satisfaction-up-despite -struggling-industry.ars, accessed February 3, 2009; "The American Customer Satisfaction Index Scores by Company, Personal Computers Through 2011," *ACSI*, http://www.theacsi.org/index.php?option=com _content&view=article&id =149&catid=&Itemid =214&c=Apple+, accessed March 20, 2012.

15. Christina Bonnington, "Tim Cook Apologizes for Mapocalypse Debacle," Wired, September 28, 2012, http://www.wired.com/gadgetlab/2012/09/tim -cook-apologizes-for-maps/, accessed February 4, 2013; Juliette Garside, "Apple Shares Slide as iPhone Misses Christmas Sales Forecast," *Guardian*, January 23, 2013, http://www.guardian.co.uk /technology/2013/jan/24/apple-results-iphone-sales, accessed February 4, 2013.

16. Gill Saporito, "Making Good, Plus a Profit," *Time* Magazine, March 22, 2015, http://time.com /author/bill-saporito/, accessed March 15, 2015.

17. Tom Raddle, "Giving USA: Americans Do-nated an Estimated $358.38 Billion to Charity in 2014; Highest Total in Report's 60-Year History," GivingUSA, June 29, 2015, http://givingusa.org /giving-usa-2015-press-release-giving-usa-americans -donated-an-estimated-358-38-billion-to-charity -in-2014-highest-total-in-reports-60-year-history/, accessed March 13, 2016.

18. Todd Henneman, "Patagonia Fills Payroll with People Who Are Passionate," Workforce, November 5, 2011, http://www.workforce.com /articles/patagonia-fills-payroll-with-people-who -are-passionate, accessed January 25, 2013.

19. Starbucks, https://news.starbucks.com/news /starbucks-hiring-initiatives, accessed March 26, 2017.

20. "Starbucks Focuses Hiring Strategy on Veter-ans and Military Spouses," Starbucks, November 6, 2013, http://news.starbucks.com/news/starbucks -focuses-hiring-strategy-on-veterans-and-military -spouses, accessed January 25, 2014.

21. "Recycling in the Restaurant," McDonald's, http:// www.aboutmcdonalds.com/mcd/sustainability /library/policies_programs/environmental _responsibility/recycling_in_the _restaurant.html, accessed February 5, 2013.

22. "'Carbon Footprint' Gaining Business Attention," press release, Conference Board, October 18, 2006, http://www.conference-board.org/UTILITIES /pressDetail.cfm?press_ID=2985, accessed February 4, 2009; Jeffery Ball, "Green Goal of 'carbon neutrality' hits limit," *The Wall Street Jour-nal*, December 30, 2008, http://online.wsj.com/article /SB123059 880241541259.html, accessed February 4, 2009; Andrew Martin, "How Green Is My Orange?" *The New York Times*, January 22, 2009, http://www .nytimes.com/2009/01/22/business/22pepsi.html? _r=1&scp=1&sq=How%20green%20is%20my %20orange&st=cse, accessed February 4, 2009.

23. Debra Shepard, "The Scoop on Scope 3 Emissions," SustainServ, June 16, 2011, http://www .sustainserv.com/de/easyblog/entry/the-scoop-on -scope-3-emissions.html, accessed February 5, 2012; Rachel King, "U.S. Corporations Size Up Their Carbon Footprints," *Bloomberg Business-week*, June 1, 2009, http://www.businessweek.com /technology/content/jun2009/tc2009061_692661 .htm, accessed February 24, 2011.

24. Jena McGregor, "The Oddest, Worst and Most Memorable CEO Apologies of the Year," *The*

Washington Post, December 23, 2014, http:// www .washingtonpost.com/blogs/on-leadership/wp/2014 /12/23/the-oddest-worst-and-most-memorable -ceo-apologies-of-the-year/, accessed March 15, 2015; Eun Kyung Kim, "Lululemon Co-founder Steps Down in Wake of 'women's bodies' Remark," *Today Money*, December 10, 2013, http://www .today.com/money/lululemon-co-founder-steps- down-wake-womens-bodies-remark-2D11721314, accessed March 15, 2015; Mark Thompson and Chris Liakos, "Volkswagen CEO Quits Over 'Grave Crisis,'" *CNN*, September 23, 2015, http://money .cnn.com/2015/09/23/news/companies/volkswagen -emissions-crisis/, accessed March 17, 2016.

25. Jan Hoffman, "Cheating's Surprising Thrill," *The New York Times*, October 7, 2013, http://well .blogs.nytimes.com/2013/10/07/in-bad-news-cheating -feels-good/, accessed January 28, 2014; Romeo Vitelli, "Is There a 'Cheater's High'?," *Psychology Today*, October 14, 2013, http://www.psychologytoday .com/blog/media-spotlight/201310/is-there-cheaters -high, accessed January 28, 2014; Nicole E. Reudy, Celia Moore, Francesca Gino, and Maurice E. Schweitzer, "The Cheater's High: The Unexpected Affective Benefits of Unethical Behavior," *Journal of Personality and Social Psychology*, September 2, 2013, http://www.apa.org/pubs/journals/releases/ psp-a0034231.pdf, accessed March 16, 2015.

26. "Corruption Perceptions Index 2015," Trans-parency International, http://www.transparency .org/cpi2015, accessed March 18, 2016.

27. Marcus Noland and Tyler Moran, "Firms with More Women in the C-Suite Are More Profitable," *Harvard Business Review*, February 8, 2016, https:// hbr.org/2016/02/study-firms-with-more-women-in -the-c-suite-are-more-profitable, accessed March 27, 2017.

28. Matthew Boyle, "In Emerging Markets, Unilever Finds a Passport to Profit," *BusinessWeek*, January 3, 2013, http://www.businessweek.com /articles/2013-01-03/in-emerging-markets-unilever -finds-a-passport-to-profit, accessed January 28, 2014; Thomas Donaldson, "Values in Tension: Eth-ics Away from Home," *Harvard Business Review*, September/October 1996.

29. Nathaniel Parish Flannery, "Has Ralph Lauren Learned That Bribery Is a Bad Business Strategy in Latin America?," *Forbes*, April 24, 2013, http://www .forbes.com/sites/nathanielparishflannery/2013/04/24 /bribery-a-bad-business-strategy-in-latin-america/, accessed January 26, 2014; Juan Gonzalez and Amy Goodman, "Walmart Is Now Under Investigation in Mexican 'Bribery Aisle' Scandal," Truthout, December 21, 2012, http://truth-out.org/news /item/13469-the-bribery-aisle-how-walmart-used -payoffs-to-bribe-its-way-through-expansion-in -mexico, accessed February 6, 2013; Joe Palazzolo, Emily Galzer, and Joann Lublin, "Prosecutors Ask to Meet Jung in Avon Bribe Probe," *The Wall Street Journal*, July 29 2012, http://online.wsj.com/article /SB10000872396390444840104577553683406542666.html, accessed February 6, 2013; "Bribe Payers Index 2011," Transparency International, http://bpi .transparency.org /results/, accessed March 24, 2012; Stephen Gandel, "Not just Wal-Mart: Dozens of U.S. companies face bribery suspicions," *Fortune*, April 26, 2012, http://fortune.com/2012/04/26/not-just-wal-mart -dozens-of-u-s-companies-face-bribery-suspicions/, accessed March 16, 2015.

30. Kay Johnson, "Marketing. Selling to the Poor," *Time* Bonus Section, May 2005; C. K. Prahalad and Allen Hammond, "Serving the World's Poor,

Profitably—The Payoff for Investing in Poor Countries," *Harvard Business School Working Knowledge*, http://hbswk.hbs.edu/item.jhtml?id =3180&t=nonprofit&noseek=one.

31. Gap, Inc. Social Reporting Award, *Business Ethics*, December 20, 2004, http://www.business -ethics.com/annual.htm#Gap%20Inc.

Pg. 70 Fact: Getting to Grips with China's Middle Class by Brendan O'Reilly, July 2, 2014, *China Outlook*, http://chinaoutlook.com/getting-to-grips- with-chinas-middle-class/, accessed November 7, 2016.

5

1. Kevin Fallon, "Fooled by 'The Onion': 9 Most Embarrassing Fails," The Daily Beast, November 27, 2012, http://www.thedailybeast.com/articles/2012 /09/29/fooled-by-the-onion-8-most-embarrassing -fails.html, accessed February 2, 2014.

2. Eugene Raudsepp, "Body Language Tactics That Sway Interviewers," *The Wall Street Journal Career Journal*, December 5, 2002, http://www .careerjournal.com/jobhunting/interviewing /20021205-raudsepp.html.

3. Michael McCarthy, "Lance Armstrong Blew His Last Chance Experts Say," *Advertising Age*, January 19, 2013, http://adage.com/article/media /lance-armstrong-blew-chance-experts/239295/, accessed February 20, 2013; Brigid Schulte, "Dominance and Empathy," *The Washington Post*, February 13, 2013, http://www.washingtonpost.com /local/body-language-experts-say-obama-exuded -dominance-and-empathy/2013/02/13/7755207e -7590-11e2-95e4-6148e45d7adb_story.html, accessed March 21, 2015.

4. Michael Purdy, "The Listener Wins," Monster, http://featuredreports.monster.com/career-advice /article/the-listener-wins, accessed August 22, 2006; The Human Side of Business, by Stephen D. Boyd, *Agency Sales* magazine, February 2004, page 35, accessed via Infotrac College Edition.

5. We Learn More by Listening Than Talking, by Harvey Mackay, *The Daily Herald*, January 16, 2005, page E6[SB14], http://old.heraldextra.com /modules.php?op=modload&name=News&file =article&sid=45313; Listening Factoids, International Listening Association, http://www .listen.org/pages/factoids.html, accessed August 22, 2006.

6. The Human Side of Business, by Stephen D. Boyd, *Agency Sales* magazine, February 2004, page 35, accessed via Infotrac College Edition; Learn to Listen: Closing the Mouth and Opening the Ears Facilitates Effective Communication, by Marjorie Brody, Incentive, May 2004, page 57, ac-cessed via Business and Company Resource Center.

7. Number of Employers Passing on Applicants Due to Social Media Posts Continues to Rise, Ac-cording to New CareerBuilder Survey, June 26, 2014, CareerBuilder, http://www.careerbuilder .com/share/aboutus/pressreleasesdetail.aspx?sd =6%2F26%2F2014&id=pr829&ed=12%2F31 % 2F2014, accessed March 22, 2015; Twitter's Growth Will Continue to Slow, Says New Fore-cast, May 27, 2014, *Forbes*, http://www.forbes .com/sites/jeffbercovici/2014/05/27/twitters-growth -will-continue-to-slow-says-new-forecast/, ac-cessed March 22, 2015; Twitter was the fastest growing social network in 2012, by Shea Bennet, MediaBistro, http://www.mediabistro.com

/alltwitter/social-networks-growth-2012_b35076, accessed February 21, 2013.

8. Forget "Best" or "Sincerely," This Email Closing Gets the Most Replies by Brendan Greenley, January 31, 2017, Boomerang Website, http://blog.boomerangapp.com/2017/01/how-to-end-an-email-email-sign-offs/#footnotes, accessed April 6, 2017.

9. Kevin Sintumuang, "Tech Etiquette: 21 Do's and Don'ts for 2015," *The Wall Street Journal*, January 2, 2015, http://www.wsj.com/articles/tech-etiquette-21-dos-and-donts-for-2015-1420222724, accessed March 22, 2015; Sarah Griffiths, "Never End a Relationship by Text or Social Media," *Daily Mail*, February 25, 2016, http://www.dailymail.co.uk/sciencetech/article-3463952/Thou-shalt-not-end-relationship-text-Psychologist-reveals-17-golden-rules-digital-etiquette.html, accessed April 7, 2016.

10. Edward P. Bailey, *Writing and Speaking at Work* (Prentice Hall, 2005), pages 82–89.

11. "Presenting Effective Presentations with Visual Aids," U.S. Department of Labor, Occupational Safety and Health Administration, http://www.osha.gov/doc/outreachtraining/htmlfiles /traintec.html, accessed August 22, 2006.

12. Philip Tucker, "Bringing the Cloud with You," Google Docs Blog, March 31, 2008, http:// googledocs.blogspot.com/2008/03/bringing-cloud-with-you.html, accessed February 13, 2009; Brian Braiker, "Living in the Clouds," *News-week*, June 10, 2008, http://www.newsweek.com/id/140864, accessed February 13, 2009; Michael Miller, "Comparing Google Docs with Competing Cloud Computing Applications," *InformIT,* February 9, 2009, http://www.informit.com/articles/article.aspx?p=1323244&seqNum=3, accessed February 13, 2009.

6

1. P. George, "The Scary Truth about Corporate Survival," *Harvard Business Review,* 94 (December 2016): 24–25.

2. "Why States Should Adopt RULLCA," Uniform Law Commission: The National Conference of Commissioners on Uniform State Laws, http://www.uniformlaws.org/Narrative.aspx?title=Why%20States%20Should%20Adopt%20RULLCA, accessed January 16, 2017.

3. "Table 12: Number of Business Tax Returns, by Size of Business for Income Years, 1990–2014 [1] Expanded," Internal Revenue Service, https://www.irs.gov/uac/soi-tax-stats-historical-table-12, accessed January 16, 2017.

4. J. Sparshott, "Big Growth in Tiny Businesses," *The Wall Street Journal,* December 28, 2016, http://www.wsj.com/articles/big-growth-in-tiny-businesses-1482953786, accessed January 16, 2017.

5. A. Shi, "The 10 Most Profitable Companies in the Fortune 500," *Fortune,* June 8, 2016, http://fortune.com/2016/06/08/fortune-500-most-profitable-companies-2016/, accessed January 16, 2017.

6. "Table 12: Number of Business Tax Returns, by Size of Business for Income Years, 1990–2014 [1] Expanded," Internal Revenue Service, https://www.irs.gov/uac/soi-tax-stats-historical-table-12, accessed January 16, 2017.

7. Ibid.

8. J. Sparshott, "Big Growth in Tiny Businesses," *The Wall Street Journal*, December 28, 2016, http://www.wsj.com/articles/big-growth-in-tiny-businesses-1482953786, accessed January 16, 2017.

9. E. Palattella, "Unpaid Wages Pile Up at Erie County Farms," *GoErie*, December 4, 2016, http://www.goerie.com/news/20161204/unpaid-wages-pile-up-at-erie-county-farms, accessed January 16, 2017.

10. "BrightStar Care Franchise is the Leader in the Fast-Growing Home Care Industry," BrightStar Care, http://franchise.brightstarcare.com/, accessed January 21, 2017; "How To Start Senior Home Care Business | Home Instead Franchises—Franchise FAQ", Home Instead Senior Care, http://franchises.homeinstead.com/franchising-faq/Pages/default.aspx, accessed January 21, 2017; E. Garone, "Iconic Franchises—Then and Now," *The Wall Street Journal*, November 29, 2016, http://www.wsj.com/articles/iconic-franchisesthen-and-now-1479697681, accessed January 21, 2017; T. Mullaney, "BrightStar CEO: Major Tech, Workforce Investments Sharpen Competitive Edge," Home Health Care News, January 3, 2017, http://homehealthcarenews.com/2017/01/brightstar-ceo-major-tech-workforce-investments-sharpen-competitive-edge/, accessed January 21, 2017; R. Simon, "Senior-Care Business Booms for Franchisers," *The Wall Street Journal*, August 10, 2016, http://www.wsj.com/articles/hot-franchising-trend-services-for-seniors-1470821404, accessed January 21, 2017.

11. "About Us," Delaware Division of Corporations, http://www.corp.delaware.gov/aboutagency.shtml, accessed March 19, 2016.

12. K. Klein, "Setting Up a One Person Corporation," *BusinessWeek,* November 7, 2007, Business-Week, http://www.businessweek.com/smallbiz/content/nov2007/sb2007117_803605.htm, accessed January 19, 2017.

13. J. Drucker and S. Frier, "For Facebook's Zuckerberg, Charity Is in Eye of Beholder," *Bloomberg,* December 2, 2015, http://www.bloomberg.com/news/articles/2015-12-02/for-facebook-s-zuckerberg-charitable-is-in-eye-of-beholder, accessed March 21, 2016; R. Rubin, L. Saunders, and D. Seetharaman, "Mark Zuckerberg Tests New Philanthropic Model," *The Wall Street Journal,* 3 December, 2015, B10; N. Singer and M. Isaac, "Mark Zuckerberg's Philanthropy Uses L.L.C. for More Control," *The New York Times,* December 2, 2015, http://www.nytimes.com/2015/12/03/technology/zuckerbergs-philanthropy-uses-llc-for-more-control.html, accessed March 21, 2016.

14. A. Hufford, "Apple CEO Cook's 2016 Pay Lower as Tech Giant Misses Targets," *The Wall Street Journal,* January 6, 2017, http://www.wsj.com/articles/apple-cuts-ceo-tim-cooks-pay-after-missing-2016-targets-1483710023, accessed January 19, 2017.

15. "A Home for Innovation: The HP Garage—the Birthplace of Silicon Valley," HP, December 2012, http://www.hp.com/hpinfo/abouthp/histnfacts/publications/garage/innovation.pdf, accessed January 21, 2017; Q. Hardy, "Meg Whitman Seeks Reinvention for HP as It Prepares for Split," *The New York Times,* October 30, 2015, https://www.nytimes.com/2015/10/31/technology/meg-whitman-seeks-reinvention-for-hp-as-it-prepares-for-split.html?_r=0, accessed January 21, 2017; R. McMillan, "H-P Is Back in Buying Mode as It Readies to Split in Two," *The Wall Street Journal,* June 4, 2015, http://www.wsj.com/articles/h-p-is-back-in-buying

-mode-as-it-readies-to-split-in-two-1433459156, accessed January 21, 2017.

16. "Why States Should Adopt RULLCA," Uniform Law Commission: The National Conference of Commissioners on Uniform State Laws, http://www.uniformlaws.org/Narrative.aspx?title=Why%20States%20Should%20Adopt%20RULLCA, accessed January 16, 2017.

17. Kelly Phillips Erb, "Small Business Startup and Survival Guide," *Forbes,* August 19, 2015, http://www.forbes.com/sites/kellyphillipserb/2015 /08/19/small-biz-startup-and-survival-guide, accessed May 10, 2016; Elizabeth Garone, "As Competition for Franchisees Heats Up, so Do Incentives," *The Wall Street Journal,* January 25, 2016, http://www.wsj.com/articles/as-competition-for-franchisees-heats-up-so-do-incentives-1453690992, accessed May 10, 2016.

18. "Why States Should Adopt RULLCA," Uniform Law Commission: The National Conference of Commissioners on Uniform State Laws, http://www.uniformlaws.org/Narrative.aspx?title=Why%20States%20Should%20Adopt%20RULLCA, accessed January 16, 2017.

19. Franchise Business Economic Outlook for 2016, January 2016, prepared by IHS Economics for the International Franchise Association Educational Foundation, IFA, http://emarket.franchise.org/FranchiseOutlookJan2016.pdf, accessed March 20, 2016; "Census Bureau's First Release of Comprehensive Franchise Data Shows Franchises Make Up More Than 10% of Employer Businesses," U.S. Census Bureau, http://www.census.gov/newsroom/releases/archives/economic_census/cb10-141.html, accessed March 20, 2016.

20. "McDonald's: Units (Locations)," *Entrepreneur,* http://www.entrepreneur.com/franchises/mcdonalds/282570, accessed January 19, 2017; "Subway: Units (Locations)," *Entrepreneur,* http://www.entrepreneur.com/franchises/subway/282839, accessed January 19, 2017; "7–11: Units (Locations)," *Entrepreneur,* http://www.entrepreneur.com/franchises/7eleveninc/282052, accessed January 19, 2017.

21. K. Taylor, "Women in Franchising: An Enthusiastic Minority," *Entrepreneur,* http://www.entrepreneur.com/article/229675, accessed April 7, 2015.

22. G. Moran, "3 Women to Watch in the Franchising Sector," *Entrepreneur,* http://www.entrepreneur.com/slideshow/240847, accessed April 7, 2015; Julie Bennett, "Franchising Attracts More Women, Minorities," *Startup Journal,* accessed through Entrepreneur.com, http://www.entrepreneur.com/franchises/franchisezone/startupjournal/article61324.html; Julie M. Young, "Female Franchisors Few and Far Between," e-magnify.com, https://www.e-magnify.com/resources_articlearchiveresults.asp?categoryID=18.

23. "Franchised Business Ownership: By Minority and Gender Groups," International Franchising Association, http://www.franchise.org/sites/default/files/ek-pdfs/html_page/MinorityReport2011_0.pdf, accessed March 20, 2016.

24. J. Bourdow and M. Brewer, "Inclusion Is a Growth Strategy," *Franchising World,* (June 2013): 15–17.

25. "DIVERSITYFRAN: Diversity in Franchising," International Franchise Association, http://www.franchise.org/diversityfran, accessed March 20, 2016; "DiversityFran Participating Companies,"

International Franchise Organization, http://www
.franchise.org/sites/default/files/uploaded_documents
/Educational_Foundation/April_%202015_Diversity
Fran%20Participating%20Companies.pdf, accessed
January 19, 2017.

26. "Subway," *Entrepreneur*, http://www.entrepreneur
.com/franchises/subway/282839-2.html, accessed
March 20, 2016.

27. E. Anderson, "Who Wants to be a McMillionaire?
Meet Britain's Hidden Army of Successful Fast
Food Owners," *Telegraph*, November 14, 2015,
http://www.telegraph.co.uk/finance/newsbysector
/retailandconsumer/11993677/Who-wants-to-be
-a-McMillionaire-Meet-Britains-hidden-army-of
-successful-fast-food-owners.html, accessed
January 22, 2017; L. Patton, "McDonald's Is Pushing Out the Small Fries," *Bloomberg Businessweek*,
September 1, 2015, https://www.bloomberg.com
/news/articles/2016-09-01/mcdonald-s-is-pushing
-out-the-small-fries, accessed January 22, 2017.

28. Franchise Rule Compliance Guide, Federal
Trade Commission, http://www.ftc.gov/bcp/edu
/pubs/business/franchise/bus70.pdf, pages 20,
102–103, and 121.

Pg. 99 Fact: John McCormack, "GE Filed 57,000-
Page Tax Return, Paid No Taxes on $14 Billion in
Profits," *The Weekly Standard*, November 17, 2011,
http://www.weeklystandard.com/blogs/ge-filed
-57000-page-tax-return-paid-no-taxes-14
-billionprofits_609137.html.

7

1. Dane Stangler, "Entrepreneurial Activity Declines
Again in 2013 as Labor Market Strengthens, according
to Kauffman Report," Kauffman Foundation, April 9,
2014, http://www.kauffman.org/newsroom/2014/04
/entrepreneurial-activity-declines-again-in-2013-as
-labor-market-strengthens, accessed July 3, 2014;
J. D. Harrison, "New Business Formation Bounces
Back; Posts First Increase Since the Recession," *The
Washington Post*, July 31, 2013, http://articles
.washingtonpost.com/2013-07-31/business/40931691
_1_job-growth-new-firms-small-business, accessed
February 5, 2014; "New Business Startups Declined
in 2011, Annual Kauffman Study Shows," March 19,
2012, Kauffman Foundation, http://www.kauffman
.org/research-and-policy/kiea-2012-infographic.aspx,
accessed June 12, 2012.

2. Walter Hamilton, "A Drop-Off in Start-ups:
Where Are All the Entrepreneurs?," September 7,
2014, *The Los Angeles Times*, http://www.latimes.
com/business/la-fi-entrepreneurs-20140907-story
.html#page=1, accessed April 5, 2015; Millennial
Branding and Internships.com Release First Ever
Study on High School Careers, February 3, 2014
http://millennialbranding.com/2014/high-school-
careers-study/: Access April 27, 2018; Make Way
For Generation Z Entrepreneurs Saying No
To College by Kaytie Zimmerman, number 17,
2017, https://www.forbes.com/sites/kaytiezim-
merman/2017/12/17/make-way-for-generation-z-
entrepreneurs-saying-no-to-college/#46e5deae47a6,
accessed April 27, 2018.

3. Matthew Miller and Duncan Greenberg (eds.),
"The Forbes 400," *Forbes*, September 17, 2008, http://
www.forbes.com/2008/09/16/forbes-400-billionaires
-lists-400list08_cx_mn _0917richamericans_land.html,
accessed February 15, 2009.

4. *Newsweek* staff, "The Big Fat Story, The Geek
Kings," *Newsweek*, June 5, 2011, http://www.newsweek
.com/big-fat-story-geek-kings-67969, accessed
February 5, 2013; "*Forbes* 400 Richest Americans,"
Forbes, September 2013, http://www.forbes.com
/profile/dustin-moskovitz/, accessed February 19,
2014; Jason Nazar, "Surprising Past Jobs of Successful Entrepreneurs," *Business Insider*, October 31,
2013, http://www.businessinsider.com/surprising
-past-jobs-of-successful-entrepreneurs-2013-10,
accessed April 5, 2015.

5. "Discover Polls Reveal True Character of the
American Entrepreneur," press release, Discover
Financial Services, October 22, 2007, http://
investorrelations.discoverfinancial.com/phoenix
.zhtml?c=204177&p=irol-newsArticle&ID
=1065373&highlight=, accessed February 15,
2009.

6. "More than Half of Small Business Owners
Work at Least Six-Day Weeks, Still Find Time for
Personal Life," Wells Fargo News Release, August
9, 2005, https://www.wellsfargo.com/press/20050809
_GallupPersonalLife; "Discover Polls Reveal True
Character of the American Entrepreneur," press
release, Discover Financial Services, October 22,
2007, http://investorrelations.discoverfinancial.com
/phoenix.zhtml?c=204177&p=irol-newsArticle&ID
=1065373&highlight=, accessed February 15, 2009;
"Small Business Owners Working Longer Hours,"
May 26, 2009, Rent to Own, http://rtoonline.com
/Content/Article/may09/smal-business-owners-work
-hours-survey-052609.asp, accessed June 12, 2012.

7. Brian Wu and Anne Marie Knott, "Entrepreneurial Risk and Market Entry," SBA Office of
Advocacy, January 2005, http://www.sba.gov/advo
/research/wkpbw249.pdf.

8. "Failure: Use It as a Springboard to Success,"
U.S. SBA Online Library, http://www.sba.gov
/library/successXIII/19-Failure-Use-it.doc, accessed
December 28, 2005.

9. Alice E. Vincent, "Rejection Letters: The Publishers Who Got It Embarrassingly Wrong . . . ," *The
Huffington Post*, November 7, 2012, http://www
.huffingtonpost.co.uk/2012/05/16 /publishers-who
-got-it-wrong_n_1520190. html#slide=more226527,
accessed March 15, 2013; "Failure: Use It as a
Springboard to Success," U.S. SBA Online Library,
http://www.sba.gov/library/successXIII/19-Failure
-Use-it.doc, accessed December 28, 2005.

10. "The Biggest Lies People Told Me About Entrepreneurship," Inc., April 4, 2017, https://www
.inc.com/cox-business/the-biggest-lie-people-told-me
-about-entrepreneurship.html, accessed April 13, 2017.

11. Keith McFarland, "What Makes Them Tick,"
Inc 500, 2005, Inc, http://www.inc.com/resources
/inc500/2005/articles/20051001/tick.html; Kwame
Kuadey, "Bootstrapping Your Startup? Make Money
Before You Spend It," Young Entrepreneurs Council, June 12, 2012, http://theyec.org /bootstrapping-
your-startup-make-money-before-you-spend-it/,
accessed June 12, 2012.

12. Benjamin Ryan, "Starved of Financing, New
Businesses Are in Decline," *Gallup Business Journal*, September 4, 2014, http://www.gallup.com
/businessjournal/175499/starved-financing-new
-businesses-decline.aspx, accessed April 5, 2015.

13. "How to Finance a New Business," *Consumer
Reports*, April 2008, http://www.consumerreports.
org/cro/money/credit-loan/how-to-finance-a-new
-business/overview/how-to-finance-a-new-business
-ov.htm, accessed March 18, 2011.

14. Adam Lashinsky, "How Alibaba's Jack Ma Is
Building a Truly Global Retail Empire," *Fortune*,
March 23, 2017, http://fortune.com/2017/03/24
/jack-ma-alibaba-china-ecommerce-world-greatest
-leaders/, accessed April 12, 2017.

15. John Tozzi, "Credit Cards Replace Small Business Loans," *BusinessWeek*, August 20, 2008, http://
www.businessweek.com/smallbiz/content/aug2008
/sb20080820_288348.htm?chan=smallbiz_smallbiz
+index+page_top+small+business+stories, accessed
February 15, 2009.

16. Patrick Clark, "What Do Small Businesses Need
Banks for, Anyway?," *BusinessWeek*, September 10,
2013, http://www.businessweek.com/articles/2013
-09-10/what-do-small-businesses-need-banks-for
-anyway, accessed February 6, 2014.

17. "Start-up Information," Delaware Small Business Development Center, updated April 28, 2008,
http://www.delawaresbdc.org/DocumentMaster.
aspx?doc=1003#6, accessed February 15, 2009.

18. Mike Freeman, "San Diego's Investing Angels,"
San Diego Union Tribune, January 32, 2013, http://
www.utsandiego.com/news/2013/jan/31/Tech-Coast
-Angels-fund-local-start-ups/?page=1#article-copy,
accessed March 24, 2013; "Financial Assistance,"
Small Business Administration, http://www.sba.gov
/services/financialassistance/index.html, accessed
February 15, 2009.

19. Darrah Brustein, "Growth-Hacking 101," *Entrepreneur*, August 5, 2016, https://www.entrepreneur.com
/article/280130, accessed April 13, 2017.

20. "Crowdfunding Industry Statistics 2015 2016,"
CrowdExpert.com, February 29, 2016, http://
crowdexpert.com/crowdfunding-industry-statistics/,
accessed April 13, 2017.

21. Jeffrey Sohl, "Angel Investor Market in Q1Q2
2011: A Return to the Seed Stage," Center for
Venture Research, University of New Hampshire,
October 11, 2011, https://paulcollege.unh.edu/sites
/paulcollege.unh.edu/files/q1q2_2011_analysis
_report_0.pdf, accessed June 12, 2012; Abby Tracy,
"Angel Investments Up 40%," Inc., March 13, 2012,
http://wire.inc.com/2012/03/13/angel-investments
-up-40/, accessed June 12, 2012.

22. "The Steady, Strategic Assent of JetBlue
Airways," Strategic Management Knowledge at
Wharton, December 14, 2005–January 10, 2006,
http://knowledge.wharton.upenn.edu/article/1342
.cfm; Bobbie Gossage, "Charging Ahead," Inc.
Magazine, January 2004, http://www.inc.com
/magazine/20040101/gettingstarted.html.

23. Amplestuff, http://www.amplestuff.com/; "Kazoo
v. Walmart," *Reveries* magazine, November 29,
2005, http://www.reveries.com/?p=232.

24. "E-Commerce Award—June 2002," Anything
Left-Handed, http://www.anythingleft-handed.
co.uk/pressreleases.html, accessed May 24, 2017.

25. Rhonda Abrams, "Focus on Success, Not
Failure," *USA Today*, May 7, 2004, http://www
.usatoday.com/money/smallbusiness/columnist
/abrams/2004-05-06-success_x.htm.

26. "Is Entrepreneurship for You?," U.S. Small
Business Administration, http://www.sba.gov
/starting_business/startup/areyouready.html,
accessed December 15, 2005.

27. "Committee Examines Ways to Ease Growing
Regulatory Burden on Small Businesses," U.S.
House of Representatives Press Release, House of
Representatives, July 30, 2008, http://www.house
.gov/smbiz/PressReleases/2008/pr-7-30-08-regulatory
.html, accessed February 15, 2009.

28. David Nather, "How Obamacare Affects Businesses—Large and Small," *Politico,* September 30, 2013, http://www.politico.com/story/2013/09/how -obamacare-affects-businesses-large-and-small -97460.html, accessed February 6, 2014; "Entrepreneurship in the 21st Century," *Conference Proceedings,* March 26, 2004, SBA Office of Advocacy and the Kauffman Foundation, http://www.sba.gov /advo/stats/proceedings_a.pdf; Sharon McLoone, "Health Care Costs Surface in Economic Stimulus Debate," *Washington Post,* February 10, 2009, http://voices.washingtonpost.com/small-business /2009/02/health_care_costs_surface_in_e.html, accessed February 15, 2009.

29. "Business Plan Basics," U.S. SBA, http://www .sba.gov/starting_business/planning/basic.html, accessed February 15, 2009.

30. "Inventor of the Week, Lemulson-MIT," http:// web.mit.edu/invent/iow/epperson.html, accessed March 15, 2013; "10 Accidental Inventions You Won't Believe," Science Channel, http://science .discovery.com/brink/top-ten/accidental-inventions /inventions-01.html, accessed March 22, 2011.

31. "2016 Frequently Asked Questions," Small Business Administration Office of Advocacy, July 20, 2016, https://www.sba.gov/advocacy/frequently -asked-questions-about-small-business, accessed April 13, 2017.

32. "Frequently Asked Questions," SBA Office of Advocacy, updated September 2008, SBA, http://www.sba.gov/advo/stats/sbfaq.pdf, accessed February 17, 2009.

33. Ibid.

34. "Small Business Drives Inner City Growth and Jobs," news release, U.S. SBA Office of Advocacy, October 11, 2005, http://www.sba.gov/advo /press /05-32.html.

35. Niels Bosma, Zoltan J. Acs, Erkko Autio, Alicia Coduras, and Jonathan Levie, "Global Entrepreneurship Monitor, 2008 Executive Report," Global Entreprenurship Research Association, London School of Economics, January 15, 2009, http://www .gemconsortium.org/article.aspx?id=76, accessed February 17, 2009.

Pg. 121 Fact: John Greathouse, "Business Tips from College Dropouts: Zuckerberg, Jobs, Gates, Dell, Ellison, Branson and Disney," *Forbes,* June 5, 2012, http://www.forbes.com/sites /johngreathouse/2012/06/05/business-tips-from -college-dropouts-zuckerberg-jobs-gates-dell -ellison-branson-and-disney/, accessed November 2012; and http://www.gemconsortium.org/docs /download/260, accessed November 2012.

8

1. N. Weinberg, "Making a Loss Look Like a Profit: Where Perrigo Led the S&P 500," *Bloomberg Businessweek,* September 13, 2016, https://www .bloomberg.com/news/articles/2016-09-13/making -a-loss-look-like-a-profit-where-perrigo-led-the-s -p-500, accessed January 24, 2017.

2. March 23, 2016; B. Berkort & D. Grover, "Pfizer's New Tax Rate Higher Than Investors Hoped, Shares Fall," *Reuters,* January 20, 2018, https://www. reuters.com/article/us-pfizer-results/pfizers-new- tax-rate-higher-than-investors-hoped-shares-fall- idUSKBN1FJ1KL, accessed February 13, 2018; T. Francis, "For Multinationals, the Tax Bill's Good

Likely Outweighs the Bad," *Wall Street Journal,* December 1, 2017, https://www.wsj.com/articles/ for-multinationals-the-tax-bills-good-likely-outweighs- the-bad-1512124200, accessed February 13, 2018; T. Francis, "What Investors Need to Know About the New Tax Law," *Wall Street Journal,* February 11, 2018, https://www.wsj.com/articles/what-investors- need-to-know-about-the-new-tax-law-1518405120, accessed February 13, 2018; T. Francis & Y. Serkez, "How the Tax Law Will Affect U.S. Firms Bringing Overseas Mone," *Wall Street Journal,* January 16, 2018, http://www.wsj.com/graphics/tax-repatriation/, accessed February 13, 2018; J. Rockoff and N. Trentmann, "New Tax Law Haunts Companies That Did 'Inversion' Deals," *Wall Street Journal,* February 11, 2018, https://www.wsj.com/articles/ new-tax-law-haunts-companies-that-did-inversion- deals-1518350401, accessed February 13, 2018; S. Schechner, "Tax Change Aims to Lure Intellectual Property Back to the U.S.," *Wall Street Journal,* January 24, 2018, https://www.wsj.com/articles/ companies-explore-whether-u-s-can-replace-double- irish-1516789801, accessed February 13, 2018; D. Wakabayashi and B. Chen, "Apple, Capitalizing on New Tax Law, Plans to Bring Billions in Cash Back to U.S.," *New York Times,* January 17, 2018, https:// www.nytimes.com/2018/01/17/technology/apple-tax- bill-repatriate-cash.html, accessed February 13, 2018.

3. T. Shumsky and D. Francis, "Accounting Choices Blur Profit Picture," *The Wall Street Journal,* June 28, 2016, http://www.wsj.com/articles/accounting-choices -blur-profit-picture-1467086625, accessed January 24, 2017.

4. Ibid.

5. A. Ross Sorkin, "Graphic: A Long Line of Accounting Scandals," Dealbook, *The New York Times,* November 20, 2012, http://dealbook .nytimes.com/2012/11/20/graphic-a-long-line-of -accounting-scandals/, accessed March 5, 2013.

6. D. Michales, "Fuzzy-Math Accounting Chided by Buffett Gets Fresh SEC Scrutiny," *Bloomberg,* March 1, 2016, http://www.bloomberg.com/news /articles/2016-03-01/fuzzy-math-accounting-chided -by-buffett-gets-fresh-sec-scrutiny, accessed March 23, 2016; G. Morgenson, "Tech Companies Fly High on Fantasy Accounting," *The New York Times,* June 18, 2015, http://www.nytimes.com/2015/06/21 /business/high-tech-fantasy-accounting.html?ref =todayspaper, accessed March 22, 2016; T. Shumsky and D. Francis, "Accounting Choices Blur Profit Picture," *The Wall Street Journal* , June 28, 2016, http://www.wsj.com/articles/accounting-choices-blur -profit-picture-1467086625, accessed January 24, 2017.

7. "Effective Rates of Corporation Tax in Ireland: Technical Paper," Irish Department of Finance, April 2014, www.budget.gov.ie/Budgets/2015 /Documents/Technical_Paper_Effective_Rates _Corporation_Tax_Ireland.pdf, accessed January 25, 2017; N. Drozdiak and S. Schechner, "Apple Ordered by EU to Repay $14.5 Billion in Irish Tax Breaks, *The Wall Street Journal,* August 30, 2016, http://www.wsj.com/articles/apple-received -14-5-billion-in-illegal-tax-benefits-from-ireland -1472551598, accessed January 25, 2017; H. McGee, "Apple Tax Appeal: The Three Arguments Government to Use, *Irish Times,* September 3, 2016, http://www.irishtimes.com/business/economy/apple -tax-appeal-the-three-arguments-government-to -use-1.2777679, accessed January 25, 2017; M. Scott, "Tim Cook, Apple Chief, Defends Tax Practices and Says Cash Will Return to U.S.," *The*

New York Times, September 1, 2016, https://www .nytimes.com/2016/09/02/technology/apple-tax -ireland-tim-cook.html?_r=0, accessed January 25, 2017; WSJ Staff, "Tim Cook's Letter to Apple Customers After EU Tax Ruling—In Full, *The Wall Street Journal,* August 30, 2016, http://blogs.wsj .com/dispatch/2016/08/30/tim-cooks-letter-to-apple -customers-after-eu-tax-ruling-in-full/, accessed January 25, 2017; WSJ Staff, "Apple's Tax in Ireland – At A Glance, *The Wall Street Journal,* August 30, 2016, http://blogs.wsj.com/briefly/2016 /08/30/apples-irish-tax-bill-at-a-glance/, accessed January 25, 2017; Apple Statement, "The Facts about Apple's Tax Payments," Apple, November 6, 2017, https://www.apple.com/au/ newsroom/2017/11/the-facts-about-apple-tax- payments/, accessed February 13, 2018; N. Drozdiak, "Apple Agrees to Deal With Ireland Over $15 Billion Unpaid Tax Issue," *Wall Street Journal,* December 4, 2017, https://www.wsj. com/articles/apple-agrees-deal-with-ireland-over- 15-billion-unpaid-tax-issue-1512392552, accessed February 13, 2018.

8. J. Jargon, "McDonald's Won't Spin Off Real Estate Holdings," *The Wall Street Journal,* November 10, 2015, http://www.wsj.com/articles/mcdonalds-wont -spin-off-real-estate-holdings-1447180384, accessed January 24, 2017; W. Ma, R. Carew, and K. Wu, "McDonald's China Franchise Deal Could Fetch Up to $2 Billion Up Front," *The Wall Street Journal,* October 4, 2016, http://www.wsj.com/articles /mcdonalds-china-franchise-deal-could-fetch-up-to-2 -billion-up-front-1475487030, accessed January 24, 2017; K. Wu and J. Jargon, "McDonald's Looks to Sell Part of Stake in Japan Business," *The Wall Street Journal,* January 12, 2017, http://www.wsj .com/articles/mcdonalds-looks-to-sell-part-of-stake -in-japan-business-1484219630, accessed January 24, 2017.

9. J. Henley, "Sweden Leads the Race to Become Cashless Society," *The Guardian,* June 4, 2016, https://www.theguardian.com/business/2016/jun/04 /sweden-cashless-society-cards-phone-apps-leading -europe, accessed January 31, 2017; J. Letzing, "Swiss Are Frank About Their Love of Cash," *The Wall Street Journal,* January 2, 2017, https://www .wsj.com/articles/swiss-are-frank-about-their-love -of-cash-1483378809, accessed January 31, 2017; C. Mims, "Why Your Business Should Ditch Cash," *The Wall Street Journal,* January 30, 2017, https:// www.wsj.com/articles/why-your-business-should -ditch-cash-1485698400, accessed January 31, 2017; E. Palma, "What Happens When We Become A Cashless Society?" *Fast Company,* May 15, 2016, https://www.fastcoexist.com/3056736/what -happens-when-we-become-a-cashless-society, accessed January 31, 2017; A. Picchi, "Stores to Customers: "Cash Not Welcome Here," *CBS News,* August 12, 2016, http://www.cbsnews.com/news /stores-to-customers-cash-not-welcome-here/, accessed January 31, 2017.

10. A. Hair and R. Winkler, "Google Creates Parent Company Called Alphabet in Restructuring," *The Wall Street Journal,* August 20, 2015, https:// www.wsj.com/articles/google-creates-new-company -alphabet-1439240645, accessed January 31, 2017; M. Chafkin and M. Bergen, "Google Makes so Much Money, It Never Had to Worry About Financial Discipline—Until Now," *Bloomberg Businessweek,* December 8, 2016, https://www.bloomberg .com/news/features/2016-12-08/google-makes-so -much-money-it-never-had-to-worry-about-financial

-discipline, accessed January 31, 2017; J. Nicas, "Google Parent Alphabet Finds New Growth beyond Search," *The Wall Street Journal*, January 26, 2017, https://www.wsj.com/articles/BT-CO-20170126 -717052, accessed January 31, 2017; L. Rao, "The Wall Street Veteran Who's Helping Google Get Disciplined," *Fortune*, September 12, 2016, http://fortune.com/google-cfo-ruth-porat-most-powerful -women/, accessed January 31, 2017.

11. "Mission and Vision," Public Company Accounting Oversight Board, https://pcaobus.org /About/History/Pages/default.aspx, accessed January 24, 2017.

12. R. Teitelbaum, "Accountants, Auditors to Get a New Ethics Rule Book," *The Wall Street Journal*, July 11, 2016, http://www.wsj.com/articles /accountants-auditors-to-get-a-new-ethics-rule -book-1468283179, accessed January 24, 2017.

13. Ibid.

14. *The Essentials of Finance and Budgeting* (Boston, MA: Harvard Business School Press, 2005), pp. 177–181.

15. S. Nassauer and P. Ziobro, "Lowe's to Cut Thousands of Store Workers, Shuffle Jobs," *The Wall Street Journal*, January 12, 2017, http://www .wsj.com/articles/lowes-to-cut-thousands-of-store -workers-shuffle-jobs-1484256389, accessed January 25, 2017.

16. W. Steve Albrecht, James D. Stice, Earl K. Stice, and Monte R. Swain, *Accounting Concepts and Applications*, 9th ed. (Boston, MA: Cengage Learning), p. 758.

Pg. 138 Fact: "Securities and Exchange Commission: A Beginner's Guide to Financial Statements," SEC, http://www.sec.gov/investor/pubs/begfinstmtguide .htm, accessed March 29, 2009. ("Read The Footnotes" finished seventh in the 2004 Kentucky Derby.)

9

1. S. Pulliam, M. Ramsey, and B. Mullins, "Elon Musk Supports His Business Empire with Unusual Financial Moves," *The Wall Street Journal*, April 27, 2016, https://www.wsj.com/articles/elon-musk -supports-his-business-empire-with-unusual-financial -moves-1461781962?mod=djem10point, accessed February 1, 2017.

2. S. Bainbridge, "A Duty to Shareholder Value," *The New York Times*, April 16, 2015, http://www .nytimes.com/roomfordebate/2015/04/16/what-are -corporations-obligations-to-shareholders/a-duty-to -shareholder-value, accessed February 1, 2017.

3. L. Strine, "The Dangers of Denial: The Need for a Clear-Eyed Understanding of the Power and Accountability Structure Established by the Delaware General Corporation Law," *Wake Forest Law Review* 50 (2015): 761.

4. See, for example, J. R. McGuigan, R. P. Rao, and C. Moyer, *Fundamentals of Contemporary Financial Management*, 2nd ed. (Stamford, CT: South-Western, Cengage Learning), p. 3; Eugene F. Brigham, *Fundamentals of Financial Management*, 11th ed. (Stamford, CT: Cengage Learning, 2005), p. 2.

5. A. Damodaran, "Annual Returns on Stock, T. Bonds and T. Bills: 1928—Current," Stern School of Business, New York University, January 5, 2017, http://pages.stern.nyu.edu/~adamodar/

New_Home_Page/datafile/histretSP.html, accessed February 2, 2017; "Risk and Return: An Introduction," Bogleheads, August 1, 2016, https://www.bogleheads.org/wiki/Risk_and_return:_an_introduction#cite_note-7, accessed February 2, 2017.

6. "Industry Browser—Services—Restaurants Industry—Company List," Yahoo! Finance, http://finance.yahoo.com/q/ks?s=MCD+Key+Statistics, accessed April 9, 2015; "McDonald's Corporation Financials," *The Wall Street Journal*, http://quotes .wsj.com/MCD/financials/Ratios, accessed April 9, 2015; "McDonald's Financial Ratios MCD," The Motley Fool, http://www.fool.com/quote/nyse /mcdonalds/mcd/financial-ratios, accessed April 9, 2015; "McDonald's Visual Financials," ADVFN, http://www.advfn.com/stock-market/NYSE/MCD /financials, accessed April 9, 2015; "Overview Industry Profile: Fast-Food & Quick-Service Restaurants," First Research, http://mergent. firstresearch-learn.com/industry _detail. aspx?pid=433&chapter=7, accessed April 9, 2015.

7. J. Ballard, "Activision Blizzard Is Set for Outperformance," *The Motley Fool*, December 28, 2016, https://www.fool.com/investing/2016/12/28 /activision-blizzard-is-set-for-outperformance.aspx, accessed February 2, 2017; D. Gallagher, "Tracking Videogame Sales Is Tougher Than You Think," *The Wall Street Journal*, July 26, 2016, C8.

8. A. Davidson, "Sustainable Investing Goes Mainstream," *The Wall Street Journal*, January 13, 2015; A. Edmans and D. Vogel, "Does Socially Responsible Investing Make Financial Sense?," *The Wall Street Journal*, February 28, 2016, http://www.wsj .com/articles/does-socially-responsible-investing -make-financial-sense-1456715888, accessed March 27, 2016; E. McCarthy, "Investor IQ: Test Your Smarts . . . on Ethical Investing, *The Wall Street Journal*, June 3, 2014, p. R8; A. Pryor, "Weekend Investor—Investing with a Mission," *The Wall Street Journal*, July 18, 2015, p. B7.

9. The approximate "finance charge" of not taking the discount on credit can be computed using the following formula:

$$= \frac{\% \text{ discount}}{(100 - \% \text{ discount})} \times \frac{365}{(\text{Credit\_Period} - \text{Discount\_Period})}$$

where % discount is the discount the buyer receives for paying on or before the last day the discount is available, and the Credit Discount Period is the number of days before payment of full invoice amount is due.

10. R. Cole, "Bank Credit, Trade Credit or No Credit: Evidence from the Surveys of Small Business Finances," Office of Advocacy, Small Business Administration, June 2010, https://www.sba.gov/sites/default /files/rs365tot.pdf, accessed February 2, 2017.

11. E. Dou and G. Wong, "Hon Hai Banks on Finance—The iPhone Assembler Now Provides Loans to Electronics Industry," *The Wall Street Journal*, November 18, 2015, p. B6.

12. "Annual Asset-Based Lending and Factoring Survey Highlights, 2014," Commercial Finance Association, March 31, 2015, https://www.cfa.com/eweb /DynamicPage.aspx?Site=cfa&WebKey=2f388eee-12cc -441b-9584-986d6261fc51, accessed February 2, 2017.

13. B. Olson, E. Glazer, and M. Jarzemsky, "Bad Loans Hit the Oil Patch," *The Wall Street Journal*, March 25, 2016, A1., 2013.

14. M. Pilon, "What Is Commercial Paper and Why Does It Matter?" *The Wall Street Journal*, October 7, 2008, http://blogs.wsj.com/wallet /2008/10/07 /what-is-commercial-paper-and-why-does-it-matter /tab/print/, accessed March 24, 2013.

15. "Commercial Paper Rates: Derived from Data Supplied by The Depository Trust & Clearing Corporation," Board of Governors of the Federal Reserve System, February 1, 2017, https://www .federalreserve.gov/releases/cp/rates.htm, accessed February 2, 2017.

16. J. White, "Cash Managers Favored Commercial Paper in January," *The Wall Street Journal*, February 6, 2013, http://blogs.wsj.com /cfo/2013 /02/06/cash-managers-favored-commercial -paper-in-january/, accessed March 24, 2013; J. Willhite, "Finance Execs Dumped Commercial Paper in December—The CFO Report, http://blogs.wsj.com/cfo/2015/01/22/finance-execs -dumped-commercial-paper-in-december/?KEYW -ORDS=%22commercial+paper%22, January 22, 2015, accessed April 9, 2015; T. Shumsky, "Companies Pare Government Bond Holdings, Favor Commercial Paper in August—CFO Journal," *The Wall Street Journal*, August 8, 2016, http://blogs.wsj.com /cfo/2016/08/08/companies-pare-government-bond -holdings-favor-commercial-paper-in-august/, accessed February 2, 2017.

17. "Alphabet, Inc. Financials," Google Finance, December 31, 2016, https://www.google.com /finance?q=NASDAQ%3AGOOGL&fstype=ii&ei =L62TWPGWCMS1jAHFtYj4Dg.

18. "Net Private Saving: Domestic Business: Undistributed Corporate Profits [B057RC1Q027SBEA]," U.S. Bureau of Economic Analysis, retrieved from FRED, Federal Reserve Bank of St. Louis, December 22, 2016, https://fred.stlouisfed.org/series /B057RC1Q027SBEA, accessed February 2, 2017.

19. "Berkshire Hathaway Inc., Historical Prices, February 3, 2004 to February 2, 2017," Google Finance, https://www.google.com/finance/histo rical?cid=4376&startdate=Feb%203%2C%20 2004&enddate=Feb%203%2C%202017&num =30&ei=CZiUWKCbK4e62Aam_4XoCQ&start =0, accessed February 3, 2017.

20. "Why Do companies Issue Debt and Bonds? Can't They Just Borrow from the Bank?, Investopedia, http://www.investopedia.com/ask/answers /05 /reasonforcorporatebonds.asp, accessed on February 3, 2017.

21. "Restructuring Information: Investor FAQ," Arch Coal, www.archcoal.com/restructuring/pdfs /FINAL%20ACI%20Agreement%20-%20Chapter %2011%20Investor%20FAQ.pdf, accessed February 3, 2017; S. Chaney, "Arch Coal Emerges from Chapter 11," *The Wall Street Journal*, October 5, 2016, https://www.wsj.com/articles /arch-coal-emerges-from-chapter-11-1475684184, accessed February 3, 2017.

22. C. Boston, "Dell Sells $20 Billion of Bonds in Year's Second-Biggest Deal," *Bloomberg*, May 17, 2016, https://www.bloomberg.com/news/articles /2016-05-17/dell-said-to-boost-bond-offering-for -emc-takeover-to-20-billion, accessed February 6, 2017; R. King, "Dell Closes $60 Billion Merger with EMC," *The Wall Street Journal*, September 7, 2016, https://www.wsj.com/articles/dell-closes -60-billion-merger-with-emc-1473252540, accessed

February 6, 2017; M. de la Merced, "How Dell Raised $67 Billion for the Biggest Tech Deal Ever," *The New York Times*, August 5, 2016, https://www.nytimes.com/2016/08/06/business/dealbook/how-dell-pieced-together-67-billion-to-buy-emc.html?_r=0, accessed February 6, 2017; M. de la Merced and Q. Hardy, "Dell in $24 Billion Deal to Go Private," *The New York Times*, February 5, 2013, https://dealbook.nytimes.com/2013/02/05/dell-sets-23-8-billion-deal-to-go-private/, accessed February 6, 2017; J. McGurk, S. McDermid, V. Amin, and I. Chan, "Making Sense of Dell + EMC + VMware," Andreessen Horowitz, October 26, 2015, http://a16z.com/2015/10/26/dell-emc-vmware/, accessed February 6, 2017; "Dell-EMC Acquisition Deal: How is the Debt Being Financed?," Zacks Equity Research, April 8, 2016, https://www.zacks.com/stock/news/212818/dellemc-acquisition-deal-how-is-the-debt-being-financed, accessed February 6, 2017; E. Platt, "Dell Bonds Draw $85bn in Investor Orders," *Financial Times*, May 17, 2016, https://www.ft.com/content/b40877ac-1c48-11e6-a7bc-ee846770ec15, accessed February 6, 2017; M. de la Merced, "Is Dell's Debt Load Pushing It Into a Deal?" *New York Times*, February 2, 2018, https://www.nytimes.com/2018/02/02/business/dealbook/is-dells-debt-load-pushing-it-into-a-deal.html, accessed February 12, 2018; D. Gallagher, "Dell's Problem: Bigger Not Always Better," *Wall Street Journal*, January 30, 2018, https://www.wsj.com/articles/dells-problem-bigger-not-always-better-1517308201, accessed February 12, 2018.

23. M. Isaac and M. de la Merced, "Uber Turns to Saudi Arabia for $3.5 Billion Cash Infusion," *The New York Times*, June 1, 2016, https://www.nytimes.com/2016/06/02/technology/uber-investment-saudi-arabia.html?_r=0, accessed February 3, 2017; D. MacMillan, "Uber Raises $3.5 Billion From Saudi Fund," *The Wall Street Journal*, June 1, 2016, https://www.wsj.com/articles/uber-raises-3-5-billion-from-saudi-fund-1464816529, accessed February 3, 2017.

24. Chris Arnold, "Financial Sectors' New Buzzword Is Deleverage," *NPR*, http://www.npr.org/templates/story/story.php?storyId=94795760, accessed August 9, 2009; James Saft, "Deleveraging, Now Only in Early Stages, Will Transform the Banking Industry," *The New York Times*, http://www.nytimes.com/2008/06/26/business/worldbusiness/26iht-col27.1.14006619.html?_r=1, accessed August 9, 2009; "Deleveraging: A Fate Worse than Debt," *Economist*, http://www.economist.com/businessfinance/displaystory.cfm?story_id=12306060, accessed August 9, 2009.

25. "Brief Summary of the Dodd-Frank Wall Street Reform and Consumer Protection Act. United States Senate Committee on Banking,: Housing and Urban Affairs, http://banking.senate.gov/public/_files/070110_Dodd_Frank_Wall_Street_Reform_comprehensive_summary_Final.pdf; Michael Rapoport and Rachael King, "For Heavily Indebted Firms Like Dell, Tax Bill Delivers a Downside," *Wall Street Journal*, December 21, 2017, https://www.wsj.com/articles/downside-of-tax-bill-hits-dell-other-heavily-indebted-companies-1513852200, accessed February 12, 2018; W. Richter, "What Will the Tax Law Do to Over-Indebted Corporate America?" *Wolf Street*, December 22, 2017, https://wolfstreet.com/2017/12/22/what-will-the-tax-law-do-to-over-indebted-corporate-america/, accessed February 12, 2018; J. Lahart, "The One Tax Change That Really Bites Businesses," *Wall Street Journal*,

December 19, 2017, https://www.wsj.com/articles/the-one-tax-change-that-really-bites-businesses-1513708835, accessed February 12, 2018.

26. "Stock Information | Dividend History," Caterpillar, December 14, 2016, http://www.caterpillar.com/en/investors/stock-information/dividend-history.html, accessed February 3, 2017; M. Bird, "Dividends Eat Up Bigger Slice of Company Profits," *The Wall Street Journal*, , https://www.wsj.com/articles/dividends-eat-up-bigger-slice-of-company-profits-1471565154, accessed February 3, 2017; B. Eisen, "Dividends Are What Matter Now," *The Wall Street Journal*, August 24, 2016, https://www.wsj.com/articles/dividends-are-what-matter-now-1472081992, accessed February 3, 2017; R. Teitelbaum, "As Dow Industrials Pass 20000, CFOs Will Reassess Buybacks," *The Wall Street Journal*, January 25, 2017, http://blogs.wsj.com/cfo/2017/01/25/as-dow-industrials-pass-20000-cfos-will-reassess-buybacks/, accessed February 3, 2017.

27. A. Kadet, "A Book Store Glut Proves Print Isn't Dead—Just Used," *The Wall Street Journal*, July 16, 2016, p. A16.

28. J. Rosevear, "Why Toyota's Japanese Factories Will Shut Down Next Week," *The Motley Fool*, February 1, 2016, http://www.fool.com/investing/general/2016/02/01/why-toyotas-japanese-factories-will-shut-down-next.aspx, accessed March 27, 2016.

29. T. Francis and V. Monga, "Businesses Ready to Ramp Up Investment," *The Wall Street Journal*, January 3, 2017, p. B1.

30. M. Campbell and P. Levring, "Denmark: Land Below Zero Where Negative Interest Rates Are Normal," *Bloomberg*, June 6, 2016, https://www.bloomberg.com/news/articles/2016-06-06/denmark-land-below-zero-where-negative-interest-rates-are-normal, accessed February 7, 2017; K. Davidson, "Would Negative Rates Work in the U.S.," *The Wall Street Journal*, April 14, 2016, https://www.wsj.com/articles/would-negative-rates-work-in-the-u-s-1460493711, accessed February 7, 2017; C. Duxbury and D. Gauthier-Villars, "Negative Rates Around the World: How One Danish Couple Gets Paid Interest on Their Mortgage," *The Wall Street Journal*, April 14, 2016, https://www.wsj.com/articles/the-upside-down-world-of-negative-interest-rates-1460643111, accessed February 7, 2017; C. Forelle, "Everything You Need to Know About Negative Rates," *The Wall Street Journal*, August 8, 2016, https://www.wsj.com/articles/everything-you-need-to-know-about-negative-rates-1456700481, accessed February 7, 2017; G. Kantchev, C. Whittall, and M. Inada, "Are Negative Rates Backfiring? Here's Some Early Evidence," *The Wall Street Journal*, August 8, 2016, https://www.wsj.com/articles/are-negative-rates-backfiring-heres-some-early-evidence-1470677642, accessed February 7, 2017; J. Mackintosh, "What Comes After Negative Rates? Helicopter Money," *The Wall Street Journal*, April 14, 2016, https://www.wsj.com/articles/what-comes-after-negative-rates-helicopter-money-1460646993, accessed February 7, 2017.

Pg. 148 Fact: "Nielsen: 50% of Global Consumers Surveyed Willing to Pay More for Goods, Services From Socially Responsible Companies, Up From 2011," Nielsen, August 6, 2013, http://www.nielsen.com/content/corporate/us/en/press-room/2013/nielsen-50-percent-of-global-consumers-surveyed-willing-to-pay-more-fo.html.

10

1. J. Zweig, "Inching Your Way Toward Wealth with Your Phone—MoneyBeat," *The Wall Street Journal*, February 3, 2017, http://blogs.wsj.com/moneybeat/2017/02/03/inching-your-way-toward-wealth-with-your-phone/, accessed February 8, 2017.

2. Ibid.

3. Financial Accounts of the United States: Flow of Funds, Balance Sheets, and Integrated Macroeconomic Accounts, L.110 Private Depository Institutions (1), Federal Reserve Statistical Release, December 8, 2016, http://www.federalreserve.gov/releases/z1/Current/z1.pdf, accessed February 8, 2017.

4. M. Farell, A. Hufford, and J. Marshall, "Snapchat Parent Snap Inc. Files for IPO," *The Wall Street Journal*, February 2, 2017, https://www.wsj.com/articles/snapchat-parent-snap-inc-files-for-ipo-1486071371, accessed February 9, 2017; S. Grocer, "Snap's IPO Filing: Everything You Need to Know," *The Wall Street Journal*, February 2, 2017, http://blogs.wsj.com/moneybeat/2017/02/02/snaps-ipo-filing-everything-you-need-to-know/, accessed February 9, 2017; J. Marshall and M. Shields, "Snap's IPO Filing Offers Peek Into Its Advertising Strategy, Snap's IPO Filing Offers Peek Into Its Advertising Strategy," *The Wall Street Journal*, February 2, 2017, https://www.wsj.com/articles/snaps-ipo-filing-offers-peek-into-its-advertising-strategy-1486078983, accessed February 9, 2017; J. Stern, "How to Use Snapchat," *The Wall Street Journal*, January 12, 2016, https://www.wsj.com/articles/snapchat-101-learn-to-love-the-worlds-most-confusing-social-network-1452628322, accessed February 9, 2017; G. Wells, "Snap Lists Sustaining User Growth as One of Its Biggest Risks," *The Wall Street Journal*, February 2, 2017, https://www.wsj.com/articles/snap-lists-sustaining-user-growth-as-one-of-its-biggest-risk-1486075541, https://www.wsj.com/articles/snap-lists-sustaining-user-growth-as-one-of-its-biggest-risk-1486075541.

5. "How Is a Credit Union Different Than a Bank?," MyCreditUnion.gov, http://www.mycreditunion.gov/about-credit-unions/Pages/How-is-a-Credit-Union-Different-than-a-Bank.aspx, accessed February 8, 2017.

6. Financial Accounts of the United States: Flow of Funds, Balance Sheets, and Integrated Macroeconomic Accounts, Table L.114 Credit Unions, Federal Reserve Statistical Release, December 8, 2016, http://www.federalreserve.gov/releases/z1/Current/z1.pdf, accessed February 8, 2017.

7. "Mortgage Debt Outstanding," Board of Governors of the Federal Reserve System, December 2016, http://www.federalreserve.gov/econresdata/releases/mortoutstand/current.htm, accessed February 8, 2017.

8. Timothy Curry and Lynn Shibut, "The Cost of the Savings and Loan Crisis: Truth and Consequences," *FDIC Banking Review*, December 2000, http://www.fdic.gov/bank/analytical/banking/2000dec/brv13n2_2.pdf, accessed March 28, 2016.

9. Ibid.

10. "Deposit Insurance FAQs," Federal Deposit Insurance Corporation, https://www.fdic.gov/deposit/deposits/faq.html, accessed February 8, 2017.

11. "Towers of Babel: Is There Such a Thing as a Skyscraper Curse?," *Economist*, March 28, 2015, http://www.economist.com/news/finance-and

-economics/21647289-there-such-thing-skyscraper
-curse-towers-babel, accessed March 30, 2016;
"World's Tallest Buildings 2016," SkyscraperPage,
March 2016, http://skyscraperpage.com
/diagrams/?searchID5200, accessed March 30,
2016; "World Skyscraper Construction 2016,"
SkyscraperPage, http://skyscraperpage.com/
diagrams/?searchID=202, accessed March 30, 2016;
J. Anderlini, "The Chinese Chronicle of a Crash
Foretold," *Financial Times*, February 24, 2016,
http://www.ft.com/intl/cms/s/0/65a584e2-da53
-11e5-98fd-06d75973fe09.html#axzz41E0r3hSt,
accessed March 30, 2016; W. Pesek, "The Bigger
Asia Builds, The Harder It Falls," *Barron's*,
January 21, 2016, http://www.barrons.com/
articles/thebigger-asia-builds-the-harder-it-
falls-1453337389, accessed March 30, 2016; R.
Dobbs, S. Lund, J. Woetzel, and M. Mutafchieva,
"Debt and (Not Much) Deleveraging," McKinsey
& Company, February 2015, http://www.mckinsey.
com/global-themes/employment-and-growth/debt
-and-not-much-deleveraging, accessed March 30,
2016.

12. "About the PCAOB," Public Company Accounting Oversight Board, https://pcaobus.org
/About, accessed February 8, 2017.

13. "Brief Summary of the Dodd-Frank Wall Street
Reform and Consumer Protection Act," United
States Senate Committee on Banking, Housing and
Urban Affairs, http://banking.senate.gov/public/
_files/070110_Dodd_Frank_Wall_Street_Reform
_comprehensive_summary_Final.pdf, accessed
April 13, 2015; "About FSOC," Financial Stability
Oversight Council, https://www.treasury.gov/initiatives
/fsoc/about/Pages/default.aspx, accessed February 8,
2017.

14. T. Higgins and C. Sweet, "Tesla Says SolarCity
Deal Would Boost Balance Sheet," *The Wall Street
Journal*, November 1, 2016, https://www.wsj.com
/articles/tesla-says-solarcity-deal-would-boost
-balance-sheet-1478035626, accessed February 8,
2017.

15. T. Higgins and C. Sweet, "Tesla, SolarCity
Merger Gets Shareholder Approval," *The Wall
Street Journal*, November 17, 2016, https://www
.wsj.com/articles/tesla-solarcity-merger-gets
-shareholder-approval-1479417860, accessed
February 8, 2017.

16. Press Release, "Chesapeake Energy Corporation Reinstates Payment of Quarterly Preferred
Stock Dividends," Chesapeake Energy, January 20,
2017, http://www.chk.com/media/news/press
-releases/Chesapeake+Energy+Corporation+
Reinstates+Payment+Of+Quarterly+Preferred+Sto
ck+Dividends+1+20+2017+, accessed February 8,
2017; L. Cook, "Oil Patch Is Bracing For Further
Cuts in Jobs," *The Wall Street Journal*, July 27,
2015, p. B1; B. Levisohn, "Chesapeake Energy:
Sending Signals—Stocks to Watch," *Barron's*,
January 23, 2017, http://blogs.barrons.com
/stockstowatchtoday/2017/01/23/chesapeake
-energy-sending-signals/, accessed February 8,
2017.

17. Some preferred stock contains a "participating" feature on its dividend. This means that if the
dividend paid to common stockholders exceeds
some specified amount, the board must also raise
the dividend to preferred stockholders. See Participating Preferred Stock, Investopedia, http://www.
investopedia.com/terms/p/participatingpreferred-
stock.asp, accessed April 13, 2015.

18. R. Atkins, "Why Investors Will Make 100-year
Loans," *Financial Times*, June 4, 2015, https:
//www.ft.com/content/9d794036-09cd-11e5-a6a8
-00144feabdc0, accessed February 8, 2017.

19. R. Lehmann, "The Coming Bond Default
Wave," *Forbes*, September 8, 2008, http://www
.forbes.com/free_forbes/2008/1013/130.html,
accessed February 8, 2017.

20. M. Krantz, "Corporate Default Rate Expected
to Jump 30%," *USA Today*, August 19, 2016, http://
www.usatoday.com/story/money/markets
/2016/08/19/corporate-default-rate-expected-jump
-30-soon/88967964/, accessed February 8, 2017.

21. P. Vigna, "The Party's Over for Corporate
Bonds, as Moody's Warns of Rising Defaults," *The
Wall Street Journal*, March 1, 2016, http://blogs.wsj.
com/moneybeat/2016/03/01/the-partys-over-for
-corporate-bonds-as-moodys-warns-of-rising
-defaults/, accessed February 8, 2017.

22. N. Friedman, "Berkshire's B Shares Are
Second Class No More—MoneyBeat," *The Wall
Street Journal*, December 14, 2016, http://blogs
.wsj.com/moneybeat/2016/12/14/berkshires
-b-shares-are-second-class-no-more/, accessed
February 9, 2017.

23. J. Brown, "What Investors Should Know
About Callable Bonds," *U.S. News & World
Report*, August 22, 2016, http://money.usnews.com
/investing/articles/2016-08-22/what-investors-should
-know-about-callable-bonds, accessed February 10,
2017; B. Eisen, "Falling Rates Create Bond-Call
Frenzy," *The Wall Street Journal*, August 8, 2016,
https://www.wsj.com/articles/falling-rates-create
-bond-call-frenzy-1470671759, accessed February 10,
2017; B. Eisen, "Bond Investors Fear These Words:
Call Me Maybe?" *The Wall Street Journal*, August 1,
2016, http://blogs.wsj.com/moneybeat/2016/08/01
/bond-investors-fear-these-words-call-me-maybe/,
accessed February 10, 2017; S. Goldfarb, "Microsoft
Sets 2017 High With $17 Billion Bond Sale," *The
Wall Street Journal*, January 30,2017, https://www
.wsj.com/articles/microsoft-sets-terms-on-17-billion
-bond-sale-1485807664, accessed February 10,
2017.

24. "Build a Diversified Portfolio with Just a Few
Vanguard Funds," The Vanguard Group, https://
personal.vanguard.com/pdf/s050.pdf?2210105586,
accessed February 9, 2017.

25. "SLIM—The Obesity Thematic ETF: Invest
in the Battle against Obesity," Janus Capital Group,
https://www.janus.com/advisor/exchange-traded
-funds/janus-obesity-thematic-etf, accessed
February 9, 2017; W. Updegrave, "Exchange-
Traded Funds: Avoid Offbeat ETFs, Stick to Investing Basics," Money, June 22, 2016, http://time.com
/money/4374957/why-you-should-avoid-etfs-investing
-basics/, accessed February 9, 2017.

26. T. Puko, M. Jarzemsky, and M. Farrell,
"Diamond in the Rough? Coal IPOs Rise," *The
Wall Street Journal*, February 4, 2017, B1.

27. "Intercontinental Exchange Fact Sheet,"
Intercontinental Exchange, February 2017, https://
www.theice.com/publicdocs/ICE_at_a_glance.pdf,
accessed February 9, 2017.

28. "List: Access Capital," NASDAQ, http://
business.nasdaq.com/list, accessed February 9,
2017.

29. "David Bowie: Sound and Vision," *The Wall
Street Journal*, January 11, 2016, http://graphics.wsj.
com/image-grid/david-bowie/, accessed March 30,

2016; J. Boulden, "David Bowie Made Financial
History with Music Bond," *CNN Money*, January 11,
2016, http://money.cnn.com/2016/01/11/media
/bowie-bonds-royalties/, accessed February 24, 2016;
A. Russell, "David Bowie Dies at 69 After Battle
With Cancer," *The Wall Street Journal*, January 11,
2016, http://www.wsj.com/articles/david-bowie-dies
-at-69-after-battle-with-cancer-1452497400, accessed
February 24, 2016; I. Fraser, "Bowie Bonds: How
David Bowie Became a Pioneer in the Worlds of
Finance and the Internet," *The Telegraph*, January
11, 2016, http://www.telegraph.co.uk/finance
/newsbysector/banksandfinance/12093143/Bowie
-Bonds-How-David-Bowie-became-a-pioneer-in-the
-worlds-of-finance-and-the-internet.html, accessed
March 30, 2016; T. Stubbington and M. Bird, "David
Bowie: The Man Who Sold the World . . . and
Bonds," *The Wall Street Journal*, January 11, 2016,
http://www.wsj.com/articles/david-bowie-the-man
-who-sold-the-worldand-bonds-1452542807,
accessed March 30, 2016.

30. L. Kramer and S. Smith, "Can Robo Advisers
Replace Human Financial Advisers?," *The Wall
Street Journal*, February 28, 2016, http://www.wsj
.com/articles/can-robo-advisers-replace-human
-financial-advisers-1456715553, accessed April 6,
2016; P. Sullivan, "The Computer as a Financial
Planner," *The New York Times*, June 20, 2015,
B5; Powell, Robert, "Behavioral Economist Richard Thaler on the Key to Retirement Savings,"
The Wall Street Journal, November 29, 2015,
accessed March 22, 2016, http://www.wsj
.com/articles/behavioral-economist-richard
-thaler-on-the-key-to-retirement-savings
-1448852602; "SmartDeposit: Auto-Deposit, But
Smarter," Betterment, https://www.betterment.
com/resources/inside-betterment/product-news
/smartdeposit-auto-deposit-but-smarter/,
accessed April 5, 2016.

31. K. Bahler, "Apple: Macbook Pro Prices Rise
Because of Brexit," *Time* Magazine, October 28,
2016, http://time.com/money/4549675/apple
-macbook-pro-prices-expensive-uk-british-pound/,
accessed February 10, 2017; T. Black & A. Webb,
"Trump's Strong Dollar Means Weaker Sales at
Apple," *Bloomberg*, February 3, 2017, https://
www.bloomberg.com/news/articles/2017-02-03
/trump-s-stronger-dollar-means-weaker-sales-at
-apple-honeywell, accessed February 10, 2017;
S. Chaudhuri, "Unilever Raises U.K. Prices as
Pound Falls," *The Wall Street Journal*, October 13,
2016, https://www.wsj.com/articles/unilever-says
-it-resolves-pricing-dispute-with-tesco-1476380119,
accessed February 10, 2017; T. Francis and
E. Sylvers, "Strong Dollar Has Companies Counting the Cost—And Opportunities," *The Wall Street
Journal*, December 7, 2016, https://www.wsj.com
/articles/strong-dollar-has-companies-counting-
the-costand-opportunities-1481106610, accessed
February 10, 2017; J. Titcomb, "Apple to Raise UK
App Prices by 25pc after Sterling's Recent Losses,"
Telegraph, January 17, 2017, http://www.telegraph
.co.uk/technology/2017/01/17/apple-raise-uk-app
-prices-25pc-post-brexit-fall-pound/, accessed
February 10, 2017.

32. L. Carlozo, "Why Warren Buffett Loves
Buy-and-Hold Stocks," *US News*, September 7,
2016, http://money.usnews.com/investing
/articles/2016-09-07/why-warren-buffett
-loves-buy-and-hold-stocks, accessed February 9,
2017.

11

1. Derek Thompson, "War and Peace in 30 Seconds: How Much Does the Military Spend on Ads?" *The Atlantic*, January 30, 2012, http://www.theatlantic.com/business/archive/2012/01/war-and-peace-in-30-seconds-how-much-does-the-military-spend-on-ads/252222/, accessed February 9, 2014; Stuart Elliott, "Army to Use Webcasts From Iraq for Recruiting," *The New York Times*, November 10, 2008, http://www.nytimes.com/2008/11/11/business/media/11adco.html, accessed February 22, 2009; "Army Strong! Army Smash!" Armchair Generalist, October 11, 2006, http://armchairgeneralist.typepad.com/my_weblog/2006/10/army_strong_arm.html, accessed April 19, 2011; "U.S. Army Searches New Agency, Defines Hispanic Market as Key Target," Portada, August 12, 2010, http://www.portada-online.com/article.aspx?aid=6604, accessed April 19, 2010; Andrew McMains, "U.S. Army Puts Marketing in Play," *AdWeek*, August 11, 2010, http://www.adweek.com/news/advertising-branding/us-army-puts-marketing-play-103040, accessed June 16, 2012.

2. Al Ries, "What Marketers Can Learn from Obama's Campaign," *Advertising Age*, November 5, 2008, http://adage.com/moy2008/article?article_id=131810, accessed February 22, 2009.

3. Thomas Moore, "Tourism Officials Report Record 42.9M Las Vegas Visitors in 2016," *Las Vegas Sun*, January 10, 2017, https://lasvegassun.com/news/2017/jan/10/tourism-officials-report-record-429m-las-vegas-vis/, accessed April 21, 2117.

4. "Consumer Satisfaction Benchmarks by Industry," *The American Customer Satisfaction Index*, http://www.theacsi.org/customer-satisfaction-benchmarks/benchmarks-by-industry, accessed April 22, 2017.

5. Rama Ramaswami, "Eight Reasons to Keep Your Customers Loyal," Multichannel Merchant, January 12, 2005, http://multichannelmerchant.com/opsandfulfillment/advisor/Brandi-custloyal, accessed February 24, 2009.

6. June Campbell, "The Psychology of Color in Marketing," 4hb, http://www.4hb.com/0107psysocolormarket.html, accessed May 22, 2017; Al Martinovic, "Color psychology in marketing," ImHosted, June 21, 2004, http://developers.evrsoft.com/article/web-design/graphics-multimedia-design/color-psychology-in-marketing.shtml; Suzanne Roman, "Colors that Sell," ImHosted, November 29, 2004, http://developers.evrsoft.com/article/web-design/graphics-multimedia-design/colors-that-sell.shtml; Pam Belluck, "Reinvent Wheel? Blue Room. Defusing a Bomb? Red Room," *The New York Times*, February 6, 2009, http://www.nytimes.com/2009/02/06/science/06color.html, accessed February 26, 2009.

7. Trefis Team, "Nike's China Problem," Trefis, March 20, 2014, http://www.trefis.com/stock/nke/articles/229536/marynikes-china-problem/2014-03-20, accessed April 18, 2015; Andria Cheng, "Shoe Makers Gunning for Olympian Feat," Market Watch, May 9, 2008, http://www.marketwatch.com/news/story/story.aspx?guid={781CC2E2-2B3F-4FF5-A0C5-0FB962D7E204}, accessed February 24, 2009; Matt Townsend and Robert Fenne, "Nike Climbs to Record as Orders Surge, Profit Rises," Bloomberg, September 24, 2010, http://www.businessweek.com/news/2010-09-24/nike-climbs-to-record-as-orders-surge-profit-rises.html, accessed April 12, 2011; Laurie Burkitt, "In China, Nike Sets Out to Alter Sports Mindset," *The Wall Street Journal*, http://online.wsj.com/article/SB10001424052970204450804576624900309968790.html, accessed June 17, 2012; Bradley McNew, "China Is Still Nike Inc.'s Greatest Opportunity for Growth," Motley Fool, September 29, 2015, http://www.fool.com/investing/general/2015/09/29/china-still-represents-nike-incs-greatest-opportun.aspx, accessed May 1, 2016; Steve Schaefer, "If China Is Collapsing, Nobody Told Nike," *Forbes*, September 25, 2015, http://www.forbes.com/sites/steveschaefer/2015/09/25/nike-earnings-china-jordan/#226bb6c44c09, accessed May 1, 2016; Trefis Team, "How China Could Be the Key Driver of Nike's Future Revenues," *Forbes*, January 13, 2013, http://www.forbes.com/sites/greatspeculations/2016/01/13/how-china-could-be-the-key-driver-of-nikes-future-revenues/#11b8ddcb4c2d, accessed September 4, 2016.

8. K. C. Ifeanyi, "Exclusive: Viacom's New Study Is A Marketer's Blueprint for Millennials," Fast Company, April 19, 2017, https://www.fastcompany.com/40406542/exclusive-viacoms-new-study-is-a-marketers-blueprint-for-millennials, accessed April 23, 2017.

9. "Facebook: Friend, Foe, or Frenemy?" *Newsweek*, May 27, 2010, http://www.newsweek.com/blogs/techtonic-shifts/2010/05/26/facebook-friend-foe-or-frenemy-.html, accessed April 11, 2010.

10. Rebecca Borison, "The Top 10 Social Media Fails of 2014," Inc., December 10, 2014, http://www.inc.com/rebecca-borison/top-10-social-media-fails-2014.html, accessed April 19, 2015; Anthony Volastro, "Don't Tell Customers They're Fat: 2013's Biggest Corporate Goofs," *NBC*, February 3, 2014, http://www.nbcnews.com/business/business-news/dont-tell-customers-theyre-fat-2013s-biggest-corporate-goofs-f2D11785316, accessed February 9, 2014; Ashley Lutz, "Abercrombie & Fitch Refuses to Make Clothes for Large Women," Business Insider, May 3, 2013, http://www.businessinsider.com/abercrombie-wants-thin-customers-2013-5, accessed February 9, 2014; Jerry Barrow, "Why This Nivea for Men Ad Is 'Uncivilized,'" *The Urban Daily*, August 17, 2011, http://theurbandaily.com/1485855/why-this-nivea-for-men-ad-is-uncivilized-opinion/, accessed June 17, 2012; "Marketing Muck-Ups: The Biggest Follies of 2011," *AdvertisingAge*, December 12, 2011, http://adage.com/article/special-report-book-of-tens-2011/marketing-muck-ups-biggest-follies-2011/231468/, accessed June 17, 2012; Phil Whaba, "Hall of Shame: The 9 Worst Marketing Fails by Retailers in 2015," *Fortune*, December 22, 2015, http://fortune.com/2015/12/22/retail-ads-worst-2015/, accessed May 1, 2016.

11. "The Problem with Sustainability Marketing? Not Enough Me, Me, Me," March 9, 2015, https://www.theguardian.com/sustainable-business/behavioural-insights/2015/mar/09/problem-sustainability-marketing-not-enough-me, accessed April 22, 2017.

12. "Environment a Fair-weather Priority for Consumers," press release, Penn, Schoen & Bergland, June 3, 2008, http://www.psbresearch.com/press_release_Jun3-2008.htm, accessed February 24, 2009; Gloria Sin, "Green Fashion: Is It More Than Marketing Hype?," *Fast Company*, May 28, 2008, http://www.fastcompany.com/articles/2008/05/green-fashion-hype.html, accessed February 24, 2009; "'Green Fashion,' Formerly Hippie, Now Hip!," CBS News, February 21, 2008, http://www.cbsnews.com/stories/2008/02/21/earlyshow/living/beauty/main3855868.shtml, accessed February 24, 2009.

Pg. 201 Fact: Marketing Charts staff, "Facebook Posts Get Half Their Reach Within 30 Minutes of Being Published, "November 2, 2012, MarketingCharts, http://www.marketingcharts.com/online/facebook-posts-get-half-their-reach-within-30-minutes-of-being-published-24453/, accessed September 2014.

12

1. Melissa Sowry, "The Ultimate Energy Drink: Cocaine?," ABCNews, September 18, 2006, http://abcnews.go.com/Health/story?id=2459718&page=1#.UU45fjcwok9, accessed March 20, 2013; "Top 25 Biggest Product Flops of All Time," DailyFinance, http://www.dailyfinance.com/photos/top-25-biggest-product-flops-of-all-time/#slide=3662621, accessed March 20, 2013.

2. "Characteristics of a Great Name," The Brand Name Awards, Brighter Naming, http://www.brandnameawards.com/top10factors.html, accessed April 10, 2005.

3. Adam Bass, "Brand Extensions: Marketing in Inner Space," Brand Channel, http://www.brandchannel.com/papers_review.asp?sp_id=296, accessed March 25, 2007; Reena Jana, "Brand Extensions We Could Do Without," BusinessWeek, August 7, 2006, http://www.businessweek.com/magazine/content/06_32/b3996420.htm; "The 20 Worst Product Failures," Sales HQ, http://saleshq.monster.com/news/articles/2655-the-20-worst-product-failures, accessed June 20, 2012.

4. Alex Palmer, "Private Label Growing Rapidly," AdWeek, September 22, 2009, http://www.adweek.com/brand-marketing/private-label-growing-rapidly-105007/, accessed June 14, 2010; Christopher Durham, "Ten Private Brand Trends that Shook North America," My[Private]Brand, December 9, 2010, http://mypbrand.com/2010/12/09/10-private-brand-trends-that-shook-north-america/, accessed May 2, 2011; "IRI: Fewer Shoppers Buying Private Label Versus Last Year," Store Brands Decisions, http://www.storebrandsdecisions.com/news/2011/04/05/iri-fewer-shoppers-buying-private-label-versus-last-year, posted April 5, 2011, accessed May 2, 2011; Christopher Durham, "Private Brand Sales Outpace National Brands—PLMA's 2013 Private Label Yearbook," My Private Brand, June 28, 2013, http://mypbrand.com/2013/06/28/private-brands-sales-outpace-national-brands-plmas-2013-private-label-yearbook/, accessed February 12, 2014.

5. "The USA Apparel Market Research Report," Informat Fashion, June 2010, http://www.infomat.com/fido/getpublication.fcn?&type=research&SearchString=apparel&id=737870ST0000927&start=1&tr=17Infomat, accessed June 14, 2010.

6. "Not on the List? The Truth About Impulse Purchases," Knowledge@Wharton, January 7, 2009, http://knowledge.wharton.upenn.edu/article.cfm?articleid=2132, accessed February 28, 2009.

7. "3M: Commitment to Sustainability," GreenBiz Leaders website, 1999.

8. "Wacky Warning Labels 2009 Winners Announced," Foundation for Fair Civil Justice, August 16, 2009,

http://www.foundationforfaircivil justice.org/news /in_depth/wacky_warning_labels_2009_winners _announced/, accessed June 14, 2010; Bob Dorigo Jones, "Wacky Warning Labels Show Toll of Frivolous Lawsuits," Bob Dorigo Jones, June 8, 2012, http://www.bobdorigojones.com/, accessed June 20, 2012; Bob Dorigo Jones, "Deadline for Entering 15th Annual Wacky Warning Labels™ Contest Is May 15," Bob Dorigo Jones, May 7, 2012, http://www.bobdorigojones.com/, accessed June 20, 2012.

9. Dawn C. Chmielewski, "Binge-viewing Is Transforming the Television Experience," *The Los Angeles Times*, February 1, 2013, http://articles.latimes .com/2013/feb/01/entertainment/la-et-ct-binge -viewing-20130201, accessed March 20, 2013; David Hinkley, "Americans Spend 34 Hours a Week Watching TV, According to Nielsen Numbers," Daily News, September 19, 2012, http://www.nydailynews .com/entertainment/tv-movies/americans-spend -34-hours-week-watching-tv-nielsen-numbers -article-1.1162285, accessed March 20, 2013; Stine Thorhauge, "How People Spend Their Time Online," Mind-Jumpers, May 24, 2012, http://www .mindjumpers.com/blog/2012/05/time-spend -online/, accessed March 20, 2013; "U.S. Consumer Online Behavior Survey Results 2007 Part One: Wireline Usage," International Data Corporation website, February 19, 2008, http://www.idc.com /getdoc.jsp?containerId=prUS21096308, accessed March 3, 2009; Dan Frommer, "Why Video On Demand Is Still Cable's Game to Lose," The Business Insider, September 5, 2008, http://www .businessinsider.com/2008/9/why-video-on -demand-is-still-cable-s-game-to-lose, accessed March 3, 2009; Glenn Abel, "Streaming Vids Boost Netflix profits," Download Movies 101, January 29, 2009, http://downloadmovies101.com/wordpress -1/2009/01/29/streaming-vids-boost-netflix-profits/, accessed March 3, 2009; "Casting the Big Movie Download Roles," eMarketer, September 7, 2007, http://www.emarketer.com/Article.aspx?id=1005346, accessed March 3, 2009; Clark Fredricksen, "Time Watching TV Still Tops Internet," December 15, 2010, eMarketer Blog, http://www.emarketer.com /blog/index.php/time-spent-watching-tv-tops -internet/, accessed May 4, 2011; "Average Time Spent Online Per U.S. Visitor in 2010," ComScore Data Mine, January 11, 2011, http://www .comscoredatamine.com/2011/01 /average-time -spent-online-per-u-s-visitor-in-2010/, accessed May 4, 2011; Erick Schonfeld, "How People Watch TV Online and Off," TechCrunch, January 8, 2012, http://techcrunch.com /2012/01/08/how-people- watch-tv-online/, accessed June 20, 2012.

10. William C. Taylor, "Permission Marketing," Fast Company, December 18, 2007, http://www. fastcompany.com/magazine/14/permission.html, accessed March 3, 2009.

11. Bruce Horowitz, "Budweiser's Clydesdale Wins Ad Meter by a Nose," USA Today, February 4, 2013, http://www.usatoday.com/story/money/ business/2013/02/04/clydesdale-ad-wins-by-a- nose/1889693/, accessed March 20, 2013; Bruce Horovitz, "'Two Nobodies from Nowhere' craft winning Super Bowl ad," *USA Today*, February 4, 2009, http://www.usatoday.com/money/advertising/ admeter/2009admeter.htm, accessed March 4, 2009; Watch the top 5 highest-rated Super Bowl LII ads by Alan Siegel, February 5, 2018, http://admeter. usatoday.com/2018/02/05/watch-the-top-5-highest- rated-super-bowl-lii-ads/, accessed May 4, 2018.

12. Professor Paul Herbig, Tristate University, International Marketing Lecture Series, Session 6, International Advertising, http://www.tristate.edu /faculty/herbig/pahimadvstg.htm, accessed June 1, 2005; Karl Moore and Mark Smith, "Taking Global Brands to Japan," The Conference Board, http:// www.conference-board.org/worldwide/worldwide _article.cfm?id=243&pg=1, accessed June 1, 2005.

13. "US Digital Display Ad Spending to Surpass Search Ad Spending in 2016," eMarketer, January 11, 2016, https://www.emarketer.com/Article/US -Digital-Display-Ad-Spending-Surpass-Search-Ad -Spending-2016/1013442, accessed April 29, 2017

14. "Mobile Gets One Out of Five Paid Search Clicks," eMarketer, May 6, 2013, http://www .emarketer.com/Article/Mobile-Gets-One-of-Five -Paid-Search-Clicks/1009865, accessed February 13, 2014; "Steady gains for mobile paid search," eMarketer, February 22, 2013, http://www.emarketer .com/Article/Steady-Gains-Mobile-Paid-Search /1009686, accessed March 20, 2013; "Search Marketing Trends: Back to Basics," eMarketer, February 2009, http://www.emarketer.com/Report. aspx?code=emarketer_2000559, accessed June 18, 2010; "eMarketer: Display ad Growth Catching Up with Search," posted by Leah McBride Mensching, December 16, 2010, sfnblog, http://www.sfnblog .com/advertising/2010/12/emarketer_display_ad _growth_catching_up.php, accessed May 11, 2011; "US Online Ad Spend Poised to Grow 20% in 2011," eMarketer, June 8, 2011, http://www.emarketer .com/Article.aspx?R=1008431, accessed June 20, 2012.

15. "Mobile Requires Revamped SEO, SEM Strategy," eMarketer, April 18, 2013, http://www.emarketer .com/Article/Search-Gets-Mobile-Makeover /1009822, accessed February 13, 2014; Pamela Parker, "eMarketer: Among Online Ads, Search to Gain Most New Dollars in 2011," SearchEngine Land, June 11, 2008, http://searchengineland.com /emarketer-among-online-ads-search-to-gain-most -new-dollars-in-2011-80707, accessed March 20, 2013; Adweek staff, "eMarketer: Search Is Vital in a Recession," Brandweek, February 25, 2009, http:// www.brandweek.com/bw/content_display /news -and-features/digital/e3i195c363ab252f 976a2 dabde4d8ef2549, accessed March 3, 2009.

16. "Online Video Advertising Moves Front and Center," eMarketer, May 14, 2013, http://www .emarketer.com/Article/Online-Video-Advertising -Moves-Front-Center/1009886, accessed February 13, 2017; "U.S. Online Advertising Video Spending 2007–2013," eMarketer, August 2008, http://www .marketingcharts.com/television/emarketer-revises -online-video-ad-spend-projections-downward-5679 /emarketer-online-video-ad-spend-us-2007-2013jpg/, accessed June 18, 2010; "Promises, Promises: Will Online Video Ads Deliver this Year?," posted by David Hallerman, December 9, 2010, The eMarketer Blog, http://www.emarketer.com/blog/index .php /promises-promises-online-video-ads-deliver -year/, accessed May 11, 2011; "US Online Ad Spend Poised to Grow 20% in 2011," eMarketer, June 8, 2011, http://www.emarketer.com/Article .aspx?R=1008431, accessed June 20, 2012.

17. "Social Media Claims More of Our Attention. But Email's Not Dead Yet," posted by Meghan Keane, August 2, 2010, eConsultancy, http:// econsultancy.com/us/blog/6366-social-media -might-claim-a-lot-of-our-attention-but-email -s-not-dead-yet, accessed May 11, 2011; Erik Qualman, "Social Media ROI Examples & Video,"

posted November 12, 2009, Socialnomics, Social Media Blog, http://socialnomics.net/2009/11/12 /social-media-roi-examples-video/, accessed June 28, 2010; Lauren Fisher, "The ROI of Social Media: 10 Case Studies," The Next Web, July 16, 2011, http://thenextweb.com/socialmedia/2011/07/16 /the-roi-of-social-media-10-case-studies/, accessed June 21, 2012.

18. "Infographic: Native Advertising Grows Despite Budget and Transparency Concerns," Adweek, February 16, 2015, http://www.adweek.com/news /technology/infographic-native-advertising-grows -despite-budget-and-transparency-concerns-162963, accessed April 25, 2015.

19. Margot Peppers, "Crocs Get a Stylish Make-over as Brand Hopes to DOUBLE Sales in Five Years— But Can the Foam Shoe Move on from Its Ugly Past?," *Daily Mail*, July 19, 2013, http://www.dailymail .co.uk/femail/article-2370360/Crocs-stylish-make -brand-hopes-DOUBLE-sales-years--foam-shoe-ugly -past.html, accessed February 15, 2013; "Pizza and a Movie, Time Pop Chart," *Time* Magazine, June 3, 2013, http://content.time.com/time/magazine/article /0,9171,2144105,00.html, accessed February 15, 2014.

20. Abram Sauer, "Brandchannel's 2004 Product Placement Awards," Brandchannel, February 21, 2005, http://www.brandchannel.com/start1.asp?fa _id =251; Dale Buss, "A Product Placement Hall of Fame," BusinessWeek Online, June 22, 1998, http://www.businessweek.com/1998/25/b3583062 .htm.

21. Angie Han, "'Transformers: Age of Extinction' Tops 2015 Product Placement Awards," SlashFilm, March 4, 2015, http://www.slashfilm.com/transformers -age-of-extinction-tops-2015-product-placement -awards/, accessed April 25, 2015; Abe Sauer, "Announcing the 2013 BrandCameo Product Placement Award Winners," BrandChannel, February 25, 2013, http://www.brandchannel.com/home/post/2013 /02/25/Brandchannel-9th-Brandcameo-Product -Placement-Awards-022513.aspx, accessed March 20, 2013. Eric Slivka, "Apple tops 2010 film product placement awards," MacRumors, February 22, 2011, http://www.macrumors.com/2011/02/22/apple-tops -2010-film-product-placement-awards/, accessed May 11, 2011.

22. Tatyana Shumsky, "United, Pepsi Outcry Unlikely to Hurt Financial Results," *The Wall Street Journal*, April 15, 2017, https://www.wsj .com/articles/united-pepsi-outcry-unlikely-to -hurt-financial-results-1492250400, accessed April 30, 2017.

23. Abe Sauer, "Product Placement Sees Global Rise as Fans Face Saturated Entertainment," BrandChannel, April 24, 2013, http://www.brandchannel. com/home/post/2013/04/24/Product-Placement-On -The-Rise-042413.aspx, accessed February 13, 2014; Abe Sauer, "Announcing the 2013 BrandCameo Product Placement Award Winners," BrandChannel, February 25, 2013, http://www.brandchannel .com/home/post/2013/02/25/Brandchannel-9th -Brandcameo-Product-Placement-Awards-022513 .aspx, accessed March 20, 2013; "PQ Media Market Analysis Finds Global Product Placement Spending Grew 37% in 2006; Forecast to Grow 30% in 2007, Driven by Relaxed European Rules, Emerging Asian Markets; Double-Digit Growth in U.S. Decelerates," PQ Media, March 14, 2007, http:// www.pqmedia.com/about-press-20070314-gppf .html, accessed September 4, 2008; Jose Fermoso, "DVR Households Swelling Ranks," Portfolio,

December 16, 2008, http://www.portfolio.com/views /blogs/the-tech-observer/2008/12/16/dvr-household s-swelling-ranks, accessed March 4, 2009; "FCC Opens Inquiry Into Stealthy TV Product Placement," *USA Today*, June 26, 2008, http://www.usatoday.com /life/television/2008-06-26-fcc-advertising_N.htm, accessed March 4, 2009; Bill Gorman, "DVRs now in 30.6% of U.S. Households," TV by the Numbers, April 30, 2009, http://tvbythenumbers.com /2009/04/30/dvrs-now-in-306-of-us-households/17779, accessed June 16, 2010; Andrew Hampp, "Product Placement Dipped Last Year for the First Time," AdAge, June 29, 2010, http://adage.com/article /madisonvine-news/product-placement-dipped -year-time/144720/, accessed May 11, 2011; Robert Seidman, "DVR Penetration Grows to 39.7% of Households, 42.2% of Viewers," TV by the Numbers, March 23, 2011, http://tvbythenumbers.zap2it.com /2011/03/23/dvr-penetration-grows-to-39-7-of -households-42-2-of-viewers/86819/, accessed May 11, 2011; Joseph Plambeck, "Product Placement Grows in Music Videos," *The New York Times*, July 5, 2010, http://www.nytimes.com/2010/07/06/business/media /06adco.html?_r=1, accessed June 21, 2012; Bill Carter and Brian Stelter, "DVRs and Streaming Prompt a Shift in the Top-Rated TV Shows," *The New York Times*, March 4, 2012, http://www.nytimes .com/2012/03/05/business/media/dvrs-and-streaming -prompt-a-shift-in-the-top-rated-tv-shows.html? pagewanted=all, accessed June 21, 2012.

24. Susan Gunelius, "Ford, Coke & AT&T Pay More to Sponsor American Idol," Bizzia, January 18, 2008, http://www.bizzia.com/brandcurve/ford-coke -att-pay-more-to-sponsor-american-idol/, accessed March 4, 2009; Amy Johannes, "Global Paid Product Placement to Reach $7.6 billion by 2010: Report," PromoMagazine, August 17, 2006, http:// promomagazine.com/research/paidplacementreport/, accessed June 16, 2010.

25. Angela Moscaritolo, "Number of U.S. Video Game Players Falls," PC Magazine, September 5, 2012, http://www.pcmag.com/article2/0,2817,240 9313,00.asp, accessed March 20, 2013; "Advertis- ers support games through new placements like branded virtual goods and opt-in videos,", eMar- keter, December 12, 2012, http://www.emarketer. com/Article/US-Gamers-Race-Mobile/1009543, accessed March 20, 2013; "Massive Summary Research—Significant Findings," Massive, http:// www.massiv-eincorporated.com/casestudiesa.html, accessed March 4, 2009; Nick Gonzalez, "Google to Buy Adscape," TechCrunch, February 16, 2007, http://www.techcrunch.com/2007/02/16/google -to-buy-adscape-for-23-million/, accessed March 5, 2009; "IN-game Advertising Is a Massive Market," *The Telegraph*, May 15, 2011, http://www.telegraph .co.uk/technology/news/5312188/In-game-advertising -is-a-massive-market.html, accessed May 16, 2011; Mike Shields, "Report: Video Game Ads to Reach $1 Bil. by 2012," AdWeek, March 4, 2008, http:// www.adweek.com/news/television/report-video -game-ads-reach-1-bil-2012-95119, accessed June 21, 2012; "Let the Games Begin Advertising!," eMar- keter, April 6, 2007, http://www.emarketer.com /Article.aspx?1004739&R=1004739, accessed June 21, 2012.

26. "Snap to It; Snapchat's Future," *The Economist*, February 4, 2017, https://www.highbeam.com/doc /1G1-479741711.html, accessed April 30, 2017; Lauren Johnson, "Taco Bell's Cinco de Mayo Snapchat Lens Was Viewed 224 Million Times," *AdWeek*, May 11, 2016, http://www.adweek.com /digital/taco-bells-cinco-de-mayo-snapchat-lens -was-viewed-224-million-times-171390/, accessed April 30, 2017.

27. Lisa Evans, "Fitness First—Wait Watching," *The Cool Hunter,* March 17, 2009, http://www . thecoolhunter.co.uk/article/detail/1504/fitness -first-wait-watching, accessed March 30, 2013; "UNICEF Finland: Mom," March 31, 2009, I Believe in Advertising, http://www.ibelieveinadv .com/2009/03/unicef-finland-mom/, accessed March 30, 2013; Melanie Wells, "Kid Nabbing," *Forbes*, February 2, 2004, http://www.forbes.com/free _forbes/2004/0202/084.html; Tremor, http://tremor. com/index.html, accessed March 5, 2009; Elaine Wong, "General Mills, Kraft Launch Word of Mouth Networks," *BrandWeek*, October 5, 2008, http://www.brandweek.com/bw/content _display/news-and-features/packaged-goods /e3i2db03fb29d573ec52722456845f5c274, accessed March 5, 2009; "The World's Weird America: How Some of Our Most Popular Products Are Seen Overseas," *Pacific Standard*, February 26, 2014, https://psmag.com/the-world-s-weird-america-how -some-of-our-most-popular-products-are-seen -overseas-1d4a6b1732c0#.38jodwtwf, accessed May 7, 2016.

28. Aaron Agius, "The 10 Best Social Media Mar- keting Campaigns of 2016 So Far," *Social Media Today*, July 28, 2016, http://www.socialmediatoday .com/marketing/10-best-social-media-marketing- campaigns-2016-so-far, accessed April 30, 2017.

29. "Economic Uncertainty to Slow Sponsorship Growth in 2012," *IEG*, January 11, 2012, http:// www.sponsorship.com/About-IEG/Press-Room /Economic-Uncertainty-To-Slow-Sponsorship -Growth-In.aspx, accessed March 20, 2013; "Spon- sorship Spending to Rise 2.2 Percent in 2009," press release, *IEG*, February 11, 2009, Sponsorship .Com, http://www.sponsorship.com/About-IEG /Press-Room/Sponsorship-Spending-To-Rise -2.2-Percent-in-2009.aspx, accessed March 5, 2009; "Sponsorship Spending to Rise 2.2 Percent in 2009," Sommerville Baddley Marketing, August 28, 2009, http://www.sbmktg.net/2009/08/sponsorship -spending-to-rise-22-percent-in-2009/, accessed June 16, 2010; "Sponsorship Spending: 2010 Proves Better Than Expected; Bigger Gains Set for 2011," press release, *IEG*, January 12, 2011, http://www .prweb.com/releases/2011/01/prweb4958744.htm, accessed May 15, 2011; "Economic Uncertainty to Slow Sponsorship Growth in 2012," *IEG*, January 11, 2012, http://www.sponsorship.com/About-IEG .aspx, accessed June 22, 2012.

30. Shawn Paul Wood, "Emissions Scandal Took the Air Out of Volkswagen Sales in November," AdWeek, December 2, 2015, http://www.adweek .com/prnewser/emissions-scandal-took-the-air-out -of-volkswagen-sales-in-november/119765, accessed May 15, 2016.

31. Bill Stoller, "Publicity from Thin Air (Don't Just Wait for News to Happen)," ArticlesClick.com, http://articlesclick.com/articles/public -relations/publicity-from-thin-air.php, accessed June 15, 2005.

32. "The Employment Situation—April 2011," Bu- reau of Labor Statistics News Release, May 6, 2011, Bureau of Labor Statistics, http://www.bls.gov/news .release/pdf/empsit.pdf, accessed May 16, 2011.

Pg. 222 Fact: Erik Qualman, "Social Media Video 2013," *Socialnomics*, January 1, 2013, http://www .socialnomics.net/2013/01/01/social-media-video -2013/, accessed September 2014.

13

1. "Supermarket Facts, Industry Overview 2008," Food Marketing Institute, http://www.fmi.org/facts _figs/?fuseaction=superfact, accessed June 30, 2010.

2. Sebastian Valencia, "Wholesale Distribution Industry Outlook: Drones," Clarkson Consulting, August 27, 2014, http://clarkstonconsulting.com /blog/wholesale-distribution-industry-outlook -drones/, accessed April 27, 2015; Doug Gross, "Amazon's Drone Delivery: How Would It Work?," *CNN*, December 2, 2013, http://www.cnn.com /2013/12/02/tech/innovation/amazon-drones -questions/, accessed April 27, 2015; Hilary Brueck, "Here's How Amazon Is Fighting for U.S. Drone Deliveries," *Fortune*, March 21, 2016, http:// fortune.com/2016/03/21/amazon-drone-lobbying/, accessed May 21, 2016.

3. Suzanne Kapner, "Brick-and-Mortar Stores Are Shuttering at a Record Pace," *The Wall Street Journal*, April 21, 2017 https://www.wsj.com /articles/brick-and-mortar-stores-are-shuttering-at -a-record-pace-1492818818, accessed May 5, 2017; Carleton English, "Weak Mall Traffic Spells Pain for Abercrombie, American Eagle & L Brands," Real Money, April 20, 2016, http://realmoney. thestreet.com/articles/04/20/2016/weak-mall-traffic -spells-pain-abercrombie-american-eagle-l-brands, accessed May 5, 2017.

4. "Apparel Drives US Retail Ecommerce Sales Growth," eMarketer, April 20, 2012, http://www .emarketer.com/newsroom/index.php/apparel -drives-retail-ecommerce-sales-growth/, accessed February 17, 2014; Susanna Kim, "Walmart Website Error Allowed Customers to Buy $600 Electronics for $8.85," *ABC News,* November 6, 2013, http://abcnews.go.com/Business/walmart- super-low-prices-website-glitch/story?id=20804317, accessed February 26, 2014; "Healthy Growth for Ecommerce as Retail Continues Shift to Web," eMarketer Newsletter, March 17, 2011, http:// www.emarketer.com/Article/Healthy-Growth -Ecommerce-Retail-Continues-Shift-Web/1008284, accessed April 6, 2013; Rachel Metz, "Report: On- line retail could reach $156B in 2009," by January 29, 2009, The Industry Standard, http://www .thestandard.com/news/2009/01/29/report-online -retail-could-reach-156b-2009, accessed March 13, 2009; Jeffrey Grau, "eMarketer revises e-commerce forecast," eMarketer, March 5, 2009, http://www .emarketer.com/Article.aspx?id=1006948; Beth Kowitt, "Inside the Secret World of Trader Joes," *Fortune*, August 23, 2010, http://money.cnn. com/2010/08/20/news/companies/inside_trader_joes _full_version.fortune/index.htm, accessed May 30, 2011; "Healthy Growth for Ecommerce as Retail Continues Shift to Web," eMarketer Blog, March 17, 2011, http://www.emarketer.com /Article.aspx?R=1008284, accessed May 30, 2011; http://mashable.com/2011/02/28 /forrester -e-commerce/.

5. "Worldwide Retail Ecommerce Sales Will Reach $1.915 Trillion This Year," eMarketer, August 22, 2016, https://www.emarketer.com/Article /Worldwide-Retail-Ecommerce-Sales-Will-Reach -1915-Trillion-This-Year/1014369, accessed May 5, 2017.

6. Miranda Hobbs, "How Does Real-time Online Support Boost Conversion Rates and Ensure a Pur- chase Sticks?," iAdvize blog, April 16, 2015, http:// www.iadvize.com/blog/en/en-conversion-rate

-optimisation-live-chat/, accessed May 5, 2017; Justyna Kraszewska, "Why Should I Set Up Chat Greetings," Live Chat, https://www.livechatinc.com/kb/why-should-i-set-up-chat-greetings/, 7.

7. Khadeeja Safdar, "Victoria's Secret Turns Its Back on the Catalog," *The Wall Street Journal*, April 8, 2016, https://www.wsj.com/articles/victorias-secret-turns-its-back-on-the-catalog-1460155651, accessed May 5, 2017.

8. Christian Storm, "30 Bizarre Vending Machines from Around the World," *Business Insider*, November 10, 2014, http://www.businessinsider.com/most-unique-vending-machines-2014-11, accessed April 27, 2015.

9. "Sales soften at Costco," Retail Analysis, IGD, March 4, 2009, http://www.igd.com/analysis/channel/news_hub.asp?channelid=1&channelitemid=9&ni dp=&nid=5616, accessed March 13, 2009.

10. Ann Lukits, "How to Get College Students to Eat Healthier," January 13, 2017, https://www.wsj.com/articles/how-to-get-college-students-to-eat-healthier-1484324984, accessed May 6, 2017.

11. Loss Leader Strategy, Investopedia website (a Forbes Digital Company), http://www.investopedia.com/terms/l/lossleader.asp, accessed March 14, 2009; Al Norman, "Walmart Not Crying Over Spilt Milk," *The Huffington Post*, August 22, 2008, http://www.huffingtonpost.com /al-norman/wal-mart-not-crying-over_b_120684 .html, accessed March 14, 2009.

12. Rafi Mohammed, "The Problem with Price Gouging Laws," *Harvard Business Review*, July 23, 2013, https://hbr.org/2013/07/the-problem-with-price-gouging-laws, accessed May 6, 2017; Jeffrey Dorfman, "Price Gouging Laws Are Good Politics But Bad Economics," *Forbes*, September 23, 2016, https://www.forbes.com/sites/jeffreydorfman/2016/09/23/price-gouging-laws-are-good-politics-but-bad-economics/#2a5aebc264d3, accessed May 6, 2017.

13. Stephanie Clifford, "Shopper Alert: Price May Drop for You Alone by Stephanie Clifford," *The New York Times*, August 9, 2012 http://www.nytimes.com/2012/08/10/business/supermarkets-try-customizing-prices-for-shoppers.html, accessed May 6, 2017.

14. Ben Kunz, "How Apple Plays the Pricing Game," *Bloomberg Businessweek*, October, 6, 2010, http://www.nbcnews.com/id/38980367/ns/business-us_business/t/how-apple-plays-pricing-game/#.UWInbjcwok9, accessed April 7, 2013.

15. Steven Greenhouse, "How Costco Became the Anti Walmart," *The New York Times*, July 17, 2005, http://www.nytimes.com/2005/07/17/business/yourmoney/17costco.html?adxnnl=1&pagewanted=1&adxnnlx=1122004143-8Vfn2DFl 1MJfern M1navLA; Matthew Boyle, "Why Costco Is So Addictive," *CNNMoney*, October 25, 2006, http://money.cnn.com/magazines/fortune/fortune_archive/2006/10/30/8391725/index.htm, accessed March 14, 2009.

Pg. 242 Fact: Russian proverb.

14

1. Stephanie Vozza, "The Surprising First Jobs of 10 Famous CEOS," Fast Company, http://www.fastcompany.com/3027074/dialed/the-surprising-first-jobs-of-10-famous-ceos#1, accessed May 1,

2015; "First Jobs of the Rich and Famous," *Parade*, http://www.parade.com/celebrity/slideshows/flashback/stars-first-jobs.html#?slideindex=0, accessed April 7, 2013; "The Importance of Being Richard Branson, Leadership and Change," Knowledge@Wharton, January 12, 2005, http://knowledge.wharton.upenn.edu/article/1109.cfm; Jeffrey Kluger, "Ambition: Why Some People Are Most Likely to Succeed," *Time* Magazine, November 14, 2005, pp. 48–59, http://www.time.com/time/archive/preview/0,10987,1126746,00.html; "Jeff Bezos," Reference for Business, http://www.referenceforbusiness.com/businesses/A-F/Bezos-Jeff.html, accessed June 24, 2012; Matt Melvin2011, "The Roller Coaster Ride of Mark Zuckerberg," Teen Ink, http://www.teenink.com/nonfiction/academic/article/292887/The.., accessed June 24, 2012; "Reagan Trail Days," The Ronald Reagan Trail, http://www.ronaldreagantrail.net/Pages/ReaganTrail.php?city=2&page=Dixon, accessed June 24, 2012; "Celebrities' First Jobs," Oprah.com, http://www.oprah.com/entertainment/Oprahs-Live-Newscast-and-Celebrities-First-Jobs, accessed September 4, 2016; David Kushner, "Will Virtual Reality Change Your Life?," *Rolling Stone*, May 23, 2016, http://www.rollingstone.com/culture/features/will-virtual-reality-change-your-life-20160523, accessed September 4, 2016.

2. Erika Anderson, "It Seemed Like a Good Idea at the Time: 7 of the Worst Business Decisions Ever Made," *Forbes*, October 4, 2013, http://www.forbes.com/sites/erikaandersen/2013/10/04/it-seemed-like-a-good-idea-at-the-time-7-of-the-worst-business-decisions-ever-made/, accessed March 1, 2014; "The Worst Business Decisions of All Time," 24/7 *The Wall Street Journal*, October 4, 2013, http://247wallst.com/2012/10/17/the-worst-business-decisions-of-all-time/3/, accessed April 7, 2013; "Top Ten Bad Business Decisions," Business Excellence, October 10, 2010, http://www.bus-ex.com/article/top-ten-bad-business-decisions, accessed June 24, 2012; Peter Roesler, "8 of the Biggest Business Mistakes in History," Inc., April 20, 2015, http://www.inc.com/peter-roesler/8-of-the-biggest-business-mistakes-in-history.html, accessed June 1, 2016.

3. "The Importance of Being Richard Branson," Leadership and Change, Knowledge@Wharton, January 12, 2005, http://knowledge.wharton.upenn.edu/article/1109.cfm.

4. "Hot Topic, Inc. Reports Fourth Quarter EPS Increases 19% to $0.32 Per Diluted Share; Provides Guidance for the 1st Quarter of 2009," News Blaze, March 11, 2009, http://newsblaze.com/story/2009031112554500001.pz/topstory.html, accessed March 25, 2009.

5. Larry Page, "Motivate Your Staff," How to Succeed in 2005, Business 2.0 magazine, December 1, 2004, http://money.cnn.com/magazines/business2/business2_archive/2004/12/01/8192529/index.htm.

6. Steve Lohr, "A New Game at the Office: Many Young Workers Accept Fewer Guarantees," *The New York Times*, December 5, 2005, http://select.nytimes.com/gst/abstract.html?res=F00F12FE385 50C768CDDAB0994DD404482.

7. Jeremy Morgan, "Uber Was Right to Hustle, but Here's Where its Leadership Blew It," *Fortune*, March 22, 2017, http://fortune.com/2017/03/20/uber-president-resigns-travis-kalanick/, accessed May 14, 2017; Dinah Eng, "For Which Wich, Success Is in the Bag," April 22, 2017, http://fortune

.com/2017/04/22/which-wich-sandwiches-jeff-sinelli/, accessed May 14, 2017.

8. "Fortune 100 Best Companies to Work for 2017," *Fortune*, http://beta.fortune.com/best-companies/, accessed May 13, 2017.

9. Ibid.

10. Ibid.

11. "Zuckerberg Claims 'We Don't Build Services to Make Money,'" by Larry Magid, February 1, 2012, *Forbes*, http://www.forbes.com/sites/larrymagid/2012/02/01/zuckerberg-claims-we-dont-build-services-to-make-money/, accessed April 7, 2013; Venessa Wong, "This CEO Gives Every Employee His Cell Number (Seriously)," *Bloomberg Businessweek*, October 22, 2012, http://www.businessweek.com/articles/2012-10-22/this-ceo-gives-every-employee-his-cell-number-seriously, accessed April 7, 2013.

12. Darrell Rigby, "Don't Get Hammered by Management Fads," *The Wall Street Journal*, May 21, 2001.

13. Catherine Rampell, "A Generation of Slackers? Not So Much," *The New York Times*, May 28, 2011, http://www.nytimes.com/2011/05/29/weekinreview/29graduates.html, accessed June 29, 2011.

14. "The Cow in the Ditch: How Anne Mulcahy rescued Xerox," Special Section: Knowledge at Wharton, November 16–29, 2005, http://knowledge.wharton.upenn.edu/index.cfm?fa=viewArticle&id=1318&specialId=41.

15. Amy Langfield, "Unused Vacation Days at 40-year High," *CNBC*, October 23, 2014, http://www.cnbc.com/id/102110867, accessed May 4, 2015; Tony Schwartz, "Relax! You'll Be More Productive," *The New York Times*, February 9, 2013, http://www.nytimes.com/2013/02/10/opinion/sunday/relax-youll-be-more-productive .html?pagewanted=all&_r=0, accessed April 8, 2013; Chris Morris, "The Average American Throws Away 4 Vacation Days a Year," *Fortune*, November 17, 2015, http://fortune.com/2015/11/17/vacation-paid-time-americans-survey/, accessed June 5, 2016; Suyin Hayes, "Lack of Sleep Costs U.S. About $411 Billion in Lost Productivity, Study Finds," *Fortune*, November 30, 2016, http://fortune.com/2016/11/30/sleep-productivity-rand-corp-411-billion/, accessed May 14, 2017; "The state of American vacation: How vacation became a casualty of our work culture," Project: Time Off, http://www.projecttimeoff.com/research/state-american-vacation-2016, accessed May 14, 2017.

15

1. Cheryl Hall, "Southwest Airlines CEO Is Defining Himself as a Leader—Without Bag Fees," *DallasNews*, April 19, 2010, http://www.dallasnews.com/business/columnists/cheryl-hall/20100417-Southwest-Airlines-CEO-is-defining-himself-5278.ece, accessed April 8, 2013; Gary Kelly and Kate McCann, "Southwest Airlines CEO on the Business of Building Trust," *McCombs School of Business*, October 11, 2005, http://www.mccombs.utexas.edu/news/pressreleases/lyceum05_kelly_wrap05.asp, accessed July 2, 2010; "Southwest Airlines Reports Fourth Quarter Profit and 37th Consecutive Year of Profitability," PRNewsWire, January 21, 2010, http://www.prnewswire.com/news-releases/southwest-airlines-reports-fourth-quarter-profit-and-37th

-consecutive-year-of-profitability-82241197. html, accessed July 2, 2010; 1106 HR Magazine: "Views from the Top," SHRM, November 1, 2006, http://www.shrm.org/Publications/hrmagazine /EditorialContent/Pages/1106ceoex.aspx, accessed July 5, 2011.

2. Anna Brown and Eileen Patten, "The Narrowing, But Persistent, Gender Gap in Pay," Fact Tank, Pew Research Center, April 3, 2017, http://www .pewresearch.org/fact-tank/2017/04/03/gender -pay-gap-facts/, accessed May 21, 2017.

3. Top CEOs Make More in Two Days Than An Average Employee Does in One Year by Grace Donnelly July 20, 2017, http://fortune. com/2017/07/20/ceo-pay-ratio-2016/, accessed May 28, 2018.

4. "America's Jobless Recovery. Not Again," *Economist*, June 3, 2011, http://www.economist .com/blogs/freeexchange/2011/06/americas-jobless- recovery, accessed July 5, 2011; Steve Lohr, "A New Game at the Office: Many Young Workers Accept Fewer Guarantees," *The New York Times*, December 5, 2005, http://select.nytimes.com/gst /abstract.html?res=F00F12FE38550C768CDDAB 0994DD404482.

5. Kathryn Dill, "Report: CEOs Earn 331 Times as Much as Average Workers, 774 Times as Much as Minimum Wage Earners," *Forbes*, April 15, 2014, http://www.forbes.com/sites/kathryndill/2014/04/15 /report-ceos-earn-331-times-as-much-as-average -workers-774-times-as-much-as-minimum-wage -earners/, accessed Mary 10, 2015.

6. Jennifer Liberto, "CEO pay is 380 times average worker's—AFL-CIO," *CNNMoney*, April 19, 2012, http://money.cnn.com/2012/04/19/news/economy /ceo-pay/index.htm, accessed April 9, 2013; Dionysus, "CEO pay vs. performance—Still a roll of the dice," posted on Economatrix, April 1, 2010, http://www .economatix.com/ceo-pay-vs-performance -still-a-roll-of-the-dice-wsj, accessed September 6, 2011; Figure 3AE from Lawrence Mishel, Jared Bernstein, and Heidi Shierholz, *The State of Working America 2009/2009: An Economic Policy Institute Book* (Ithaca, NY: ILR Press, An Imprint of Cornell University Press, 2009), http://www .stateofworkingamerica.org/tabfig/2008/03/SWA08 _Chapter3_Wages_r2_Fig-3AE.jpg, accessed July 1, 2010; Pradnya Joshi, "We Knew They Got Raises. But This?," *The New York Times*, July 2, 2011, http://www.nytimes.com/2011/07/03 /business/03pay.html, accessed July 5, 2011; Marla Dickerson, "U.S. CEO's Pay 231 Times Higher Than That of Average Workers," *Los Angeles Times*, May 2, 2012, http://articles.latimes .com/2012/may/02/business/la-fi-mo-us-ceo-pay -231times-more-than-average-workers-20120502, accessed June 30, 2012; Scott Thurm, "CEO Pay Moves with Corporate Results," *The Wall Street Journal*, May 23, 2012, http://online.wsj.com /article/SB1000142405270230401940457741 62 10712022298.html, accessed July 2, 2012; Scott Thrum, "'Pay for Performance' No Longer a Punchline," *The Wall Street Journal*, March 20, 2013, http://www.wsj.com/articles/SB10001424127 88732437320457837244079319544, accessed June 12, 2016; Paul Hodgson, "Top CEOs Make More Than 300 Times the Average Worker," *Fortune*, June 22, 2015, http://fortune.com/2015/06/22/ceo -vsworker-pay/, accessed June 12, 2016.

7. "In 2011 the Baby Boomers Start to Turn 65: 16 Statistics About the Coming Retirement Crisis That Will Drop Your Jaw," The Ameri- can Dream, December 30, 2010, http:// endoftheamericandream.com/archives/in-2011the -baby-boomers-start-to-turn-65-16-statisticsabout -the-coming-retirement-crisis-thatwill-drop-your -jaw, accessed July 5, 2011.

8. Steve Greenhouse, "The Age Premium: Retain- ing Older Workers," *The New York Times*, May 14, 2014, https://www.nytimes.com/2014/05/15/business /retirementspecial/the-age-premium-retaining-older -workers.html, accessed May 15, 2017.

9. "Facing Young Workers' High Job Expectations," *Los Angeles Times*, June 27, 2005; Bruce Tulgan, *Not Everyone Gets a Trophy* (San Francisco: Jossey-Bass [Wiley imprint], 2009).

10. Betsy Morris, "How Corporate America Is Be- traying Women," *Fortune*, January 10, 2005; "Jane Drain—Women Leaving Your Workforce," Smart Manager, http://www.smartmanager.com.au /web/au/smartmanager/en/pages/89_jane_drain— women_leaving_workforce.html, accessed July 5, 2011; Tiziana Barghini, "Educated Women Quit Work as Spouses Earn More," Reuters, March 8, 2012, http://www.reuters.com/article/2012/03/08 /us-economy-womenidUSBRE8270AC20120308, accessed June 25, 2012; "Highly Achieved Women Leaving the Traditional Workforce, Final Report March 2008," U.S. Department of Labor, http:// www.choose2lead.org/Publications/Are%20We %20Losing%20the%20Best%20and%20the%20 Brightest.pdf, accessed June 25, 2012.

11. Featured Employee Rap Sheet, Hot Topic, http://www.hottopic.com/community/rapsheets /emp_jodi.asp?LS=0&, accessed April 11, 2006; Steve Lohr, "A New Game at the Office: Many Young Workers Accept Fewer Guarantees," *The New York Times*, December 5, 2005, http:// select.nytimes.com/gst/abstract.html?res =F00F12FE38550C768CDDAB0994DD404482; Andrea Shim, "Work-life Benefits Fall Victim to Sloweconomy," *Los Angeles Times*, April 4, 2009, http://www.latimes.com/business/la-fi -flexible42009apr04,0,4344887.story, accessed April 4, 2009; Sue Shellenbarger, "Pending Job Flexibility Act Received Mixed Reviews," *WSJ Career Journal*, http://www.careerjournal.com /columnists/workfamily/20010426-workfamily .html, accessed August 9, 2005.

12. Keith W. Hammonds, "Why We Hate HR," Fast Company, December 19, 2007, http:// www.fastcompany.com/magazine/97/open _hr.html?page=0%2C1, accessed April 4, 2009.

13. Mary Beth Marklein, "One-third of Young People Have a Bachelor's," *USA Today*, November 5, 2012, http://www.usatoday.com/story/news/nation /2012/11/05/college-graduates-pew/1683899/, accessed April 9, 2013; "Table 1. The 30 Fastest Growing Occupations Covered in the 2008–2009 Occupational Outlook Handbook," Economic news release, Bureau of Labor Statistics, December 18, 2007, http://www.bls.gov/news.release/ooh.t01. htm, accessed April 7, 2009; "Census Bureau Data Underscore Value of College Degree," U.S. Census Bureau News, October 26, 2006, http://www.census .gov/Press-Release/www/rel-eases/archives/education /007660.html, accessed April 7, 2009; Derek Quizon, "Increasing Share of Adults Have College Degrees, Census Bureau Finds," *The Chronicle of Higher Education*, April 26, 2011, http://chronicle. com/article/Increasing-Share-ofAdults/127264/, accessed July 5, 2011.

14. "SHRM Human Capital Benchmarking Study," 2008 Executive Summary, page 14, SHRM, http://www.shrm.org/Research/Documents /2008%20Executive%20Summary_FINAL.pdf, accessed April 7, 2009; "Effective Recruiting Tied to Stronger Financial Performance," news release, Watson Wyatt Worldwide, August 16, 2005, http:// www.watsonwyatt.com/news/press.asp?ID=14959, accessed April 7, 2009.

15. "CareerBuilder Releases Annual List of Strangest Interview and Body Language Mistakes," CareerBuilder January 12, 2017, http://www .careerbuilder.com/share/aboutus/pressreleasesdetail .aspx?ed=12%2F31%2F2017&id=pr984&sd =1%2F12%2F2017, accessed May 20, 2017; "Top 10 Unbelievable Interview Blunders," CareerBuild- er, http://employer.careerbuilder.com/jobposter /small-business/article.aspx?articleid=ATL _0174INTERVIEWBLUNDERS, accessed May 20, 2017.

16. Jeanne Sahadi, "Top Five Resume Lies," *CNN Money*, December 9, 2004, http://money.cnn .com/2004/11/22/pf/resume_lies/.

17. Elaine Pofeldt, "Source: Shocker: 40% of Workers Now Have 'Contingent' Jobs, Says U.S. Government," May 25, 2015, https://www.forbes .com/sites/elainepofeldt/2015/05/25/shocker-40-of -workers-now-have-contingent-jobs-says-u-s -government/, accessed May 20, 2017.

18. Ibid.

19. Matt DeLuca, "Orientation: Not Just a Once- over-Lightly Anymore," HRO Today, April/May 2005, http://www.hrotoday.com/Magazine .asp?artID=928; by Leslie Gross Klaff, "New Em- phasis on First Impressions," Workforce Manage- ment, March 2008, http://www.workforce.com /archive/feature/25/41/58/index.php, accessed April 7, 2009; Leon Rubis, "Show and Tell—Disney Institute's Four-Day Seminar on HR Management," HR magazine, April 1998; Daryl Stephenson, "New Employee Experience Aims for Excitement Beyond the First Day," Boeing Frontiers Online, May 2002, http://www.boeing.com/news/frontiers /archive/2002/may/i_mams.html.

20. Sean McFadden, "Labor-Intensive," *Boston Business Journal*, November 19, 2004, http://www .bizjournals.com/boston/stories/2004/11/22/smallb1 .html; Stanley Holmes and Wendy Zelner, "The Costco Way; Higher Wages Mean Higher Profits. But Try Telling Wall Street," *Business-Week*, April 12, 2004; Todd Raphael, "Study: Moderation in Hiring Practices Boosts Business Performance," *Workforce Management*, August 19, 2005, http:// www.workforce.com/section/00/article/24/14/03 .html.

21. Carroll Lachnit, "Appreciating Benefits as Times Gets Tough," Blog: The Business of Management, Workforce Management, March 24, 2009, http://www.workforce.com /article/20090324/BLOGS02/303249999 /appreciatingbenefits-as-times-gets-tough, accessed April 9, 2009.

22. John Simons, "IBM, a Pioneer of Remote Work, Calls Workers Back to the Office," *The Wall Street Journal*, May 18, 2017, https://www.wsj .com/articles/ibm-a-pioneer-of-remote-work-calls -workers-back-to-the-office-1495108802, accessed May 21, 2017.

23. Sue Shellenbarger, "Perking Up: Some Com- panies Offer Surprising New Benefits," *The Wall Street Journal*, March 18, 2009, http://online.wsj

.com/article/SB123733195850463165.html, accessed April 9, 2009.

24. "Questions and Answers About Flexible Work Schedules: A Sloan Work and Family Research Network Fact Sheet," Sloan Work and Family Research Network, updated September 2008, http://wfnetwork.bc.edu/pdfs/flexworksched.pdf, accessed April 9, 2009; Andrea Shim, "Work-life Benefits Fall Victim to Slow Economy," *Los Angeles Times*, April 4, 2009, http://www.latimes.com /business/la-fi-flexible4-2009apr04,0,4344887.story, accessed April 4, 2009.

25. Kenneth Rapoza, "One in Five Americans Work from Home, Numbers Seen Rising Over 60%," *Forbes*, February 18, 2013, http://www. forbes.com/sites/kenrapoza/2013/02/18/onein-five-americans-work-from-home-numbersseen-rising-over-60/, accessed March 30, 2014; Rick Hampson, "The Work-from-home Tug of War," *USA Today*, March 11, 2013, http://www.usatoday .com/story/news/nation/2013/03/11/the-work -from-home-tug-ofwar/1979457/, accessed March 30, 2014; "Global Workplace Analytics and the Telework Research Network," Telework Research Network, http://www.teleworkresearchnetwork .com/pros-cons, accessed April 10, 2013; Mary C. Noonan and Jennifer L. Glass, "The Hard truth About Telecommuting," *Monthly Labor Review,* June 2012, http://www.bls.gov/opub/mlr/2012/06 /art3full.pdf, accessed April 10, 2013; Ted Samson, "Give telecommuting the green light," InfoWorld, June 7, 2007, http://www.infoworld.com/d/green -it/givetelecommuting-green-light-628, accessed April 10, 2009; Brendan I. Koerner, "Home Sweet Office: Telecommute Good for Business, Employees, and Planet," Wired, September 22, 2008, http://www.wired.com/culture/culturereviews /magazine/16-10/st_essay, accessed April 10, 2009; Ginger Christ, "Skype: More Companies Allow Telecommuting," *Dayton Business Journal*, April 5, 2011, http://www.bizjournals.com /dayton/news/2011/04/05/more-companies -allowtelecommuting.html, accessed July 5, 2011; "Costs and Benefits, Advantages of Telecommuting for Companies," Telework Research Network, http://www.teleworkresearchnetwork.com /costsbenefits, accessed July 5, 2011.

26. Michelle V. Rafter, "The New Job Sharers," Workforce Management, May 2008, http://www .workforce.com/archive/feature/25/53/28/index.php, accessed April 10, 2009; Stephen Miller, "Study Attempts to Dispel Five Myths of Job Sharing," Society for Human Resource Management, May 9, 2007, http://moss07.shrm.org/Publications /HRNews/Pages/XMS_021497.aspx, accessed April 10, 2009.

27. Jacquelyn Smith, "Here's What Hiring Managers REALLY Think of Your Tattoos," *Business Insider,* January 5, 2016, http://www.businessinsider.com/what -hiring-managers-really-think-of-yourtattoos-2016-1, accessed June 12, 2016.

28. Rex Nutting, "5.1 million jobs lost in this recession so far," MarketWatch, April 3, 2009, http:// www.marketwatch.com/news/story/51-million -jobs-lost-recession/story. aspx?guid={CF54164C -6F7B-4501-B6FB-D7D1C8D710B9}&dist=msr_8, accessed April 10, 2009; "Boost Employee Morale After Layoffs," Workforce Management, http:// www.workforce.com/archive/article/22/14/10.php, accessed April 10, 2009.

29. "Charges Alleging Sexual Harassment FY 2010–FY 2015," EEOC, https://www.eeoc.gov/eeoc/ statistics/enforcement/sexual_harassment_new.cfm, accessed June 12, 2016.

30. Sexual Harassment," US Equal Employment Opportunity Commission, updated March 11, 2009, http://www.eeoc.gov/types/sexual_harassment.html, accessed April 10, 2009.

Pg. 266 Fact: Kate Taylor, "Why Millennials Are Ending The 9 To 5," *Forbes*, August 23, 2013, http://www.forbes.com/sites/katetaylor/2013/08/23/why-millennials-are-ending-the-9-to5/#256850533d75, accessed September 4, 2016.

Pg. 267 Fact: "Frivolous Lawsuits," America's Best, April 2008, http://www.americasbestcompanies .com/magazine/articles/frivolous-lawsuits.aspx, accessed November 27, 2012.

Pg. 270 Fact: Walter Hamilton, "Few Firms Recruiting Liberal Arts Majors," *Los Angeles Times*, May 21, 2014, http://www.latimes.com /business/la-fi-companies-hiring-liberal-arts-majors -jobs20140521-story.html, accessed May 10, 2015.

Pg. 278 Fact: "Occupational Safety and Health Administration Statistics," Occupational Safety and Health Administration, https://www.osha.gov /oshstats/commonstats.html, accessed September 2014.

16

1. John Markoff, "The iPad in Your Hand: As Fast as a Supercomputer of Yore," *The New York Times*, May 9, 2011, http://bits.blogs.nytimes. com/2011/05/09/the-ipad-in-your-hand-as-fast-as-a -supercomputer-of-yore/, accessed April 2, 2013; S. Caldwell, "An Apple Pencil-Drawn Review of the Apple Pencil," iMore, March 7, 2016, http://www .imore.com/review-apple-pencil-drawn-review -apple-pencil, accessed April 1, 2016; R. Smith, "More on Apple's A9X SoC: 47mm2@TSMC, 12 GPU Cores, No L3 Cache," Anandtech, November 30, 2015, http://www.anandtech.com/show/9824 /more-on-apples-a9x-soc, accessed April 1, 2016.

2. J. Paparrizos, R. White, and E. Horvitz, "Screening for Pancreatic Adenocarcinoma Using Signals From Web Search Logs: Feasibility Study and Results," *Journal of Oncology Practice* 12, no. 8 (2016): 737–744.

3. J. Markoff, "Microsoft Finds Cancer Clues in Search Queries," *The New York Times*, June 7, 2016, https://www.nytimes.com/2016/06/08 /technology/online-searches-can-identify-cancer -victims-study-finds.html?_r=0, accessed February 11, 2017.

4. "2016 Global Internet Phenomena: Latin America & North American," Sandvine Intelligent Broadband Networks, June 2016, https://www .sandvine.com/downloads/general/global-internet -phenomena/2016/global-internet-phenomena -report-latin-america-and-north-america.pdf, accessed February 11, 2017.

5. "The Size of the World Wide Web (The Internet)," WorldWideWebSize, February 11, 2017, http://ww.worldwidewebsize.com/, accessed February 11, 2017.

6. J. Horrigan and M. Duggan, "Home Broadband 2015," Pew Research Center, December 21, 2015, http://www.pewinternet.org/2015/12/21/ home-broadband-2015/, accessed April 1, 2016; "Demographics of Internet and Home Broadband Usage in the United States," Pew Research Center, January 12, 2017, http://www.pewinternet.org/ fact-sheet/internet-broadband/, accessed February 11, 2017.

7. "Demographics of Mobile Device Ownership and Adoption in the United States," Pew Research Center, January 12, 2017, http://www.pewinternet .org/fact-sheet/mobile/, accessed February 11, 2017.

8. Ibid.

9. "About Us, The Internet2 Community: Enabling the Future," Internet2, May 2016, http:// www.internet2.edu/about-us/, accessed February 11, 2017.

10. Ibid.

11. E. Boyd, "Internet2 Technology Update," Internet 2, January 21, 2008, https://www.internet2 .edu/presentations/jt2008jan/20080121-boyd.ppt, accessed February 11, 2017.

12. J. Cox, "The Rise of 'Have I Been Pwned?'," an Invaluable Resource in the Hacking Age," *Motherboard*, March 10, 2016, https://motherboard.vice .com/en_us/article/the-rise-of-have-i-been-pwned -an-invaluable-resource-in-the-hacking-age-troy -hunt, accessed February 13, 2017; T. Hunt, "Have I been pwned?" FAQs, https://haveibeenpwned. com/FAQs, accessed February 13, 2017; K. Rogers, "If Mark Zuckerberg Can Be Hacked on Twitter, So Can You," *The New York Times*, June 6, 2016, https://www.nytimes.com/2016/06/07/technology/if -mark-zuckerberg-can-be-a-hacking-victim-so-can -you.html, accessed February 13, 2017.

13. S. Rosenbush, "Cloud Adoption Among Large Companies Set to Accelerate, McKinsey Studies Find—CIO Journal," *The Wall Street Journal*, September 15, 2016, http://blogs.wsj.com /cio/2016/09/15/cloud-adoption-among-large -companies-set-to-accelerate-mckinsey-studies -find/, accessed February 12, 2017.

14. J. Anders, "Amazon's Andy Jassy on the Promise of the Cloud," *The Wall Street Journal*, October 30, 2016, https://www.wsj.com/articles /amazons-andy-jassy-on-the-promise-of-the -cloud-1477880220, accessed February 12, 2017.

15. J. Greene, "Amazon to Offer Cloud-Migration Service," *The Wall Street Journal*, March 15, 2016, p. B4.

16. S. Ovide and C. Boulton, "Flood of Rivals Could Burst Amazon's Cloud," *The Wall Street Journal*, July 26, 2014, p. B4.

17. E. Rusli, "Next in Tech: Research Labs Jump to Cloud–Startups Use Software, Robots to Slash Costs for Basic Experiments," *The Wall Street Journal*, July 1, 2014, B4.

18. T. Sultana, "Big Data Is Driving Safety on Freight Railroads," RealClearTechnology, January 27, 2016, http://www.realcleartechnology .com/articles/2016/01/27/big_data_is_driving _safety_on_freight_railroads_1271.html, accessed February 12, 2017.

19. Q. Hardy, "As a Data Deluge Grows, Companies Rethink Storage," *The New York Times*, March 14, 2016, https://www.nytimes.com/2016/03/15/technology /as-a-data-deluge-grows-companies-rethink-storage .html?_r=0, accessed February 12, 2017.

20. Ibid.

21. N. Singer, "Bring Big Data to the Fight Against Benefits Fraud," *The New York Times*, February 20, 2015, http://www.nytimes.com/2015/02/22 /technology/bringing-big-data-to-the-fight-against -benefits-fraud.html, accessed April 15, 2015.

22. L. Lagnado, "Doctors Test Tools to Predict Your Odds of a Disease," *The Wall Street Journal*, May 30, 2016, https://www.wsj.com/articles /doctors-test-tools-to-predict-your-odds-of-a -disease-1464633980, accessed February 12, 2017.

23. Effy Oz, *Management Information Systems*, 5th ed., Course Technology (Stamford, CT: Cengage Learning, 2006), pp. 332–338; Jack Copeland, "What Is Artificial Intelligence," AlanTuring.Net, May 2000, http://www.cs.usfca.edu/www.AlanTuring .net/turing_archive/pages/Reference%20Articles /what_is_AI/What%20is%20AI07.html.

24. David M. Kroenke, *Experiencing MIS* (Upper Saddle River, NJ: Pearson Prentice Hall, 2008): 340–341; "What Are Expert Systems?," Thinkquest.org, http://library.thinkquest.org/11534 /expert.htm, accessed May 24, 2009.

25. D. Nations, "What Is Enterprise 2.0? Enterprise 2.0 Explained," About Tech, http://webtrends .about .com/od/office20/a/enterprise-20.htm, accessed April 16, 2015; D. Nation, "What Is Web 2.0—How Web 2.0 Is Defining Society," About Tech, http://webtrends.about.com/od/web20/a /what-is-web20.htm, accessed April 16, 2015.

26. IAB Internet Advertising Revenue Report: 2016 First Sixth Months Results, PricewaterhouseCooper, November 1, 2016, http://www.iab .com/wp-content/uploads/2016/04/IAB_Internet _Advertising_Revenue_Report_HY_2016___.pdf, accessed February 12, 2017.

27. A. Andriotis and P. Rudegeair, "Credit-Card Fraud Keeps Rising, Despite New Security Chips," *The Wall Street Journal*, February 1, 2017, https:// www.wsj.com/articles/credit-card-fraud-keeps -rising-despite-new-security-chipsstudy -1485954000, accessed February 14, 2017; R. Holmes, "Hootsuite's CEO on What He Learned from Getting Hacked on Social Media," *Harvard Business Review*, October 6, 2016, https://hbr .org/2016/10/hootsuites-ceo-on-what-he-learned -from-getting-hacked-on-social-media, accessed February 14, 2017.

28. "Q4 2016 Fact Sheet," PayPal.com, https:// www.paypalobjects.com/digitalassets/c/website /marketing/global/shared/global/media-resources /documents/paypal-fastfacts-q4-and-fy-final.pdf, accessed February 12, 2017.

29. "Disney Bets Big on Visitor-Tracking Technology," *Bloomberg Businessweek* /MSN Money, March 10, 2014, http://money.msn.com/technology -investment/post--disney-bets-big-on-visitor-tracking -technology, accessed March 31, 2014.

30. Apple Mac Owners Held to Ransom by KeRanger Malware, *The Telegraph*, March 7, 2016; Why Ransomware Is on the Rise, by J. O'Connell, *Phys.org*, February 25, 2016; "Ransomware" a Growing Threat to Small Businesses, by R. Simon, *The Wall Street Journal*, April 15, 2015, http://www .wsj.com/articles/ransomware-a-growing-threat -to-small-businesses-1429127403, accessed April 2, 2016; How My Mom Got Hacked, by A. Simone, *The New York Times*, January 2, 2015, http://www .nytimes.com/2015/01/04/opinion/sunday/how-my -mom-got-hacked.html?_r=0, accessed April 2, 2016.

31. D. Gudkova, M. Vergelis, and N. Demidova, "Spam and phishing in Q3 2016," Securelist, https://securelist.com/analysis/quarterly-spam -reports/76570/spam-and-phishing-in-q3-2016/, accessed February 13, 2017.

32. C. Metz, "Google Says Its AI Catches 99.9 Percent of Gmail Spam," *Wired*, July 9, 2015, https://www.wired.com/2015/07/google-says-ai -catches-99-9-percent-gmail-spam/, accessed February 13, 2017.

33. M. Maunder, "Wide Impact: Highly Effective Gmail Phishing Technique Being Exploited," Wordfence, January 12, 2017, https://www.wordfence .com/blog/2017/01/gmail-phishing-data-uri /#officialupdate, accessed February 13, 2017.

34. J. Condliffe, "The 25 Most Popular Passwords of 2015: We're All Such Idiots," Gizmodo, January 22, 2016, http://gizmodo.com/the-25-most-popular -passwords-of-2015-were-all-such-id-1753591514, accessed April 2, 2016; L. Graham, "MasterCard to Replace Passwords with Selfies," *CNBC*, February 24, 2016, http://www.cnbc.com/2016/02 /24/mastercard-to-replace-passwords-with-selfies .html, accessed April 2, 2016; T. Mickle & R. McMillan, "Can Apple Unlock Promise of Facial Recognition?" *Wall Street Journal*, September 13, 2017, https://www.wsj.com/articles/can-apple-unlock- promise-of-facial-recognition-1505320165, accessed February 10, 2018.

35. "Pharming: Is Your Trusted Website a Clever Fake?" Microsoft, January 3, 2007, http://www .microsoft.com/protect/yourself/phishing /pharming .mspx; "Online Fraud: Pharming," Symantic, http:// www.symantec.com/norton/cybercrime/pharming .jsp, accessed May 24, 2009; "Advisory: Watch Out for Drive-by-Pharming Attacks," Pharming. org, http://www .pharming.org/index.jsp, accessed May 24, 2009.

36. M. Huffman, "'Smishing' Emerges as New Threat to Cell Phone Users," *Consumer Affairs*, http://www.consumeraffairs.com/news04/2006/11 /smishing.html, accessed May 22, 2009; E. Millis, "'SMiShing' Fishes for Personal Data Over Cell Phone," *CNet*, February 24, 2009, http://news .cnet.com/8301-1009_3-10171241-83.html, accessed April 2, 2013; L. Musthaler, "How to Avoid Becoming a Victim of SMiShing (SMS phishing)," NetworkWorld, March 7, 2013, http://www .networkworld.com/newsletters/techexec/2013/0308 13bestpractices.html, accessed April 2, 2013.

37. "Create Strong Passwords," Microsoft Safety & Security Center, http://www.microsoft.com/security /online-privacy/passwords-create.aspx, accessed April 2, 2013.

38. T. Simonite, "You've Been Misled About What Makes a Good Password," *MIT Technology Review*, October 19, 2015, https://www.technologyreview .com/s/542576/youve-been-misled-about-what -makes-a-good-password/, accessed February 13, 2017.

39. R. Myers, "The Best Password Manager (and Why You Need One): 1Password," September 12, 2016, http://thesweetsetup.com/apps/best-password -manager-and-why-you-need-one/, accessed February 13, 2017.

40. West Brother, "Editorial: The Trolley Problem," East-West Brothers Garage, October 24, 2016, http://www.eastwestbrothersgarage.com/2016/10 /editorial-trolley-problem.html, accessed February 14, 2017; D. Morris, "Mercedes' Self-Driving Cars Will Save Passengers, Not Bystanders," *Fortune*, October 15, 2016, http://fortune. com/2016/10/15/mercedes-self-driving-car-ethics /, accessed February 14, 2017; F. Pasquale, "Get Off the Trolley Problem: Self-driving cars shouldn't have to choose who to protect in a crash," *Slate*,

October 18, 2016, http://www.slate.com/articles /technology/future_tense/2016/10/self_driving_cars _shouldn_t_have_to_choose_who_to_protect_in_a _crash.html, accessed February 14, 2017; M. Taylor, "Self-Driving Mercedes-Benzes Will Prioritize Occupant Safety over Pedestrians," *Car and Driver Blog*, October 7, 2016, http://blog. caranddriver.com/self-driving-mercedes-will -prioritize-occupant-safety-over-pedestrians/, accessed February 14, 2017.

41. W. Oremus, "The Skimming Scam," *Slate*, August 25, 2015, http://www.slate.com/articles/life /travel_explainer/2015/08/credit_cards_passports _and_rfid_fraud_are_special_blocking_wallets _necessary.html, accessed February 13, 2017.

42. Ibid.

43. "Seizing Opportunity Through License Compliance: BSA Global Software Survey," BSA: The Software Alliance, May 2016, http://globalstudy.bsa .org/2016/downloads/studies/BSA_GSS _US.pdf#page=5, accessed February 13, 2017.

44. J. F. Gantz, A. Florean, R. Lee, V. Lim, B. Sikdar, et al., "The Link Between Pirated Software and Cybersecurity Breaches: How Malware in Pirated Software Is Costing the World Billions," National University of Singapore and IDC, March 2014, http://news.microsoft.com/download/ presskits/dcu/docs/idc_031814.pdf, accessed April 16, 2015.

45. Ibid.

17

1. H. Martin, "Here's What Happens on the Airplane before You Board your Flight," *The Los Angeles Times*, December 26, 2016, http://www .latimes.com/business/la-fi-airline-turn-around -20161226-story.html, accessed February 15, 2017.

2. M. Perry, "Technology Has Advanced So Rapidly That a Laptop Computer Today Is 96% Cheaper than a 1994 Model and 1,000x Better," AE ideas, May 25, 2016, http://www.aei.org/publication /technology-has-advanced-so-rapidly-that-a-laptop -computer-today-is-96-cheaper-than-a-1994-model -and-1000x-better/, accessed February 15, 2017.

3. "Establishment DataEmployment-Table B-1a. Employees on Nonfarm Payrolls by Industry Sector and Selected Industry Detail, Seasonally Adjusted," Current Employment Statistics—CES (National): Bureau of Labor Statistics, February 3, 2017, https://www.bls.gov/web/empsit/ceseeb1a.htm, accessed February 15, 2017.

4. Starbucks' Secret Menu—The Drinks You Didn't Know You Can Ask For," *The Telegraph*, February 15, 2017, http://www.telegraph.co.uk /finance/picture-galleries/11375182/Revealed-The -drinks-you-didnt-know-you-could-order-at-Starbucks.html, accessed February 15, 2017.

5. J. Beck, "Starbucks Orders and the Mass Customization of American Food," *The Atlantic*, May 13, 2016, https://www.theatlantic.com /health/archive/2016/05/food-customization-america /482073/, accessed February 15, 2017.

6. D. Cardwell, "Apple Becomes a Green Energy Supplier, With Itself as Customer," *The New York Times*, August 23, 2016, https://www.nytimes. com/2016/08/24/business/energy-environment

/as-energy-use-rises-corporations-turn-to-their
-own-green-utility-sources.html?_r=0, accessed
February 15, 2017.

7. S. Chaudhuri, "IKEA Gets Deeper Into the
Woods," *The Wall Street Journal*, July 31, 2015,
B6; J. Hansegard, "IKEA Slides Into Cramped
Quarters," *The Wall Street Journal*, October 1,
2015, p. B1; B. Kowitt, "How Ikea Took Over the
World," *Fortune*, March 10, 2015, http://fortune.
com/ikea-world-domination/, accessed February
18, 2017; O. Roeder, "The Weird Economics of
Ikea," *FiveThirtyEight*, October 21, 2016, https://
fivethirtyeight.com/features/the-weird-economics-
of-ikea/, accessed February 18, 2017.

8. "Activate Pre-Owned Vehicle," OnSta, https://
www.onstar.com/us/en/get-onstar/pre-owned.html,
accessed April 3, 2016.

9. "Boeing: Services—Training & Resourcing,
Boeing," February 16, 2017, http://www.boeing
.com/commercial/services/flight-operations
-solutions/training-and-resourcing/, accessed
February 16, 2017.

10. D. Collier and J. Evans, *OM*, 2nd ed. (Mason,
OH: South-Western, Cengage Learning, 2010): 27–28.

11. D. Berman, "Where Netflix Sees Potential—
and Risks," *The Wall Street Journal*, October 31,
2016, R4.

12. E. Humes, "Your iPhone's 500,000-Mile
Journey to Your Pocket," *Wired*, April 12,
2016, https://www.wired.com/2016/04/iphones
-500000-mile-journey-pocket/, accessed February
16, 2017.

13. "Outsourcing: Ripoff Nation," BW Smallbiz
Front Line, Winter 2006, *BusinessWeek*, http://
www.businessweek.com/magazine/content/06_52
/b4015435.htm?chan=rss_topStories_ssi_5; Steve
Dickinson, "Outsourcing in China: Five Basic Rules
for Reducing Risk," Ezine Articles, http://ezinearticles
.com/?Outsourcing-in-China:-Five-Basics-for
-Reducing-Risk&id=17214.

14. David Stodder, "ERP and Cloud Computing:
Delivering a Virtual Feast," *Information Week*,
May 20, 2010, http://www.informationweek.com
/news/software/bi/224701329, accessed December
6, 2011.

15. M. Bitner, "Servicescapes: The Impact of
Physical Surroundings on Customers and Employees, *Journal of Marketing*, April 1992: 57–71.

16. "Taco Bell New Urban Restaurant Concept
Redefines Fast Food Experience," pres release,
Taco Bell, September 15, 2015, https://www
.tacobell.com/news/taco-bell-new-urban-restaurant
-concept-redefines-fast-food-experience, accessed
February 17, 2017; J. Jargon, "Taco Bell to Open
Upscale 'Cantina' Restaurants," *The Wall Street
Journal*, September 15, 2015, https://www.wsj.com
/articles/taco-bell-to-open-upscale-cantina-restaurants
-1442330973, accessed February 17, 2017.

17. A. Khouri, "Chalupas and Beer? Taco Bell to
Serve Alcohol at New Cantina Restaurants," *The
Los Angeles Times*, September 15, 2015, http://
www.latimes.com/business/la-fi-taco-bell-cantinas
-20150915-story.html, accessed February 16, 2017.

18. J. Wakefield, "Foxconn Replaces '60,000 Factory Workers with Robots,'" *BBC News*, May 25,
2016, http://www.bbc.com/news/technology
-36376966, accessed February 17, 2017.

19. T. Chen, "In China, a Robot's Place Is in the
Kitchen," *The Wall Street Journal*, July 24, 2016,

https://www.wsj.com/articles/in-china-a-robots
-place-is-in-the-kitchen-1469393604, accessed
February 17, 2017.

20. O. Zaleski, "Inside Silicon Valley's Robot
Pizzeria," *Bloomberg*, June 24, 2016, https://www
.bloomberg.com/news/articles/2016-06-24/inside
-silicon-valley-s-robot-pizzeria, accessed
February 17, 2017.

21. G. Fowler, "Robot Baristas Serve Up the Future of Coffee at Cafe X," *The Wall Street Journal*,
January 30, 2017, https://www.wsj.com/articles
/robot-baristas-serve-up-the-future-of-coffee
-at-cafe-x-1485781201, accessed February 17,
2017.

22. Associated Press, "Robot Revolution
Sweeping Chinese Factory Floors," *CBS News*,
September 23, 2015, http://www.cbsnews.com/
news/robot-revolution-sweeping-chinese-factory
-floors/, accessed February 17, 2017.

23. J. Wakefield, "Foxconn Replaces '60,000 Factory Workers with Robots,'" *BBC News*, May 25,
2016, http://www.bbc.com/news/technology
-36376966, accessed February 17, 2017.

24. "Mine of the FutureTM" Rio Tinto, 2014,
http://www.riotinto.com/documents/Mine_of_The
_Future_Brochure.pdf, accessed February 18,
2017; F. Els, "Rio's Now Mining Iron Ore for
$14.30 a Tonne," *Mining*, August 3, 2016, http://
www.mining.com/rios-now-mining-iron-ore-14-30
-tonne/, accessed February 18, 2017; Nick G., "Automation and Asteroids: How Rio Tinto is Changing
the Future of Mining—Technology and Operations Management," *Harvard Business School*,
November 18, 2016, https://rctom.hbs.org
/submission/automation-and-asteroids-how-rio
-tinto-is-changing-the-future-of-mining/, accessed
February 18, 2017; T. Simonite, "Mining 24 Hours
a Day with Robots," *MIT Technology Review*,
December 28, 2016, https://www.technologyreview
.com/s/603170/mining-24-hours-a-day-with-robots/,
accessed February 18, 2017; D. Stringer and R.
Keenan, "Creating the World's Biggest Robots
Proves Challenging for Miners," *Bloomberg*,
June 16, 2016, https://www.bloomberg.com/news
/articles/2016-06-17/world-s-biggest-robots-delay
-dims-zeal-to-automate-mine-trains, accessed
February 18, 2017.

25. S. McCartney, "Overhead Bins That Actually
Fit Bags," *The Wall Street Journal*, October 14,
2015, https://www.wsj.com/articles/overhead
-bins-that-actually-fit-bags-1444840178, accessed
February 17, 2017.

26. S. Chaudhuri, "At IKEA, Ensuring 'Quality as
an Enabler of Lower Cost'—Corporate Intelligence," *The Wall Street Journal*, June 17, 2015,
http://blogs.wsj.com/corporate-intelligence/2015
/06/17/at-ikea-ensuring-quality-as-an-enabler-of
-lower-cost/, accessed February 17, 2017.

27. Ibid.

28. K, Simon, "How Mistake Proof Are Your Processes?" iSixSigma, https://www.isixsigma.com
/tools-templates/poka-yoke/how-mistake-proof-
are-your-processes/, accessed February 17, 2017;
M. Hendricks, "Make No Mistake," *Entrepreneur
magazine*, October 1996, http://www.entrepreneur
.com/magazine/entrepreneur/1996/october/13430
.html, accessed February 17, 2017.

29. Steven Rosenbush and Laura Stevens, "At
UPS, the Algorithm Is the Driver—Turn Right,
Turn Left, Turn Right: Inside Orion, the 10-year

Effort to Squeeze Every Penny from Delivery
Routes," *The Wall Street Journal*, February 17,
2015, pp. B1, B4; http://www.pressroom.ups
.com/Media+Kits /ORION; Alex Konrad, "Meet
ORION, Software That Will Save UPS Millions by
Improving Drivers' Routes," *Forbes*, November 1,
2013, http://www.forbes.com/sites/alexkonrad
/2013/11/01/meet-orion-software-that-will-save
-ups-millions-by-improving-drivers-routes
/?partner=yahootix, accessed February 27,
2015.

30. "Baldrige Award Process Fees," *Baldrige Performance Excellence Program*, http://www.nist.gov
/baldrige/enter/award_fees.cfm, accessed February
17, 2017.

31. Drones Are Becoming the Oil Industry's
Guardian Angels, HPE Matter, Summer 2015,
https://www.hpematter.com/issue-no-5-summer
-2015-idea-economy/drones-are-becoming-oil
-industrys-guardian-angels, accessed April 3,
2016; V. Addison, "Drones Take Flight in Oil,
Gas Sector," *Exploration & Production*, March 6,
2015, http://www.epmag.com/drones-take-flight
-oil-gas-sector-785996, accessed April 3, 2016;
O. Solon, "Flying Robots Replace Oil Rough-
necks," *Bloomberg*, August 21, 2015; T. Woody,
"Drones Are Becoming Energy's New Roust-
abouts," *The New York Times*, April 21, 2014,
http://www.nytimes.com/2014/04/22/business
/energy-environment/drones-are-becoming
-energys-new-roustabouts.html, accessed April
3, 2016.

32. "ISO Standards," ISO, http://www.iso.org
/iso/home/standards.htm, accessed February 17,
2017.

33. "The ISO Survey of Management System
Standard Certifications 2015: Executive Summary,"
International Organization for Standardization,
December 31, 2015, www.iso.org/iso/the_iso_survey
_of_management_system_standard_certifications
_2015.pdf, accessed February 17, 2017; "The ISO
Survey," International Organization for Standardization, http://www.iso.org/iso/home/standards
/certification/iso-survey.htm, accessed February
17, 2017.

34. "At Vuitton, Growth in Small Batches—Lux-
ury-Goods Maker's New French Factory Adds to
Capacity but Sticks to Strategy of Tight Rein," *The
Wall Street Journal*, June 27, 2011, p. B1.

35. P. Kowsmann, "Fast Fashion: How a Zara
Coat Went From Design to Fifth Avenue in 25
Days," *The Wall Street Journal*, December 6, 2016,
https://www.wsj.com/articles/fast-fashion-how-a
-zara-coat-went-from-design-to-fifth-avenue-in
-25-days-1481080981, accessed February 17,
2017.

36. A. Coolidge, "New Technology Helps Kroger
Speed Up Checkout Times," *USA Today*, June 20,
2013, http://www.usatoday.com/story/money
/business/2013/06/20/new-technology-helps
-kroger-speed-up-checkout-times/2443975/,
accessed April 1, 2014.

37. T. Mann, "GE Strikes Deal to Install LED
Lighting at 5,000 J.P. Morgan Bank Branches,"
The Wall Street Journal, February 18, 2016,
https://www.wsj.com/articles/ge-strikes-deal
-to-install-led-lighting-at-5-000-j-p-morgan
-bank-branches-1455836163, accessed February
17, 2017.

38. "Sustainability Initiatives Cut Costs 6–10%,"
Environmental Leader, http://www.environmental-

leader.com/2009/06/09/sustainability-initiatives-cut-costs-by-6-10/, accessed April 6, 2013.

39. ISO 14000—Environmental Management—ISO, http://www.iso.org/iso/home/standards/management-standards/iso14000.htm, accessed April 17, 2015.

Personal Finance Appendix

1. "Infographic: Financial Capability in the United States 2016, from the National Financial Capability Study" FINRA Investor Education Foundation, www.usfinancialcapability.org/downloads/2015_Study_Infographic.pdf, accessed February 24, 2017; "Stress in America: Part 1," American Psychological Association, February 15, 2017, www.apa.org/news/press/releases/stress/2016/coping-with-change.pdf, accessed February 24, 2017.

2. J. Berman, " Where Millennials Go for Financial Advice," *Wall Street Journal*, December 14, 2015, R8.

3. J. Duffy, "The Best Personal Finance Services of 2017, January 10, 2017, *PC Mag*, PCMag.com, http://www.pcmag.com/article2/0,2817,2407617,00.asp, accessed February 24, 2017.

4. "Gain Total Control of Your Money," YNAB, https://www.learnvest.com/wp-content/uploads/2016/12/LearnVest-Financial-Plan-Sample-Only.pdf, accessed February 24, 2017.

5. D. Bach, *The Automatic Millionaire*, Broadway Books (New York): 2004.

6. S. Matz, J. Gladstone & D. Stillwell, "Money Buys Happiness When Spending Fits Our Personality," *Psychological Science*, v. 27 no. 5 (2016): 715-725.

7. K. Newman, "How Spending Influences Happiness," *Greater Good*, June 6, 2016, http://greatergood.berkeley.edu/article/item/how_spending_influences_happiness, accessed February 24, 2017.

8. "Hardships, Early Withdrawals and Loans,", Internal Revenue Service, May 26, 2016, https://www.irs.gov/retirement-plans/hardships-early-withdrawals-and-loans, accessed February 24, 2017.

9. Bach, David, *The Automatic Millionaire*, New York: Broadway Books, 2004.

10. FDIC: What's Covered, https://www.fdic.gov/deposit/covered/, accessed February 24, 2017; FDIC: How Are My Deposit Accounts Insured by the FDIC?, https://www.fdic.gov/deposit/covered/categories.html,accessed February 24, 2017.

11. What's In Your FICO Score? myFICO.com, http://www.myfico.com/CreditEducation/WhatsInYourScore.aspx, accessed February 24, 2017; P. Curry, "How Credit Scores Work, How

a Score Is Calculated," Bankrate.com, http://www.bankrate.com/brm/news/credit-scoring/20031104a1.asp, , accessed February 24, 2017.

12. About Credit Scores, Money-Zine.com, http://www.money-zine.com/financial-planning/debt-consolidation/about-credit-scores/, accessed February 24, 2017.

13. How Your Credit Score Affects Your Mortgage, U.S. News and World Report, March 2, 2011, http://money.usnews.com/money/blogs/my-money/2011/03/02/how-your-credit-score-affects-your-mortgage, accessed February 24, 2017.

14. C. Tsosie, "Credit Card Late Fees Could Rise In 2017," NerdWallet, December 22, 2016, https://www.nerdwallet.com/blog/credit-cards/credit-card-late-fee-in-2017/, accessed February 24, 2017.

15. C. Prater, "12 Consumer Protections in the Credit CARD Act," CreditCards.com, January 28, 2016, http://www.creditcards.com/credit-card-news/help/card-act-12-consumer-protections-6000.php, accessed February 24, 2017.

16. We're On Your Side," Consumer Financial Protection Bureau, https://www.consumerfinance.gov/, accessed February 24, 2017.

17. L. McFadden, "What the Dodd-Frank Law Means for You," Bankrate.com, June 25, 2010, http://www.bankrate.com/financing/credit-cards/what-the-dodd-frank-act-means-for-you/, accessed April 21, 2013.

18. A. Carrns, "A Little Nagging Can Help Reduce Credit Card Debt," *New York Times*, September 9, 2016, https://www.nytimes.com/2016/09/10/your-money/a-little-nagging-can-help-reduce-credit-card-debt.html, accessed February 24, 2017.

19. P. Lach, "What's the 'Long Run' for Investing? Longer Than You Think," *Wall Street Journal*, February 15, 2017, http://blogs.wsj.com/experts/2017/02/15/whats-the-long-run-for-investing-longer-than-you-think/, accessed February 25, 2017.

20. C. Lee and J. Hook, "Fresh Downgrade Threat to U.S. Debt," *The Wall Street Journal*, June 9. 2011, http://online.wsj.com/article/SB10001424052702304778304576373992711772366.html, accessed April 21, 2013.

21. Can Robo Advisers Replace Human Financial Advisers? by J. F. Podovin, *The Wall Street Journal*, February 28, 2016, http://www.wsj.com/articles/can-robo-advisers-replace-human-financial-advisers-1456715553, accessed April 6, 2016; The Computer as a Financial Planner, by P. Sullivan, *The New York Times*, June 20, 2015, B5; Behavioral Economist Richard Thaler on the Key to Retirement Savings, by Robert Powell, *The Wall Street Journal*, November 29, 2015, http://www.wsj.com /articles/behavioral-economist-richard-thaler-on-the-key-to-retirement-savings-1448852602, accessed March 22, 2016; SmartDeposit: Auto- Deposit, But Smarter, *Betterment*, https://www.betterment.com/resources/inside-betterment /product-news/smartdeposit-auto-deposit-but-smarter/, accessed April 5, 2016.

22. Table 5. Quartiles and Selected Deciles of Usual Weekly Earnings of Full-Time Wage and Salary Workers by Selected Characteristics, Fourth Quarter 2016 Averages, Not Seasonally Adjusted, Economic News Release, Bureau of Labor Statistics, January 24, 2017, http://www.bls.gov/news.release/wkyeng.t05.htm, accessed February 25, 2017.

23. Table A-4. Employment Status of the Civilian Population 25 Years and Over by Educational Attainment, Economic News Release, Bureau of Labor Statistics, February 3, 2017, http://www.bls.gov/news.release/empsit.t04.htm/, accessed February 25, 2017.

24. J. Oates & N. Leppink, "U.S. Department of Labor Advisory: Joint Guidance for States Seeking to Implement Subsidized Work-Based Training Programs for Unemployed Workers," U.S. Department of Labor, January 29, 2010, http://wdr.doleta.gov/directives/attach/TEGL/TEGL12-09acc.pdf, accessed February 25, 2017; S. Greenhouse, "The Unpaid Intern, Legal or Not," *New York Times*, April 2, 2010, http://www.nytimes.com/2010/04/03/business/03intern.html, accessed February 25, 2017.

25. M. Kirchner, "Venmo Doesn't Make People Jerks," *New York* magazine, May 23, 2016, http://nymag.com/selectall/2016/05/its-not-venmos-fault-if-your-friends-are-jerks.html, accessed February 25, 2017; K. Paul, "Venmo is Turning Our Friends into Petty Jerks," *Quartz*, May 19, 2016, — Quartz, https://qz.com/687395/venmo-is-turning-our-friends-into-petty-jerks/, , accessed February 25, 2017; S. Pizzi, "Technology is Changing Student Spending," *Villanovan*, February 27, 2017, http://www.villanovan.com/news/view. php/1027533/Technology-is-changing-student-spending, accessed February 25, 2017.

26. While earnings on traditional IRA contributions Are always tax deferred, there are income-based Limits on the deductibility of contributions. Thus, High-income taxpayers are unable to deduct any Money they contribute to a traditional IRA. For More specifics, see the IRS guideline: http://www.irs.gov/Retirement-Plans/Individual-Retirement-Arrangements-(IRAs)-1, accessed April 28, 2014.

27. "IRS Announces 2017 Pension Plan Limitations; 401(k) Contribution Limit Remains Unchanged at $18,000 for 2017," IRS, October 27, 2016, https://www.irs.gov/uac/newsroom/irs-announces-2017-pension-plan-limitations-401k-contribution-limit-remains-unchanged-at-18000-for-2017, accessed February 25, 2017.

Pg. 333 Fact: Bankrate.com credit card calculator—How much will the minimum credit card payment cost me?, http://www.bankrate.com/calculators/credit-cards/credit-card-payoff-calculator.aspx.

GLOSSARY

401(k), 403(b), and 457 plans
Employee payroll-deduction retirement plans that offer tax benefits.

absolute advantage
The benefit a country has in a given industry when it can produce more of a product than other nations using the same amount of resources.

accounting
A system for recognizing, organizing, analyzing, and reporting information about the financial transactions that affect an organization.

accounting equation
Assets = Liabilities + Owners' Equity

accredited investor
An organization or individual investor who meets certain criteria established by the SEC and so qualifies to invest in unregistered securities.

accrual-basis accounting
The method of accounting that recognizes revenue when it is earned and matches expenses to the revenues they helped produce.

acquisition
A corporate restructuring in which one firm buys another.

active listening
Attentive listening that occurs when the listener focuses his or her complete attention on the speaker.

active voice
Sentence construction in which the subject performs the action expressed by the verb (e.g., The accountant did the taxes.). The active voice works better for the vast majority of business communication.

activity-based costing (ABC)
A technique to assign product costs based on links between activities that drive costs and the production of specific products.

administrative law
Laws that arise from regulations established by government agencies.

advergaming
Video games created as a marketing tool, usually with brand awareness as the core goal.

advertising
Paid, nonpersonal communication, designed to influence a target audience with regard to a product, service, organization, or idea.

affirmative action
Policies meant to increase employment and educational opportunities for minority groups—especially groups defined by race, ethnicity, or gender.

agent
A party who agrees to represent another party, called the principal.

agents/brokers
Independent distributors who do not take title of the goods they distribute (even though they may take physical possession on a temporary basis before distribution).

angel investors
Individuals who invest in start-up companies with high growth potential in exchange for a share of ownership.

annual percentage rate (APR)
The interest expense charged on a credit card, expressed as an annual percentage.

applications software
Software that helps a user perform a desired task.

apprenticeships
Structured training programs that mandate that each beginner serve as an assistant to a fully trained worker before gaining full credentials to work in the field.

arbitration
A process in which a neutral third party has the authority to resolve a dispute by rendering a binding decision.

articles of incorporation
The document filed with a state government to establish the existence of a new corporation.

asset management ratios
Financial ratios that measure how effectively a firm is using its assets to generate revenues or cash.

assets
Resources owned by a firm.

autocratic leaders
Leaders who hoard decision-making power for themselves and typically issue orders without consulting their followers.

automation
Replacing human operation and control of machinery and equipment with some form of programmed control.

balance of payments
A measure of the total flow of money into or out of a country.

balance of payments deficit
Shortfall that occurs when more money flows out of a nation than into that nation.

balance of payments surplus
Overage that occurs when more money flows into a nation than out of that nation.

balance of trade
A basic measure of the difference in value between a nation's exports and imports, including both goods and services.

balance sheet
A financial statement that reports the financial position of a firm by identifying and reporting the value of the firm's assets, liabilities, and owners' equity.

Baldrige National Quality Program
A national program to encourage American

firms to focus on quality improvement.

Banking Act of 1933

The law that established the Federal Deposit Insurance Corporation (FDIC) to insure bank deposits. It also prohibited commercial banks from selling insurance or acting as investment banks.

behavioral segmentation

Dividing the market based on how people behave toward various products. This category includes both the benefits that consumers seek from products and how consumers use the products.

benefits

Noncash compensation, including programs such as health insurance, vacation, and childcare.

bias

A preconception about members of a particular group. Common forms of bias include gender bias; age bias; and race, ethnicity, or nationality bias.

board of directors

The individuals who are elected by stockholders of a corporation to represent their interests.

bond

A formal debt instrument issued by a corporation or government entity.

boycott

A tactic in which a union and its supporters and sympathizers refuse to do business with an employer with which they have a labor dispute.

brand

A product's identity—including product name, symbol, design, reputation, and image—that sets it apart from other players in the same category.

brand equity

The overall value of a brand to an organization.

brand extension

A new product, in a new category, introduced under an existing brand name.

breach of contract

The failure of one party to a contract to perform his or her contractual obligations.

breakeven analysis

The process of determining the number of units a firm must sell to cover all costs.

broadband Internet connection

An Internet connection that is capable of transmitting large amounts of information very quickly.

budget (personal)

A detailed forecast of financial inflows (income) and outflows (expenses) to determine your net inflow or outflow for a given period of time.

budget deficit

Shortfall that occurs when expenses are higher than revenue over a given period of time.

budget surplus

Overage that occurs when revenue is higher than expenses over a given period of time.

budgeted balance sheet

A projected financial statement that forecasts the types and amounts of assets a firm will need to implement its future plans and how the firm will finance those assets. (Also called a pro forma balance sheet.)

budgeted income statement

A projection showing how a firm's budgeted sales and costs will affect expected net income. (Also called a pro forma income statement.)

budgeting

A management tool that explicitly shows how a firm will acquire and use the resources needed to achieve its goals over a specific time period.

business

Any organization or activity that provides goods and services in an effort to earn a profit.

business buyer behavior

Describes how people act when they are buying products to use either directly or indirectly to produce other products.

business cycle

The periodic contraction and expansion that occur over time in virtually every economy.

business environment

The setting in which business operates. The five key components are: economic environment, competitive environment, technological environment, social environment, and global environment.

business ethics

The application of right and wrong, good and bad, in a business setting.

business format franchise

A broad franchise agreement in which the franchisee pays for the right to use the name, trademark, and business and production methods of the franchisor.

business intelligence system

A sophisticated form of decision support system that helps decision makers discover information that was previously hidden.

business law

The application of laws and legal principles to business relationships and transactions.

business marketers (also known as business-to-business or B2B)

Marketers who direct their efforts toward people who are buying products to use either directly or indirectly to produce other products.

business plan

A formal document that describes a business concept, outlines core business objectives, and details strategies and timelines for achieving those objectives.

business products

Products purchased to use either directly or indirectly in the production of other products.

business technology

Any tools—especially computers, telecommunications, and other digital products—that businesses can use to become more efficient and effective.

business-to-business (B2B) e-commerce

E-commerce in markets where businesses buy from and sell to other businesses.

business-to-consumer (B2C) e-commerce

E-commerce in which businesses and final consumers interact.

buzz marketing

The active stimulation of word-of-mouth via unconventional, and often relatively low-cost, tactics. Other terms for buzz marketing are "guerrilla marketing" and "viral marketing."

C corporation

The most common type of corporation, which is a legal business entity that offers limited liability to all of its owners, who are called stockholders.

cafeteria-style benefits

An approach to employee benefits that gives all employees a set dollar amount that they must spend on company benefits, allocated however they wish within broad limitations.

cannibalization

When a producer offers a new product that takes sales away from its existing products.

capital budgeting

The process a firm uses to evaluate long-term investment proposals.

capital gain

The return on an asset that results when its market price rises above the price the investor paid for it.

capital structure

The mix of equity and debt financing a firm uses to meet its permanent financing needs.

capitalism

An economic system—also known as the private enterprise or free market system—based on private ownership, economic freedom, and fair competition.

carbon footprint

Refers to the amount of harmful greenhouse gases that a firm emits throughout its operations, both directly and indirectly.

case law (also called common law)

Laws that result from rulings, called precedents, made by judges who initially hear a particular type of case.

cash budget

A detailed forecast of future cash flows that helps financial managers identify when their firm is likely to experience temporary shortages or surpluses of cash.

cash equivalents

Safe and highly liquid assets that many firms list with their cash holdings on their balance sheet.

cause-related marketing

Marketing partnerships between businesses and nonprofit organizations, designed to spike sales for the company and raise money for the nonprofit.

certificate of deposit (CD)

An interest-earning deposit that requires the funds to remain deposited for a fixed term. Withdrawal of the funds before the term expires results in a financial penalty.

channel intermediaries

Distribution organizations that facilitate the movement of products from the producer to the consumer.

channel of distribution

The network of organizations and processes that links producers to consumers.

Chapter 7 bankruptcy

A form of bankruptcy that discharges a debtor's debts by liquidating assets and using the proceeds to pay off creditors.

Chapter 11 bankruptcy

A form of bankruptcy used by corporations and individuals that allows the debtor to reorganize operations under a court-approved plan.

Chapter 13 bankruptcy

A form of bankruptcy that allows individual debtors to set up a repayment plan to adjust their debts.

Civil Rights Act of 1964

Federal legislation that prohibits discrimination in hiring, firing, compensation, apprenticeships, training, terms, conditions, or privileges of employment based on race, color, religion, sex, or national origin.

closed shop

An employment arrangement in which the employer agrees to hire only workers who already belong to the union.

cloud computing

The use of Internet-based storage capacity, processing power, and computer applications to supplement or replace internally owned information technology resources.

cobranding

When established brands from different companies join forces to market the same product.

code of ethics

A formal, written document that defines the ethical standards of an organization and gives employees the information they need to make ethical decisions across a range of situations.

cognitive dissonance

Consumer discomfort with a purchase decision, typically for a higher-priced item.

collective bargaining

The process by which representatives of union members and employers attempt to negotiate a mutually acceptable labor agreement.

commercial banks

Privately owned financial institutions that accept demand deposits and make loans and provide other services for the public.

commercial paper

Short-term (and usually unsecured) promissory notes issued by large corporations.

common market

A group of countries that have eliminated tariffs and harmonized trading rules to facilitate the free flow of goods among the member nations.

common stock

The basic form of ownership in a corporation.

communication

The transmission of information between a sender and a recipient.

communication barriers

Obstacles to effective communication, typically defined in terms of physical, language, body language, cultural, perceptual, and organizational barriers.

communication channels

The various ways in which a message can be sent, ranging from one-on-one in-person meetings to Internet message boards.

communism

An economic and political system that calls for public ownership of virtually all enterprises, under the direction of a strong central government.

company matching

An amount contributed by the employer to an employee's retirement account, matching the employee's retirement contributions either dollar for dollar or based on a percentage of each dollar contributed by the employee.

comparative advantage

The benefit a country has in a given industry if it can make products at a lower opportunity cost than other countries.

compensation

The combination of pay and benefits that employees receive in exchange for their work.

compensatory damages

Monetary payments that a party who breaches a contract is ordered to pay in order to compensate the injured party for the actual harm suffered by the breach of contract.

compressed workweek

A version of flextime scheduling that allows employees to work a full-time number of hours in less than the standard workweek.

computer virus

Computer software that can be spread from one computer to another without the knowledge or permission of the computer users by attaching itself to emails or other files.

computer-aided design (CAD)

Drawing and drafting software that enables users to create and edit blueprints and design drawings quickly and easily.

computer-aided design/computer-aided manufacturing (CAD/CAM)

A combination of software that can be used to design output and send instructions to automated equipment to perform the steps needed to produce this output.

computer-aided engineering (CAE)

Software that enables users to test, analyze, and optimize their designs.

computer-aided manufacturing (CAM)

Software that takes the electronic design for a product and creates the programmed instructions that robots must follow to produce that product as efficiently as possible.

computer-integrated manufacturing (CIM)

A combination of CAD/CAM software with flexible manufacturing systems to automate almost all steps involved in designing, testing, and producing a product.

conceptual skills

The ability to grasp a big-picture view of the overall organization, the relationships among its various parts, and its fit in the broader competitive environment.

conglomerate merger

A combination of two firms that are in unrelated industries.

consideration

Something of value that one party gives another as part of a contractual agreement.

constitution

A code that establishes the fundamental rules and principles that govern a particular organization or entity.

consumer behavior

Description of how people act when they are buying, using, and discarding goods and services for their own personal consumption. Consumer behavior also explores the reasons behind people's actions.

consumer marketers (also known as business-to-consumer or B2C)

Marketers who direct their efforts toward people who are buying products for personal consumption.

consumer price index (CPI)

A measure of inflation that evaluates the change in the weighted-average price of goods and services that the average consumer buys each month.

consumer products

Products purchased for personal use or consumption.

consumer promotion

Marketing activities designed to generate immediate consumer sales, using tools such as premiums, promotional products, samples, coupons, rebates, and displays.

consumerism

A social movement that focuses on four key consumer rights: (1) the right to be safe, (2) the right to be informed, (3) the right to choose, and (4) the right to be heard.

contingency planning

Planning for unexpected events, usually involving a range of scenarios and assumptions that differ from the assumptions behind the core plans.

contingent workers

Employees who do not expect regular, full-time jobs, including temporary full-time workers, independent contractors, and temporary agency or contract agency workers.

contract

An agreement that is legally enforceable.

contraction

A period of economic downturn, marked by rising unemployment and falling business production.

controlling

Monitoring performance and making adjustments as needed.

convertible security

A bond or share of preferred stock that gives its holder the right to exchange it for a stated number of shares of common stock.

copyright

The exclusive legal right of an author, artist, or other creative individual to use, copy, display, perform, and sell their own creations and to license others to do so.

corporate bylaws

The basic rules governing how a corporation is organized and how it conducts its business.

corporate philanthropy

All business donations to nonprofit groups, including money, products, and employee time.

corporate responsibility

Business contributions to the community through the actions of the business itself rather than donations of money and time.

corporation

A form of business ownership in which the business is considered a legal entity that is separate and distinct from its owners.

cost

The value of what is given up in exchange for something.

countertrade

International trade that involves the barter of products for products rather than for currency.

coupon rate

The interest paid on a bond, expressed as a percentage of the bond's par value.

covenant

A restriction lenders impose on borrowers as a condition of providing long-term debt financing.

craft union

A union comprising workers who share the same skill or work in the same profession.

credit

Allows a borrower to buy a good or acquire an asset without making immediate payment, and to repay the balance at a later time.

credit card

A card issued by a bank or finance company that allows the cardholder to make a purchase now and pay the credit card issuer later.

credit score

A numerical measure of a consumer's creditworthiness.

credit union

A depository institution that is organized as a cooperative, meaning that it is owned by its depositors.

crime

A wrongful act against society, defined by law and prosecuted by the state.

critical path method (CPM)

A project-management tool that illustrates the relationships among all the activities involved in completing a project and identifies the sequence of activities likely to take the longest to complete.

critical path

The sequence of activities in a project that is expected to take the longest to complete.

current yield

The amount of interest earned on a bond, expressed as a percentage of the bond's current market price.

customer benefit

The advantage that a customer gains from specific product features.

customer loyalty

When customers buy a product from the same supplier again and again—sometimes paying even more for it than they would for a competitive product.

customer relationship management (CRM)

The ongoing process of acquiring, maintaining, and growing profitable customer relationships by delivering unmatched value.

customer satisfaction

When customers perceive that a good or service delivers value above and beyond their expectations.

cybermediary

An Internet-based firm that specializes in the secure electronic transfer of funds.

data

Raw, unprocessed facts and figures.

data mining

The use of sophisticated statistical and mathematical techniques to analyze vast amounts of data to discover hidden patterns and relationships, thus creating valuable information.

data warehouse

A large, organization-wide database that stores data in a centralized location.

database

A file consisting of related data organized according to a logical system and stored on a hard drive or some other computer-accessible media.

debit card

A card issued by the bank that allows the customer to make purchases as if the transaction involved cash. In a debit card purchase, the customer's bank account is immediately reduced when the purchase is made.

debt financing

Funds provided by lenders (creditors).

decision support system (DSS)

A system that gives managers access to large amounts of data and the processing power to convert these data into high-quality information, thus improving the decision-making process.

deflation

A period of falling average prices across the economy.

degree of centralization

The extent to which decision-making power is held by a small number of people at the top of the organization.

demand

The quantity of products that consumers are willing to buy at different market prices.

demand curve

The graphed relationship between price and quantity from a customer demand standpoint.

democratic leaders

Leaders who share power with their followers. While they still make final decisions, they typically solicit and incorporate input from their followers.

demographic segmentation

Dividing the market into smaller groups based on measurable characteristics about people, such as age, income, ethnicity, and gender.

demographics

The measurable characteristics of a population. Demographic factors include population size and density as well as specific traits such as age, gender, and race.

departmentalization

The division of workers into logical groups.

depository institution

A financial intermediary that obtains funds by accepting checking and savings deposits and then lending those funds to borrowers.

depression

An especially deep and long-lasting recession.

direct channel

A distribution process that links the producer and the customer with no intermediaries.

direct cost

Costs that are incurred directly as the result of some specific cost object.

direct investment

(or foreign direct investment) When firms either acquire foreign firms or develop new facilities from the ground up in foreign countries.

discount rate

The rate of interest that the Federal Reserve charges when it loans funds to banks.

discretionary payments

Expenditures for which the spender has significant control in terms of the amount and timing.

disinflation

A period of slowing average price increases across the economy.

distribution strategy

A plan for delivering the right product to the right person at the right place at the right time.

distributive bargaining

The traditional adversarial approach to collective bargaining.

distributorship

A type of franchising arrangement in which the franchisor makes a product and licenses the franchisee to sell it.

divestiture

The transfer of total or partial ownership of some of a firm's operations to investors or to another company.

Dodd-Frank Act

A law enacted in the aftermath of the financial crisis of 2008–2009 that strengthened government oversight of financial markets and placed limitations on risky financial strategies such as heavy reliance on leverage.

Dow Jones Industrial Average (DJIA)

An index that tracks stock prices of 30 large, well-known U.S. corporations.

dynamic delivery

Vibrant, compelling presentation delivery style that grabs and holds the attention of the audience.

e-commerce

The marketing, buying, selling, and servicing of products over a network (usually the Internet).

economic system

A structure for allocating limited resources.

economics

The study of the choices that people, companies, and governments make in allocating society's resources.

economy

A financial and social system of how resources flow through society, from production to distribution, to consumption.

effectiveness

Using resources to create value by providing customers with goods and services that offer a better relationship

between price and perceived benefits.

efficiency

Producing output or achieving a goal at the lowest cost.

electronic bill presentment and payment

A method of bill payment that makes it easy for the customer to make a payment, often by simply clicking on a payment option contained in an email.

electronic communications network (ECN)

An automated, computerized securities trading system that automatically matches buyers and sellers, executing trades quickly and allowing trading when securities exchanges are closed.

e-marketplace

A specialized Internet site where buyers and sellers engaged in business-to-business e-commerce can communicate and conduct business.

embargo

A complete ban on international trade of a certain item, or a total halt in trade with a particular nation.

employment at will

A legal doctrine that views employment as an entirely voluntary relationship that both the employee and employer are free to terminate at any time and for any reason.

enterprise resource planning (ERP)

Software-based approach to integrate an organization's (and in the sophisticated versions, a value chain's) information flows.

entrepreneurs

People who risk their time, money, and other resources to start and manage a business.

environmental scanning

The process of continually collecting information from the external marketing environment.

Equal Employment Opportunity Commission (EEOC)

A federal agency designed to regulate and enforce the provisions of Title VII.

equilibrium price

The price associated with the point at which the quantity demanded of a product equals the quantity supplied.

equity financing

Funds provided by the owners of a company.

equity theory

A motivation theory that proposes that perceptions of fairness directly affect worker motivation.

ethical dilemma

A decision that involves a conflict of values; every potential course of action has some significant negative consequences.

ethics

A set of beliefs about right and wrong, good and bad.

European Union (EU)

The world's largest common market, composed of 28 European nations.

everyday-low pricing (EDLP)

Long-term discount pricing, designed to achieve profitability through high sales volume.

exchange rate

A measurement of the value of one nation's currency relative to the currency of other nations.

exchange traded fund (ETF)

Shares traded on securities markets that represent the legal right of ownership over part of a basket of individual stock certificates or other securities.

expansion

A period of robust economic growth and high employment.

expectancy theory

A motivation theory that concerns the relationship among individual effort, individual performance, and individual reward.

expenses

Resources that are used up as the result of business operations.

expert system (ES)

A decision support system that helps managers make better decisions in an area where they lack expertise.

exporting

Selling products in foreign nations that have been produced or grown domestically.

external locus of control

A deep-seated sense that forces other than the individual are responsible for what happens in his or her life.

external recruitment

The process of seeking new employees from outside the firm.

extranet

An intranet that allows limited access to a selected group of stakeholders, such as suppliers or customers.

factor

A company that provides short-term financing to firms by purchasing their accounts receivables at a discount.

factors of production

Four fundamental elements—natural resources, capital, human resources, and entrepreneurship—that businesses need to achieve their objectives.

federal debt

The sum of all the money that the federal government has borrowed over the years and not yet repaid.

Federal Deposit Insurance Corporation (FDIC)

An independent agency created by Congress to maintain stability and public confidence in the nation's financial system, primarily by insuring bank deposits.

Federal Reserve Act of 1913

The law that established the Federal Reserve System as the central bank of the United States.

finance

The functional area of business that is concerned with finding the best sources and uses of financial capital.

Financial Accounting Standards Board (FASB)

The private board that establishes the generally accepted accounting principles used in the practice of financial accounting.

financial accounting

The branch of accounting that prepares financial statements for use by owners, creditors, suppliers, and other external stakeholders.

financial budgets

Budgets that focus on the firm's financial goals and identify the resources needed to achieve these goals.

financial capital

The funds a firm uses to acquire its assets and finance its operations.

financial diversification

A strategy of investing in a wide variety of securities in order to reduce risk.

financial leverage

The use of debt in a firm's capital structure.

financial markets

Markets that transfer funds from savers to borrowers.

financial ratio analysis

Computing ratios that compare values of key accounts listed on a firm's financial statements.

Financial Services Modernization Act of 1999

An act that overturned the section of the Banking Act of 1933 that prohibited commercial banks from selling insurance or performing the functions of investment banks.

firewall

Software and/or hardware designed to prevent unwanted access to a computer or computer system.

first-line (supervisory) management

Managers who directly supervise nonmanagement employees.

fiscal policy

Government efforts to influence the economy through taxation and spending.

fixed costs

Costs that remain the same when the level of production changes within some relevant range.

flextime

A scheduling option that allows workers to choose when they start and finish their workdays, as long as they complete the required number of hours.

foreign franchising

A specialized type of foreign licensing in which a firm expands by offering businesses in other countries the right to produce and market its products according to specific operating requirements.

foreign licensing

Authority granted by a domestic firm to a foreign firm for the rights to produce and market its product or to use its trademark/patent rights in a defined geographical area.

foreign outsourcing

(also contract manufacturing) Contracting with foreign suppliers to produce products, usually at a fraction of the cost of domestic production.

franchise

A licensing arrangement under which a franchisor allows franchisees to use its name, trademark, products, business methods, and other property in exchange for monetary payments and other considerations.

franchise agreement

The contractual arrangement between a franchisor and franchisee that spells out the duties and responsibilities of both parties.

Franchise Disclosure Document (FDD)

A detailed description of all aspects of a franchise that the franchisor must provide to the franchisee at least 14 calendar days before the franchise agreement is signed.

franchisee

The party in a franchise relationship that pays for the right to use resources supplied by the franchisor.

franchisor

The business entity in a franchise relationship that allows others to operate its business using resources it supplies in exchange for money and other considerations.

free trade

The unrestricted movement of goods and services across international borders.

free-rein leaders

Leaders who set objectives for their followers but give them freedom to choose how they will accomplish those goals.

General Agreement on Tariffs and Trade (GATT)

An international trade treaty designed to encourage worldwide trade among its members.

general partnership

A partnership in which all partners can take an active role in managing the business and have unlimited liability for any claims against the firm.

generally accepted accounting principles (GAAP)

A set of accounting standards that is used in the preparation of financial statements.

geographic segmentation

Dividing the market into smaller groups based on where consumers live. This process can incorporate countries, cities, or population density as key factors.

goods

Tangible products.

grace period

The period of time that the credit card holder has to pay outstanding balances before interest or fees are assessed.

green marketing

Developing and promoting environmentally sound products and practices to gain a competitive edge.

grievance

A complaint by a worker that the employer has violated the terms of the collective bargaining agreement.

gross domestic product

(GDP) The total value of all final goods and services produced within a nation's physical boundaries over a given period of time.

hacker

A skilled computer user who uses his or her expertise to gain unauthorized access to the computer (or computer system) of others, sometimes with malicious intent.

hardware

The physical tools and equipment used to collect, input, store, organize, and process data and to distribute information.

high/low pricing

A pricing strategy designed to drive traffic to retail stores by special sales on a limited number of products, and higher everyday prices on others.

horizontal analysis

Analysis of financial statements that compares account values reported on these statements over two or more years to identify changes and trends.

horizontal merger

A combination of two firms that are in the same industry.

human resource (HR) management

The management function focused on maximizing the effectiveness of the workforce by recruiting world-class talent, promoting career development, and determining workforce strategies to boost organizational effectiveness.

human skills

The ability to work effectively with and through other people in a range of different relationships.

hyperinflation

An average monthly inflation rate of more than 50%.

immediate predecessors

Activities in a project that must be completed before some other specified activity can begin.

implicit cost

The opportunity cost that arises when a firm uses owner-supplied resources.

importing

Buying products domestically that have been produced or grown in foreign nations.

income statement

The financial statement that reports the revenues, expenses, and net income that resulted from a firm's operations over an accounting period.

independent wholesaling businesses

Independent distributors that buy products from a range of different businesses and sell those products to a range of different customers.

indirect costs

Costs that are the result of a firm's general operations and are not directly tied to any specific cost object.

industrial union

A union comprising workers employed in the same industry.

inflation

A period of rising average prices across the economy.

information

Data that have been processed in a way that make them meaningful to their user.

infrastructure

A country's physical facilities that support economic activity.

initial public offering (IPO)

The first time a company issues stock that may be bought by the general public.

institutional investor

An organization that pools contributions from investors, clients, or depositors and uses these funds to buy stocks and other securities.

integrated marketing communication

The coordination of marketing messages through every promotional vehicle to communicate a unified impression about a product.

intellectual property

Property that is the result of creative or intellectual effort, such as books, musical works, inventions, and computer software.

intercultural communication

Communication among people with differing cultural backgrounds.

interest-based bargaining

A form of collective bargaining that emphasizes cooperation and problem solving in an attempt to find a "win–win" outcome.

internal locus of control

A deep-seated sense that the individual is personally responsible for what happens in his or her life.

internal recruitment

The process of seeking employees who are currently within the firm to fill open positions.

International Monetary Fund (IMF)

An international organization of 188 member nations that promotes international economic cooperation and stable growth.

Internet

The world's largest computer network; essentially a network of computer networks all operating under a common set of rules that allow them to communicate with each other.

Internet2 (I2)

A new high-tech Internet with access limited to a consortium of member organizations (and other

organizations these members sponsor). I2 utilizes technologies that give it a speed and capacity far exceeding the current Internet.

intranet

A private network that has the look and feel of the Internet and is navigated using a web browser, but which limits access to a single firm's employees (or a single organization's members).

inventory

Stocks of goods or other items held by organizations.

investing

Reducing consumption in the current time period in order to build future wealth.

investment bank

A financial intermediary that specializes in helping firms raise financial capital by issuing securities in primary markets.

IRA

An individual retirement account that provides tax benefits to individuals who are investing for their retirement.

ISO 14000

A family of generic standards for environmental management established by the International Organization for Standardization.

ISO 9000

A family of generic standards for quality management systems established by the International Organization for Standardization.

job analysis

The examination of specific tasks that are assigned to each position, independent of who might be holding the job at any specific time.

job description

An explanation of the responsibilities for a specific position.

job enrichment

The creation of jobs with more meaningful content, under the assumption that challenging, creative work will motivate employees.

job specifications

The specific qualifications necessary to hold a particular position.

joint ventures

When two or more companies join forces—sharing resources, risks, and profits, but not actually merging companies—to pursue specific opportunities.

just-in-time (JIT) production

A production system that emphasizes the production of goods to meet actual current demand, thus minimizing the need to hold inventories of finished goods and work in process at each stage of the supply chain.

labor union

A group of workers who have organized to work together to achieve common job-related goals, such as higher wages, better working conditions, and greater job security.

Labor–Management Relations Act (Taft–Hartley Act)

Law passed in 1947 that placed limits on union activities, outlawed the closed shop, and allowed states to pass right-to-work laws that made union shops illegal.

laws

Rules that govern the conduct and actions of people

within a society that are enforced by the government.

leading

Directing and motivating people to achieve organizational goals.

lean production

An approach to production that emphasizes the elimination of waste in all aspects of production processes.

leverage ratios

Ratios that measure the extent to which a firm relies on debt financing in its capital structure.

liabilities

Claims that outsiders have against a firm's assets.

licensing

Purchasing the right to use another company's brand name or symbol.

limit order

An order to a broker to buy a specific stock only if its price is below a certain level, or to sell a specific stock only if its price is above a certain level.

limited liability

When owners are not personally liable for claims against their firm. Owners with limited liability may lose their investment in the company, but their other personal assets are protected.

limited liability company (LLC)

A form of business ownership that offers both limited liability to its owners and flexible tax treatment.

limited liability partnership (LLP)

A form of partnership in which all partners have the right to participate in management and have limited liability for company debts.

limited partnership

A partnership that includes at least one general partner who actively manages the company and accepts unlimited liability and one limited partner who gives up the right to actively manage the company in exchange for limited liability.

line-and-staff organizations

Organizations with line managers forming the primary chain of authority in the company, and staff departments working alongside line departments.

line extensions

Similar products offered under the same brand name.

line managers

Managers who supervise the functions that contribute directly to profitability: production and marketing.

line of credit

A financial arrangement between a firm and a bank in which the bank pre-approves credit up to a specified limit, provided that the firm maintains an acceptable credit rating.

line organizations

Organizations with a clear, simple chain of command from top to bottom.

liquid asset

An asset that can quickly be converted into cash with little risk of loss.

liquidity ratios

Financial ratios that measure the ability of a firm to obtain the cash it needs to pay its short-term debt obligations as they come due.

lockout

An employer-initiated work stoppage.

logistics

A subset of supply chain management that focuses largely on the tactics involved in moving products along the supply chain.

loss

When a business incurs expenses that are greater than its revenue.

loss-leader pricing

Closely related to high/low pricing, loss-leader pricing means pricing a handful of items—or loss leaders—temporarily below cost to drive traffic.

M1 money supply

Includes all currency plus checking accounts and traveler's checks.

M2 money supply

Includes all of M1 money supply plus most savings accounts, money market accounts, and certificates of deposit.

macroeconomics

The study of a country's overall economic dynamics, such as the employment rate, the gross domestic product, and taxation policies.

malware

A general term for malicious software, such as spyware, computer viruses, and worms.

management

Achieving the goals of an organization through planning, organizing, leading, and controlling organizational resources including people, money, and time.

management development

Programs to help current and potential executives develop the skills they need to move into leadership positions.

managerial (or management) accounting

The branch of accounting that provides reports and analysis to managers to help them make informed business decisions.

market makers

Securities dealers that make a commitment to continuously offer to buy and sell the stock of a specific corporation listed on the NASDAQ exchange or traded in the OTC market.

market niche

A small segment of a market with fewer competitors than the market as a whole. Market niches tend to be quite attractive to small firms.

market order

An order telling a broker to buy or sell a specific security at the best currently available price.

market segmentation

Dividing potential customers into groups of similar people, or segments.

market share

The percentage of a market controlled by a given marketer.

marketing

An organizational function and a set of processes for creating, communicating, and delivering value to customers and for managing customer relationships in ways that benefit the organization and its stakeholders.

marketing concept

A business philosophy that makes customer satisfaction—now and in the future—the central focus of the entire organization.

marketing mix

The blend of marketing strategies for product, price, distribution, and promotion.

marketing plan

A formal document that defines marketing objectives and the specific strategies for achieving those objectives.

marketing research

The process of gathering, interpreting, and applying information to uncover marketing opportunities and challenges, and to make better marketing decisions.

Maslow's hierarchy of needs theory

A motivation theory that suggests that human needs fall into a hierarchy and that as each need is met, people become motivated to meet the next-highest need in the pyramid.

mass customization

The creation of products tailored for individual consumers on a mass basis.

master budget

A presentation of an organization's operational and financial budgets that represents the firm's overall plan of action for a specified time period.

matrix organizations

Organizations with a flexible structure that brings together specialists from different areas of the company to work on individual projects on a temporary basis.

maturity date

The date when a bond will come due.

mediation

A method of dealing with an impasse between labor and management by bringing in a neutral third party to help the two sides reach agreement by reducing tensions and making suggestions for possible compromises.

merchant wholesalers

Independent distributors who take legal possession, or title, of the goods they distribute.

merger

A corporate restructuring that occurs when two formerly independent business entities combine to form a new organization.

microeconomics

The study of smaller economic units such as individual consumers, families, and individual businesses.

middle management

Managers who supervise lower-level managers and report to a higher-level manager.

mission

The definition of an organization's purpose, values, and core goals, which provides the framework for all other plans.

mixed economies

Economies that embody elements of both planned and market-based economic systems.

modes of transportation

The various transportation options—such as planes, trains, and railroads—for moving products through the supply chain.

monetary policy

Federal Reserve decisions that shape the economy by influencing interest rates and the supply of money.

money

Anything generally accepted as a medium of exchange, a measure of value, or a means of payment.

money market mutual funds

A mutual fund that pools funds from many investors and uses these funds to purchase very safe, highly liquid securities.

money supply

The total amount of money within the overall economy.

monopolistic competition

A market structure with many competitors selling differentiated products. Barriers to entry are low.

monopoly

A market structure with one producer completely dominating the industry, leaving no room for any significant competitors. Barriers to entry tend to be virtually insurmountable.

multichannel retailing

Providing multiple distribution channels for consumers to buy a product.

multilevel marketing (MLM)

Involves hiring independent contractors to sell products to their personal network of friends and colleagues and to recruit new salespeople in return for a percentage of their commissions.

mutual fund

An institutional investor that raises funds by selling shares to investors and uses the accumulated funds to buy a portfolio of many different securities.

national brands

Brands that the producer owns and markets.

National Labor Relations Act (Wagner Act)

Landmark pro-labor law enacted in 1935. This law made it illegal for firms to discriminate against union members and required employers to recognize certified unions and bargain with them in good faith.

natural monopoly

A market structure with one company as the supplier of a product because the nature of that product makes a single supplier more efficient than multiple, competing ones. Most natural monopolies are government sanctioned and regulated.

negligence

An unintentional tort that arises due to carelessness or irresponsible behavior.

net asset value per share

The value of a mutual fund's securities and cash holdings minus any liabilities, divided by the number of shares of the fund outstanding.

net income

The difference between the revenue a firm earns and the expenses it incurs in a given time period.

net present value (NPV)

The sum of the present values of expected future cash flows from an investment, minus the cost of that investment.

noise

Any interference that causes the message you send to be different from the message your audience understands.

nondiscretionary payments

Expenditures that the spender has little or no control over.

nonprofit corporation

A corporation that does not seek to earn a profit and differs in several fundamental respects from C corporations.

nonprofits

Business-*like* establishments that employ people and produce goods and services with the fundamental goal of contributing to the community rather than generating financial gain.

nonverbal communication

Communication that does not use words. Common forms of nonverbal communication include gestures, posture, facial expressions, tone of voice, and eye contact.

North American Free Trade Agreement (NAFTA)

The treaty among the United States, Mexico, and Canada that eliminated trade barriers and investment restrictions over a 15-year period starting in 1994.

observation research

Marketing research that does not require the researcher to interact with the research subject.

odd pricing

The practice of ending prices in numbers below even dollars and cents in order to create a perception of greater value.

offshoring

Moving production or support processes to foreign countries.

oligopoly

A market structure with only a handful of competitors selling products that can be similar or different. Barriers to entry are typically high.

on-the-job training

A training approach that requires employees to simply begin their jobs—sometimes guided by more experienced employees—and to learn as they go.

open market operations

The Federal Reserve function of buying and selling government securities, which include treasury bonds, notes, and bills.

open shop

An employment arrangement in which workers are not required to join a union or pay union dues.

operating budgets

Budgets that communicate an organization's sales and production goals and the resources needed to achieve these goals.

operational planning

Very specific, short-term planning that applies tactical plans to daily, weekly, and monthly operations.

operations management

Managing all of the activities involved in creating value by producing goods and services and distributing them to customers.

opportunity cost

The opportunity of giving up the second-best choice when making a decision.

organization chart

A visual representation of the company's formal structure.

organizing

Determining a structure for both individual jobs and the overall organization.

orientation

The first step in the training and development process, designed to introduce employees to the company culture and provide key administrative information.

out-of-pocket cost

A cost that involves the payment of money or other resources.

outsourcing

Arranging for other organizations to perform supply chain functions that were previously performed internally.

over-the-counter (OTC) market

The market where securities that are not listed on exchanges are traded.

owners' equity

The claims a firm's owners have against their company's assets (often called "stockholders' equity" on balance sheets of corporations).

par value (of a bond)

The value of a bond at its maturity; what the issuer promises to pay the bondholder when the bond matures.

partnership

A voluntary agreement under which two or more people act as co-owners of a business for profit.

passive voice

Sentence construction in which the subject does not do the action expressed by the verb; rather, the subject is acted upon (e.g., The taxes were done by our accountant.). The

passive voice tends to be less effective for business communication.

patent

A legal monopoly that gives an inventor the exclusive right over an invention for a limited time period.

penetration pricing

A new product pricing strategy that aims to capture as much of the market as possible through rock-bottom prices.

performance appraisal

A formal feedback process that requires managers to give their subordinates feedback on a one-to-one basis, typically by comparing actual results to expected results.

personal selling

The person-to-person presentation of products to potential buyers.

pharming

A scam that seeks to steal identities by routing Internet traffic to fake websites.

phishing

A scam in which of official-looking emails are sent to individuals in an attempt to get them to divulge private information such as passwords, usernames, and account numbers.

physical distribution

The actual, physical movement of products along the distribution pathway.

picketing

A union tactic during labor disputes in which union members walk near the entrance of the employer's place of business, carrying signs to publicize their position and concerns.

planned obsolescence

The strategy of deliberately designing products to fail in order to shorten the time between purchases.

planning

Determining organizational goals and action plans for how to achieve those goals.

poka-yokes

Simple methods incorporated into a production process designed to eliminate or greatly reduce errors.

positioning statement

A brief statement that articulates how the marketer would like the target market to envision a product relative to the competition.

preferred stock

A type of stock that gives its holder preference over common stockholders in terms of dividends and claims on assets.

present value

The amount of money that, if invested today at a given rate of interest (called the discount rate), would grow to become some future amount in a specified number of time periods.

primary data

New data that marketers compile for a specific research project.

primary securities market

The market where newly issued securities are traded. The primary market is where the firms that issue securities raise additional financial capital.

principal

A party who agrees to have someone else (called an agent) act on his or her behalf.

principal–agent relationship

A relationship in which one party, called the principal, gives another party, called the agent, the authority to act in place of, and bind, the principal when dealing with third parties.

private placement

A primary market issue that is negotiated between the issuing corporation and a small group of accredited investors.

privatization

The process of converting government-owned businesses to private ownership.

probationary period

A specific time frame (typically three to six months) during which a new hire can prove his or her worth on the job before he or she becomes permanent.

process

A set of related activities that transform inputs into outputs, thus adding value.

producer price index (PPI)

A measure of inflation that evaluates the change over time in the weighted-average wholesale prices.

product

Anything that an organization offers to satisfy consumer needs and wants, including both goods and services.

product consistency

How reliably a product delivers its promised level of quality.

product differentiation

The attributes that make a good or service different from other products that compete to meet the same or similar customer needs.

product features

The specific characteristics of a product.

product life cycle

A pattern of sales and profits that typically changes over time.

product line

A group of products that are closely related to each other, either in terms of how they work or the customers they serve.

product mix

The total number of product lines and individual items sold by a single firm.

product placement

The paid integration of branded products into movies, television, and other media.

productivity

The basic relationship between the production of goods and services (output) and the resources needed to produce them (input) calculated via the following equation: output/input = productivity.

profit

The money that a business earns in sales (or revenue), minus expenses, such as the cost of goods and the cost of salaries. Revenue − Expenses = Profit (or Loss).

profit margin

The gap between the cost and the price of an item on a per-product basis.

profitability ratios

Ratios that measure the rate of return a firm is earning on various measures of investment.

promotion

Marketing communication designed to influence

consumer purchase decisions through information, persuasion, and reminders.

promotional channels

Specific marketing communication vehicles, including traditional tools, such as advertising, sales promotion, direct marketing, and personal selling, and newer tools such as product placement, advergaming, and Internet minimovies.

property

The legal right of an owner to exclude nonowners from having control over a particular resource.

protectionism

National policies designed to restrict international trade, usually with the goal of protecting domestic businesses.

psychographic segmentation

Dividing the market into smaller groups based on consumer attitudes, interests, values, and lifestyles.

public offering

A primary market issue in which new securities are offered to any investors who are willing and able to purchase them.

public relations (PR)

The ongoing effort to create positive relationships with all of a firm's different "publics," including customers, employees, suppliers, the community, the general public, and the government.

publicity

Unpaid stories in the media that influence perceptions about a company or its products.

pull strategy

A marketing approach that involves creating demand

from the ultimate consumers so that they "pull" your products through the distribution channels by actively seeking them.

pure competition

A market structure with many competitors selling virtually identical products. Barriers to entry are quite low.

pure goods

Products that do not include any services.

pure services

Products that do not include any goods.

push strategy

A marketing approach that involves motivating distributors to heavily promote—or "push"—a product to the final consumers, usually through heavy trade promotion and personal selling.

quality level

How well a product performs its core functions.

quality of life

The overall sense of well-being experienced by either an individual or a group.

quotas

Limitations on the amount of specific products that may be imported from certain countries during a given time period.

radio frequency identification (RFID)

A technology that stores information on small microchips that can transmit the information when they are within range of a special reader.

recession

An economic downturn marked by a decrease in the GDP for two consecutive quarters.

recovery

A period of rising economic growth and employment.

registration statement

A long, complex document that firms must file with the SEC when they sell securities through a public offering.

reserve requirement

A rule set by the Fed, which specifies the minimum amount of reserves (or funds) a bank must hold, expressed as a percentage of the bank's deposits.

retailers

Distributors that sell products directly to the ultimate users, typically in small quantities, that are stored and merchandized on the premises.

retained earnings

The part of a firm's net income it reinvests.

revenue

Increases in a firm's assets that result from the sale of goods, provision of services, or other activities intended to earn income.

revolving credit agreement

A guaranteed line of credit in which a bank makes a binding commitment to provide a business with funds up to a specified credit limit at any time during the term of the agreement.

right-to-work law

A state law that makes union shops illegal within that state's borders.

risk

The degree of uncertainty regarding the outcome of a decision.

risk-return trade-off

The observation that financial opportunities that offer high rates of return are generally riskier than opportunities that offer lower rates of return.

robot

A reprogrammable machine that is capable of manipulating materials, tools, parts, and specialized devices in order to perform a variety of tasks.

S corporation

A form of corporation that avoids double taxation by having its income taxed as if it were a partnership.

salaries

The pay that employees receive over a fixed period, most often weekly or monthly.

sale

A transaction in which the title (legal ownership) to a good passes from one party to another in exchange for a price.

sales promotion

Marketing activities designed to stimulate immediate sales activity through specific short-term programs aimed at either consumers or distributors.

Sarbanes-Oxley Act

Federal legislation passed in 2002 that sets higher ethical standards for public corporations and accounting firms. Key provisions limit conflict-of-interest issues and require financial officers and CEOs to certify the validity of their financial statements.

savings account

An interest-bearing account holding funds not needed to meet regular expenditures.

savings and loan association

A depository institution that has traditionally obtained most of its funds by accepting savings deposits, which have been used primarily to make mortgage loans.

scope of authority (for an agent)

The extent to which an agent has the authority to act for and represent the principal.

SCORE (Service Corps of Retired Executives)

An organization—affiliated with the Small Business Administration—that provides free, comprehensive business counseling for small business owners from qualified volunteers.

secondary data

Existing data that marketers gather or purchase for a research project.

secondary securities market

The market where previously issued securities are traded.

Securities Act of 1933

The first major federal law regulating the securities industry. It requires firms issuing new stock in a public offering to file a registration statement with the SEC.

Securities and Exchange Act of 1934

A federal law dealing with securities regulation that established the Securities and Exchange Commission to regulate and oversee the securities industry.

Securities and Exchange Commission

The federal agency with primary responsibility for regulating the securities industry.

securities broker

A financial intermediary that acts as an agent for investors who want to buy and sell financial securities. Brokers earn commissions and fees for the services they provide.

securities dealer

A financial intermediary that participates directly in securities markets, buying and selling stocks and other securities for its own account.

services

Intangible products.

servicescape

The environment in which a customer and service provider interact.

sexual harassment

Workplace discrimination against a person based on his or her gender.

Six Sigma

An approach to quality improvement characterized by very ambitious quality goals, extensive training of employees, and a long-term commitment to working on quality-related issues.

skimming pricing

A new product pricing strategy that aims to maximize profitability by offering new products at a premium price.

Small Business Administration (SBA)

An agency of the federal government designed to maintain and strengthen the nation's economy by aiding, counseling, assisting, and protecting the interests of small businesses.

Small Business Development Centers (SBDCs)

Local offices—affiliated with the Small Business Administration—that provide comprehensive management assistance to current and prospective small business owners.

social audit
A systematic evaluation of how well a firm is meeting its ethics and social responsibility goals.

social responsibility
The obligation of a business to contribute to society.

socialism
An economic system based on the principle that the government should own and operate key enterprises that directly affect public welfare.

sociocultural differences
Differences among cultures in language, attitudes, and values.

software
Programs that provide instructions to a computer so that it can perform a desired task.

sole proprietorship
A form of business ownership with a single owner who usually actively manages the company.

spam
Unsolicited email advertisements usually sent to very large numbers of recipients, many of whom may have no interest in the message.

span of control
Span of management; refers to the number of people a manager supervises.

specific performance
A remedy for breach of contract in which the court orders the party committing the breach to do exactly what the contract specifies.

speed-to-market
The rate at which a new product moves from conception to commercialization.

sponsorship
A deep association between a marketer and a partner (usually a cultural or sporting event), which involves promotion of the sponsor in exchange for either payment or the provision of goods.

spontaneous financing
Financing that arises during the natural course of business without the need for special arrangements.

spyware
Software that is installed on a computer without the user's knowledge or permission to track the user's behavior.

staff managers
Managers who supervise the functions that provide advice and assistance to the line departments.

stakeholders
Any groups that have a stake—or a personal interest—in the performance and actions of an organization.

Standard & Poor's 500
A stock index based on prices of 500 major U.S. corporations in a variety of industries and market sectors.

standard of living
The quality and quantity of goods and services available to a population.

statement of cash flows
The financial statement that identifies a firm's sources and uses of cash in a given accounting period.

statute of frauds
A requirement that certain types of contracts must be in writing in order to be enforceable.

statute of limitations
The time period within which a legal action must be initiated.

statutory close (or closed) corporation
A corporation with a limited number of owners that operates under simpler, less formal rules than a C corporation.

statutory law
Law that is the result of legislative action.

stock (or securities) exchange
An organized venue for trading stocks and other securities that meet its listing requirements.

stock index
A statistic that tracks how the prices of a specific set of stocks have changed.

stockholder
An owner of a corporation.

store brands
Brands that the retailer both produces and distributes (also called private-label brands).

strategic alliance
An agreement between two or more firms to jointly pursue a specific opportunity without actually merging their businesses. Strategic alliances typically involve less formal, less encompassing agreements than partnerships.

strategic goals
Concrete benchmarks that managers can use to measure performance in each key area of the organization.

strategic planning
High-level, long-term planning that establishes a vision for the company, defines long-term objectives and priorities, determines broad action steps, and allocates resources.

strategies
Action plans that help the organization achieve its goals by forging the best fit between the firm and the environment.

strike
A work stoppage initiated by a union.

structured interviews
An interviewing approach that involves developing a list of questions beforehand and asking the same questions in the same order to each candidate.

supply
The quantity of products that producers are willing to offer for sale at different market prices.

supply chain
All organizations, processes, and activities involved in the flow of goods from the raw materials to the final consumer.

supply chain management (SCM)
Planning and coordinating the movement of products along the supply chain, from the raw materials to the final consumers.

supply curve
The graphed relationship between price and quantity from a supplier standpoint.

survey research

Marketing research that requires the researcher to interact with the research subject.

sustainable development

Doing business to meet the needs of the current generation, without harming the ability of future generations to meet their needs.

SWOT analysis

A strategic planning tool that helps management evaluate an organization in terms of internal strengths and weakness, and external opportunities and threats.

system software

Software that performs the critical functions necessary to operate the computer at the most basic level.

tactical planning

More specific, shorter-term planning that applies strategic plans to specific functional areas.

target market

The group of people who are most likely to buy a particular product.

tariffs

Taxes levied against imports.

technical skills

Expertise in a specific functional area or department.

telecommuting

Working remotely—most often from home—and connecting to the office via phone lines and/or broadband networks.

Theory X and Theory Y

A motivation theory that suggests that management attitudes toward workers fall into two opposing categories based on management assumptions about worker capabilities and values.

time value of money

The principle that a dollar received today is worth more than a dollar received in the future.

title

Legal ownership.

Title VII

A portion of the Civil Rights Act of 1964 that prohibits discrimination in hiring, firing, compensation, apprenticeships, training, terms, conditions, or privileges of employment based on race, color, religion, sex, or national origin for employers with 15 or more workers.

top management

Managers who set the overall direction of the firm, articulating a vision, establishing priorities, and allocating time, money, and other resources.

tort

A private wrong that results in physical or mental harm to an individual, or damage to that person's property.

total quality management (TQM)

An approach to quality improvement that calls for everyone within an organization to take responsibility for improving quality and emphasizes the need for a long-term commitment to continuous improvement.

trade credit

Spontaneous financing granted by sellers when they deliver goods and services to customers without requiring immediate payment.

trade deficit

Shortfall that occurs when the total value of a nation's imports is higher than the total value of its exports.

trade promotion

Marketing activities designed to stimulate wholesalers and retailers to push specific products more aggressively over the short term.

trade surplus

Overage that occurs when the total value of a nation's exports is higher than the total value of its imports.

trademark

A mark, symbol, word, phrase, or motto used to identify a company's goods.

trading bloc

A group of countries that have reduced or even eliminated tariffs, allowing for the free flow of goods among the member nations.

U.S. Treasury bills (T-bills)

Short-term marketable IOUs issued by the U.S. federal government.

underwriting

An arrangement under which an investment banker agrees to purchase all shares of a public offering at an agreed-upon price.

unemployment rate

The percentage of people in the labor force over age 16 who do not have jobs and are actively seeking employment.

Uniform Commercial Code (UCC)

A uniform act governing the sale of goods, leases, warranties, transfer of funds, and a variety of other business-related activities.

union shop

An employment arrangement in which a firm can hire nonunion workers, but these workers must join the union within a specified time period to keep their jobs.

universal ethical standards

Ethical norms that apply to all people across a broad spectrum of situations.

utility

The ability of goods and services to satisfy consumer "wants."

value

The relationship between the price of a good or a service and the benefits that it offers its customers.

value chain

The network of relationships that channels the flow of inputs, information, and financial resources through all of the processes directly or indirectly involved in producing goods and services and distributing them to customers.

variable costs

Costs that vary directly with the level of production.

venture capital firms

Companies that invest in start-up businesses with high growth potential in exchange for a share of ownership.

vertical integration

Performance of processes internally that were previously performed by other organizations in a supply chain.

vertical merger

A combination of firms at different stages in the production of a good or service.

vesting period

A specified period of time for which an employee must work for an employer in order to receive the full advantage of certain retirement benefits.

viral marketing

An Internet marketing strategy that tries to involve customers and others not employed by the seller in activities that help promote the product.

voluntary export restraints (VERs)

Limitations on the amount of specific products that one nation will export to another nation.

wages

The pay that employees receive in exchange for the number of hours or days that they work.

Web 2.0

Websites that incorporate interactive and collaborative features to create a richer, more interesting, and more useful experience for their users.

wheel of retailing

A classic distribution theory that suggests that retail firms and retail categories become more upscale as they go through their life cycles.

whistle-blowers

Employees who report their employer's illegal or unethical behavior to either the authorities or the media.

wholesalers

Distributors that buy products from producers and sell them to other businesses or nonfinal users such as hospitals, nonprofits, and the government.

World Bank

An international cooperative of 189 member countries, working together to reduce poverty in the developing world.

World Trade Organization (WTO)

A permanent global institution to promote international trade and to settle international trade disputes.

World Wide Web

The service that allows computer users to easily access and share information on the Internet in the form of text, graphics, video, apps, and animation.

worm

Malicious computer software that, unlike viruses, can spread on its own without being attached to other files.

INDEX

CHAPTER 1 LEARNING OBJECTIVES / KEY TERMS

1-1 **Define business and discuss the role of business in the economy.** A business is any organization or activity that provides goods and services in an effort to earn a profit. *Profit* is the money that a business earns in sales, minus expenses, such as the cost of goods and the cost of salaries. Profit potential provides a powerful incentive for people to start their own businesses, or to become *entrepreneurs*. Successful businesses create wealth, which increases the standard of living for virtually all members of a society.

value The relationship between the price of a good or a service and the benefits that it offers its customers. (p. 2)

business Any organization or activity that provides goods and services in an effort to earn a profit. (p. 5)

profit The money that a business earns in sales (or revenue), minus expenses, such as the cost of goods and the cost of salaries. Revenue — Expenses = Profit (or Loss). (p. 5)

loss When a business incurs expenses that are greater than its revenue. (p. 5)

entrepreneurs People who risk their time, money, and other resources to start and manage a business. (p. 5)

standard of living The quality and quantity of goods and services available to a population. (p. 5)

quality of life The overall sense of well-being experienced by either an individual or a group. (p. 5)

1-2 **Explain the evolution of modern business.** Business historians typically divide the history of American business into five distinct eras, which overlap during the periods of transition.

- *Industrial Revolution:* From the mid-1700s to the mid-1800s, technology fueled a period of rapid industrialization. Factories sprang up in cities, leading to mass production and specialization of labor.
- *Entrepreneurship Era:* During the second half of the 1800s, large-scale entrepreneurs emerged, building business empires that created enormous wealth, but often at the expense of workers and consumers.
- *Production Era:* In the early 1900s, major businesses focused on further refining the production process, creating huge efficiencies. The assembly line, introduced in 1913, boosted productivity and lowered costs.
- *Marketing Era:* After World War II, consumers began to gain power. As goods and services flooded the market, the marketing concept emerged: a consumer-first orientation as a guide to business decision making.
- *Relationship Era:* With the technology boom in the 1990s, businesses began to look beyond the immediate transaction, aiming to build a competitive edge through long-term customer relationships.

1-3 **Discuss the role of nonprofit organizations in the economy.** Nonprofit organizations often work hand in hand with business to improve the quality of life in our society. Nonprofits are business-like establishments that contribute to economic stability and growth. Similar to businesses, nonprofits generate revenue and incur expenses. Their goal is to use any revenue above and beyond expenses to advance the goals of the organization, rather than to make money for its owners. Some nonprofits—such as museums, schools, and theaters—can act as economic magnets for communities, attracting additional investment.

The Relationship between Nonprofits and Businesses

Advance Goals of Organization

Generate Revenue Incur Expenses Provide Employment

Create Profit for Owners

nonprofits Business-like establishments that employ people and produce goods and services with the fundamental goal of contributing to the community rather than generating financial gain. (p. 6)

1-4 **Outline the core factors of production and how they affect the economy.** The four factors of production are the fundamental resources that both businesses and nonprofits use to achieve their objectives.

1. *Natural resources:* All inputs that offer value in their natural state, such as land, fresh water, wind, and mineral deposits. The value of natural resources tends to rise with high demand, low supply, or both.

2. *Capital:* The manmade resources that an organization needs to produce goods or services. The elements of capital include machines, tools, buildings, and technology.

3. *Human resources:* The physical, intellectual, and creative contributions of everyone who works within an economy. Education and motivation have become increasingly important as technology replaces manual labor jobs.

4. *Entrepreneurship:* Entrepreneurs take the risk of launching and operating their own businesses. Entrepreneurial enterprises can create a tidal wave of opportunity by harnessing the other factors of production.

© Cengage

factors of production Four fundamental elements—natural resources, capital, human resources, and entrepreneurship—that businesses need to achieve their objectives. (p. 7)

1-5 Describe today's business environment and discuss each key dimension. Accelerating change marks every dimension of today's business environment.

- *Economic environment:* In late 2008, the U.S. economy plunged into a deep financial crisis. The value of the stock market plummeted, companies collapsed, and the unemployment rate soared. The president, Congress, and the Federal Reserve took unprecedented steps—including a massive economic stimulus package—to encourage a turnaround. The U.S. economy eventually recovered, but the entire world economy began to stagger in early 2016 as economic instability in China caused frightening ripples around the globe.

- *Competitive environment:* As global competition intensifies, leading-edge companies have focused on long-term customer satisfaction as never before.

- *Technological environment:* The recent digital technology boom has transformed business, establishing new industries and burying others.

- *Social environment:* The U.S. population continues to diversify. Consumers are gaining power, and society has higher standards for business behavior. Sustainability has become a core marketplace issue.

- *Global environment:* The U.S. economy works within the context of the global environment. The worldwide recession has dampened short-term opportunities, but China and India continue their rapid economic development.

The Business Environment

business environment The setting in which business operates. The five key components are economic environment, competitive environment, technological environment, social environment, and global environment. (p. 8)

speed-to-market The rate at which a new product moves from conception to commercialization. (p. 10)

business technology Any tools—especially computers, telecommunications, and other digital products—that businesses can use to become more efficient and effective. (p. 12)

World Wide Web The service that allows computer users to easily access and share information on the Internet in the form of text, graphics, video, apps, and animation. (p. 12)

e-commerce Business transactions conducted online, typically via the Internet. (p. 12)

demographics The measurable characteristics of a population. Demographic factors include population size and density, as well as specific traits such as age, gender, and race. (p. 12)

free trade An international economic and political movement designed to help goods and services flow more freely across international boundaries. (p. 15)

General Agreement on Tariffs and Trade (GATT) An international trade agreement that has taken bold steps to lower tariffs and promote free trade worldwide. (p. 15)

1-6 Explain how current business trends might affect your career choices. With automation picking up speed, many traditional career choices have become dead ends. But some things—including empathy, creativity, change management, and great communication—can't be digitized. Having these skills can provide you with personal and financial opportunity.

© Cengage

2-1 **Define economics and discuss the evolving global economic crisis.** Economics—the study of how people, companies, and governments allocate resources—offers vital insights regarding the forces that affect every business on a daily basis. Understanding economics helps businesspeople make better decisions, which can lead to greater profitability, both short-term and long-term. Macroeconomics is the study of broad economic trends. Microeconomics focuses on the choices made by smaller economic units, such as individual consumers, families, and businesses.

In September 2008, the U.S. economy plunged into a deep economic crisis. The banking system hovered on the edge of collapse, property values plummeted, and home foreclosure rates soared. Massive layoffs put more than a million Americans out of work. By the end of the year, the stock market had lost more than a third of its value. To prevent total financial disaster, the federal government and the Federal Reserve intervened in the economy at an unprecedented level by bailing out huge firms that faced total collapse. In early 2009, Congress passed a colossal economic stimulus package, designed to turn around the economy and position the United States for long-term economic growth. In mid-2010, the economy began a painfully slow turnaround. By 2014, the economic recovery had clearly taken hold.

economy A financial and social system of how resources flow through society, from production to distribution, to consumption. (p. 18)

economics The study of the choices that people, companies, and governments make in allocating society's resources. (p. 18)

macroeconomics The study of a country's overall economic dynamics, such as the employment rate, the gross domestic product, and taxation policies. (p. 18)

microeconomics The study of smaller economic units such as individual consumers, families, and individual businesses. (p. 19)

2-2 **Analyze the impact of fiscal and monetary policy on the economy.** Fiscal policy and monetary policy refer to efforts to shape the health of the economy. Fiscal policy involves federal government taxation and spending decisions designed to encourage growth and boost employment. Monetary policy refers to decisions by the Federal Reserve that influence the size of the money supply and the level of interest rates. Both the federal government and the Federal Reserve attempted to play a pivotal role in mitigating the impact of the recent financial crisis and establishing a framework for recovery via fiscal and monetary policy. These tools can also help sustain economic expansions.

fiscal policy Government efforts to influence the economy through taxation and spending. (p. 22)

budget surplus Overage that occurs when revenue is higher than expenses over a given period of time. (p. 22)

budget deficit Shortfall that occurs when expenses are higher than revenue over a given period of time. (p. 22)

federal debt The sum of all the money that the federal government has borrowed over the years and not yet repaid. (p. 22)

monetary policy Federal Reserve decisions that shape the economy by influencing interest rates and the supply of money. (p. 23)

commercial banks Privately owned financial institutions that accept demand deposits and make loans and provide other services for the public. (p. 23)

money supply The total amount of money within the overall economy. (p. 24)

money Anything generally accepted as a medium of exchange, a measure of value, or a means of payment. (p. 24)

M1 money supply Includes all currency plus checking accounts and traveler's checks. (p. 24)

M2 money supply Includes all of M1 money supply plus most savings accounts, money market accounts, and certificates of deposit. (p. 24)

open market operations The Federal Reserve function of buying and selling government securities, which include treasury bonds, notes, and bills. (p. 24)

Federal Deposit Insurance Corporation (FDIC) A federal agency that insures deposits in banks and thrift institutions for up to $250,000 per customer, per bank. (p. 25)

discount rate The rate of interest that the Federal Reserve charges when it loans funds to banks. (p. 25)

reserve requirement A rule set by the Fed, which specifies the minimum amount of reserves (or funds) a bank must hold, expressed as a percentage of the bank's deposits. (p. 26)

2-3 **Explain and evaluate the free market system and supply and demand.** Capitalism, also known as the *free market system*, is based on private ownership, economic freedom, and fair competition. In a capitalist economy, individuals, businesses, or nonprofit organizations privately own the vast majority of enterprises. As businesses compete against each other, quality goes up, prices remain reasonable, and choices abound, raising the overall standard of living.

The interplay between the forces of supply and demand determines the selection of products and prices available in a free market economy. *Supply* refers to the quantity of products that producers are willing to offer for sale at different market prices at a specific time. *Demand* refers to the quantity of products that consumers are willing to buy at different market prices at a specific time. According to economic theory, markets will naturally move toward the point at which supply and demand are equal: the *equilibrium point*.

economic system A structure for allocating limited resources. (p. 26)

capitalism An economic system—also known as the private enterprise or free market system—based on private ownership, economic freedom, and fair competition. (p. 26)

pure competition A market structure with many competitors selling virtually identical products. Barriers to entry are quite low. (p. 27)

monopolistic competition A market structure with many competitors selling differentiated products. Barriers to entry are low. (p. 28)

oligopoly A market structure with only a handful of competitors selling products that can be similar or different. Barriers to entry are typically high. (p. 28)

monopoly A market structure with one producer completely dominating the industry, leaving no room for any significant competitors. Barriers to entry tend to be virtually insurmountable. (p. 28)

natural monopoly A market structure with one company as the supplier of a product because the nature of that product makes a single supplier more efficient than multiple, competing ones. Most natural monopolies are government sanctioned and regulated. (p. 28)

supply The quantity of products that producers are willing to offer for sale at different market prices. (p. 29)

supply curve The graphed relationship between price and quantity from a supplier standpoint. (p. 29)

demand The quantity of products that consumers are willing to buy at different market prices. (p. 29)

demand curve The graphed relationship between price and quantity from a customer demand standpoint. (p. 30)

equilibrium price The price associated with the point at which the quantity demanded of a product equals the quantity supplied. (p. 30)

2-4 Explain and evaluate planned market systems. In planned economies, the government—rather than individual choice—plays a pivotal role in controlling the economy. The two main types of planned economies are socialism and communism. While planned economies are designed to create more equity among citizens, they tend to be more prone to corruption and less effective at generating wealth than market-based economies.

socialism An economic system based on the principle that the government should own and operate key enterprises that directly affect public welfare. (p. 30)

communism An economic and political system that calls for public ownership of virtually all enterprises, under the direction of a strong central government. (p. 31)

2-5 Describe the trend toward mixed market systems. Most of today's nations have mixed economies, falling somewhere along a spectrum that ranges from pure planned at one extreme to pure market at the other. Over the past 30 years, most major economies around the world have moved toward the market end of the spectrum, although recently—in the wake of the global financial crisis—the United States has added more planned elements to the economy.

mixed economies Economies that embody elements of both planned and market-based economic systems. (p. 31)

privatization The process of converting government-owned businesses to private ownership. (p. 32)

2-6 Discuss key terms and tools to evaluate economic performance. Since economic systems are so complex, no single measure captures all the dimensions of economic performance. But each measure yields insight on overall economic health.

- *Gross domestic product (GDP):* The total value of all goods and services produced within a nation's physical boundaries over a given period of time.
- *Unemployment rate:* The percentage of the labor force reflecting those who don't have jobs and are actively seeking employment.

- *Business cycle:* The periodic expansion and contraction that occur over time in virtually every economy.
- *Inflation rate:* The rate at which prices are rising across the economy. The government tracks the consumer price index and the producer price index.
- *Productivity:* The relationship between the goods and services that an economy produces and the inputs needed to produce them.

gross domestic product (GDP) The total value of all final goods and services produced within a nation's physical boundaries over a given period of time. (p. 33)

unemployment rate The percentage of people in the labor force over age 16 who do not have jobs and are actively seeking employment. (p. 33)

business cycle The periodic contraction and expansion that occur over time in virtually every economy. (p. 34)

contraction A period of economic downturn, marked by rising unemployment and falling business production. (p. 34)

recession An economic downturn marked by a decrease in the GDP for two consecutive quarters. (p. 34)

depression An especially deep and long-lasting recession. (p. 34)

recovery A period of rising economic growth and employment. (p. 34)

expansion A period of robust economic growth and high employment. (p. 34)

inflation A period of rising average prices across the economy. (p. 35)

hyperinflation An average monthly inflation rate of more than 50%. (p. 35)

disinflation A period of slowing average price increases across the economy. (p. 35)

deflation A period of falling average prices across the economy. (p. 35)

consumer price index (CPI) A measure of inflation that evaluates the change in the weighted-average price of goods and services that the average consumer buys each month. (p. 35)

producer price index (PPI) A measure of inflation that evaluates the change over time in the weighted-average wholesale prices. (p. 35)

productivity The basic relationship between the production of goods and services (output) and the resources needed to produce them (input) calculated via the following equation: output/input = productivity. (p. 36)

CHAPTER 3 LEARNING OBJECTIVES / KEY TERMS

3-1 Discuss business opportunities in the world economy. Advancing technology and falling trade barriers have created unprecedented international business opportunities. Despite the global economic crisis that began in 2008, high-population developing countries—such as China, India, Indonesia, and Brazil—continue to offer the most potential due to both their size and their relatively strong economic growth rates.

3-2 Explain the key reasons for international trade. The benefits of international trade for individual firms include access to factors of production, reduced risk, and an inflow of new ideas from foreign markets. Overall, industries tend to succeed on a global basis in countries that enjoy a competitive advantage. A country has an absolute advantage in a given industry when it can produce more of a good than other nations, using the same amount of resources, and a country has a comparative advantage when it can make products at a lower opportunity cost than other nations. Unless they face major trade barriers, the industries in any country tend to produce products for which they have a comparative advantage.

opportunity cost The opportunity of giving up the second-best choice when making a decision. (p. 42)

absolute advantage The benefit a country has in a given industry when it can produce more of a product than other nations using the same amount of resources. (p. 42)

comparative advantage The benefit a country has in a given industry if it can make products at a lower opportunity cost than other countries. (p. 42)

3-3 Describe the tools for measuring international trade. Measuring the impact of international trade on individual nations requires a clear understanding of balance of trade, balance of payments, and exchange rates.

● *Balance of trade:* A basic measure of the difference between a nation's exports and imports.

● *Balance of payments:* A measure of the total flow of money into or out of a country, including the balance of trade, plus other financial flows, such as foreign loans, foreign aid, and foreign investments.

● *Exchange rates:* A measure of the value of one nation's currency relative to the currency of other nations. The exchange rate has a powerful influence on the way global trade affects both individual nations and their trading partners.

balance of trade A basic measure of the difference in value between a nation's exports and imports, including both goods and services. (p. 43)

trade surplus Overage that occurs when the total value of a nation's exports is higher than the total value of its imports. (p. 43)

trade deficit Shortfall that occurs when the total value of a nation's imports is higher than the total value of its exports. (p. 43)

balance of payments A measure of the total flow of money into or out of a country. (p. 43)

balance of payments surplus Overage that occurs when more money flows into a nation than out of that nation. (p. 43)

balance of payments deficit Shortfall that occurs when more money flows out of a nation than into that nation. (p. 43)

exchange rate A measurement of the value of one nation's currency relative to the currency of other nations. (p. 43)

countertrade International trade that involves the barter of products for products rather than for currency. (p. 44)

3-4 Analyze strategies for reaching global markets. Firms can enter global markets by developing foreign suppliers, foreign customers, or both. Two strategies for acquiring foreign suppliers are outsourcing and importing. Key strategies for developing foreign markets include exporting, licensing, franchising, and direct investment. Exporting is relatively low cost and low risk, but it offers little control over the way the business unfolds. Direct investment, at the other end of the spectrum, tends to be high cost and high risk, but it offers more control and higher potential profits.

Market Development Options

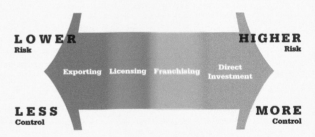

LOWER Risk — HIGHER Risk

Exporting Licensing Franchising Direct Investment

LESS Control — MORE Control

foreign outsourcing (also contract manufacturing) Contracting with foreign suppliers to produce products, usually at a fraction of the cost of domestic production. (p. 45)

importing Buying products domestically that have been produced or grown in foreign nations. (p. 45)

exporting Selling products in foreign nations that have been produced or grown domestically. (p. 45)

foreign licensing Authority granted by a domestic firm to a foreign firm for the rights to produce and market its product or to use its trademark/patent rights in a defined geographical area. (p. 45)

foreign franchising A specialized type of foreign licensing in which a firm expands by offering businesses in other countries the right to produce and market its products according to specific operating requirements. (p. 46)

© Cengage

direct investment (or foreign direct investment) When firms either acquire foreign firms or develop new facilities from the ground up in foreign countries. (p. 47)

joint ventures When two or more companies join forces—sharing resources, risks, and profits, but not actually merging companies—to pursue specific opportunities. (p. 47)

partnership A voluntary agreement under which two or more people act as co-owners of a business for profit. (p. 47)

strategic alliance An agreement between two or more firms to jointly pursue a specific opportunity without actually merging their businesses. Strategic alliances typically involve less formal, less encompassing agreements than partnerships. (p. 47)

3-5 **Discuss barriers to international trade and strategies to surmount them.** Most barriers to trade fall into the following categories: sociocultural differences, economic differences, and legal/political differences. Each country has a different mix of barriers. Often countries with the highest barriers have the least competition, which can be a real opportunity for the first international firms to break through. The best way to surmount trade barriers is to cultivate a deep understanding of a country before beginning business. And since conditions change rapidly in many nations, learning and responding are continual processes.

sociocultural differences Differences among cultures in language, attitudes, and values. (p. 47)

infrastructure A country's physical facilities that support economic activity. (p. 48)

protectionism National policies designed to restrict international trade, usually with the goal of protecting domestic businesses. (p. 50)

tariffs Taxes levied against imports. (p. 50)

quotas Limitations on the amount of specific products that may be imported from certain countries during a given time period. (p. 50)

voluntary export restraints (VERs) Limitations on the amount of specific products that one nation will export to another nation. (p. 50)

embargo A complete ban on international trade of a certain item, or a total halt in trade with a particular nation. (p. 51)

3-6 **Describe the free-trade movement and discuss key benefits and criticisms.** Over the past two decades, the emergence of regional trading blocs, common markets, and international trade agreements has moved the world economy much closer to complete free trade. Key players include:

- GATT and the WTO
- The World Bank
- The International Monetary Fund (IMF)
- The North American Free Trade Agreement (NAFTA)
- The European Union (EU)

The free trade movement has raised the global standard of living, lowered prices, and expanded choices for millions of people, but critics are troubled by the growing economic gap between the haves and the have-nots, worker abuse, large-scale pollution, and cultural homogenization.

European Union 2018

*Note: The United Kingdom is scheduled to depart the European Union on March 29, 2019.

free trade The unrestricted movement of goods and services across international borders. (p. 51)

General Agreement on Tariffs and Trade (GATT) An international trade treaty designed to encourage worldwide trade among its members. (p. 51)

World Trade Organization (WTO) A permanent global institution to promote international trade and to settle international trade disputes. (p. 51)

World Bank An international cooperative of 189 member countries, working together to reduce poverty in the developing world. (p. 52)

International Monetary Fund (IMF) An international organization of 188 member nations that promotes international economic cooperation and stable growth. (p. 52)

trading bloc A group of countries that have reduced or even eliminated tariffs, allowing for the free flow of goods among the member nations. (p. 53)

common market A group of countries that have eliminated tariffs and harmonized trading rules to facilitate the free flow of goods among the member nations. (p. 53)

North American Free Trade Agreement (NAFTA) The treaty among the United States, Mexico, and Canada that eliminated trade barriers and investment restrictions over a 15-year period starting in 1994. (p. 53)

European Union (EU) The world's largest common market, composed of 28 European nations. (p. 53)

CHAPTER 4 LEARNING OBJECTIVES / KEY TERMS

CHAPTER REVIEW

4-1 Define ethics and explain the concept of universal ethical standards. Ethics is a set of beliefs about right and wrong, good and bad. Who you are as a human being, your family, and your culture all play a role in shaping your ethical standards. The laws of each country usually set minimum ethical standards, but truly ethical standards typically reach beyond minimum legal requirements. Despite some significant cultural and legal differences, people around the globe tend to agree on core values, which can serve as a starting point for universal ethical standards across a wide range of situations: trustworthiness, respect, responsibility, fairness, caring, and citizenship.

ethics A set of beliefs about right and wrong, good and bad. (p. 58)

universal ethical standards Ethical norms that apply to all people across a broad spectrum of situations. (p. 60)

4-2 Describe business ethics and ethical dilemmas. Business ethics is the application of right and wrong, good and bad, in a business setting. Ethical dilemmas arise when you face business decisions that throw your values into conflict. These are decisions that force you to choose among less-than-ideal options because whatever choice you make will have some significant negative consequences.

business ethics The application of right and wrong, good and bad, in a business setting. (p. 60)

ethical dilemma A decision that involves a conflict of values; every potential course of action has some significant negative consequences. (p. 60)

4-3 Discuss how ethics relates to both the individual and the organization. Ethical choices begin with ethical individuals. To help people make good choices, experts have developed frameworks for reaching ethical decisions. While the specifics vary, the core principles of most decision guides are similar:

- Do you fully understand each dimension of the problem?
- Who would benefit? Who would suffer?
- Are the alternative solutions legal? Are they fair?
- Does your decision make you comfortable at a "gut feel" level?
- Could you defend your decision on the nightly TV news?
- Have you considered and reconsidered your responses to each question?

While each person is responsible for his or her own actions, the organization can also have a dramatic influence on the conduct of individual employees. An ethical culture—which includes ethical leadership from top executives, and accountability at every level of the organization—has an outsized impact on individual conduct. But formal ethics programs also play a crucial role. A written code of ethics—a document that lays out the values and priorities of the organization—is the cornerstone of a formal ethics program. Other key elements include ethics training and a clear enforcement policy for ethical violations.

Ethical Dilemma

code of ethics A formal, written document that defines the ethical standards of an organization and gives employees the information they need to make ethical decisions across a range of situations. (p. 64)

whistle-blowers Employees who report their employer's illegal or unethical behavior to either the authorities or the media. (p. 64)

4-4 Define social responsibility and examine the impact on stakeholder groups. Social responsibility is the obligation of a business to contribute to society. Enlightened companies carefully consider the priorities of all stakeholders—groups who have an interest in their actions and performance—as they make key decisions. Core stakeholder groups for most businesses are listed below, along with key obligations.

- *Employees:* Treat employees with dignity, respect, and fairness. Ensure that hard work and talent pay off. Help workers balance emerging work–life priorities.
- *Customers:* Provide quality products at a fair price. Ensure that customers are safe and informed. Support consumer choice and consumer dialogue.
- *Investors:* Create an ongoing stream of profits. Manage investor dollars according to the highest legal and ethical standards. Support full disclosure.
- *Community:* Support nonprofit groups that improve the community and fit with your company. Minimize the negative environmental impact of your business.

The Spectrum of Social Responsibility

© Cengage

CHAPTER **REVIEW**

CHAPTER 4 LEARNING OBJECTIVES / KEY TERMS

social responsibility The obligation of a business to contribute to society. (p. 64)

stakeholders Any groups that have a stake—or a personal interest—in the performance and actions of an organization. (p. 65)

consumerism A social movement that focuses on four key consumer rights: (1) the right to be safe, (2) the right to be informed, (3) the right to choose, and (4) the right to be heard. (p. 65)

planned obsolescence The strategy of deliberately designing products to fail in order to shorten the time between purchases. (p. 67)

Sarbanes-Oxley Act Federal legislation passed in 2002 that sets higher ethical standards for public corporations and accounting firms. Key provisions limit conflict-of-interest issues and require financial officers and CEOs to certify the validity of their financial statements. (p. 68)

corporate philanthropy All business donations to nonprofit groups, including money, products, and employee time. (p. 68)

cause-related marketing Marketing partnerships between businesses and nonprofit organizations, designed to spike sales for the company and raise money for the nonprofit. (p. 68)

corporate responsibility Business contributions to the community through the actions of the business itself rather than donations of money and time. (p. 69)

sustainable development Doing business to meet the needs of the current generation, without harming the ability of future generations to meet their needs. (p. 69)

carbon footprint Refers to the amount of harmful greenhouse gases that a firm emits throughout its operations, both directly and indirectly. (p. 70)

green marketing Developing and promoting environmentally sound products and practices to gain a competitive edge. (p. 70)

4-5 **Explain the role of social responsibility in the global arena.** Social responsibility becomes more complex in the global arena, largely due to differences in the legal and cultural environments. Bribery and corruption are key issues, along with concern for human rights and environmental standards.

Social Responsibility Issues in the Global Arena

4-6 **Describe how companies evaluate their efforts to be socially responsible.** Many companies—even some entire industries—monitor themselves. The process typically involves establishing objectives for ethics and social responsibility and then measuring achievement of those objectives on a systematic, periodic basis. Other groups play watchdog roles as well. Key players include activist customers, investors, unions, environmentalists, and community groups.

WATCHDOG GROUPS
• Activist Customers
• Investors
• Unions
• Environmentalists
• Community Groups

social audit A systematic evaluation of how well a firm is meeting its ethics and social responsibility goals. (p. 73)

5-1 **Explain the importance of excellent business communication.** Effective communication happens when *relevant meaning* is transmitted from the sender to the receiver. Skillful communicators save time and money, and develop deeper, more trusting relationships with their colleagues. Anything that interferes with the correct transmission of your message is a barrier to communication. Barriers can be physical, verbal, nonverbal, cultural, perceptual, or organizational. To communicate effectively, you should be able to identify and surmount any barriers that stand between you and your audience. The result? Greater chance of long-term success in every aspect of business.

Barriers to Communication Can Be Daunting

physical barriers, language barriers, body language barriers, cultural barriers, perceptual barriers, organizational barriers

communication The transmission of information between a sender and a recipient. (p. 76)

noise Any interference that causes the message you send to be different from the message your audience understands. (p. 77)

communication barriers Obstacles to effective communication, typically defined in terms of physical, language, body language, cultural, perceptual, and organizational barriers. (p. 77)

intercultural communication Communication among people with differing cultural backgrounds. (p. 78)

5-2 **Describe the key elements of nonverbal communication.** The key elements of nonverbal communication include eye contact, tone of voice, facial expressions, gestures, and posture. Studies suggest that, on average, only 7% of meaning during face-to-face communication comes from the verbal content of the message, which magnifies the importance of every element of nonverbal communication. Active listening also plays an influential role. The starting point is empathy: a genuine attempt to understand and appreciate the speaker. You should signal your focus to the speaker through verbal cues, such as "I understand your point," and nonverbal cues, such as nods, eye contact, and leaning forward. The result will be better relationships and better information for you.

Eye contact
Tone of voice
Facial expressions
Gestures
Posture

93% of meaning comes from nonverbal communication

nonverbal communication Communication that does not use words. Common forms of nonverbal communication include gestures, posture, facial expressions, tone of voice, and eye contact. (p. 78)

active listening Attentive listening that occurs when the listener focuses his or her complete attention on the speaker. (p. 79)

5-3 **Compare, contrast, and choose effective communication channels.** Communication channels differ significantly in terms of richness: the amount of information that they offer the audience. The spectrum ranges from written communication at the low end to face-to-face meetings at the high end. The best choice depends on your objective, your message, and your audience. To ensure that your communication achieves your goals, always consider the needs and expectations of your audience. If you tailor each message with the audience in mind, you'll give yourself a competitive edge in terms of the time, attention, and response of your audience.

Communication Channels Have Different Levels of Richness

Very High
High
Moderate
Low
Very Low

Face-to-Face Meeting | In-Person Presentation | Tele-phone | Voice Mail | Email | Memos/Reports | Texting

communication channels The various ways in which a message can be sent, ranging from one-on-one in-person meetings to Internet message boards. (p. 80)

© Cengage

5-4 **Choose the right words for effective communication.** The right words can make the difference between a message your audience absorbs and a message your audience ignores. Keep these considerations in mind: analyze your audience, be concise, avoid slang, avoid bias, and use the active voice.

bias A preconception about members of a particular group. Common forms of bias include gender bias; age bias; and race, ethnicity, or nationality bias. (p. 82)

active voice Sentence construction in which the subject performs the action expressed by the verb (e.g., The accountant did the taxes.). The active voice works better for the vast majority of business communication. (p. 83)

passive voice Sentence construction in which the subject does not do the action expressed by the verb; rather, the subject is acted upon (e.g., The taxes were done by our accountant.). The passive voice tends to be less effective for business communication. (p. 83)

5-5 **Write more effective business memos, letters, and emails.** Here, too, you should begin with the needs of your audience; their anticipated response should drive the structure of your writing. Determine the "bottom line" of your communication, and be sure to deliver it up front. Your message itself should have a natural tone and must be completely free of grammatical errors.

Sample Emails: Same Message, Different Approach

If the recipient will feel neutral...

Main point in the first sentence

Subject line specifies the key issue

TO: Online Poker Team
FROM: Yumi Tanaka, VP Product Development
RE: Game Development Team Restructuring

To help meet our goal of developing three more innovative games this year, I plan to reassign each member of the online poker team to a new team that needs to brainstorm more effectively. Please let me know sometime in the next two days if you have a preference regarding your new assignment.

Thank you for arranging to present the new version of your online poker game to the sales force last week. I am confident that this game your team developed will be a huge hit with our key customers.

Positive close reinforces goodwill

If the recipient will feel negative...

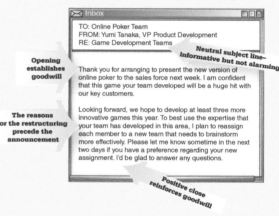

Opening establishes goodwill

The reasons for the restructuring precede the announcement

Neutral subject line—informative but not alarming

TO: Online Poker Team
FROM: Yumi Tanaka, VP Product Development
RE: Game Development Teams

Thank you for arranging to present the new version of online poker to the sales force next week. I am confident that this game your team developed will be a huge hit with our key customers.

Looking forward, we hope to develop at least three more innovative games this year. To best use the expertise that your team has developed in this area, I plan to reassign each member to a new team that needs to brainstorm more effectively. Please let me know sometime in the next two days if you have a preference regarding your new assignment. I'd be glad to answer any questions.

Positive close reinforces goodwill

5-6 **Create and deliver successful verbal presentations.** A great presentation begins with a hook that draws your audience in and engages their attention. The body of the presentation typically focuses on three key points, supported by credible information and persuasive arguments. The close summarizes the key points and often refers back to the opening hook. Dynamic delivery is simply a matter of practice, with a focus on knowing your material.

dynamic delivery Vibrant, compelling presentation delivery style that grabs and holds the attention of the audience. (p. 90)

6-1 **Describe the characteristics of the four basic forms of business ownership.** A sole proprietorship is a business that is owned, and usually managed, by a single person. A partnership is a voluntary arrangement under which two or more people act as co-owners of a business for profit. A corporation is a legal entity created by filing a document (known in most states as the "articles of incorporation") with a state agency. A corporation is considered to be separate and distinct from its owners, who have limited liability for the debts of their company. A limited liability company (LLC) is a relatively new form of business ownership that, like a corporation, offers limited liability to all of its owners. However, LLCs offer more flexibility in tax treatment and have simpler operating requirements.

sole proprietorship A form of business ownership with a single owner who usually actively manages the company. (p. 93)

partnership A voluntary agreement under which two or more people act as co-owners of a business for profit. (p. 93)

general partnership A partnership in which all partners can take an active role in managing the business and have unlimited liability for any claims against the firm. (p. 93)

corporation A form of business ownership in which the business is considered a legal entity that is separate and distinct from its owners. (p. 93)

articles of incorporation The document filed with a state government to establish the existence of a new corporation. (p. 93)

limited liability When owners are not personally liable for claims against their firm. Owners with limited liability may lose their investment in the company, but their other personal assets are protected. (p. 94)

limited liability company (LLC) A form of business ownership that offers both limited liability to its owners and flexible tax treatment. (p. 94)

6-2 **Discuss the advantages and disadvantages of a sole proprietorship.** A sole proprietorship is the simplest and least expensive form of ownership to establish. It offers the single owner the flexibility of running the business without having to seek the approval of other owners. If the business is successful, the sole proprietor retains all of the profits. Finally, the earnings of a sole proprietorship are taxed only as income of the owner, with no separate tax levied on the business itself. One key disadvantage of a sole proprietorship is that the single owner has unlimited liability for the debts of the business. Sole proprietors also often work long hours and assume heavy responsibilities, and they may have difficulty raising funds for expansion. Another drawback of sole proprietorships is their limited life.

6-3 **Evaluate the pros and cons of the partnership as a form of business ownership.** The most basic type of partnership is a *general partnership*, in which each co-owner may take an active role in management. Compared to the sole proprietorships, a general partnership offers the advantages of pooled financial resources and the benefits of a shared workload that can take advantage of complementary skills. The earnings of general partnerships are taxed only as income to the partners; there is no separate income tax on the business itself. One major disadvantage of a general partnership is that each owner has unlimited liability for the debts of the company. Moreover, disagreements among partners can complicate decision making. Finally, the death or withdrawal of a partner can create instability and uncertainty in the management and financing of the company.

There are two other common types of partnerships. A *limited partnership* must have at least one general partner and at least one limited partner. General partners actively manage the company and have unlimited liability for the company's debts. Limited partners have limited liability but may not actively manage the partnership. In a *limited liability partnership*, all partners may manage their company and are protected by some degree of limited liability for the debts of their firm.

limited partnership A partnership that includes at least one general partner who actively manages the company and accepts unlimited liability and one limited partner who gives up the right to actively manage the company in exchange for limited liability. (p. 97)

limited liability partnership (LLP) A form of partnership in which all partners have the right to participate in management and have limited liability for company debts. (p. 98)

6-4 **Explain why corporations have become the dominant form of business ownership.** The most common form of corporation is the C corporation. All stockholders (the owners of a C corporation) have limited liability for company debts. C corporations can raise financial capital by issuing bonds or shares of stock, giving them an advantage when it comes to financing growth. Other advantages include unlimited life, easy transfer of ownership, and the ability to take advantage of professional management. But forming a corporation can be more complex and expensive than forming a partnership. Another drawback is that any profits distributed to stockholders are taxed twice—once as income to the corporation, then again as income to the stockholders. Corporations are also subject to extensive government regulation.

C corporation The most common type of corporation, which is a legal business entity that offers limited liability to all of its owners, who are called stockholders. (p. 98)

corporate bylaws The basic rules governing how a corporation is organized and how it conducts its business. (p. 99)

stockholder An owner of a corporation. (p. 99)

institutional investor An organization that pools contributions from investors, clients, or depositors and uses these funds to buy stocks and other securities. (p. 99)

board of directors The individuals who are elected by stockholders of a corporation to represent their interests. (p. 100)

S corporation A form of corporation that avoids double taxation by having its income taxed as if it were a partnership. (p. 102)

statutory close (or closed) corporation A corporation with a limited number of owners that operates under simpler, less formal rules than a C corporation. (p. 102)

nonprofit corporation A corporation that does not seek to earn a profit and differs in several fundamental respects from C corporations. (p. 102)

acquisition A corporate restructuring in which one firm buys another. (p. 102)

horizontal merger A combination of two firms that are in the same industry. (p. 103)

vertical merger A combination of firms at different stages in the production of a good or service. (p. 103)

conglomerate merger A combination of two firms that are in unrelated industries. (p. 103)

merger A corporate restructuring that occurs when two formerly independent business entities combine to form a new organization. (p. 103)

divestiture The transfer of total or partial ownership of some of a firm's operations to investors or to another company. (p. 103)

6-5 **Explain why limited liability companies are becoming an increasingly popular form of business ownership.** Limited liability companies (LLCs) are attractive because they avoid the problem of double taxation endemic to C corporations, while giving all owners the protection of limited liability. In this sense, LLCs are similar to S corporations, but without the restrictions on ownership. LLCs also face fewer regulations than corporations and give the owners the flexibility to either manage the company themselves or hire professional managers.

6-6 **Evaluate the advantages and disadvantages of franchising.** A franchise is a licensing arrangement under which one party (the *franchisor*) allows another party (the *franchisee*) to use its name, trademark, patents, copyrights, business methods, and other property in exchange for monetary payments and other considerations. The franchisor gains revenue without the need to invest its own money. The franchisee gains the right to use a well-known brand name and proven business methods and often receives training and support from the franchisor. On the downside, franchisors often find that dealing with a large number of franchisees can be complex and challenging. For franchisees, the main drawbacks are the monetary payments (fees and royalties) they must pay to the franchisor and the loss of control over management of their business.

TYPES OF MERGERS AND ACQUISITIONS

Type of Merger	Definition	Common Objective	Example
Horizontal Merger	A combination of firms in the same industry.	Increase size and market power within the industry. Improve efficiency by eliminating duplication of facilities and personnel.	U.S.-based Sherwin-Williams, which makes paints and paint-related products, acquired U.S.-based Valspar, a paint, coating, and finishes company, for $11.3 billion.
Vertical Merger	A combination of firms that are at different stages in the production of a good or service, creating a "buyer-seller" relationship.	Provide tighter integration of production and increased control over the supply of crucial inputs.	China National Chemical Corporation, a Fortune 500 firm and the largest chemical firm in China, acquired Swiss-based Sygenta AG, which sells pesticides and soybean seeds, for $43 million.
Conglomerate Merger	A combination of firms in unrelated industries.	Reduce risk by making the firm less vulnerable to adverse conditions in any single market.	Chinese-based Midea, a maker of consumer appliances and heating, ventilation, and air-conditioning systems, acquired Kuka AG, a German-based robotics and automation systems company, for $5 billion.

franchise A licensing arrangement under which a franchisor allows franchisees to use its name, trademark, products, business methods, and other property in exchange for monetary payments and other considerations. (p. 106)

franchisor The business entity in a franchise relationship that allows others to operate its business using resources it supplies in exchange for money and other considerations. (p. 106)

franchisee The party in a franchise relationship that pays for the right to use resources supplied by the franchisor. (p. 106)

distributorship A type of franchising arrangement in which the franchisor makes a product and licenses the franchisee to sell it. (p. 106)

business format franchise A broad franchise agreement in which the franchisee pays for the right to use the name, trademark, and business and production methods of the franchisor. (p. 106)

franchise agreement The contractual arrangement between a franchisor and franchisee that spells out the duties and responsibilities of both parties. (p. 109)

Franchise Disclosure Document (FDD) A detailed description of all aspects of a franchise that the franchisor must provide to the franchisee at least 14 calendar days before the franchise agreement is signed. (p. 110)

© Cengage

7-1 **Explain the key reasons to launch a small business.** Launching a business is tough, but the advantages of business ownership can far outweigh the risk and hard work. Most people who take the plunge are seeking some combination of greater financial success, independence, flexibility, and challenge. But some are seeking survival and simply have no other options.

entrepreneurs People who risk their time, money, and other resources to start and manage a business. (p. 113)

7-2 **Describe the typical entrepreneurial mindset and characteristics.** Not all small business owners are entrepreneurs. The difference is attitude: from day one, true entrepreneurs aim to dominate their industry. The entrepreneurial personality typically includes some combination of the following characteristics: vision, self-reliance, energy, confidence, tolerance of uncertainty, and tolerance of failure. While these qualities are very helpful, they aren't essential: it's clearly possible to succeed with a number of different personality types.

internal locus of control A deep-seated sense that the individual is personally responsible for what happens in his or her life. (p. 116)

external locus of control A deep-seated sense that forces other than the individual are responsible for what happens in his or her life. (p. 116)

7-3 **Discuss funding options for small business.** For many entrepreneurs, finding the money to fund their business is the top challenge of their start-up year. The vast majority of new firms are funded by the personal resources of the founder, including personal accounts (e.g., credit cards), family, and friends. Other key funding sources include bank loans, angel investors, and venture capital firms.

angel investors Individuals who invest in start-up companies with high growth potential in exchange for a share of ownership. (p. 118)

venture capital firms Companies that invest in start-up businesses with high growth potential in exchange for a share of ownership. (p. 119)

7-4 **Analyze the opportunities and threats that small businesses face.** Small businesses enjoy some key advantages but also face daunting obstacles as they fight for a foothold in the turbulent marketplace.

Opportunities:
- *Market niches:* Many small firms are uniquely positioned to exploit small, but profitable, market niches.
- *Personal customer service:* With a smaller customer base, small firms can develop much more personal relationships with individual customers.
- *Lower overhead costs:* Many small firms can hold down overhead costs by hiring fewer managers and fewer specialized employees.
- *Technology:* The Web has played a powerful role in opening new opportunities for small business in both local and global markets.

Threats:
- *High risk of failure:* Starting a new business involves a lot of risk, but the odds improve significantly after the five-year mark.
- *Lack of knowledge and experience:* Entrepreneurs often have expertise in a particular area but lack the background to run a successful business.
- *Too little money:* Lack of start-up money is a major issue for most new firms, since ongoing profits don't usually begin for months, or even years.
- *Bigger regulatory burden:* Small firms spend 45% more per employee than big firms, simply complying with federal regulations.
- *Higher health insurance costs:* Small-scale health plans are much more expensive, making it harder to offer employees competitive coverage.

market niche A small segment of a market with fewer competitors than the market as a whole. Market niches tend to be quite attractive to small firms. (p. 119)

CHAPTER REVIEW / CHAPTER 7 LEARNING OBJECTIVES / KEY TERMS

Entrepreneurial Characteristics

Arek Malang/Shutterstock.com

NEW BUSINESS SURVIVAL RATES

Year in Business	Survival Rate	Change vs. Prior Year (percentage points)
Year 1	100.0%	—
Year 2	78%	−22
Year 3	66%	−12
Year 4	56%	−10
Year 5	50%	−6
Year 6	45%	−5
Year 7	42%	−3
Year 8	40%	−2
Year 9	37%	−3
Year 10	35%	−2

Source: Entrepreneurship and the U.S. Economy, Bureau of Labor Statistics, http://www.bls.gov/bdm/entrepreneurship/bdm_chart3.htm, accessed May 18, 2016.

7-5 **Discuss ways to become a new business owner and tools to facilitate success.** Many people who are interested in owning their own business prefer to start from scratch and build their company from the ground up. But buying an established business, or even a franchise, can be an excellent choice as well. Each choice involves a range of pros and cons, but broadly speaking, it's less risky to buy an established business or franchise, but more satisfying (at least for some people) to start a new venture from scratch. Whichever path you choose—whether you're an ambitious entrepreneur or simply a small business owner—several strategies can help you succeed over the long term: gain experience in your field, learn from others, educate yourself, access SBA resources, and develop a business plan.

BUSINESS LAUNCH OPTIONS

- Starting from scratch
- Buying an established business
- Buying a franchise

STRATEGIES FOR SUCCESS:

- Gain experience
- Learn from others
- Educate yourself
- Access SBA resources
- Develop a plan

Small Business Administration (SBA) An agency of the federal government designed to maintain and strengthen the nation's economy by aiding, counseling, assisting, and protecting the interests of small businesses. (p. 122)

Small Business Development Centers (SBDCs) Local offices—affiliated with the Small Business Administration—that provide comprehensive management assistance to current and prospective small business owners. (p. 123)

SCORE (Service Corps of Retired Executives) An organization—affiliated with the Small Business Administration—that provides free, comprehensive business counseling for small business owners from qualified volunteers. (p. 123)

business plan A formal document that describes a business concept, outlines core business objectives, and details strategies and timelines for achieving those objectives. (p. 123)

7-6 **Explain the size, scope, and economic contributions of small business.** Small businesses play a vital role in the American economy, generating about half of the U.S. gross domestic product and accounting for more than two-thirds of all new jobs over the past two decades. In addition to fueling employment growth, small businesses contribute innovations to the economy at a much higher rate than their big business counterparts. They also form the backbone of many inner-city economies, finding opportunities—and offering products and services—in places where most large firms opt not to operate. The entrepreneurship rate around the world varies dramatically from country to country, ranging from a high of 39.9% in Nigeria and Zambia to a low of 3.4% in Italy, Russia, and Japan. The differences among countries seem to depend largely on the national per capita income, the opportunity costs for entrepreneurs, and the national culture and political environment.

8-1 **Define accounting and describe how accounting information is used by a variety of stakeholders.** Accounting is a system for recognizing, organizing, analyzing, and reporting information about the financial transactions that affect an organization. This information is important to many different stakeholder groups. Owners want to know whether their firm made a profit or suffered a loss. Creditors want to make sure that the firm has the capacity to repay any loans they make. Employees want to know whether their company is performing well enough to provide job security and a good pay raise. The IRS wants to know the amount of taxable income the firm earns during each period.

accounting A system for recognizing, organizing, analyzing, and reporting information about the financial transactions that affect an organization. (p. 128)

8-2 **Identify the purposes and goals of generally accepted accounting principles.** Generally accepted accounting principles (GAAP) are rules that govern the practice of financial accounting. The goal of GAAP is to ensure that the information generated by financial accounting is relevant, reliable, consistent, and comparable.

financial accounting The branch of accounting that prepares financial statements for use by owners, creditors, suppliers, and other external stakeholders. (p. 130)

generally accepted accounting principles (GAAP) A set of accounting standards that is used in the preparation of financial statements. (p. 130)

Financial Accounting Standards Board (FASB) The private board that establishes the generally accepted accounting principles used in the practice of financial accounting. (p. 131)

8-3 **Describe the key elements of the major financial statements.** The balance sheet shows the firm's financial position at a specific point in time by reporting the value of its assets, liabilities, and owners' equity. The income statement shows the net income (profit or loss) the firm earns over a stated time period by deducting expenses from revenues. The statement of cash flows shows the inflows and outflows of cash that result from a firm's operations, financing activities, and investing activities in a given time period and the net change in the amount of cash the firm has over that time period.

balance sheet A financial statement that reports the financial position of a firm by identifying and reporting the value of the firm's assets, liabilities, and owners' equity. (p. 132)

accounting equation Assets = Liabilities + Owners' Equity (p. 132)

assets Resources owned by a firm. (p. 132)

liabilities Claims that outsiders have against a firm's assets. (p. 132)

owners' equity The claims a firm's owners have against their company's assets (often called "stockholders' equity" on balance sheets of corporations). (p. 133)

income statement The financial statement that reports the revenues, expenses, and net income that resulted from a firm's operations over an accounting period. (p. 134)

revenue Increases in a firm's assets that result from the sale of goods, provision of services, or other activities intended to earn income. (p. 134)

accrual-basis accounting The method of accounting that recognizes revenue when it is earned and matches expenses to the revenues they helped produce. (p. 135)

expenses Resources that are used up as the result of business operations. (p. 135)

net income The difference between the revenue a firm earns and the expenses it incurs in a given time period. (p. 136)

statement of cash flows The financial statement that identifies a firm's sources and uses of cash in a given accounting period. (p. 136)

8-4 **Describe several methods stakeholders can use to obtain useful insights from a company's financial statements.** In addition to looking at the numbers in financial statements, it's also important to check out the independent auditor's report, read the management discussion, and examine the endnotes that accompany these statements. The auditor's report indicates whether the financial statements were prepared in accordance with GAAP and fairly present the financial condition of the company. The management discussion provides insights by top management to put the numbers in context. Endnotes often disclose key information that isn't directly available in the statements themselves. It's also a good idea to compare the figures reported in current statements to those from earlier statements to see how key account values have changed.

horizontal analysis Analysis of financial statements that compares account values reported on these statements over two or more years to identify changes and trends. (p. 141)

8-5 **Explain how the budget process can help managers plan, motivate, and evaluate their organization's performance.** Budgeting facilitates planning by translating goals into measurable quantities and requiring managers to identify the specific resources needed to achieve them. The budgeting process can help with both motivation and evaluation. Employees tend to be more highly motivated when they understand the goals they are expected to accomplish and believe they are ambitious but achievable. Managers can compare actual performance to budgeted figures to determine whether various departments and functional areas are making adequate progress toward achieving their organization's goals.

© Cengage

CHAPTER 8 LEARNING OBJECTIVES / KEY TERMS

CHAPTER REVIEW

budgeting A management tool that explicitly shows how a firm will acquire and use the resources needed to achieve its goals over a specific time period. (p. 141)

operating budgets Budgets that communicate an organization's sales and production goals and the resources needed to achieve these goals. (p. 142)

financial budgets Budgets that focus on the firm's financial goals and identify the resources needed to achieve these goals. (p. 142)

master budget A presentation of an organization's operational and financial budgets that represents the firm's overall plan of action for a specified time period. (p. 142)

8-6 **Explain the role of managerial accounting and describe the various cost concepts identified by managerial accountants.** Managerial accounting provides information to an organization's managers and other internal stakeholders so that they can make better decisions. One key type of information provided by managerial accounting involves the classification and measurement of costs. Explicit (or out-of-pocket) costs involve monetary payments. Implicit costs arise when a company gives up an opportunity to use an asset in an alternative way. Fixed costs don't change when a firm changes its rate of output. Variable costs rise when production increases and fall when it decreases. Direct costs are tied to the production of a specific good, while indirect costs are incurred as the result of a firm's overall operations and are not tied directly to a specific good.

Development of the Master Budget

COMPARISON OF FINANCIAL AND MANAGERIAL ACCOUNTING

	Financial Accounting	Managerial Accounting
Purpose	Primarily intended to provide information to external stakeholders, such as stockholders, creditors, and government regulators. Information provided by financial accounting is available to the general public.	Primarily intended to provide information to internal stakeholders, such as the managers of specific divisions or departments. This information is proprietary—meaning that it isn't available to the general public.
Type of Information Presented	Focuses almost exclusively on financial information.	Provides both financial and nonfinancial information.
Nature of Reports	Prepares a standard set of financial statements.	Prepares customized reports to deal with specific problems or issues.
Timing of Reports	Presents financial statements on a predetermined schedule (usually quarterly and annually).	Creates reports upon request by management rather than according to a predetermined schedule.
Adherence to Accounting Standards?	Governed by a set of generally accepted accounting principles (GAAP).	Uses procedures developed internally that are not required to follow GAAP.
Time Period Focus	Summarizes past performance and its impact on the firm's present condition.	Provides reports dealing with past performance but also involves making projections about the future when dealing with planning issues.

managerial (or management) accounting The branch of accounting that provides reports and analysis to managers to help them make informed business decisions. (p. 143)

cost The value of what is given up in exchange for something. (p. 144)

out-of-pocket cost A cost that involves the payment of money or other resources. (p. 144)

implicit cost The opportunity cost that arises when a firm uses owner-supplied resources. (p. 144)

fixed costs Costs that remain the same when the level of production changes within some relevant range. (p. 145)

variable costs Costs that vary directly with the level of production. (p. 145)

direct cost Costs that are incurred directly as the result of some specific cost object. (p. 145)

indirect costs Costs that are the result of a firm's general operations and are not directly tied to any specific cost object. (p. 145)

activity-based costing (ABC) A technique to assign product costs based on links between activities that drive costs and the production of specific products. (p. 145)

9-1 **Identify the goal of financial management and explain the issues financial managers confront as they seek to achieve this goal.** Historically, the goal of financial management has been to *maximize the value of the firm to its owners*. But many of today's businesses have adopted a broader perspective, believing that they have responsibilities not just to stockholders but also to customers, employees, and other stakeholders. Treating these other stakeholders well often builds value, which benefits stockholders, but other stakeholder groups also sometimes have goals that conflict with those of stockholders. When this happens, financial managers generally adopt the policies they believe are most consistent with the interests of ownership. Another challenge that financial managers face is the need to find the appropriate balance between risk and return. The *risk-return trade-off* suggests that sources and uses of funds that offer the potential for high rates of return tend to be riskier than those that offer lower returns.

financial capital The funds a firm uses to acquire its assets and finance its operations. (p. 148)

finance The functional area of business that is concerned with finding the best sources and uses of financial capital. (p. 149)

risk The degree of uncertainty regarding the outcome of a decision. (p. 151)

risk-return trade-off The observation that financial opportunities that offer high rates of return are generally riskier than opportunities that offer lower rates of return. (p. 151)

9-2 **Describe the tools financial managers use to evaluate their company's current financial condition and develop financial plans.** One way financial managers evaluate the firm's current financial condition is by computing ratios based on key accounts listed on their firm's financial statements. Financial managers look at four basic types of ratios. *Liquidity ratios* indicate whether the firm will have enough cash to pay its short-term liabilities as they come due. *Asset management ratios* tell financial managers how effectively a firm is using various assets to generate revenues for their firm. *Leverage ratios* measure the extent to which a firm relies on debt in its capital structure. *Profitability ratios* measure the firm's overall success at using resources to create a profit for its owners.

The budgeted income statement, the budgeted balance sheet, and the cash budget are the key tools that financial managers use to develop and present their financial plans. The budgeted income statement develops a forecast of net income for the planning period. The budgeted balance sheet forecasts the types and amounts of assets the firm will need to implement its plans, and the amount of additional financing necessary to obtain those assets. The cash budget identifies the timing of cash inflows and outflows to help the firm identify when it will have shortages and surpluses of cash.

financial ratio analysis Computing ratios that compare values of key accounts listed on a firm's financial statements. (p. 151)

liquid asset An asset that can quickly be converted into cash with little risk of loss. (p. 152)

liquidity ratios Financial ratios that measure the ability of a firm to obtain the cash it needs to pay its short-term debt obligations as they come due. (p. 152)

asset management ratios Financial ratios that measure how effectively a firm is using its assets to generate revenues or cash. (p. 152)

financial leverage The use of debt in a firm's capital structure. (p. 152)

leverage ratios Ratios that measure the extent to which a firm relies on debt financing in its capital structure. (p. 153)

profitability ratios Ratios that measure the rate of return a firm is earning on various measures of investment. (p. 153)

budgeted income statement A projection showing how a firm's budgeted sales and costs will affect expected net income. (Also called a pro forma income statement.)(p. 154)

budgeted balance sheet A projected financial statement that forecasts the types and amounts of assets a firm will need to implement its future plans and how the firm will finance those assets. (Also called a pro forma balance sheet.)(p. 154)

cash budget A detailed forecast of future cash flows that helps financial managers identify when their firm is likely to experience temporary shortages or surpluses of cash. (p. 154)

9-3 **Evaluate the major sources of funds available to meet a firm's short-term and long-term financial needs.** Established firms have several sources of short-term funds, including bank loans, trade credit, factoring, and commercial paper. Trade credit arises when suppliers ship materials, parts, or goods to a firm without requiring immediate payment. Banks extend short-term loans to firms with good credit ratings. Factors provide immediate cash to firms by purchasing their accounts receivable at a discount. Major corporations sometimes raise funds by selling commercial paper, which are short-term IOUs.

Firms that want to build up their permanent financial base have two basic options. First, they can rely on equity financing, which consists of funds provided by owners. The second option is long-term debt financing.

trade credit Spontaneous financing granted by sellers when they deliver goods and services to customers without requiring immediate payment. (p. 156)

spontaneous financing Financing that arises during the natural course of business without the need for special arrangements. (p. 156)

factor A company that provides short-term financing to firms by purchasing their accounts receivables at a discount. (p. 156)

line of credit A financial arrangement between a firm and a bank in which the bank pre-approves credit up to a specified limit, provided that the firm maintains an acceptable credit rating. (p. 157)

revolving credit agreement A guaranteed line of credit in which a bank makes a binding commitment to provide a business with funds up to a specified credit limit at any time during the term of the agreement. (p. 157)

commercial paper Short-term (and usually unsecured) promissory notes issued by large corporations. (p. 157)

retained earnings The part of a firm's net income it reinvests. (p. 158)

covenant A restriction lenders impose on borrowers as a condition of providing long-term debt financing. (p. 159)

9-4 **Identify the key issues involved in determining a firm's capital structure.** Capital structure refers to the mix of equity and debt financing a firm uses to meet its financing needs. Debt financing enables the firm to finance activities without requiring the owners to put up more money. When the firm earns more on borrowed funds than it pays in interest, the excess goes to the owners, thus magnifying the return on their investment. And the interest payments on debt are tax deductible. However, the interest payments and the requirement to repay the amount borrowed can put a strain on companies when business conditions are poor. Equity financing is safer and more flexible than debt financing. But dividend payments are not tax deductible. And issuing new stock can dilute the ownership share of existing stockholders.

equity financing Funds provided by the owners of a company. (p. 159)

debt financing Funds provided by lenders (creditors). (p. 159)

capital structure The mix of equity and debt financing a firm uses to meet its permanent financing needs. (p. 159)

Dodd-Frank Act A law enacted in the aftermath of the financial crisis of 2008–2009 that strengthened government oversight of financial markets and placed limitations on risky financial strategies such as heavy reliance on leverage. (p. 163)

9-5 **Describe how financial managers acquire and manage current assets.** Firms must have cash, but cash earns little or no interest. Firms with a surplus of cash often hold cash equivalents such as T-bills, commercial paper, and money market mutual funds to earn interest. Accounts receivable are what customers who buy on credit owe to a firm. Firms must establish credit policies that balance the higher sales generated by accounts receivable against these risks that credit customers might not make their payments. Inventories are the stocks of materials, work in process, and finished goods a firm holds. For many firms, the costs of storing, handling, and insuring inventory items are significant. In recent years, many firms have become very aggressive about keeping inventories as low as possible.

cash equivalents Safe and highly liquid assets that many firms list with their cash holdings on their balance sheet. (p. 163)

U.S. Treasury bills (T-bills) Short-term marketable IOUs issued by the U.S. federal government. (p. 164)

money market mutual funds A mutual fund that pools funds from many investors and uses these funds to purchase very safe, highly liquid securities. (p. 164)

9-6 **Explain how financial managers evaluate capital budgeting proposals to identify the best long-term investment options for their company.** Capital budgeting is the process financial managers use to evaluate major long-term investment opportunities. Capital budgeting investments are expected to generate cash flows for many years, so financial managers must take the time value of money into account. The time value of money recognizes that the sooner a cash flow is received, the sooner it can be reinvested to earn more money. Financial managers take the time value of money into account by computing the present values of all cash flows the proposal will generate. The present value of a sum of money received in the future is the amount of money today that will become that future amount if it is invested at a specified rate of interest. The net present value (NPV) of the project is the sum of the present values of all the estimated future cash flows, minus the initial cost of the investment. If the NPV of a project is positive, it will increase the value of the firm. If the NPV is negative, it will decrease the value of the firm.

capital budgeting The process a firm uses to evaluate long-term investment proposals. (p. 165)

time value of money The principle that a dollar received today is worth more than a dollar received in the future. (p. 167)

certificate of deposit (CD) An interest-earning deposit that requires the funds to remain deposited for a fixed term. Withdrawal of the funds before the term expires results in a financial penalty. (p. 167)

present value The amount of money that, if invested today at a given rate of interest (called the discount rate), would grow to become some future amount in a specified number of time periods. (p. 167)

net present value (NPV) The sum of the present values of expected future cash flows from an investment, minus the cost of that investment. (p. 168)

CHAPTER 10 LEARNING OBJECTIVES / KEY TERMS

10-1 **Explain the role of financial markets in the U.S. economy and identify the key players in these markets.** Financial markets transfer funds from savers (individuals and organizations willing to defer the use of some of their income in order to earn a financial return and build their wealth) to borrowers (individuals and organizations that need additional funds to achieve their financial goals in the current time period). Key players in these markets included depository institutions and nondepository institutions. Depository institutions, such as banks, credit unions, and savings and loan associations, accept checking or savings deposits (or both) from individuals, businesses, and other institutions and then lend these funds to borrowers. Nondepository institutions include institutional investors, such as mutual funds, pension funds, and insurance companies, that don't accept deposits but amass financial capital from other sources and use these funds to acquire a portfolio of many different assets.

financial markets Markets that transfer funds from savers to borrowers. (p. 170)

depository institution A financial intermediary that obtains funds by accepting checking and savings deposits and then lending those funds to borrowers. (p. 171)

credit union A depository institution that is organized as a cooperative, meaning that it is owned by its depositors. (p. 171)

savings and loan association A depository institution that has traditionally obtained most of its funds by accepting savings deposits, which have been used primarily to make mortgage loans. (p. 172)

securities broker A financial intermediary who acts as an agent for investors who want to buy and sell financial securities. Brokers earn commissions and fees for the services they provide. (p. 173)

securities dealer A financial intermediary who participates directly in securities markets, buying and selling stocks and other securities for its own account. (p. 173)

investment bank A financial intermediary that specializes in helping firms raise financial capital by issuing securities in primary markets. (p. 173)

10-2 **Identify the key laws that govern the way financial markets operate and explain the impact of each law.** The Federal Reserve Act of 1913 created the Federal Reserve System (called the Fed) and gave it the primary responsibility for regulating our nation's banking system. The Banking Act of 1933 (also called the Glass-Steagall Act) established the Federal Deposit Insurance Corporation, which insures deposits in banks and other depository institutions. It also prohibited banks from dealing in securities or selling insurance. The Securities Act of 1933 regulated the way corporate securities were issued, and the Securities Exchange Act of 1934 established the Securities and Exchange Commission and gave it the authority to oversee securities markets. The Financial Services Modernization Act of 1999 reversed the Glass-Steagall Act's prohibition of banks selling insurance or securities. The Dodd-Frank Act of 2010 gave the Fed the authority to regulate nondepository financial institutions. It also established the Financial Stability Oversight Council to identify emerging risks in the financial sector so that action could be taken to rein in risky practices before they lead to a crisis.

Federal Reserve Act of 1913 The law that established the Federal Reserve System as the central bank of the United States. (p. 174)

Banking Act of 1933 The law that established the Federal Deposit Insurance Corporation (FDIC) to insure bank deposits. It also prohibited commercial banks from selling insurance or acting as investment banks. (p. 174)

Securities Act of 1933 The first major federal law regulating the securities industry. It requires firms issuing new stock in a public offering to file a registration statement with the SEC. (p. 175)

Securities and Exchange Act of 1934 A federal law dealing with securities regulation that established the Securities and Exchange Commission to regulate and oversee the securities industry. (p. 175)

Securities and Exchange Commission The federal agency with primary responsibility for regulating the securities industry. (p. 175)

Financial Services Modernization Act of 1999 An act that overturned the section of the Banking Act of 1933 that prohibited commercial banks from selling insurance or performing the functions of investment banks. (p. 175)

10-3 **Describe and compare the major types of securities that are traded in securities markets.** Common stock represents basic ownership in a corporation. Common stockholders have voting rights and the right to receive a dividend if the corporation's board declares one. Some corporations also issue preferred stock. Preferred stockholders don't normally have voting rights but are entitled to receive their stated dividend before any dividend can be paid to common stockholders and have a preferred claim on assets over common stockholders should the company go bankrupt. Bonds are formal IOUs issued by corporations or government entities. Firms must pay interest on the bonds they issue and must pay the face value of the bond to the bondholder when the bond matures.

common stock The basic form of ownership in a corporation. (p. 176)

capital gain The return on an asset that results when its market price rises above the price the investor paid for it. (p. 176)

preferred stock A type of stock that gives its holder preference over common stockholders in terms of dividends and claims on assets. (p. 177)

bond A formal debt instrument issued by a corporation or government entity. (p. 177)

maturity date The date when a bond will come due. (p. 177)

par value (of a bond) The value of a bond at its maturity; what the issuer promises to pay the bondholder when the bond matures. (p. 177)

coupon rate The interest paid on a bond, expressed as a percentage of the bond's par value. (p. 178)

current yield The amount of interest earned on a bond, expressed as a percentage of the bond's current market price. (p. 178)

© Cengage

convertible security A bond or share of preferred stock that gives its holder the right to exchange it for a stated number of shares of common stock. (p. 178)

financial diversification A strategy of investing in a wide variety of securities in order to reduce risk. (p. 179)

mutual fund An institutional investor that raises funds by selling shares to investors and uses the accumulated funds to buy a portfolio of many different securities. (p. 179)

net asset value per share The value of a mutual fund's securities and cash holdings minus any liabilities, divided by

the number of shares of the fund outstanding. (p. 179)

exchange traded fund (ETF) Shares traded on securities markets that represent the legal right of ownership over part of a basket of individual stock certificates or other securities. (p. 180)

10-4 **Explain how securities are issued in the primary market and traded on secondary markets.** Primary securities markets are where corporations sell newly issued securities to raise financial capital. In public offerings, the securities are sold to the general public. In private placements, the securities are sold to a select group of accredited investors. Previously issued securities are traded in secondary securities markets. There are two types of secondary markets: securities exchanges and the over-the-counter market. Securities exchanges list and trade the stocks of corporations that satisfy their listing requirements and pay listing fees. Stocks of corporations not listed on an exchange are traded in the over-the-counter market through a network of securities dealers.

primary securities market The market where newly issued securities are traded. The primary market is where the firms that issue securities raise additional financial capital. (p. 180)

secondary securities market The market where previously issued securities are traded. (p. 181)

public offering A primary market issue in which new securities are offered to any investors who are willing and able to purchase them. (p. 181)

private placement A primary market issue that is negotiated between the issuing corporation and a small group of accredited investors. (p. 181)

initial public offering (IPO) The first time a company issues stock that may be bought by the general public. (p. 181)

underwriting An arrangement under which an investment banker agrees to purchase all shares of a public offering at an agreed-upon price. (p. 181)

registration statement A long, complex document that firms must file with the SEC when they sell securities through a public offering. (p. 181)

accredited investor An organization or individual investor who meets certain criteria established by the SEC and so qualifies to invest in unregistered securities. (p. 181)

stock (or securities) exchange An organized venue for trading stocks and

other securities that meet its listing requirements. (p. 182)

market makers Securities dealers that make a commitment to continuously offer to buy and sell the stock of a specific corporation listed on the NASDAQ exchange or traded in the OTC market. (p. 183)

over-the-counter (OTC) market The market where securities that are not listed on exchanges are traded. (p. 183)

electronic communications network (ECN) An automated, computerized securities trading system that automatically matches buyers and sellers, executing trades quickly and allowing trading when securities exchanges are closed. (p. 183)

10-5 **Compare several strategies that investors use to invest in securities.** Income investors choose securities, such as bonds and preferred stocks, that generate relatively steady and predictable flows of income. Market timers try to time their purchases of specific stocks to buy low and sell high on a short-term basis. Value investors try to find undervalued stocks. Growth investors often look for stocks in small companies with innovative products and the potential for exceptional growth. Investors using a buy-and-hold approach invest in a broad portfolio of securities with the intention of holding them for a long period of time.

market order An order telling a broker to buy or sell a specific security at the best currently available price. (p. 184)

limit order An order to a broker to buy a specific stock only if its price is below a

certain level, or to sell a specific stock only if its price is above a certain level. (p. 185)

10-6 **Interpret the information provided in the stock quotes available on financial websites.** Investors can track broad movements in stock prices by following stock indices such as the Dow Jones Industrial or the Standard & Poor's 500. Many websites provide in-depth information about individual stocks, including each stock's current price, volume (number of shares traded), market capitalization (total market value of all outstanding shares), earnings per share, and other key statistics.

stock index A statistic that tracks how the prices of a specific set of stocks have changed. (p. 187)

Dow Jones Industrial Average (DJIA) An index that tracks stock prices of 30 large, well-known U.S. corporations. (p. 187)

Standard & Poor's 500 A stock index based on prices of 500 major U.S. corporations in a variety of industries and market sectors. (p. 187)

© Cengage

CHAPTER 11 LEARNING OBJECTIVES / KEY TERMS

11-1 **Discuss the objectives, the process, and the scope of marketing.** Marketing means delivering value to your customers with the goal of satisfying their needs and achieving long-term profitability for your organization. Goods and services meet customer needs by providing "utility" (or satisfaction) on an ongoing basis. Marketing has moved well beyond the scope of traditional goods and services, to include people, places, events, and ideas. Much nontraditional marketing involves both public and private not-for-profit organizations, which measure their success in nonmonetary terms. Over the past century, marketing has evolved through a number of phases. The marketing era gave birth to the marketing concept, which is still in force today: a philosophy that customer satisfaction—now and in the future—should be the central focus of the entire organization.

The Evolution of Marketing

The focus of marketing has evolved over time.

While individual firms differ in their approach to marketing, the prevailing view at leading-edge firms has changed over time as shown here.

marketing An organizational function and a set of processes for creating, communicating, and delivering value to customers and for managing customer relationships in ways that benefit the organization and its stakeholders. (p. 190)

utility The ability of goods and services to satisfy consumer "wants."(p. 190)

marketing concept A business philosophy that makes customer satisfaction—now and in the future—the central focus of the entire organization. (p. 193)

11-2 **Identify the role of the customer in marketing.** Successful marketers always place the customer front and center, with a focus on customer relationship management: acquiring, maintaining, and growing profitable customer relationships by consistently delivering unmatched value. Effective data management and one-on-one personalization are key customer relationship tools. The result of an effective customer-first strategy is loyal customers, who may even be willing to pay more for your product.

customer relationship management (CRM) The ongoing process of acquiring, maintaining, and growing profitable customer relationships by delivering unmatched value. (p. 194)

value A customer perception that a product has a better relationship than its competitors between the cost and the benefits. (p. 194)

customer satisfaction When customers perceive that a good or service delivers value above and beyond their expectations. (p. 194)

customer loyalty When customers buy a product from the same supplier again and again—sometimes paying even more for it than they would for a competitive product. (p. 195)

11-3 **Explain each element of marketing strategy.** Marketing strategy essentially involves determining who your *target audience* is and how you will reach it. Choosing the right target begins with *market segmentation*: dividing your market into segments, or groups, of people with similar characteristics. Then you need to determine the best *marketing mix*—the most effective combination of product, pricing, distribution, and promotion strategies to reach your target market. Finally, you must continually monitor each element of the *marketing environment* to ensure that you respond quickly and effectively to change.

Marketing Strategy

marketing plan A formal document that defines marketing objectives and the specific strategies for achieving those objectives. (p. 195)

market segmentation Dividing potential customers into groups of similar people, or segments. (p. 195)

target market The group of people who are most likely to buy a particular product. (p. 195)

consumer marketers (also known as business-to-consumer or B2C) Marketers who direct their efforts toward people who are buying products for personal consumption. (p. 196)

business marketers (also known as business-to-business or B2B) Marketers who direct their efforts toward people who are buying products to use either directly or indirectly to produce other products. (p. 196)

demographic segmentation Dividing the market into smaller groups based on measurable characteristics about people, such as age, income, ethnicity, and gender. (p. 196)

geographic segmentation Dividing the market into smaller groups based on where consumers live. This process can incorporate countries, cities, or population density as key factors. (p. 196)

© Cengage

psychographic segmentation
Dividing the market into smaller groups based on consumer attitudes, interests, values, and lifestyles. (p. 196)

behavioral segmentation Dividing the market based on how people behave toward various products. This category includes both the benefits that consumers seek from products and how consumers use the products. (p. 197)

marketing mix The blend of marketing strategies for product, price, distribution, and promotion. (p. 197)

environmental scanning The process of continually collecting information from the external marketing environment. (p. 200)

market share The percentage of a market controlled by a given marketer. (p. 200)

11-4 **Describe the consumer and business decision-making process.** Understanding how customers make decisions will help you meet their needs. When people buy for their own personal consumption, a number of forces influence them, including cultural, social, personal, and psychological factors. For high-risk decisions, they generally follow a decision process, but for low-risk decisions, they often just follow rules of thumb. When people buy for business, they typically are more methodical, driven by product specifications.

consumer behavior Description of how people act when they are buying, using, and discarding goods and services for their own personal consumption. Consumer behavior also explores the reasons behind people's actions. (p. 201)

cognitive dissonance Consumer discomfort with a purchase decision, typically for a higher-priced item. (p. 202)

business buyer behavior Describes how people act when they are buying products to use either directly or indirectly to produce other products. (p. 202)

11-5 **Discuss the key elements of marketing research.** Marketing research involves gathering, interpreting, and applying information to uncover opportunities and challenges. Primary and secondary data offer complementary strengths and weaknesses. Observation research tools involve gathering data without interacting with the research subjects, while survey tools involve asking research subjects direct questions.

marketing research The process of gathering, interpreting, and applying information to uncover marketing opportunities and challenges, and to make better marketing decisions. (p. 202)

secondary data Existing data that marketers gather or purchase for a research project. (p. 204)

primary data New data that marketers compile for a specific research project. (p. 204)

observation research Marketing research that does not require the researcher to interact with the research subject. (p. 204)

survey research Marketing research that requires the researcher to interact with the research subject. (p. 205)

11-6 **Explain the roles of social responsibility and technology in marketing.** The surging social responsibility movement and dramatic advances in technology have had a significant influence on marketing. In addition to seeking long-term profitability, socially responsible marketers actively contribute to meeting the needs of the broader community. Key areas of concern include fair labor practices (especially in foreign markets), environmentalism, and involvement in local communities. The digital boom of the past decade has revolutionized marketing, shifting the balance of power from producers to consumers. The Internet has also created marketing opportunities, helping businesses realize new efficiencies, facilitating more customized service, and generating new promotional opportunities.

green marketing Developing and promoting environmentally sound products and practices to gain a competitive edge. (p. 205)

mass customization The creation of products tailored for individual consumers on a mass basis. (p. 206)

CHAPTER 12 LEARNING OBJECTIVES / KEY TERMS

12-1 Explain "product" and identify product classifications.

A product can be anything that a company offers to satisfy consumer needs and wants; the possibilities include not only physical goods but also services and ideas. A product also includes all the attributes that consumers associate with it, such as name, image, and guarantees. Goods and services fall along a spectrum from pure goods to pure services. Most products fall somewhere between the two ends, incorporating elements of both goods and services. Products typically encompass three layers: the core benefit, the actual physical good or delivered service, and the augmented product. Customers buy consumer products for personal consumption, and they buy business products to contribute to the production of other products.

product Anything that an organization offers to satisfy consumer needs and wants, including both goods and services. (p. 208)

pure goods Products that do not include any services. (p. 210)

pure services Products that do not include any goods. (p. 210)

consumer products Products purchased for personal use or consumption. (p. 210)

business products Products purchased to use either directly or indirectly in the production of other products. (p. 210)

12-2 Describe product differentiation and the key elements of product planning.

Product differentiation means making your product different from—and better than—the competition. Product planning offers the opportunity to achieve differentiation through elements such as better quality, better features and benefits, and a stronger brand. These elements are the foundation of an effective product strategy.

product differentiation The attributes that make a good or service different from other products that compete to meet the same or similar customer needs. (p. 212)

quality level How well a product performs its core functions. (p. 213)

product consistency How reliably a product delivers its promised level of quality. (p. 213)

product features The specific characteristics of a product. (p. 213)

customer benefit The advantage that a customer gains from specific product features. (p. 213)

product line A group of products that are closely related to each other, either in terms of how they work or the customers they serve. (p. 214)

product mix The total number of product lines and individual items sold by a single firm. (p. 214)

cannibalization When a producer offers a new product that takes sales away from its existing products. (p. 214)

brand A product's identity—including product name, symbol, design, reputation, and image—that sets it apart from other players in the same category. (p. 214)

brand equity The overall value of a brand to an organization. (p. 214)

line extensions Similar products offered under the same brand name. (p. 215)

brand extension A new product, in a new category, introduced under an existing brand name. (p. 215)

licensing Purchasing the right to use another company's brand name or symbol. (p. 215)

cobranding When established brands from different companies join forces to market the same product. (p. 215)

national brands Brands that the producer owns and markets. (p. 215)

store brands Brands that the retailer both produces and distributes (also called private-label brands). (p. 216)

12-3 Discuss innovation and the product life cycle.

Innovation can range from small modifications of existing products to brand-new products that change how people live. Either way, for a business to thrive over the long term, effective new product development is vital. The new product development process is meant to streamline product development. The six steps include idea generation, idea screening, analysis, development, testing, and commercialization. After introduction, successful new products move through a life cycle. During the *introduction* phase, a product first hits the market. Marketing generates awareness and trial. During the *growth* phase, sales rise rapidly and profits usually peak. Competitors enter the category. Marketing focuses on gaining new customers. During the *maturity* phase, sales usually peak, while profits fall. Competition intensifies as growth stops. Marketing aims to capture customers from competitors. During the *decline* phase, sales and profits drop. Marketers consider discontinuing products.

product life cycle A pattern of sales and profits that typically changes over time. (p. 219)

12-4 Analyze and explain promotion and integrated marketing communications.

Promotion is marketing communication that influences consumers by informing, persuading, and reminding them about products. The most effective promotion builds strong, ongoing relationships between customers and companies. The current promotional environment is changing rapidly. Thanks to technology, consumers have more control over how, when, and even *if* they receive promotional messages. Media have splintered across entertainment options, and consumer viewing patterns have changed. In response, marketers are seeking increasingly creative means to reach their target customers. Their goal is to zero in on the right customers, at the right time, with the right message. The goal of integrated marketing communications (IMC) is to ensure that consumers receive a unified, focused

© Cengage

message regardless of the message source. To make this happen, marketers must break through the clutter, coordinating their messages through various promotional vehicles. Everyone who manages the marketing messages must have information about the customer, the product, the competition, the market, and the strategy of the organization. And clearly, solid teamwork is crucial. The result of effective IMC is a relevant, coherent image in the minds of target customers.

promotion Marketing communication designed to influence consumer purchase decisions through information, persuasion, and reminders. (p. 220)

integrated marketing communication The coordination of marketing messages through every promotional vehicle to communicate a unified impression about a product. (p. 221)

12-5 Discuss development of the promotional message. The promotional message should be a big idea—a meaningful, believable, and distinctive concept that cuts through the clutter. Finding the big idea begins with the positioning statement—a brief statement that articulates how you want your target market to envision your product relative to the competition. A creative development team—often spearheaded by advertising agency professionals—uses the positioning statement as a springboard for finding a big idea. The ideas themselves are typically based on either a rational or an emotional premise, with humor as a recurrent favorite.

positioning statement A brief statement that articulates how the marketer would like the target market to envision a product relative to the competition. (p. 221)

12-6 Discuss the promotional mix and the various promotional tools. The promotional mix is the combination of promotional tools that a marketer chooses to best communicate the big idea to the target audience. In today's rapidly changing promotional environment, new promotional tools have emerged, and secondary promotional tools have burst into the mainstream. Examples include Internet advertising (especially paid search advertising, search engine optimization), social media, product placement, advergaming, buzz marketing, and sponsorships. Yet traditional promotional tools retain enormous clout in terms of both spending and impact on the market. Mainstream advertising has split among a growing array of media options. Sales promotion, designed to stimulate immediate sales, represents a quickly growing area. Public relations, designed to generate positive, unpaid media stories about a company or its products, also aims to boost brand awareness and credibility. Personal selling, designed to close sales and build relationships, continues to play a dominant role in the promotional mix. Selecting the right mix of promotional tools poses an ongoing challenge for many marketers.

promotional channels Specific marketing communication vehicles, including traditional tools, such as advertising, sales promotion, direct marketing, and personal selling, and newer tools such as product placement, advergaming, and Internet minimovies. (p. 223)

product placement The paid integration of branded products into movies, television, and other media. (p. 224)

advergaming Video games created as a marketing tool, usually with brand awareness as the core goal. (p. 225)

buzz marketing The active stimulation of word of mouth via unconventional, and often relatively low-cost, tactics. Other terms for buzz marketing are "guerrilla marketing" and "viral marketing."(p. 226)

sponsorship A deep association between a marketer and a partner (usually a cultural or sporting event), which involves promotion of the sponsor in exchange for either payment or the provision of goods. (p. 227)

advertising Paid, nonpersonal communication, designed to influence a target audience with regard to a product, service, organization, or idea. (p. 227)

sales promotion Marketing activities designed to stimulate immediate sales activity through specific short-term programs aimed at either consumers or distributors. (p. 228)

consumer promotion Marketing activities designed to generate immediate consumer sales, using tools such as premiums, promotional products, samples, coupons, rebates, and displays. (p. 228)

trade promotion Marketing activities designed to stimulate wholesalers and retailers to push specific products more aggressively over the short term. (p. 230)

public relations (PR) The ongoing effort to create positive relationships with all of a firm's different "publics," including customers, employees, suppliers, the community, the general public, and the government. (p. 230)

publicity Unpaid stories in the media that influence perceptions about a company or its products. (p. 230)

personal selling The person-to-person presentation of products to potential buyers. (p. 231)

push strategy A marketing approach that involves motivating distributors to heavily promote—or "push"—a product to the final consumers, usually through heavy trade promotion and personal selling. (p. 233)

pull strategy A marketing approach that involves creating demand from the ultimate consumers so that they "pull" your products through the distribution channels by actively seeking them. (p. 233)

13-1 Define distribution and differentiate between channels of distribution and physical distribution. Distribution is the element of the marketing mix that involves getting the right product to the right customers in the right place at the right time. A channel of distribution is the path that a product takes from the producer to the consumer, while physical distribution is the actual movement of products along that path. Distributors add value by reducing the number of transactions—and the associated costs—required for goods to flow from producers to consumers. Distributors can also add a range of different utilities:

- *Form utility:* Provides customer satisfaction by converting inputs into finished products.
- *Time utility:* Adds value by making products available at a convenient time for consumers.
- *Place utility:* Satisfies customer needs by providing the right products in the right place.
- *Ownership utility:* Adds value by making it easier for customers to actually possess the goods and services that they purchase.
- *Information utility:* Boosts customer satisfaction by providing helpful information.
- *Service utility:* Adds value by providing fast, friendly, personalized service.

distribution strategy A plan for delivering the right product to the right person at the right place at the right time. (p. 236)

channel of distribution The network of organizations and processes that links producers to consumers. (p. 236)

physical distribution The actual, physical movement of products along the distribution pathway. (p. 236)

direct channel A distribution process that links the producer and the customer with no intermediaries. (p. 236)

channel intermediaries Distribution organizations that facilitate the movement of products from the producer to the consumer. (p. 237)

retailers Distributors that sell products directly to the ultimate users, typically in small quantities, that are stored and merchandized on the premises. (p. 239)

wholesalers Distributors that buy products from producers and sell them to other businesses or nonfinal users such as hospitals, nonprofits, and the government. (p. 239)

13-2 Describe the various types of wholesale distributors. Wholesalers buy products from the producer and sell them to other businesses and organizations. The two key categories of wholesalers are:

- *Merchant wholesalers,* who take legal title to the goods they distribute. Full-service merchant wholesalers provide a wide array of services, whereas limited-service merchant wholesalers offer more focused services.
- *Agents and brokers,* who connect buyers and sellers in exchange for commissions but without taking legal ownership of the goods they distribute.

independent wholesaling businesses Independent distributors that buy products from a range of different businesses and sell those products to a range of different customers. (p. 239)

merchant wholesalers Independent distributors who take legal possession, or title, of the goods they distribute. (p. 239)

agents/brokers Independent distributors who do not take title of the goods they distribute (even though they may take physical possession on a temporary basis before distribution). (p. 239)

13-3 Discuss strategies and trends in store and nonstore retailing. Retailers are the final stop before the consumer on the distribution path. The two main retail categories are *store* and *nonstore*, but the line between the two has blurred as more and more retailers are pursuing a multichannel approach, with online and offline outlets supporting each other. Key nonstore retail approaches include online retailing, direct-response retailing, direct selling, and vending. As competition intensifies, a growing segment of retailers (both store and nonstore) have distinguished themselves by offering their customers an entertainment-like experience.

multichannel retailing Providing multiple distribution channels for consumers to buy a product. (p. 240)

wheel of retailing A classic distribution theory that suggests that retail firms and retail categories become more upscale as they go through their life cycles. (p. 242)

multilevel marketing (MLM) Involves hiring independent contractors to sell products to their personal network of friends and colleagues and to recruit new salespeople in return for a percentage of their commissions. (p. 243)

13-4 Explain the key factors in physical distribution. As marketers manage the movement of products through the supply chain, they must make decisions regarding each of the following factors:

- *Warehousing:* How many warehouses do we need? Where should we locate our warehouses?
- *Materials handling:* How should we move products within our facilities? How can we best balance efficiency with effectiveness?
- *Inventory control:* How much inventory should we keep on hand? How should we store and distribute it? What about taxes and insurance?

CHAPTER **REVIEW**

CHAPTER 13 LEARNING OBJECTIVES / KEY TERMS

- *Order processing:* How should we manage incoming and outgoing orders? What would be most efficient for our customers and suppliers?
- *Customer service:* How can we serve our customers most effectively? How can we reduce waiting times and facilitate interactions?
- *Transportation:* How can we move products most efficiently through the supply chain? What are the key tradeoffs?

Elements of the Supply Chain

Raw Materials

Logistics (transportation, coordination, etc.)

Warehouse/Storage

Production

Warehouse/Storage

Logistics (transportation, coordination, etc.)

Distributors—Marketing and Sales

supply chain All organizations, processes, and activities involved in the flow of goods from the raw materials to the final consumer. (p. 243)

supply chain management (SCM) Planning and coordinating the movement of products along the supply chain, from the raw materials to the final consumers. (p. 243)

logistics A subset of supply chain management that focuses largely on the tactics involved in moving products along the supply chain. (p. 243)

modes of transportation The various transportation options—such as planes, trains, and railroads—for moving products through the supply chain. (p. 244)

13-5 **Outline core pricing objectives and strategies.** Many marketers continually evaluate and refine their pricing strategies to ensure that they meet their goals. Even the goals themselves may shift in response to the changing market. Key objectives and strategies include:

- Building profitability
- Driving volume
- Meeting the competition
- Creating prestige

penetration pricing A new product pricing strategy that aims to capture as much of the market as possible through rock-bottom prices. (p. 245)

everyday-low pricing (EDLP) Long-term discount pricing, designed to achieve profitability through high sales volume. (p. 245)

high/low pricing A pricing strategy designed to drive traffic to retail stores by special sales on a limited number of products, and higher everyday prices on others. (p. 246)

loss-leader pricing Closely related to high/low pricing, loss-leader pricing means pricing a handful of items—or loss

leaders—temporarily below cost to drive traffic. (p. 246)

skimming pricing A new product pricing strategy that aims to maximize profitability by offering new products at a premium price. (p. 247)

13-6 **Discuss pricing in practice, including the role of consumer perceptions.** While most marketers are familiar with economics, they often don't have the information they need to apply the theories to their specific pricing strategies. Because of those limitations, most companies *consider* market-based factors—especially customer expectations and competitive prices—but they *rely* on cost-based pricing: What should we charge to cover our costs and make a profit? Common approaches

include breakeven analysis and fixed margin pricing. Many marketers also account for consumer perceptions, especially the link between price and perceived quality, and odd pricing. If no other information is available, consumers will often assume that higher-priced products are higher quality. *Odd pricing* means ending prices in dollars and cents rather than round numbers (e.g., $999.99 versus $1,000) in order to create a perception of greater value.

breakeven analysis The process of determining the number of units a firm must sell to cover all costs. (p. 248)

profit margin The gap between the cost and the price of an item on a per-product basis. (p. 249)

odd pricing The practice of ending prices in numbers below even dollars and cents in order to create a perception of greater value. (p. 250)

© Cengage

CHAPTER 14 LEARNING OBJECTIVES / KEY TERMS

14-1 **Discuss the role of management and its importance to organizational success.** The formal definition of management is to achieve the goals of an organization through planning, organizing, leading, and controlling organizational resources. Managers provide vision for their company and inspire others to follow their lead. Most medium-size and large companies have three basic management levels: top management, middle management, and first-line (or supervisory) management. Managers must draw on a wide range of skills, but most of their abilities cluster into three key categories: *technical skills, human skills,* and *conceptual skills*. All three skill sets are essential for management success, but in different proportions at each managerial level.

management Achieving the goals of an organization through planning, organizing, leading, and controlling organizational resources including people, money, and time. (p. 252)

planning Determining organizational goals and action plans for how to achieve those goals. (p. 252)

organizing Determining a structure for both individual jobs and the overall organization. (p. 252)

leading Directing and motivating people to achieve organizational goals. (p. 252)

controlling Monitoring performance and making adjustments as needed. (p. 252)

top management Managers who set the overall direction of the firm, articulating a vision, establishing priorities, and allocating time, money, and other resources. (p. 253)

middle management Managers who supervise lower-level managers and report to a higher-level manager. (p. 253)

first-line (supervisory) management Managers who directly supervise nonmanagement employees. (p. 253)

technical skills Expertise in a specific functional area or department. (p. 254)

human skills The ability to work effectively with and through other people in a range of different relationships. (p. 254)

conceptual skills The ability to grasp a big-picture view of the overall organization, the relationships among its various parts, and its fit in the broader competitive environment. (p. 254)

14-2 **Explain key theories and current practices of motivation.** Research suggests that people's thoughts and feelings play a vital role in motivation. Key theories that incorporate this perspective include Maslow's Hierarchy of Needs Theory, Theory X and Theory Y, job enrichment, expectancy theory, and equity theory. In today's business environment, leading-edge firms nourish distinctive, positive cultures that tend to create productive employees who are deeply attached to both their work and their companies. Many also focus on training and education, which are especially motivating for the growing cadre of employees who identify themselves based on their field of expertise rather than their organization.

Maslow's hierarchy of needs theory A motivation theory that suggests that human needs fall into a hierarchy and that as each need is met, people become motivated to meet the next-highest need in the pyramid. (p. 256)

Theory X and Theory Y A motivation theory that suggests that management attitudes toward workers fall into two opposing categories based on management assumptions about worker capabilities and values. (p. 256)

job enrichment The creation of jobs with more meaningful content, under the assumption that challenging, creative work will motivate employees. (p. 256)

expectancy theory A motivation theory that concerns the relationship among individual effort, individual performance, and individual reward. (p. 257)

equity theory A motivation theory that proposes that perceptions of fairness directly affect worker motivation. (p. 257)

14-3 **Outline the categories of business planning and explain strategic planning.** The four main categories of business planning are *strategic planning, tactical planning, operational planning,* and *contingency planning*. Strategic planning, handled by top managers, sets the broad direction of the organization, typically over a five-year horizon. Strategic planning guides the entire planning process, since all other plans—and most major management decisions—stem from the strategic plan. Given fierce competition and often-unpredictable change, most large firms revise their strategic plans on a yearly basis.

strategic planning High-level, long-term planning that establishes a vision for the company, defines long-term objectives and priorities, determines broad action steps, and allocates resources. (p. 259)

tactical planning More specific, shorter-term planning that applies strategic plans to specific functional areas. (p. 260)

operational planning Very specific, short-term planning that applies tactical plans to daily, weekly, and monthly operations. (p. 260)

CHAPTER REVIEW / KEY TERMS

CHAPTER 14 LEARNING OBJECTIVES

contingency planning Planning for unexpected events, usually involving a range of scenarios and assumptions that differ from the assumptions behind the core plans. (p. 260)

mission The definition of an organization's purpose, values, and core goals, which provides the framework for all other plans. (p. 261)

SWOT analysis A strategic planning tool that helps management evaluate an organization in terms of internal strengths and weakness, and external opportunities and threats. (p. 261)

strategic goals Concrete benchmarks that managers can use to measure performance in each key area of the organization. (p. 262)

strategies Action plans that help the organization achieve its goals by forging the best fit between the firm and the environment. (p. 262)

14-4 Discuss the organizing function of management. The organizing function of management means creating a logical structure for people, their jobs, and their patterns of interaction. In choosing the right structure for a specific company, management must consider many different factors, including the goals and strategies of the firm, its products, and its size. Management must also make decisions about the degree of centralization, the span of management control, and the type of departmentalization. Company structures tend to follow one of three different patterns: line organizations, line-and-staff organizations, and matrix organizations.

organization chart A visual representation of the company's formal structure. (p. 263)

degree of centralization The extent to which decision-making power is held by a small number of people at the top of the organization. (p. 264)

span of control Span of management; refers to the number of people a manager supervises. (p. 264)

departmentalization The division of workers into logical groups. (p. 264)

line organizations Organizations with a clear, simple chain of command from top to bottom. (p. 265)

line-and-staff organizations Organizations with line managers forming the primary chain of authority in the company, and staff departments working alongside line departments. (p. 265)

line managers Managers who supervise the functions that contribute directly to profitability: production and marketing. (p. 266)

staff managers Managers who supervise the functions that provide advice and assistance to the line departments. (p. 266)

matrix organizations Organizations with a flexible structure that brings together specialists from different areas of the company to work on individual projects on a temporary basis. (p. 266)

14-5 Explain the role of managerial leadership and the key leadership styles. Effective business leaders motivate others to achieve the goals of their organization. Most experts agree that true leaders are trustworthy, visionary, and inspiring. Other key leadership traits include empathy, courage, creativity, intelligence, fairness, and energy. While leaders have a range of different styles, three main approaches include autocratic, democratic, and free-rein. The best leaders tend to use all three approaches, shifting style in response to the needs of the followers and the situation.

autocratic leaders Leaders who hoard decision-making power for themselves and typically issue orders without consulting their followers. (p. 267)

democratic leaders Leaders who share power with their followers. While they still make final decisions, they typically solicit and incorporate input from their followers. (p. 267)

free-rein leaders Leaders who set objectives for their followers but give them freedom to choose how they will accomplish those goals. (p. 267)

14-6 Describe the management control process. Controlling means monitoring performance of the firm—or individuals within the firm—and making improvements when necessary. As the environment changes, plans change. And as plans change, the control process must change to ensure that the company achieves its goals. The control process has three main steps:

1. Establish clear performance standards.
2. Measure actual performance against standards.
3. Take corrective action if necessary.

15-1 **Explain the importance of human resources to business success.** A world-class workforce can lead straight to world-class performance. Human resource managers can directly contribute to that goal by recruiting top talent, promoting career development, and boosting organizational effectiveness. Yet human resource departments typically face numerous challenges in making this happen.

human resource (HR) management
The management function focused on maximizing the effectiveness of the workforce by recruiting world-class talent, promoting career development, and determining workforce strategies to boost organizational effectiveness. (p. 271)

15-2 **Discuss key human resource issues in today's economy.** As the economy and society continue to change rapidly, a number of issues have emerged that directly affect human resources. As the Great Recession struck, massive layoffs thrust human resources into turmoil. The growing wage gap between senior managers and the average employee has created tension for a number of stakeholders. Older workers have begun to retire, while younger workers bring optimism, open minds, technological know-how, and an unprecedented sense of entitlement to the workforce. Many women are leaving traditional jobs. Workers are actively seeking more flexibility and a better work–life balance. And the number of costly employee lawsuits has skyrocketed in the past couple of decades.

15-3 **Outline challenges and opportunities that the human resources function faces.** While HR workers tend to have strong people skills, many lack the business acumen to contribute directly to broad company objectives, and other departments often view HR as either irrelevant or adversarial. HR can respond to these issues by demonstrating that they understand the strategic goals of the company, the core customers, and the competition. The best HR departments use this knowledge to raise the value of the firm's human capital, which in turn increases the value of the firm itself.

15-4 **Discuss human resource planning and core human resources responsibilities.** Human resource planning objectives must flow from the company's master plan, and the HR strategies must reflect company priorities. The first step should be to determine where the firm currently stands in terms of human resources and to forecast future needs. Other key areas of focus follow:

- *Recruitment:* The key to recruitment is finding *qualified* candidates who fit well with the organization. The right people can come from either internal or external labor pools.

- *Selection:* Choosing the right person from a pool of candidates typically involves applications, interviews, tests, and references. The terms of the job offer itself play a role as well.

- *Training:* The training process begins with orientation but should continue throughout each employee's tenure. Options include on-the-job training, off-the-job training, and management development.

- *Evaluation:* Performance feedback should happen constantly. But most firms also use formal, periodic performance appraisals to make decisions about compensation, promotions, training, transfers, and terminations.

- *Compensation:* Compensation includes both pay and benefits. Interestingly, companies that offer higher compensation generally outperform their competitors in terms of total return to shareholders.

- *Separation:* Employees leave their jobs for both positive and negative reasons. When the separation is not voluntary—e.g., layoffs or termination—fairness and documentation are critical.

Considerations for Compensation

Variable Pay System
- Commission
- Bonuses
- Profit sharing
- Stock options
- Pay for knowledge

job analysis The examination of specific tasks that are assigned to each position, independent of who might be holding the job at any specific time. (p. 274)

job description An explanation of the responsibilities for a specific position. (p. 274)

job specifications The specific qualifications necessary to hold a particular position. (p. 274)

internal recruitment The process of seeking employees who are currently within the firm to fill open positions. (p. 275)

external recruitment The process of seeking new employees from outside the firm. (p. 275)

structured interviews An interviewing approach that involves developing a list of questions beforehand and asking the same questions in the same order to each candidate. (p. 276)

probationary period A specific time frame (typically three to six months) during which a new hire can prove his or her worth on the job before he or she becomes permanent. (p. 277)

contingent workers Employees who do not expect regular, full-time jobs, including temporary full-time workers, independent contractors, and temporary agency or contract agency workers. (p. 277)

orientation The first step in the training and development process, designed to introduce employees to the company culture and provide key administrative information. (p. 278)

on-the-job training A training approach that requires employees to simply begin their jobs—sometimes guided by more experienced employees—and to learn as they go. (p. 278)

apprenticeships Structured training programs that mandate that each beginner serve as an assistant to a fully trained worker before gaining full credentials to work in the field. (p. 278)

management development Programs to help current and potential executives develop the skills they need to move into leadership positions. (p. 279)

performance appraisal A formal feedback process that requires managers to give their subordinates feedback on a one-to-one basis, typically by comparing actual results to expected results. (p. 279)

compensation The combination of pay and benefits that employees receive in exchange for their work. (p. 280)

wages The pay that employees receive in exchange for the number of hours or days that they work. (p. 280)

salaries The pay that employees receive over a fixed period, most often weekly or monthly. (p. 280)

benefits Noncash compensation, including programs such as health insurance, vacation, and childcare. (p. 280)

cafeteria-style benefits An approach to employee benefits that gives all employees a set dollar amount that they must spend on company benefits, allocated however they wish within broad limitations. (p. 281)

flextime A scheduling option that allows workers to choose when they start and finish their workdays, as long as they complete the required number of hours. (p. 281)

compressed workweek A version of flextime scheduling that allows employees to work a full-time number of hours in less than the standard workweek. (p. 281)

telecommuting Working remotely—most often from home—and connecting to the office via phone lines and/or broadband networks. (p. 282)

15-5 **Explain the key federal legislation that affects human resources.** Perhaps the most influential piece of employment legislation is the Civil Rights Act of 1964. Title VII of this act prohibits discrimination in hiring, firing, compensation, apprenticeships, training, terms, conditions, or privileges of employment based on race, color, religion, sex, or national origin. Additional legislation prohibits discrimination based on pregnancy, age, and disability. The Equal Employment Opportunity Commission (EEOC) enforces the provisions of Title VII. Affirmative action programs—while controversial—have received support from the U.S. Supreme Court. And human resource managers must guard against sexual harassment in the organization, since it violates Title VII.

Civil Rights Act of 1964 Federal legislation that prohibits discrimination in hiring, firing, compensation, apprenticeships, training, terms, conditions, or privileges of employment based on race, color, religion, sex, or national origin. (p. 283)

Title VII A portion of the Civil Rights Act of 1964 that prohibits discrimination in hiring, firing, compensation, apprenticeships, training, terms, conditions, or privileges of employment based on race, color, religion, sex, or national origin for employers with 15 or more workers. (p. 283)

Equal Employment Opportunity Commission (EEOC) A federal agency designed to regulate and enforce the provisions of Title VII. (p. 283)

affirmative action Policies meant to increase employment and educational opportunities for minority groups—especially groups defined by race, ethnicity, or gender. (p. 284)

sexual harassment Workplace discrimination against a person based on his or her gender. (p. 284)

16-1 **Explain the basic elements of computer technology—including hardware, software, and networks—and describe key trends in each area.** Hardware is the physical equipment used to collect, store, organize, and process data and to distribute information. Software consists of computer programs that provide instructions to a computer. System software performs the critical functions necessary to operate the computer at the most basic level. Applications software helps users perform a desired task. Most firms (and many households) now use networks to enable users to communicate with each other quickly and efficiently and share both files and hardware resources. The Internet is a vast network of computer networks. The part of the Internet used most by the general public is the World Wide Web, which consists of billions of documents written and linked together using Hypertext Markup Language (HTML). Many organizations have developed intranets that have the same look and feel as the Internet but are limited to servers within an organization. Extranets are intranets that provide limited access to specific stakeholders, such as customers or suppliers.

hardware The physical tools and equipment used to collect, input, store, organize, and process data and to distribute information. (p. 287)

software Programs that provide instructions to a computer so that it can perform a desired task. (p. 288)

system software Software that performs the critical functions necessary to operate the computer at the most basic level. (p. 288)

applications software Software that helps a user perform a desired task. (p. 288)

Internet The world's largest computer network; essentially a network of computer networks all operating under a common set of rules that allow them to communicate with each other. (p. 288)

broadband Internet connection An Internet connection that is capable of transmitting large amounts of information very quickly. (p. 289)

Internet2 (I2) A new high-tech Internet with access limited to a consortium of member organizations (and other organizations these members sponsor). I2 utilizes technologies that give it a speed and capacity far exceeding the current Internet. (p. 289)

intranet A private network that has the look and feel of the Internet and is navigated using a web browser, but which limits access to a single firm's employees (or a single organization's members). (p. 291)

extranet An intranet that allows limited access to a selected group of stakeholders, such as suppliers or customers. (p. 291)

16-2 **Discuss the reasons for the increasing popularity of cloud computing.** Cloud computing means going beyond a company's firewall to store data and run applications using Internet-based resources. Cloud computing allows firms to obtain storage space, processing power, and software without investing heavily in internally owned IT resources. Cloud computing also makes it easier for people in different organizations to collaborate, since resources in the cloud are not tied to a specific type of hardware or operating system. But several high-profile security breaches of cloud services in recent years have caused serious concerns. However, for many organizations, moving to the cloud may actually increase data security.

cloud computing The use of Internet-based storage capacity, processing power, and computer applications to supplement or replace internally owned information technology resources. (p. 292)

16-3 **Describe how data become information and how decision support systems can provide high-quality information that helps managers make better decisions.** Data are raw facts and figures. Data become information when they are processed, organized, and presented in a way that is meaningful to a decision maker. Many companies develop decision support systems (DSS) that give managers access to large amounts of data and the processing power to convert the data into high-quality information. Some firms also develop expert systems to help decision makers when they must deal with problems beyond their expertise. To develop an expert system, programmers ask experts in the relevant area to provide step-by-step instructions describing how they solve a problem. The programmers then write software that mimics the expert's approach and guides the decision maker toward a good solution.

High-Quality Information Is	
1. Accurate	Free from errors and omissions
2. Relevant	Concerns issues that are important to the decision maker
3. Timely	Available in time to make a difference to the decision maker
4. Understandable	Presented in a way that allows decision makers to grasp its meaning and significance
5. Secure	Stored and presented in a way that prevents hackers and other unauthorized parties from obtaining access to it

data Raw, unprocessed facts and figures. (p. 293)

information Data that have been processed in a way that make them meaningful to their user. (p. 293)

database A file consisting of related data organized according to a logical system and stored on a hard drive or some other computer-accessible media. (p. 293)

decision support system (DSS) A system that gives managers access to large amounts of data and the processing power to convert these data into high-quality information, thus improving the decision-making process. (p. 294)

business intelligence system A sophisticated form of decision support system that helps decision makers discover information that was previously hidden. (p. 294)

data warehouse A large, organization-wide database that stores data in a centralized location. (p. 294)

© Cengage

data mining The use of sophisticated statistical and mathematical techniques to analyze vast amounts of data to discover hidden patterns and relationships, thus creating valuable information. (p. 294)

expert system (ES) A decision support system that helps managers make better decisions in an area where they lack expertise. (p. 295)

16-4

Explain how Internet-based technologies have changed business-to-consumer and business-to-business commerce. Information technology, and especially the Internet, has revolutionized the way firms interact with their customers in both the business-to-consumer (B2C) and business-to-business (B2B) markets. In the B2C market, the Internet has enabled firms to reach broader markets, advertise in new ways, and take customer relationship marketing to a new level. One strategy has been to create more interactive websites that encourage customers to collaborate and provide content—an approach referred to as *Web 2.0.* In the B2B market, e-marketplaces enable firms to negotiate with suppliers or customers more effectively and share information that leads to better coordination and collaboration.

e-commerce The marketing, buying, selling, and servicing of products over a network (usually the Internet). (p. 295)

business-to-consumer (B2C) e-commerce E-commerce in which businesses and final consumers interact. (p. 295)

business-to-business (B2B) e-commerce E-commerce in markets where businesses buy from and sell to other businesses. (p. 295)

Web 2.0 Websites that incorporate interactive and collaborative features to create a richer, more interesting, and more useful experience for their users. (p. 296)

viral marketing An Internet marketing strategy that tries to involve customers and others not employed by the seller in activities that help promote the product. (p. 297)

cybermediary An Internet-based firm that specializes in the secure electronic transfer of funds. (p. 298)

electronic bill presentment and payment A method of bill payment that makes it easy for the customer to make a payment, often by simply clicking on a payment option contained in an email. (p. 298)

e-marketplace A specialized Internet site where buyers and sellers engaged in business-to-business e-commerce can communicate and conduct business. (p. 298)

radio frequency identification (RFID) A technology that stores information on small microchips that can transmit the information when they are within range of a special reader. (p. 299)

16-5

Describe the problems posed by the rapid changes in Internet-based technologies, and explain ways to address these problems. The rapid development of Internet-based technologies has created several challenges and raised some controversial issues. The Internet has made it easier for malware such as computer viruses and spyware to land in your computer, undermining the security of your information and the stability of your system. Performing regular backups and keeping antivirus and antispyware software and operating systems updated can reduce these threats. Spam is unsolicited commercial email, usually sent to vast numbers of people with little regard for whether they have any interest in the message. Spam filters are available, but spammers are good at finding ways to fool the filters. Phishing and pharming are scams that use fake websites to trick people into divulging private information. One of the most controversial impacts of information technology has been the loss of personal privacy. Another issue involves intellectual property. The Internet makes it possible to share videos, music, and computer programs with large numbers of people, leading to a surge in the illegal sharing of copyrighted material.

malware A general term for malicious software, such as spyware, computer viruses, and worms. (p. 299)

spyware Software that is installed on a computer without the user's knowledge or permission to track the user's behavior. (p. 299)

computer virus Computer software that can be spread from one computer to another without the knowledge or permission of the computer users by attaching itself to emails or other files. (p. 300)

worm Malicious computer software that, unlike viruses, can spread on its own without being attached to other files. (p. 300)

spam Unsolicited email advertisements usually sent to very large numbers of recipients, many of whom may have no interest in the message. (p. 301)

phishing A scam in which official-looking emails are sent to individuals in an attempt to get them to divulge private information such as passwords, usernames, and account numbers. (p. 301)

pharming A scam that seeks to steal identities by routing Internet traffic to fake websites. (p. 301)

hacker A skilled computer user who uses his or her expertise to gain unauthorized access to the computer (or computer system) of others, sometimes with malicious intent. (p. 302)

firewall Software and/or hardware designed to prevent unwanted access to a computer or computer system. (p. 302)

intellectual property Property that is the result of creative or intellectual effort, such as books, musical works, inventions, and computer software. (p. 304)

17-1 **Define operations management and describe how the role of operations management has changed over the last five decades.** Operations management oversees all the activities involved in producing and distributing goods and services. When operations managers do their job well, their firms produce the *right* goods and services in the *right* quantities and distribute them to the *right* customers at the *right* time—all while keeping quality high and costs low.

Operations management has undergone profound changes over the past half century. One change has been a switch in focus from efficiency to effectiveness. *Efficiency* means achieving a goal at the *lowest cost*. *Effectiveness* means *creating value* by satisfying wants. Other key changes include more emphasis on the provision of services, a switch from mass production to customized production, a focus on global markets (and global competition), reliance on complex value chains, and recognition of the need to protect the environment.

operations management Managing all of the activities involved in creating value by producing goods and services and distributing them to customers. (p. 306)

efficiency Producing output or achieving a goal at the lowest cost. (p. 306)

effectiveness Using resources to create value by providing customers with goods and services that offer a better relationship between price and perceived benefits. (p. 307)

goods Tangible products. (p. 308)

services Intangible products. (p. 308)

17-2 **Discuss the key responsibilities of operations managers.** Operations managers often play a role in the design of products by helping designers understand the challenges and constraints involved in producing high-quality products on time and within budget. Once the design is finalized, operations managers must determine the best production processes to convert inputs into outputs; design a facility layout that creates an efficient flow of materials, parts, and work in process through the production process; select the best locations for facilities; make decisions about how much inventory to hold; determine how to allocate resources needed to complete complex projects; and manage value chains to coordinate the functions of all of the organizations and processes directly or indirectly involved in producing goods and services and distributing them to customers.

process A set of related activities that transform inputs into outputs, thus adding value. (p. 310)

inventory Stocks of goods or other items held by organizations. (p. 312)

critical path method (CPM) A project-management tool that illustrates the relationships among all the activities involved in completing a project and identifies the sequence of activities likely to take the longest to complete. (p. 313)

immediate predecessors Activities in a project that must be completed before some other specified activity can begin. (p. 314)

critical path The sequence of activities in a project that is expected to take the longest to complete. (p. 314)

value chain The network of relationships that channels the flow of inputs, information, and financial resources through all of the processes directly or indirectly involved in producing goods and services and distributing them to customers. (p. 315)

vertical integration Performance of processes internally that were previously performed by other organizations in a supply chain. (p. 315)

outsourcing Arranging for other organizations to perform supply chain functions that were previously performed internally. (p. 315)

offshoring Moving production or support processes to foreign countries. (p. 315)

enterprise resource planning (ERP) Software-based approach to integrate an organization's (and in the sophisticated versions, a value chain's) information flows. (p. 316)

17-3 **Describe how operations managers face the special challenges posed by the provision of services.** Customers often participate in the provision of services, so service providers have only limited control over ways in which their processes are carried out, how long they take to complete, and whether the result is satisfactory. A *servicescape* is the environment in which the customer and service provider interact. A well-designed servicescape can create a better service experience for both the customer and the provider.

Another challenge facing service providers involves determining the proper capacity of service facilities. If the capacity of a service facility is too small, customers facing long waits during peak periods may take their business elsewhere. But a facility large enough to handle peak capacity is more expensive to build and operate and may have substantial excess capacity during off-peak periods. Many service firms try to spread out demand so that big surges don't occur by offering price discounts to customers during off-peak times.

servicescape The environment in which a customer and service provider interact. (p. 316)

17-4 **Explain how changes in technology have revolutionized operations management.** Rapid changes in both machinery and equipment and in software and information technologies have revolutionized operations management. The biggest change in machinery and equipment has been the increasing use of automation, which means replacing human operation and control of machinery and equipment with programmed control. The development of software applications to allow computer-aided design (CAD), computer-aided engineering (CAE), and computer-aided manufacturing (CAM) has given firms the flexibility to design, test, and produce goods more quickly and efficiently than ever before. When these powerful software applications are integrated with robots and other automated equipment, the result is called *computer-integrated manufacturing*. This tight integration allows firms to produce customized goods quickly and at low cost, a process called *mass customization*.

automation Replacing human operation and control of machinery and equipment with some form of programmed control. (p. 318)

robot A reprogrammable machine that is capable of manipulating materials, tools, parts, and specialized devices in order to perform a variety of tasks. (p. 318)

computer-aided design (CAD) Drawing and drafting software that enables users to create and edit

blueprints and design drawings quickly and easily. (p. 318)

computer-aided engineering (CAE) Software that enables users to test, analyze, and optimize their designs. (p. 318)

computer-aided manufacturing (CAM) Software that takes the electronic design for a product and creates the programmed instructions that robots must follow to produce that product as efficiently as possible. (p. 319)

computer-aided design/computer-aided manufacturing (CAD/CAM) A combination of software that can be used to design output and send instructions to automated equipment to perform the steps needed to produce this output. (p. 319)

computer-integrated manufacturing (CIM) A combination of CAD/CAM software with flexible manufacturing systems to automate almost all steps involved in designing, testing, and producing a product. (p. 319)

17-5 **Describe the strategies operations managers have used to improve the quality of goods and services.** In recent years, U.S. firms have adopted programs such as total quality management (TQM) and Six Sigma to improve quality. TQM and Six Sigma both view quality improvement as a continuous process that is the responsibility of everyone within the organization. Both approaches also empower workers and make use of teams to solve quality-related problems. But Six

Sigma incorporates more specific quality goals and relies on more sophisticated techniques that require a higher degree of expertise.

Another way firms have tried to improve efficiency has been to launch programs designed to achieve certification or recognition from outside authorities. Two common approaches are to participate in the Baldrige National Quality Program and to seek certification under the International Organization for Standardization's ISO 9000 standards.

total quality management (TQM) An approach to quality improvement that calls for everyone within an organization to take responsibility for improving quality and emphasizes the need for a long-term commitment to continuous improvement. (p. 320)

poka-yokes Simple methods incorporated into a production process designed to eliminate or greatly reduce errors. (p. 321)

Six Sigma An approach to quality improvement characterized by very ambitious quality goals, extensive training of employees, and a long-term commitment to working on quality-related issues. (p. 321)

Baldrige National Quality Program A national program to encourage American firms to focus on quality improvement. (p. 321)

ISO 9000 A family of generic standards for quality management systems established by the International Organization for Standardization. (p. 322)

17-6 **Explain how lean and green practices can help both the organization and the environment.** *Lean production* refers to a set of strategies and practices that eliminate waste to make organizations more efficient, responsive, and flexible. Inventory control is one of the key areas where waste often occurs. Many lean firms use just-in-time production methods to minimize the amount of parts, work in process, and finished products they hold in inventory.

Many firms have also become "greener" by finding environmentally friendly ways to produce and distribute their goods and services. Green practices include designing facilities to be more energy efficient; using renewable energy; making use of recyclable materials; switching to paints, lubricants, cleaning fluids, and solvents that are less harmful to the environment; and providing labeling to help consumers find out which products are the most environmentally friendly.

lean production An approach to production that emphasizes the elimination of waste in all aspects of production processes. (p. 323)

just-in-time (JIT) production A production system that emphasizes the

production of goods to meet actual current demand, thus minimizing the need to hold inventories of finished goods and work in process at each stage of the supply chain. (p. 324)

ISO 14000 A family of generic standards for environmental management established by the International Organization for Standardization. (p. 325)

A-1 **Apply the principles of budgeting to your personal finances.** A budget is a detailed schedule that documents your expected financial inflows (revenues earned and received) and outflows (expenses incurred and paid) in order to determine your net inflow or outflow for a given period of time. You can use your budget to develop your financial plan and to monitor your progress toward achieving your financial goals. One key part of the budgeting process is accurate estimation of revenues. The other key to setting up a budget is to assess your expenses. Consideration should also be given to understanding factors that affect your spending habits. Certain types of expenditures, called "discretionary costs," can be adjusted fairly easily. Other expenditures, called "nondiscretionary costs," are more difficult to cut—at least in the short run.

budget (personal) A detailed forecast of financial inflows (income) and outflows (expenses) to determine your net inflow or outflow for a given period of time. (p. 328)

discretionary payments Expenditures for which the spender has significant control in terms of the amount and timing. (p. 330)

nondiscretionary payments Expenditures that the spender has little or no control over. (p. 330)

A-2 **Identify strategies to help build a sufficient savings.** A savings account is an interest-bearing account that is intended to satisfy obligations that cannot be handled by a checking account. Many financial experts suggest that your savings account should be able to cover six months of your expenses. One technique for establishing a sizable savings balance is to "pay yourself first." This technique is accomplished by automatically depositing a predetermined amount into your savings account with each paycheck.

savings account An interest-bearing account holding funds not needed to meet regular expenditures. (p. 331)

Federal Deposit Insurance Corporation (FDIC) An independent agency created by Congress to maintain stability and public confidence in the nation's financial system, primarily by insuring bank deposits. (p. 331)

A-3 **Explain the importance of using credit wisely.** Credit refers to your ability to obtain goods or resources without having to make immediate payment. One of the most important determinants of the amount of credit you can obtain is your credit score, which is a numerical indicator of your creditworthiness. Currently, the most commonly used credit scoring system is the Fair, Isaac and Company (FICO) scale. The FICO scale runs from 300 to 850.

A credit card allows its holder to make a purchase now and pay the credit card issuer later. Credit cards are more convenient and safer than carrying a lot of cash. They also make it easy to track your expenditures, since you have access to a monthly summary of charges. And many cards offer perks, such as discounts on certain products, extended warranties on purchases, or frequent-flier miles. Another benefit of the *responsible* use of credit cards is that it can improve your credit score by allowing you to establish a history of prompt payments.

One downside of having a credit card is that the "buy now, pay later" aspect of credit card use makes it hard for some people to maintain financial discipline. Another problem is that interest rates on unpaid card balances tend to be very high. Many card issuers also impose a variety of fees that can make a noticeable dent in your wallet. And making late payments or failing to pay what you owe can damage your credit history, hurting your chances of getting additional credit when you need it.

Before you accept a credit card, you should read and understand all of the main conditions for using that card. Among the major areas to consider are (1) the grace period, the period of time that you have to pay your balance before interest or fees are assessed, (2) the APR (annual interest rate on unpaid balances) as well as any other fees that may be assessed if a payment is not received within a grace period or if credit limits are exceeded when using the credit card, and (3) other fees, such as annual fees, over-the-credit-limit fees, and balance-transfer fees.

The first rule when you have credit card difficulties is to just stop using the card. Then commit to setting up (and sticking to) a budget and putting a consistent amount of money toward retiring the debt on that card. Another useful tip is to use cash or a debit card instead. Many people tend to spend more when they pay with a credit card than if they pay with cash.

credit Allows a borrower to buy a good or acquire an asset without making immediate payment and to repay the balance at a later time. (p. 331)

credit score A numerical measure of a consumer's creditworthiness. (p. 331)

credit card A card issued by a bank or finance company that allows the cardholder to make a purchase now and pay the credit card issuer later. (p. 332)

grace period The period of time that the credit card holder has to pay outstanding balances before interest or fees are assessed. (p. 332)

annual percentage rate (APR) The interest expense charged on a credit card, expressed as an annual percentage. (p. 332)

debit card A card issued by the bank that allows the customer to make purchases as if the transaction involved cash. In a debit card purchase, the customer's bank account is immediately reduced when the purchase is made. (p. 333)

© Cengage

WHAT FICO CREDIT SCORES MEAN

Score	Creditworthiness	Percentage of Consumers
Below 500	Very poor	5.7%
500–599	Poor to below average	18.5%
600–699	Below average to fair	22.3%
700–799	Fair to good	35%
800 or Better	Excellent	18.6%

A-4 Discuss key wealth-building principles and the financial instruments that may be part of a wealth-building strategy. Investing involves reducing consumption today in order to build future wealth. One key to investing is consistency—make it a habit to invest something every month. Another key is to begin as soon as possible, even if you can only invest a little. The time value of money says that a dollar invested today is worth more than a dollar invested later, because the earlier a dollar is invested, the longer it can earn a return.

There are several different types of financial assets you might want to consider. Each has its own advantages and disadvantages. One tradeoff involves risk and return. Investments that offer the potential for high returns tend to be riskier than investments that offer lower returns.

Corporate stock represents shares of ownership in a corporation. Investing in stock offers the possibility of receiving dividends, which are a distribution of a company's profits to its stockholders. It also offers the potential for capital gains, which are increases in the market value of stocks. However, neither dividends nor capital gains are guaranteed. *Corporate bonds* are formal IOUs issued by corporations. Bonds typically pay a stated rate of interest until they mature (come due). Once a bond matures, the issuer is obligated to pay the bondholder an amount known as the "principal" (or face value) of the bond.

Certificates of deposit are offered by banks and other depository institutions. They are similar to savings accounts but are issued for a fixed term—ranging from a few months to as long as five years. One advantage of CDs is that they are insured by the Federal Deposit Insurance Corporation (FDIC). Because of this insurance and their predictable rate of return, CDs are considered to be among the safest investment options. But they generally pay less interest than bonds and most other investments.

Government securities are IOUs issued by a government entity. States and municipalities often issue bonds. The federal government issues several types of government securities, ranging from short-term T-bills to long-term bonds. T-bills usually offer relatively low interest rates but have usually been considered very safe investments. The big increase in federal debt in recent years has led some investors to rethink this view.

Mutual funds offer investors shares that represent ownership in a variety of financial securities, such as stocks, corporate bonds, and government securities. These funds are professionally managed. The managers select the specific securities that the fund holds. *Exchange-traded funds* are "market baskets" of securities that are traded much like individual shares of stock.

Investors have several options when it comes to building up wealth for their retirement. One approach is to open an individual retirement account (IRA). There are several types of IRAs, the most popular being the traditional IRA and the Roth IRA. Contributions to a traditional IRA are tax deductible, but withdrawals are taxed. Contributions to a Roth IRA aren't tax deductible, but the distributions paid to retirees are tax exempt. One drawback of IRAs is that the amount investors can contribute each year is relatively small. In 2016, the maximum contribution for both types of plans was 5,500. (Individuals over the age of 50 could contribute up to 6,500.) 401(k), 403(b), and 457 employee contribution retirement plans are named for the sections of the tax code where they are defined. These retirement accounts are funded by payroll deductions. Like IRAs, these plans have both traditional and Roth versions. But compared to IRAs, they have much higher contribution limits. Another possible advantage is that many companies match (contribute) the employee contribution either dollar for dollar or a percentage of each dollar you contribute, up to a limit.

investing Reducing consumption in the current time period in order to build future wealth. (p. 334)

IRA An individual retirement account that provides tax benefits to individuals who are investing for their retirement. (p. 338)

401(k), 403(b), and 457 plans Employee payroll-deduction retirement plans that offer tax benefits. (p. 338)

company matching An amount contributed by the employer to an employee's retirement account, matching the employee's retirement contributions either

dollar-for-dollar or based on a percentage of each dollar contributed by the employee. (p. 338)

vesting period A specified period of time for which an employee must work for an employer in order to receive the full advantage of certain retirement benefits. (p. 340)

A1-1 **Describe how unions in the United States are organized.** A labor union is a group of workers who have organized in order to pursue common job-related objectives, such as securing better wages and benefits, safer working conditions, and greater job security. Unions can be organized either as craft unions, which consist of members who share the same skill or profession, or as industrial unions, which consist of workers in the same industry. The most basic unit of a union is the local union. This is the level at which most members have an opportunity to get directly involved in union activities. Most locals belong to a national (or international) union. The national union provides training, legal support, and bargaining advice to locals; organizes new locals; and sometimes takes an active role in the collective bargaining process. Many national unions belong to the AFL-CIO, which serves as the national voice for the labor movement.

labor union A group of workers who have organized to work together to achieve common job-related goals, such as higher wages, better working conditions, and greater job security. (p. A1-2)

craft union A union comprising workers who share the same skill or work in the same profession. (p. A1-2)

industrial union A union comprising workers employed in the same industry. (p. A1-2)

A1-2 **Discuss the key provisions of the laws that govern labor–management relations.** Until the 1930s, no federal laws dealt specifically with the rights of workers to organize unions or the way unions could carry out their functions. During the Great Depression of the 1930s, several pro-labor laws were enacted. The most important of these was the National Labor Relations Act, often called the "Wagner Act." This law prevented employers from discriminating against union members and required employers to recognize and bargain with certified unions. It also established the National Labor Relations Board to investigate charges of unfair labor practices. After World War II, Congress enacted the Labor–Management Relations Act, more commonly called the "Taft–Hartley Act." This law sought to limit the power of unions. It identified several unfair labor practices by unions and declared them illegal and allowed workers to vote to decertify a union that represented them. It also made closed shops (in which employers could only hire workers who already belonged to a union) illegal. Finally, it allowed states to pass right-to-work laws that made union shops (in which all workers had to join the union within a specified time in order to keep their jobs) illegal.

employment at will A legal doctrine that views employment as an entirely voluntary relationship that both the employee and employer are free to terminate at any time and for any reason. (p. A1-4)

National Labor Relations Act (Wagner Act) Landmark pro-labor law enacted in 1935. This law made it illegal for firms to discriminate against union members and required employers to recognize certified unions and bargain with them in good faith. (p. A1-5)

Labor–Management Relations Act (Taft–Hartley Act) Law passed in 1947 that placed limits on union activities, outlawed the closed shop, and allowed states to pass right-to-work laws that made union shops illegal. (p. A1-5)

closed shop An employment arrangement in which the employer agrees to hire only workers who already belong to the union. (p. A1-5)

union shop An employment arrangement in which a firm can hire nonunion workers, but these workers must join the union within a specified time period to keep their jobs. (p. A1-5)

right-to-work law A state law that makes union shops illegal within that state's borders. (p. A1-5)

open shop An employment arrangement in which workers are not required to join a union or pay union dues. (p. A1-5)

A1-3 **Explain how labor contracts are negotiated and administered.** The process by which representatives of labor and management attempt to negotiate a mutually acceptable labor agreement is called "collective bargaining." There are two broad, basic approaches to collective bargaining. In distributive bargaining, the process tends to be adversarial. The sides begin with predetermined positions and an initial set of demands. They then use persuasion, logic, and even threats to gain as much as they can. The other approach is called "interest-based bargaining." In this approach, the two sides do not present initial demands. Instead, they raise issues and concerns and try to work together to develop mutually beneficial solutions.

Negotiations sometimes break down. An impasse occurs when it becomes obvious that a settlement is not possible under current conditions. When an impasse is reached, the union may call a strike, or the employer may call a lockout. However, both sides may agree to either mediation or arbitration to try to settle their differences and reach agreement without resorting to such work stoppages. Mediators can only make suggestions and encourage the two sides to settle. If one or both sides reject the mediator's efforts, then the process is likely to fail. In contrast, an arbitrator has the authority to render a binding decision. Arbitration is common in the public sector but rare in the private sector.

When workers believe they have been unfairly treated under terms of the contract, they may file a grievance. Most labor agreements contain a formal grievance procedure that identifies a specific series of steps involved in settling a complaint. The final step usually involves binding arbitration.

collective bargaining The process by which representatives of union members and employers attempt to negotiate a mutually acceptable labor agreement. (p. A1-6)

distributive bargaining The traditional adversarial approach to collective bargaining. (p. A1-6)

interest-based bargaining A form of collective bargaining that emphasizes cooperation and problem solving in an attempt to find a "win–win" outcome. (p. A1-7)

strike A work stoppage initiated by a union. (p. A1-7)

© Cengage

lockout An employer-initiated work stoppage. (p. A1-7)

picketing A union tactic during labor disputes in which union members walk near the entrance of the employer's place of business, carrying signs to publicize their position and concerns. (p. A1-7)

boycott A tactic in which a union and its supporters and sympathizers refuse to do business with an employer with which they have a labor dispute. (p. A1-7)

mediation A method of dealing with an impasse between labor and management by bringing in a neutral third party to help the two sides reach agreement by

reducing tensions and making suggestions for possible compromises. (p. A1-8)

arbitration A process in which a neutral third party has the authority to resolve a dispute by rendering a binding decision. (p. A1-8)

grievance A complaint by a worker that the employer has violated the terms of the collective bargaining agreement. (p. A1-8)

A1-4 **Evaluate the impact that unions have had on their members' welfare and the economy, and explain the challenges that today's unions face.** Most studies find that union workers earn higher wages and receive more benefits than nonunion workers with similar skills, performing the same type of job. Union contracts and the grievance procedure also provide union members with more protection from arbitrary discipline (including firings) than nonunion workers enjoy. However, unionized industries in the private sector haven't provided much job security. Total employment in many highly unionized industries has fallen dramatically in recent years.

Many critics argue that unions undermine worker productivity by imposing rules and restrictions that reduce the ability of firms to innovate and require employers to use more labor than necessary to produce goods and provide services. But union supporters suggest that unions reduce worker turnover and encourage worker training, thus increasing productivity. Research on this topic has not yielded clear-cut evidence in support of either position.

One of the major problems facing unions is the continuing decline in union membership in the private sector. There are several reasons for this decline. In part, it represents a change in the structure of the U.S. economy. But another reason has been the increasing willingness of employers to use antiunion tactics to discourage union membership. The AFL-CIO and national unions

MAJOR LABOR LEGISLATION IN THE UNITED STATES

Date	Law	Major Provisions
1932	Norris–LaGuardia Act	▪ Stated that workers had a legal right to organize ▪ Made it more difficult to get injunctions against peaceful union activities
1935	National Labor Relations Act (or Wagner Act)	▪ Made it illegal for employers to discriminate based on union membership ▪ Established the National Labor Relations Board to investigate unfair labor practices ▪ Established a voting procedure for workers to certify a union as their bargaining agent ▪ Required employers to recognize certified unions and bargain with them in good faith
1938	Fair Labor Standards Act	▪ Banned many types of child labor ▪ Established the first federal minimum wage (25 cents per hour) ▪ Established a standard 40-hour workweek ▪ Required that hourly workers receive overtime pay when they work in excess of 40 hours per week
1947	Labor–Management Relations Act	▪ Identified unfair labor practices by unions and declared them illegal ▪ Allowed employers to speak against unions during organizing campaigns ▪ Allowed union members to decertify their union, removing its right to represent them ▪ Established provisions for dealing with emergency strikes that threatened the nation's health or security
1959	Labor–Management Reporting and Disclosure Act (or Landrum–Griffin Act)	▪ Guaranteed rank-and-file union members the right to participate in union meetings ▪ Required regularly scheduled secret ballot elections of union officers ▪ Required unions to file annual financial reports ▪ Prohibited convicted felons and Communist Party members from holding union office

have placed greater emphasis on organizing activities in recent years in an attempt to reverse this trend. Until recently, these efforts met with little success. However, between 2006 and 2007 there was a slight increase in private-sector union membership for the first time in 25 years. This was followed by an even larger increase in membership between 2007 and 2008. These

developments raised hopes among union leaders that they had turned the corner. However, union membership fell substantially from 2009 to 2016, when only 6.4% of workers in private industry belonged to unions. The steep decline in private-sector unions is the main reason overall union membership dropped from 20.1% of all wage and salary workers in 1983 to 10.7% in 2016.

© Cengage

APPENDIX LEARNING OBJECTIVES / KEY TERMS

A2-1 **Explain the purposes of laws and identify the major sources of law in the United States.** Laws are those rules—enforced by a government—that set parameters for the conduct and actions of people within a society. These rules promote order and stability, protect individuals from physical or mental harm, protect property from damage or theft, promote behavior that society deems desirable, and deter behavior that society deems undesirable. Laws come from several sources. Constitutional law is based on a constitution, such as the U.S. Constitution or a state constitution. Statutory law is enacted by a legislative body, such as Congress or a state legislature.

Administrative laws are established and enforced by government agencies. Case law (also called *common law*) is law based on court decisions known as *precedents*.

There are two branches of law in the United States. *Civil law* deals with disputes between private parties. These disputes are settled in the courts when one of the parties (called the *plaintiff*) initiates a lawsuit against the other (called the *defendant*). *Criminal law* involves cases in which the state investigates and prosecutes alleged wrongdoers accused of a violation of their public duty. The most serious crimes are called *felonies*. Less serious crimes are called *misdemeanors*.

laws Rules that govern the conduct and actions of people within a society that are enforced by the government. (p. A2-2)

constitution A code that establishes the fundamental rules and principles that govern a particular organization or entity. (p. A2-2)

statutory law Law that is the result of legislative action. (p. A2-3)

Uniform Commercial Code (UCC) A uniform act governing the sale of goods,

leases, warranties, transfer of funds, and a variety of other business-related activities. (p. A2-3)

administrative law Laws that arise from regulations established by government agencies. (p. A2-3)

case law (also called common law) Laws that result from rulings, called precedents, made by judges who initially hear a particular type of case. (p. A2-4)

tort A private wrong that results in physical or mental harm to an individual, or damage to that person's property. (p. A2-4)

negligence An unintentional tort that arises due to carelessness or irresponsible behavior. (p. A2-5)

crime A wrongful act against society, defined by law and prosecuted by the state. (p. A2-5)

A2-2 **Describe the characteristics of a contract and explain how the terms of contracts are enforced.** A contract is an agreement that is enforceable in a court of law. A valid contract is characterized by (1) mutual assent; (2) consideration; (3) legal capacity; and (4) legal purpose. In addition, according to the *statute of frauds*, certain types of contracts, such as those that will take more than a year to complete, or those involving the sale of goods worth more than $500, must be in writing.

A breach of contract occurs if one of the parties does not live up to the terms of the agreement. When one party breaches a contract, the other party can sue in a civil court. If the court agrees that a party breached the contract, it orders some type of remedy. The most common remedy is compensatory damages, which means the party who breached the contract must pay money to the injured party to compensate for the actual harm suffered. In cases where the contract calls for the sale of a unique good, the courts may apply a remedy known as "specific performance," which requires the party who breached the contract to do exactly what the contract says. Finally, the courts may issue injunctions (court orders) that prevent the party who breached the contract from taking some action.

DIFFERENCES BETWEEN CIVIL AND CRIMINAL LAW CASES

	Civil Law	Criminal Law
Nature of Action and Parties Involved	Lawsuits to settle disputes between private parties	Federal or state government prosecution of parties charged with wrongdoings against society
Examples of Cases	Intentional torts such as slander, libel, invasion of privacy, wrongful death; unintentional torts arising from negligence; breach of contract	Felonies such as robbery, theft, murder, arson, identity theft, extortion, embezzlement, as well as less serious crimes called misdemeanors
Possible Outcomes	Liable or not liable	Guilty or not guilty
Standard of Proof (What is Needed for the State or Plaintiff to Win the Case)	Preponderance of evidence (a much less stringent requirement than beyond reasonable doubt)	Proof beyond a reasonable doubt
Goal of Remedy	Compensate injured party for harm suffered	Punish wrongdoer and deter similar behavior
Common Remedies	Monetary damages (payments of money to compensate the injured party), injunctions against certain types of behavior, or requirements for specific performance	Fines and/or imprisonment; in the most serious felonies, such as premeditated murder, capital punishment (the death penalty) may be imposed

business law The application of laws and legal principles to business relationships and transactions. (p. A2-5)

contract An agreement that is legally enforceable. (p. A2-6)

consideration Something of value that one party gives another as part of a contractual agreement. (p. A2-6)

statute of frauds A requirement that certain types of contracts must be in writing in order to be enforceable. (p. A2-6)

breach of contract The failure of one party to a contract to perform his or her contractual obligations. (p. A2-6)

statute of limitations The time period within which a legal action must be initiated. (p. A2-7)

compensatory damages Monetary payments that a party who breaches a contract is ordered to pay in order to compensate the injured party for the actual harm suffered by the breach of contract. (p. A2-7)

specific performance A remedy for breach of contract in which the court orders the party committing the breach to do exactly what the contract specifies. (p. A2-7)

A2-3 **Describe how both title and risk pass from the seller to the buyer when a sale occurs.** A sale occurs when title to a good or a piece of real property passes from one party to another in exchange for a price. Sales of goods are covered by Article 2 of the Uniform Commercial Code, which has been adopted by every state in the United States except Louisiana. Sales of services are based on precedents established by common law. A sales contract must contain the same basic elements as other contracts. However, the UCC has relaxed the requirements for some of these elements. For example, under the UCC, courts may recognize a sales contract even if certain key facts of the agreement (such as the price of the

good) aren't explicitly spelled out. In such cases, the UCC provides guidelines for supplying the missing details. One key sales contract issue involves when title actually passes from one party to another. If the contract is silent about this, the UCC generally holds that title passes when the seller has completed all duties related to the delivery of the good. Another key issue involves which party bears the risk if the goods are lost, damaged, or destroyed during the transfer from seller to buyer. If the contract doesn't specify which party assumes the risk, the UCC normally places the risk on the party that is most likely to have insurance against a loss, or on the party that is in the better position to prevent a loss.

sale A transaction in which the title (legal ownership) to a good passes from one party to another in exchange for a price. (p. A2-7)

title Legal ownership. (p. A2-7)

A2-4 **Provide an overview of the legal principles governing agency, intellectual property, and bankruptcy.** A principal–agent relationship exists when one party (the principal) gives another party (the agent) the authority to act and enter into binding agreements on the principal's behalf. As long as agents act within their scope of authority, principals are legally liable for any contracts their agents enter into while representing them. Not all employees have the authority to act as agents, but many do. A loan officer at a bank and a salesperson at a store are both employees of, and agents for, their companies.

Intellectual property refers to the rights of inventors, innovators, authors, and artists to own their creations and prevent others from copying, distributing, displaying, performing, or selling these creations without their permission. Patents protect the intellectual property rights of inventors. Most patents give the inventor exclusive rights to their invention for 20 years. Copyrights protect the intellectual property rights of authors, artists, and other creative individuals. Copyrights normally extend for 70 years beyond the

author's or artist's life. Trademarks, which are marks, symbols, words, phrases, or mottos that identify a company's goods, are another form of intellectual property. Registered trademarks are protected for 10 years, and the protection can be extended for an unlimited number of additional 10-year periods.

Bankruptcy provides a way for debtors who are unable to meet their obligations to discharge their debts and get a fresh start. There are several different types of bankruptcy procedures. In a Chapter 7 bankruptcy, the debtor's assets are liquidated, and the proceeds are used to pay the creditors. Once this is done, the debtor's obligations are considered fully discharged, even if (as is almost certainly the case) the proceeds are insufficient to make full payment. Chapter 11 bankruptcy occurs when a debtor reorganizes under a court-approved plan. This approach is usually used by corporations, though it is also possible for individuals to file under Chapter 11. Finally, Chapter 13 bankruptcy allows individuals to adjust their debt payments under a court-approved schedule.

principal–agent relationship A relationship in which one party, called the principal, gives another party, called the agent, the authority to act in place of, and bind, the principal when dealing with third parties. (p. A2-8)

principal A party who agrees to have someone else (called an agent) act on his or her behalf. (p. A2-8)

agent A party who agrees to represent another party, called the principal. (p. A2-8)

scope of authority (for an agent) The extent to which an agent has the authority to act for and represent the principal. (p. A2-8)

Chapter 7 bankruptcy A form of bankruptcy that discharges a debtor's debts by liquidating assets and using the proceeds to pay off creditors. (p. A2-9)

Chapter 11 bankruptcy A form of bankruptcy used by corporations and individuals that allows the debtor to reorganize operations under a court-approved plan. (p. A2-10)

Chapter 13 bankruptcy A form of bankruptcy that allows individual debtors to set up a repayment plan to adjust their debts. (p. A2-10)

property The legal right of an owner to exclude nonowners from having control over a particular resource. (p. A2-10)

intellectual property Property that results from intellectual or creative efforts. (p. A2-11)

patent A legal monopoly that gives an inventor the exclusive right over an invention for a limited time period. (p. A2-11)

trademark A mark, symbol, word, phrase, or motto used to identify a company's goods. (p. A2-11)

copyright The exclusive legal right of an author, artist, or other creative individual to use, copy, display, perform, and sell their own creations and to license others to do so. (p. A2-12)

© Cengage